INTERPRETATIONS OF

AMERICAN HISTORY

PATTERNS AND PERSPECTIVES

Seventh Edition

Volume I: Through Reconstruction

EDITED BY

FRANCIS G. COUVARES

MARTHA SAXTON

GERALD N. GROB

GEORGE ATHAN BILLIAS

THE FREE PRESS   *New York London Toronto Sydney Singapore*

THE FREE PRESS
A Division of Simon & Schuster Inc.
1230 Avenue of the Americas
New York, NY 10020

Manufactured in the United States of America

10 9 8 7 6 5 4 3 2 1

Library of Congress Cataloging-in-Publication Data

Interpretations of American history : patterns and perspectives / edited by Francis G.
Couvares . . . [et al.].—7th ed.
p.   cm.
Includes bibliographical references and index.
Contents: v.   1. Through Reconstruction— v.   2. From Reconstruction.
1. United States—History.   2. United States—Historiography.   I. Couvares, Francis G.,
1948–
E178.6.I53 2000
973—dc21   00-024709

ISBN 0-684-86773-7

To Gerald F. Linderman and Alexander Saxton,
teachers and historians

ACKNOWLEDGMENTS

For all their generous help we would like to thank David Blight, Kevin Boyle, Rhea Cabin, Betty Couvares, Enrico Ferorelli, Eric Foner, Dan Freedberg, Naana Frimpong, Hugh Hawkins, Chris Kuipers, Bruce Laurie, Gordie Levin, Douglas Little, Kim Palmer, Lisa Raskin, Mary Renda, Kevin Sweeney, Lauren Winner, and Nancy Woloch.

CONTENTS

INTRODUCTION

These volumes, as their title suggests, reflect our understanding that history is an act of interpretation. They also reflect the dramatic changes in the practice of history over the last thirty years. Thirty years ago the subjects historians most often interpreted were politics, diplomacy, and war. Those privileged to do the interpreting were mostly white and male. Since then, civil rights, antiwar, and women's movements have reshaped dramatically what historians and readers consider suitable topics of study and have brought into the profession women, African Americans, Hispanics, and Native Americans. Contemporary American historians write about nearly everything that has affected nearly everybody—from agriculture to housework, illness to leisure, banking systems to sewer systems. Their expansive new history touches nearly every American and invites each to make a personal interpretation of history.

But the influx of a wide variety of new historians has, in a way, only linked the past more strongly to the present. Over a hundred years ago, the Italian philosopher Benedetto Croce observed that "Every true history is contemporary history."[1] He was trying to cast doubt on arguments of late-nineteenth-century historians (called "historicists" or "positivists") that history was a science and could recover objective truths if properly practiced. Croce insisted that the past "in itself" is unknowable. History rather reflects the need of historians (and readers) to make sense out of their own worlds. Opening up the practice of history to groups previously excluded from the profession has demonstrated the validity of Croce's view in new ways. Views of the past vary not only with generations but also because of divergent experiences stemming from the historian's sex, ethnicity, class, and race. This does not mean that we cannot find out anything solid about

---

[1]Benedetto Croce, in *History: Its Theory and Practice* (New York, 1921), develops ideas he first articulated in 1893. For a sampling of the work of Croce and other philosophers of history in the first half of the twentieth century, see Hans Meyerhoff, ed., *The Philosophy of History in Our Time* (New York, 1959), and Patrick Gardiner, ed., *Theories of History* (Glencoe, Ill., 1959). See also Fritz Stern, ed., *Varieties of History: From Voltaire to the Present* (Cleveland and New York, 1956). An excellent guide through these philosophical thickets, designed especially for students, is Michael Stanford, *A Companion to the Study of History* (Oxford, 1994).

the past. But it does mean that no account of the past is free of the perspectives, prejudices, and priorities of its author.

When we read history we are reading a particular historian's encounter with the world. The historian is devoted to the "facts," spends hours, indeed years of his or her life combing through the archives, and believes that the story she or he comes away with represents reality. But in writing, the historian renders this material into a story. The designing of this narrative reflects the author's social circumstances and views of the good, the true, and the beautiful. Thus, historians can be characterized by nationality, or school of thought, or theoretical and methodological preference. One historian is, we say, a Jeffersonian liberal, another a nationalist, another a Progressive, still another a feminist or postmodernist. Perry Miller's account of the Puritans, for example, seems to reflect his sense of alienation from twentieth-century American liberalism; Kenneth Stampp's account of Reconstruction is shaped by his engagement with the civil rights movement; Oscar Handlin's saga of immigration reflects his own ethnic experience; Kathryn Sklar's ideas about Progressivism are informed by her feminism.

If history is partly craft and partly polemic, however, it is also partly science. An error as common as thinking history is "just the facts" is thinking it is "just your story." Whereas the nineteenth-century positivists thought that scientific method could guarantee objective truth in history just as in physics, some present-day postmodern literary theorists maintain that history is entirely opinion. Postmodern criticism has encouraged historians to be more attentive to the possible layers of meaning in their documents, and also to their own use of language in writing history. But those postmodernists who assert that historians cannot arrive at truth, or that history is no different from fiction, err as much as the positivists in the opposite direction. However parallel some of the techniques of ideologue, novelist, and historian, the historian is constrained by the record in a way the other two are not. As one literary critic has recently written, the historian's "allegiance is to fact."[2] Historians willingly acknowledge that no account is absolutely true, and certainly no account is ever final, but they also insist that some histories are better than others. Something other than the historian's political, moral, or esthetic preferences comes into play in judging one history better than another, something, for want of a better term, objective. While committed to a particular interpretation, the historian remains faithful to the evidence and determined to test the accuracy, the reliability, and the adequacy of every historical account.

---

[2]Sue Halpern, "The Awful Truth," *New York Review of Books* (September 25, 1997): 13.

History succeeds when it tells us how things really were, yet at the same time reminds us that the only access we have to that past is through the imagination of a finite and very contemporary human being. History reveals the contours of a landscape from a distinct perspective, but it does not invent the landscape.[3]

One important check on possible imaginative excess is that historians constantly criticize, correct, and supplement each other's views. That is, historians get closer to the truth by arguing with one another. The shape and dimensions of a selected landscape come more clearly into view the more historians bring different perspectives and common skills to the tasks of documentation, description, and narration. So history is historiography, the study of history and its changing interpretations.[4] Every historian begins work by immersing himself or herself in the subject and remains in dialogue with others interested in similar matters. Most books by serious historians include historiographical essays that locate the work within the context of related works.

Historiography reminds us that history is not a closed book, not a collection of inarguable facts or a seamless story. Historiography is a reminder that there is always something to argue about in history, something that makes us think about the conduct of our contemporary lives. Thus, in a world of liberation movements and resurgent nationalism, it matters how we tell the story of the American Revolution or the growth of America's overseas empire. In a society riven by conflicts over racial justice, sexual exploitation, and growing disparities between

---

[3]The most recent denial of history's truth claims is Peter Novick, *That Noble Dream: The "Objectivity Question" and the American Historical Profession* (Cambridge, 1988). Dorothy Ross, "Grand Narrative in American Historical Writing: From Romance to Uncertainty," *American Historical Review*, 100 (June 1995): 651–77, offers brilliant critiques of historians' narrative strategies and somewhat elusive postmodernist suggestions about alternatives. Arguments for a middle ground between "objectivism" and Novick's "relativism" can be found in James T. Kloppenberg, "Objectivity and Historicism: A Century of American Historical Writing," *American Historical Review*, 94 (October 1989): 1011–30; Thomas L. Haskell, "Objectivity Is Not Neutrality: Rhetoric vs. Practice in Peter Novick's *That Noble Dream*," *History & Theory*, 29 (1990): 129–57; David Hollinger, *In the American Province: Studies in the History and Historiography of Science* (Bloomington, Ind., 1985); and the "*AHR* Forum: Peter Novick's *That Noble Dream*: The Objectivity Question and the Future of the Historical Profession," *American Historical Review*, 96 (June 1991): 675–708, with contributions from Hollinger and others, and with a reply from Novick. See also Joyce Appleby, Lynn Hunt, and Margaret Jacoby, *Telling the Truth About History* (New York, 1994); Alan B. Spitzer, *Historical Truth and Lies about the Past: Reflections on Dewey, Dreyfus, de Man, and Reagan* (Chapel Hill, N.C., 1996); and Richard J. Evans, *In Defense of History* (New York, 1999). A more conservative and alarmist defense of objectivity is Keith Windschuttle, *The Killing of History: How Literary Critics and Social Theorists are Murdering Our Past* (New York, 1997).

[4]J. H. Hexter defines it as "the craft of writing history" or the "rhetoric of history," in "The Rhetoric of History", originally published in the *International Encyclopedia of the Social Sciences*, Vol. 6 (New York, 1968), pp. 368–94, and republished in revised form in his *Doing History* (Bloomington, Ind., 1971), pp. 15–76.

rich and poor, it matters how we narrate the history of labor, or the New Deal, or the rights movements of the 1960s and 1970s. Knowing that black state governments in the Reconstruction era were no more or less corrupt than those that preceded or succeeded them makes it impossible to justify the black disfranchisement of the 1880s and 1890s. It may also affect the way we think about the politics of race in our own day. Knowing that great numbers of turn-of-the-century migrants to America returned to their homelands may require us to revise how we explain the motivation of immigrants or the timing and completeness of their assimilation. It may also change the way we think of the dual loyalties of contemporary migrants.

Historical scholarship is thus in continual flux. Even in fields of study where new evidence scarcely ever comes to light, consensus is always elusive. But for careful students of historiography, disagreement is more interesting than agreement could ever be, for the conflict holds the secret to understanding not just the past but, just possibly, the present and future as well.

With these comments in mind, what follows is a sketch of the evolution of American history as a discipline over the course of the last two centuries.[5] As with all attempts to fit diverse strands of thought and experience into a single story, ambiguities haunt this narration or are suppressed in the interest of a continuous story line. As much as possible, the following tries to balance human complexity with narrative simplicity.

Broadly speaking, the writing of American history has passed through four stages: the providential, the rationalist, the nationalist, and the professional. The ministers and magistrates of the seventeenth and eighteenth centuries, and all the women who wrote history through the Civil War, wrote a form of providential history. The Puritan practitioners who originated this form had no doubt about what they were doing and why. They wished to justify the ways of God to man, and vice-versa. Their history was a holy chronicle, revealing His Providence toward His Chosen People and their efforts to build a New Canaan in the wilderness. The preeminent work in this tradition was William Bradford's *Of Plimouth Plantation*. Written over the course of the 1630s and 1640s when Bradford was governor of the colony, the book recounts the fate of a tiny band of Pilgrims who fled England for Holland and then for the New World. They rested in the certainty that God's hand led them forward, that their disasters were His rebukes, their successes His merciful rewards. Governor John Winthrop of Massachusetts wrote such a history, as did Cotton Mather in the next

---

[5]On the development of the historical profession in America, see John Higham, *History: Professional Scholarship in America* (New York, 1973). See also works cited in footnote 3.

century. Mary Rowlandson's eyewitness account of her own captivity employed the same providential themes. Well into the nineteenth century, male and female historians, including Mercy Otis Warren, Elizabeth Peabody, and Hannah Adams, viewed the story of America as an extension of the history of the Protestant Reformation. The Revolution became for them a triumph of reformed Christianity over paganism and Catholicism. And the United States as a whole took the place of New England as the model of Christian virtue for the corrupt Old World to emulate.[6]

In the late eighteenth century, as the European Enlightenment came to America, history took on a secular and naturalistic cast. A new class of intellectuals, profoundly influenced by Newton, Locke, and the French philosophes, had come to see history, like the physical universe, as subject to natural law. These rationalist historians flourished alongside and sometimes superseded the clerics who had once dominated the educated class in the colonies. The new story they told was of progress and reason—and, indeed, "the progress of reason"—in human affairs. Although some Protestant ministers responded vibrantly to the new intellectual currents,[7] most historians in the late eighteenth century were lawyer-politicians, planter-aristocrats, merchants, or professionals—one, Judith Sargent Murray, was the daughter and wife of ministers. Among the most prominent were Thomas Hutchinson, leading merchant and royal governor of Massachusetts; William Smith, physician, landowner, and lieutenant governor of New York; and Robert Beverly and William Byrd of Virginia, both planter-aristocrats and office-holders. These men possessed classical educations, fine private libraries, and the leisure time to use both. Their writing was more refined and allusive than the studiously plain prose of their Puritan predecessors. They wrote history for their own satisfaction, but also to explain to the enlightened world the success of men like themselves: free, bold, intelligent, and ambitious—men who built fortunes and governed provinces that embodied a perfect balance between liberty and order.

Thomas Jefferson's *Notes on the State of Virginia* (written in the midst of revolutionary turmoil and finally published in 1785) is a highly evolved product of this rationalist tradition. America is for Jefferson, as it was for the Puritans, a model for the world, but natural law takes the place of divine providence in directing its affairs. Self-interest, not piety, motivates men; reason, not faith, allows them to discover and pursue their destiny. The fruits of liberty include not only astonishing material prosperity and advances in knowledge but moral

---

[6]Nina Baym, *American Women Writers and the Work of History* (New Brunswick, N.J., 1995), particularly "History from a Divine Point of View," pp. 46–66.

[7]See Edmund S. Morgan, *The Gentle Puritan: A Life of Ezra Stiles, 1727–1795* (New Haven, Conn., 1962).

progress as well. The new nation is destined to open the way toward a new era in human history not only because its natural resources are vast but because free people are virtuous and possessed of the moral energy to change the world. Some evangelical Protestants called Jefferson a "confirmed infidel" and a "howling atheist" for his emphasis on human as opposed to divine agency. But Jefferson's most potent enemies were political: in the 1790s he led the Republican opposition to the Federalist party of Washington and Adams. During the brutal presidential election campaigns of 1800 and 1804, both of which Jefferson won, Federalist writers combed the *Notes* to find ammunition against Jefferson the infidel, the apologist for slavery, the lover of French revolutionary excess. Their charges reveal, among other things, that history had already become politicized. History was a story about how wealth, power, rights, and wrongs came to be in this world—how causes produced effects, and how human actions could change those effects. But the story for the rationalists was no more open-ended than it was for the providentialists: it still pointed upward. Through most of the nineteenth century and into the early twentieth, American history was the story of the progress of the "Empire of Liberty."

As the nineteenth century wore on, historians began to temper their Enlightenment assurance about human beings' capacity for rational improvement. They came increasingly to view races as having different capacities, and to see America as the triumph of Anglo-Saxon people over inferior races. Similar strains of thinking in Europe helped to justify colonization. George Bancroft, the most distinguished American historian of the mid-nineteenth century, organized the history of America around three themes: progress, liberty, and Anglo-Saxon destiny. Bancroft deviated from his own rationalist background after studying in Germany, where he absorbed the romantic emphasis on the inborn virtues of the "folk." The idea that Teutonic peoples (which included Anglo-Saxons) were racially destined to spread freedom across the globe was central to this romantic nationalism. According to Bancroft, the Anglo-Saxons developed the most distinctive tradition of free institutions, and American democracy produced the most advanced forms. In twelve volumes published between 1834 and 1882, Bancroft chronicled the march of history, which corresponded to the spread of American democratic institutions throughout the world and culminated at home in Jacksonian democracy.[8]

Even women historians such as Hannah Adams, Susanna Rowson, Elizabeth Peabody, and Emma Willard, whose evangelical commitments made them political enemies of the Jacksonian Democratic

---

[8]On Bancroft and other romantic historians see David Levin, *History as Romantic Art* (New York, 1963).

party, manifested romantic nationalist thinking not unlike Bancroft's. In her *Pioneer Women of the West* (1852), Elizabeth Ellet focused on conflict between white settlers and indigenous people. As Nina Baym put it in 1995, Ellet "is as close to a genocidal writer as one is likely to find."[9] Some women, however, did break the barriers of gender and nationalist history. Helen Hunt Jackson explored white-Indian relations in both fiction and history. Her *Century of Dishonor* (1881)—which she sent to every member of Congress—documented the American nation's shameful dealings with Indians. Intent on reaching a wider popular audience she then published a novel, *Ramona*, which dramatized white appropriation of Indian lands and other cruelties. At the same time, white and Indian anthropologists began studying native cultures, some because they thought Indians were disappearing, others because they wished to counteract racist myths by displaying the vigor and richness of Indian cultures.[10] Unfortunately, neither criticism nor ethnographic knowledge seriously affected the trajectory of mainstream history. Not until the arrival of the inclusionary politics of the late twentieth century would the work of anthropologists and ethnographers find its way into the pages of mainstream history.

By the 1870s, Bancroft's self-congratulatory epic history had become second nature to most Americans who thought about the past. But changes were afoot in the discipline. The first change was in leadership: amateur writers increasingly gave way to professional historians. As college education became more common among middle-class Americans, and as industrialization reinforced the value of technical and scientific knowledge, historians increasingly concerned themselves with specialized training, research methodology, and educational credentials. History was now a profession like any other—that is, it was practiced by the only sort of people who had access to advanced education: white men. Many of them were trained in Germany, but in 1876 Johns Hopkins University became the first exclusively graduate research institution in the United States. Soon thereafter, graduate study spread to the midwestern land-grant universities and the Ivy League. These newly minted historians usually planned careers in the same university system that had trained them. They prided themselves on rigorous research and a capacity to distinguish scientifically verified truth from romantic notion. Reflecting on these developments in 1894, Henry Adams imagined this new professional historian "dreaming of the immortality that would be achieved

---

[9]Baym, *The Work of History*, pp. 219, 238. Other enemies of Jackson, such as historians Francis Parkman and W. H. Prescott, wrote a similar kind of romantic-racial epic: see Levin, *History as Romantic Art.*

[10]See Robert F. Berkhofer, Jr., *The White Man's Indian: Images of the American Indian from Columbus to the Present* (New York, 1968).

by the man who should successfully apply Darwin's method to the facts of human history."[11]

Along with Frederick Jackson Turner, Adams exemplified the first generation of professional historians, which held sway from about 1870 to 1910. A scion of the great family that had produced presidents and statesmen, Adams might appear at first to be a throwback to the era of patrician amateurs. Politics was the career he had hoped for, while history seemed an avocation. But as his political hopes dimmed, his professional ambitions ignited. In 1870 he was invited to Harvard to teach the first seminar ever devoted to historical research at that institution. Adams taught the meticulous methods of German scholarship and insisted that history's goal was to develop knowledge every bit as sound as that in physics. His exhaustively researched, nine-volume history of the Jefferson and Madison administrations represented the fruit of his own commitment to that scientific method and has remained a classic. Although he left Harvard after a few years, his career symbolized the passing of the guard from patrician amateurs to professionals, which would permanently transform the discipline from his time forward.

If Turner inherited Adams's mantle, he could not have been more different from him in background and personal circumstances. Born of modest means in a rural town in Wisconsin, he attended the University of Wisconsin, received a Ph.D. in history at Johns Hopkins, and went on to teach at Wisconsin and Harvard. Different from Adams in so many ways, Turner shared his belief that history should be a science. He fulfilled Adams's prophecy in using Darwin's evolutionary theory to reveal the contours of American history. Just as one species surpassed another, he argued in his famous "The Significance of the Frontier in American History," so one frontier environment succeeded another in the course of American expansion. As successive frontiers grew more remote from European antecedents, they increasingly nurtured the distinctive American virtues—self-reliance, egalitarianism, tolerance, practicality, realism.[12] Although he embodied the new scientific history, Turner's sweeping generalizations and his assumptions about the "progress of the race" linked him to his nationalist predecessors. Like them he conflated America with capitalism, democracy, and the heroic deeds of the pioneers. Turner's epic was, like that of his predecessors, a hymn to America's glory.

-----

[11]Henry Adams, "The Tendency of History," *Annual Report of the American Historical Association for the Year 1894* (Washington, D.C., 1895), p. 19.

[12]Turner's essay, originally delivered as his presidential address to the American Historical Association in 1893, can be found in *The Frontier in American History* (New York, 1920). For more on Turner, see John Higham, *Writing American History: Essays on Modern Scholarship* (Bloomington, Ind., 1970), pp. 118–29; see also the discussion in Volume I, Chapter 7.

Between 1910 and 1945 a second generation of professional scholars—the Progressive historians—rose to prominence. As their name implies, they were identified with the Progressive movement in politics, which took aim at corporate arrogance and political corruption in early-twentieth-century America.[13] They observed that modernity—industrialization, urbanization, and class conflict—had fundamentally transformed the society. If democracy was to survive, people needed a history of changing institutions and economic interests, not fables about liberty and justice. Progressives saw history as politics, not science (or art). To be sure, science was needed to produce usable facts, and art to persuade people to act on them, but it was political action that Progressive historians wanted their history to provoke. Neither genteel amateurs nor morally neutral scientists, Progressives were muscular intellectuals—or, as they would have gladly called themselves, reformers.

In 1913, the most famous Progressive historian, Charles A. Beard, published *An Economic Interpretation of the Constitution*, quite possibly the most influential book ever written in American history. It argued that the Constitution was the product not of wise men intent on balancing liberty and order, but of a clique of wealthy merchants and landowners who wanted a central government strong enough to defend their privileges against the unruly masses. A series of books culminating in *The Rise of American Civilization* (1927), which Beard wrote with his wife Mary Ritter Beard, elaborated the thesis that American history was a succession of conflicts between economic interest groups. Although critics found flaws in his economic determinism and faith in Progressive reform, Beard managed to inspire a generation to seek in history answers to the questions that pressed most insistently upon the democratic citizenry.

With a literary flair that exceeded that of either Turner or Beard, Vernon L. Parrington brought the Progressive interpretation to intellectual history in *Main Currents in American Thought*. His story was arrestingly simple: all of American history was shaped by the contest between Jeffersonian and Hamiltonian ways of thinking. Jefferson, champion of the people, represented decentralized agrarian democracy; Hamilton, tribune of the privileged, stood for centralized commercial aristocracy. From the moment the Revolution ended, these two ideas fought for control of American minds. In whatever guise—Federalist versus Republican, Whig versus Jacksonian, Progressive versus Conservative—all these conflicts reflected a continuous economic dynamic that animated American history. The function of history was to uncover the economic basis of political ideas and thereby to educate the citizenry. Like the patricians and the nationalists, Parrington

---

[13]See Volume II, Chapter 6.

wanted his fellow citizens to see that, despite periods of reaction, the direction of their history was upward, but determined in the end by the forces of reform.

Progressive history challenged the profession in another way: it insisted that historical knowledge is relative. In an essay published in 1935 entitled "That Noble Dream," Charles Beard observed that one bar to objectivity is that the historian's documentation is always partial. More important, like Croce he insisted that the historian is never neutral and therefore must write an interpretation, not a scientific re-creation, of the past. The noble but illusory dream of objectivity must be discarded by any serious and honest historian. Acknowledging one's politics and prejudices does not weaken the value of the historian's work, Beard insisted, but rather strengthens it. An interpretation—which he defined as an "overarching hypothesis or conception employed to give coherence and structure to past events"—should be measured not by whether it is correct or incorrect but by whether it is useful to people who are trying to improve their world.[14] Carl L. Becker, a Progressive historian of early America, made the promotion of relativism one of the central purposes of his career. In his famous 1931 presidential address to the American Historical Association, "Everyman His Own Historian," and in other essays, Becker repeated that, however indispensable the scientific pursuit of facts, history meant nothing unless it were yoked to the political necessities of real people. History's obligation is not to the dead but to the living; its account of the past is "perhaps neither true nor false, but only the most convenient form of error."[15]

Female and African American scholars challenged the profession in still other ways, though historians were not yet ready to respond. For example, Mary Ritter Beard, who published many works with her husband and many books about women on her own, culminating in *Woman as a Force in History* in 1946, achieved little or no recognition from the profession. After having a baby, she entered Columbia graduate school with her husband in 1902, but dropped out two years later and subsequently nurtured a hostility for academics and for college education for women. Women with careers, she wrote scornfully, were "capitalist entrepreneurs or retainers of the bourgeoisie." She chose to wear her amateur status like a crown in the face of a profession that re-

---

[14]Charles A. Beard, "That Noble Dream," *American Historical Review*, 41 (October 1935): 74–87.

[15]This and related essays may be found in *Everyman His Own Historian* (New York, 1935). See also Phil L. Snyder, ed., *Detachment and the Writing of History: Essays and Letters of Carl L. Becker* (Ithaca, N.Y., 1958). For more on historical relativism, see Higham, *History*. A neorelativist argument can be found in Peter Novick, *That Noble Dream*, and other works cited in note 3, above. Still very useful as a philosophical guide is Jack W. Mieland, *Scepticism and Historical Knowledge* (New York, 1965).

fused to welcome her.[16] Other women in the Progressive era who chose to write women's history similarly saw their work ignored by their male colleagues.[17]

African American historians fared little better. At the American Historical Association meeting in 1909, W.E.B. Du Bois, having earned a Ph.D. from Harvard, offered a startling reinterpretation of Reconstruction that focused on the lives of poor blacks and whites. In the face of a daunting tradition condemning Reconstruction, he argued that it had briefly provided the South with democratic government, public schools, and other needed social legislation. Like other Progressives, Du Bois found economic causes underlying political events; unlike them, however, he included black people as legitimate historical subjects. This simple act of inclusion irrevocably altered his assessment of Reconstruction. Published in 1935, his book attracted many favorable reviews but was ignored by most historians. Du Bois's views did not enter the mainstream of the profession until John Hope Franklin's and Kenneth Stampp's revisionist interpretations appeared in the 1960s.[18]

The Progressives' economic determinism and their relativism both had an enormous impact on the history profession, but neither Beard nor Becker held the center stage exclusively or for long. At the very moment of their triumph—each elevated to the presidency of the American Historical Association, each hailed as a great mind and, more important, a sound political guide amidst the darkness and confusion of the Great Depression years—critics of both Progressive and relativist assertions began to multiply. In part the critics were responding to the rise of totalitarianism, which made faith in progress seem naive and relativism seem cowardly. That Charles Beard quite conspicuously continued to oppose American involvement in the Second World War, at a time when most left-wing intellectuals were rapidly shifting from pacifist to interventionist positions, seemed to many intellectuals to emphasize the narrowmindedness of the Progressive point of view. In the face of Hitler and Stalin, and especially after the horrors of Auschwitz, Dresden, and Hiroshima, American historians asked themselves if Progressive history had ill-prepared them and their fellow citizens for the harrowing obligations of the twentieth century. But it was not just the weight of tragic events that shifted the historiographical terrain.

---

[16]Ann J. Lane, *Mary Ritter Beard, a Sourcebook* (New York, 1977), pp. 33, 53–54.

[17]Helen Sumner's *Women and Industry in the U.S.* and Edith Abbott's *Women in Industry*, both published in 1910, were barely noticed by the male profession.

[18]W.E.B. Du Bois, *Black Reconstruction in America, 1860–1880* (New York, 1992), pp. vii–viii, xvi. For more on the historiography of Reconstruction, see Chapter 11 in this volume.

In the 1930s and 1940s younger historians increasingly found the Progressive historians' psychology shallow, their social analysis predictable, and their moral judgments superficial. Like the philosophers and theologians who were criticizing liberalism for its facile optimism and obtuseness in the face of human tragedy, they criticized Progressive historians for underestimating humankind's propensity for evil, overestimating its capacity for good, and turning history into a simple morality play. More important, they found the Progressive insistence on explaining most events as the product of conflict between rich and poor, East and West, reactionaries and reformers, and so forth to be more hindrance than help in making sense of specific historical problems. More and more historians were insisting that, for better *and* worse, consensus rather than conflict marked American political history; that the absence of European-style class conflict had indelibly shaped American institutions and ideas. In Europe the crises of depression and war led many historians in radical directions; here, under the influence of the Cold War, they led toward what came to be called "consensus history."

The caricature of consensus historians is that they asserted the unity and homogeneity of America's past, the stability of basic institutions, and the existence of a homogeneous national character. When they did acknowledge that conflict occurred between sections, classes, and groups, the consensus historians insisted that such struggles were fought within a common liberal framework and that the protagonists were never really in disagreement over fundamentals. Moreover, this caricature continues, consensus historians doubted the value of social change and, having observed a world brutalized by fascism and communism, feared mass movements of any kind. In this reading, consensus historians were neoconservatives who trimmed the sails of history to the anticommunist winds of the McCarthy era. In fact, so-called consensus historians were remarkably diverse, and many were liberals. Some were, indeed, "Cold War liberals" who believed that a defense of American values and institutions was more important than social criticism at a moment when totalitarianism threatened to take over the world. However, there was no simple correlation between Cold War attitudes and consensus historiography. Arthur M. Schlesinger, Jr., who never departed from the Progressive camp, was the leading "Cold War liberal" in the history profession. On the other hand, the distinguished Columbia University historian Richard Hofstadter, who was called a consensus historian and was definitely a critic of Progressive historiography, was equally if not more critical of the consensus he found in American history.

Some consensus historians did tell a comforting tale for Cold War America. In his influential *The Liberal Tradition in America*, Louis Hartz argued that because America lacked a feudal tradition it escaped the struggles between reactionaries, liberals, and socialists that characterized the history of most European countries. The United States instead had a three-century-long tradition of liberal consensus, wherein all Americans subscribed to the Lockean tenets of individualism, private property, natural rights, and popular sovereignty. The differences among Americans, Hartz maintained, were over means rather than ends. And thus America had very little class conflict and little ground for the breeding of class-based ideologies. Socialism could mean little in America because nearly everyone had access to a middle-class way of life. Conservatism too could mean little because the only thing to conserve—the only continuous tradition—was liberalism.[19]

Another consensus historian whose work was labeled "neoconservative" was Daniel Boorstin. In his three-volume epic story of settlement, westward migration, and community-building, Boorstin echoed the Progressive Turner in many ways. But in contrast to Turner, Boorstin described characters who were largely uninterested in politics and ideology. Most of them were pragmatic, energetic, healthy-minded "Versatiles," ready to conquer a continent, invent the balloon-frame house, experiment with popular democracy, and in the process develop the freest and most prosperous society on earth. Boorstin's approach was social-historical. Like the more radical social historians who would soon transform the discipline, Boorstin insisted that American society and culture were decisively shaped by millions of ordinary folk, not by elites. But for Boorstin, those anonymous masses were middle-class at heart and yearned for nothing so much as a house with a picket fence and a little room to breathe. Distinct from most of the other consensus historians, Boorstin preached a political message that might be called conservative populism.

If Hartz's insistence on ideological homogeneity and Boorstin's populist social history seemed conservative, it was not so easy to gauge the political tonality of Richard Hofstadter's work. Beginning in 1948 with the publication of *The American Political Tradition and the Men Who Made It,* Hofstadter argued that the liberal tradition had failed because it could not escape the acquisitive and individualistic assumptions that had originally shaped it. Supposed reformers such as the Populists and Progressives looked back with nostalgia to an era of self-made men; neither faced up to the fundamental problems of an industrialized and corporate America. Even Franklin Delano Roosevelt, who did not share the nostalgia common to the Progressive tradition, was primarily a pragmatist whose attraction lay in the force of his personality rather than in any consistent ideology or philosophy. In *The Age of Reform: From Bryan to F.D.R.* Hofstadter exposed what he saw as the curious blend of racism, nativism, and provincialism that shaped the Populists and would later manifest itself in national paranoid scares such as McCarthyism in the 1950s. All such movements meant "to restore the

---

[19]Louis Hartz, *The Liberal Tradition in America: An Interpretation of American Political Thought Since the Revolution* (New York, 1955).

conditions prevailing before the development of industrialism and the commercialization of agriculture."[20] Hofstadter maintained that American political conflicts mostly reflected not the clash of economic interests but the search by different ethnic and religious groups for a secure status in society. By the latter third of the nineteenth century, Hofstadter asserted, professional scions of Anglo-Saxon Protestant families were finding themselves displaced from traditional positions of leadership by a nouveau-riche plutocracy, on the one hand, and urban immigrant political machines, on the other. Responding to this displacement, the elite launched a moral crusade to resuscitate older Protestant and individualistic values—the Progressive movement. In this campaign "to maintain a homogeneous Yankee civilization," Hofstadter wrote, "I have found much that was retrograde and delusive, a little that was vicious, and a good deal that was comic."[21]

Hofstadter emerged from within the Progressive historiographical tradition, briefly flirted with Marxism in the 1930s, and thereafter considered himself a liberal partisan. In a sense, his entire career can be seen as a lover's quarrel with liberalism, in the course of which he relentlessly exposed its inadequacies, delusions, and failures. The implication of Hofstadter's interpretation was indeed striking: the United States had never had a viable or effective progressive tradition. Those who professed liberalism—Populists, Progressives, and even New Dealers—were mostly well-to-do, middle-to-upper-class reformers, alienated from their society by technological and industrial changes and resentful of those who had succeeded in the scramble for money and status. While Hofstadter himself wrote from the left of the political spectrum, he resisted completely the temptation to find heroic victories for the people in what he saw as a depressing chronicle of consensus based on common cupidity. America was more illiberal than either the Progressive historians or he himself would prefer; they wrote history that fostered the illusion of liberal reform, but he would not.

Hofstadter's powerful critique of American liberalism was shaped not only by his evolving political views, but also by his reading of twentieth-century social science research. Based on that reading he began to address in new ways a familiar set of questions about American society. Who were American reformers and what did they want? Hofstadter used the findings of social scientists to explain the significance of status in shaping social behavior. If abolitionists, Populists, and Progressives had not in fact democratized America, just what had they accomplished? Hofstadter looked to the sociology of bureaucracy and complex organizations, as well as research into the modernization of

---

[20]Richard Hofstadter, *The Age of Reform: From Bryan to F.D.R.* (New York, 1955), p. 62.

[21]Ibid., p. 11.

societies in the European and non-European world, to illuminate an era in which Americans were moving from small towns to big cities, from simple and homogeneous to complex and pluralistic social structures. To explain the reformers' passions he employed social-psychological concepts such as projection, displacement, scapegoating, and the authoritarian personality.

If Hofstadter derived critical insights from social science, another consensus historian, Edmund S. Morgan, looked elsewhere. A student of Perry Miller, the distinguished Harvard historian of early American religion and culture, Morgan echoed his mentor's distrust of Progressive history and of liberalism generally. Liberalism, Miller had believed, possessed few intellectual resources with which to criticize the modern pursuit of individualism, self-expression, and material success. In the premodern and therefore preliberal Puritan world, Morgan (like Miller) found depths of wisdom that seemed lacking in the twentieth century. Wary of those who applied present-day assumptions to the task of understanding the past, Morgan refused to see Puritans as cartoon bluenoses, sexually repressed and obsessed with sin. And he refused to see colonial dissidents as anticipators or forerunners of latter-day democratic liberalism. Thus, in his earliest works he portrayed Anne Hutchinson and Roger Williams not as progressive critics of Puritan oligarchy, but as self-righteous zealots, nihilists even. In contrast, Governor John Winthrop was not a repressive Puritan oligarch but a man striving to live responsibly in a deeply imperfect world, a world that required order more than individual freedom for visionaries.[22]

If Progressives and Marxists insisted that economic interests and material forces shaped history, Morgan would follow his mentor Perry Miller in insisting that ideas mattered. Winthrop and his adversaries were obsessed with ideas, led by them, willing to suffer and even die for them. In 1967, in a striking demonstration of this belief, Morgan admitted that he had been wrong about Roger Williams. *Roger Williams: The Church and the State* argued that Williams's ideas were momentous. He had understood that conscience was not a mask for anarchy but a vehicle of reason, that conscientious protest was an act "not so much of defiance as of discovery." What Roger Williams discovered—what John Winthrop could not—was that separation of church and state was absolutely necessary, first and foremost, to preserve religion from being corrupted by the state, and second, to protect the state from becoming the engine of religious intolerance. Thus, the historian who had begun his career by rebuking modern liberals for misrepresenting the strange world of seventeenth-century Puritanism found himself in the 1960s affirming the connection between Puri-

---

[22]See especially Edmund S. Morgan, *The Puritan Dilemma: The Story of John Winthrop* (Boston, 1958).

tanism and the tradition of civil-libertarian protest that became a hall-mark of the later democratic republic.[23] Perhaps the America he and his students encountered in the 1960s forced this most scrupulous of historians to reflect on what Croce called the contemporaneous character of history.

Morgan's work spanned a great variety of subjects, from Puritan thought, to the Revolution, to slavery. Although he never abandoned his faith in the power of ideas, by the late 1960s his research into the origins of slavery had plunged him deeply into social history, that is, into the realm of group experience and collective fate that seemed very far away from the world of intellectuals and political leaders that had once so occupied him. Executing a dazzling intellectual pirouette, Morgan came to insist that there was nothing incompatible between asserting that consensus dominated mainstream American political and intellectual history and insisting that the most egregious form of oppression—slavery—lay at the heart of the American social experience. Indeed, he claimed, it was precisely because white America relied on slavery to keep the lowest of the low under control, thereby minimizing class conflict among the free, that liberal democracy was able to flower in the late-eighteenth and nineteenth centuries.

Morgan's *American Slavery, American Freedom* is the book named "most admired" more frequently than any other in a recent poll of American historians.[24] Morgan's complex argument cannot be summarized here, but its power can be attributed to its capacity to span the "historiography wars" that marked the history profession in the 1960s and for several decades thereafter. What historian John Higham called the "Cult of American Consensus" had made American history tame and predictable.[25] Within that perspective, eighteenth-century America appeared to be the spawning ground for middle-class democracy; the Revolution was a uniquely intellectual movement; radical abolitionists, Reconstructionists, socialists, and so forth were maladjusted sufferers from status anxiety; and the Cold War was a noble (if reluctant) effort to save the world from totalitarianism. In the face of this antiseptic treatment of the past, dissenters predictably arose. A new generation of neo-Progressives began to insist that conflict not consensus marked the American past.

The assault on consensus history reflected the erosion of political consensus in 1960s America. Already in the late 1950s, the emergence of the civil rights movement signaled the beginning of a new aware-

---

[23]Edmund S. Morgan, *Roger Williams: The Church and the State* (New York, 1967).

[24]Edmund S. Morgan, *American Slavery, American Freedom: The Ordeal of Colonial Virginia* (New York, 1975). The historians' poll and commentary on it can be found in the *Journal of American History*, 81 (December 1994).

[25]John Higham, "The Cult of 'American Consensus': Homogenizing Our History," *Commentary*, 27 (February 1959): 93–100.

ness of inequality and division in American society. For a time, the movement could be subsumed under the rubric of liberal reform, welcomed as a perfection of liberal democracy rather than a fundamental challenge to it. But by the mid-1960s, the racial animosity and poverty that had once been invisible, and for a time appeared readily curable, came to seem more endemic and intractable. Radical inequality would require radical measures—at least, some insisted, measures more radical than integration or the war on poverty. When New Left critics of American society looked back for radical antecedents in contemporary historical accounts, they found chronicles of consensus. But not for long. Increasingly, younger historians found in older Progressive historical works and in neo-Marxist scholarship from Europe the inspiration to rewrite American history as a chronicle of struggle—for working-class power, for racial equality, for women's rights, for ethnic identity, and for all forms of social justice. The Vietnam War added immense energy to this endeavor. As college campuses became centers of protest against the war, historians absorbed the growing suspicion that the U.S. foreign policy establishment served interests quite distinct from "the national interest." They focused their scholarly sights on all forms of concentrated power—corporations, political parties, government bureaucracies, professional organizations, and the like—that seemed to profit from inequality and promote injustice not only in America but around the world.

External pressures only reinforced internal tendencies toward radical critique already under way in the history profession. Some of these were methodological, involving the increased interaction of history with social science, the increased interest in comparative history, and the new use of quantitative methods. While some consensus historians, such as Hofstadter and Hartz, had already begun to pay attention to social science research and comparative approaches, the move to quantification was new. With the exception of economic historians, most historians had no acquaintance with the use of scientifically measurable historical data. One of the attractions of quantitative techniques was quite old-fashioned: like the positivists of the late-nineteenth and early-twentieth centuries, modern-day quantifiers sought the authority of science. They also wanted to strengthen their claim to the growing pools of research money available in the postwar United States from both government and private funders of social science research. At the same time, the urge to quantify was related to a democratic urge to capture the reality of ordinary lives through social history. Peasants, workers, slaves, migrants—whole categories of human beings were invisible because they had been "inarticulate," that is, illiterate and ignored by those who left written documents. Quantitative history suggested a way to make them speak: through records that traced collective behavior and from which ideas, values, intentions, and beliefs might be inferred. Thus John Demos could bring surprisingly to view the interior lives of the earliest settlers of Plymouth colony through the analysis of wills, deeds, contracts, and probate records.[26] On a much broader canvas, Paul Kleppner's quantitative analysis of voting records revealed the ethnic motives of voters in the nineteenth-century Midwest, and Stephen Thernstrom discovered as a result of computer analysis of manuscript censuses and other data the astounding geographical (and limited social) mobility of working-class New Englanders in the industrial era.[27]

Quantitative historians drew inspiration not only from the social and behavioral sciences but also from the work of historians associated with the French journal *Annales*. Led by Lucien Febvre and Marc Bloch, who had begun using quantitative techniques in the 1930s and 1940s, these French historians strove for "total history": a history that recorded the myriad experiences of masses of people, not just the dramatic events that featured prominent actors. In the hands of a leading figure in the *Annales* school, Fernand Braudel, history became a slow, majestic procession of material change—change in population, agricultural production, prices, trade, and so forth—that created, unbeknownst to any individual, the true conditions of life in medieval and early modern Europe. This version of social history was "history with the politics left out," indeed, history with all of the usual markers of individual consciousness left out.[28]

Others trying to write a new social history took a very different tack. For them social history meant history from the bottom up. Though sometimes inspired by the quantifiers' capacity to occupy a distant perch and from there comprehend a vast historical terrain, these new social historians were more interested in small-bore institutional change and group action. They refused to believe that the masses were inaccessible to creative historical research. In fact, social historians began to find copious evidence of conscious thought and action among the lower orders. Slave narratives, diaries of farm wives and artisan workers, letters and articles in obscure newspapers, broadsides and pamphlets, court and police records, institutional memoranda and reports—these and many other sources, having been uncovered or used in new ways, began to give up their secrets. Inspired by the civil rights and antiwar movements, new social historians rewrote American history as a history of struggle. Neo-Progressives, in

---

[26]John Demos, *A Little Commonwealth: Family Life in Plymouth Colony* (New York, 1970).

[27]Paul Kleppner, *The Third Electoral System: 1853–1892: Parties, Voters, and Political Cultures* (Chapel Hill, N.C., 1979); Stephen Thernstrom, *Poverty and Progress: Social Mobility in a Nineteenth-Century City* (Cambridge, Mass., 1964) and *The Other Bostonians: Poverty and Progress in an American Metropolis* (Cambridge, Mass., 1973).

[28]Of Braudel's many works, perhaps the most accessible is *Capitalism and Material Life, 1400–1800* (New York, 1967).

a way, they were far more radical than Beard and Becker. Piecemeal political reform would not easily remake a society hideously distorted by
racism and sexism, dominated by immense corporations, regulated by
"therapeutic" bureaucracies, and dedicated to the systematic exploitation of the Third World. Not Progressive reform, but militant, even
revolutionary activism—like that of artisan revolutionaries in the
1770s, the abolitionists and radical Reconstructionists in the nineteenth century, and the most militant unionists in the 1930s—were
the models for latter-day radicals in the 1960s and 1970s.[29]

As Chapter 3 in Volume II makes clear, among the first subjects to
respond to this approach was labor history or, as it came increasingly
to be called, working-class history. Inspired especially by the English
neo-Marxist E. P. Thompson, new labor historians rewrote the history
of unions and unionization, but more important, of working-class families and communities, working-class politics and culture. The people
whom they studied, far from seeming to be either aspirants to middle-
class status or alien radicals, came to seem at once both more militantly class-conscious and more deeply rooted in American society
and culture. Other fields, such as immigration history, African American history, and women's history, similarly experienced a dramatic renaissance. Both white and black scholars helped to turn the history of
slavery into one of the most exciting and fruitful fields of history. Recovering the seminal scholarship of African American historians such
as W.E.B. Du Bois and Eric Williams,[30] and plunging into previously ignored archival sources, the historians of the 1960s found not passivity
but agency among slaves, not absorption of their descendants into
white culture but cultural resistance and the endurance of African traditions and practices. They insisted that the Civil War had been fought
to abolish slavery, that African Americans played a crucial part in its
conduct and success, and that only force and betrayal—not the alleged
cultural deprivation or political immaturity of blacks—had led to the
failure of Reconstruction.

Women's historians began to effect a similarly profound change in
the standard narrative of American history. If women had been excluded from electoral politics, diplomacy, corporate management, the
academy, the clergy, and other public and therefore conventionally
male realms of power and respectability, they had no less been excluded from the pages of American history. Inspired by the women's
liberation movement and by the simultaneous and notable arrival of

---

[29]A sweeping narrative (and celebration) of the rise of radical history can be found
in Jonathan M. Wiener, "Radical Historians and the Crisis in American History, 1959–
1980," *Journal of American History*, 76 (September 1989): 399–434, part of a "Round
Table" that includes criticism and commentary from a variety of historians and a response from Wiener.

[30]See these and other works cited in Volume I, Chapters 4 and 9.

history from the bottom up in the 1960s and 1970s, male and especially female historians began to hear the voices of women and transfer them to the pages of history.[31] In the suffrage movement and the labor movement; in the records of settlement houses and women's academies and colleges; in the records of births and marriages, of prostitution arrests and temperance campaigns; in the copious records of literary and moral reform publications, in which women argued both for equality and for recognition of their distinctive feminine gifts; and in many other sources, historians of women rewrote the story of America from its very beginnings up to the recent past. They did not merely give women a place in the existing narratives; rather, they reconceived whole fields of history. Thus, for example, the culture of slavery appears to be a realm not simply of *either* accommodation *or* resistance, but—when women are brought centrally into its historical reconstruction—a realm of endurance and cultural creativity.[32] Likewise, the history of Progressive reform becomes the story of women, denied direct access to political office, asserting their right to set the public agenda and to demand maternalist state action in the interest of reforming the social household.[33]

In these and many other ways, historians of women and of African Americans joined a broader wave of socially critical scholarship that had moved very far away from even the history of the most progressive men of earlier generations. The findings of these scholars were so diverse that by the 1980s interpretive coherence vanished from the profession. Many historians feared that fragmentation threatened to consign scholars to increasingly microscopic and specialized enclaves, making it impossible to communicate with one another, let alone a broader public. To others this lack of coherence seemed a healthy state of ferment and pluralistic openness: "Maybe drift and uncertainty," one such historian remarked, ". . . are preconditions for creativity."[34] It is probably true that coherence and fragmentation, harmony and polytonality, the pursuit of the microscopic and the synthetic, are parallel rather than alternative practices within the history profession.

Today it seems that every man and woman has become his or her own historian in a way even Carl Becker would have found surprising

---

[31] See Volume II, Chapter 10.

[32] See Volume I, Chapter 9.

[33] See Volume II, Chapter 6, and also Volume I, Chapter 8.

[34] On the perils of fragmentation, see Thomas Bender, "Wholes and Parts: The Need for Synthesis in American History," *Journal of American History*, 73 (June 1986): 120–36. See the ensuing debate on Bender's essay in "A Round Table: Synthesis in American History," *Journal of American History*, 74 (June 1987): 107–30. See also John Higham, "The Future of American History," *Journal of American History*, 80 (March 1994): 1289–1309. The quotation is from Jackson Lears, "Mastery and Drift," *Journal of American History*, 84 (December 1997): 979–88.

(and cheering). A real measure of success in democratizing the academy in the wake of civil rights and women's rights movements has unseated dominant perspectives and opened the way for diverse schools of interpretation in history and other disciplines. But a diversity of perspectives does not rule out a broadly synthetic multicultural history. The ambition to make sense of a complex past—to narrate a big story—should not be conflated with an urge to drown difference in a wave of false or oppressive homogeneity. To the contrary, if men and women desire "to chart their lives by what they believe to be true," then in that task history "offers a variety of tools for effecting liberation from intrusive authority, outworn creeds, and counsels of despair."[35]

A final note about the way in which each chapter in this collection presents competing interpretations of a common historical phenomenon: while it is certainly true that interpretive argument is among the most common and necessary of practices in the discipline, it is equally true that the "either-or" format can distort the true nature of historians' arguments. Indeed, burlesquing this format is a happy pastime common in graduate student lounges all over the country ("Fat-Free Mozzarella: Noble Experiment or Tragic Error?"). We have, in fact, tried wherever possible in this edition to offer differences in interpretation that are not polar or mutually exclusive, but rather partially overlapping and complementary. Sharp differences there are, and sometimes hot debate produces light. But historians usually do not differ by excluding each other's evidence or utterly demolishing each other's arguments. More often they try to incorporate as much of the former and recast as much of the latter as possible in their efforts to better explain a historical phenomenon. Thus, for example, whereas once Progressive historians might have portrayed the New Deal as a radical advance in liberal reform, and New Left historians as a triumph of corporate hegemony, both William Leuchtenberg and Alan Dawley in their essays in Volume II acknowledge a good deal of common ground, even while clearly disagreeing over important points. Whether the New Deal was "radical within limits" or "conservative with radical implications" remains truly a matter of opinion, but the common ground shared by these two historians makes clear the cumulative and "objective" quality of scholarship on the subject. In coming to a judgment on this and other questions posed in the chapters below, we hope that students will find in the debates, and the historiographical essays that precede them, a pathway to understanding the world they live in and an encouragement to change that world for the better.

---

[35]Appleby et al., *Telling the Truth About History*, pp. 301, 308.

2

THE PURITANS:
ORTHODOXY OR DIVERSITY?

Puritanism occupies a crucial position in the mainstream of American thought. "Puritanism" identifies the religious philosophy and intellectual outlook that characterized New England's first settlers. But, for some, it has also come to stand for an important thread in the development of American civilization. Indeed, one historian of colonial America has gone so far as to remark, "Without some understanding of Puritanism . . . there is no understanding of America."[1]

Just what Puritanism means, however, is a matter of dispute. To one group of historians the Puritans were reactionary bigots—people opposed to freedom of thought, religious liberty, and the idea of democratic government. For these historians Massachusetts represents a perfect case study of the kind of undemocratic colony the Puritans founded. Massachusetts was a theocracy—a state in which the civil government was under the control of the ministers or churches. Resisting change and repressing all dissenting views, Puritan oligarchs banished independent thinkers like Anne Hutchinson and Roger Williams whose radical religious ideas represented a threat to the stability of the colony. They rejected the new ideas of Newtonian science and remained indifferent to cultural matters; they imposed a "glacial period" on the intellectual life of the colony from the 1630s to the outbreak of the American Revolution.

A second group of historians, however, took a much more sympathetic view of the Puritans and the society they created. To them the Puritans were the torchbearers of religious liberty and political freedom—brave pioneers of American democracy. The strict discipline and control exercised by the Puritan oligarchy in Massachusetts was necessitated by the demands of a frontier environment. Within these parameters, the Puritan clergy did everything possible to stimulate intellectual activity, founding the first college and public school system in the American colonies.

This favorable image of the Puritans survived well into the nineteenth century because the writing of American history and literature was dominated by the descendants of Puritans. The so-called filiopi-

---

[1]Perry Miller, *The American Puritans* (New York, 1956), p. ix.

etist school of historians, reflecting both ancestor worship and provincial pride, identified the Puritans as the source of all virtues attributed to the American people—thrift, hard work, and moral earnestness. The accepted view among these historians was that America's contemporary political and religious liberty sprang from the seventeenth-century Puritan tradition.

John Gorham Palfrey took this approach in his five-volume *History of New England* (1858–90). A descendant of early seventeenth-century New England stock, Harvard graduate, and Unitarian clergyman from Boston, Palfrey deeply admired his ancestors, and his work was one long paean of praise in their behalf. "In the colonial history of New England," he wrote, "we follow the strenuous action of intelligent and honest men in building up a free, strong, enlightened, and happy state."[2]

In the 1920s there was a marked change in attitude toward New England Puritanism as historians and commentators began to reexamine different aspects of American culture. Disillusioned with the ambiguous results of World War I and worried by the Russian Revolution, they turned to history with the hope of discovering what was unique and indigenous in the American tradition and in search of a heritage that seemed a logical predecessor to the current national character.

The rise of intellectual history in the post–World War I period was as important a force as cultural nationalism in directing attention of scholars to the study of Puritanism. Throughout the nineteenth and early twentieth centuries, historians who wrote about Puritanism dealt almost exclusively with its political and institutional aspects, not ideas and culture. In the 1920s, however, American historians threw off the old distrust of the study of ideas that had characterized much of nineteenth-century scholarship. Historians now forged ahead on the assumption that the study of Puritan thought was crucial.

The pro-Puritan and anti-Puritan tendencies continued to shape historians' views into the late twentieth century. The Progressive historians who tended to read the social conflicts of their own day back into the nation's past were strongly anti-Puritan. They rewrote American history in terms of economic conflict—as a continuous struggle between the forces of liberalism and conservatism, aristocracy and democracy, and the rich and the poor. The Progressives saw the Puritans as reactionaries.

Three Progressive scholars—James Truslow Adams, Vernon L. Parrington, and Thomas J. Wertenbaker—led an anti-Puritan school of historians in the 1920s. They pictured Puritans as reactionary, authoritarian, bigoted, and hypocritical. These scholars prided themselves on being "realists," and in the debunking era of the postwar period they

---

[2]John Gorham Palfrey, *History of New England*, 5 vols. (Boston, 1875), Vol. IV, p. x.

found a receptive audience when they attacked the myth that the Puritans had founded American democracy.

James Truslow Adams inaugurated this cult of anti-Puritanism with his book *The Founding of New England*, published in 1921. Adams thought Puritans repressed private choice and were intolerant in public life of any deviation from the ruling orthodoxy.[3] No detail of the Puritans' personal conduct was too small to escape a ruling by the oligarchy: "The cut of clothes, the names he bore, the most ordinary social usages, could all be regulated in accordance with the will of God," concluded Adams.[4] In Adams's opinion the Puritan leaders' desire for control was economically, not religiously motivated. Once in America, "They looked with fear, as well as jealousy, upon any possibility of allowing control of policy of law and order, and of legislation concerning persons and property, to pass to others."[5]

Vernon L. Parrington's first volume of his literary history, *Main Currents in American Thought*, published in 1927—*The Colonial Mind*—helped to redirect Puritan studies toward intellectual history. To Parrington, orthodox Puritanism was a reactionary theology. A succession of liberal heroes, like Roger Williams and Anne Hutchinson, who rose up to oppose such reactionary views represented the liberal tradition that America was destined to follow. "In banishing the Antinomians and Separatists and Quakers, the Massachusetts magistrates cast out the spirit of liberalism."[6] For Parrington, then, Puritanism played no part in the native tradition of American liberalism.

The anti-Puritan writers of the 1920s were followed in the 1930s by a host of historians at Harvard University who were more sympathetic to seventeenth-century Puritanism. Three of these scholars—Samuel Eliot Morison, Clifford K. Shipton, and Perry Miller—proceeded to rehabilitate the somewhat battered reputation of the early Puritan leaders. Rather than seeing the Puritans through the lens of twentieth-century liberalism, the Harvard historians studied these early pioneers in the context of their own age and background.

In 1930, Samuel Eliot Morison published his *Builders of the Bay Colony*, a book that proved to be the turning point in this fresh appraisal of the Puritans. In elegant writing, Morison transformed the rigidly stereotyped Puritans presented by Adams, Parrington, and Wertenbaker into living human beings. As he recalled two decades later, his was a lonely voice at the time "crying in the wilderness against the common notion of the grim Puritan . . . steeple-hatted [and] long-faced living in a log cabin and planning a witch-hunt . . . as a holi-

---

[3]James T. Adams, *The Founding of New England* (Boston, 1921), p. 143.

[4]Ibid., p. 79.

[5]Ibid., p. 143.

[6]Vernon L. Parrington, *Main Currents in American Thought*, 3 vols. (New York, 1927–30), Vol. I, p. iv.

day diversion."[7] Morison humanized many of the major Puritan figures by showing that they were not averse to the simple pleasures of life—sex, strong drink, and colorful clothes—but that their dedication and unswerving zeal to serve God provided them with even greater satisfaction.

In a second work, *The Puritan Pronaos*, published in 1936, Morison emphasized the intellectual content of Puritanism. From the Reformation, the Puritans had gained such a love for education and learning that they insisted upon founding elementary and grammar schools and setting up a university even while they were still clearing the forests in Massachusetts. The Puritan creed, he concluded, was "an intellectualized form of Christianity that steered a middle course between a passive acceptance of ecclesiastical authority on the one hand and ignorant emotionalism on the other, and stimulated mental activity on the part of those who professed it."[8]

Clifford K. Shipton, the second of the Harvard historians, produced a series of articles in the 1930s whose general theme was expressed in the title of one of them—"A Plea for Puritanism." One of the most militant defenders of the Puritan contribution to American democratic thought, Shipton was particularly concerned about what he felt was an unfair portrayal of the Puritan clergy as undemocratic and bigoted leaders. The clergy were the most learned class in the Puritan colonies, according to Shipton; they were always open-minded and receptive to new ideas. "Far from being narrow bigots, the ministers were the leaders in every field of intellectual advance in New England."[9]

The work of Perry Miller, the third of the Harvard historians, constituted a landmark in American intellectual history. In the 1930s Miller published two works, *Orthodoxy in Massachusetts* and *The New England Mind: The Seventeenth Century*, which dissected the principal ideas in Puritan thought. Miller argued that reason had played a major role in Puritan theology. Puritans looked upon man as an essentially rational and responsible being despite their belief that he was tainted by original sin. By holding such views the Puritans were taking part in the great intellectual revolution that was being fought all over Europe—the revolt against scholasticism. "Puritanism," according to Miller, "was one of the major expressions of the Western intellect, [in] that it [had] achieved an organized synthesis of concepts which are fundamental to our culture."[10]

---

[7]Samuel Eliot Morison, "Faith of a Historian," *American Historical Review*, 56 (January 1951): 272.

[8]Samuel Eliot Morison, *The Puritan Pronaos* (New York, 1936), p. 264. This work was reissued under the title *The Intellectual Life of Colonial New England* (New York, 1956).

[9]Clifford K. Shipton, "A Plea for Puritanism," *American Historical Review* (April 1935): 467.

[10]Perry Miller, *The New England Mind: The Seventeenth Century* (New York, 1939), p. viii.

In *Orthodoxy in Massachusetts,* published in 1933, Miller showed the seriousness with which people in the early 1600s took their religious ideas and their willingness to create a church and a life that conformed to those ideas. In fact, most of the problems the Puritans encountered in putting their ideas of church government into practice in Massachusetts arose more from their experiences in New England than in opposition from old England. Much of what Miller had to say in this work was not new, but he demonstrated as never before that the history of the Bay Colony during its first two decades could be "strung on the thread of an idea."[11]

Six years later, Miller produced *The New England Mind: The Seventeenth Century,* a more detailed analysis of the ideas of New England Puritanism. Miller took up Puritanism's principal concepts and showed how each was related to the whole and to the Puritan view of human beings. He described the interlocking system of covenants—the covenant of grace, social covenant, and church covenant—that formed the core of Puritan theology. He demonstrated more conclusively than earlier scholars that the doctrine of the covenant was the keystone of Puritanism and argued that this covenant theology made room for man's activity in the process of his own salvation. Thus Puritanism, rather than being fatalistic in outlook, was a stimulus to action. Running throughout this work was the major theme of the transformation of Puritan thought as New World experiences and the passage of time made an impact upon the ideas the settlers had originally brought over with them.[12]

In the second volume of *The New England Mind,* published in 1953 and subtitled *From Colony to Province,* Miller explored change as the second and third generations of Puritans became more provincial and began grappling with the day-to-day problems in the New World. Material success, which sprang from the Puritan idea of a calling—faithfully doing God's appointed work here on earth—undermined spiritual life; Christian brotherhood and Puritan consensus gave way to personal squabbles, theological conflicts were replaced by political struggles, and secular values triumphed over religious aims. Miller's description of the metamorphosis of the Puritan mind from the arrival of the first settlers in the 1620s to the beginnings of Enlightenment thought in the 1720s thereby became a tale of irony as well as change.

Miller's works lifted the study of New England Puritanism out of the narrow framework of national history and placed it within the much broader context of world history. He was able to discover hitherto unsuspected connections between the ideas in America and those

---

[11]Perry Miller, *Orthodoxy in Massachusetts 1630–1680* (Cambridge, Mass., 1933), p. xii.

[12]Miller, *The New England Mind,* passim.

in the rest of the world—among New England Puritanism and Renaissance humanism, the Reformation, and scholasticism. In his hands the study of Puritanism became more than a history of the ideas of the New England founders; it became instead a study of an important epoch in the intellectual history of the Western world. The first selection in this chapter presents Miller's point of view and is drawn from a book of readings he wrote with Thomas H. Johnson.

In the decades since the 1960s, the direction of the study of American Puritanism has entered upon an entirely new phase marked by four main lines of approach. First came the direct revisionist critiques of Miller's monumental work, often by intellectual historians. The second group of contributions were studies by scholars of literature who, in the 1970s, brought literary analysis to bear on Puritan texts and sometimes expanded upon or attacked Miller's hypothesis. Then came the contributions of the "new social historians," who began in the 1960s to study the experience of women within the Puritan world and Puritanism within the microcosm of New England communities. This mounting scholarship was as diversified as it was massive: Between 1960 and 1987 it was estimated that more than one thousand books, articles, and dissertations were written on the Puritans.[13] Finally, in the 1990s, Puritan studies have entered what David Hall has called a postrevisionist phase in which historians are working to integrate the insights of the revisionists into a satisfying whole—both vindicating and reshaping Miller's own views.

The first historians after Miller worked, by necessity, in his shadow. Some revered him not only as the most important Puritan scholar but also as the greatest American historian of the twentieth century. They considered his reconstruction of the Puritan intellectual world to be the towering achievement of American scholarship in our time. According to other scholars, however—especially the "new social historians" of the 1960s—Miller's perspective was flawed, his conclusions unsound, and his writings too highly praised.

Miller's opponents criticized him for focusing on elites and giving little attention to the thinking, beliefs, and behavior of the common people. His view of Puritanism, they argued, was unrepresentative; it was reconstructed from the writings of well-educated Puritan clergymen rather than from those of the average layman. Second, Miller concentrated on the inner life of abstract ideas and disregarded the social and economic forces from which such ideas sprang. Third, he assumed a unity in Puritan experience that was belied by a multiplicity of believers and sects. Fourth, he erroneously held that the New England Puritans had formulated their covenant theology to free themselves from the terrible uncertainty of a strict, predestinarian Calvinism, that

---

[13]David D. Hall, "On Common Ground: The Coherence of American Puritan Studies," *William and Mary Quarterly*, 3d Ser., 44 (1987): 193.

is, a religious view in which God had, at the beginning of time, already determined who would be saved and who would be damned. And finally, he incorrectly pictured Puritanism as being in a process of gradual spiritual decline; he postulated a "declension" of the New England mind and a trend toward secularism and materialism as religious orthodoxy weakened during the seventeenth century.

Intellectual historians in the 1950s and 1960s argued that Miller had overintellectualized the Puritan experience at the expense of their emotional engagement. Others showed that there was no "declension" in church membership among women, only men. And Michael Walzer, a political scientist, made the case for Puritans as radicals attempting to change not only society and politics, but also religion.[14]

The intellectual historian David D. Hall, one of Miller's sharpest critics in the 1970s, examined the relationship between Puritan ideas and the New England social and economic environment. His study of the Puritan ministry in *The Faithful Shepherd* showed that the migration from England posed new problems for ministers, forcing many to rethink the older teachings inherited from English Puritanism. But, Hall concluded, the ideas and values derived from the mother country were probably more influential in shaping the New England ministers.[15]

Many other intellectual historians challenged Miller's interpretation on different grounds in the 1970s. Robert Middlekauff, for example, in a thoughtful multiple biography of members of the Mather family, disagreed with Miller's depiction of a "declension" in the Puritan sense of mission. Examining three generations of Mather ministers—Richard, Increase, and Cotton—Middlekauff found a different pattern, one that showed a spiritual strengthening and growing piety over time.[16]

---

[14]Alan Simpson, *Puritanism in Old and New England* (Chicago, 1955); Norman Pettit, *The Heart Prepared* (New Haven, 1966); Robert G. Pope, *The Half-Way Covenant* (Princeton, N.J., 1969); and Michael Walzer, *Revolution of the Saints* (Cambridge, Mass., 1965).

[15]David D. Hall, *The Faithful Shepherd* (Chapel Hill, N.C., 1972). In "Understanding the Puritans," in Herbert J. Bass, ed., *The State of American History* (Chicago, 1970), pp. 330–49, Hall summarized some of the critical reaction to Miller's account of the relationship between Puritanism and Calvinism. James Hoopes, a supporter of Miller, organized a conference on his work in 1982 at Babson College, taking up the issue of "declension" and popular religious beliefs in New England. Hoopes argued for the internal coherence of Miller's work. James Hoopes, "Art as History: Perry Miller's New England Mind," *American Quarterly,* 34 (1984): 3–25. Scholars including David D. Hall, Joyce Appleby, P. M. G. Harris, and Margaret Sobczak attacked "declension." In 1982, Francis T. Butts defended Miller, claiming the revisionists were attacking a caricature rather than Miller's real assumptions. Joyce Appleby, "History as Art: Another View"; David D. Hall, "A Readers' Guide to the New England Mind: The Seventeenth Century"; P. M. G. Harris, "Of Two Minds, Falsely Sundered: Faith and Reason, Duality and Complexity, Art and Science in Perry Miller and in Puritan New England"; and Margaret Sobczak, "Hoopes' Symposium on Perry Miller." *American Quality,* 34 (1984): 25–48.

[16]Robert Middlekauff, *The Mathers* (New York, 1972).

Historians critical of Miller, such as Philip Gura, objected that Miller, in his *New England Mind*, in particular, had treated Puritan literature as though it were the product of a single homogeneous group. Philip Gura, like others before him, noted the well-known presence of prominent dissenters from the tradition. Such persons as Roger Williams and Anne Hutchinson and such groups as Quakers, certain Baptist sects, and some millennarians constituted a long line of radicals who were just as Puritan as John Winthrop's mainstream orthodox establishment. The second selection in this chapter is from Gura's book, *A Glimpse of Sion's Glory*.[17]

Other intellectual historians attacked the Miller thesis from different angles. Theodore D. Bozeman in *To Live Ancient Lives* provided an important corrective to Miller's "errand" hypothesis. Miller had argued in his influential essay "Errand into the Wilderness" that the Puritans intended the Massachusetts Bay Colony to be a shining example to save England from its excesses by providing a perfect model of society. Bozeman insisted, however, that a careful reading of the primary sources, taking seriously the Puritans' own words, failed to justify such a conclusion.[18]

Some intellectual historians, such as David D. Hall, focused upon the lay or popular beliefs of New Englanders to challenge Miller's depiction of one New England mind. In *Worlds of Wonder, Days of Judgment*, Hall demonstrated the importance of folk beliefs, the appeal of "magic," the popular "wonder" books of the era, rates of literacy, and common rituals of the conversion process to show how broad was their role in shaping the religious beliefs in America. By revealing the impact of popular beliefs and practices on New England culture, Hall showed that organized religion was only one way in which the Puritans viewed their place in the cosmos.[19]

By introducing popular culture into the religious perspective, Hall completely changed the parameters of the debate about Puritanism and scored a permanent blow for the Miller critics. Whether scholars defended, extended, or criticized Miller's work, they had to take into account the new broadened picture of New England culture. So Harry S. Stout read several thousand sermons in manuscript and showed that Miller's picture of the pervasiveness of Puritanism in New England so-

---

[17]Philip Gura, *A Glimpse of Sion's Glory* (Middletown, Conn., 1984).

[18]Theodore D. Bozeman, *To Live Ancient Lives* (Chapel Hill, N.C., 1988).

[19]Francis T. Butts, "The Myth of Perry Miller," *American Historical Review*, 87 (1982): 665–94. For a penetrating critique of Miller that points out some fundamental flaws in his work, see Arihu Zakai, "'Epiphany in Matadi': Perry Miller's Orthodoxy in Massachusetts and the Meaning of American History," *Reviews in American History*, 13 (1985): 627–40.

ciety and culture held up. Norman Piering suggested that the inner life of New Englanders developed over a long time, and that new theories of the mind led to a more subjective life that subsequently gave rise to more complicated theories. James Hoopes, though not addressing Miller directly, formulated a view of conversion (the crucial event in Puritan life as self-interpretation), and sought to connect Puritanism with some of the more modern notions of self. Charles L. Cohen likewise analyzed the conversion experience along the lines of ideas about the self. His work, like that of Stout, Fiering, Hoopes, Bozeman, and others, showed that the intellectual history approach that had generally fallen into disrepute proved to be one of the most fruitful perspectives employed in the study of Puritanism throughout the 1980s.[20]

The second line of approach in post-Miller Puritan studies used the methods of literary criticism to analyze religious and social phenomena. These scholars, who were not focused specifically on doing battle with Miller, brought about a dramatic change in the understanding of the Puritan imagination and the relationship between literature and ideas by employing new theories such as deconstruction, semiotics, and gender analysis. They suggested that the ideas developed in New England had given rise to a powerful myth—the myth of New England as the place God had chosen to create His millennial kingdom on earth as the New Jerusalem. The Puritan vision originated the notion of New England as a separate and exceptional place. This regional self-identity, in turn, produced the national myth of American exceptionalism, the idea that America was unique and fundamentally different from Europe and the rest of the world. Perry Miller himself, of course, had been an exemplar of American exceptionalism, and many literary scholars drew their inspiration from him. Criticism in this vein also shone light for the first time on negative aspects of American exceptionalism, particularly its racism and violence.

Sacvan Bercovitch, perhaps better than any other literary scholar, expanded upon Miller's notion of a Puritan mission and the concept of American identity. In his *Puritan Origins of the American Self*, Bercov-

---

[20]David D. Hall, *Worlds of Wonder, Days of Judgment* (New York, 1989); Harry S. Stout, *The New England Soul* (New York, 1986); Norman Piering, *Moral Philosophy at Seventeenth-Century Harvard* (Chapel Hill, N.C., 1981); James Hoopes, *Consciousness in New England* (Baltimore, 1989); Charles L. Cohen, *God's Caress* (New York, 1986); David D. Hall, "Religion and Society: Problems and Reconsiderations," in Jack P. Greene and J. R. Pole, eds., *Colonial British America* (Baltimore, 1984), p. 325. Michael McGiffert, a historian of religion, showed how preachers in Elizabethan England groped their way to new concepts of the covenant of grace and the covenant of works in the late seventeenth century. See Michael McGiffert, "Grace and Works: The Rise and Division of Covenant Theology in Elizabethan Puritanism," *Harvard Theological Review*, 7S (1982): 463–502; "Tyndale's Conception of Covenant," *Journal of Ecclesiastical History*, 32 (1981): 167-84. See also the important work of another historian of religion, Charles Hambrick-Stowe, *The Practice of Piety* (Chapel Hill, N.C., 1980).

itch explored the essence of Puritan rhetoric through literary analysis of language, symbolism, and myth. To Bercovitch, early New England rhetoric provided the religious framework for the production of values, later to become secular, with which America would become identified: human perfectibility, individualism, technological progress, and democracy. In Bercovitch's view, such American writers as Ralph Waldo Emerson came directly from the Puritan rhetorical tradition.[21]

In a later study, *The American Jeremiad*, Bercovitch revised Miller's somewhat pessimistic view of this kind of political sermon, which stressed the failings of the people of New England as a way to explain their political and social difficulties. Where Miller's interpretation of the jeremiad led to "declension" or a falling away from early piety, Bercovitch concluded that the Puritan cry of "declension" was part of a strategy designed to revitalize the idea of an "errand into the wilderness." Where Miller saw decline in the seventeenth century, Bercovitch argued that Puritanism succeeded in giving rise to a "myth" of an eternal American mission that has characterized middle-class culture.[22]

Very recently, Michael Kauffman, in *Institutional Individualism*, has taken issue with Bercovitch's discovery that in the Puritans' strenuous denial of the self, paradoxically, lay the birth of the modern individual. Kauffman believes this anachronistic claim misreads the Puritans' idea of identity. Kauffman argues instead that individuals in early New England formed their identities in the specific context of their institutions. This institutionally dependent identity preceded a modern notion of the independent, striving individual.[23]

Some literary scholars uncovered and pursued the dark side to Berkovitch's narrative, finding violent intolerance toward the "other" implicated in the same myth. Richard Slotkin's *Regeneration Through Violence* explores these themes, particularly as Puritan and later national ideology sanctioned Indian killing. Following on Slotkin, Ann Kibbey, a feminist literary scholar, found in the way Puritans constructed supernatural power a link to violence, particularly toward Indians. In 1998, Jill Lepore, in a sweeping literary analysis of the New England histories of King Philip's War in 1676–77, connected these writings to the development of American identity. She argues that "wounds and words—the injuries and their interpretation—cannot be

---

[21]Sacvan Bercovitch, *Puritan Origins of the American Self* (New Haven, Conn., 1975).

[22]Sacvan Bercovitch, *The American Jeremiad* (Madison, Wisc., 1978). For a searching review essay from which much of this discussion is drawn, see Gordon S. Wood, "Struggle Over the Puritans," *New York Review of Books*, Nov. 8, 1989.

[23]Michael Kauffman, *Institutional Individualism, Conversion, Exile, and Nostalgia in Puritan New England* (Middletown, Conn., 1998).

separated, that acts of war generate acts of narration, and that both types of acts are often joined in a common purpose: defining the geographical, political, cultural, and sometimes racial and national boundaries between peoples."[24]

Patricia Caldwell, a literary scholar and student of Miller's disciple Alan Heimert, used the tools of her discipline in the 1980s to reinforce the Miller thesis concerning the importance of the Puritan conversion experience. She, too, supported the concept of a Puritan literary tradition that served as the foundation for a distinctly American literature. Her thesis in this regard was reflected in the subtitle of her book *The Puritan Conversion Narrative: The Beginnings of American Expression.*[25]

Some literary scholars, like intellectual historians, did not agree with Miller. Andrew Delbanco, for example, denied that there was any grand "errand" or journey toward the millennium in the minds of the Puritans when they came to America. The Puritans, according to him, were fleeing the chaos they found in England and in themselves.[26]

The third major development in Puritan studies was the appearance of the "new social historians" from the 1960s on. They rejected Miller's approach that claimed the early history of New England could be strung "on the thread of an idea." Writing New England's local history from the bottom up, these scholars studied secular records—wills, deeds, tax lists, town records, and registers of births, marriages, and deaths—to reconstruct the development of Puritan communities and to understand the communitarian values that shaped them. They were concerned with precise conclusions and insights from other disciplines such as social psychology, historical demography, and cultural anthropology.

A whole host of community studies of New England written between the 1960s and the end of the 1980s analyzed the impact of Puritanism on the everyday life of the early settlers. Historians explored a number of themes that Miller had either failed to look at, such as family dynamics, inheritance patterns, and witchcraft, or that he had written about without providing a socioeconomic base, such as the idea of a declension, or a falling away from communitarian ideals. While all of this history revised the belief that intellectual history alone was a sufficient way to understand the Puritans, some of the revisionists chal-

---

[24]Richard Slotkin, *Regeneration Through Violence, the Mythology of the American Frontier* (Middletown, Conn., 1973); Ann Kibbey, *The Interpretation of Material Shapes in Puritanism: A Study of Rhetoric, Prejudice and Violence* (New York, 1986); Jill Lepore, *The Name of War, King Philip's War and the Origins of American Identity* (New York, 1998).

[25]Patricia Caldwell, *The Puritan Conversion Narrative: The Beginnings of American Expression* (New York, 1983).

[26]Andrew Delbanco, *Puritan Ordeal* (Cambridge, Mass., 1989).

lenged Miller's idea with their research, while others ended up confirming or elaborating on observations he had made.

Sumner Chilton Powell's *Puritan Village*, for instance, demonstrated that local English institutions were transformed by the Puritans to produce a new kind of community in Sudbury, Massachusetts. As with Miller's Puritanism, what was transplanted was transformed. Arguing instead for continuity, David Grayson Allen showed the persistence of English laws and customs in the New World in his *In English Ways*.[27]

Kenneth Lockridge traced the evolution of local institutions in Dedham, Massachusetts, over a one-hundred-year period. He concluded that the town during its first fifty years was a "Christian Utopian Closed Corporate community." But in the second fifty years, conflicts eroded the prevailing consensus, shattered the Puritan vision of a perfect society, and gave rise to a modern provincial town. Lockridge's story refined the declension theme by providing it with an economic and political base.[28]

In another view of the religious and social stresses caused by increasing economic success, Paul Boyer and Stephen Nissenbaum studied witchcraft in *Salem Possessed*. Severe tensions developed in Salem because of the emerging merchant capitalism resulting from rising commercialism, the explosive rate of population growth, and the decreasing availability of land. These material developments conflicted with accepted Puritan values and helped provoke the outbreak of witchcraft hysteria, which, according to Boyer and Nissenbaum, was caused by these stresses rather than by the Puritan dogmatism and bigotry emphasized in the older and more traditional interpretations.[29]

Virginia DeJohn Anderson focused on a community within a community, some seven hundred of the Great Migration generation. Applying new social historical methods to a theme Perry Miller had explored, Anderson was searching for the origins of Puritan exceptionalism. She looked to the experience of crossing the ocean, town planting, and community building to explain the distinctive legacy of the Puritans. Meanwhile, others, in the revisionist tradition of David Cressy, were challenging precisely this notion and arguing, as the Pro-

---

[27]Sumner Chilton Powell, *Puritan Village* (Middletown, Conn., 1963), and David Grayson Allen, in *English Ways* (Chapel Hill, N.C., 1981). The literature on Puritan community studies is voluminous, and the studies cited are merely representative of certain theses or generalizations. Among the first of the community studies to challenge Miller's findings directly was Darrett Rutman, *Winthrop's Boston* (Chapel Hill, N.C., 1965). See also his *American Puritanism: Faith and Practice* (Philadelphia, 1970). For the relationship between law and society, see David T. Konig, *Law and Society in Puritan Massachusetts, Essex County, 1629—1692* (Chapel Hill, N.C., 1982).

[28]Kenneth Lockridge, *A New England Town* (New York, 1970).

[29]Paul Boyer and Stephen Nissenbaum, *Salem Possessed* (Cambridge, Mass., 1979).

gressives had, that there was nothing particularly religious about the motivation of the emigrants and that there was nothing particularly Puritan about most of the residents of New England.[30]

Studies of the colonial family by the new social historians also provided important insights into the Puritan value system and behavior. John Demos in his study of the Plymouth colony in the seventeenth century, *A Little Commonwealth,* pioneered an exploration of Puritan child-rearing practices and resorted to the techniques of demography, social psychology, and archeology to arrive at his conclusions. Philip Greven in *Four Generations* argued, as did Demos, that the family was the key institution in socializing the individual within the Puritan community. Greven studied changes within the family household and community structure in Andover, Massachusetts, over four generations and concluded that landholding practices, geographical mobility, birth-and-death rates, marriage customs, and intergenerational relationships all helped to shape the outlines of this Puritan town in new ways.[31]

But there was increasing disenchantment with the large number of community studies that had appeared by the end of the 1980s. Although the studies were interesting individually, there was growing skepticism about their offering collectively much in the way of new generalizations about Puritanism, or about anything else for that matter. No community could be taken as being typical of a region or colony or as representative of the American colonies as a whole. As Darrett Rutman pointed out, moreover, American colonial historians assumed that Puritanism led to communal cohesiveness, while English historians saw Puritans as being a divisive force in the villages of the mother country. Thus, the definition of the term "Puritan" itself came under question. To use community studies to discover more about Puritanism, Rutman concluded, "new social historians" would have to explore outward links—economic, governmental, political, religious, and intellectual—between individual communities and surrounding places.[32]

Historians of women who had been influenced by the new social history looked at Puritan life from the standpoint of gender to understand more about power relations among Puritans and women's roles

---

[30]Virginia DeJohn Anderson, *New England's Generation, the Great Migration and the Formation of Society and Culture in the Seventeenth Century* (New York, 1991); David Cressy, *Coming Over: Migration and Communication Between England and New England* (New York, 1987).

[31]John Demos, *A Little Commonwealth* (New York, 1970), and Philip Greven, *Four Generations* (Ithaca, 1970). The work on this subject by the "new social historians" was preceded by Edmund S. Morgan's insightful *Puritan Family* (Boston, 1944).

[32]Darrett Rutman, "Assessing the Communities of Early America," *William and Mary Quarterly,* 3d series (1986): pp. 163–78.

in preserving communitarian values, and to challenge Miller's idea of a single New England spirituality. Lyle Koehler, in *A Search for Power*, argued, as the title suggests, that Anne Hutchinson's banishment solidified a tendency among Puritan men to subjugate women. They responded by seeking power in a variety of ways, including defying sexual prohibitions. Many historians thought his argument was too much influenced by contemporary assumptions and preferred Laurel Thatcher Ulrich's *Goodwives* which focused on women's experience in the family and household economy and among neighbors. She retrieved women's experience by looking at several well-defined biblical roles. By studying northern New England she showed that strict Puritan theology was diluted in daily life by English village culture. Robert Saint George, in an article on slander in Puritan communities, observed how women took a significant role policing the moral bounds of the community. Mary Maples Dunn, however, looked at Puritan sources for women's religious and moral activism and compared these, unfavorably, with the experience of Quaker women.[33]

Looking at the law from the perspective of gender provided insight into Puritan methods of enforcing their moral—particularly, their sexual—code. Nancy Hull, studying the Puritan legal system and its effect on women, found them particularly susceptible to being punished for sexual transgressions, and disproportionate punishment increased dramatically when the women were black. Later, Cornelia Dayton Hughes, studying women and the law in the highly orthodox New Haven colony, found that women under the Puritans in the seventeenth century fared better in the legal process than they did in the more secular atmosphere of the eighteenth century.[34]

In 1987, Carol Karlsen was the first, astonishingly, to analyze witchcraft from the standpoint of gender. In her innovative study, *The Devil in the Shape of a Woman*, she employed tools from psychology and cultural anthropology, as had John Demos in his earlier study, *Entertaining Satan*. Her work revealed how Puritan ideology, despite its emphasis on the equality of male and female souls in the eyes of God, saw specific spiritual vulnerabilities in women that led to a greater likelihood that

---

[33]Lyle Koehler, *A Search for Power: The "Weaker Sex," in Seventeenth Century New England* (Urbana, 1980); Laurel Thatcher Ulrich, *Goodwives, Image and Reality in the Lives of Women in Northern New England, 1650–1750* (New York, 1982); Robert Saint George, "Heated Speech, and Literacy in Seventeenth-Century New England," in *Seventeenth Century New England* (Boston, 1985); Mary Maples Dunn, "Saints and Sinners, Congregational and Quaker Women in the Early Colonial Period," *American Quarterly*, 30 (1978): 582–601. See also Jennifer Monaghan, "Literacy Instruction and Gender in Colonial New England," *American Quarterly*, 40 (March 1988): 18–41, for a discussion of how and why so many Puritan women learned to read.

[34]Nancy E. Hull, *Female Felons* (Urbana, Ill., 1987); Cornelia Dayton Hughes, *Women Before the Bar, Gender, Law and Society in Connecticut, 1639–1789* (Chapel Hill, N.C., 1995).

they would be perceived as practicing witchcraft. Her study also found a significant correlation between displays of women's independence—especially ownership of property—and witchcraft accusations. Very recently, Elizabeth Reis, in *Damned Women*, has explored the ideological origins of Puritan views of women's characteristic weaknesses that opened them to charges of witchcraft.[35]

Other "new social historians" employed interdisciplinary approaches to demonstrate Puritan strategies of obtaining consensus and conformity. Kai T. Erikson, for example, used sociological and psychological theories to study those groups that Puritans defined as deviants. He then showed what constituted the "boundaries" of acceptable behavior within Puritan society. Michael Zuckerman, using cultural anthropology, concluded that a kind of communal consensus created peace, order, and harmony within a number of eighteenth-century towns based in part on a carry-over of Puritan cultural ideals. These communities remained "peaceable kingdoms" until the eve of the Revolution, according to Zuckerman, despite underlying social tensions.[36]

All of these different lines of approach to Puritanism resulted in shattering or questioning Miller's synthesis, but they gave rise to problems of their own. Social historians, particularly those involved in community studies to explore Puritanism, appeared to have foundered on the problem of how representative these communities were. Intellectual historians dismantled Miller's notion of the covenant as a compromise provoked by the unbearably high anxiety engendered by predestination, but no one could come up with a convincing theory that seemed to define Puritans as a group and what held New England together. Literary historians with their new perspectives provided new overviews of New England and its mythology, but their analytic methods, such as deconstruction and the absence of economic and social evidence, did not persuade most traditional historians.

In a new work on Puritans, a recent scholar has looked back on this welter of studies and described certain of its underlying asumptions. Darren Staloff argues that the revisionist or anti-Miller synthesis is an essentially conservative view of the Puritans, one that he attempts to disprove.[37] Revisionists, such as David Hall, have rejected the notion of

---

[35]Carol Karlsen, *The Devil in the Shape of a Woman, Witchcraft in Colonial New England* (New York, 1987); John Demos, *Entertaining Satan: Witchcraft and the Culture of Early New England* (New York, 1982); Elizabeth Reis, *Damned Women, Sinners and Witches in Puritan New England* (Ithaca, N.Y., 1997).

[36]Kai T. Erikson, *Wayward Puritans* (New York, 1966), and Michael Zuckerman, *Peaceable Kingdoms* (New York, 1970).

[37]Darren Staloff, *The Making of an American Thinking Class, Intellectuals and Intelligentsia in Puritan Massachusetts* (Oxford, 1998). Staloff's invaluable Appendix B (pp. 192–205) is the basis for these remarks on postrevisionism and Perry Miller.

a broad consensus on Puritanism that left out the bottom half of the population entirely and homogenized many differences of belief among the others. Scholars continue to argue, as they did against Miller, that there has been an overemphasis on ideas and an underemphasis on the social and economic differences among dissenters. In Staloff's new attempt at a synthesis, taking into consideration the social, political, and institutional influences on Puritanism is necessary, but so is acknowledging the immense importance of the Puritan clergy. Staloff sees this group's struggle for power and status as directly linked to a mobilization of middling and lower orders into the Puritan cause. "The flowering of Puritan divinity was then, in part at least, the religious mobilization of the 'popular' elements of the political nation by a semi-underground ministry."[38] Staloff attempts to fold in the arguments of the (now older) "new" social historians such as Michael Walzer about the democractic urgency of Puritanism, by finding political radicalism in the Puritan emphasis on the authority of the Bible over church hierarchy. Puritan ministers interpreted the Bible, to be sure, and therein lay the source of their own power. But ultimately, in the emphasis on literacy and the individual's ability to read and understand scripture for himself, the Puritan message could undermine all temporal authority. This radical realization of Puritanism could only have happened in the New World. "The most profound political result of the truncation of the English social order [in America] was the dramatic increase in the power of the educated gentry, professionals, and clergy who crossed the Atlantic." "New England is thus key to unfolding the radical nature of Puritan dissent. . . . A postrevisionist interpretation puts New England back at the center of Miller's Calvinist internationale."[39]

Staloff sustained Miller's conviction that New England Congregationalism was a unique and a vital strain of American culture. His rendition gave precedence to a relatively small group of individuals whose concern about their own status overlapped fortuitously with the democratic desires of middling and lower sorts. How long this synthesis will hold against criticisms that it has placed too much emphasis on ideas, rather than material realities, that it gives pride of place to the machinations of a small, relatively elite group, or that it unduly exalts the importance of Puritans in shaping New England and vice versa remains to be seen.

Already Louise Breen has argued against this postrevisionist synthesis. The "social context drove the theological debate," she insisted. "Few Puritans lived without the temptation to free themselves from the confining intellectual and social bonds" of Winthrop's city on a

---

[38]Staloff, *Thinking*, p. 202.
[39]Ibid., p. 204.

hill. The poor do not seem to be mobilized to the cause of the clergy here and the radicalism is economic, ideological, and divisive. And Thomas N. Ingersoll, in his marvelously titled 1999 article, "'Riches and Honor Were Rejected by Them as Loathsome Vomit': The Fear of Levelling in New England," presented the Puritan clergy lumping together with horror radical religious sectarians and the undeferential poor. He showed these two often overlapping groups managing to inch the Puritan elite, kicking and screaming, toward greater democracy.[40]

Questions persist about Puritanism and its relation to New England and America. Were Puritans bigots, obsessed with ridding themselves of the "other," or consensus-minded community-builders? Were the Puritans pious idealists concerned mainly with maintaining their special Protestant way of life? Or were they practical-minded pioneers, simply seeking to make their way and establish viable settlements in the New World? Were they part of a conservative social and religious movement dedicated to stability at all costs? Or were they a radical movement that needed the institutional vacuum of the New World to realize its potential for religious and intellectual innovation? Was Puritanism as a cultural movement restricted to its own time in terms of its influence? Or did it give rise to a New England myth and later a national myth of manifest destiny? Was Puritan devotion repressive or essentially progressive in its effect on daily life? These are some of the questions that occur in trying to determine the precise role of the Puritans and their proper place in American history.

---

[40]Louise Breen, "Religious Radicalism in the Puritan Officer Corps: Heterodoxy, the Artillery Company, and Cultural Integration in Seventeenth Century Boston," quoted in Thomas N. Ingersoll, "'Riches and Honor Were Rejected by Them as Loathsome Vomit': The Fear of Levelling in New England," in Carla Gardina Pestana and Sharon Salinger, eds., *Inequality in Early America* (Hanover, N.H., 1999), p. 48.

PERRY MILLER AND
THOMAS H. JOHNSON

PERRY MILLER (1905–63) was professor of American literature at Harvard University until his death. He was the author of numerous articles and books, including The New England Mind, 2 vols. *(1939–53),* Errand into the Wilderness *(1956),* Jonathan Edwards *(1949), and* The Life of the Mind in America: From the Revolution to the Civil War *(1965).* THOMAS H. JOHNSON *(1902–86) taught for many years at the Lawrenceville School in New Jersey as well as at a number of universities. He was the author of* Emily Dickinson: An Interpretive Biography *(1955) and* The Oxford Companion to American History *(1966).*

Puritanism may perhaps be described as that point of view, that philosophy of life, that code of values, which was carried to New England by the first settlers in the early seventeenth century. Beginning thus, it has become one of the continuous factors in American life and American thought. Any inventory of the elements that have gone into the making of the "American mind" would have to commence with Puritanism. It is, indeed, only one among many: if we should attempt to enumerate these traditions, we should certainly have to mention such philosophies, such "isms," as the rational liberalism of Jeffersonian democracy, the Hamiltonian conception of conservatism and government, the Southern theory of racial aristocracy, the Transcendentalism of nineteenth-century New England, and what is generally spoken of as frontier individualism. Among these factors Puritanism has been perhaps the most conspicuous, the most sustained, and the most fecund. Its role in American thought has been almost the dominant one, for the descendants of Puritans have carried at least some habits of the Puritan mind into a variety of pursuits, have spread across the country, and in many fields of activity have played a leading part. The force of Puritanism, furthermore, has been accentuated because it was the first of these traditions to be fully articulated, and because it has inspired certain traits which have persisted long after the vanishing of the original creed. Without some understanding of Puritanism, it may safely be said, there is no understanding of America.

Yet important as Puritanism has undoubtedly been in shaping the nation, it is more easily described than defined. It figures frequently in

Perry Miller and Thomas H. Johnson, eds., *The Puritans* (New York: Anerican Book Company, 1938), pp. 1–19. Reprinted with omissions by permission of the American Book Company.

controversy of the last decade, very seldom twice with exactly the same connotation. Particularly of recent years has it become a hazardous feat to run down its meaning. In the mood of revolt against the ideals of previous generations which has swept over our period, Puritanism has become a shining target for many sorts of marksmen. Confusion becomes worse confounded if we attempt to correlate modern usages with anything that can be proved pertinent to the original Puritans themselves. To seek no further, it was the habit of proponents for the repeal of the Eighteenth Amendment during the 1920s to dub Prohibitionists "Puritans," and cartoonists made the nation familiar with an image of the Puritan: a gaunt, lank-haired killjoy, wearing a black steeple hat and compounding for sins he was inclined to by damning those to which he had no mind. Yet any acquaintance with the Puritans of the seventeenth century will reveal at once, not only that they did not wear such hats but also that they attired themselves in all the hues of the rainbow, and furthermore that in their daily life they imbibed what seem to us prodigious quantities of alcoholic beverages, with never the slightest inkling that they were doing anything sinful. True, they opposed drinking to excess, and ministers preached lengthy sermons condemning intoxication, but at such pious ceremonies as the ordination of new ministers the bill for rum, wine, and beer consumed by the congregation was often staggering. Increase Mather himself—who in popular imagination is apt to figure along with his son Cotton as the archembodiment of the Puritan—said in one of his sermons:

> Drink is in it self a good creature of God, and to be received with thankfulness, but the abuse of drink is from Satan; the wine is from God, but the Drunkard is from the Devil.

Or again, the Puritan has acquired the reputation of having been blind to all aesthetic enjoyment and starved of beauty; yet the architecture of the Puritan age grows in the esteem of critics and the household objects of Puritan manufacture, pewter and furniture, achieve prohibitive prices by their appeal to discriminating collectors. Examples of such discrepancies between the modern usage of the word and the historical fact could be multiplied indefinitely. It is not the purpose of this volume to engage in controversy, nor does it intend particularly to defend the Puritan against the bewildering variety of critics who on every side today find him an object of scorn or pity. In his life he neither asked nor gave mercy to his foes; he demanded only that conflicts be joined on real and explicit issues. By examining his own words it may become possible to establish, for better or for worse, the meaning of Puritanism as the Puritan himself believed and practiced it.

Just as soon as we endeavor to free ourselves from prevailing conceptions or misconceptions, and to ascertain the historical facts about seventeenth-century New Englanders, we become aware that we face still another difficulty: not only must we extricate ourselves from interpretations that have been read into Puritanism by the twentieth century, but still more from those that have been attached to it by the eighteenth and nineteenth. The Puritan philosophy, brought to New England highly elaborated and codified, remained a fairly rigid orthodoxy during the seventeenth century. In the next age, however, it proved to be anything but static; by the middle of the eighteenth century there had proceeded from it two distinct schools of thought, almost unalterably opposed to each other. Certain elements were carried into the creeds and practices of the evangelical religious revivals, but others were perpetuated by the rationalists and the forerunners of Unitarianism. Consequently our conception of Puritanism is all too apt to be colored by subsequent happenings; we read ideas into the seventeenth century which belong to the eighteenth, and the real nature of Puritanism can hardly be discovered at all, because Puritanism itself became two distinct and contending things to two sorts of men. The most prevalent error arising from this fact has been the identification of Puritanism with evangelicalism in many accounts, though in histories written by Unitarian scholars the original doctrine has been almost as much distorted in the opposite direction.

Among the evangelicals the original doctrines were transformed or twisted into the new versions of Protestantism that spawned in the Great Awakening of the 1740s, in the succeeding revivals along the frontier and through the back country, in the centrifugal speculations of enraptured prophets and rabid sects in the nineteenth century. All these movements retained something of the theology or revived something of the intensity of spirit, but at the same time they threw aside so much of authentic Puritanism that there can be no doubt the founding fathers would vigorously have repudiated such progeny. They would have had no use, for instance, for the camp meeting and the revivalist orgy; "hitting the sawdust trail" would have been an action exceedingly distasteful to the most ardent among them. What we know as "fundamentalism" would have been completely antipathetic to them, for they never for one moment dreamed that the truth of scripture was to be maintained in spite of or against the evidences of reason, science, and learning. The sects that have arisen out of Puritanism have most strikingly betrayed their rebellion against the true spirit of their source by their attack upon the ideal of a learned ministry; Puritans considered religion a very complex, subtle, and highly intellectualized affair, and they trained their experts in theology with all the care we would lavish upon preparing men to be engineers or chemists. For the same reasons, Puritans would object strenuously to almost all recent attempts to "humanize" religion, to smooth over hard doctrines, to introduce sweetness and light at the cost of hard-headed realism and invincible logic. From their point of view, to bring Christ down to earth in such a fashion as is implied in statements we sometimes encounter—that He was the "first humanitarian" or that He would certainly endorse this or that political party—would seem to them frightful blasphemy. Puritanism was not only a religious creed, it was a philosophy and a metaphysic; it was an organization of man's whole life, emotional and intellectual, to a degree which has not been sustained by any denomination stemming from it. Yet because such creeds have sprung from Puritanism, the Puritans are frequently praised or blamed for qualities which never belonged to them or for ideas which originated only among their successors and which they themselves would have disowned.

On the other hand, if the line of development from Puritanism tends in one direction to frontier revivalism and evangelicalism, another line leads as directly to a more philosophical, critical, and even skeptical point of view. Unitarianism is as much the child of Puritanism as Methodism. And if the one accretion has colored or distorted our conception of the original doctrine, the other has done so no less. Descendants of the Puritans who revolted against what they considered the tyranny and cruelty of Puritan theology, who substituted taste and reason for dogma and authority and found the emotional fervor of the evangelicals so much sound and fury, have been prone to idealize their ancestors into their own image. A few decades ago it had become very much the mode to praise the Puritans for virtues which they did not possess and which they would not have considered virtues at all. In the pages of liberal historians, and above all in the speeches of Fourth of July orators, the Puritans have been hymned as the pioneers of religious liberty, though nothing was ever farther from their designs; they have been hailed as the forerunners of democracy, though if they were, it was quite beside their intention; they have been invoked in justification for an economic philosophy of free competition and laissez-faire, though they themselves believed in government regulation of business, the fixing of just prices, and the curtailing of individual profits in the interests of the welfare of the whole.

The moral of these reflections may very well be that it is dangerous to read history backwards, to interpret something that was by what it ultimately became, particularly when it became several things. . . . The Puritans were not a bashful race, they could speak out and did; in their own words they have painted their own portraits, their majestic strength and their dignity, their humanity and solidity, more accurately than any admirer had been able to do; and also they have betrayed the motes and beams in their own eyes more clearly than any enemy has been able to point them out.

Puritanism began as an agitation within the Church of England in the latter half of the sixteenth century. It was a movement for reform of that institution, and at the time no more constituted a distinct sect or denomination than the advocates of an amendment to the Constitution of the United States constitute a separate nation. In the 1530s the Church of England broke with the pope of Rome. By the beginning of Elizabeth's reign it had proceeded a certain distance in this revolt, had become Protestant, had disestablished the monasteries and corrected many abuses. Puritanism was the belief that the reform should be continued, that more abuses remained to be corrected, that practices still survived from the days of popery which should be renounced, that the Church of England should be restored to the "purity" of the first-century church as established by Christ Himself. In the 1560s, when the advocates of purification first acquired the name of Puritans, no one, not even the most radical, knew exactly how far the process was to go or just what the ultimate goal would be; down to the days of Cromwell there was never any agreement on this point, and in the end this failure of unanimity proved the undoing of English Puritanism. Many Puritans desired only that certain ceremonies be abolished or changed. Others wanted ministers to preach more sermons, make up their own prayers on the inspiration of the moment rather than read set forms out of a book. Others went further and proposed a revision of the whole form of ecclesiastical government. But whatever the shade or complexion of their Puritanism, Puritans were those who wanted to continue a movement which was already under way. Their opponents, whom we shall speak of as the Anglicans—though only for the sake of convenience, because there was at that time not the remotest thought on either side of an ultimate separation into distinct churches, and Puritans insisted they were as stoutly loyal to the established institution as any men in England—the Anglicans were those who felt that with the enthronement of Elizabeth and with the "Elizabethan Settlement" of the church, things had gone far enough. They wanted to call a halt, just where they were, and stabilize at that point.

Thus the issue between the two views, though large enough, still involved only a limited number of questions. On everything except matters upon which the Puritans wanted further reformation, there was essential agreement. The Puritans who settled New England were among the more radical—though by no means the most radical that the movement produced—and even before their migration in 1630 had gone to the lengths of formulating a concrete platform of church organization which they wished to see instituted in England in place of the episcopal system. Joining battle on this front gave a sufficiently extended line and provided a vast number of salients to fight over; the gulf between the belief of these Puritans and the majority in the Church of England grew so wide that at last there was no bridging it at all. But notwithstanding the depth of this divergence, the fact still remains that only certain specific questions were raised. If we take a comprehensive survey of the whole body of Puritan thought and belief as it existed in 1630 or 1640, if we make an exhaustive enumeration of ideas held by New England Puritans, we shall find that the vast majority of them were precisely those of their opponents. In other words, Puritanism was a movement toward certain ends within the culture and state of England in the late sixteenth and early seventeenth centuries; it centered about a number of concrete problems and advocated a particular program. Outside of that, it was part and parcel of the times, and its culture was simply the culture of England at that moment. It is necessary to belabor the point, because most accounts of Puritanism, emphasizing the controversial tenets, attribute everything that Puritans said or did to the fact that they were Puritans; their attitudes toward all sorts of things are pounced upon and exhibited as peculiarities of their sect, when as a matter of fact they were normal attitudes for the time. Of course, the Puritans acquired their special quality and their essential individuality from their stand on the points actually at issue, and our final conception of Puritanism must give these concerns all due importance. Yet if first of all we wish to take Puritan culture as a whole, we shall find, let us say, that about 90 percent of the intellectual life, scientific knowledge, morality, manners and customs, notions and prejudices, was that of all Englishmen. The other 10 percent, the relatively small number of ideas upon which there was dispute, made all the difference between the Puritan and his fellow Englishmen, made for him so much difference that he pulled up stakes in England, which he loved, and migrated to a wilderness rather than submit them to apparent defeat. Nevertheless, when we come to trace developments and influences on subsequent American history and thought, we shall find that the starting point of many ideas and practices is as apt to be found among the 90 percent as among the 10. The task of defining Puritanism and giving an account of its culture resolves itself, therefore, into isolating first of all the larger features which were not particularly or necessarily Puritan at all, the elements in the life and society which were products of the time and place, of the background of English life and society rather than of the individual belief or peculiar creed of Puritanism.

Many of the major interests and preoccupations of the New England Puritans belong to this list. They were just as patriotic as Englishmen who remained at home. They hated Spain like poison, and France only a little less. In their eyes, as in those of Anglicans, the most important issue in the Western world was the struggle between Catholicism and Protestantism. They were not unique or extreme in thinking that religion was the primary and all-engrossing business of man, or that all human thought and action should tend to the glory of God. . . .

In its major aspects the religious creed of Puritanism was neither peculiar to the Puritans nor different from that of the Anglicans. Both were essentially Protestant; both asserted that men were saved by their faith, not by their deeds. The two sides could agree on the general statement that Christians are bound to believe nothing but what the Gospel teaches, that all traditions of men "contrary to the Word of God" are to be renounced and abhorred. They both believed that the marks of a true church were profession of the creed, use of Christ's sacraments, preaching of the word—Anglican sermons being as long and often as dull as the Puritan—and the union of men in profession and practice under regularly constituted pastors. The Puritans always said that they could subscribe to the doctrinal articles of the Church of England; even at the height of the controversy, even after they had left England rather than put up with what they considered its abominations, they always took care to insist that the Church of England was a "true" church, not Anti-Christ as was the Church of Rome, that it contained many saints, and that men might find salvation within it. Throughout the seventeenth century they read Anglican authors, quoted them in their sermons, and even reprinted some of them in Boston.

The vast substratum of agreement which actually underlay the disagreement between Puritans and Anglicans is explained by the fact that they were both the heirs of the Middle Ages. They still believed that all knowledge was one, that life was unified, that science, economics, political theory, aesthetic standards, rhetoric and art, all were organized in a hierarchical scale of values that tended upward to the end-all and be-all of creation, the glory of God. They both insisted that all human activity be regulated by that purpose. Consequently, even while fighting bitterly against each other, the Puritans and Anglicans stood shoulder to shoulder against what they called "enthusiasm." The leaders of the Puritan movement were trained at the universities, they were men of learning and scholars; no less than the Anglicans did they demand that religion be interpreted by study and logical exposition; they were both resolute against all pretenses to immediate revelation, against all ignorant men who claimed to receive personal instructions from God. They agreed on the essential Christian contention that though God may govern the world, He is not the world itself, and that though He instills His grace into men, He does not deify them or unite them to Himself in one personality. He converses with men only through His revealed word, the Bible. His will is to be studied in the operation of His providence as exhibited in the workings of the natural world, but He delivers no new commands or special revelations to the inward consciousness of men. The larger unanimity of the Puritans and the Anglicans reveals itself whenever either of them was called upon to confront enthusiasm [as seen in] . . . Governor John Winthrop's account of the so-called Antinomian affair, the crisis produced in the little colony by the teachings of Mistress Anne Hutchin-

son in 1636 and 1637. . . . Beneath the theological jargon in which the
opinions of this lady appear we can see the substance of her contention, which was that she was in direct communication with the
Godhead, and that she therefore was prepared to follow the prompt-
ings of the voice within against all the precepts of the Bible, the
churches, reason, or the government of Massachusetts Bay. Winthrop
relates how the magistrates and the ministers defended the community against this perversion of the doctrine of regeneration, but the
tenor of his condemnation would have been duplicated practically
word for word had Anne Hutchinson broached her theories in an Anglican community. The Anglicans fell in completely with the Puritans
when both of them were confronted in the 1650s by the Quakers. All
New England leaders saw in the Quaker doctrine of an inner light, accessible to all men and giving a perfect communication from God to
their inmost spirits, just another form of Anne Hutchinson's blasphemy. John Norton declared that the "light of nature" itself taught us
that "madmen acting according to their frantick passions are to be restrained with chaines, when they can not be restrained otherwise. . . . "
Enthusiasts, whether Antinomian or Quaker, were proposing doctrines that threatened the unity of life by subduing the reason and the
intellect to the passions and the emotions. Whatever their differences,
Puritans and Anglicans were struggling to maintain a complete harmony of reason and faith, science and religion, earthly dominion and
the government of God. When we immerse ourselves in the actual
struggle, the difference between the Puritan and the Anglican may
seem to us immense; but when we take the vantage point of subsequent history, and survey religious thought as a whole over the last
three centuries, the two come very close together on essentials.
Against all forms of chaotic emotionalism, against all oversimplifica-
tions of theology, learning, philosophy, and science, against all materialism, positivism or mechanism, both were endeavoring to uphold a
symmetrical union of heart and head without impairment of either. By
the beginning or middle of the next century their successors, both in
England and America, found themselves no longer capable of sustaining this unity, and it has yet to be reachieved today, if achieved again it
ever can be. The greatness of the Puritans is not so much that they
conquered a wilderness, or that they carried a religion into it, but that
they carried a religion which, narrow and starved though it may have
been in some respects, deficient in sensuous richness or brilliant color,
was nevertheless indissolubly bound up with an ideal of culture and
learning. In contrast to all other pioneers, they made no concessions to
the forest, but in the midst of frontier conditions, in the very throes of
clearing the land and erecting shelters, they maintained schools and a
college, a standard of scholarship and of competent writing, a class of
men devoted entirely to the life of the mind and of the soul.

Because the conflict between the Puritans and the Churchmen was as much an intellectual and scholarly issue as it was emotional, it was in great part a debate among pundits. This is not to say that passions were not involved; certainly men took sides because of prejudice, interest, irrational conviction, or for any of the motives that may incite the human race to conflict. The disagreement finally was carried from the field of learned controversy to the field of battle. There can be no doubt that many of the people in England, or even in New England, became rabid partisans and yet never acquired the erudition necessary to understand the intricate and subtle arguments of their leaders. A great number, perhaps even a majority, in both camps were probably not intelligent or learned enough to see clearly the reasons for the cause they supported. . . .

The wonder is that by and large the populace did yield their judgments to those who were supposed to know, respected learning and supported it, sat patiently during two-and three-hour sermons while ministers expounded the knottiest and most recondite of metaphysical texts. The testimony of visitors, travelers, and memoirs agrees that during the Puritan age in New England the common man, the farmer and merchant, was amazingly versed in systematic divinity. A gathering of yeomen and "hired help" around the kitchen fire of an evening produced long and unbelievably technical discussions of predestination, infant damnation, and the distinctions between faith and works. In the first half of the seventeenth century the people had not yet questioned the conception of religion as a difficult art in which the authority of the skilled dialectician should prevail over the inclinations of the merely devout. This ideal of subjection to qualified leadership was social as well as intellectual. Very few Englishmen had yet broached the notion that a lackey was as good as a lord, or that any Tom, Dick, or Harry, simply because he was a good, honest man, could understand the Sermon on the Mount as well as a master of arts from Oxford, Cambridge, or Harvard. Professor Morison has shown that the life of the college in New England was saved by the sacrifice of the yeomen farmers, who contributed their pecks of wheat, wrung from a stony soil, taken from their none too opulent stores, to support teaching fellows and to assist poor scholars at Harvard College, in order that they and their children might still sit under a literate ministry "when our present Ministers shall lie in the Dust."

When we say the the majority of the people in the early seventeenth century still acceded to the dictation of the learned in religion and the superior in society, we must also remark that the Puritan leaders were in grave danger of arousing a revolt against themselves by their very own doctrines. Puritans were attacking the sacerdotal and institutional bias which had survived in the Church of England; they were maintaining a theology that brought every man to a direct experience of the spirit and removed intermediaries between himself and the deity. Yet the authority of the infallible church and the power of the bishops had for centuries served to keep the people docile. Consequently when the Puritan leaders endeavored to remove the bishops and to deny that the church should stand between God and man, they ran the hazard of starting something among the people that might get out of hand. Just as the Puritan doctrine that men were saved by the infusion of God's grace could lead to the Antinomianism of Mrs. Hutchinson, and often did warrant the simple in concluding that if they had God's grace in them they needed to pay no heed to what a minister told them, so the Puritan contention that regenerate men were illuminated with divine truth might lead to the belief that true religion did not need the assistance of learning, books, arguments, logical demonstrations, or classical languages. There was always a possibility that Puritanism would raise up a fanatical anti-intellectualism, and against such a threat the Puritan ministers constantly braced themselves. It was no accident that the followers of Mrs. Hutchinson, who believed that men could receive all the necessary instructions from within, also attacked learning and education, and came near to wrecking not only the colony but the college as well. . . .

[T]he New England leaders were face to face with a problem as old as the history of the Christian church. Throughout the Middle Ages there had been such stirrings among the people as those to which Mrs. Hutchinson or the Fifth Monarchy Men gave voice. The great scholastic synthesis always remained incomprehensible to the vulgar, who demanded to be fed again and again with the sort of religious sustenance they craved. The Reformation drew upon these suppressed desires. Common men turned Protestant primarily because Protestantism offered them a religion which more effectively satisfied their spiritual hunger. Yet in Europe theologians and metaphysicians retained the leadership and kept Protestantism from becoming merely an emotional outburst. They supplied it with a theology which, though not so sophisticated as scholastic dogma, was still equipped with a logic and organon of rational demonstration. Though Protestantism can be viewed as a "liberation" of the common man, it was far from being a complete emancipation of the individual. It freed him from many intellectual restraints that had been imposed by the church, but it did not give him full liberty to think anything he pleased; socially it freed him from many exactions, but it did not permit him to abandon his traditional subjection to his social and ecclesiastical superiors. The original settlers of New England carried this Protestantism intact from Europe to America. Except for the small band that was driven into exile with Anne Hutchinson, and one or two other groups of visionaries who also were hustled across the borders into Rhode Island, the rank and file did follow their leaders, meekly and reverently. Captain Johnson probably represents the average layman's loyalty to the clergy. The New England "theocracy" was simply a Protestant version of the European social ideal, and except for its Protestantism was thoroughly medieval in character.

It was only as the seventeenth century came to a close that the imported structure began to show the strain. In Europe social tradition had conspired with the ministers to check enthusiasts in religion and "levellers" in society; in England the authorities, whether Anglican or Puritan, royal or Cromwellian, were able to suppress the assault upon the scholarly and aristocratic ideal. In America the character of the people underwent a change; they moved further into the frontier, they became more absorbed in business and profits than in religion and salvation, their memories of English social stratification grew dim. A preacher before the General Court in 1705 bewailed the effects of the frontier in terms that have been echoed by "Easterners" for two hundred years and more; men were no longer living together, he said, in compact communities, under the tutelage of educated clergymen and under the discipline of an ordered society, but were taking themselves into remote corners "for worldly conveniences." "By that means [they] have seemed to bid defiance, not only to Religion, but to Civility it self: and such places thereby have become Nurseries of Ignorance, Profaneness and Atheism." In America the frontier conspired with the popular disposition to lessen the prestige of the cultured classes and to enhance the social power of those who wanted their religion in a more simple, downright and "democratic" form, who cared nothing for the refinements and subtleties of historic theology. Not until the decade of the Great Awakening did the popular tendency receive distinct articulation through leaders who openly renounced the older conception, but for half a century or more before 1740 its obstinate persistence can be traced in the condemnations of the ministers.

The Puritan leaders could withstand this rising tide of democracy only by such support as the government would give them—which became increasingly less after the new charter of 1692 took away from the saints all power to select their own governors and divorced the state and church—or else by the sheer force of their personalities. As early as the 1660s and '70s we can see them beginning to shift their attentions from mere exposition of the creed to greater and greater insistence upon committing power only to men of wisdom and knowledge. . . . By the beginning of the eighteenth century the task of buttressing the classified society, maintaining the rule of the well-trained and the culturally superior both in church and society seems to have become the predominant concern of the clergy. Sermon after sermon reveals that in their eyes the cause of learning and the cause of a hierarchical, differentiated social order were one and the same. . . . Leadership by the learned and dutiful subordination of the unlearned—as long as the original religious creed retained its hold upon the people these exhortations were heeded; in the eighteenth century, as it ceased to arouse their loyalties, they went seeking after gods that were utterly strange to Puritanism. They demanded fervent rather than learned ministers and asserted the equality of all men.

Thus Puritanism appears, from the social and economic point of view, to have been a philosophy of social stratification, placing the command in the hands of the properly qualified and demanding implicit obedience from the uneducated; from the religious point of view it was the dogged assertion of the unity of intellect and spirit in the face of a rising tide of democratic sentiment suspicious of the intellect and intoxicated with the spirit. It was autocratic, hierarchical, and authoritarian. It held that in the intellectual realm holy writ was to be expounded by right reason, that in the social realm the expounders of holy writ were to be the mentors of farmers and merchants. Yet in so far as Puritanism involved such ideals it was simply adapting to its own purposes and ideals of the age. Catholics in Spain and in Spanish America pursued the same objectives, and the Puritans were no more rigorous in their application of an autocratic standard than King Charles himself endeavored to be—and would have been had he not been balked in the attempt.

PHILIP F. GURA

PHILIP F. GURA (1950–   ) is professor of English at the University of North Carolina. His books include The Wisdom of Words: Language, Theology and Literature in the New England Renaissance *(1981) and* A Glimpse of Sion's Glory: Puritan Radicalism in New England 1620–1660 *(1984).*

Between 1630 and 1660, among the approximately twenty thousand colonists who settled in New England were many individuals, ministers as well as laymen, whose Puritanism was not consonant with the official ideology of the Bay Colony. . . . The Massachusetts Puritans attempted to limit the colony's population to those whose religious views were compatible to their own, and as the decade of the 1630s wore on, compatibility more and more meant agreement with the principles of nonseparating congregationalism. Nevertheless, the great Puritan migration that, beginning in 1629, brought to New England a cross section of old England's population, included many who had been influenced by theological views more radical than those officially sanctioned in Massachusetts and who subsequently sought to promulgate them in the communities where they settled. By the 1640s New England's congregationalists (as well as their conservative English critics) complained that the colonies harbored self-declared (or scarcely disguised) separatists, antinomians, familists, Seekers, anabaptists, Ranters, Adamites, and Quakers, all implicitly aligned against the established church system because of their insistence that an individual's personal religious experience supersede the demands of ecclesiastical tradition and civil law. In many cases, theirs were the same Protestant principles Winthrop and others earlier had defended in England yet, under pressure to settle a wilderness and codify their ecclesiology, soon enough condemned as seditious or heretical.

The experiences of the Husbandmen and other radical Puritans in seventeenth-century New England have not been studied with any completeness because of a prevailing disposition among historians of colonial America to regard American Puritanism as relatively homogeneous and the American sectarians only as weak, if prophetic, advocates of religious toleration. To be sure, accounts of early New England history invariably mention such prominent dissenters as Roger Williams, Anne Hutchinson, and the Quakers; still, no historian has attempted to document either the widespread presence of radical Puritans in New England or their complex and extended relationship to their English counterparts. A number of studies—most notably those of Christopher Hill and Keith Thomas—do describe the radical Protestant sects that flourished in England between the death of Queen Elizabeth and the Restoration, but historians of American Puritanism have insistently portrayed it as but one branch of an English plant and not itself a vigorous if slender rootstock that brought forth the same exotic varietals as its English counterpart. Williams, Hutchinson, and the Quakers, as significant as were their challenges to the New England Way, offer only the most memorable examples of an inescapable fact: between 1630 and 1660 the doctrinal and ecclesiastical, as well as the imaginative, development of American Puritanism was nurtured in soil thoroughly turned by radical elements in the New Englanders' midst.

This resistance to an acknowledgment of the radicals' effect upon New England Puritanism can be traced to the still-pervasive influence of Perry Miller, who in his magisterial account of "the New England mind"—what he termed his "map of the intellectual terrain of the seventeenth century"—continually emphasized what he considered the

New England Puritans' supreme achievement. To him this achievement was the theological and ecclesiastical synthesis known as nonseparating congregationalism, an ecclesiastical system under which
individual congregations maintained their autonomy while at the
same time claiming their continued allegiance to the hierarchy of the
Church of England. But in his desire to illustrate the extent to which
the American Puritans were successful in promulgating and defending
this world-view, Miller was too willing to believe that "after the New
England divines had weathered the storm of 1637–1638 they were
never seriously threatened by any form of Antinomianism, though
they were horrified by the sectarian outbursts in England . . . and magnified the few Quakers who ventured within their jurisdiction." He
sketched the contours of his "map" of New England's intellectual development under the assumption, too readily accepted by other scholars, that "the first three generations in New England paid almost
unbroken allegiance to a unified body of thought, and that individual
differences among particular writers or theorists were merely minor
variations within a general frame." In the two decades since Miller's
death, it has become all too clear that the "liberty" he took of "treating the whole literature as though it were the product of a single intelligence" reveals more about his own desire for order than it does of the
full complexity of the New England mind in the seventeenth century.

Miller's eagerness to identify those characteristics that distinguished American Puritanism from its English and Continental counterparts and his insistence that the American wilderness guaranteed
such distinctions, led him to claim that through the early eighteenth
century the "official cosmology" of the Bay Colony remained un-
marked by any challenge to its legitimacy. Even in *From Colony to
Province* (1953), a study devoted to the institutional development of
New England Puritanism, he maintained that "such developments as
took place [in the colonists' ideology]" only affected "lesser areas of
church polity, political relations, or the contests of groups and interests." Miller admitted that some of these developments had been "intense and shattering experiences" for those who were involved in them,
yet, he believed, these events did not cause "any significant alterations" in the "doctrinal frame of reference" within the colony. But the
sheer intellectual vigor of Miller's narrative in this work (and in other
works of his that deal with seventeenth-century New England) under-
cuts his assumption: the intensity of the conflicts over matters of
church polity and colonial politics, as well as over theological doctrine,
indicates that, no matter how decidedly the Puritan authorities "triumphed" in these "contests of groups and interests," the various challenges to the magistrates' authority initiated by dissenting colonists
had an undeniable effect upon the future course of New England's history. Miller viewed New England dissent as a sideshow to the events on
the main stage of New England's intellectual and social history.

I will argue, in contrast, that in large measure New England Puritanism developed as it did because of, and not in spite of, the criticism of the colony from those in the population whose vision of the kingdom of God in America differed significantly from John Winthrop's. . . .

A perusal of church, town, and colony records of seventeenth-century New England reveals . . . a surprisingly wide range of theological opinion in the colonies before the Restoration and a complex relation of such diversity to the internal development of American Puritan doctrine. *Heterogeneity,* not unanimity, actually characterized the colony's religious life. Darrett Rutman, who has gone as far as anyone to challenge Miller's conclusions about the existence of a unified body of thought called "American Puritanism," noted that, contrary to the observations of Miller and other historians, "orthodox New England possessed the semblance but not the substance of unity." In such works as *Winthrop's Boston: Portrait of a Puritan Town* and *American Puritanism: Faith and Practice,* Rutman argues that, even among the ministers in the colony, "disparity of doctrine and even practice was the rule, not the exception." For him, American Puritanism can best be explained as chance confluence of diverse cultural and religious forces; "if what eventually emerged was uniquely American," he writes, "it was only because one found here a continuing juxtaposition of varied elements which could not be duplicated anywhere." In New England "there was no Puritan way, no constant to be injected" by the settlers into the waiting body of the new continent. There were merely the "actions, reactions, interactions" of the heterogeneous population themselves.

Rutman's astute assessment addresses itself specifically to the range of theological opinion in colonial New England; his conclusions are derived from detailed demographic analyses. If he fails finally to explore the significance of the dialectic between the dissenters and more moderate Puritans in New England for the development of Puritan doctrine, or the dissenters' role in what in effect was a transatlantic debate about the nature and extent of the Puritan renovation of society, Rutman at least calls attention to the ideological blinders that narrowed Miller's delineation of the intellectual contours of the New England mind. As one recent student has said of the Antinomian Controversy—in seventeenth-century New England the most important radical challenge to the ideology of nonseparating congregationalism: "it was apparent from the outset that not all who came to the Bay Colony had been listening to the same spirit or brought the same notions about the nature of the New England enterprise." Here, in the very complexity of English Puritanism on the eve of the colonization of New England, we must seek an understanding of the true import of what Miller and others hitherto have dismissed as "minor" events in the development of American Puritanism.

In 1936 Charles M. Andrews noted that the large influx of settlers to New England between 1630 and 1640 had "brought an unusual number of ministers . . . whose interpretations of scripture and the purpose of God in his relations with men . . . represented many shades of opinion." It is also important to recognize that the New England mind was formed as much, if not more, by the laity, by what another historian has called "the spontaneous, irrepressible aggregation of like-minded saints in shifting voluntary groups . . . seeking comfort and enlightenment for themselves from the Gospel." A full understanding of seventeenth-century New England Puritanism depends on an acknowledgment that many of those who migrated to America did not share a fixed ideology or commitment to an agreed-upon ecclesiastical program as much as a common spiritual hunger and a disenchantment with the Church of England's refusal to address the nation's spiritual famine. Further, English Puritans—including those who later emigrated to the New World—had not tempered their intellectual and social bonds at any single ideological forge but over the spiritual flames of countless private devotional meetings or "conventicles" throughout England. From these private meetings, which perhaps more than any institution or idea provided Puritans with a group identity, sprang not only the likes of John Winthrop, Thomas Hooker, Thomas Shepard, and others who became staunch supporters of nonseparating congregationalism, but also those individuals who by the mid-1640s had helped to generate a myriad of radical Puritan sects that threatened to fulfill the prophecy of Acts 17:6 and turn the known world upside down. In England the soon-to-be settlers' experience as "Puritans" had been as varied as the regions from which they came. This fact must inform any examination of the variety of American Puritanism.

From what we know of the persistence of English local institutions in the various New England towns that have been examined by such historians as T. H. Breen and David Grayson Allen, it should come as no surprise that once in the New World many Puritans sought to replicate the form and quality of their previous religious experience. They replicated precisely what one would expect from English Puritanism between 1630 and 1660: everything from the most structured presbyterianism to the religious and social radicalism of antinomians, Seekers, and Ranters. Moreover, in the free air of the New World, English Puritans had every right to anticipate that what they had learned in the privacy of their conventicles would form the basis of a new social order. History would prove their dreams illusory. Many individuals, once as powerless before the bishops as other of their brethren, who had justified their resistance to the Church of England through appeals to individual religious experience similar to those that led others to more radical positions, in the New World assumed a more conservative posture. They came to believe that, no matter what their experience with more radical forms of Puritan thought in England, they must establish and maintain strict doctrinal orthodoxy to achieve civil order in a new society. Most historians have minimized the resistance to the institution of such a unified body of doctrine in New England. It is clear, nevertheless, that the experience of English Puritanism was too varied to have been so easily transformed without serious challenge by those whose understanding of the logic of the Gospel plan differed at many points from that of the leaders of the more conservative colonies. Miller would have us marvel at how compelling the colonists found the New England Way. Rather, we should ask why anyone who had experienced the range of English Puritan thought, and the spiritual and social liberation it offered, would accept the ideological limitations of New England congregationalism.

Consider Samuel Gorton, founder of Warwick, Rhode Island, a radical spiritist with many connections to the sectarian underground in England, particularly to the General Baptist groups. Frequently linked to such prominent English radicals as John Saltmarsh and William Dell, Gorton was instrumental in preparing the way for the reception of the Quakers in his colony. Or John Clarke, of Newport, also in the Rhode Island colonies, a Particular Baptist who, along with Obadiah Holmes and John Crandall, openly challenged the relationship of church and state in Massachusetts. He maintained close contact with his doctrinal counterparts in London, particularly Henry Jessey and John Tombes, two of the signers of the famous Baptist Confession of 1644. Then, too, there was William Pynchon, first settler of Springfield in the Connecticut Valley of Massachusetts, who took his inspiration from such English latitudinarians or "Socinians" as Anthony Wotton and John Goodwin. Pynchon's tracts published in the 1650s display his advocacy of an enlightened rationalism in religion, particularly as a basis for toleration of diverse Christian opinions; his settlement in the Valley initiated that region's long-standing challenge to the supremacy, religious and otherwise, of the clergy of eastern Massachusetts. William Aspinwall, one of the antinomians disarmed in 1637, later returned to England to become a prolific pamphleteer for the cause of the Fifth Monarchy; his conception of a divinely instituted church state was reviewed and accepted by some of the most advanced radicals of the 1650s. One of his followers, Thomas Venner, left his trade as a wine cooper in Boston to lead the major Fifth Monarchy uprising in London in 1661; he was hanged, drawn, and quartered, and his head was placed on a pike atop one of the city gates. These are but a few of the more prominent spokesmen for Puritan radicalism in New England. Many have received insufficient attention.

The response of the Bay Colony and of Connecticut to the presence of such radicals was complicated by the fact that some of the points of doctrine which from the outset of the migration had been central to the evolution of the New England Way encouraged the same radical conclusions about church and society advanced by the sectarians, both at home and in England. Note, in particular, the colonists' fervent millennialism and their belief in both a gathered church of Christian saints and, more important, the animating power of the Holy Spirit. These emphases within New England Puritanism, especially the Puritans' stress on the witness of the Spirit in each saint and on the saint's obligation to bring Christ's kingdom to earth, were irreducible elements of the religious culture within which the colonists had lived in old England. It was by fully addressing the ideological implications of such beliefs that the leaders of Massachusetts and Connecticut could implement their own more conservative plans for the renovation of the English church. The nature and extent of the dialogue between representatives of nonseparating congregationalism and those among the settlers who, at least initially, refused to relinquish their own very different plans for the establishment of a Christian commonwealth lies at the center of any appreciation of the complexity of New England's religious culture in the mid-seventeenth century.

The radicals' ideas, in addition to affecting the officially sanctioned theology of New England Puritanism, contributed significantly to the social and political development of the New England colonies. This was particularly so in the ways in which Massachusetts and Connecticut congregationalists protected themselves against the further spread of radical ideas, and in their response to the increasing criticism of their repressive policies levelled at them by their English brethren. Further, the radicals' various challenges to the New England Way also had profound effect on the Puritans' imaginative conception of themselves and their social experiment. It is the underlying premise of Sacvan Bercovitch's *The American Jeremiad* that since their earliest days in the New World the Puritans had adhered to a "myth of America" that involved the creation and maintenance of an ideological community most clearly defined not by its territorial or political integrity but by its members' incessant rhetorical self-justification of a divinely ordained purpose. Scholars of American Puritanism, including Miller and Bercovitch himself, have described the development of this myth of American exceptionalism in terms of the colonists' adoption and subtle modification of the principles of nonseparating congregationalism, particularly in light of an increasing awareness of their physical and ideological distance from old England. But what is apparent in the colonists' elaborate definitions and justifications of their ecclesiastical polity and evident in their polemics against dissenters is that the New Englander's ideological self-image was shaped less by any set of ecclesiastical principles than by an unyielding effort to neutralize the influence of those who argued for a much more radical reorganization of the society. The "middle-class culture" that defined New England from its earliest days was the result not merely, as Bercovitch suggests, of the

New Englanders' freedom from the feudal restrictions of Europe, of a corrupt opportunism in the face of New World opportunity, or of an antipathy to the Arminian tendencies of the Church of England, but also of a sharp and continual debate with those who from their English Puritan experience had formed a particularly democratic notion of their errand into America's wilderness.

I am concerned with the social and political, as well as with the religious, implications of the radical Puritans' presence in New England. Like Miller . . . and Bercovitch, I recognize the importance for American history of the ideological consensus that later generations of Americans discerned in the first decades of New England's settlement. But, once aware of the nature and extent of the radical challenges to this consensus, we have every right to ask why seventeenth-century New England did not become *more* radicalized and *more* democratic than it did. Such scholars of English Puritanism as William Haller and Christopher Hill have taught us that the Puritan sectarians fundamentally challenged many of the traditional assumptions on which their society was based. In the religious sphere they raised searching questions about the proper relationship of church and state, the minister and his congregation, the word of the Bible and the witness of the Spirit. They also reexamined the moral bases of society: they challenged the established relationship of the sexes in both the religious and domestic spheres; they questioned the very existence of heaven and hell, and of sin, and wondered aloud if in an age of impending apocalypse an educated ministry was at all necessary. As Haller himself noted many years ago, to attempt to reform the Church of England in the seventeenth century was quite simply "to attempt the reorganization of society." Why, then, did the New England Puritans, three thousands miles away from the iron grasp of the bishops, refuse to incorporate into their society more of the ideas the radicals advocated? If, as the Woburn, Massachusetts, militia-captain Edward Johnson wrote, New England was "the place where the Lord will create a new Heaven, and a new Earth in, new Churches and a new Commonwealth together," what prevented the colony from being modeled after the spiritual utopia of a John Saltmarsh, or the political democracy of a John Lilburne?

Such speculation is not out of line, for a large number of those who came to New England in the 1630s and 1640s, before the advent of the English civil wars had shifted the Puritans' focus back to England, clearly believed that their transatlantic voyage had been undertaken for much more than an escape from ecclesiastical persecution. Since the 1620s they had heard countless Puritan preachers remind them of the Books of Daniel and Revelation, in which it was apparent that "there be many Prophesies and Promises . . . that are not yet fulfilled; and the fulfilling whereof will bring the *Church* into a more glorious condition than ever it was yet in the World." For many who came to America in those two decades it seemed perfectly plausible that in their new home such prophecy would be fulfilled. From New England one could view not only the return of Christ, but the staging of his triumph over Satan's legions. New Englanders were not hesitant to raise Christ's standard and march in the vanguard of his armies, for they believed that they were a chosen people. As Edward Johnson put it, "God hath . . . caused the dazeling brightnesse of his presence to be contracted in the burning-Glasse of [their] zeal." New England was destined to be more than a shining beacon upon a hill. Its spiritual ardor would set Christ's fire to the whole world, its flames never quenched "till it hath burnt up Babilon Root and Branch."

Thomas Tillam, who later returned to England a fervent Fifth Monarchist, in a poem written "Upon the first sight of New-England, June 29, 1638," hailed a "holy-land wherein our holy lord/Hath planted his most true and holy word" for the sake of a society in which he and his fellow colonists, "free from all annoye," could "Injoye" Christ's presence in every aspect of their lives. A similar eschatological hope compelled Ezekiel Rogers of Rowley to remind Governor Winthrop in 1639 that the "worke of the Lorde in bringing so many pretious ones to this place is not for nothing." Like Boston's minister, the renowned John Cotton, who that same year began to preach the sermons that would comprise *An Exposition upon the Twelfth Chapter of the Revelation*, Rogers looked forward to the reappearance of Christ on earth and the bestowal of his blessing on "none but [the] downright godly ones" who had prayed for his reappearance; Rogers was sure that the Saviour first would be seen in New England. By 1647 Samuel Symonds of Ipswich knew enough of New England to proclaim that the days of the New Jerusalem had indeed commenced: "Is not government in church and Common weale (according to gods own rules) that new heaven and earth promised, in the fullnes accomplished when the Jewes come in; and the first fruites begun in this poore of New Engl[and] . . .?" Similarly, Sir Symonds D'Ewes, writing in his autobiography in 1638 from the perspective of England, believed the New England experiment of paramount importance, "a true type of heaven itself" in which the colonists, "in the main, aim simply at God's glory, and to reduce the public service of God to that power and purity which it enjoyed in primitive times." In 1651 his sentiment was echoed by none other than Oliver Cromwell, who begged John Cotton to write to tell him "What is the Lord a-doing? What prophecies are now fulfilling?"

New England, then, was settled in the belief that it was to become nothing less than a fulfillment of biblical prophecy, a land in which the life of the spirit informed all behavior and so would mark the spot of the New Jerusalem. Within such a context of millennial expectation the Puritan radicals presented plans, which they believed to be as firmly grounded in Scripture as the more conservative Puritans did theirs, for the religious and social reformation that would initiate Christ's holy commonwealth.

The radicals' challenge to the church and state in England was effectively defused by the political and religious settlement of the Restoration. By the 1660s in the New World, however, compromise had taken a different form: the dissenters seemingly had become *bona fide* members of the congregational order on which Winthrop, Hooker, Shepard, and others had expended so much intellectual effort. In New England, where the Church of England never had been institutionalized, one found instead the gradual evolution of an ideological system that, while it could not fully satisfy the spiritist longings of the radicals, harnessed enough of the potential energy of their ideas to garner the support of the majority of the settlers. Only at the fringes of Massachusetts and Connecticut—in the Rhode Island communities (which one observer called "the receptacle of all sorts of riff-raff people, and . . . the sewer of New England") and to the north in what eventually became New Hampshire and Maine—did the inhabitants continue to press for a different social order from that overseen by Winthrop or Thomas Dudley. At the meetings of the Synod of 1662, which set the direction of the New England Way for the next fifty years, those who represented congregationalism—"a speaking *Aristocracy* in the face of a silent Democracy," in the words of the Hartford minister Samuel Stone—emerged with enough power to end the plans of more radical Puritans for the establishment of a New Canaan.

The manner in which the supporters of both the Synods of 1648 and 1662 gathered such power to themselves of course is of great interest, for the compromises over polity and doctrine to which the colonies' leaders were forced by their more radical brethren also led to the American Puritans' most impressive achievement, the sublimation of radical ideology into the emerging "myth of America" described by scholars like Bercovitch and Robert Middlekauff in their accounts of the New England mind. Through the rhetorical power of the ministers' jeremiads and the subtle redefinition of New England's errand within the terms of scriptural typology, much of the original force of the radicals' criticism of seventeenth-century society was subsumed into the millennial component of Puritan thought that always had formed a significant part of the Puritans' understanding of their position in the New World.

The full co-optation of the radicals' program into what Bercovitch elsewhere calls "the American self" had to await the second generation of American Puritans, who had missed both the excitement of life in outlawed conventicles and the heady delight of viewing the New World as "a new Indes of heavenly treasure" where "yet more . . . may be." But even as the foundation of the New England Way was being laid in the years before 1660, Puritans in both old and New England had begun to worry whether the colony was fulfilling the divine destiny to which it was called. In 1644, for example, Roger Williams thought it a "monstrous Paradox" that within the Bay Colony "Gods children should persecute Gods children" and reported "the Speech of an honourable Knight of the Parliament" who, on hearing of the intolerance of the Massachusetts leaders, exclaimed: "What, Christ persecute Christ in New England?" Isaac Penington, arguing against John Norton's defense of the colony's persecution of the Quakers in the 1650s, asked New Englanders to consider whether they really had felt themselves "to grow in the inward life, upon [their] coming into *New-England*, or did that [life] begin to flag and wither, and [their] growth chiefly consist in form and outward order?" Even Peter Bulkeley, minister to the frontier outpost of Concord and a strong supporter of Shepard, warned that unless the colonists rearranged their priorities "God [may] remove thy Candlesticke out of the midst of thee" and change Massachusetts from "a Citie upon an hill, which many seek unto," to "a Beacon upon the top of a mountaine, desolate and forsaken." Though John Cotton, as his grandson Cotton Mather reported, may indeed have written to John Davenport that in New England "*the order of the churches and commonwealth . . . brought to his mind the new heaven and the new earth,*" it is essential to realize that his sentiment simply was not shared by all the population. Some had very different expectations for the future of the colony.

In the place of the spiritual and, by implication, political democracy the radicals demanded, the New Englanders erected only a half-way house on the road to a more democratic society—the congregationalism that played so large a part in the liberation of radical ideology in England but which, when institutionalized as it was in New England, more often than not produced supporters as harsh and intolerant as the English prelates. But some historians—Stephen Foster, for example—argue that the colonists "actually put into practice the Independents' most visionary and apparently unachievable goals," specifically, an "insistence on the rule of the saints, on government of and by the regenerate." More important, for the first four decades of New England's history individuals and groups who represented the full range of English Puritan thought fertilized the New England mind with much more novel, and sometimes downright startling, ideas carried with them from their English experience.

3

AMERICAN INDIANS: RESISTANCE OR ACCOMMODATION?

"I am an *Indian*," wrote Virginia planter-historian Robert Beverley in his 1705 preface to his *The History and Present State of Virginia*, "and don't pretend to be exact in my language: But I hope the Plainness of my Dress, will give [the reader] the kinder Impressions of my Honesty, which is what I pretend to."[1] Beverley's appropriation of Indianness and his personal definition of it hints at some of the unique problems in attempting to track the historiography of American Indians. Historians of Indians, in addition to bringing to bear the weight of their various political agendas, have also, perhaps more than historians of any other subject in our history, brought their personal desires, identifications and hatreds to studying indigenous peoples. Beverley was an unusual eighteenth-century observer-ethnographer, in his relatively of matter-of-fact and even positive description of the Powhatan of Virginia, but he was not unusual in regarding them as a way to reflect aspects of himself, in this case, his unadorned prose and person. Other historians of the period remarked on the Indians' vanity and love of adornment as well as their extraordinary eloquence, so while Beverley's motives in characterizing his subjects are benign, they clearly do not reflect anything established about the Powhatan.

The difficulty of historians in trying to write about Indians without projecting onto them a dizzying variety of their own aspirations, fears, and odium has spawned a secondary historiography of its own, a history of how to explain European-American attitudes toward Indians. Gustav Jahoda's contribution, *Images of Savages, Ancient Roots of Modern Prejudices in Western Cultures*, and Robert Berkhoff's *The White Man's Burden*[2] are only two of the most recent in a long procession of volumes probing the origins and development of Europeans' often toxic views of Native Americans.

In addition to the psychological difficulties historians have encountered in assessing the history of indigenous American people,

---

[1] Robert Beverley, *The History and Present State of Virginia*, Louis B. Wright, ed. (Chapel Hill, N.C., 1947), p. 9.

[2] Gustav, Jahoda (New York, London, 1999).

there have been and continue to be formidable methodological problems involved in establishing even the most basic facts. Emotionally charged disputes over how many Native Americans lived in continental North America continue. Those who incline toward higher numbers see themselves not only as righting an incorrect perception but also as supplying potent evidence about the magnitude of the demographic disaster that began with Columbus's landing on San Salvador. Much more than scholars in other fields, historians have had to look to archeology, paleontology, and anthropology and await the establishment of fields like environmental history and biolinguistics in order to further their research. Even so, substantial questions remain unanswered, such as whether the Iroquois came from elsewhere or evolved their complex society in the territory they occupied when the Europeans first encountered them and whether the confederacy, which lived in Eastern Virginia when the English arrived, was of long standing or the product of Powhatan's power and will.

Contributing to our ignorance about many aspects of Indian history has been the fact that the Indian point of view was, for more than two centuries after Jamestown, of little concern to most historians, for whom Indians represented primarily an obstacle in working out the chroniclers' own destiny. Although there are a handful of important exceptions, it is largely only in the last thirty years that historians have become interested in trying to write history from an Indian perspective.

This sudden growth and enrichment of a field with imaginative and wide-ranging scholarship has come about for a variety of reasons that underlie the growth of social history and the creation of new fields, such as women's history and African-American history. Revulsion at American colonialism in Vietnam and at the nation's treatment of indigenous people overlapped.[3] AIM, the American Indian Movement, initiated an era in 1969 in which activists went to the streets and to the courts to draw attention to their grievances and seek justice for centuries of racism, exploitation, and the resulting poverty, joblessness, and despair that was endemic on reservations.[4]

Four particularly significant volumes initiated a widespread change in the depth and seriousness of Indian studies. Vine Deloria, Jr., a Standing Rock Sioux law school student, published *Custer Died for Your Sins: An Indian Manifesto* in 1969 in which he satirized the work of anthropologists descending upon reservations each summer. "Their concern is not the ultimate policy that will affect the Indian people, but merely the creation of new slogans and doctrines by which they can climb the university totem pole."[5] Deloria, who has remained en-

---

[3]See especially Richard Drinnon, *Facing West: The Metaphysics of Indian Hating and Empire Building* (Norman, Okla., 1980).

[4]For an account of AIM see Paul Chaat Smith and Robert Allen Warrior, *Like a Hurricane, The Indian Movement from Alcatraz to Wounded Knee* (New York, 1996).

gaged in the struggle for Indian rights throughout his life, started off his career challenging non-Indian academics to reconsider their motives and methods for studying indigenous people. Deloria saw the scholar, not the subject, empowered by knowledge about Indians. In DeLoria's reading, the contemporary form of expropriation of Indian identity was no longer as personal traits like valor and simplicity but as data for careerists.

The methodological sophistication of Anthony F. C. Wallace's *Death and Rebirth of the Seneca* (1969), which used history, anthropology, and psychoanalytic techniques, indicated the insights a multidisciplinary approach could produce. Gary Nash's *Red, White, and Black: The Peoples of Early America* (1973) for the first time placed Indians as major players in the colonial story. This pathbreaking synthesis of early American histories discarded the myth of the "discovery" of the continent and introduced readers to the variety of native people here when the European explorers arrived. Nash wrote, "The history of the American peoples begins not in 1492 . . . but more than 30 centuries before the birth of Christ." And two years later Francis Jennings's provocative and polemical *The Invasion of America: Indians, Colonialism, and the Cant of Conquest* challenged more complacent interpretations of white-Indian relations, commanding a wealth of detail to argue that land lust created the climate in which Puritans massacred Indians and called it God's will. Jennings relegated missionary efforts to the status of hypocritical coverups for Puritan expansion.[6]

Wallace was not the first scholar to combine anthropology and history and Jennings was hardly the first to criticize the treatment of native peoples. A minority of scholars and concerned writers had attacked European policies toward Indians since Bartolome de Las Casas published *The Devastation of the Indies* in 1552. But the 1970s was the first time scholars in large numbers devoted themselves to trying to write history from the point of view of the Indians. This effort has continued unabated. How has Indian historiography developed and what happened to produce this change?

Puritan historians, who, like Increase and Cotton Mather, might also be ministers, saw their world as one in which God repeatedly tested his chosen people. Indians constituted one of the greatest tests—as serious as witchcraft—a scourge inflicted upon the settlers to remind them to return to the paths of righteousness. God's favor in allowing his people to conquer both the Pequots in 1636 and the Wampanoags in 1676

---

[5]Thomas Biolsi and Larry J. Zimmerman, *Indians and Anthropology, Vine Deloria Jr. and the Critique of Anthropology* (Tucson, Ariz., 1997), p. 3.

[6]Anthony F. C. Wallace, *Death and Rebirth of the Seneca* (New York, 1969). Gary B. Nash, *Red, Black and White, The Peoples of Early North America* (Englewood Cliffs, N.J.,1974), p. 7. Francis Jennings, *The Invasion of America: Indians, Colonialism, and the Cant of Conquest* (New York, 1975).

demonstrated both His love and forbearance toward His people as well as His frustration with them for frequently abandoning His way. And the Puritans' conviction of their own superior claim to God's attention justified their occupation of Indian lands. As Cotton Mather wrote of the plague that struck down the Massachusetts Indians shortly before Bradford's Pilgrims landed at Plymouth, "The *Indians* in these Parts had newly . . . been visited with such a prodigious Pestilence; as carried away not a *Tenth*, but *Nine Parts* of *Ten* (yea, 'tis said *Nineteen* of *Twenty*) among them: So that the *Woods* were almost cleared of those pernicious Creatures, to make Room for a *better Growth*."[7]

Looking at Indians, according to some scholars, such as Richard Slotkin, Puritans saw through their own prism of regulated behavior and repressed impulses. They projected onto native people their own imaginings of wild freedom: sexual license, unrestrained cruelty, male laziness, and devil-worship. These beliefs accompanied and justified their economic and political motives.[8] As Captain John Underhill wrote in a firsthand account of the massacre of approximately five hundred Pequots, mostly old people, women and children, "Sometimes the Scripture declareth women and children must perish with their parents. . . . We had sufficient light from the word of God for our proceedings."[9]

Seventeenth-century chroniclers, however, were not all ethnocentric zealots. Robert Beverley's ethnography was remarkable for its respect and compassion. In concluding the section on Indians in his *The History and Present State of Virginia*, he wrote that Indians had a number of reasons to "lament the arrival of the *European*s, by whose means they seem to have lost their Felicity, as well as their Innocence. The *English* have taken away a great part of their Country, and consequently made every thing less plenty amongst them. They have introduc'd Drunkenness and Luxury amongst them, which have multiply's their Wants, and put them upon desiring a thousand things, they never dreamt of before." Concluding, he wrote that he would go on to describe Virginia "as it is now improv'd, (I should rather say alter'd) by the *English*." Beverley was among the first to suggest that what Europeans brought to the New World was not to the advantage of indigenous peoples, and not necessarily an improvement over what had gone before.

Writing about the same time as Beverley, William Byrd, a planter and Indian trader, observed that there were only about two hundred Nottoways left, and they formed the largest remaining group of indigenous

---

[7]Cotton Mather, *Magnalia Christi Americana* (Cambridge, Mass., London, 1977), p. 129.

[8]Richard Slotkin, *Regeneration Through Violence, The Mythology of the American Frontier, 1600–1860* (Hanover, N.H., 1973), p. 76. Gustav Jahoda, *Images of Savages, Ancient Roots of Modern Prejudices in Western Cultures* (New York, London, 1999).

[9]Captain John Underhill, *Newes from America: or, a new and Experimentall Discovery of New England*, quoted in Slotkin, *Regeneration Through Violence*.

people in Virginia. Byrd wrote of his wish that his English forebears had acted more like the French: that is, marrying Indian women and drawing them into English society rather than excluding them. He believed that this way the indians would have had no cause to complain about losing their lands since they would have come to the English as doweries. "Nor wou'd the shade of the Skin have been any reproach at this day; for if Moor may be washt white in three generations, Surely an Indian might be blancht in two."[10] Apart from the fact that Indian ideas about land tenure did not include doweries, Byrd's fantasy represented a common tendency among writers on Indians: once their military threat was distant, Americans were likely to view them with respect and nostalgia.

After the Revolution, historians had to assimilate local histories to a national purpose and deal, somehow, with the stunning contradiction between the young nation's declared promises of equality and freedom and its treatment of Native Americans, not to mention African-Americans. Edmund Randolph, twice a member of the Continental Congress, and Governor of Virginia, wrote in the first decade of the nineteenth century a history that ascribed to Virginia preeminence in the Revolution and nation-building. In his treatment of Indians he took a number of positions, none of them new, that would be repeated throughout the nineteenth century to support the federal policy of displacing Indians and occupying their lands. In discussing Virginia's refusal to honor Cherokee land claims, Randolph wrote, "She [Virginia] supposed that it was no less absurd to recognize the extravagant hunting rights of savages than the idle assumption of the Pope to grant the Western world between two nations." White Americans discredited Indian land claims by insisting that to hold land legitimately it had to be farmed European style. Hence, Randolph wrote that while settlers had broken the law by settling beyond the Proclamation Line after the end of the Seven Years War, they "had laid a stock of merit in forming a barrier against the incursions of the Indians." Virginia, therefore, had to grant squatters' right to the "occupancy to the vacant western lands."[11] Those frontiersmen who used violence to dispossess Indians of lands legally granted to them were technically in the wrong, but actually were to be commended as brave souls doing a service to civilization. He managed at the same time to sustain the contradictory but powerful myth that the lands Americans occupied were empty.

From the time Randolph wrote his history until 1890, the U.S. government was almost continuously at war with Native Americans on some part of the continent. The years up through 1840 were devoted to subduing and removing the Shawnee confederation, including

---

[10]William Byrd, *The Writings of Colonel William Byrd*, John Bassett, ed. (New York, 1901), pp. 8, 9, 56, 98–99, 102.

[11]Edmund Randolph, *History of Virginia* (Charlottesville, Va., 1970), pp. 259, 272.

the Miamis, Wyandots, Delawares and Mingos under Tecumseh and Black Hawk and the Fox and Sauk from the Ohio Valley. Andrew Jackson intervened in the Creeks' civil war and conducted a long and bloody war in Florida with the Seminoles. Jackson removed the Cherokee, Choctaw, and Chickasaw without a war.

In 1839, George Bancroft's comprehensive *History of the United States* was published. He wrote extensively on the indigenous groups east of the Mississippi, but in the end, he recapitulated what others had said before him. He discoursed on the "absence of all reflective consciousness, and of all logical analysis of ideas" in the savage mind. He picked up a colonial theme that would be repeated throughout the nineteeth century, that Indians had no religion. They believed in a spirit that pervaded all things, therefore they had no conception of an absolute self-existent being. All of their deficiencies in reason and "moral qualities" meant that civilization wiped out the Indians because they "could not change [their] habits."[12]

Writers about Indians had two responses to the trials Indians were undergoing. All assumed that the Indian way of life was doomed, and most assumed that along with his culture, the Indian was doomed as well. For some, like the historian John Gorham Palfrey, the demise of Indians and their way of life was no loss. Palfrey's Indians were vacant-minded, primitive, irreligious, unfeeling, and deeply inferior to Europeans in their physical and mental capacities.[13] Even the fact that they never raped white women meant that they were "cold," not ethical. For others, such as the antebellum historian Francis Parkman, the presumed disappearance of Indians was a tragedy and a reason to memorialize their ways in prose. Parkman's major work, *The Conspiracy of Pontiac and the Indian War after the Conquest of Canada*, first published in 1851, was, in part, a long excursus on why Indians were unable to survive in the Anglo-Saxon world of bustle and enterprise. The cause was a characterological difference. Parkman thought the Frenchman frivolous and distracted by sex, the Mexican dirty and lazy, and the Indian proud, stubborn, and inflexible. In a remarkable paragraph, Parkman outlined his assessment of why the Indian had to die out. "Races of inferior energy have possessed a power of expansion and assimilation to which he is a stranger; and it is this fixed and rigid quality which has proved his ruin. He will not learn the arts of civlization, and he and his forest must perish together. The stern, unchanging features of his mind excite our admiration from their very immutability;

---

[12]Quoted in Roy Harvey Pearce, *Savagism and Civilization: A Study of the Indian Movement and the American Mind* (Berkeley, Calif., 1953, 1988), p. 162; see also Introduction for discussion of George Bancroft.

[13]John Gorham Palfrey, *A Compendious History of new England, from the Discovery by Europeans to the First General Congress of the Anglo-American Colonies*, 5 vols. (Boston, 1873), Vol. I, pp. 35–36.

and we look with deep interst on the fate of this unclaimable son of the wilderness, the child who will not be weaned from the breast of his rugged mother."[14]

Like Randolph, Palfrey subscribed to the theory that Indian population, at least in the East, had been very thin—fifty thousand, Palfrey estimated—and "wide tracts now known as Vermont, Northern New Hampshire and Western Massachusetts, were then almost, if not absolutely without inhabitants." He ascribed the small population to the inhospitable terrain as well as the fact that these were people "destitute of the resources of art." They were, according to Palfrey, devoid of the desire for property that "enforces industry and creates civilization." In fact, an Indian man "lived the laziest of lives. When not engaged in war or hunting, he would pass weeks in sleep, or in sitting silent, with his elbows on his knees." His wife was his "drudge and slave."[15] The logic seemed to be that since we had just fought a war to end slavery, Indian males who held their women in bondage deserved the wars they got.

The first serious dissent from this white supremacist history came from a New England poet and novelist, Helen Hunt Jackson, who had been deeply moved by the testimony of Standing Bear, a Ponca, who lectured on the tribulations of his tribe resisting removal from their home in Nebraska to a reservation in Oklahoma. In 1881 Jackson published *Century of Dishonor*, a compendium of the United States' injustices toward various groups, including the Cherokee, the Lakota, the Delawares, the Nez Perces, the Utes, and the Cheyennes. At her own expense, she sent a copy to each member of Congress. Subsequently appointed commissioner of Indian affairs by President Chester A. Arthur, she went on a fact-finding tour of California and used the material gathered for *Ramona*, a novel, in which she dramatized for readers points she had made in nonfiction earlier. Although *Ramona* was fiction and *Century of Dishonor* was weak scholarship, they did create an alternative vision of Indians as victims rather than aggressors. In the wake of the especially strong antipathy to Indians that Custer's defeat at the Little Bighorn in 1876 had generated, this was a significant feat.[16]

By the beginning of the twentieth century, Native Americans had fallen to their smallest numbers—a recent estimate is 237,196, down

---

[14]Francis Parkman, *The Conspiracy of Pontiac and the Indian War after the Conquest of Canada* (New York, 1991), p. 389. For Frenchmen see *The Oregon Trail*, pp. 217–18; for the Mexicans, pp. 10, 272. For Anglo-American industry, pp. 83–84, 88; see also pp. 403–22 Ch. III, "The French, English and Indians." See also introduction.

[15]John Gorham Palfrey, *A Compendious History of New England, from the Discovery By Europeans to the First General Congress of the Anglo-American Colonies*, 5 vols. (Boston, 1873), Vol. I, pp. 35–36.

[16]Helen Hunt Jackson, *Ramona*, introduction by Michael Dorris (New York, 1988), pp. viii–ix.

from around 4.4 million at contact.[17] They did seem to be vanishing. What disease, warfare, and despair had not already done the Dawes Severalty Act (1887) accelerated. This law prohibited the Indian practice of holding land in common and broke up reservations into plots of 160 acres, selling to white settlers what was referred to as "surplus." The Dawes Act was meant to integrate Indians into the larger society, but because the land they were allotted was so marginal and because they were so easily defrauded of what little land remained to them, the policy rapidly became a disaster.

Indians also sustained in the late 1800s a concerted attack on their cultures and traditions. Reformers concerned with Indians shared ideas with Progressives who were working to Americanize immigrants. Just as Progressives tried to win immigrants away from garlic, cabbage, and their native languages, reformers wanted to wean Indians from the "blanket," that is, teaching them to reject communalism and indigenous languages and customs. As one reformer and teacher said, "We must either butcher them or civilize them, and what we do we must do quickly."[18]

By the time that Frederick Jackson Turner enunciated his famous thesis[19] in 1893, the last holdouts, the Lakota and the Apache, had been coerced onto reservations. Turner, the first professional historian to deal with the Indians, however backhandedly, reflected the nation's sense that Indians had effectively disappeared. In his essay on the frontier, he noted that they had contributed to the martial spirit of the American democrats who moved across the continent, settling its empty spaces. While he said almost nothing about Indians themselves, Turner posited that American men regressed into a kind of Indianness in settling new lands. However, these primitive settlements rapidly evolved into higher and more complex forms of society, recapitulating the growth of Western civilization. In Turner's model, life in the wilderness honed manliness, but it was only a brief stop on the way to the final destination: higher civilization. As in Edmund Randolph' s work, Indians were both there and not there for Turner.[20] Their presence was sufficiently threat-

---

[17]Nancy Shoemaker, *American Indian Population Recovery in the Twentieth Century* (Albuquerque, N.M., 1999), p. 4; Edward G. Gray, *New World Babel, Languages & Nations in Early America* (Princeton, N.J., 1999), p. 18.

[18]David Wallace Adams, *Education for Extinction, American Indians and the Boarding School Exprerience* (Lawrence, Kans., 1995). Another important book on this topic is Fred Hoxie's *A Final Promise: The Campaign to Assimilate the Indians, 1880–1920* (Lincoln, Neb., 1984).

[19]Frederick Jackson Turner, "The Significance of the Frontier in American History," in *The Frontier in American History* (Tucson, Ariz., 1986).

[20]Frederick Jackson Turner, *The Frontier in American History* (Tucson, 1820, 1947, 1987), pp. 15, 32; Richard White and Patricia Limerick, *The Frontier in American Culture* (Berkeley, 1994), p. 29.

ening to evoke bravery among backwoodsmen, yet, somehow, the land the settlers took had been vacant. "So long as free land exists, the opportunity for a competency exists," explained Turner.

At the same time that Indians were disappearing from the national narrative, they were becoming the foundation of American anthropology. Turner's effort to write scientific history was in step with work of the pioneer anthropologist Henry Lewis Morgan, who had proposed a similar model in *Ancient Society*, which traced the course of progress from barbarity to civilization. Morgan, Adolphe Bandelier, and Henry Rowe Schoolcraft, all of whom began to publish in the antebellum period, studied Indian cultures as cultures, not simply as obstacles to the expansion of the nation, although in their parallel analyses of savagery, it was clear that the Indian and his culture should not survive.[21] Early anthropologists studied indigenous people in what one scholar has called a "salvage operation."[22] They believed that the cultures, but not necessarily the people, they were studying were disappearing, and this gave their studies a certain urgency. As James Mooney wrote in the first chapter (suggestively entitled "Paradise Lost") of *The Ghost Dance*, "Perhaps the most sadly prophetic form of the myth [of world renewal] was found among the Winnebago . . . [which] held that the tenth generation of their people was near its close, and that at the end of the thirteenth the red race would be destroyed. By prayers and ceremonies they were then endeavouring to placate their angry gods and put farther away the doom that now seems rapidy closing in on them."[23]

There were Native Americans among the earliest anthropologists, including Arthur Parker, a Seneca; James R. Murie, a Pawnee, educated at Hampton Institute, who became an ethnographer; John Joseph Matthews, an Osage educated at Oxford who became an ethnographer; and Francis La Flesche, an Omaha who wrote extensively on Osage religion.[24] Fluent in Osage, La Flesche had for sources the last remaining priests in the Mississippian tradition, heirs of the mound builders at Cahokia.[25] Unlike non-Indians, he was motivated to expose the complexity and richness of Osage belief in order to contradict the stereo-

---

[21]Roy Harvey Pearce, *Savagism and Civilization, A Study of the Indian and the American Mind* (Berkeley, 1988), pp. 120–29.

[22]Elsie Clews Parsons, ed., *American Indian Life* (Lincoln and London, 1991), Joan Mark, "Introduction," p. ix.

[23]James Mooney, *The Ghost Dance* (North Dighton, Mass., 1996), p. 23.

[24]Jonathan W. Bolton and Claire M. Wilson, *Scholars, Writers, and Professionals* (New York, 1994), pp. 92, 100.

[25]Anthropologists' interest was in Indian cultures before European contact, so they usually found elderly informants and elicited details about traditional life as it no longer existed on reservations. A classic example of this, although by a poet, not an anthropologist, is John Neihardt's transcription of the Sioux holy man Black Elk's words published in 1932. See John G. Neihardt, *Black Elk Speaks* (Lincoln, Neb., 1979).

type of Indian religion as childlike or "murky," as Parkman described it. Whether other scholars and reformers were pro- or anti-Indian, they all, he felt, believed Indians incapable of thinking and speaking for themselves. He died in 1932 without having had the occasion to make an overall synthesis of his work, so it has only recently been integrated and published.[26]

Morgan and Schoolcraft as young men were members of the Grand Order of the Iroquois, whose constitution, which Morgan wrote, gave as its purpose, "To encourage a kinder feeling towards the Indian, founded upon a truer knowledge of his civil and domestic institutions, and of his capabilities for future elevation."[27] Morgan studied Iroquois kinship systems, branching out to other cultures, including the Ojibwa, and eventually concluding that all Native American societies were organized around kinship relations rather than property relations.[28] The title of Morgan's other major work, *Ancient Society, or Researches in the Lines of Human Progress from Savagery through Barbarism to Civilization*, published in 1877, was an evolutionary view of societies, but also a warning against the dominant role of property in contemporary industrial life.

The growth and excitement surrounding anthropology encouraged many young, aspiring intellectuals to enter the field, and by the 1920s Elsie Clews Parsons, Alfred L. Kroeber, Frank Speck, and John Swanton had become scholars of Indian cultures. John Collier, a Progressive, entered Columbia, where Franz Boaz and the others trained. After visiting the Taos Pueblo, Collier became dedicated to working for Indian reform, supported at a grass roots level by the General Federation of Women's Clubs before he got a position in Franklin Roosevelt's administration. He insisted on the misguidedness of trying to extinguish Indian cultures and sending Indians away from the reservations to boarding schools and the disaster that the Dawes Act had produced. He revolted from the Progressives' assimilationist paradigm, and as Roosevelt's commissioner of Indian affairs, he worked to reverse the Dawes Act and the efforts to destroy Indian culture and institutions. While some Indians approved of his initiatives, others opposed a Washington-directed program, not specifically tailored by and for each tribe.

During Collier's tenure as commissioner, Angie Debo, a professor of history at the University of Oklahoma, published a book on the people whom allotment (the five tribes were exempt from the Dawes Act, but the Curtis Act of 1898 abolished their tribal governments and

---

[26]Francis La Flesche, *The Osage and the Invisible World*, ed. and with an introduction by Garrick Bailey (Norman, Okla., 1995), pp. 3, 10, 11.

[27]Henry Lewis Morgan, *The Indian Journals, 1859–1862* (New York, 1959) p. 2.

[28]Ibid., pp. 9–13.

forced allotment on them) had harmed the most dramatically, the Cherokee, Creek, Seminole, Chickasaw, and Choctaw of Oklahoma. As Debo wrote, "The orgy of exploitation that resulted is almost beyond belief." She agreed with Collier completely about the importance of retaining Indian culture: "The policy of the United States in liquidating the institutions of the Five Tribes was a gigantic blunder that ended a hopeful experiment in Indian development, destroyed a unique civilization, and degraded thousands of individuals."[29]

Debo's book was first published in 1940 to little reaction, but after World War II more historians became dissatisfied with leaving work on indigenous people to the anthropologists. Native American contributions to the war had been disproportionately high, from volunteering for service to buying Liberty Bonds, and the fame of Navajo code talkers helped bring the strenuous Indian war effort into the nation's consciousness. Nazism's unspeakable ideology and practices altered for many—especially in the academy—the spirit in which they approached different cultures.

Ironically, because so many Native Americans had been drawn off the reservation and into the armed services or defense industry jobs, it seemed propitious to the Eisenhower administration to pursue a policy that came to be called "termination," which hoped to end reservations and fully assimilate Indians into the wider culture. Termination seemed to make an ideological fit with the consensus ideas of the 1950s, which posited a relatively seamless past, homogenous Americans united and progressing toward greater freedom and a higher standard of living. In 1954 Eisenhower signed a bill that gave the Menominee full control of their own affairs and full citizenship. Proponents of termination saw it as a logical extension of the Dawes Act, which had been wrongly but understandably interrupted because of the stress of the Depression. They offered Indians the chance to sue to reclaim the value of lands wrongfully taken from them. The initial attempts of Indians to recover under these measures were almost never successful. It was frustration over these failures, as well as the disruption and misery produced by termination and relocation of Indians to cities, that was in part responsible for the development of the Indian rights movement of the 1960s and 1970s.[30]

In the climate of postwar revulsion toward Nazism, scholars of Indians, who almost by definition could not be consensus historians, not only looked at their subjects differently, but they also began to reevaluate themselves and their profession. Roy Harvey Pearce's book *Sav-*

---

[29]Angie Debo, *And Still The Waters Run, The Betrayal of the Five Civilized Tribes* (Princeton, N.J., 1940), pp. x–xi.

[30]Albert Hurtado and Peter Iverson, *Major Problems in American Indian History* (Lexington, Mass., 1994), pp. 483–84, 490.

agism and Civilization, published in 1953, studied literature about Native Americans in an attempt to understand the cultural ideas dominating scholarship about them. Pearce exposed the connections among ideas, information, and power. He looked at writing about indigenous people in the colonial, national, and modern eras, identified each one's construction of Indians, and related those ideas to actions and policies that affected them. In his groundbreaking study, Pearce illuminated as almost[31] no one else before him what Robert Beverley meant when he claimed to be an Indian, and what had bedeviled studies of Indians from the start. "Studying the savage, trying to civilize him, destroying him, in the end they had only studied themselves, strengthened their own civilization, and given those who were coming after them an enlarged certitude of another, even happier destiny—that manifest in the progress of American civilization over all obstacles."[32] Pearce was a professor of literature, and it took historians some years to recognize the significance of his work. Anthropologists, on the other hand, were more receptive to Pearce's interest in myth and symbol and more actively concerned with the theoretical questions of where the scholar stands in relation to his subject. In 1954, anthropologists would found the journal *Ethnohistory,* which has been a central conduit of the new ideas and approaches toward Native Americans from anthropologists, ethnographers, and historians as well that began pouring out in the next decades.[33]

In the years since Pearce's book, growth of Native American history has been at first slow and then exponential. If he had lived in these years the Crow leader Plenty Coups might not have said what he did in 1925: "I do not care at all what historians have to say about the Crow Indians."[34] The scholarship of the past quarter century has added immeasurably to our understanding of Indian cultures. For example, Daniel Richter's *The Ordeal of the Longhouse* discusses the origins of the famous Iroquois League and their politics and military conflicts with the French and English from the sixteenth to the eighteenth century. Tom Hatley's *Dividing Paths* looks at the Cherokee in what became South Carolina, focusing on how they served as a reflection of colonists' fears and dreams about themselves. Joel Martin's *Sacred Re-*

---

[31]A near contemporary was Wilcomb Washburn, *The Governor and The Rebel* (Chapel Hill, 1957), in which Washburn portrays the colonial rebel leader Nathaniel Bacon as a violent racist and Governor Berkeley as a protector of the Indians. "What has caused English and America historians to overlook the frontiersman's aggressiveness? The reason lies partly in the white historian's unconscious immersion in his racial bias" (p. 162).

[32]Roy Harvey Pearce, *Savagism and Civilization, A Study of the Indian and the American Mind* (Berkeley, 1988), p. xvii.

[33]Ibid., p. xiii.

[34]Quoted in Frederick E. Hoxie, *Parading Through History, The Making of the Crow Nation in America, 1805–1935* (New York, 1995), p. 1.

volt examines the traditionalists' Red Stick movement among the Creek, arguing for its religious and emotional validity as a source of cultural renewal. James Merrell in *The Indians' New World* looks at the ways in which the Catawba of South Carolina managed to accommodate themselves flexibly to the European market and politics. In *The Middle Ground*, Richard White shows how imperial politics and rivalries forced Europeans and Indians to cooperate in creating new cultural meanings and forms in the Great Lakes area, forms that would not survive American domination. And in a recent article Ronald Karr has studied the question of why the English unleashed genocidal violence against the Pequots in 1637. His answer concerning the Puritans' willingness to use "unconventional" warfare against the Pequots helps to explain the escalation in warfare by subsequent Indian enemies.[35]

Women have contributed substantially to understanding changing gender relations among Native Americans. Karen Anderson's study of the Huron conversion to Catholicism demonstrates how Native American women suffered important losses of power.[36] Sylvia Van Kirk has studied the Hudson's Bay Company through several generations, showing how a dependence on the skills and crafts of Native American wives gave way in the nineteenth century to the importation of British wives and increasingly racist attitudes toward Native Americans and *metis* or mixed bloods.[37] Jean O'Brien's recent book studies Indian loss of land in colonial Massachusetts and the changes it wrought in living and working arrangements.[38] We have vastly increased our knowledge of the fur trade, ecology, religions, gender relations, agriculture, hunting, military tactics, and a host of other pursuits.

In a sense, any history treating Indians in the United States must deal with how Indian and white cultures interact, as this theme has played itself out since the first contact. One relatively recent approach to this study is how European and Indian cultures have influenced each other and shared similar experiences over the last four hundred years. Colin Calloway's excerpt from his larger book *New Worlds for All* begins to discuss the ways in which the cultures interacted during and after the Revolution and through the relentless economic development that has characterized America. Like Gary Nash, Calloway is

---

[35]Daniel Richter, *The Ordeal of the Longhouse* (Chapel Hill, 1992); Tom Hatley, *Dividing Paths* (New York, 1993); Joel Martin, *Sacred Revolt* (Boston, 1991); James Merrell, *The Indians' New World* (Chapel Hill, 1989); Richard White, *The Middle Ground* (New York, 1991); Ronald Dale Karr, "'Why Should You Be So Furious?': The Violence of the Pequot War," *Journal of American History.* Vol. 85, No. 3, December 1998: 876–908.

[36]Karen Anderson, *Chain Her By One Foot* (New York, 1991).

[37]Sylvia Van Kirk, *Many Tender Ties* (Norman Okla., 1983).

[38]Jean M. O'Brien, *Dispossession by Degrees, Indian Land and Identity in Natick, Massachusetts, 1650–1790* (New York, 1997). See also Theda Perdue's study *Cherokee Women, Gender and Culture Change, 1700–1835* (Lincoln, Neb., 1998).

trying to write history in which Indians are an integral part of the American narrative, not brought in only to be pushed out again after providing a moment of local color. Calloway's focus, like that of such historians as Anthony Wallace, James Merrell, and James Axtell, is on how native cultures adapted to European impositions, how they selected and used facets of the dominant culture while rejecting others.

Gregory Evans Dowd's work concerns Indian groups working together, sharing and coordinating responses to the wider society in which they lived. At contact there were some 329 distinct language groups among Native Americans. Although Europeans lumped them together they did not think of themselves as one group, indeed many were enemies. European culture perpetually confronted them with choices about how to sustain their identities, first as a unique people, second as something broader called "Indians," and finally as Americans. Some anthropologists and historians, such as Joel Martin and Gregory Dowd, have focused on ways in which Indians resisted, singly or in groups, white culture, and how they came to see themselves as "Indians."

It is ironic that a central problem facing many Indian groups today is establishing their legal identity as Indians in order to prosecute their various unfulfilled claims based on treaties with the United States. In a cultural context that has traditionally rejected and tried to wipe out most of the characteristics that count as "Indian," such as language, religious traditions, and communal property, this has proved anything but easy. Robert Beverley could assert that he was an Indian, but a jury found in 1978 that the Mashpee community on Cape Cod were not Indians, or anyway, not a tribe. They had several African-American ancestors, many were Baptists, and they no longer spoke Mashpee.[39] Given the pressures on indigenous peoples to convert to Christianity, to "give up the blanket," to join the economy as individual accumulators of property, and to sell whatever land they possessed, it is no longer entirely clear to an outsider what an Indian is, but our legal traditions are the ones that have the power to decide. As historians, after centuries, finally take this question seriously, it raises a related question that has always been at the heart of our inability to see Indians for themselves: what is an American?

---

[39]Jack Campisi, *The Mashpee Indians, Tribe on Trial* (Syracuse, N.Y., 1991), pp. 27–28, 59.

COLIN G. CALLOWAY (1953–   ) is professor of history and Native American studies at Dartmouth College. His books include The Western Abenakis of Vermont, 1600–1800 *(1990),* The American Revolution in Indian Country *(1995),* New Worlds for All *(1997), and* First Peoples: A Documentary Survey of American Indian History *(1999).*

When Europeans first encountered Indian peoples, they saw no churches and little they recognized as organized worship. They met shamans and witnessed dances but dismissed Native American belief systems as primitive superstition or devil worship; Indian ceremonies struck them as heathen rituals. In the eyes of the Christian invaders, Indians had no real religion; converting them to Christianity would be a simple matter of filling a dark void with the light of the Gospel. Indian people, for their part, must have been mystified by the odd behavior of European "holy men," who came into their villages carrying Bibles and preaching about sin and damnation but who surely committed daily acts of sacrilege by failing to observe the rituals and proper behavior that maintained relationships between humans and spirits in the Indian world. Indian peoples responded to spirits and believed in the power of dreams to foretell the future and guide their lives. Father Jacques Frémin said the Senecas had "only one single divinity . . . the dream"; Jean de Brébeuf said dreams were "the principal God of the Hurons." Christians, too, believed in visions, but missionaries insisted that Indian people follow the injunctions of the Bible, not the messages in their dreams. In the new religious climate created by European invasion, many Indian people read the Bible and attended church services, but many continued to dream as well.

The soldiers of Christ were entering a world of deeply held religious beliefs every bit as complex and sophisticated as their own, but one they would rarely fathom or even try to understand. Native religions did not possess a specific theology; nor did they require that "believers" give verbal confessions of faith and live in obedience to a set of religious tenets stipulated by the church. Nevertheless, religion and ritual permeated the everyday lives of Indian peoples. European missionaries, convinced that there was only one true religion and it was theirs, tended to see things as black or white, good or evil. Indians who converted to Christianity must demonstrate unquestioning faith; Indians who resisted were clinging to heathen ways. For Christian mis-

Calloway, *New Worlds for All*, pp. 66–91, © 1997 Colin G. Calloway.

sionaries, conversion was a simple matter: Indian people who had been living in darkness and sin would receive the light and accept salvation. It proved to be not that simple. . . .

Indian religions tended to be much less exclusive and intolerant than Christianity, and Indian people often explored, considered, and incorporated elements of its teaching. Sometimes, Indians converted to Christianity and abandoned old beliefs. Often, old and new beliefs continued to exist side by side. Sometimes, Christianity itself changed as Indian people adopted it. They reshaped it to fit their notions of the world, eventually making it into an Indian as well as a European religion. Some Indians even used Christianity, and the missionaries who taught it to them, as a way of resisting white culture, of remaining Indian. . . .

The historical reputation of Christian missionaries has declined considerably in recent years. There was a time when, relying primarily on records written by missionaries and sharing their assumption that Christianity was synonymous with civilization, historians portrayed them as many missionaries thought of themselves. Courageous and selfless servants of Christ dedicated their lives to doing God's work and saving heathen souls. Indians gave up pagan ways, found contentment in their new lives, and experienced the joy that comes with the promise of everlasting life. Indian converts lived in peace and harmony with their priest or padre in idyllic mission communities within the sound of church bells.

Today, we are more inclined to question the missionaries' assumptions, finding their arrogance repellent and despising them as agents of cultural genocide. Indian people were wrenched from their homes and concentrated into mission villages, where they died of new diseases or had their traditional beliefs beaten out of them. Missionaries exploited their labor, stole their lands, and subjected them to sexual abuse. Oppression and chaos, not peace and harmony, characterized life in the missions. Christianity was a weapon of conquest, not a path to salvation.

Depending on time and place, circumstance and individual experience, one could provide examples to support any or all views of missionaries and their work. Indians were deeply spiritual people, but Europeans in those times, whatever we think of their assumptions and actions, were also spiritual, the products of powerful religious movements that enjoined them to go out and convert others.

For some Indian people, the missionaries brought them a new religion that changed their lives on earth and gave them reason to believe in eternal life in the hereafter. These individuals renounced their old ways and embraced the new, worked hard to make their mission villages into model Christian communities, and found meaning and hope in the church. . . .

Many more Indians kept the missionaries at arm's length, weighing their words but evading their evangelism by various strategies of passive resistance. "However much they are preached at," wrote a French officer in the Seven Years' War, "they listen very calmly & without ill-will, but they always return to their usual refrain, that they are not sufficiently intelligent to believe and follow what they are told, that their forefathers lived like them & that they adopt their way of life." The Indian custom of listening politely while missionaries regaled them with the word of God led many priests to misinterpret silence as tacit agreement and to see conversions where none occurred.

Other people did not listen quietly. They fought tooth and nail against the alien religion that threatened their world, resisting every effort to separate them from their cultural and spiritual roots, and saw missionaries as malevolent forces. The Reverend Samuel Kirkland encountered one Seneca in the 1760s who was of the "fixed opinion that my continuance there would be distructive to the nation, & finally over throw all the traditions & usages of their Forefathers & that there would not be a warrior remaining in their nation in the course of a few years." Another Seneca took a shot at the persistent missionary. . . .

Thousands of Indian people, however, selected a middle path of their own making. They heard the missionaries' message, asked questions, and found areas of common ground between old and new beliefs. According to David Weber, many of the Indians whom Spain claimed as converts "simply added Jesus, Mary, and Christian saints to their rich pantheons and welcomed the Franciscans into their communities as additional shamans." In a new world of suffering and uncertainty, people listened to preachers who assured them that terrestrial pain was temporary, life in paradise an eternity. Why not pray to the Christians' God? They had nothing to lose, so long as they did not abandon their own prayers, rituals, and beliefs. . . .

The collision and confluence of religious beliefs in North America did not occur in a vacuum. Indian people were dying of new diseases, succumbing to the inroads of alcohol, losing their economic independence, fighting new wars with deadly new weapons, struggling to hold on to their lands, and watching the physical world change around them. Converts most commonly came from communities that were falling apart. Christianity promised relief from the pain and suffering, but religious change also added to the turmoil.

Indian people and Christian missionaries shared areas of understanding. Both, for instance, attributed "natural" events to "supernatural" phenomena, although most Indian peoples saw no such arbitrary distinction between the two. At the same time, however, they saw their place in the world in radically different ways. For Christians, man was at the top of the hierarchy of creation and Europe at the pinnacle of civilization. Indian people shared their world with animals, plants, and their spirits. Where Europeans saw a religious void, Indian people had daily rituals and cycles of ceremonies that sustained life,

propitiated spirits, and offered thanks, which helped maintain balance
and order in the universe and gave meaning to the world. Missionaries
who insisted that Indian people stop practicing such ceremonies were
asking them to invite disaster.

Indian hunters often relied on the power of their dreams to help
them locate their prey and foretell the kill. Hunting was a ceremonial
activity as much as an economic necessity, since only if the proper rituals were observed would the animals consent to let themselves be
taken, or agree to return. Traveling in the Carolina backcountry in
1701, John Lawson reported how the Indians he met carefully preserved and then burned the bones of the animals they killed, believing
"that if they omitted that Custom, the Game would leave their Country, and they should not be able to maintain themselves by their Hunting." At a time when Indian people were becoming increasingly
dependent on European trade goods, and commercial hunting to satisfy
the demands of the European fur and deerskin trades threatened to undermine such ritual observances, European missionaries tried to sever
Indians' ties to the animal world and to separate them from the world
of dreams. . . .

As Carolyn Merchant points out, Christianity was altering the
symbolic superstructure of the Indians' economy: "An ethic of moral
obligation between human and God replaced the ethic of reciprocity
between human and animal." God was above nature; the new religious
teachings required no respect for animals and the natural world. Old
hunting rituals continued, "but they ceased to function as a restraining environmental ethic." The way was open for Indian peoples to become commercial hunters, responding to the lure of the marketplace
rather than listening to the spirits of the animals.

Farther west, on the northern shores of the Great Lakes in Ontario,
Huron people also found ways to accommodate Christianity. The
Hurons were trading partners of the French, and Jesuit priests were eager to carry the word of God to the Huron villages and establish a base
for future missions. The Hurons were a people in crisis in the 1630s.
Recurrent epidemics of disease cut Huron population in half between
1634 and 1640, but the mortality rate among children was much
higher. Many Hurons blamed the Jesuits for the disaster: "With the
Faith, the scourge of God came into the country," wrote Jesuit Father
François Joseph Bressani, "and, in proportion as the one increased, the
other smote them more severely." The Hurons believed that the Jesuits were sorcerers who, like shamans, could use their power for good
or evil. But the need to maintain trading alliances with the French prevented them from exacting vengeance on the missionaries; indeed, the
French would not sell guns to non-Christians in the first half of the
seventeenth century, and many Hurons accepted baptism to secure
firearms. Meanwhile, as traditional curing practices and ceremonies
proved ineffective against the new killer diseases, Huron villages filled

with the sick and dying. People looked in desperation for new answers or at least for some source of hope, and parents brought their children to the Jesuit fathers for baptism. The Jesuits recorded only twenty-two Huron baptisms in 1635, but baptisms increased dramatically as the Huron population plummeted. . . .

Only the Tahontaenrat Hurons survived as a group; the rest of the people scattered throughout the Great Lakes region. Many of them became incorporated into the villages of their Iroquois enemies; some survived at the mission town of Lorette on the St. Lawrence.

In New England, meanwhile, Indian peoples encountered a different brand of Christianity as English missionaries introduced them to the tenets of Puritanism. Puritan missionaries demanded what amounted to cultural suicide from their Indian converts, insisting that they live like their English neighbors if they intended to practice the Christian religion. Nevertheless, many Indian people accepted conversion as they sought spiritual meaning in an increasingly chaotic world. Thomas Mayhew Jr. began preaching to the Wampanoag Indians on Martha's Vineyard in the 1640s but with relatively little success. Then, epidemic diseases swept the island in 1643 and 1645. The shamans, the traditional spiritual leaders and healers, were unable to cure the sick. Scores of Indian people looked to Christianity to provide new explanations, if not new cures, and to fill a void left by the decline of traditional communal rituals. The Indians built their own church community and passed the Gospel from generation to generation.

But the Indian converts on Martha's Vineyard did not become English or cease being Indian. Some Indians who worshiped in Christian churches continued to live in wigwams. They made Christianity an Indian religion. Indian men served as preachers, pastors, and deacons; Indian women found that Christianity honored their traditional roles, offered them the opportunity to learn to read and write, and provided solace and support as their island society threatened to unravel amid alcoholism and violence. Christian Indians took Christian names, but they continued to be called by their Indian ones. A deacon named Paul, for instance, kept his Wampanoag name, Mashquattuhkooit. In time, some Christian Indian families began to use given names and surnames, in the European style. But the surnames were based on traditional names—the descendants of Hiacoomes, the first Indian convert on Martha's Vineyard, became known by the surname Coomes. . . .

On the mainland, John Eliot hoped to prevent any such "compromises." Eliot came to America in 1631, began to learn the Massachusett Indian language in 1643, and started preaching three years later. He compiled a dictionary and grammar of Massachusett and by 1663, with the assistance of Indian translators, had translated the entire Bible into Massachusett. For Eliot, enabling Indians to read the Bible was a vital first step on the road to "civilization." Eliot also established a total of fourteen "praying towns," model Christian communities where Indian converts lived quarantined from the negative influences of unconverted relatives or unsavory English characters. He laid down harsh penalties for Indians who disobeyed his rules. Men must work hard; women must learn to spin and weave. They must wear their hair English-style, stop using bear's grease as protection against mosquitoes, and give up plural wives. Discarded wives and children presumably suffered misery and poverty so that their now-monogamous ex-husbands and fathers could live Christian lives. Eliot's program promoted social revolution and cultural disintegration.

Not surprisingly, many Indian people refused to accept such an assault on their way of life. Indian communities that had not yet experienced devastation proved more resistant to Puritan teachings. At their height, Eliot's praying towns held only about eleven hundred people, and the extent of individual conversions among these people, and how many accepted Eliot's complete program of social change, remains uncertain. At Natick, Eliot's showpiece praying-town, some Indian converts were given a Christian funeral service, but were interred in traditional fashion with wampum, beads, and other earthly items. As Daniel Mandell notes, "The desire to maintain an Indian community in an English/Christian world extended even to the grave." . . .

For those who did accept Christianity, conversion may have meant something different from what it meant to Eliot. Massachusett Indians believed in a creator, but their world was inhabited by countless *manitowuk*, spirits who directed the course of their daily lives. Adding God or Christ did not necessarily disrupt their worldview. . . .

Some people may have embraced Christianity as a way of fending off annihilation as the world crumbled about them. Missions offered Indian people a haven from some of the turmoil and provided them knowledge and skills to deal with the strange new world that was being created. Learning to read was a way of acquiring knowledge about the English as well as about God; it could be used to understand treaties, laws, and deeds in addition to the Bible. It may also have carried status and involved ritual and spiritual qualities of which Eliot would not have been aware. Some women may have been attracted to Christianity because it redefined gender roles or simply because they wanted to learn to spin. For all these people, conversion to Christianity had meaning; but that was not necessarily the same meaning that it had for Eliot.

However complete their conversion, the inhabitants of the praying towns could not find shelter from the storms around them. During King Philip's War (1675–76), Indians from Natick supported the English, but the colonists viewed all Indians with fear and suspicion. Praying-town residents were rounded up and incarcerated on Deer Island in Boston Harbor. Eliot's mission program fell to pieces. . . .

Like Eliot in New England, Spanish missionaries in the South labored to save Indian souls with an assault on Indian culture that severed kinship relations, restricted sexual practices, altered settlement patterns, and promoted new divisions of labor. Jesuit Father Juan Rogel declared in 1570: "If we are to gather fruit, the Indians must join in and live in settlements and cultivate the soil." Spanish missionaries regarded resettling Indian people as peasants living in sedentary communities as a prerequisite to Christianity. Under the Spanish mission system, Indian people built the missions, raised and tended the crops and stock that fed the mission community, and performed the routine services that sustained the mission. But the reality the missions achieved rarely matched the goal they pursued. The Spanish missions also produced massive population decline, food shortages, increased demands for labor, and violence.

At its height in the mid-seventeenth century, the Spanish mission system in the colony of La Florida included seventy friars in forty missions stretching from St. Augustine to the coast of South Carolina in the north and the Apalachicola River near present-day Tallahassee in the west. . . . But Indians resented and resisted Franciscan efforts. Guale Indians rebelled against their missionaries in 1597; Christian Apalachees revolted in 1638 and 1647; Timucuans, in 1656. British and Indian raids from the north at the beginning of the eighteenth century effectively brought the mission system to an end. The net result of Spanish missionary efforts in the area was abandoned missions, fragmented communities, and refugee converts huddled around St. Augustine.

Following Juan de Oñate's colonizing expedition into New Mexico in 1598, Spanish Franciscan missionaries established themselves in almost every pueblo along the Rio Grande. The Spanish Crown saw missions as a line of defense, protecting the colony from Indian enemies and European rivals. The Pueblos may have seen them in somewhat similar terms: the missions could stand against Apache enemies and against potentially aggressive Spanish soldiers and colonists. But Spanish priests not only invaded kivas (underground ceremonial chambers), they desecrated kachina masks and tried to suppress Native rituals and sexual practices. Many Pueblos refused to accept a new faith that threatened their social and spiritual order; others continued to practice their ancestral ways behind closed doors or, more accurately, in underground kivas. Some fled west to the Hopis and other more distant Pueblos; others retaliated in periodic outbreaks of violence. Drought, falling populations, and increasing Navajo and Apache raids indicated that the new religion was not a source of powerful spiritual protection, and that people should return to their ancient ways, if they ever had left them. In 1680, Popé, a Tewa medicine man from San Juan, synchronized an uprising of the different Pueblos that drove out the Spaniards for a dozen years. The Indians killed and mutilated many of the friars who had been trying to stamp out their religion and desecrated the alien paraphernalia of Catholicism.

The Spaniards returned, but they had learned from the experience. Where their predecessors had tried to eradicate all Native rituals, friars now more often turned a blind eye to such practices—a shift, as historian John Kessel describes it, "from crusading intolerance to pragmatic accommodation." Indian people meanwhile became resigned to the Spaniards and adopted more subtle tactics of resistance. When Diego de Vargas returned on his campaign of reconquest in 1692, Luis, a Picuri Pueblo leader, appeared before him dressed in animal skins and wearing a band of palm shell around his head; but he also wore a rosary round his neck and carried a silver cross, an Agnus Dei, and a cloth printed with the image of Our Lady of Guadeloupe. A century of contact with Spanish missionaries had left its imprint. Many Pueblos accepted the outward forms of Hispanic Christianity while keeping the friars away from clan, kiva, and kachina, the things that constituted the core of their religion and their Pueblo identity. Many Pueblos became nominally Catholic, attending mass and observing Christian holidays, but they continued to practice traditional rituals and kept their worldview intact. . . .

The Hopis were more insulated than other Pueblos from Spanish crusading. Their villages sat atop isolated mesas in northern Arizona, and they were better able to keep Spanish priests at arm's length. Hopi religious leaders not only resisted those Spanish missionaries who made the trek to their villages, they even on occasion debated and denounced the padres in public confrontations. . . .

The Franciscan friar Junípero Serra brought Catholicism to the Indians of California in 1769. Traveling north to the San Francisco Bay area, his expedition established the first Catholic mission at San Diego. Other missions followed until a chain of twenty-one missions stretched more than 650 miles. By 1800, Indian neophytes—as the converts were called—numbered some twenty thousand, testimony to the disintegration of Native societies under the hammerblows of new diseases as much as to the power of Christianity. But the fact that Indian neophytes adopted Christian symbols and stories did not necessarily mean they accepted conversion on Spanish terms. They may have seen in the pageantry and paraphernalia of Catholic services new sources of spiritual power which they could acquire without jeopardizing their old beliefs. Spanish missionaries congregated Indian peoples into new communities and used Indian labor to support the mission system while they themselves labored to save Indian souls. The friars segregated unmarried men and women into separate dormitories at night to enforce Catholic moral codes, imposed strict labor regimens, and resorted to whipping, branding, and solitary confinement to keep the Indians on the path to "civilization and salvation." . . .

Indian populations plummeted. Many Indians ran away from the missions; others turned to violence: several hundred Indians launched an unsuccessful attack on the San Diego mission in 1775.

Missionary efforts elsewhere met with limited success, although not always for the same reasons. Moravian missionaries won many converts among the Delaware Indians in Pennsylvania and Ohio in the eighteenth century, and some Delawares clearly embraced the Christian way of life that missionaries such as John Heckewelder and David Zeisberger brought them. But the Moravians and their converts were building peaceful mission havens in what was fast becoming a war zone. The colonial and revolutionary wars that raged in the Ohio Valley in the second half of the century disrupted the missionaries' work, dislocating their communities, and brought disaster to the converts. In 1782, American militiamen butchered ninety-six pacifist and unarmed Moravian Indians in their village at Gnadenhütten. The Moravians and their converts migrated to Canada in the years after the American Revolution. . . .

Converted and unconverted Indians alike noted differences between Christianity as preached and as practiced. Indians commonly countered missionary arguments by declaring, "We are better Christians than you." Those, like Occom, who converted during the Great Awakening found fault with the established church. Many Narragansetts converted to Christianity in the 1740s, embracing a religious movement that challenged the intellectual elitism of Puritanism. It more closely resembled their traditional religion, emphasizing visions, the spoken rather than the written word, and religious leadership based on a "calling" rather than on formal education. The Narragansetts built their own church and had Narragansett ministers. Samuel Niles, the first Narragansett minister, said that his people regarded educated ministers as "Thieves, Robbers, Pirates, etc. . . . They steal the word. God told the Prophets the words they Spoke: and these Ministers Steal that Word." . . .

Indians spread Christianity in less direct ways than operating as missionaries. Iroquois Indians who converted to Catholicism in the seventeenth century formed new mission communities at places like Caughnawaga near Montreal. In the early years of the nineteenth century, Iroquois from Caughnawaga migrated to the Rocky Mountain region to work in the fur trade as trappers and guides. Some of them intermarried with local Indian women and brought their Indian Catholicism to the tribes there.

Though many Indian people looked to Christianity for help in times of crisis, Christianity often generated additional crises and tensions in Indian communities. Rituals such as the Green Corn Ceremony united Indian communities, bringing people together in seasonal ceremonies of prayer, thanksgiving, and world renewal; Christian missionaries prohibited their converts from participating in such "pagan rituals," thereby severing ties of community and identity. Missionaries also attempted to set up new patterns of work and behavior between the sexes. In gender-egalitarian societies like the Hurons and the Montagnais, where women enjoyed an influence unknown in Europe, French missionaries tried to subordinate women, to reorder Indian society along more "civilized" lines.

Some communities split between traditional and Christian factions. The Hurons were bitterly factionalized by the time the Iroquois attacked them in 1648–49. Delawares who converted to the Moravian faith lived in separate villages from their unconverted relatives and sometimes experienced ridicule and resentment from them. Formerly viewed with respect by other Iroquois, Oneida headmen by 1772 felt "despised by our brethren, on account of our christian profession." Some opportunistic Indian leaders embraced Christianity to add spiritual sanction in their political challenge to established leaders. At Natick in the seventeenth century, Waban used Christianity as a core around which to organize a faction challenging the leadership of Cushamekin, which rested on more traditional spiritual foundations. Men like Waban employed the missionaries as allies to serve their own political interests.

Some communities split even further as factions formed around different denominations. In about 1700, the Christian Wampanoag community at Gay Head on Martha's Vineyard split into Baptist and Congregational churches. Most Mohawks became nominal Anglicans in the early eighteenth century; their relatives who accepted the Catholic faith moved away to form new communities near the French at St. Regis (present-day Akwesasne) and Caughnawaga. The surface harmony Richard Smith witnessed at Oquaga in 1769 concealed widening divisions between Anglican and Presbyterian factions within the community.

All across America, Christian and Indian peoples and elements mingled. In Quebec and northern New England, Abenaki Indians took French saints' names as surnames, wore crucifixes around their necks, spoke French, prayed to Catholic saints, and even hung wampum belts on Catholic statues. As did Spanish officers in the Southwest, French officers in the Northeast acted as godparents at baptisms of Abenaki children. Sebastian Rasles said the Abenakis' faith was "the bond that unites them to the French," and Abenakis themselves rejected English missionary efforts, asserting their loyalty to the French: "We have promised to be true to God in our Religion, and it is this we profess to stand by." But Abenakis also kept traditional rituals alive. When French priests frowned on dancing to drums, they danced to rattles instead.

The missionary experience also left an imprint on some missionaries, however. Men who went into Indian country to convert the "heathen" sometimes found themselves slowly being converted to an Indian way of life they were dedicated to destroy. . . .

As they did in China and Paraguay, Jesuit missionaries modified their practices to accommodate the culture of the native peoples whom they hoped to make into Catholics. They realized that their best strategy lay in first winning acceptance and support in the communities where they lived and preached, building on common ground and avoiding head-on confrontations with Native practices that did not clash openly with Christian teachings. They adapted their messages to suit Indian styles of oratory, looking for parallels in Indian belief systems and behaving as much as possible according to Native protocol. When Father Nau wanted to establish a mission among the Iroquois in 1735, he recognized that he would need to conform to Iroquois ways: he accepted adoption into the Bear clan, because, he explained, "a missionary would not be an acceptable person in the village were he not a member of the tribe."

Missionaries sought to discredit traditional spiritual leaders, yet took over many of their functions in Indian society—they dispensed advice, spoke in council, shared what they had, and ministered to the sick. Sebastian Rasles lived almost thirty years among the Abenaki Indians at Norridgewock in Maine. He dedicated himself to converting the Indians to Christianity and changing their way of life forever. It was, he wrote, "necessary to conform to their manners and customs, to the end that I might gain their confidence and win them to Jesus Christ." Yet, in a letter to his brother the year before he died, Rasles confided that the conversion process had been mutual: "As for what concerns me personally, I assure you that I see, that I hear, that I speak, only as a savage." The English hated Rasles, feared that he used his influence among the Indians to incite attacks on English settlements, and put a price on his head. In 1724, they raided Norridgewock, burned the village, killed Rasles, and mutilated his body.

David Brainerd, a young Presbyterian minister preaching to Indians along the Susquehanna River in the 1740s, found that their responses prompted him to question and reevaluate his mission. Munsee Indians rejected Christianity as a corrupting influence and told Brainerd they preferred to "live as their fathers lived and go where their fathers were when they died." Delawares in western Pennsylvania seemed equally unreceptive. The blank stares of the Indians whose souls he had set out to save drove Brainerd into a critical period of soul searching, reassessing his goals and even wondering about his God. More receptive Indian audiences brought a renewed commitment before Brainerd's early death from tuberculosis, but the Indians he met clearly molded the young missionary's character and influenced "everything from his evangelistic method to his psychological health." . . .

As James Axtell explains, the direction of religious change in North America was "decidedly unilinear," largely because Indian religions, unlike Christianity, were tolerant of other faiths. Indian religions were always on the defensive, and any changes that occurred in colonial religion "were minor and self-generated," not in response to

Native pressures to convert. Nevertheless, being on the defensive did not totally rob Indians of the initiative. Frequently, they used elements of Christianity for their own purposes: "By accepting the Christian priest as the functional equivalent of a native shaman and by giving traditional meanings to Christian rites, dogmas, and deities," writes Axtell, "the Indians ensured the survival of native culture by taking on the protective coloration of the invaders' culture."

Periodically, new religious movements developed in Indian country, and messiahs preached a return to traditional ways of life. By the second half of the eighteenth century, as Gregory Dowd has argued, Indian peoples in the eastern woodlands who fought to preserve their remaining lands from European and American expansion also struggled to recover their world by restoring and reviving traditional rituals. Some messiahs and prophets preached total rejection of the white man and his ways. Indian people could become whole again only if they denounced alcohol, trade goods, and Christianity. Others offered a more flexible approach. In 1799, a Seneca Indian named Handsome Lake, who had given in to alcoholism and despair as his world crumbled around him, experienced a vision. He renounced alcohol and began to preach a program of social reform and cultural rejuvenation, urging his people to abandon what was evil but take what was best from white culture. He also offered them a religion that blended elements of Christian teaching, possibly picked up from neighboring Quakers, with traditional rituals such as the Green Corn Ceremony and the Midwinter Ceremony. Handsome Lake revived and restructured traditional religion for a new world. The Longhouse religion, as it became known, thrived and spread and continues today.

Time and again in North America, Christian missionaries established a foothold in Indian communities during a crisis, reaped a harvest of converts, and then were pushed back or held at arm's length as Indian people kept or revived ancient beliefs. Indian people learned that the best way to preserve their religious beliefs was to hide them from evangelizing Europeans, a strategy that, ironically, often convinced outsiders that the Indians' religion had died out. The result often lay somewhere between total acceptance and total rejection. In southwestern pueblos, kivas still exist alongside Catholic churches, and Indian people often participate in Christian as well as traditional ceremonies. At Gay Head and Mashpee, in Massachusetts, where Indians became Christians as early as the seventeenth century, Native folk beliefs about ghosts, witches, and spirits survived into the twentieth century. In such instances, Christianity did not eradicate old beliefs; rather, it supplemented and even strengthened them, providing a new, broader spiritual basis. The new world that emerged was one in which Christian and traditional beliefs alike, sometimes separately and sometimes together, guided and gave meaning to people's lives.

GREGORY EVANS DOWD is associate professor of history at the University of Notre Dame where he teaches American Indian, colonial, and revolutionary history. He is the author of A Spirited Resistance, the North American Indian Struggle for Unity *(1992).*

One night in 1760 the gathered people of the village of Tioga witnessed their fate in the heavens. Here, on a mountain-fringed plain beside Pennsylvania's flooding Susquehanna River, not far from the present border of New York, the villagers looked into the night sky, where two violent horses did battle in the face of the moon. Having galloped in an ascent from the east, one of the horses overpowered its western enemy. The scene left the Indians below surprised and "vexed." As they set out to discover its meaning, word of the vision swept through the villages of the valley.

The people on the plain were Munsees, speakers of a dialect of the Delaware language. They inhabited one of perhaps a dozen villages that the British increasingly, though still loosely, identified as constituent parts of the Delaware "tribe," "nation," or "people." They lived on the Susquehanna River, as they had for some twenty years before those celestial horses reared in the moonlight. The Tiogans had earlier come west to the Susquehanna from the Upper Delaware. Before long, most of them would again move, this time from the Susquehanna to the Upper Ohio, pushed further west by the British colonists until, eighteen years after the vision, Tioga burned under a visitation by the revolutionaries who called themselves "Americans." But looking upward in 1760, in the final North American stages of the Seven Years' War, the Tiogans, recently enemies to the British, saw a force from the east triumph in the night.

The Tiogans' vision swirled out of a larger storm of nativistic visions blowing in the late eighteenth century across the Indians' Appalachian borderland with Anglo-America. With the Tiogans, other peoples saw the Anglo-American East rise as a spiritual as well as physical menace to the Indian West. As occurred among the Tiogans, other visions would gain acceptance not merely through the agency of a single prophet but through the religious experiences of companies of people. . . .

Not all Indians shared in or accepted word of the visions. Even as Tiogans in enmity with British colonists spread their fearful nativistic

Dowd, *A Spirited Resistance*, pp. xvii–xxii, 2–4, 16–22, 191, 200–201, © 1992 Gregory Evans Dowd.

message, other Munsees, including Tiogans, made peace with the British, sought their material assistance, and worked toward a policy of accommodation within an imperial system. Accommodation played a constant counterpoint to nativism, often predictably dissonant, sometimes surprisingly harmonious. Like nativism, accommodation had adherents across the length of the shifting and often broken Indian border with Anglo-America; it played a critical, if paradoxical, role in the formation of the pan-Indian movement it often, though not always, opposed.

There would be a generation, roughly, between the outbreak of the American Revolution and the signing of the Treaty of Greenville in 1795, when advocates of both nativism and accommodation could play down their differences, form an alliance, and advance together the cause of Indian unity in resistance to the expansion of the states. Those twenty-odd years saw the pan-Indian quest reach its greatest fulfillment. Militant religion, while in something of a hiatus during those years, both provided and continued to extend the intertribal networks upon which unity depended.

There would also be times, however—during the formative period of the Seven Years' War and, especially, the decade that followed it, and during the two decades that culminated in the War of 1812—when the advocates of nativism and accommodation could not easily cooperate, when they could not work toward the same end while understanding things differently, and when they fought bitterly against each other, dividing their own peoples from within even as the nativist militants attempted to unite all Indian peoples from without. During these periods, constellations of individuals who possessed special knowledge of the Great Spirit—those who came to be called "prophets" by the Anglo-Americans—rose to provide spiritual guidance to militant followers charting the waters of intertribal diplomacy. These prophets intensified nativism's religious dimension and generated a great deal of civil conflict, fiercely dividing villages and even households. Their ascendance raised a paradox: commanding unity abroad, they discovered enemies at home.

Studies of individual prophets and local episodes have shed much light on their role in "revitalizing" village or even "tribal" culture. Anthony F. C. Wallace has advanced the most powerful of theoretical formulations regarding the rise of prophets since Max Weber launched his theory of charismatic authority. Both scholars focus on the condition of the culture and the personality of the prophets; however, Weber emphasizes the dramatic transformative qualities of charismatic leaders, whereas Wallace stresses the role of the individual prophet in precipitating the "reformulation" or "revitalization" of his or her culture. According to Wallace's theory, when an entire culture is under stress, "a single individual" may experience dreams and visions that, if preached and accepted, mark the "occasion of a new synthesis of values and meanings" for the culture as a whole. Wallace studies single communities, evoking the social and, with more emphasis, the psychological dimensions of religious movements. But less attention has been paid, by Wallace or others, to the relationships that prophecy forged among different Indian peoples even as the peoples revitalized, or divided, from within. An exploration of the intertribal, even diplomatic, character of prophecy in the late eighteenth and early nineteenth centuries suggests that the revitalization movements that Wallace treats largely as discrete, if parallel, were often not only related but were interdependent and intertwined. If Wallace insists that we examine the condition of the community as much as the personality of the prophet, I ask that we examine many Indian communities in relation to one another—that we realize that the late eighteenth century was, until very recently, the period of North America's most widespread intertribal activity.

In shifting the focus from the village or "tribe" to intertribal relations over a good part of the continent, striking patterns come into resolution. Indian prophets arose not singly but in groups, and in doing so they integrated dissidents of various peoples into far-flung and often militant networks. Their followers throughout the Anglo-Indian borderlands, from the Senecas in New York to the emerging Seminoles in Florida, were not the disciples of single charismatic leaders alone, but were the adherents of a broadly interconnected movement that produced many visionaries even as it divided communities. The visions of one inspired visions in others. A prophet's ecstatic confrontation with the spirits, moreover, should be explored not so much as the critical moment in a single village's or a particular people's "revitalization," but as one of many events in the long career of a widespread, often divisive, yet intertribal movement that shook the local foundations of Indian government while spreading the truly radical message that Indians were one people.

That message, often sacred in character, both drew upon and faced challenges from the past. On the one hand, the past left to the visionaries and their adherents the strength of traditional religious symbols—displayed in pictures, stories, dances, and songs—shared in a variety of forms throughout much of eastern Native North America. With this shared symbolic lexicon, the disciples of the vision came to an understanding of events that spanned impressive geographic, linguistic, and political barriers. The shared understanding, by peoples of widely separated regions, of symbols whose meanings sprang out of deeper understandings of the workings of the world, provided an essential principle for the pan-Indian movement of the late eighteenth and early nineteenth centuries. The principle was that the power of the British and Anglo-American invaders could be met with sacred power. The past, in other words, provided an approach to events that permitted many Indians to challenge Anglo-American expansion with a religious, militant, armed, and self-consciously "Indian" movement for thoroughgoing autonomy.

The past also, however, presented challenges. The heritage of Indian diversity and of highly localized, familial, and ethnically oriented government yielded neither easily nor completely. In fact, while nativists attempted to organize a pan-Indian movement, rival movements for centralization on a regional or "tribal" level were also underway. The problem of ethnic and regional diversity was compounded by deliberate Anglo-American efforts to keep the Indians divided and to influence Indian politics, often through the "traditional" channels of governance, that is, through the emerging "tribal" leadership.

Indians struggling for intertribal fellowship had more obstacles to confront than inherited ethnic rivalries or linguistic differences. They had more to worry about than potential adversaries such as Anglo-American diplomats, traders, missionaries, or gunmen, all of whom were troubling enough. They had also to redefine, or at least to expand, the fundamentals of social and political identity. Previously characterized in the Eastern Woodlands largely by language and lineage, such identity now had to be construed in new ways. In reaching beyond both the boundaries of clan or village and the less easily defined boundaries of people, chiefdom, nation or confederacy to include all Native Americans, the seekers of Indian unity threatened to subvert both the authority of clan or village leaders and the concentrating authority of those whom the Anglo-Americans called "tribal" chiefs. In this manner, the advocates of pan-Indian unity departed from the local practices of the past, while defying local authorities who could strongly claim the past as their own.

Tensions thus arose within all levels of Indian political organization—village, clan, chiefdom, people, and confederacy—as factions divided against one another both over the manifestations of colonial power within the "tribal" councils and over the movement's attempt to circumscribe, or undermine, that power. Indians who identified with "tribal" leaders generally emphasized the interests of their particular people; these often cooperated with, although they were only rarely controlled by, the imperial powers. In the terms of this book, they were advocates of *accommodation*. Others cast their lot with the movement's militants, here termed *nativists*, holding less regard for "tribal" affiliation. Still others occupied positions between the two poles or shifted from one position to the other. Sometimes, as during the American Revolution, when there was little reason for conflict between the two positions, it was easy to occupy the center. At other times, as in the years immediately following the Seven Years' War or those culminating in the War of 1812, the center could not hold.

Within such contexts, the cost of both the nativistic movement for Indian unity and the accommodating drive for tribal centralization became internal strife. By the end of the nineteenth century's second decade, four of the peoples who inhabited the long border with Anglo-America between Lake Erie and the Gulf of Mexico, the four who are most examined in this work—Delawares, Shawnees, Cherokees, and Creeks—had paid the cost in full measure. . . .

A "nativistic movement," in the language of Ralph Linton, the anthropologist who brought the term into prominence in the 1940s, is a "conscious, organized attempt on the part of a society's members to revive or perpetuate selected aspects of its culture." Linton's definition carefully recognizes that nativists concern themselves "with particular elements of culture, never with cultures as wholes," that they seek, in other words, no complete resurrection of a dead past. Nonetheless, the association of "nativism" with notions of revival or persistence, with the past rather than with the present or the future, has led some scholars to abandon the term *nativism*, feeling that it embodies, "in the word itself," the suggestion that these movements are "solely reversionary, regressive flights from the present into the past." These scholars properly object to the easy characterization of anticolonial religions as fatalistic and backward.

Nativism, however, need not suggest conservatism and regression—not if we abandon theories of cultural evolution that hold imperialist cultures as advanced and the native cultures of colonized lands as laggard. The term *nativist*, it seems to me, connotes atavism only if we accept the view that the native inhabitants of such lands were peoples at a tardy stage in a predictable process of cultural development. Once we discard that view, many of the objectionable connotations of the term go with it.

In the sense that it appears in this book, the term *nativism* has not to do with stages in time (a native past *against* a modern present) but with people in a landscape (a native adaptation to the pressures of an encroaching power). Nativists did not retreat wildly into a pristine tradition that never was, hopelessly attempting to escape a world changed by colonial powers. Rather, they identified with other native inhabitants of the continent, they self-consciously proclaimed that selected traditions and new (sometimes even imported) modes of behavior held keys to earthly and spiritual salvation, and they rejected the increasing colonial influence in native government, culture, and economy in favor of native independence. What is more, there are good reasons to employ the term *nativism* for the movement described herein, because it sought native-directed solutions, based primarily upon a cosmology composed by Native Americans, to the problem of European, and more particularly Anglo-American, ambition.

From an investigation of war, diplomacy, and ceremony among the

Delawares and Shawnees in the Upper Ohio region, the Cherokees at the headwaters of the Tennessee, and the Creek peoples of the Gulf Plains, we begin to sketch the emergence of both militant Indian identity and its Native American opposition. The story cannot be entirely restricted to four peoples—Senecas, Mohawks, Ottawas, Chickasaws, Choctaws and others inevitably force their way in, as do the belligerent empire builders, impoverished backcountry yeomen, and devout missionaries from the East. But by charting the interactions of the four groups under study, particularly of the Shawnees with each of the others, we gain a view of the rough pattern of internal conflict and external cooperation, the pattern along which Indians cut their identities as they worked and dreamed in the very teeth of a new, and ultimately hostile, people. . . .

American Indians of the mid-eighteenth century did not have to incline toward Christianity to believe that God was angry with them; they needed only to attend to the words of numerous prophets and shamans who accused them of the neglect of ritual and warned of an impending doom. While these holy men and women absorbed some of their notions from Christian missionaries, soldiers, captives, traders, and runaway slaves . . . they transformed these imported notions into new forms, forms they included within their own developing tradition of opposition to Anglo-American domination.

The prophets often called for the abandonment of things European, but they did not see this, as we tend to, as a call for a collapse backward into an actual or imagined precolonial condition. Rather, they experimented with "new" ritual in "traditional" ways. They introduced new cultural forms according to old processes. The peoples of the Eastern Woodlands under study here—the Delawares, Shawnees, Cherokees, and Creeks—had never inhabited isolated, tightly integrated cultures, however much they might identify themselves, as peoples, against all others. Theirs were societies whose openness to innovation emerges clearly in many of the "traditional" forms most studied by historians and anthropologists. Is not, for example, the willful adoption of captured adult enemy women—itself by now a highly studied Eastern Woodland "tradition"—an invitation to cultural innovation? And did not the traditional ceremonies originate, according to myth, in the heroic journeys of members of the communities, highly creative acts (however they may have been inspired)? Eighteenth-century prophets who offered new ceremonies to their people did so after having taken such heroic journeys in conscious imitation of ancient myths, after having embarked on traditional quests for power.

Power lay at the center of all concerns. Nothing was more important for life than power. Power meant the ability to live, to grow crops, to woo lovers, to slay animals, to defeat enemies. More esoterically, power meant the ability to heal the sick, to converse with animals, or to visit "God." But most fundamentally, power meant the ability of an individual to influence other people and other beings. Power meant successful interaction.

Power was widely distributed throughout the Indians' universe, but some things possessed more power than others. To secure power and to gain the favor of powerful beings, Indians celebrated rituals and ceremonies. To neglect ritual, conversely, was both to lose power and to incite the wrath of offended spirits. Eighteenth-century participants in the pan-Indian movement would resort frequently to ritual. The success of their movement would depend on the conviction that they could gain power through ritual and righteousness.

Throughout the Eastern Woodlands, Native Americans commonly believed that their rituals and ceremonies had once been gifts, donated by benevolent forces. According to some myths, culture heroes had received these ceremonies after crossing into other dimensions of the universe. Such passages were always dangerous and themselves demanded ritual. . . .

Several curious Cherokee warriors, James Mooney learned in the late nineteenth century, had long ago sought to enter the upper world. After a hard journey eastward, they came to the horizon's border with the sky vault, made of an immense, bowl-shaped stone that "was always swinging up and down, so that when it was up there was an open place like a door" through which the morning sun appeared. "They waited until the sun had come out and then tried to get through while the door was still open, but just as the first one was in the doorway the rock came down and crushed him." Unaided by sacred power, their bravery alone could not gain them passage.

In the Shawnee version of the story, the hero had better luck; a powerful being came to his aid. He met a spiritual "grandfather," who, "knowing his errand, gave him 'medicine' to transform him into a spirit, that he might pass through the celestial courts." The hero strictly followed his grandfather's advice, learned "the mysteries of heaven and the sacred rights of worship," and returned with these gifts to his people. Successful passage to and from the upper world, then, required supernatural aid and ceremony. Such travel entailed risks but could bring great rewards. . . .

Ritual loomed so large in the culture of Indian war because ritual delivered the assistance of sacred powers. In preparing to enter hostile territory, Indians appealed to the underworldly forces for protection. In divining their chances for victory, warriors sought information from the spirits. In scalping and burning their captives—acts that damned

the spirit of the enemy and liberated the tormented spirits of kins-
men—villagers mastered the destinies of the dead. In transforming
captives into slaves or adopted kin, Indians employed rituals to permit
others to live among them. Rites of passage—not just of birth, matu-
rity, marriage, and death, but of all passages and communications from
one order to another—abounded in the culture of fighting, just as they
did in the cultures of hunting and planting. Among Eastern Woodlands
peoples, the concern for order or, better, for the ability to master these
passages and communications became acute as disorder seized the Appalachian borderlands and Gulf Plains in the eighteenth century.
Among none of the peoples, however, would there emerge a consen-
sual explanation for the disasters.

Those seeking to explain their misfortunes and disorders had
much to explain. Militant, nativistic factions among many of the peoples on the Anglo-American borderlands quickly identified one source
of their agonies: the prolific and aggressive people to the east. Anglo-
American incursions precipitated the forced migrations of the nations
from their beloved lands, and these Indians knew it. The trans-
Appalachian traders distributed the whiskey and rum that destroyed
the people, and these Indians knew it. The penetrating armies from the
east galled their warriors, their women, and their children, and left
widespread starvation by destroying Indian corn; these Indians knew
that, too.

There is a broad and diverse literature that suggests that the cata-
strophes suffered by Indian peoples led to a decline in native spirituality, at least along traditional lines, though scholars have even
employed the term *secularization* to describe the event. The primary
cause of the alleged process was the failure of healers and shamans to
cure and prevent the spread of disease. The death of these specialists
before they had the chance to pass on their esoteric secrets to successors, it has been further argued, caused a thinning of inherited traditional wisdom. When entire communities fell before a plague or an
invading army, the traditional beliefs, the "collective wisdom," fell
with them.

The argument deserves scrutiny. Spirituality, or religious conviction, is notoriously difficult to measure, even among societies that left
behind genuine and now-public archives. Indian communities, moreover, had a greater variety of religious resources upon which to draw
than the advocates of religious declension have noted. To begin with,
few communities existed in utter isolation from others; they were accustomed to exchanges both of thought and of practice. The most profound of these exchanges resulted from the mourning-war complex
and its attendant captivities. Young adult women—fully integrated
into the culture of one people but then captured, adopted, and loved by
another—would become active transmitters of culture to their chil-

dren, friends, co-workers in the fields, and, in some societies, their pa-
tients. Captured children and the occasional adult male adoptee would
also render permeable the lines drawn between peoples. Less profound
exchanges would come about in trade, diplomacy, warfare, and more
casual encounters. But all of these exchanges rendered a certain dynamism to any Indian community's belief system. Perhaps more important, they gave the Indian communities structures that, far from
encouraging stasis, promoted intersocietal exchange. By capturing the
intended mothers of their children from among speakers of radically
different languages, communities invited change as well as exchange,
however unconsciously. One result was the diffusion of notions we
would call religious, such as the widely shared mourning-war complex
itself. The breadth of native religious notions imparted to Indian spirituality the resilience to absorb potent shocks dealt by the forces of
colonialism.

We should be careful about equating the loss of a ceremony, of a
shaman, or even, horrible as it was, of entire communities as crippling
blows to native spirituality as a whole. These were wrenching events,
but survivors often held on. Having been raised in religious systems
that were largely integrated with the patterns of daily life, yet flexible
enough to incorporate notions borrowed from captives and others, the
survivors could enrich their ordinary ritual repertoire with ceremonies
and esoteric practices borrowed from outside of their communities,
but borrowed in a traditionally sanctioned manner. They could, as
their mythical forebears had, seek entry to the sky world, to obtain
new ceremonies from the sacred forces in visions. This would be the
path of the prophets. They could also learn from surviving neighbors,
particularly as they might gather with refugees from other disasters in
the creation of new communities. . . .

Finally, and most critically, responses to the disasters that scholars
have laid at the base of religious decline were not uniform; even
within a village there were always a variety of possibilities. The disasters did not promote a steady, level evaporation of ancient beliefs;
rather they promoted conflicts within communities over how best to
cope. Thus when prophets called for a restoration of a religion "lost,"
their concern for the sacred may have intensified as they struck out
against members of their community who sought a different method
of meeting the challenge of colonialism. Prophetic declamations of
spiritual loss reflect more accurately the increasing divisiveness of Native America than they do its uniform "despiritualization."

Rather than a loss of a sense of the sacred among Indians, what the
disasters of colonialism brought about was a debate over the efficacy of
sacred power. Those whose spirituality intensified could agree with
those whose spirituality diminished that their people were, quite literally, losing ground. For some, it was apparent that the Anglo-Ameri-

cans were simply more powerful and that the Indians' sacred powers had failed them. These Indians sought survival and even gain in cooperation, at least of a limited kind, with the Anglo-American or European powers. Others, in a more moderate stance, sought to decipher the secrets of Anglo-American strength, and made efforts to incorporate those secrets into their own way of living. Then there were those who understood that they had failed in their commitments to the sacred powers, particularly the Great Spirit, the remote Creator who became increasingly important, probably under the influence of Christianity. In this understanding—which itself also entailed a radical reorientation, for it meant calling into question the identity of townspeople and relatives who cooperated too fully with the Anglo-Americans—lay the central premise of the militant, pan-Indian religious movements of the late eighteenth and early nineteenth centuries.

The questioning of one's neighbors' identity often involved violent charges of witchcraft. Witches, who were effectively performers of anti-rituals, had done the most to lose their peoples the favor of the other powers of the universe, particularly the Great Spirit. Short of witchcraft, other impurities, abominations, and neglects of ritual had blocked the peoples' access to sacred power. Thus, if Indians would gather to invoke the proper rituals—and these included new rituals obtained from the sacred powers by rising generations of prophets—to reject abomination, to kill witches, and thus to purify themselves, supernatural favor would return. They would recapture sacred power. To regain their access to sacred power, Indians had to perform rituals in a state of cleanliness. They had to reject the abominations that blocked their approach to the supernatural; but first they had to expose them.

One source of impurity became obvious to many who had suffered at the hands of English-speaking traders, soldiers, and settlers. At southern Green Corn ceremonies, Adair noticed that celebrants refused to buy a ceremonial ingredient, bear's oil, from the traders because "the Indians are so prepossessed with a notion of white people being all impure and accursed, that they deem their oil as polluting on those sacred occasions." Another Briton, who recorded his observations in the years before the Revolution, captured the Delaware Indians' sense of irony, reporting that he had "heard the Delawares, on being asked what made them more wicked than the other indians, answer, it was owing to their having been so much with the white people." In the same period, Neolin, the renowned Delaware Prophet, encouraged his followers to give up "all the Sins & Vices which the Indians have learned from the White People." Whether Neolin actually meant all white people or just the British is unclear. In fact he was apparently fond of the French. But Neolin did go further than most and planned to end, eventually, the use of all European-made trade goods. He recognized that he could not accomplish this immediately but claimed that dependence on the traders could be ended within seven years of his first vision in 1761. When the Indians, said Neolin, began to turn conscientiously away from the ways of the English, "then will the great Spirit give success to our arms; then he will give us strength to conquer our enemies, to drive them from hence." Of course Neolin's very insistence that Indians abandon the English reveals the local resistance to his argument. Not all Delawares would follow him.

The beliefs of Neolin and others like him would culminate, in the early nineteenth century, in the preachings of the Shawnee Tenskwatawa and the other itinerant prophets who, from the Great Lakes to the Gulf of Mexico, joined him and his brother Tecumseh. In Neolin's generation and Tenskwatawa's, and to a surprising extent in the generation in between, these beliefs supplied the ideological core of militant Indian resistance, a resistance not only to Anglo-American expansion but also to direct Anglo-American influence in Indian government and society.

Not all Indians agreed with or could abide by these nativists' developing constructions of the Indian and the Anglo-American. In Neolin's day and even more so in Tenskwatawa's, Indian peoples throughout the trans-Appalachian borderlands found themselves polarized between the "nativistic" advocates of resistance to dependence on AngloAmerica and proponents of "accommodation" with the expansionist settlers to the east.

These conflicts reflected social divisions, and a kind of political stratification, that had emerged in the course of the Indians' dealings with Europeans. Leaders with good contacts among the Euro-American powers used their influence to consolidate power at home; sometimes, as Richard White has brilliantly detailed among the Choctaws, they did so in an arguably "traditional" manner. Not surprisingly, the European and Euro-American empire builders generally recognized these strategists as tribal leaders and attempted to shore up their dominance. Having some clout with colonial powers, accommodating leaders did not share the intensity of the nativists' opposition to direct Euro-American influence. Rather, they sought benefits—not always for themselves and their kin but often more broadly for their people—from their ability to manipulate that influence.

Leaders who supported accommodation could and often did seek to defend both Indian land and formal political independence. At times, when proponents of accommodation drew arms from European opponents of the Anglo-Americans, as they did from the British during the Revolution and later from the British and the Spanish in the late 1780s and early 1790s, they won the nativists' cooperation. In these periods, although with different outlooks, accommodation and nativism worked together in the movement for Indian unity. But when the exponents of accommodation despaired of European support, as most did after 1795, when they committed themselves to cooperation with the erstwhile Anglo-American enemy, they incurred the opposition of the developing nativistic movement. While nativists sought consistently to block Anglo-American influence in Indian councils, and in that manner to prevent the sale of Indian lands, supporters of accommodation cooperated, if only reluctantly, with the Anglo-Americans.

On the critical issue of Indian identity, the seekers of accommodation often took what at first blush seems a more traditional stand than the nativists, although this pattern actually underscores their as well as the nativists' departure from the past. As William McLoughlin has demonstrated in his studies of the Cherokees, these leaders developed a largely tribal, even a national, orientation, centralizing governments and consolidating authority. But the nativists expanded their identity even further, beyond the boundaries of clan and people, to include all Indians. Nativists deployed a new theory of polygenesis, stressing both the common origin of all Indians and the spiritual impurity of Anglo-Americans. To follow the Anglo-Americans' ways too closely, according to this Indian theory of the separate creation, was to violate the structure of the universe and thus to lose sacred power. . . .

Kenny no doubt felt that he had bested a heathen, convincing him that God was angry with the Indians for their resistance to Christianity. But within a few months, when a full-blown nativist revolt wiped out most of Britain's garrisons in the trans-Appalachian North, when hot ball rained from Indian muskets into the muddy works about Fort Pitt, and when Kenny and others fled back across the Alleghenies to safety, he may have wondered. Kenny may not have realized it, but in telling Armstrong that the Indians should quit their evil practices, he was only suggesting to the warrior what the nativists already believed: it was time for all Indians to behave independently of the English, time to challenge the wisdom of leaders who yielded too much to the colonizers, time to drive out the invaders. The twin notions, that Indians should identify with one another and that they should identify the British colonists with evil, notions that would find vivid expression in the visions of prophets, did not result only from the prophets' ecstatic spiritual journeys. They did not come blindingly out of the cloudless sky or rear suddenly in the moonlight like the celestial war horses of Tioga. They grew out of centuries of thought, and decades of experience.

*   *   *

The nativists failed. Measured by their own goals, the failure was complete. The union of all Indians, the rescue by sacred power, and the demise or containment of the Anglo-Americans did not come about. We might expect the failure to have led to repudiation; instead the ideas continued to animate isolated groups of believers on both sides of the Mississippi. Notions of Indian unity, of separation from Americans, and of the possible rescue by the sacred powers inspired resisters of removal under Black Hawk in Illinois as well as the far more powerful Seminoles of Florida, but the notions also lived on in the memory of people who would never again bear arms against the United States. As nativistic notions persisted, so did their Native American antitheses.

Nativism lived on in large measure because its opposition had failed just as bitterly. Within a generation of the murder of Francis and the battle death of Tecumseh, the United States had driven most of its Indian allies as well as its Indian enemies west of the Mississippi. There, and in scattered hollows throughout the East, the debates of the ages of Pontiac and Tecumseh found resonance: some continued to seek an accommodation with the United States, others argued for the irreconcilable differences separating all Indians, whatever their particular people, from the nation that stole their lands. . . .

The nativists' failure . . . could be laid to other Indians' violations. In the nativists' view, their failure was not one of their prophets' misunderstandings, but of the Indians' seduction by the Anglo-Americans. The nativists could see that they had not been rescued by the sacred powers, but they could also maintain that the ways of their Indian opponents had proved no more effective in preserving their lands and people. The United States, by driving its friends as well as its enemies across the Mississippi, gave force to nativistic arguments that Indians would never be welcome either in the neighborhood of whites or in the Christian heaven. It is not surprising, therefore, that Shawnees west of the Mississippi, despite the disastrous failure of their forebears' nativism, continued to speak of separate heavens for Indians and whites. It is not surprising that they spoke of an "anti-christian sage," unnamed in our record, who had . . . opposed the work of missionaries.

In the manner of the earlier prophets, the sage had collapsed with all the appearance of death, "and became stiff and cold, except a spot upon his breast, which still retained the heat of life." Awakening, he told his friends and family that he "had ascended to the Indian's heaven." There his grandfather gave him a warning, a warning flushed with the memory of numerous Shawnee "removals." As Anglo-America had forced them repeatedly from their homes and had failed to honor promises made even to its Indian allies, so, the grandfather warned the new prophet, would Christian promises yield no salvation, no heavenly mansion: "Beware of the religion of the white man: . . . every Indian who embraces it is obliged to take the road to the white man's heaven; and yet no red man is permitted to enter there, but will have to wander about forever without a resting place."

4

THE ATLANTIC WORLD AND THE ORIGINS OF SLAVERY: PREJUDICE OR PROFIT?

Why did Europeans enslave Africans? Did Europeans think blacks inferior and therefore deserved slavery? Was slavery initially motivated by the enormous profits to be made from exploitation, and did the brand of inferiority follow? Did the profits from the slave trade create the capital that financed the Industrial Revolution in England or was the trade marginal to the growth of the English economy? Did Africans profit in the trade or were they simply victims of European exploitation? How many Africans were actually taken? From which ethnic groups? Where did they end up? How did this affect their history in the New World? These are just a few of the questions historians have asked in looking at the slave trade.

Tracing the origins of slavery has been one of historians' most difficult tasks for two kinds of reasons, social and methodological, and all historians of the slave trade have battled to overcome both types of problems. Questions about slavery and the corresponding guilt of a slaveholding society are uniquely difficult to approach evenhandedly. Current political concern about race, poverty, and a host of related issues is read back into the way historians reconstruct the slave trade and the origins of slavery in this country. Historians of slavery and its beginnings often find their work fueling contemporary political arguments in ways they may not have anticipated or desired. Furthermore, a historian's desire either to expose or to minimize racism can color the way he or she views it as a historical phenomenon.

The sheer difficulty of procuring data about a trade that lasted from the 1440s to the 1860s and involved eight European nations or principalities, the North American colonies, a wide variety of African nations, the islands of the Caribbean, and Central and South America is formidable. Apart from ethnocentrism and the tendency of historians to focus on narrow, manageable questions, the methodological problems involved in studying the slave trade in its entirety have been all but overwhelming. Many questions could not even be posed, much less answered, until scholars began, in the early twentieth century, the painstaking process of building an empirical database about the capture and sale of Africans. The long view of the study of the slave trade shows its focus moving from England, the Caribbean islands, and the American colonies, usually under the rubric of mercantilism or the "triangular trade," and gradually widening in scope until it encompassed the economic, social, and political development of Western Europe, the Caribbean, all the Americas, and Africa—the entire "Atlantic World."

The earliest historians of the slave traffic were British abolitionists, such as Thomas Clarkson, who wrote in the decades around the American Revolution, at the height of the trade when seventy-five thousand slaves were arriving in the New World every year. Because of their political aims these writers tended to emphasize the tortures of the "middle passage" from Africa to the New World, exaggerating its already horrific conditions and leaving myths that subsequent historians have had to correct.[1] Up until the Civil War, American writers discussed the trade either to justify slavery as the rescue and redemption in Christianity of "heathen" Africans or to prove its immorality. In the decades after the Civil War the topic rested while southern and northern whites made peace with one another by agreeing to shelve Reconstruction efforts to guarantee former slaves their rights as citizens.

The first professional American historian to delve into the origins of slavery was W. E. B. Du Bois, pioneer in this subject. Du Bois, who graduated from Fisk and got his doctorate from Harvard, and has been called the foremost African American intellectual of the twentieth century, was interested in exploring the economics of slavery and countering the self-congratulatory histories that ascribed the regulation of the slave trade to ethical principles. In 1892, the year before Frederick Jackson Turner announced his thesis about the relationship between American democracy and the frontier, Du Bois read a paper on the North American slave trade to the American Historical Association. His account, drawn from British documents, looked at the Anglo-American portion of the trade in search of the motives behind restricting it. He concluded that American attempts to regulate the slave trade before the Revolution derived from fear of the potentially rebellious slave population, not from moral qualms. Indeed, after the Revolution, South Carolina, which had lost about twenty-five thousand slaves during the conflict, began purchasing slaves with renewed enthusiasm.

Du Bois laid out many of the terms of debate for subsequent historians of slavery, and his conclusion, in line with Progressive thinking of his day, has provided areas for exploration for generations of scholars: "Here was a rich new land, the wealth of which was to be had in return for ordinary manual labor. Had the country been conceived of

---

[1]Herbert Klein, *The Atlantic Slave Trade* (New York, 1999), p. xviii.

as existing primarily for the benefit of its actual inhabitants, it might have waited for natural increase or immigration to supply the needed hands. Both Europe and the earlier colonists themselves regarded this land as existing chiefly for the benefit of Europe, and designed to be exploited, as rapidly and ruthlessly as possible, of the boundless wealth of its resources. This was the primary excuse for the rise of the African slave-trade to America."[2]

The second historian to explore the trade was the son of a plantation owner, Ulrich B. Phillips, who like Du Bois was interested in the economics of the trade and of slavery itself, but whose underlying ideas about race and the ethical issues slavery raised were dramatically different. Phillips, in his introduction to his work, published in 1918, encapsulated his racial view by recalling a visit to a southern military training camp:

> The men of the two races are of course quartered separately; but it is a daily occurrence for white Georgian troops to go to the negro companies to seek out their accustomed friends and compare home news and experiences. The negroes themselves show the same easygoing, amiable, serio-comic obedience and the same personal attachments to white men, as well as the same sturdy light-heartedness and the same love of laughter and rhythm, which distinguished their forbears. The non-commissioned officers among them show a punctilious pride of place which matches that of the plantations foremen of old; and the white officers who succeed best in the command of these companies reflect the planter's admixture of tact with firmness of control, the planter's patience of instruction, and his crisp though cordial reciprocations of sentiment. . . . A hilarious party dashes in pursuit of a fugitive, and gives him lashes with a belt "moderately laid on." When questioned, the explanation given is "a awnroolly nigger" whose ways must be mended. . . . The grim realities of war . . . [are] remote in the thought of these men. . . . It may be that the change of African nature by plantation slavery has been exaggerated. At any rate a generation of freedom has wrought less transformation in the bulk of the blacks than might casually be supposed.[3]

Phillips, surveying contemporary race relations, found them fundamentally good, despite some momentary "asperities." They were good because they duplicated the harmonious relations of the plantation, where white planters tactfully and affectionately managed their happy-go-lucky slaves, who manifested unthinking loyalty to what-

---

[2]W. E. B. Du Bois, *The Suppression of the African Slave Trade* (Baton Rouge, La., 1896, 1969), p. 194.

[3]Ulrich Bonnell Phillips, *American Negro Slavery, A Survey of the Supply, Employment and Control of Negro Labor as Determined by the Plantation Regime* (New York, 1918), pp. viii–ix.

ever white man took charge. This was a remarkable finding shortly after a period that has been called the nadir of black-white relations and
that was marked by frequent lynchings, including the murder of black
soldiers returning from service in World War I.

Phillips, like Du Bois, thought the trade built up England's economic power, which was particularly visible in such trading cities as
Liverpool and Bristol. He also pointed to the profits the trade brought
other European countries and "Yankees." He differed from Du Bois
most starkly in arguing that slave owners themselves suffered from the
system. The trade "immensely stimulated the production of the staple
crops. On the other hand it kept the planters constantly in debt for their
dearly bought labor, and it left a permanent and increasingly complex
problem of racial adjustments."[4] In other words, planters (as opposed to
slave traders) were not acting as economically rational men. Like Du
Bois, Phillips placed the actual voyage slaves made on a continuum of
misery with the importation of poor Europeans, but unlike Du Bois, he
asserted that poor Irish suffered more from the trans-Atlantic journey
than did Africans. He quoted the South Carolinian slave trader Henry
Laurens, who protested that it made no economic sense for traders to
mistreat slaves, since they had an investment in their well-being.[5]

As to the question Du Bois raised of the basis for regulation of the
trade, Phillips saw northern abolitionism as hypocritical; it derived
from the North's particular economic conditions. In the South, he argued, one could not treat slavery as a theory—it was an overwhelming
fact. "The negroes of the rice coast were so outnumbering and so
crude," Phillips wrote, "that an agitation applying the doctrine of inherent liberty and equality to them could only have had the effect of
discrediting the doctrine itself."[6]

Phillips's racial attitudes were consistent with those of many if
not most white people of the period. For example, his contempt for
Africa encouraged him to see Africans both as the instigators of the
slave trade and as such incapable businessmen that they gained, in the
long run, little or nothing by it and destabilized their world at the
same time. "In the irony of fate those Africans who lent their hands to
the looting got nothing but deceptive rewards, while the victims of
rapine were quite possibly better off on the American plantations than
the captors who remained in the African jungle."[7] Like Du Bois, he argued that Africans were enslaved because colonists needed labor, and
Africans were available, not because of any preexisting racial attitudes.

---

[4]Phillips, *Slavery*, pp. 44–45.
[5]Ibid., p. 36.
[6]Ibid., p. 125.
[7]Ibid., pp. 44–45.

Slavery, however, did not *cause* whites to see blacks as inferior—for Phillips, they simply *were,* for the most part, and slavery gave their lives, which would otherwise be chaotic and hence full of fear and misery, the gifts of order and security.

Du Bois and Phillips, like other historians in this period studying the colonial economy, looked at slavery as an aspect of the mercantile system that ordered economic relations between England and her colonies. Through mercantilism England attempted to insure that the raw riches of its colonies would benefit exclusively the mother country. England insisted on the extraction and importation of colonial resources that it used in manufacturing products—many of which were then exported to the colonies. The American colonies were not to trade with any country except England. In studying mercantilism, most historians touched lightly on the slave trade, usually ignoring American participation in and profits from it and locating it under the rubric "The Triangular Trade," whereby English traders took American rum to Africa in exchange for slaves and brought them back to the Caribbean for molasses, which they brought to the American colonies where it was made into rum. Most historians left aside the larger geopolitical concerns of Europe and Africa in this period, as well as the effects on the world economy of the exploitation of African labor and the resources of Caribbean islands and South and Central America. The main question the study of mercantilism raised for Americans was whether it benefited the colonies or stunted their economic development.

Nationalist historians, such as George Bancroft, argued that the mercantile system kept the colonies' manufacturing capacities primitive and contributed to the grievances bringing on the Revolution. Later historians in the early and mid-twentieth century rejected this idea, arguing that mercantilism was largely beneficial to the New World,[8] that the system operated fairly loosely, and that colonies ignored many of its more restrictive aspects, smuggling goods to countries that were officially prohibited as trading partners, particularly French- and Dutch-owned islands in the Caribbean. In either view, slavery was mostly incidental to the social picture and to the functioning of the economic system. In Du Bois's reckoning, on the other hand, slavery was the most essential ingredient of this trade, and it prodigiously benefited both the colonies and the mother country. In Phillips's view as well, the trade was of tremendous economic and social importance. And while slavery and the slave trade were better for England and the North than for the South, nevertheless, in the Deep South, he believed, conditions warranted a slave system to get the difficult work of converting swampy acreage into producing plantations done.

---

[8]Lawrence Gipson, *The British Empire Before the American Revolution,* 15 vols. (Caldwell, Idaho, 1936–1970).

The study of slavery as a key to the economic connections among and growth of all the early modern nation-states picked up slowly after the First World War. The imperialism of its combatants and its deathly consequences impelled a few historians to look more closely into the slave trade. Most notably, Elizabeth Donnan's massive *Documents Illustrative of the History of the Slave Trade to America*, published in the early years of the Depression, and the works of anthropologist Melville Herskovitz initiated the study of the links between African cultures and the culture of American slaves. At approximately the same time, the French scholars Padre Rinchon and Gaston-Martin began gathering archival evidence in France and Great Britain that would illuminate the great demographic changes that the trade caused.

In 1944, Eric Williams, an Oxford-trained Trinidadian scholar and statesman, published *Capitalism and Slavery*, a work that enlarged on the themes Du Bois had first outlined, placing slavery in the context of worldwide—not simply triangular—economic forces. Williams had studied (and, no doubt, smarted under) Sir Reginald Coupland at Oxford, who wrote admiringly about the moral mission of English colonialism, its shouldering the burden of "weak and backward black people." He lauded abolitionism as Great Britain's most dazzling display of its national virtue. At the time Williams wrote *Capitalism and Slavery*, however, the West Indies were fighting against English imperialism. It was in part to bolster West Indian demands for self-government that Williams argued, even more explicitly than Du Bois had, that race had nothing to do with the enslavement of Africans; it was about British self-interest. Williams ridiculed British claims that a civilizing mission inspired their bringing Africans from Africa. Profits from slavery were always at the core of the trade.[9]

In a daring move, Williams argued that slavery had provided the capital for England's Industrial Revolution, by dramatically evoking the growing prosperity of the slave-trading centers of Liverpool and Bristol. While some subsequent historians would disagree that the capital accumulated from the slave trade directly financed the Industrial Revolution, others would agree with Williams, and virtually all scholars acknowledge that Williams had opened up the study of the slave trade and provided questions for decades to come. Indeed, in 1987, more than forty years after the publication of *Capitalism and Slavery*, scholars held a conference to debate once again the issues Williams raised.[10]

---

[9]Barbara Solow and Stanley Engerman, eds., *British Capitalism and Caribbean Slavery, The Legacy of Eric Williams* (New York, 1987), p. 26.

[10]The findings of that conference are published in Solow and Engerman, *British Capitalism and Caribbean Slavery*.

Williams saw nothing preordained in the selection of Africans as slaves. As others would after him, he looked at the failed efforts to enslave Native Americans and at the system of indenture, which supplied limited labor needs but could not provide for the huge plantations that grew sugar in the Caribbean and rice and cotton in the American colonies. Williams stated bluntly, challenging historians to one of the most important debates in American history: "Slavery was not born of racism; rather racism was the consequence of slavery. Unfree labor in the New World was brown, white, black, and yellow; Catholic, Protestant and pagan."[11] The determinants in singling out Africans were price, quality, and manageability. Indentured servants could escape and blend into the white populace, find their own land and farm. Furthermore, they were expensive. African slaves cost the same as ten years' labor from indentured servants, were good workers, and could not escape easily, nor disappear once free. They were easy to distinguish in countries where black skin increasingly signified slave status.

In support of Williams's preponderant emphasis on the business of slavery and in sympathy with the post–World War II civil rights movement, American scholars, including Oscar and Mary Handlin and Kenneth Stampp, insisted that racism derived from slavery, and that it was an acquired prejudice that grew with the material degradation of Africans in America.[12] Other scholars, however, were not satisfied with the material explanation for slavery. They explored the idea that racial prejudice made Europeans think that the enslavement of black people in perpetuity was their proper destiny. In working to uncover white attitudes that could account for transporting and inflicting lifetime slavery on some 8 million to 12 million black people, scholars have produced a rich understanding of early modern European thought and supplied a history of the development of racial thinking. The study of racial ideology had produced a wealth of knowledge on the etiology of racism and its employment in service of political and economic goals.

In 1959, Carl Degler challenged Williams's view that the economics of slavery led to racism, asserting that whites believed themselves superior to blacks from the moment they arrived on this continent. The problem of racism, he claimed, was deeper and more complicated than Williams or his followers had recognized. Because Degler and his adversaries all argued from the same small collection of Chesapeake

---

[11]Williams, *Slavery*, p. 7.

[12]Kenneth Stampp, *The Peculiar Institution* (New York, 1956); Oscar and Mary Handlin, "Origins of the Southern Labor System," *The William and Mary Quarterly*, Third Ser. VII (1950): 210–11.

documents, however, the argument seemed to be going nowhere until Winthrop Jordan published *White Over Black* in 1968. In this learned and thoughtful study of European attitudes toward blackness, Jordan demonstrated convincingly that racial prejudice preceded African slavery. Jordan argued that once enslaved, Negroes became more and more degraded in the eyes of whites, but the initial enslavement, he thought, had more to do with English racial attitudes than simple greed.

Almost simultaneously, Philip Curtin published *The Atlantic Slave Trade: A Census*, a work that widened yet again the horizon on which historians would consider the origin and development of slavery.[13] Curtin, while not specifically addressing the racism- or slavery-first debate, implicitly seemed to be coming in on the side emphasizing the economics of slavery. For Curtin, the slave trade was almost as old as human history. An improvised, ad hoc affair, it changed and adapted to circumstances and therefore required careful empirical study.

Curtin, whose work emerged during the era of civil rights protests, saw ethnocentrism in earlier considerations of the slave trade. He pointed out that traditional national histories had always treated the slave trade as peripheral to "their social and political development," whereas, like Williams, Curtin saw the slave trade having central significance. He also objected to most studies for only looking at slavery and the trade in their own localities, missing the broader picture. Curtin's work posited the existence of an Atlantic World, in which scholars now locate early modern history, populated by a widely diverse group of trading and military powers—sometimes allies and sometimes competitors in exploiting the riches of the New World.

Curtin posed—and at least hesitantly answered—a number of absolutely basic questions about the trade. From which parts of Africa did slaves come? How many were taken? When? To what destinations were they carried? Consulting all the available published sources from the mid-1400s to the 1860s, Curtin estimated the total number of slaves transported at somewhere between 9.5 million and 11 million Africans. Among other themes, Curtin touched on changing African demography, European economic interests, mortality in crossing the Atlantic, and the ethnic variations among slaves imported into America. Curtin's figures and his methods of arriving at them laid the foundation for a host of new studies corroborating and challenging his findings. The debate over

---

[13]Carl Degler, "Slavery and the Generation of American Race Prejudice," *Comparative Studies in Society and History*, II (1959–60), pp. 48–66; Kenneth Stampp, *The Peculiar Institution* (New York, 1956); Winthrop Jordan, *White Over Black: American Attitudes Toward the Negro, 1550–1812* (Chapel Hill, N.C., 1968); Philip Curtin, *The Atlantic Slave Trade: A Census* (New York, 1969).

these numbers was intense and bitter, showing how politically charged even the most "objective" data can appear.[14]

Following on Curtin in 1972, Richard Dunn published a book that would take a while to catch the attention of American historians, but that exerted a strong influence on them once it did. Dunn's *Sugar and Slaves*, a discussion of the British experience in the West Indies, was important in expanding the horizons of American historians beyond the Chesapeake to antecedents in the English Caribbean. African slavery was established firmly in Barbados in the 1640s when planters replaced tobacco with sugar production and consolidated their small farms into large ones. "Sugar did have a truly revolutionary impact upon the European pattern of colonization in the Indies," he found. "All of the English and French islands inexorably followed the Barbadian example, changing from European peasant societies into slave-based plantation colonies."[15] Dunn's careful depiction of the rise of plantation agriculture in the West Indies invited American historians to include the Caribbean experience in tallying up the influences creating American racial slavery.

Dunn's work was also a reminder of how dependent North American economic growth was on supplying the slave islands of the Caribbean. Most of the colonists' trade was with the West Indies. It was vital because the West Indians used every inch of land to grow sugar and imported all their cattle, a variety of vegetables, corn, wood for barrels and building, and other staples from the mainland colonies.

Dunn also offered a view of the origins of slavery that emphasized the unique Caribbean environment. In *Sugar and Slaves* Dunn depicted living "beyond the line," living in what he described as the Far West of sixteenth- and seventeenth-century European civilization. "The . . . record plainly showed that Spaniards, Englishmen, Frenchmen, and Dutchmen who sojourned in the tropics all tended to behave in far more unbuttoned fashion than at home. White men who scrambled for riches in the torrid zone exploited their Indian and black slaves more shamelessly than was possible with the underprivileged laboring class in Western Europe."[16] The islands meant to European men the license to use brute force and to be openly rapacious. They fought among themselves and exploited whomever it was possible to exploit.

The influence of Dunn's work extended as far as Puritan studies.

---

[14]For challenges to Curtin see Joseph Inikori and Stanley Engerman, eds., *The Atlantic Slave Trade, Effects of Economies, Societies, and Peoples in Africa, the Americas, and Europe* (Durham, N.C., 1992).

[15]Richard Dunn, *Sugar and Slaves, The Rise of the Planter Class in the English West Indies, 1624–1713* (New York, 1972), p. 20.

[16]Ibid., p. 12.

Karen Ordahl Kupperman traced the Puritans' settlement of Providence Island in the Caribbean and their effort to run a successful plantation. Her work shows that the Puritans' vaunted aversion to slavery seems to have been environmentally rather than morally determined.[17]

The conjunction of Curtin's work with Dunn's and innovative comparative studies, such as the one Herbert Klein edited in 1978, The *Middle Passage: Comparative Studies in the Atlantic Slave Trade,* confirmed that the origins and economics of slavery would be studied in a broader and broader context. Klein's contributors studied the French slave trade with the Portuguese in Angola and Brazil and the English in Virginia and in Jamaica. Similar collections looked at the Dutch and Spanish as well, and Hugh Thomas's massive 1997 volume *The Slave Trade* implicated the Danes, the Genoese, and the Germans in the trade, leaving little of the European world untouched by the legacy. Nor was it just the European world: in a recent work, Curtin pointed out that the Portuguese, the earliest Europeans to trade in African slaves, were originally looking for gold when they discovered an already established trade in slaves. They began establishing sugar plantations on Madeira, and then São Tomé in the Gulf of Guinea— plantations that would become models for later European plantations farther west. Luck, opportunism, and a tendency to follow preestablished patterns—not racism—were, in this view, important factors in determining the outlines of the slave trade and slavery.[18]

At the same time that this worldwide view of slavery has expanded our understanding of the breadth and interconnectedness of the Atlantic World, the actual economic workings of the slave trade have become more and more well-defined. Many now agree that Williams overstated the theory that the profits from slavery accounted for England's early Industrial Revolution. They say that the colonial trade just was not very important and "did little to stimulate the economy as a whole. . . . For the development of the core economies, the data suggest that 'the periphery was peripheral.'"[19] Conversely, however, a new and even broader claim has arisen: that slavery accounts for modern capitalism itself.

According to a collection edited by Barbara Solow in 1991,[20] there

---

[17]Karen Ordahl Kupperman, "Errand to the Indies: Puritan Colonization from Providence Island through the Western Design," *William and Mary Quarterly,* 3rd Ser., V. 45 (1988), 70–99.

[18]Philip D. Curtin, *The Rise and Fall of the Plantation Complex* (New York, 1990), pp. 24, 43.

[19]John J. McCusker and Russell Menard, *The Economy of British America, 1607 to 1789* (Chapel Hill, N.C., 1985), p. 43.

[20]P.C. Emmer, "The Dutch and the Second Atlantic System," in Barbara Solow, ed., *Slavery and the Rise of the Atlantic System* (Cambridge, Mass., 1991), p. 77.

were actually two Atlantic systems. The first, presided over by Spain and Portugal, acquired wealth for those countries but was not able to create "an expanding type of plantation economy" that characterized the second Atlantic system. This second system was responsible for the breakthrough into "the new era of international capitalism." It remained for the English, Dutch, and colonial American entrepreneurs to invent a world in which the market dominated all other considerations. And slavery created the wealth in products that contributed to making this happen. "It was black labour that grew the commodities that entered international trade. Sugar alone provided 60% of British America's exports to Britain before the Revolution. The exports of the British colonies in the West Indies and the American South were overwhelmingly slave produced; 78% of New England's exports and 42% of those of the Middle Colonies went to supply the slave plantations of the British West Indies before the Revolution." As these authors conclude, "The mere existence of imperialism or colonialism does not explain how the metropolis exploited the periphery. . . . It was the coerced labor of African slaves that allowed Europe to benefit so greatly from its conquests in the New World."[21] Simply dominating another place does not create the flow of wealth that induces people to devote increasing amounts of energy to developing the possibilities of the market. Slave labor and the extraordinary profits it produced demonstrated the desirability of pouring more and more of society's resources into the workings of the market.

Even critics of Williams's thesis agree that the colonies may have contributed in at least three ways to the growth of English capitalism if they did not finance the Industrial Revolution directly. First, their consumer demands encouraged innovation in the British economy; second, colonial raw materials put British workers into jobs processing those raw materials; and third, trading with the colonies helped make British financial institutions and practices more sophisticated and thus able to mobilize larger and larger amounts of capital.[22]

Paradoxically, while scholars were attributing to slavery the development of capitalism, an immensely important study was attributing to capitalism the demise of slavery. David Brion Davis, in *The Problem of Slavery in the Age of Revolution, 1770–1823*, argued that slavery had existed since the beginning of history, but it was only with the advent of capitalism that a variety of persuasive antislavery ideologies succeeded in mobilizing large numbers of people to overthrow it. In Davis's view, this was because antislavery rhetoric covertly, but significantly, served to justify the emerging capitalist system of wage labor. In a brilliant, subtle argument Davis linked the

---

[21]Solow, *Slavery*, p. 20.
[22]McCusker and Menard, *Economy*, pp. 44–45.

two phenomena without rendering abolitionists tools of capitalism or hypocrites.[23]

The study of race and its connection to slavery gained new vitality and a somewhat altered course in 1975, when Edmund Morgan published *American Slavery, American Freedom*. A meticulous and beautifully written study of the Chesapeake region, this book pulled together a wide array of scholarly concerns in an extraordinarily imaginative synthesis. For Morgan, prejudice was a condition but not a sufficient condition for slavery. He documented extensive black and white contact and peaceful exchange in the colony's early days, which countered Jordan's idea that English prejudice was already violent enough to lead immediately to black slavery. He detailed English treatment of Native Americans, suggesting that the colonists' arrogant but relatively futile efforts to exploit Indians were a warmup exercise for the Africans to come, but that African slavery was initially an opportunistic solution to the problem of a labor shortage.

In Morgan's analysis, slavery was the result of many factors combined, including elite English attitudes toward manual labor, a short supply of indentured servants, and elite fears of their unruliness. Bacon's Rebellion of 1676, an uprising of discontented whites and blacks, engendered deep fear in the hearts of English planters, who decided to use the perpetual degradation of blacks as a way to unite poor and elite whites in shared racial privileges. In this way, Morgan suggested, racism was not simply a static attitude of English colonists. Instead, it was a phenomenon that could be aroused and manipulated to gain certain ends, while it could also lie dormant for periods of time. In other words, it was a condition that itself had a history. Two of Morgan's invaluable contributions to the historiography of the origins of slavery were the dependent relationship he demonstrated between white freedom and black slavery and insistence that racism itself has a history. This complemented Davis's suggestion that ideology takes on more or less authority according to the economic and political circumstances in which it is articulated.

Reinforcing Morgan's thesis about the flexibility of racial beliefs was William McKee Evans's 1980 article, "From the Land of Canaan to the Land of Guinea: The Strange Odyssey of the Sons of Ham." In it, he proved that in every culture, slave owners say more or less the same demeaning things about their slaves regardless of what race they are. What Jordan and Degler thought was a particular psychological attitude was but a recurrent and predictable historical phenomenon.[24]

---

[23]David Brion Davis, *The Problem of Slavery in the Age of Revolution, 1770–1823* (Ithaca, N.Y., 1975).

[24]For this synopsis, see William A Green, "Race and Slavery: Considerations on the Williams Thesis," in Barbara Solow and Stanley Engerman, *British Capitalism and Caribbean Slavery* (New York, 1987), p. 35.

Evans described a broad process, similar to Morgan's in a precisely evoked local context, which historians would soon be calling the "social construction of race." The study of the social construction of race follows from Morgan's discovery that racial thinking is malleable and can be used as a tool to express the ideas and justify the needs of the dominant classes. It follows from this assumption that race in itself has no meaning. It only acquires meaning in a social context, for instance, slavery.

Race can also be constructed to reflect less sinister or even positive ends, or merely to give order to randomly observed facts about a group. In their book on the origins of slavery in the Chesapeake, which is excerpted in this section, T. H. Breen and Stephen Innes argued that racial thinking can be studied most fruitfully in local contexts, and they documented the absence of any set pattern of racist ideas in the seventeenth-century Chesapeake. In *"Myne Owne Ground"*[25] they studied the dynamic relations between whites and blacks in Virginia's eastern shore, showing racial thinking to have been variable. They also attempted to view Africans as they might have viewed themselves rather than focusing exclusively on the way whites regarded them. Their effort gave voice to the ideas and perceptions that countered prevalent racism, showing even more plainly the contingent and impermanent nature of racial thinking. That one African named his plantation "Angola" and owned several slaves himself suggests the fluidity of early Chesapeake race relations.

This attempt to unpack the full range of ideas about race and show how they came about characterizes much of the recent literature on slavery, including Ira Berlin's *Many Thousands Gone*, in which he introduces a creole generation of Africans arriving on the New World's many shores. Colonists in the New World often reacted to Berlin's arriving creole generation of cosmopolitan, multilingual Africans, experienced in the Atlantic World, as just another ethnic group crossing the Atlantic, trying to make its way. This view of race did not deny racism or its effects, but tried to go beyond them and into the world, to paraphrase Eugene Genovese's classic study, the Africans made for themselves.[26] It attempted to see what different meanings accrued to blackness at different times and in different places and to see how and when blackness has been overlooked as well.

Berlin, like Morgan, Barbara Fields,[27] Kathleen Brown,[28] and other

[25]T. H. Breen and Stephen Innes, *"Myne Own Ground": Race and Freedom on Virginia's Eastern Shore, 1640–1676* (New York, 1980).

[26]Eugene Genovese, *Roll Jordan, Roll, The World the Slaves Made* (New York, 1972).

[27]Barbara Fields, *Slavery and Freedom on the Middle Ground: Maryland During the Nineteenth Century* (New Haven, Conn., 1985).

[28]Kathleen Brown, *Good Wives, Nasty Wenches and Anxious Patriarchs: Gender, Race and Power in Colonial Virginia* (Chapel Hill, N.C., 1996).

historians of the social construction of race, noted that color difference acquired meaning through the way people behaved with one another, or sometimes, exploited one another, and attributed what went on to color difference. There was nothing fixed in the creole generation about racial differences—nothing sure one could say about how this person or that would behave, whether he or she would succeed or fail. North America was, Berlin said, initially, like most other societies, a society with slaves, not a slave society. One might become a slave, but one might also become free. It was only in the eighteenth century, when color and slavery were firmly joined by practice and law, that racial theories began to acquire the veneer of truth. By then they expressed the redundant. Black people were of necessity slaves. They were degraded. Then and inevitably, because they were degraded they were slaves.

Leon Higginbotham, Jr., a legal scholar, used laws to sustain the view of Winthrop Jordan that racial prejudice was the necessary ingredient in determining who would be enslaved in the Chesapeake. He made a powerful case, but Breen and Innes's insistence that legal evidence must be seen in the context of other kinds of social, political, and economic evidence to give a true picture is equally compelling. Their interpretation is that while African slavery was likely—indeed probably inevitable—because of the example of the Caribbean, prejudice was not enough without the accretion of a number of other factors to solidify racial plantation slavery in the Chesapeake.

Contemporary politicians and activists inevitably read today's battles into debates over the slave trade and the evolution of racism. Historical questions involving race and slavery are caught up in every phase of the continuing African American struggle for justice. Indeed, it would be hard to overestimate the moral and political importance of this issue in contemporary America. As long as racial prejudice plays a substantial role in our society, historians will argue about what weight to give it in the origins and development of slavery. And although contemporary historians generally agree that racism and slavery were inextricably entwined, many Americans will continue to ask: did slavery produce racism, or racism the slave?

TIMOTHY BREEN AND
STEPHEN INNES

*TIMOTHY BREEN (1942–   ) is the William Smith Mason Professor
of American History at Northwestern University. He is the author of*
The Character of the Good Ruler *(1974),* Shaping Southern Society
(1980), Puritans and Adventurers *(1980), and* Tobacco Culture *(1985).*
STEPHEN INNES is professor of history at the University of Virginia.
He is the author of Labor in a New Land *(1983) and editor of* Work and
Labor in Early America *(1988).*

Slavery is an American embarrassment. The nation's historic
treatment of black men and women has compromised its perfectionist
and egalitarian ideals. The American conflict between slavery and
freedom has its roots in the seventeenth century. It was then that Europeans first displayed a dramatically heightened devotion to liberty in
Europe itself while enthusiastically building a far-flung mercantile
empire based on slave labor. As David B. Davis observes, despite the
visionary expectations of many of North America's first colonizers,
"Far from bringing a message of hope and redemption, America provided an unlimited field for the exploitation of man's fellow beings."

We would be confronted with a considerable anomaly if some form
of bonded labor had *not* taken root in early Virginia. Chattel slavery
existed in every colony in the New World from Canada to Rio de la
Plata. Men had been enslaving one another for over three thousand
years, receiving philosophic justification from every major Western
thinker from Plato to Locke. Not until the mid-eighteenth century,
with the emergence of Quaker abolitionist organizations, was sustained and coherent objection raised against the institution. The historian's task, therefore, is not to explain *why* slavery took hold in the
English colonies, but rather to examine the particular evolutionary
forms this labor system assumed in the West Indies, the Chesapeake,
and the Carolinas. And to avoid parochialism, we must remember to
view North American slavery fully within the context of the developing South Atlantic trading system.

At its height the South Atlantic slave trade linked the four conti-
nents that face on the Atlantic Ocean. After a hesitant beginning in

---

the late fifteenth century, the trade achieved its mature form by 1600. Europeans brought iron bars, textiles, firearms, and liquor to the western coasts of Africa, receiving consignments of slaves in return. The slaves were transported to Brazil, the Caribbean, and after 1640, to continental North America. The highly profitable tropical staples produced by this slave labor—sugar, tobacco, indigo, cotton—were then shipped back to European markets. The slave trade peaked during the late eighteenth century, with annual volume figures exceeding seventy thousand in the 1780s, and it was not finally extinguished until the mid-nineteenth century—after over ten million people had been transported. The largest forced migration in human history, the slave trade involved the union of European capital and African labor in the newly colonized American tropics. The Atlantic slave trade drew on an African slave trade ancient in origins and it linked these small-scale, domestic, and variegated African forms of bondage with radically different large-scale plantation labor systems in the Americas.

The arrival of black slaves in mid-seventeenth-century Virginia confronted English settlers with problems for which there were no obvious Old World solutions. First, slavery was moribund in England itself, and had been since the thirteenth century. Slavery remained on the English statute books in the institution of villenage, dating back to Roman times. However, during the period from the late fourteenth to the seventeenth century, personal feudal services gave way to impersonal rents, contractual obligations, and money payments. Villenage in practice became extinct in all but the remotest parts of England. Slavery, as a legal status, only occasionally received statutory implementation. A temporary law of 1547 mandated that beggars fleeing from enforced service were to be branded on the forehead with the letter "S," indicating that they would be "slaves" until death. A second problem for the Virginia colonists resulted from their sense of cultural superiority, particularly as it related to vaguely racialist conceptions of the "genius" of the English people. This cultural chauvinism made it unlikely that the colonists would accept blacks *into* their society in any kind of participatory fashion. To accept massive numbers of people so profoundly alien to English traditions risked permanent disjunctions within the social order. Their unfamiliarity with the institution of slavery and their xenophobia presented the colonists with two equally undesirable alternatives. They could reintroduce the institution as the special and exclusive province for Africans and Indians, or they could attempt to moderate their cultural parochialism and bring blacks into their society after a period of apprenticeship as bonded laborers.

We know the tack they ultimately took. But, as this study reveals, the route to this decision was more circuitous than many have imagined. The process of black debasement and degradation was not linear and foreordained. As the following examination of free blacks in seventeenth-century Northampton County, Virginia, suggests, Englishmen and Africans could interact with one another on terms of relative equality for two generations. The possibility of a genuinely multiracial society became a reality during the years before Bacon's Rebellion in 1676. Not until the end of the seventeenth century was there an inexorable hardening of racial lines. We argue that it was not until the slave codes of 1705 that the tragic fate of Virginia's black population was finally sealed. An awareness of the awesomeness of this tragedy—for white and black alike—must not blind us to the variety of human relationships possible during the preceding eighty years. Only by maintaining sensitivity to the expectations and goals of the people who in fact lived in seventeenth-century Virginia—from their, not our own, vantage point—will we be able fully to understand this impending transformation. . . .

Patriarch on Pungoteague Creek

Anthony Johnson would have been a success no matter where he lived. He possessed immense energy and ingenuity. His parents doubtless never imagined that their son would find himself a slave in a struggling, frontier settlement called Virginia. Over his original bondage, of course, Johnson had no control. He did not allow his low status in the New World to discourage him, however, and in his lifetime he managed to achieve that goal so illusive to immigrants of all races, the American dream. By the time Johnson died he had become a freeman, formed a large and secure family, built up a sizable estate, and in the words of one admiring historian, established himself as the "black patriarch" of Pungoteague Creek, a small inlet on the western side of Northampton County.

Despite his well-documented accomplishments, Johnson has fared poorly in the hands of historians. For the most part, the reasons for this oversight are obvious. Before the American Revolution, Virginians paid scant attention to the colony's past. The seventeenth century seemed filled with failures, massacres, and stupidity, and even if Robert Beverley or William Stith had examined the manuscript records of Northampton County, they would not have found Johnson's story edifying. At the end of the eighteenth century, Virginians invented a history filled with dashing cavaliers who, according to local legend, had been exiled to the Chesapeake for their loyalty to Charles I. Again, there was no place for Johnson, a black man, in this nostalgic reconstruction.

Race Relations as Status and Process

The status of black people in seventeenth-century Virginia has generated fierce debate among historians. In part, the intense interest in the
subject, especially since World War II, resulted from contemporary
concerns about race relations. The efforts of black Americans to
achieve full equality inevitably raised questions about the origins of
racial discrimination in this country, and scholars became curious
whether the racist attitudes they encountered in their own society
could be traced back to the first colonists. What exactly had been the
relationship between black slavery and white prejudice? Which came
first? Since Virginia was the earliest English mainland colony to legal-
ize bondage on the basis of race, it seemed logical that the records of
this colony would provide the answers. . . .

Three aspects of the literature on the seventeenth century deserve
special reconsideration: first, a teleological assumption that since
black people have generally been ill-treated in our society, the colonial
historian's primary responsibility is collecting early cases of discrimination in hopes of better understanding later more virulent forms of
racism; second, a perception of race that regards a man's color as sufficient explanation for his values as well as behavior; and third, a tendency to substitute abstract, often lifeless categories such as slavery
for the study of actual race relations. Certainly a successful recasting
of the debate over the character of race relations in seventeenth-century Virginia must take these themes into account.

Let us turn initially to the problem of teleology. . . . Contemporary
historians sometimes assume that decisions made in early colonial
times were directly responsible for current racial tensions in the United
States. They take for granted an unilinear development from 1619 to the
present, a long chain of unhappy events leading inevitably to chattel
slavery, lynching, and institutional racism. Such a view of the past at
least offers a convenient sorting device. If one knows in advance how
the story will turn out, then one has little problem establishing a research design. Teleology provides direction, and the historian's job—
whether he admits it or not—becomes one of busily collecting examples
of racial discrimination. Lawyers call this approach the "leading case"
method; Herbert Butterfield labeled an analogous approach the "Whig
interpretation of history." In any form, it grossly simplifies causal links,
making actual men and women living 300 years ago the servants of historical forces about which they possessed not the slightest knowledge.

The teleological interpretation becomes particularly obtrusive
when we turn to the sparse records of early Virginia. It is not difficult
to select laws from the colony's published statues that specifically
deny to black people rights enjoyed by whites. Someone with a sharp

eye can even ferret out signs of racial discrimination long before the appearance of the first statutory references to slavery in the 1660s. The point here is not to assert that discrimination was insignificant in early Virginia or that the blacks were treated better than we imagined. Rather, we want to stress that there was nothing inevitable about the course of race relations, and when we study free black colonists within the context of their own society, we discover that they lived their lives, made personal decisions, and planned for the future in the belief that they could in fact shape their physical and social environment. If one misses this point and insists that these people were the victims of forces beyond their control, then one will not be able to make much sense out of the behavior of Northampton's free blacks.

A second assumption running through current writing on race relations is that in colonial times, if not in all of American history, blacks and whites formed solid, largely self-contained blocs. For obvious reasons this might be termed the monolithic perception of race. The literature contains many examples of this type of thinking. The very title of Jordan's *White Over Black* suggests the persistence of sharp racial boundaries over more than two centuries. And in a more recent, widely discussed publication, the racial categories are spelled out even more definitively. As A. Leon Higginbotham, Jr., explains in the introduction to *In the Matter of Color*, "In treating the first 200 years of black presence in America, this book will demonstrate how the entire legal apparatus was used by those with the power to do so [i.e., the whites] to establish a solid legal tradition for the absolute enslavement of blacks." In studies like these, race itself becomes a sufficient cause for behavior. The logic, of course, is circular. White men and women think white thoughts and hold white prejudices because they are white. On the other hand, blacks subscribe to black thought patterns, and thus, once we know a person's skin color, we can explain his or her attitudes on a broad range of racially sensitive issues.

This form of argumentation creates considerable interpretive problems, not the least of which is that it flies in the face of social reality. To be sure, at a very high level of abstraction a scholar may generalize about the experiences of blacks and whites, treating them, in other words, as ideal types. However, the closer we examine specific biracial communities, either in the present or past, the more we discover that gross generalizations about race are misleading, if not altogether incorrect. We find ourselves confronted with too many exceptions, with blacks and whites who stubbornly refuse to behave as blacks and whites are supposed to behave. Sociologist William Julius Wilson recognized this difficulty and explained that "It is difficult to speak of a uniform black experience when the black population can be meaningfully stratified into groups." The same case for differential behavior within a racial group can be advanced for whites. According to George M. Fredrickson, "Recent sociological investigations suggest that there is no simple cause-and-effect relationship between stereotyped opinions about a given group and discriminatory actions or policies. It is quite possible for an individual to have a generalized notion about members of another race or nationality that bears almost no relation to how he actually behaves when confronted with them." Someone who understands the diversity of human responses to external factors will realize that certain activities—black slave-holding for example—do not need to be explained away as examples of social pathology.

Other factors besides race influenced the frequency and intensity of human interaction. Since whites and blacks came into regular contact throughout the colonial period, there is no legitimacy to the claim that each group developed cultural and social forms in relative isolation. As Herbert G. Gutman explained with specific reference to slaves, "The African slave learned much about New World cultures from those who first owned him, and the significant culture change that occurred between 1740 and 1780 has been obscured because so much of that interaction had been encased in snug and static historical opposites such as 'slave' and 'planter' or 'black' and 'white'." Gutman's observation holds for the seventeenth century and for free blacks as well as slaves. At any given time, the character of race relations in early American was a function of *demography* (how many persons of each race were present in the society?), *spatiality* (how was the black and white population distributed over a region?), *ethnicity* (where exactly in Europe and Africa did these people originate?), and *wealth* (how did economic standing affect racial attitudes?). When one includes such elements in an analysis of a multiracial society like Northampton, one finds that allegedly sharp racial boundaries were actually blurred and constantly shifting.

Several examples taken from the historiography of seventeenth-century Virginia reveal the subtle—and sometimes not so subtle—ways in which the monolithic perception of race influences the scholar's imagination. We shall consider the value of colony law for the study of race relations, the controversy over arms and race, the problem of mixed racial groups of runaways, and finally, the manner in which the Northampton County clerk noted a person's race in the local records. First, there is the law itself. Historians have gained much of their knowledge about race relations in colonial times from statute law, in this case from William Waller Hening's collection of Virginia laws published early in the nineteenth century. A question immediately occurs about the limitations of this particular source. Presumably statutes passed in the House of Burgesses tell us something significant about perceptions of race in colonial Virginia. But what is it? Whose perceptions are reflected in the collected laws? If the answer is all "white" Virginians—and that is usually assumed to be the case—then the source most certainly has been misinterpreted.

When Winthrop Jordan wrote his book on American attitudes toward the Negro, he was keenly aware of this problem. He attempted to negotiate it by admitting that "while statutes usually speak falsely as to actual behavior, they afford probably the best single means of ascertaining what a society thinks behavior ought to be." He also noted that unlike the settlers in French, Spanish, and Portuguese colonies, "Englishmen had representative assemblies in America [which] makes it possible for the historian to ascertain communal attitudes." In other words, English colonial society revealed its collective attitudes through the deliberations of representative assemblies. Since the particular political society or community we have been studying obviously did not include blacks, we must infer that the laws provide meaningful insight only into the white mind of Virginia. The problem here is that many whites were indentured servants, who were so unhappy about their condition in the New World that they regularly resisted the authority of their masters. In 1670, in fact, Governor William Berkeley and the members of the House of Burgesses became sufficiently worried about the unruliness of the colony's landless white freemen that they disfranchised them. Moreover, we know that blacks and whites cooperated under certain conditions—some even united in an attempt to overthrow the royal governor. While it is likely that poor whites and indentured servants shared the race prejudices of the great planters who actually wrote the laws, we cannot assume on the basis of statutes alone the existence of an undifferentiated white response to black Virginians.

Clearly, assumptions about race solidarity have influenced our understanding of the blacks' right to bear arms. Historians recognize that a gun was an essential possession in seventeenth-century Virginia. This was a violent society, and an unarmed black risked intimidation, if not physical harm, from aggressive whites as well as hostile Indians. A gun gave a man a sense of personal independence, a voice in local affairs that carried weight even when logic failed. It seemed self-evident to modern commentators that the House of Burgesses would not arm the members of an oppressed race. Unfortunately for curious scholars, Virginia lawmakers did not pay much attention to this issue before the 1660s. The only act in which Negroes and firearms were linked passed the legislature in 1640. It simply advised "all masters of families [to] . . . use their best endeavours for the firnishing of themselves and all those of their families who shall be capable of arms (excepting negros) with arms both offensive and defensive." Largely on the basis of this act, historians have drawn a number of conclusions about race relations in early Virginia. Moreover, the claims made for this particular piece of legislation have undergone a striking inflation over the last thirty years. Oscar and Mary Handlin gave only passing mention to the topic in their essay "Origins of the Southern Labor System," which first appeared in 1950. After reviewing the Virginia laws, they found no evidence of a trend toward the systematic disarmament of blacks, and they did not even bother to quote the 1640 act. Carl Degler, however, disagreed with the Handlins' analysis. He argued that the arms law demonstrated how "Negroes and slaves were singled out for special status in the years before 1650."

In an article published four years later, Winthrop Jordan decided that the statute was even more significant than Degler had thought. "Virginia law," he explained, "set Negroes apart . . . by denying them the important right and obligation to bear arms. Few restraints could indicate more clearly the denial to Negroes of membership in the white community." In other words, this law provided important insight into the growth of white prejudice, and we can only infer that the possession of guns must have been a means of establishing well-defined racial boundaries. Degler later returned to the subject in a comparative study of race relations in Brazil and the United States. By this time, he had transformed the 1640 act from proscriptive legislation into a description of actual social practice. The whites of Virginia owned guns; the blacks did not. We have moved in this escalating interpretation from a single, somewhat ambiguous case of racial discrimination to a general statement about white attitudes toward all blacks and, finally, to a complete disarmament of the colony's black population.

Considering the notoriety of the 1640 legislation, we should begin our reassessment with the text of the law itself. Even a cursory reading of the act reveals that the claims that have been made for it are unsupported. There is no indication here, for example, of an effort by the white colonists to disarm the black population, be they free or enslaved. The legislation speaks specifically in terms of families. Masters are expected by a certain future date to have armed everyone "of their families" except Negroes. These black men presumably were slaves or indentured servants working on particular plantations. The law does not prohibit a black master such as Anthony Johnson from possessing a firearm, nor for that matter, does it order all blacks regardless of their status to surrender their weapons to the state. And finally, the law does not make it illegal for blacks to engage in offensive or defensive warfare. It is true that the members of the House of Burgesses separated *some* blacks out for special treatment, but little more can be said with authority about the act. The Handlins were correct. The 1640 law seems to have been an *ad hoc* decision related more directly to taxation than to domestic security, and since the legislature did not raise the question of the blacks' right to bear arms again for more than two decades, it does not appear warranted to interpret the act as strong evidence of white over black.

Examples drawn from different types of colonial records sustain these suspicions. In July 1675 the Northampton County court issued a warrant against William Harman, a successful free black farmer, "concerninge a Gunne found in the possession of the said Harman." A white planter named William Grey had appeared before the local justices complaining that the firearm belonged to him. Harman insisted that he had legally purchased the gun from Grey's wife, and after hearing the evidence the members of the court found for Harman. The black man kept the weapon, while an unhappy Grey paid court costs. Nothing was said in this case about the defendant's race, and if we are surprised by the Northampton judgment, it is probably because historians have misinterpreted the 1640 act rather than because black Virginians were actually disarmed.

The problems with the monolithic interpretation of race relations become even more evident when we consider the active role that armed blacks played during Bacon's Rebellion. Again, the failure to appreciate their participation in this political upheaval can be traced back to the 1640 legislation. Thomas Grantham, an English sea captain, arrived in Virginia just as the rebel forces were crumbling. Nathaniel Bacon had recently died, and apparently sensing an opportunity for easy glory, Grantham volunteered to negotiate in Governor Berkeley's name with several rebel bands that remained in the field. At the plantation of Colonel John West, supposedly the rebel army's "Chiefe Garrison and Magazine," the Captain found about four hundred "English and Negroes in Armes." Grantham no doubt exceeded his authority when he told "the negroes and Servants that they were all pardoned and freed from their Slavery." But despite the "faire promises" and despite a large quantity of brandy, "eighty Negroes and Twenty English . . . would not deliver their Arms." Such figures reveal the danger of attempting to describe social practice on the basis of statute law.

With hindsight the Governor's supporters may have wished that they had, in fact, disarmed the blacks in 1640. In an act entitled "Preventing Negroes Insurrections," the House of Burgesses in 1680 ordered that "it shall not be lawful for any negroe or other slave to carry or arme himselfe with any club, staffe, gunn, sword or any other weapon of defense or offence." The Virginia legislators made no reference to a failure to enforce the earlier law. And even in 1680, with the memory of armed blacks in open rebellion fresh in their minds, the Burgesses did not attempt to disarm *all* black men. The act specifically concerned "negroe slaves," and it does not appear that freemen such as William Harman ran much danger of being left weaponless. Indeed, it was not until 1738 that the Virginia legislators declared that "all such free mulattos, negros, or Indians, as are or shall be listed [in the militia]

. . . shall appear without arms." By that time, of course, the social and demographic elements affecting the character of race relations had changed substantially, and the monolithic view of race may have corresponded to social reality more closely in this period than it did in the mid-seventeenth century.

The racially determinative interpretation of behavior has also affected our understanding of the ways in which Virginia courts punished runaway laborers. In the mid-seventeenth century, dependent workers—slaves and servants—frequently left their masters' service without permission. They did so for a variety of reasons. They resented the terrible work conditions, especially poor diet and clothing; stories of better opportunities in other colonies also lured them away. Since tobacco was a labor intensive crop and since good workers were both rare and expensive, the House of Burgesses devised ways to track down and punish servants who slipped away. None of these controls was sufficient, however, to discourage desperate men and women from attempting to escape from the drudgery of plantation life. Sometimes blacks and whites ran away together, and when local authorities managed to recapture them, they meted out stiff punishments. The cases involving blacks and whites have played a major role in shaping our understanding of early American race relations. They have provided scholars with unusual situations in which persons of different races violated the same statutes. Historians have discovered that in general the court's treatment of offenders varied, depending on a person's skin color, the white runaways faring better than did the blacks. This has been interpreted as clear evidence of the white community's race prejudice, a deep-seated antipathy toward blacks that generated systematic discrimination long before the legislature got around to writing Negro slavery into law.

Two cases adjudicated in 1640 have received particular attention. Because of their historiographical importance, we should consider them closely. In one case, three of Hugh Gwyn's servants appeared before a colony court. They had run away to Maryland, causing Gwyn considerable "loss and prejudice." The two white laborers, one a Scot and the other a Dutchman, were given thirty lashes, a harsh punishment even in seventeenth-century Virginia, as well as four years' extra service. The third man in this trio, "a negro named *John Punch,*" received not only the "thirty stripes" but also was ordered to "serve his said master or his assigns for the time of his natural Life here or elsewhere." As Carl Degler points out, Punch's treatment appears gratuitously severe. The black endured the pain and embarrassment of a public whipping, but unlike the white culprits, he lost his freedom for life. "No white servant in America," Winthrop Jordan observed, "so far as is known, ever received a like sentence."

The second case involved a complicated conspiracy. In July 1640 Captain William Pierce complained before open court that six of his servants and a Negro owned by a "Mr. Reginolds" had attempted to flee to "the *Dutch* plantation," presumably New Netherland. The group planned their escape with great care. The enterprise required courage, patience, and secrecy. The conspirators communicated between two plantations, gathered "corn powder and shot and guns," and then stole a skiff belonging to Pierce. They set off on a "Saturday night," and by the time they were apprehended they had sailed a considerable distance down the Elizabeth River. The chief organizer, a Dutchman named Christopher Miller, received the harshest punishment, a whipping, branding, shackling, and extended service. The other five white servants were given somewhat milder sentences, but they too suffered terribly for their bid for freedom. "Emanuel the Negro" was given thirty stripes, a letter "R" burnt into his cheek, and shackling for at least a year—all things which had been inflicted upon his co-conspirators as well. Unlike the whites, however, Emanuel did not have to serve extra time. Degler argues, no doubt correctly, that the black runaway "was already serving his master for a life-time—i.e., he was a slave." The court's actions demonstrated that some colonists, simply because of the color of their skins, found themselves reduced to a status below that of any white Virginian.

This analysis is persuasive to a point. Court decisions inform us about the interests and beliefs of the colony's white leaders, those planters who by 1640 owned large gangs of dependent laborers. Unfortunately, in their attempt to document the growing separation of the races, historians have ignored the highly instructive interracial cooperation to which these cases also speak. The conspiracy of the Elizabeth River servants is a good example of a much overlooked form of race relations. No one in Virginia regarded the crime of running away lightly. The chances of failure were great, and the seven laborers must have known that they risked extraordinarily severe punishments. Certainly, they could expect no compassion, for as the court explained, they had created "a dangerous precident for the future time." The conspirators trusted one another. They had no other choice. Without secrecy, the project was doomed, and so far as the six whites were concerned, it did not much matter if Emanuel was black so long as he faithfully executed his instructions.

The need for cooperation increased once the group set out on its journey. The laborers had lived in the colony only a short time, and their knowledge of the winds and currents was consequently limited. The irresponsibility of any man placed the lives of all in jeopardy. The importance of strong personal ties would not have been reduced if these runaways had taken to the woods, where Indians waited to capture or kill the fugitives. Moreover, if the workers did not husband their provisions well, they could starve.

Despite these formidable obstacles, blacks and whites persisted in running away together. In 1661 the House of Burgesses attempted to stop these joint ventures by ordering "That in case any English servant shall run away in company with any negroes who are incapable of making satisfaction by addition of time [i.e., slaves], *Bee itt enacted* that the English so running away in company with them shall serve for the time of the said negroes absence as they are to do for their owne." There is no evidence that this legislation was an effective deterrent. The possibility of large-scale, interracial cooperation continued to worry the leaders of Virginia. When a group of fugitive slaves frustrated all attempts to retake them in 1672, the planters' greatest concern was that "other negroes, Indians or servants . . . [might] fly forth and joyne with them." These cases, of course, reveal only extreme actions, desperate attempts to escape, but for every group of mixed runaways who came before the courts there were doubtless many more poor whites and blacks who cooperated in smaller, less daring ways on the plantation. These forms of interaction did not mean that white servants such as Christopher Miller necessarily regarded Negroes as their equals, nor for that matter, that Emanuel thought any better of Miller because he was white. The low legal status of an Emanuel or John Punch, however, did not preclude their forging close relationships with certain white colonists.

A final example taken from the records of the Northampton County court reveals how thoroughly modern perceptions of race solidarity have permeated our understanding of black and white in seventeenth-century Virginia. As we have seen, researchers using these and similar documents from other parts of the colony have collected cases in which a clerk jotted next to a man or woman's name the word "Negro." Without such racial indicators, it would be virtually impossible for scholars to write about race relations. Indeed, it is only because of this assistance that we know for certain that a John Punch or an Anthony Johnson was black. No doubt, because the term "Negro" appeared so regularly throughout the pages of various colony and local records, historians assumed that seventeenth-century clerks were racists. No one stated the point quite so baldly, but they obviously believed that Virginia officials classified people chiefly in terms of race. And thus, if a name appeared on a tax list or in a court proceeding without clear racial designation, one stated with a high degree of confidence that the person in question was white. It was difficult for the historian to imagine that in a society supposedly so anxious about setting the blacks apart from the whites any other system of record keeping would have been in operation. The problem with this racial logic is that in Northampton at least, the clerks did not always conduct their affairs by twentieth-century rules. Sometimes they carefully inserted "Negro" near an individual's name, but often, they simply recorded a person's identity without a racial tag. Perhaps the clerks were lazy; perhaps they regarded it a waste of time to write out "Negro" when everyone in the county knew full well that William Harman and Francis Payne were blacks? Or perhaps, they were not as racially conscious as some have surmised. Whatever their reasoning, many routine items—the sale of land and livestock, for example—did not carry the convenient racial indicators. Once the historian realizes that certain men and women were black, even when they were not so described, he can follow their lives more fully, studying economic transactions as well as the sexual and criminal activities that presently occupy a disproportionate place in the analysis of early American race relations.

A third general problem in the literature on race relations in colonial Virginia requires only brief mention. There is a tendency in some recent studies to substitute classificatory categories for real human beings. The reasons for this are complex. Such a strategy clearly lends itself to certain types of quantitative analysis, but whatever the justification, it usually leaves one with a sense that one knows a great deal more about an abstract category—slavery, the family, the plantation—and not much about the cultural and social interdependencies that gave meaning to people's lives. We may read at length, for example, about the institutional development of slavery without ever learning how specific, often idiosyncratic, patterns of master-slave relations shaped the planter's world as well as that of the dependent laborer. It is the human content of social arrangements that helps us to understand in what ways Caribbean slavery differed from that of the Chesapeake, or how nineteenth-century Virginia slavery contrasted with that of the seventeenth-century colony. These observations about the contextual definition of slavery obviously hold for the free blacks. Freedom, like slavery, acquired social meaning not through statute law or intellectual treatises, but through countless human transactions that first defined and then redefined the limits of that condition.

A .   L E O N   H I G G I N B O T H A M ,   J R .

A. LEON HIGGINBOTHAM, Jr. (1928–99), was, until the time of his death, Public Service Professor of Jurisprudence at the John F. Kennedy School of Jurisprudence at Harvard and Of Counsel to Paul, Weiss,

Rifkind, Wharton and Garrison. He was former chief judge of the U.S. Court of Appeals for the Third Circuit and the author of In the Matter of Color *(1978).*

Last Among Equals

When the first Africans arrived at Virginia in August 1619, they were initially accorded an indentured servant status similar to that of most Virginia colonists. In two letters, John Rolfe, Secretary and Recorder of the Virginia colony, reported on the arrival of the Africans. One letter stated that a Dutch man-of-war "brought not any thing but 20. and odd Negroes, which the Governor and Cape Marchant bought for victualles." The other letter, describing the same event, stated: "[A]bout the last of August, came in a dutch man of warre that sold us twenty Negars." The references in the letters to "buying" and "selling" do not necessarily mean that these Africans were being sold into chattel slavery. During that period, the majority of the population in Virginia consisted of servants. It was common practice to refer to the transaction of acquiring a servant as "buying" a person. Buying in that sense simply meant buying the person's services and not actually buying the person's body. Thus, it would appear that, in 1619, the first Africans became one more group in a majority servant class made up of whites and Native Americans.

There are two reasons, however, why the Africans probably did not join this servant class as full equals. First, most but not all white servants came to the colony voluntarily and engaged in service with a written contract of indenture for a specific period. At the expiration of the period of their indenture, whites were released into freedom. The master of a white indentured servant could not, at his sole desire and discretion, prolong the period of servitude. In fact, court approval was necessary for masters and servants to extend the original indenture. Only if the white servant had broken the contract of indenture, or if the servant had in some way violated the laws of the colony, could the period of servitude be extended, either as compensation to the master for the servant breaking the contract or as punishment by society for the servant violating the law. By contrast, as far as we know, the Africans came involuntarily or under duress, and presumably were sold into service *without* a written contract of indenture for a specific period. So, in theory, their period of servitude may have been for as long as the purchaser desired, or even for life.

The second reason why the new Africans probably did not occupy the exact same socioeconomic position as other white servants is that—as Winthrop Jordan has demonstrated—since the fifteenth cen-

tury, Englishmen had regarded blackness as "the handmaid and symbol of baseness and evil, a sign of danger and repulsion." There is no
reason to suppose that, in August 1619, the English colonists of Virginia would have immediately abandoned their historical tendency of
associating blackness with inferiority in favor of a more enlightened
view of seeing these particular black Africans as fully human. It is
more likely that, in the eyes of the English colonists, the Africans represented a dark and inferior quantity. As members of the servant class
they probably were last among equals.

Blackness As Sin

Notwithstanding the colonists' predilection for seeing Africans as less
than human, from 1619 and for approximately two decades thereafter,
the legal system did not appear to actively promote rigid, invidious
distinctions between the new African settlers and their European
counterparts. The first reference to a black person in a judicial proceeding occurred in 1624, when the Council and General Court of Virginia mentioned, in the case of *Re Tuchinge,* in sum: "John Phillip A
negro Christened in England 12 yeers since, sworne and exam sayeth,
that beinge in a ship with Sir Henry Maneringe, they tooke A spanish
shipp aboute Cape Sct Mary, and Caryed her to mamora."

The case apparently involved the trial of a white man, Symon
Tuchinge, for the illegal seizure of a Spanish ship and the kidnapping
of various persons. Given that Phillip was referred to specifically by
the court as black, it is logical to assume that the defendant, whose
race was not similarly specified, was white. This conclusion is supported by the fact that other witnesses were not identified by race.

Phillip's testimony against the white man was accepted presumably because, as the court explained, Phillip had been "Christened in
England." Prior to 1680, the colonies would often follow the Spanish
and English practice that blacks who had been baptized into the Christian religion were to be accorded the privileges of a free person.

Had the legal process in 1624 in Virginia not yet begun to institu-
tionalize the precept of black inferiority, however, one would have expected the case to have been reported quite differently from the way it
was actually reported. Specifically, had Virginia law been free of any
theory of racial subordination, the case would have been reported as
follows: "John Phillip sworne and exam sayeth, that beinge in a ship
with Sir Henry Maneringe, they tooke A spanish shipp aboute Cape
Sct Mary, and Caryed her to mamora." There would have been no description of Phillip as a "Negro" and having been "Christened," just as
there had been no mention of the white defendant's race or his reli-

gion. In a jurisdiction where black did *not* carry the stigma of inferiority, Phillip's race and religion would *not* be material to the determination of whether his testimony was admissible in court because the blemish of his race would *not* need to be washed clean by the grace of his Christian religion. In a jurisdiction such as Virginia, however, where black was already the stigma of inferiority, Phillip's race and religion *were* material to the determination of whether his testimony was to be admitted, because in a real sense, his race was a sin for which he could obtain forgiveness only by becoming a Christian.

By explicitly describing Phillip's race and religion, the court implicitly revealed that, in 1624 Virginia, the legal process was ready to perceive and to treat blacks, by reason of the color of their skin, as different from white colonists. Granted, at first, the consequences of that difference were not immutable. If blackness was a sin, at least it could be absolved by Christianity. But the sinner who obtains Christian forgiveness for his sin always pays a price for that forgiveness. The price is that he has to admit that his sin caused him to be, in some way, a less perfect or inferior image of God. For the African, the sin that caused him to be a less perfect or inferior image of God was his race. So, to the African, Christian forgiveness *and all its attendant legal rights and privileges here on earth* came only at the price of admitting to himself and to society that he was inferior. What's more, the legal process, supported by public opinion and cloaked with the mysticism of Christian religion, reinforced this sense of black inferiority by the identification of the black race in judicial decisions and in legislative enactments. In short, by 1624, the legal process had begun to lay the foundation for the precept of black inferiority and white superiority; the process had "crossed," in the words of historian Lerone Bennett, Jr., "a great divide," and had placed white colonists on one side and Africans on the other side.

The case of *Re Davis*, decided in 1630, illustrates that great divide in very stark terms. The full official court report reads as follows: "Sept. 17. 1630 *Hugh Davis* to be soundly whipt before an assembly of negroes & others for abusing himself to the dishon[o]r of God and shame of Christianity by defiling his body in lying with a negro. w[hi]ch fault he is to actk next *Sabbath* day."

This case demonstrates the evolution of the precept of inferiority in at least three ways. First, though the court did not state that Hugh Davis was white, his race may be inferred from the fact that he is not identified as a "Negro," whereas the person with whom he presumably "defiled" his body was specifically identified as a "negro." The very statement that Davis "abused himself," and that "he defiled his body by lying with a negro," means that he engaged in sexual relations with someone inferior, someone less than human. In short, Davis's crime was not fornication, but bestiality. Second, the statement of the court that Davis had abused himself "to the dishon[o]r of God and shame of Christianity" means that the blacks' inferiority was not simply a custom of society, but also a tenet of Christianity. Finally, the court ordered Davis to be "whipt before an assembly of *negroes & others.*" One must assume that the "others" referred to most probably were white colonists. Therefore, the only reason why the court specified that the assembly was also to include "negroes" was because generally white colonists were not whipped in front of blacks. For Davis, a white colonist, to be whipped in front of blacks would have been especially humiliating, because he would have been debased in front of individuals who were his legal inferiors.

The *Davis* case, decided a mere six years after the *Tuchinge* case, marked an important step in the development of the precept of black inferiority in the common law of Virginia. In *Tuchinge*, the court had remarked upon Phillip's "otherness" by simply identifying him as a "Negro Christened." The precept that Phillip's race marked him as inferior was not stated, but instead remained implicit in the fact that his race alone was identified. By contrast, in *Davis*, the precept of black inferiority was no longer implied, but stated explicitly in the fact that a white colonist "defiled" his body by engaging in sexual relations with an African. In *Tuchinge*, the court recognized that Phillip's inferiority was not so immutable that it could not be mitigated by his Christianity. Phillip, having become a Christian, was permitted to give testimony in court against a white man. God was the African's savior from inferiority. In *Davis*, however, Christianity, instead of supplying a balm for the injury of black inferiority, provided the very instrument which confirmed its existence. Davis's crime of engaging in sexual relations with a black was a crime against Christianity. God now became witness to the African's inferiority. But in *Tuchinge*, the black man's relative equality was measured by his presence in court as a witness against the white man's transgression. By contrast, in *Davis*, the black person's irredeemable inferiority was measured by his presence as the reason for the white man's punishment.

Ten years later, in 1640, the courts in Virginia took the next step in the development of the precept of black inferiority. In *Re Sweat*, the court considered the case of Robert Sweat, a white colonist who had impregnated a black woman servant belonging to a Lieutenant Sheppard. As punishment for Sweat and the unnamed black woman, the court ruled: "[T]he said negro woman shall be whipt at the whipping post and the said *Sweat* shall tomorrow in the forenoon do public penance for his offence at *James city* church in the time of devine service according to the laws of *England* in that case p[ro]vided."

Sweat, at one level, can be interpreted simply as a case about the invasion of property rights. The black woman servant belonged not to Sweat, but to Lieutenant Sheppard. Sweat impregnated her. During her pregnancy and post-childbirth period, she probably became less valuable to Sheppard. Therefore, Sweat had to pay a price for diminishing the value of Sheppard's property, and the woman servant had to pay a price for allowing her value to Sheppard to be diminished. If the case was, however, only about the invasion of Sheppard's property rights, then Sweat and the woman servant would have been made to pay compensation to Sheppard: Sweat would have had to pay monetary damages to Sheppard, and the woman servant would have had to increase the period of servitude she owed to Sheppard. Instead, Sweat and the woman servant were administered respective forms of punishment, as if this were a criminal prosecution and not a property rights dispute.

That the woman was punished and not made to increase her period of servitude can be explained simply by the fact that she "belonged" to Sheppard and was probably already a servant for life. That Sweat was also not made to pay some form of compensation to Sheppard cannot be easily explained by interpreting the case solely in the context of property rights. Instead, a more complete explanation suggests itself if the case is viewed also as an expression of the precept of black inferiority. By engaging in sexual relations, Sweat and the black woman did much more than diminish Sheppard's property rights. Sweat "defiled his body" and shamed God by sleeping with someone less than human. For that, he needed to be punished by doing public penance in church in order to mortify him and to require him to ask God's forgiveness. The black woman, in turn, defied society and rejected her inferiority by sleeping with her superior. For that, she needed to be punished at the whipping post, so that the mark of her inferiority that she had failed to imprint in her mind would now be whipped into her skin.

For blacks, the lesson of their inferiority was one that was written not only on their own bodies, but also on the bodies of their children. *In Re Graweere* in 1641 described how John Graweere, a black servant belonging to a white colonist named William Evans purchased the freedom of his young child from a Lieutenant Sheppard, the owner of the child's mother. After Graweere purchased his child from Sheppard, it seems that a question arose as to whether the child belonged to him or to Evans, his master. Graweere argued that the child should be freed, so that he would "be made a christian and be taught and exercised in the church of *England*." The court ruled in Graweere's favor and ordered: "that the child shall be free from the said *Evans* or his assigns and to be and remain at the disposing and education of the said

Graweere and the child's godfather who undertaketh to see it brought up in the christian religion as aforesaid."

This case is correctly interpreted as significant evidence that, by 1641, the legal process had not contemplated the institution of hereditary slavery. Graweere, himself, may have been a servant for life, but he was able to break the grip of servitude on his posterity by purchasing his child's freedom. Moreover, the facts of the case reveal that Graweere enjoyed certain benefits not usually afforded to slaves. Evans, Graweere's master, permitted him to own and raise hogs under an arrangement whereby Graweere paid half of the profits from his hog business to Evans and kept the other half for himself. However, this case presents more than mere evidence of the ambiguous socioeconomic position of black servants in 1641 Virginia.

In Re Graweere also offers an illustration of how the precept of black inferiority operates. The court sided with Graweere's position, by freeing his child, so that he could be raised as a Christian. But nowhere in the opinion was it stated that Graweere himself was a Christian. A close reading of the opinion reveals that Graweere was probably *not* a Christian. There are two reasons for this conclusion. First, Graweere is described only as "a negro servant unto *William Evans.*" During that period, it was common practice to distinguish between "negroes" and "Christian negroes," since certain rights and privileges flowed from a black person being a Christian. Recall the *Tuchinge* case in which the court accepted a black witness's testimony, because he had been baptized a Christian himself. Yet in this case, which turned almost entirely on the very issue of religion, Graweere's own faith was not explicitly mentioned. Surely, Graweere's position to raise his child as a free Christian would have been strengthened in the mind of the court had he been a Christian. Additionally, the court's decision to free the child would have been even more rational had the court stated that Graweere was a "Christian negro." Graweere presumably did not claim that he was a Christian, and the court did not so state in its opinion.

The second reason for that conclusion is: If Graweere was a Christian, or if he desired to convert to the Christian religion, one would assume that he could have petitioned the court to purchase *his own* freedom from Evans, because the court permitted him to purchase the freedom of his child on the promise the child was to be raised as a Christian. In other words, if, as the opinion clearly suggests, religion was the decisive argument that convinced the court to free the child, the same argument would also presumably be convincing in gaining Graweere his own freedom. The most probable reason why that argument did not apply to Graweere's situation was because, even though he wanted his child raised as a Christian, he himself was *not* a Christian.

If this argument is correct, then it inevitably raises a critical question: Why did the court permit a non-Christian black servant to gain the freedom of his child on the promise that the child would be raised and educated as a Christian? Put more simply, how could the court expect a non-Christian parent to educate a Christian child? The answer is suggested by the cryptic last statement in the court's opinion. The court wrote that the child was to "remain at the disposing and education of the said *Graweere and the child's godfather* who undertaketh to see it brought up in the christian religion as aforesaid." The godfather to whom the court refers was a Christian to be sure, either a black Christian or a white Christian. It is unlikely that the godfather was black, because that would have presented a much too obvious way for black servants to achieve their freedom in 1641. Blacks could have petitioned the court, *en masse*, for freedom by getting themselves baptized with black Christian godfathers and promising to follow in the ways of Christianity. The system of non-indentured black servants could not have possibly survived and flourished for as long as it did had the legal process permitted blacks and their children to gain freedom merely with the help of fellow blacks who were Christians.

The only remaining possibility was that the godfather of Graweere's child was white. As implausible as it may at first sound, this does more completely explain the court's willingness to free the child. After all, if the precept of black inferiority meant anything, it certainly meant that, in the court's estimation, the child's Christian education would have been better safeguarded if entrusted to the care of a white colonist than if placed in the hands of a black servant, Christian or otherwise.

In short, this case exemplifies how the legal process, in a subtle but pernicious manner, reinforced the precept of black inferiority and white superiority in the minds and hearts of the colonists. The black parent was not completely denied dominion over his child, but he was made to understand that, alone, he was too inferior to protect the freedom and save the soul of his child. The white godfather, in turn, was given control over the child, not because of any parental rights, but because of the superiority of his race.

The cases of *Tuchinge, Davis, Sweat,* and *Graweere* were not the only judicial decisions in Virginia involving blacks during the first stage in the development of the precept of black inferiority. Moreover, as was characteristic of the first stage, these four decisions were relatively benign in their treatment of blacks in comparison with later developments in Virginia law. While these cases exemplify how the legal process began to recognize the precept of black inferiority, it should also be noted that the common law at that time had not yet evolved a seamless rationale for the principles of racial subordination that would permit judges in successive decisions to apply the precept of black inferiority to different factual scenarios in a consistent fashion. In other words, the legal process had not yet merged the precept of black inferiority with the doctrine of *stare decisis*.

These qualifications notwithstanding, reviewing the decisions in *Tuchinge, Davis, Sweat*, and *Graweere* is crucial to a proper understanding of the precept of black inferiority and white superiority. Taken together, these cases reveal four essential steps that were taken in the first stage of development of the precept of black inferiority and white superiority: establish white superiority; establish black inferiority; enforce the notions publicly; and enforce the notions by way of theology.

First: convince the white colonists, regardless of their social or economic status, that they are superior to the black colonists. In that way, white servants, who may in reality have more in common with black servants, will identify with propertied whites, with whom they may have little in common other than race. For example, in *Davis* and in *Sweat*, the white colonists who engaged in sexual relations with black women were made to understand that they had defiled their own bodies. Had the defendants been propertied whites, it is difficult to imagine that they would have been punished for sleeping with their black servants or their slaves. During the antebellum period, when slavery was certainly firmly rooted in Virginia, a white master had the right to demand sexual compliance from his female slaves, just as surely as he had the right to ride his mares. This practice, encouraged *openly* as a matter of right in 1831 Virginia was, to be sure, already tolerated secretly as a matter of privilege in 1630. This was precisely the position advanced on the floor of the Virginia legislature in 1831 by a Mr. Gholson, in response to statements proposing abolition: "Why, I really have been under the impression that I *owned* my slaves. I lately purchased *four women* and ten children, in whom I thought I obtained a great bargain, for I really supposed they were *my property*, as were my *brood mares*." The only logical conclusion to be drawn from *Davis* and *Sweat*, then, is that the defendants were probably poor whites or servants who had managed to sleep with black women belonging to others. In spite of their relatively modest socioeconomic positions, the legal process sought to convince these whites that they were superior to blacks.

Second: convince blacks that they are inferior to all others. In that way, they will feel hopeless about their fate, they will become submissive to the propertied whites, and they will not hope to form alliances with white servants. For example, in *Davis*, the simple act of a white man's sleeping with a black woman was described in the space of a single-sentence judicial opinion as the white man abusing himself, dishonoring God, shaming Christianity, and defiling his body. For blacks, the lesson must have been clear: If there was only shame and dishonor and, therefore, no joy or trust in the secret sexual bonding of black and white, then there would have been even more shame and dishonor and, therefore, even less joy or trust in these two groups forging an open political, social, or economic bond.

Third: enforce the inferiority of blacks and the superiority of whites in the most open and public manner. In that way, both blacks and whites will understand the precept as clear evidence of societal custom. For example, in *Davis,* the white defendant was condemned to be whipped "before an assembly of negroes & others." Similarly, in *Sweat* the black woman was sentenced to be whipped "at the whipping post," and the white defendant, to do public penance in church. These forms of public punishment were not only designed to exact retribution from the offenders, but also to deter others from engaging in similar behavior. It must be remembered that, at the time, Virginia had already begun to erect the social and color ladder, with propertied whites at the top, poor and servant whites in the middle, and Native Americans and Africans at the bottom. For a white man to engage in sexual relations with a black woman constituted a private slip down to the bottom-most rung of the ladder. For a white man to be punished publicly for his private fall was society's way of reminding one and all of the terrible cost in status that would accompany any failure to observe the precept of black inferiority.

Fourth: explain the inferiority of blacks and the superiority of whites by reference to Christianity. In that way, both blacks and whites will respect the precept as the natural expression of divine will. For example, in *Tuchinge,* the black witness avoided a disability of inferiority only by the grace of Christianity. In *Davis,* the white colonist was said to have dishonored God and shamed Christianity by his sexual relations with a black. In *Sweat,* the white offender was sentenced to public penance in church. In *Graweere,* the black child was saved from servitude only by the intervention of a white Christian godfather. The colonists realized that, while a foolish few might be tempted to sacrifice their public status in the service of private desires, almost no one would be willing to set his face against God for the sake of a people whose black color was itself a sin.

In one passage in his *Notes on the State of Virginia,* Thomas Jefferson explained in great detail the various physical and mental differences between blacks and whites that he believed rendered blacks inferior and whites superior. After listing those differences, Jefferson concluded: "I advance it therefore as a suspicion only, that the blacks, whether originally a distinct race, or made distinct by time and circumstances, are inferior to the whites in the endowments both of body and mind." That passage, though written in 1782, best sums up the first stage in the legal development of the precept of black inferiority in Virginia between 1619 and 1662.

During that stage, the colonists seemed to believe, "as suspicion only," that blacks were inferior to whites. Their ambivalence was reflected in the uncertain socioeconomic status of the black servants in the colony, and in the relatively benign manner in which the legal process defined and enforced their condition of servitude. By 1662, however, the legal process would begin to put in place the components of lifetime and hereditary slavery for blacks. With that, Virginia would move into the second stage in the development of the precept of black inferiority.

5

THE AMERICAN REVOLUTION: SOCIAL OR IDEOLOGICAL?

The American Revolution is the single most significant event in this country's history. Within twenty years—1763 to 1783—Americans declared their independence, waged a war of liberation, transformed colonies into states, and created a new nation. But scholars disagree about using the term "revolutionary" to describe how new or different these developments were. Some historians argue that the Revolution was solely aimed at achieving the limited goal of independence from Britain. According to this view, there was a consensus among Americans about keeping things as they were once the break with Britain had been accomplished. Others claim that the Revolution was accompanied by a violent social upheaval—a class conflict—as the radical lower classes sought to gain a greater degree of democracy in what had been a basically undemocratic society in the colonial era. The question is, then, was the Revolution revolutionary at home, or was it to accomplish independence from an increasingly oppressive monarchy?

Throughout most of the nineteenth century scholars reflected one of the underlying assumptions of that era—that the main theme of American history was the quest for liberty. Within this context the Revolution was inevitably viewed as a struggle of liberty versus tyranny between America and Britain.

George Bancroft, one of the outstanding exponents of this point of view, set forth his thesis in his ten-volume *History of the United States,* published between the 1830s and 1870s. To Bancroft the Revolution represented one phase of a master plan by God for the march of all mankind toward a golden age of greater human freedom. The Revolution was "radical in its character," according to Bancroft, because it hastened the advance of human beings toward a millennium of "everlasting peace" and "universal brotherhood."[1]

In the nineteenth century, Americans desired a national historian who would tell the epic story of the Revolution in patriotic terms, and

---

[1]George Bancroft, *History of the United States of America,* 10 vols. (Boston, 1852), Vol. 4, pp. 12–13.

Bancroft fulfilled this longing. In addition, in a turbulent period, divided by the bitter politics of the Jacksonian era and the brutality of the Civil War, Bancroft reminded Americans that they had once fought as a united people for beliefs they held in common.[2]

Around the turn of the twentieth century a reaction set in against Bancroft's ultrapatriotic interpretation. With the growing rapprochement between Britain and America there was a tendency to view past relations between the two countries in a more favorable light. Populism and Progressivism, popular reactions against the concentration of power and wealth in the hands of a relatively small number of leaders in industrialized America, influenced some historians to view the Revolution as an uprising by the lower classes against the control of the upper classes. Two schools of professional historians working from the 1880s to the 1940s revised Bancroft's interpretation.

One group—the imperial school—believed that political and constitutional issues brought on the Revolution. The other—the Progressive historians—held that the primary causes were social and economic. While these two groups of historians disagreed with Bancroft on the precise causes and nature of the Revolution, they were often in agreement with his conclusion that the movement was, indeed, a revolutionary one.

The imperial school of historians headed by George L. Beer, Charles M. Andrews, and Lawrence H. Gipson set the Revolution in the broader context of the history of the British Empire as a whole. The imperial historians concluded that Britain's colonial policies were not as unjust as Bancroft had declared. Beer claimed that the colonists prospered under a system that was both liberal and enlightened. Andrews, writing in the 1930s, saw benefits as well as burdens in Britain's Navigation Acts because of the protection provided for America's goods and ships. And Gipson claimed the British were justified in taxing the Americans and tightening the Navigation Acts after 1763, because largely British blood and money had been expended in defending the North American colonies in the "Great War for Empire," 1754–63.

All three believed that constitutional issues lay at the bottom of the dispute. Andrews, for example, argued that the colonies kept moving steadily in the direction of greater self-government; the mother country toward greater control over the empire.[3] The disagreement, while constitutional in nature, was the very essence of revolution: a deep-seated conflict between two incompatible societies.

The Progressive historians, on the other hand, emphasized the

---

[2]Wesley F. Craven, "The Revolutionary Era," in *The Reconstruction of American History,* John Higham, ed. (New York, 1962), pp. 46–47.

[3]Charles M. Andrews, "The American Revolution: An Interpretation," *American Historical Review,* 31 (January 1926): 231.

growing economic split caused by the competition between the colonies and mother country. Progressive historians such as Carl L. Becker, Charles A. Beard, Arthur M. Schlesinger, Sr., and J. Franklin Jameson placed great stress upon class conflict in colonial America in part because they saw their own era in terms of an unending struggle by the people to free themselves from the shackles of the large corporate monopolies and trusts. They insisted that political or constitutional ideas had an underlying economic basis.

Carl L. Becker, one of the first and most effective of the Progressive historians, took the position that the American Revolution should be considered not as one revolution but two. The first was an external revolution—the colonial rebellion against Britain—caused by a clash of economic interests between the colonies and mother country. The second was an internal revolution—a conflict between America's social classes—to determine whether the upper or lower classes would rule once the British departed. In his first major study of the Revolution, *The History of Political Parties in the Province of New York, 1760–1776*, published in 1909, Becker summed up his thesis of a dual revolution in a memorable phrase. New York politics before the Revolution, he wrote, revolved around two questions—the "question of home rule" and the "question . . . of who should rule at home."[4]

Arthur M. Schlesinger's *The Colonial Merchants and the American Revolution*, published in 1918, continued in the vein of Charles A. Beard's famous *An Economic Interpretation of the Constitution*. Schlesinger noted that the usually conservative merchant class played a leading role in bringing on the Revolution. Why? Disenchantment of the merchants with British rule, said Schlesinger, arose from the economic reverses they suffered as a result of the strict policy of imperial control enacted by the mother country after the French and Indian War. Merchants' resistance against the mother country grew less intense after 1770, he noted, for fear of what might happen to their position and property if the more radical lower classes—"their natural enemies in society"—should gain the upper hand. The merchant class later became, in Schlesinger's words, "a potent factor in the conservative counterrevolution that led to the establishment of the United States Constitution."[5] To Schlesinger the Constitution was the antithesis of the Revolution.

J. Franklin Jameson's *The American Revolution Considered as a Social Movement*, published in 1926, described the sweeping social and economic reforms that took place during the war. Social democ-

---

[4]Carl L. Becker, *The History of Political Parties in the Province of New York, 1760–1776* (Madison, Wisc., 1909), p. 22.

[5]Arthur M. Schlesinger, *The Colonial Merchants and the American Revolution, 1763–1776* (New York, 1918), p. 606.

racy grew as property qualifications for voting and officeholding were lowered, slavery and the slave trade were abolished in some states, and the Anglican Church was disestablished in many parts of the country. The late Merrill Jensen, a distinguished scholar, and numerous other historians active from 1945 to the present maintained the Progressive approach to the Revolution.

After World War II, however, a new group of scholars—the neoconservative school of historians—emerged to challenge the interpretation set forth by the Progressive historians. The neoconservative historians, unlike the Progressives, believed that American society was essentially democratic in the colonial period. Most colonists possessed enough land to meet the necessary qualifications for voting. Colonial society was not closed but characterized by a high degree of social mobility. Thus the common man in the colonial era was satisfied with his lot in society and felt no urge to participate in class conflict in order to achieve a greater degree of democracy.

Neoconservative scholars argued that the Revolution was basically a conservative movement. Americans fought the Revolution to preserve a social order that was already democratic. When British reforms after 1763 threatened to upset the existing democratic social order in America, the colonists rose up in rebellion. In the struggle between the colonies and the mother country the Americans emerged as the "conservatives" because they were trying to keep matters as they were before 1763.

The neoconservative interpretation of the Revolution that arose after 1945 reflected the conservative climate of opinion that pervaded the United States after World War II. The Cold War made some Americans increasingly preoccupied with the problem of national security. Neoconservative historians, led by Robert E. Brown and Daniel J. Boorstin, mirrored this concern by playing down any past differences among Americans in order to present an image of a strong and united nation.

Robert E. Brown, in *Middle-Class Democracy and the Revolution in Massachusetts,* challenged the Progressive thesis that the Revolution was, in part, a class conflict over the question of who should rule at home. After studying the structure of society in prewar Massachusetts, Brown concluded that the vast majority of adult males in that colony were farmers with the necessary property qualifications for voting. Middle-class democracy in Massachusetts existed, Brown maintained, and the purpose of the Revolution was to preserve that democratic social order.

Similarly, Daniel J. Boorstin argued that the Revolution was a conservative movement on the imperial as well as the local level because Americans were fighting to retain traditional rights and liberties granted to them under the British constitution. In *The Genius of American Politics,* he argued that when the British introduced changes in the government of the empire after the French and Indian War, Americans resisted these disturbing innovations on the grounds that they were contrary to the British constitution. In refusing to accept the principle of taxation without representation, Boorstin wrote, the patriots were insisting upon an old liberty, not a new right.

Edmund S. Morgan, the distinguished colonial historian, also drew on consensus themes—the agreement among Americans on principles, and the continuity of ideas—in his *Birth of the Republic 1763–1789*. From the time of the Stamp Act in 1765 to the writing of the Constitution in 1787, according to Morgan, the majority of Americans consistently sought to realize three principles: the protection of property and liberty, the achievement of human equality, and, after the break from Britain, a form of American nationalism that would embrace the ideas of both liberty and equality. Morgan concluded that the Progressive historians had grossly exaggerated the divisions among the American people during the revolutionary era, and that the "most remarkable and exciting fact was union."[6]

In the 1960s three groups challenged the consensus school. Certain intellectual historians saw the Revolution as a radical rather than a conservative movement. Neo-Progressive and New Left historians used different approaches to search for the social and economic origins of the revolutionary movement. And a revived interest in studies of the Loyalists provided a third perspective.

The trend toward greater emphasis upon intellectual history resulted in part as a reaction against the Progressive scholars, who had generally shown a profound distrust of ideas as determining forces in history. Strongly influenced by the thought of Freud and Marx, the Progressive historians looked upon ideas as rationalizations of the deep-seated self-interest that motivated human behavior. They insisted that the upper classes in colonial America had manipulated ideas to suit the interests of their class.

Bernard Bailyn was the foremost among post–World War II scholars who rejected this view and saw the Revolution as a radical intellectual movement. In *The Ideological Origins of the American Revolution*, Bailyn took the position that ideas expressed in pamphlet literature before the Revolution constituted its major determinants.[7] Bailyn argued that an elaborate theory of politics lay at the heart of the American revolutionary ideology—an ideology that came to be called republicanism, and whose roots could be traced back to the antiauthoritarian or opposition Whig party tradition in England. Man had a natural lust for power, this theory held, and power by its very nature was a corrupting force and could be attained only by depriving others

---

[6]Edmund S. Morgan, *The Birth of the Republic 1763–1789* (Chicago, 1956), p. 163.

[7]Bernard Bailyn, *The Ideological Origins of the American Revolution* (Cambridge, Mass., 1967).

of their liberty. To protect liberty against the corrupting force of power, all elements of the body politic had to be balanced against each other in order to prevent one from gaining dominance over the others. The best solution was a balanced constitution, but the malignant influence of power was such that no system of government whatsoever could be safe or stable for very long.

The colonists, according to Bailyn, were convinced that there was a sinister plot against liberty in both England and America. In England it was the king's ministers who were conspiring against liberty. They usurped the prerogatives of the Crown, systematically encroached upon the independence of the Commons, and upset the balance of the British constitution in their corrupt drive for power. Americans believed the conspiracy had succeeded in England, and America represented the last bastion for the defense of English liberties and the freedom of all mankind.

Bailyn took issue with the Progressive historians who declared that the patriot leaders were indulging in mere rhetoric when they employed such words as "conspiracy," "corruption," and "slavery." The colonists meant what they said; the fear of conspiracy against constitutional authority was built into the very structure of politics, and these words represented "real fears, real anxieties, [and] a sense of real danger."[8]

To Bailyn the true revolution took place inside men's minds. Before the Revolution the Americans felt a sense of inferiority because they lacked a titled aristocracy, cosmopolitan culture, stratified society, and an established church. After the Revolution, on the other hand, they came to look upon these differences as good and as advantages rather than defects. These differences, Americans felt, would enable them to establish a republican government that would correspond with their republican society.

Gordon S. Wood extended this argument in the *Creation of the American Republic, 1776–1787*, which explained how the colonists' antiauthoritarian tradition was transformed after independence into a distinctive American republican ideology. These two works written in the 1960s gave rise to what came to be called the "republican synthesis" and, coupled with J. G. A. Pocock's *Machiavellian Moment*, published in the 1970s, claimed that this republican ideology dominated the political culture throughout the whole sweep of American history from the 1760s to the Civil War. The republican synthesis moved John Locke's thought on natural rights from the center of revolutionary thought and replaced it with the republican notions of disinterested virtue and the common good. Ideas of repubicanism constituted a major historiographical breakthrough: this proved to be the most widely

----

[8]Ibid., p. ix.

accepted interpretation in the voluminous literature written from the mid-1960s to the mid-1980s.[9]

Alongside these historians of the republican synthesis emerged a group who thought it useful to see the Revolution in a comparative context. The outstanding comparative historian was Robert R. Palmer, who concluded that the period from the American Revolution in 1776 to the European revolutions in 1848 constituted a series of democratic revolutions. He saw the American Revolution, then, as part of the process of democratization that was taking place throughout the entire Western world at that time. In his magisterial two-volume work, *The Age of the Democratic Revolution*, published in the late 1950s and early 1960s, Palmer was able to gain new insights into the process of revolution by resorting to the method of comparative history.[10]

Meanwhile a reaction to the republican synthesis was setting in the 1970s and 1980s from a variety of groups. Bailyn, who had revised the neoconservatives by making the Revolution seem radical again, was subjected to revisionist assaults, as were Wood and Pocock. Adherents of the republican synthesis were scored for errors of both commission and omission. Bailyn was criticized, for example, because he seemed to suggest that there was an ideological consensus among American Whigs, and that they all held the same republican ideas in common. Other scholars quickly pointed out there were other ideologies at work—evangelical Protestantism, class-based perspectives, or different political orientations—and that America's political culture was more diversified and less homogeneous. Those upholding the republican synthesis relied heavily on the classical republican tradition—which emphasized citizenship and public participation and had roots stretching back to antiquity and the Renaissance. Pocock, in fact, declared the Revolution to be "the last great act of the Renaissance." Supporters of the republican synthesis were criticized, moreover, for omitting a discussion of the various theories of political economy, including Lockean liberalism, that were so important to those of the revolutionary generation.[11]

---

[9]Gordon S. Wood, *Creation of the American Republic, 1776–1787* (Chapel Hill, N. C., 1969), and J. G. A. Pocock, *The Machiavellian Moment* (Princeton, N. J., 1975).

[10]Robert R. Palmer, *The Age of the Democratic Revolution*, 2 vols. (Princeton, N. J., 1959 and 1964).

[11]For an attack on the idea of an ideological consensus, see some of the essays in Alfred A. Young, ed., *The American Revolution: Explorations in the History of American Radicalism* (De Kalb, Ill., 1976). For two books that take up the issue of whether liberalism or republicanism was dominant in the revolutionary era, see Joyce Appleby, *Capitalism and a New Social Order* (New York, 1984), and Lance Banning, *The Jeffersonian Persuasion* (Ithaca, N.Y., 1978). See the Appleby book cited above and Drew R. McCoy, *The Elusive Republic* (Chapel Hill, N.C., 1980), for discussions of the important role of political economy in the revolutionary and postrevolutionary period. For the Pocock quotation, see "Virtue and Commerce in the Eighteenth Century," *Journal of Interdisciplinary History*, 3 (1972): 12.

Rhys Isaac, for example, undermined the idea of an ideological consensus by analyzing different powerful religious ideologies at work before, during, and after the Revolution. Focusing on prerevolutionary Virginia as a case study, Isaac showed that deep ideological differences existed between the Anglicans and Baptists. Deploying the imaginative techniques of such cultural anthropologists as Clifford Geertz, Isaac analyzed these two religious subcultures, finding two contrasting worldviews: the tradition-oriented Anglican gentry who represented the established order, and the humble evangelical Baptists who challenged the ruling Anglican establishment. His work did more than destroy the idea of a possible ideological consensus: it showed that by omitting much serious discussion of religious beliefs, Bailyn and Wood had overlooked the important role religion played in the formation of political beliefs during the Revolution.[12]

T. H. Breen, in *Tobacco Culture* (1985), an original view of the mental world of the Tidewater planters, argued that they constructed an idiosyncratic culture based on their ability to grow excellent tobacco. During the decade-long depression in tobacco prices that preceded the Revolution, this world fell apart as London creditors pressured growers. Planters became revolutionaries as their British factors destroyed their sense of self-worth, which derived from being "crop masters"—a non-market conceit, but one that could only be confirmed by market success. In Breen's work, ideas and economics blended unexpectedly to produce one particular group of revolutionaries.[13]

A group of New Left historians, emerging in the 1960s, blended with the neo-Progressive historians and challenged the ideological interpetation of the Revolution. The neo-Progressives and New Left historians were influenced not only by the earlier Progressive historians, but by the social and political concerns of the times in which they lived. These scholars brought to the study of the Revolution a renewed awareness of the existence of minority groups and disadvantaged groups in American history. The protest movements in the 1960s, 1970s, and 1980s on behalf of specific groups—the poor, blacks, ethnic minorities, and women—made these scholars sensitive to the claims of social groups that had been oppressed in the past. The work of the New Left reflected in many instances the intense interest in social justice so evident during the decades in which these historians wrote. The chief sources of the revolutionary movement, they argued, were to be found in the profound economic and social dislocations within eighteenth-century America. The tensions generated by such changes

---

[12]Rhys Isaac, *Transformation of Virginia, 1740–1790* (Chapel Hill, N. C., 1982).

[13]T. H. Breen, *Tobacco Culture, the Mentality of the Great Tidewater Planters on the Eve of Revolution* (Princeton, N. J., 1985).

led to social unrest and protest on the part of the lower social orders during the Revolution. The neo-Progressive historians portrayed the Revolution as a democratic movement stimulated in part by these growing social inequalities and aimed at broadening participation in American political life.

The leading neo-Progressive historian to inherit the mantle of Beard was Merrill Jensen, who viewed the Revolution in terms of conflict—particularly political and economic clashes—both between the colonies and the mother country and within the colonies themselves.[14] (Gary B. Nash's 1990 book recounting the failure of abolitionism during the revolutonary period began as lectures in honor of Jensen.[15]) On the whole, the neo-Progressives were not successful in linking the widening economic inequalities directly to the Revolution itself, but they successfully challenged the notion of widespread ideological agreement among the colonists.

Gary B. Nash, a historian in the neo-Progressive/New Left tradition, discussed in his *Urban Crucible* (which is excerpted in this chapter) an ideology found among laboring class and artisan groups on the eve of the Revolution that had not been treated by either Bailyn or Wood. Viewing the lives of urban dwellers in three cities—Boston, New York, and Philadelphia—from the 1680s to the Revolution, Nash concluded that social changes had turned these seaport communities into "crucibles of revolutionary agitation." The increasing poverty and the narrowing of economic opportunities resulted in resentment and rising class consciousness among segments of the artisan class.[16]

Among the most aggressive spokesmen of the New Left was Jesse Lemisch, who was one of the first to argue that the history of the Revolution had been written too much from the viewpoint of the elites. If viewed from the "bottom up," the Revolution might be shown to be more radical and characterized by greater class conflict than the neoconservatives realized. To make this point, Lemisch wrote an article arguing that American seamen were deeply distressed by the Royal Navy's practice of impressment. Yet scholars all but ignored this issue because it was seldom protested by members of the middle and upper classes. Lemisch observed that ordinary colonists might have supported the Revolution for other reasons that historians had also failed to investigate. This opened the possibility of viewing the Revolution as a radical movement undertaken by lower social groups

---

[14]Merrill Jensen, *The Founding of a Nation* (New York, 1968) and *The American Revolution within America* (New York, 1974). For Jensen's students, see Jackson Turner Main, *The Sovereign States, 1775–1783* (New York, 1973), as but one example among many.

[15]Gary B. Nash, *Race and Revolution* (Madison, Wisc., 1990)

[16]Gary B. Nash, *Urban Crucible* (Cambridge, Mass., 1979).

in the society to remedy specific grievances they suffered under British rule.[17]

One of the most important books written by members of the New Left to challenge the neoconservative historians and adherents of the "republican synthesis" was a collection of essays edited by Alfred E. Young entitled *The American Revolution: Explorations in the History of American Radicalism*, published in 1976. Many scholars in this volume took issue with Bailyn's interpretation in particular. They rejected the idea of an ideological consensus and the notion of the Revolution as mainly ideological in its origins. Some pictured the Revolution as a social movement—an internal struggle within the colonies—caused in part by class antagonisms. Others, however, held that the Revolution was ideological in nature, but not as presented by Bailyn. They saw serious differences in ideology between local leaders who shared a Whig view and the middle and lower orders of society who held different political beliefs. The volume also contained essays about the widely diverse effect of the Revolution on blacks, women and Native Americans.[18]

The New Left historian Edward Countryman went farther than Jensen in tracing the Revolution to a distinct drive for democracy. Countryman concluded that the radical leaders of New York carried through a revolutionary redefinition of politics and society in the late 1770s. Using a sophisticated quantitative analysis, he revealed how the unruly crowds of the prerevolutionary period evolved into the popularly based committees of correspondence of the independence movement. His study showed also how closely economic issues—taxes, price controls, and monetary policies—were linked not only to clashing interest groups but to conflicting visions of what republican society and government ought to be. Countryman's depiction of the collapse of the old elite order in New York after the war began undermined any idea of continuing the old consensus approach for that state.[19]

A third challenge to the neoconservative interpretation came from the historians who studied the Loyalists. The neoconservatives had traced a line of continuity in political and constitutional principles from the late colonial era through the writing of state constitutions to the Constitution in 1787. Given the premise of a conservative Revolution, the neoconservatives could not fit the Loyalists comfortably within their interpretation. How could conservatives like the Loyalists oppose a conservative Revolution? For this reason, the neoconser-

---

[17]Jesse Lemisch, "The American Revolution Seen from the Bottom Up," in *Towards a New Past*, Barton J. Bernstein, ed. (New York, 1968), pp. 3–45.

[18]Young, ed., *The American Revolution*, passim.

[19]Edward Countryman, *A People in Revolution* (Baltimore, 1981).

vatives either failed to mention the Loyalists or made only superficial references to them.[20]

During the decades from the 1960s to 1990, however, there was a revival of interest in the Loyalists. The most important work to appear during the 1960s was William H. Nelson's *The American Tory*. Although Nelson's book was a form of intellectual history, it also reflected the contemporary tendency to concentrate on social history and the inclination to use concepts drawn from other academic disciplines. Nelson presented the arresting hypothesis that the Loyalists constituted a collection of isolated "cultural minorities"—social groups that had never been assimilated into American society. These cultural enclaves, therefore, looked to Britain for protection against the threatening Whig majorities that surrounded them. Nelson applied the sociological tool of negative reference group theory to these ethnic minorities, which included Quakers and German Pietists in the middle colonies, and certain racial minorities—slaves and certain Indian tribes.[21]

Wallace Brown analyzed the social origins of the Loyalists. Contrary to the findings of earlier historians, Brown argued that the Loyalists were not primarily elite but came mainly from the lower and middle classes. Loyalism, moreover, was "a distinctly urban and seaboard phenomenon—except in New York and North Carolina where there existed "major rural inland pockets." Brown's statistics showed that they composed only between 7.6 and 18 percent of the white population.[22]

Mary Beth Norton followed the fortunes of the Loyalists after their exile in England. Loyalists came to recognize how "American" they were when they felt ill at ease and out of place in English society. Once again the negative reference group theory proved useful.[23]

Innovative historians in the 1970s and 1980s brought three new major approaches to the study of the Revolution. The first were the

---

[20]Daniel J. Boorstin, in *The Americans: The Colonial Experience* (New York, 1958), *The Americans: The National Experience* (New York, 1965), and "The American Revolution: Revolution Without Dogma," in *The Genius of American Politics* (Chicago, 1953), pp. 66–98, does not discuss the Loyalists. Louis Hartz, *The Liberal Tradition in America* (New York, 1955), p. 58, and Clinton Rossiter, *Seedtime of the Republic* (New York, 1953), pp. 3, 155, 319, 322, 340, and 349, says very little. Edmund S. Morgan in *Birth of the Republic, 1763–1789* (Chicago, 1977 edition), pp. 99 and 119–120, made only a slight mention, but Benjamin F. Wright, *Consensus and Continuity* (Boston, 1958), hardly accounted for the Loyalists at all.

[21]William H. Nelson, *The American Tory* (New York, 1961).

[22]Wallace Brown, *The King's Friends* (Providence, R.I., 1965), pp. v, 250, 257–58, 261–67. Another work that treated the Loyalists throughout the original thirteen states was Robert Calhoun, *The Loyalists of Revolutionary America, 1760–1781* (New York, 1973). One especially insightful biography of a Loyalist among many was Bernard Bailyn, *The Ordeal of Thomas Hutchinson* (Cambridge, Mass., 1974).

[23]Mary Beth Norton, *The British Americans* (Boston, 1972).

"new social historians" who saw the Revolution through community studies or the eyes of forgotten Americans. The second was a group of scholars who explored the Revolution from a psychological point of view. The third was the group of "new military historians" who looked at the military as a microcosm of colonial society and studied the dynamics between it and the civilian world.

The new social historians were united loosely by their desire to examine America's social structure and its changes over time. They often directed their attention to small communities. Their work in many instances was characterized by quantitative techniques and research in such nontraditional sources as wills, deeds, and tax lists to get at the inner lives of the inarticulate masses who left few personal memoirs. By employing such records they hoped to re-create the universe in which ordinary citizens lived.

Like the New Left historians, they sometimes were interested in specific socially or politically disadvantaged groups: the poor, blacks, and women. And like the "new intellectual historians" they followed changes in the attitudes and behavior of groups over long periods of time.

Robert Gross's *The Minutemen and Their World* analyzed Concord, Massachusetts. Much of Gross's work was quantitative; he reconstructed the life of the community not from traditional literary sources but from church records, wills, deeds, petitions, tax lists, and minutes of town meetings. Rather than making sweeping statements about the Revolution as a broad social movement, Gross demonstrated how the events affected the lives of individuals within a single town. His conclusion was conservative: that the townspeople had gone to war not to promote social change, but to stop it. Ironically enough, the results of the Revolution opened the way to unintended innovations that profoundly altered Concord's way of life.[24]

The new social historians, among many others, paid particular attention to certain social and racial groups such as blacks, women, and Indians to examine how they were affected by the Revolution. Donald L. Robinson in *Slavery in the Structure of American Politics, 1765–1820* dealt with the institution of slavery over a long period of time. Edmund S. Morgan, more than a new social historian and no longer a consensus historian, produced the most searching study, *American Slavery—American Freedom*, dealing with the paradox of how slavery and freedom developed side-by-side in the colonies. Recently, Sylvia Frey has painstakingly re-created the world of American blacks during the Revolution in *Water from the Rock*. And Gary B. Nash's *Race and Revolution* looks at northerners' responsibility for

---

[24]Robert Gross, *The Minutemen and Their World* (New York, 1976).

failing to achieve the abolition of slavery nationwide at the time of the Revolution.[25]

Mary Beth Norton's *Liberty's Daughters* and Linda K. Kerber's *Women of the Republic* looked at women in the Revolution and postrevolutionary period, finding the outlines of a role for them as "republican mothers" or mothers of the virtuous citizens the new nation needed to maintain its purity in a corrupt world. This interpretation has been useful in linking women to the national body politic. However, Joan Hoff Wilson found convincingly that the Revolution itself meant no change in the lives of women.[26] Since then, historians have looked at women's participation in the Revolution as spinners of homespun, boycotters of English goods, and food rioters seeking a moral economy.[27]

The new social history encouraged studies of Indians and the Revolution. Barbara Graymount's *The Iroquois in the American Revolution* was among the first full-scale ethnohistories of Indian participation in the war.[28] Gregory Evans Dowd, Richard White, and James Merrell have discussed the Revolution's effects on certain Indian groups, and in 1995 Colin Calloway published *The American Revolution in Indian Country*, a broad and ambitious look at the Revolution as it played out in various Indian communities.[29]

The third trend of the tumultuous 1970s–1990s took place as scholars explored the nature of the Revolution in psychological terms. Several scholars made use of psychohistory—a subdiscipline that had recently come into prominence. They suggested the Americans may have been caught up in a serious identity crisis as a people on the eve of the Revolution.

Historians using psychology saw Americans as profoundly con-

---

[25]Donald L. Robinson, *Slavery in the Structure of American Politics, 1765–1820* (New York, 1971); Edmund S. Morgan, *American Slavery—American Freedom* (New York, 1975); Sylvia Frey, *Water from the Rock* (Princeton, N. J., 1991); Gary Nash, *Race and Revolution* (Madison, Wisc., 1990).

[26]Mary Beth Norton, *Liberty's Daughters* (Boston, 1980); Linda Kerber, *Women of the Republic* (Chapel Hill, N.C., 1980); Joan Hoff Wilson, "The Illusion of Change: Women and the Revolution," in Alfred F. Young, ed., *The American Revolution: Explorations in the History of American Radicalism* (De Kalb, Ill., 1976).

[27]Ronald Hoffman and Peter J. Albert, eds., *Women in the Age of the American Revolution* (Charlottesville, Va., 1989); Barbara Clark Smith, "Food Rioters and the American Revolution, *The William and Mary Quarterly*, 3rd Ser. V. LI, No. 1, 3–38.

[28]Barbara Graymount, *The Iroquois in the American Revolution* (Syracuse, N.Y., 1972).

[29]Gregory Evans Dowd, *A Spirited Resistance: The North American Indian Struggle for Unity, 1745–1815* (Baltimore, 1992;) Richard White, *The Middle Ground: Indians, Empire and Republics in the Great Lakes Region, 1640–1815* (Cambridge, Mass., 1991); James Merrell, *The Indians' New World: Catawbas and Their Neighbors from European Contact through the Era of Removal* (Chapel Hll, N.C., 1989); Colin Calloway, *The Revolution in Indian Country* (New York, 1995).

flicted about the mother country. Colonial society underwent a process of "Anglicization" in the eighteenth century, and according to this hypothesis, Americans became more self-consciously English as they copied British ways. In becoming Anglicized, however, Americans turned their backs on certain indigenous native styles, habits, and traditions they had developed earlier. On the one hand, they admired the mother country so much that they imitated British ways. On the other, they resented the idea of emulating the British because they were seeking to establish a separate sense of American identity. Jack P. Greene, John M. Murrin, and Robert M. Weir, among others, treated the theme of an identity crisis in several essays.[30]

Other attempts at psychohistory explored the colonial relationship within a more Freudian framework. This hypothesis employed familiar sex role models—Britain as a mother country, the English king as a father figure, and the colonists as rebellious adolescents—and suggested they were all locked in an oedipal conflict. That contemporaries viewed the Revolution in such terms was clear. John Adams explained in 1765 that the colonists indeed might be children, but "have not children a right to complain when their parents are attempting to break their limbs?" Thomas Paine put it more eloquently in 1777 when he wrote, "To know whether it be the interest of the continent to be independent, we need only ask this simple question: Is it the interest of a man to be a boy all his life?" Such scholars as Winthrop D. Jordan, Edwin G. Burrows, Michael Wallace, and Bruce Mazlish explored the psychological dimensions of the Revolution along such lines.[31]

One of the most interesting attempts at psychohistory was Jay Fliegelman's *Prodigals and Pilgrims*, published in the early 1980s. Fliegelman postulated the rise of an antipatriarchal movement in Britain, France, and America during the revolutionary era. Involved

---

[30]Jack P. Greene, "Search for Identity: An Interpretation of the Meaning of Selected Patterns of Social Response in Eighteenth-Century America," *Journal of Social History,* 3 (1980): 189–220; John M. Murrin, "The Legal Transformation: The Bench and Bar of Eighteenth-Century Massachusetts," in *Essays in Politics and Development: Colonial America,* Stanley N. Katz, ed. (Boston, 1971); Jack P. Greene, "An Uneasy Connection: An Analysis of the Pre-Conditions of the American Revolution," in *Essays on the American Revolution,* Stephen G. Kurtz and James H. Hutson, eds. (Chapel Hill, N.C., 1973); Rowland Berthoff and John M. Murrin, "Feudalism, Communalism, and the Yeoman Freeholder: The American Revolution Considered as a Social Accident," ibid., pp. 256–88; and Robert M. Weir, "Who Shall Rule at Home: The American Revolution as a Crisis of Legitimacy for the Colonial Elite," *Journal of Interdisciplinary History,* 6 (1976): 679–700.

[31]Winthrop D. Jordan, "Familial Politics: Thomas Paine and the Killing of the King, 1776," *Journal of American History,* 60 (1973): 249–308; Edwin G. Burrows and Michael Wallace, "The American Revolution: The Ideology and Psychology of National Liberation," *Perspectives in American History,* 6 (1972): 167–306; and Bruce Mazlish, "Leadership in the American Revolution: The Psychological Dimension," in Elizabeth H. Kagan, comp., *Leadership in the American Revolution* (Washington, D.C., 1974).

in this movement were new noncoercive assumptions regarding the rights of children and the duties of parents. The aim of the movement was to try to perfect and improve the purely voluntary contractual relationship existing between the two generations. Prolonged submission to parental rule was to give way. The young were to be properly prepared to take their place in the world—a world assumed to be filled with great temptations and corruption—and to be released freely, without rancor, and with no expectations of continuing gratitude. It was within this frame of reference, Fliegelman argued, that the dispute between Britain and America should be cast. By discussing political issues in such terms, Fliegelman related the public discourse to private attitudes regarding patriarchy, authority, and child-rearing, and uncovered an important strain of thought that illuminated, if it did not fully explain, the imperial crisis in a strikingly different way.[32]

A fourth innovation in historiography of the Revolution was the interest in military history. The "new military historians," an offshoot of the "new social historians," broke away from the old-fashioned drum-and-trumpet narrative approach to war and wedded military and social history. They removed military history from the narrow confines of the battlefield and placed it within a much broader context—that of the relationship between warfare and society as a whole.

Many new military historians believed that the way a nation waged war shed important light on the values held by its people. John Shy, in a book of brilliant essays, maintained that the pattern of military events during the Revolutionary War helped to shape the way the American people came to view themselves and their relationship to the rest of the world. To Shy the war was not an instrument of policy or a sequence of military operations solely, but rather a social process of education.[33] Another leader in the field, Don Higginbotham, analyzed the ideas, attitudes, and traditions that helped determine how the war was fought. He showed how the armies were projections of the societies from which they sprang: the Continental Army beginning as citizen-soldier amateurs, while the British forces were composed of professional fighting men led by aristocratic officers.[34]

Charles Royster's *A Revolutionary People at War* probed the

---

[32]Jay Fliegelman, *Prodigals and Pilgrims* (Cambridge, Mass., 1982).

[33]John Shy, *A People Numerous and Armed* (New York, 1976), p. 224. For the British army in America before the Revolution and the colonists' reaction to its presence, see Shy's *Toward Lexington* (Princeton, 1965).

[34]Don Higginbotham, *War of American Independence* (New York, 1971). For a fine set of selected essays, see also Don Higginbotham, ed., *Reconsideration of the Revolutionary War* (Westport, Conn., 1978), one of which deals with the issue of the militia's use in conventional warfare.

American character and employed the Continental Army as a touchstone to reveal the complex views that the army and society had of each other. He dismissed the materialistic interpretation of many recent studies that concluded men were motivated to enter the service by self-interest. In a subtle and imaginative analysis, Royster showed how the early people's army gave way increasingly to a more European-style professional army—though one that never lost the force of revolutionary ideals. Once independence was achieved, the belief grew that victory had been won by a virtuous people, and not simply by the army. The American people thus reclaimed the war from the army, and ungratefully shunted the army aside, leaving behind an ambiguous military legacy.[35]

While the New Left, the new social historians, the new military historians, and the psychohistorians had provided invaluable case studies and insights into the Revolution, the problem of a general synthesis remained. In 1991, Gordon Wood picked up the challenge and published *The Radicalism of the American Revolution*, in which he argued, as the title suggests, that the Revolution ushered in a new American no longer hampered by habits of deference, feelings of inferiority, or hesitations about economic advancement. This new man (and he was male) felt himself to be anyone's equal and quickly exchanged his republican insistence on suppressing his self-interest for the common good for a more liberal focus on his individual rights and economic well-being.[36]

Wood quickly drew fire for his interpretation. At a forum sponsored by the *William and Mary Quarterly*, Joyce Appleby, Michel Zuckerman, and Barbara Smith attacked Wood for disregarding the various groups new social historians had painfully recovered and leaving out of his sweeping conclusions the struggling poor, blacks, and women. Inclusion of these groups, they argued, would have altered his conclusions and made class conflict and the struggle for power more central to the founding of America. They found him emphasizing ideas at the expense of material realities. They also attacked him for what they saw as his abandonment of the republican ideal in his earlier *Creation of the American Republic* and praising, instead, liberal consensus. In the words of Barbara Smith, Wood celebrated "a lack of public life, [and] the transformation of people into consumers rather than public persons."[37]

---

[35]Charles Royster, *A Revolutionary People at War* (Chapel Hill, N.C., 1979). See also Royster's *Light-Horse Harry Lee and the Legacy of the American Revolution* (New York, 1981).

[36]Gordon Wood, *The Radicalism of the American Revolution* (New York, 1991).

[37]Forum, "How Revolutionary Was the Revolution? A Discussion of Gordon S. Wood's *The Radicalism of the American Revolution*," *William and Mary Quarterly*, 3rd Ser. XLI (1992): 691.

Wood, like Bailyn before him, insisted on the Revolution's radical transformation of ideas about property, work, and the self. Property no longer meant simply land, it also meant personal wealth "dynamic, fluid, and evanescent . . . which" he claimed "could not create personal authority or identity." Work, not leisure, suddenly defined Americans, and, most important, the Revolution gave Americans a sense of equality and "self-worth."[38]

In the wake of this debate, historians have tried to understand what seems in retrospect like a republican juggernaut that rudely displaced many other elements and ideologies that contributed to the Revolution. In 1992, Daniel Rogers suggested that republicanism had been a useful concept, partly due to its elasticity and vagueness. He contended that historians had needed it to be more useful and expanatory than it really could be. He noted that for New Left historians it had been a stand-in for an antimarket mentality. They had seen it as a respectably radical and thoroughly American set of ideas that seemed to suggest virtue among laboring people in a way that embracing liberal ideas about rights and self-interest never could. As Gordon Wood put it in 1998, "Suddenly, the left had something in the American political tradition to appeal to other than the rapacious, money-making justifications of liberal capitalism."[39] And for materialists in general it seemed to define an ideology that somehow came from a material base, even though that base was never specified. For historians of women, such as Mary Beth Norton and Linda Kerber, who posited republican motherhood, republicanism's lack of definition had offered women an ill-defined but important link to the body politic. Rogers wrote that its success as a tool "stands as a measure . . . of how deeply responsive the interpretive disciplines are, not to evidence . . . but to their interpretive problematics."[40] Having seemed to explain every thing, republicanism's utility was circumscribed.

In the wake of the declining possibilities of republicanism, some historians looked to less comprehensive, more traditional approaches to understanding aspects of the Revolution. Alison Olson looked at colonial legislatures and discovered that they were indeed becoming more powerful during the colonial period. While she draws no overall conclusions from her evidence, it shows colonial institutions becoming more responsive and democratic on the eve of the Revolution.[41]

Looking once more at the ideological background of the Revolu-

---

[38]Ibid, 711, 710.

[39]Gordon Wood, Preface to the 1998 Edition of *Creation of the American Republic* (Chapel Hill, N.C., 1998), p. vi.

[40]Daniel Rogers, "Republicanism: The Career of a Concept," *Journal of American History*, Vol. 79, No. 1 (June 1992): 38.

[41]Alison Olson, "Eighteenth Century Colonial Legislatures and Their Constituents," *Journal of American History*, Vol. 79, No. 2 (September 1992): 543–67.

tion, several historians have studied religion and its effects on the coming of the conflict. James D. German, denying the presumed identity of republicanism and Puritanism, found that New England Calvinism, far from discouraging self-interest, saw it as an expression of the "disinterested love to being in general" and hence welcomed capitalism as no threat to the kingdom of God.[42]

As Gordon Wood now writes, "It is important to remember that the boxlike categories of 'republicanism' and 'liberalism' are essentially the inventions of us historians, and as such they are dangerous if heuristically necessary distortions of a very complicated past reality."[43] In the twilight of the explanatory power of republicanism, scholars of ideas are studying ideological beliefs that flourished alongside republicanism, not seeking to replace it. Eric Foner, building on insights of Orlando Patterson in his work on the interdependence of freedom on slavery, has shown how much the fact of chattel slavery influenced Americans' understandings of the meanings of freedom in the late eighteenth and early nineteenth centuries. David Hackett Fischer, in *Paul Revere's Ride*, weighs in with a variant ideology found in prerevolutionary Boston. Revere's idea of liberty, he writes, did not derive from either republicanism *or* "English opposition Ideology" *or* "Lockean liberalism," but "New England's tradition of ordered freedom, which gave heavy weight to collective rights and individual responsibilities—more so than is given by our modern calculus of individual rights and collective responsibilities."[44]

T. H. Breen, in a recent essay included in this chapter, has moved to restore Locke to a place of importance in the minds of American colonists. Taking the view that colonial America must be seen in its relationship with Great Britain and in comparison with other parts of the Empire such as Scotland and Ireland, Breen has argued that England's growing chauvinism and nationalism made colonists aware that they were not considered "Englishmen." This repudiation made them find Locke's emphasis on the natural rights of *all* men congenial to their purposes—more so than an appeal to the rights of Englishmen. It also explains the overdetermined nature of their outraged response to Great Britain's provocative policies in the years before the Revolution.

---

[42]James D. German, "The Social Utility of Wicked Self-Love: Calvinism, Capitalism, and Public Policy in Revolutionary New England," *Journal of American History*, Vol. 82, No. 3 (December 1995): 965–98, 998; on religion and the Revolution see also Peter Albert and Ronald Hoffman, eds., *Religion in a Revolutionary Age* (Charlottesville, Va., 1994), and Jonathan Clark, *The Language of Liberty, 1660–1832, Political Discourse and Social Dynamics in the Anglo-American World* (Cambridge, Mass., 1994).

[43]Gordon Wood, *Creation*, p. xi.

[44]Orlando Patterson, *Slavery and Social Death, A Comparative Study* (Cambridge, Mass., 1982); Eric Foner, *The Story of Freedom* (New York, 1998); David Hackett Fischer, *Paul Revere's Ride* (Oxford, 1994), p. xvii.

They felt not only the sting of extra taxes and the burdens of maintaining the British military presence, but also the humiliation of rejection from participation in an "Englishness" they believed they shared.[45] Breen concluded his essay noting that "it was not until after the Revolution, when Americans confronted the exclusionary and racist logic of their own nationalism, that ordinary men and women had reason to be thankful that whatever their country had become, it had commenced as a society committed to rights and equality, radical concepts then and now." While he revised Bailyn and Wood and challenged the "republican synthesis" in his emphasis on Locke, Breen concurred with Wood's conclusion that the Revolution provided the ideology that would eventually serve all Americans fighting to be included in the Declaration's promise of equality and rights. While Breen's revision returns to an earlier view of the ideological origins of the Revolution, nevertheless he agrees with Bailyn, Wood, and, in a modulated way, Bancroft that the Revolution had, in the long run, radical results.

In summary it should be noted that historians who have addressed themselves to the question of whether the Revolution was revolutionary must answer a number of related questions. Was American society truly democratic during the colonial period? Or was American society undemocratic during the colonial era, thus resulting in a dual revolution: a struggle to see who would rule at home as well as a fight for home rule? What was the true nature of the Revolution? Was there a radical ideological change in the ideas that most Americans held regarding their image of themselves and of their institutions? Or did most of the changes take place within the political and social sphere rather than in the world of ideas? Was the "republican synthesis," with its emphasis on republican ideology, a convincing interpretation of this cataclysmic event? What were the results of the Revolution for women? What motivated men to go off to fight in the Revolutionary War—was it materialism or idealism? The answers to these questions will determine the answer to the broader question of whether the American Revolution was revolutionary or nonrevolutionary.

---

[45]T. H. Breen, "Ideology and Nationalism on the Eve of the American Revolution: Revisions *Once More* in Need of Revising," *Journal of American History*, Vol. 84, No. 1 (June 1997): 13–39.

GARY B. NASH (1933–   ) is professor of history at the University of California, Los Angeles, and director of the National Center for History in the Schools. He is the author of Quakers and Politics *(1968),* Red, White and Black *(1974),* The Urban Crucible *(1979),* Race, Class and Politics *(1986),* Freedom by Degrees, *with Jean R. Soderlund (1991),* Race and Revolution *(1990), and coauthor of* History of Trial *(1998).*

Although eighteenth-century America was predominantly a rural, agricultural society, its seaboard commercial cities were the cutting edge of economic, social, and political change. Almost all the alterations that are associated with the advent of capitalist society happened first in the cities and radiated outward to the smaller towns, villages, and farms of the hinterland. In America, it was in the colonial cities that the transition first occurred from a barter to a commercial economy; where a competitive social order replaced an ascriptive one; where a hierarchical and deferential polity yielded to participatory and contentious civic life; where factory production began to replace small-scale artisanal production; where the first steps were taken to organize work by clock time rather than by sidereal cycles. The cities predicted the future, even though under one in twenty colonists lived in them in 1700 or 1775 and even though they were but overgrown villages compared to the great urban centers of Europe, the Middle East, and China.

Considering the importance of the cities as dynamic loci of change, it is surprising that historians have studied them so little. Even the fascination with urban history in the last few decades has done little to remedy this. We have at our disposal a shelfful of books on the early American inland villages, whose households numbered only in the hundreds, but have comparatively little to inform us about the colonial urban centers. . . .

This book proceeds from a different conception of how urban societies changed in the eighteenth century and is based largely on different sources. It stems from my interest in the social morphology of America's colonial cities and how it was that urban people, at a certain point in the preindustrial era, upset the equilibrium of an older system of social relations and turned the seaport towns into crucibles of revolutionary agitation. More particularly, I have tried to discover how people worked, lived, and perceived the changes going on about them, how class relationships shifted, and how political consciousness grew, especially among the laboring classes.

What has led early American historians to avoid questions about class formation and the development of lower-class political consciousness is not only an aversion to Marxist conceptualizations of history but also the persistent myth that class relations did not matter in early America because there were no classes. Land, it is widely held, was abundant and wages were high because labor was always in great demand. Therefore, opportunity was widespread and material well-being attainable by nearly everybody. If being at the bottom or in the middle was only a way station on a heavily traveled road to the top, then the composition of the various ranks and orders must have been constantly shifting and class consciousness could be only an evanescent and unimportant phenomenon. Thus, our understanding of the social history of the colonial cities has been mired in the general idea that progress was almost automatic in the commercial centers of a thriving New World society.

Only recently has the notion of extraordinary elasticity within classes and mobility between them begun to yield to a more complex analysis of how demographic trends, economic development, the spread of a market economy, and a series of costly wars produced a social, political, and ideological transformation. Historians have begun to create a far more intricate picture of social change by studying the extent of vertical and horizontal mobility, the degree of stratification, the accumulation and distribution of wealth, the social origins of the elite, the changing nature of economic and political power, and the shaping of class, ethnic, and religious consciousness. Historians are also coming to understand the need to retreat from discussing how *the* community was affected and to consider instead how different groups within the community were affected. Armies were supplied by some urban dwellers and manned by others, and those who gained or lost were not randomly selected. Price inflation and monetary devaluation caused problems for the whole society but the burdens were not distributed evenly. A sharp rise in overseas demand for American grain might increase the profits of inland farmers and seaboard merchants but could undercut the household budget of urban laborers and artisans.

Much of this book is about those who occupied the lower levels of urban society, the people who frequently suffered the unequal effects of eighteenth-century change. This is no mere quest for aesthetic balance or for simple justice in recreating the past. Examination of the circumstances of life for the great mass of common people in every period and place and inquiry into their ways of thinking and acting are essential if we are ever to test and correct the hallowed generalizations made from the study of the select few upon which our understanding of history is primarily based. What is more, I proceed from the conviction that the success of any society is best measured not by examining the attainments and accumulations of those at the top but by assaying the quality of life for those at the bottom. If this be thought the maxim of a utopian socialist, it was also the notion of an eighteenth-century English aristocrat whose writings circulated in Boston. "Every Nation," wrote Sir Richard Cox, "has the Reputation of being rich or poor from the Condition of the lowest Class of its Inhabitants."

In examining the lives of the lower classes in the eighteenth-century American cities I have repeatedly encountered evidence of social situations for which there is no accounting in the standard scholarship. Boston, I have found, was not only the commercial and intellectual center of New England Puritanism, as we have been taught, but also, by the 1740s, the New England center of mass indebtedness, widowhood, and poverty. By the end of the Seven Years War in 1763 poverty on a scale that urban leaders found appalling had also appeared in New York and Philadelphia. The narrowing of opportunities and the rise of poverty are two of the subthemes of this book. This is not to deny that compared with most places from which the colonists came—at least those who were white and free—the material circumstances of life were far more favorable than they had previously known. Comparisons between life in the colonial cities and life in Europe, however, like comparisons today between the plight of the urban poor in Chicago and Calcutta, miss the mark. An indebted shoemaker in Boston in 1760 took little satisfaction that for many of those who worked with hammer and awl life was worse and the future even bleaker in Dublin or London. People's sense of deprivation is not assuaged by referring them to distant places or ancient times. Like those above them, they measure the quality of their lives within their own locales and make comparisons primarily with the world of their parents.

To study those who resided at the bottom of the seaport societies it is also necessary to study those in the middle and at the top. Whether it is the reaction of the poor to the new formulae for dealing with urban poverty or the role of the crowd in the Stamp Act demonstrations of 1765, nothing is explicable without understanding the ideology and conduct of men at the higher levels. It was, after all, with those who possessed economic, political, and social power that the lower orders ultimately had to resolve matters. All urban people were linked together in a social network where power was unevenly distributed, and one part of this social organism cannot be understood in isolation from the others. Above all, this book is about the relationships among urban people who occupied different rungs of the social ladder.

The concept of class is central to this book. Therefore, it is important to specify that the term has a different meaning for the preindustrial period than for a later epoch. I employ it as both a heuristic and a historical category. It is a term which enables us to perceive that urban people gradually came to think of themselves as belonging to economic groups that did not share common goals, began to behave in class-specific ways in response to events that impinged upon their well-being, and manifested ideological points of view and cultural characteristics peculiar to their rank. This is not to say that all carpenters or all shopkeepers occupied the same position along the spectrum of wealth or that all ship captains or all caulkers thought alike or that merchants and shoemakers consistently opposed each other because they occupied different social strata. Nor can class be determined simply by notations on a tax assessor's list or by occupations given in inventories of estate. Moreover, evidence is abundant that vertical consciousness was always present in a society where movement up and down the social ladder never stopped and where the natural tendency of economic networks was to create a common interest among, for example, the merchant, shipbuilder, and mariner.

Thus, we must recognize the problems in employing the concept of class in eighteenth-century society, for the historical stage of a mature class formation had not yet been reached. To ignore class relations, however, is a greater problem. The movement between ranks and the vertical linkages that were a part of a system of economic clientage did not foreclose the possibility that horizontal bonds would grow in strength. People who had always thought of themselves as belonging to the lower, middling, or upper ranks, but saw no reason that this implied social conflict, would gradually associate these rough identifiers of social standing with antagonistic interests and make them the basis for political contention. One of the main tasks of this book is to show that many urban Americans, living amidst historical forces that were transforming the social landscape, came to perceive antagonistic divisions based on economic and social position; that they began to struggle around these conflicting interests; and that through these struggles they developed a consciousness of class. This is quite different, as E. P. Thompson points out, than arguing "that classes exist, independent of historical relationship and struggle, and that they struggle *because* they exist, rather than coming into existence out of that struggle."

Hence, I am concerned with the evolving relations among different groups of urban people who were subject to historically rooted changes that may have been as perplexingly intricate to them as they have been to historians since. It is not my argument that by the end of the colonial period class formation and class consciousness were fully developed, but only that we can gain greater insight into the urban social process between 1690 and 1776 and can understand more fully the origins and meaning of the American Revolution if we analyze the changing relations among people of different ranks and examine the emergence of new modes of thought based on horizontal rather than vertical divisions in society. The shift in social alignments would continue after the Revolution, not moving with telic force toward some rendezvous with destiny in the industrial period but shaped by historical forces that were largely unpredictable in 1776.

This book is also comparative in its approach. Examining concurrently the process of change in Boston, New York, and Philadelphia has enabled me to comprehend how particular factors intertwined in each city to hasten or retard the formation of class consciousness and to give a particular texture to social discourse and political behavior. I have chosen these three cities not only because they were the largest northern maritime centers, as well as the seats of provincial government, but also because their populations differed significantly in racial and ethnic origins, in religious composition, and in the legacies of their founding generations. It should be apparent in what follows that class consciousness developed according to no even-paced or linear formula. It emerged and receded depending upon conditions, leadership at both the top and bottom, cultural traditions, and other factors. The comparative approach has also convinced me that the Marxist maxim that the mode of production dictates the nature of class relations has only limited analytic potential for explaining changes during some historical eras. It is not different modes of production that account for the striking differences among the three port towns in the historical development of class consciousness but the different experiences of people who lived within three urban societies that shared a common mode of production. Thus, it is necessary to go beyond determining objective class structures and objective productive relations to examining "the specific activities of men [and women] in real social and economic relationships, containing fundamental contradictions and variations and therefore always in a state of dynamic process." Bostonians, New Yorkers, and Philadelphians experienced their situations differently between 1690 and 1776 because discrete factors impinged upon them, ranging from their proximity to Anglo-French theaters of war to the development of their hinterlands to their cultural heritage.

In inquiring into the history of the common people of the northern port towns I have adopted the term "laboring classes." I do so in order to take account of the fact that before the American Revolution—in fact, for more than half a century after the Revolution—there was no industrial working *class* composed of a mass of wage laborers who toiled in factories where a capitalist class wholly owned and controlled the productive machinery. My concern is with broad groupings of people who worked with their hands but were differentiated by skills and status. Thus, the laboring *classes* included slaves, whose bondage was perpetual, indentured servants, whose unfree status was temporary, and free persons, whose independence could be altered only in unusual circumstances. The laboring ranks also ascended from apprentice to journeyman to master craftsman. Likewise, there were gradations among ill-paid merchant seamen, laborers, and porters at the bottom; struggling shoemakers, tailors, coopers, and weavers who were a step higher; more prosperous cabinetmakers, silversmiths, instrument-makers, and housewrights; and entrepreneurial bakers, distillers, ropewalk operators, and tallow chandlers. There was, in short, no unified laboring class at any point in the period under study. That does not mean that class formation and the shaping of class consciousness was not happening in the era culminating with the American Revolution.

Despite the importance attached to economic and social change, this book argues that ideology in many instances was far more than a reflection of economic interests and acted as a motive force among urban people of all ranks. But it needs to be emphasized at the outset that ideology is not the exclusive possession of educated individuals and established groups. Nor do I believe that those at the top established an ideology that was then obligingly adopted by those below them. Slaves, indentured servants, the laboring poor, women, and the illiterate also had an ideology, although many of these people did not express ideas systematically in forms that are easily recoverable by historians two hundred years later. What I mean by ideology is awareness of the surrounding world, penetration of it through thought, and reasoned reactions to the forces impinging upon one's life. People living in communities as small as the prerevolutionary port towns, linked together as they were by church, tavern, workplace, and family, exchanged views, compared insights, and through the face-to-face nature of their associations, arrived at certain common understandings of their social situations. The world for them may have always been half-seen and imperfectly comprehended, but, as is universally true, they acted upon reality as they understood it, whether they were university trained and rich or could barely keep their shop books by crooked hand in a rented room.

It is not possible to fathom the subterranean social changes that transformed the urban centers of colonial America or to peer into the minds of the mass of urban dwellers who have been obscured from historical sight by consulting only the sources that are most accessible to the historian—newspapers, municipal records, business accounts, diaries and correspondence, and published sermons, political tracts, and legislative proceedings. As vital as these sources are, they are insufficient to the task, for they most often came from the hands of upper-class merchants, lawyers, clergymen, and politicians, who, though they tell us much, do not tell all. These sources are particularly silent on the lives of those in the lower reaches of the urban hierarchy and they are only occasionally helpful in revealing the subsurface social processes at work. This is not surprising, for on the one hand the gentry was not interested in illuminating the lives of laboring-class city dwellers and on the other hand they were often unaware of, mystified by, or eager to obscure the changing social, economic, and political relationships in their cities. Buried in less familiar documents, virtually all of them unpublished and many of them fragmentary and difficult to use, are glimpses of the lives of ordinary people. The story of how life was lived and conditions changed in the colonial cities can be discerned, not with mathematical precision or perfect clarity but in general form, from tax lists, poor relief records, wills, inventories of estate, deed books, mortgages, court documents, and portledge bills and wage records. This book draws extensively upon such sources as well as upon more traditional forms of evidence. It also infers lower-class thought from lower-class action, which is justifiable when the action is adequately recorded and is repetitive. . . .

It is not within the compass of this book to analyze the revolutionary process that occurred after the outbreak of fighting in eastern Massachusetts in the spring of 1775. It is enough to note that the work of a new generation of historians has begun to demonstrate that much of the complexity and significance of the American Revolution is missed by portraying it primarily as a movement for independence and the creation of republican institutions. It was certainly that, but it was also a social upheaval involving "the rapid and often violent mobilization into public life of many different groups," the challenging of gentry control of public affairs, and the proposing of remedies for the social ills that many believed had beset American society.

The burden of this book has been to show how the growth and commercial development of the northern seaport towns brought about multifaceted change involving the restructuring of social groups, the redistribution of wealth, the alteration of labor relations, the emergence of states of consciousness that cut horizontally through society, and the mobilization into political life of the lower ranks of laboring people. Haltingly it was recognized by many in the cities that the ligaments of the corporate society of the past had been torn in ways that struck at their opportunities, well-being, and sense that equity prevailed. In this century-long process there emerged no perfect crystallization of classes or class consciousness. But both master craftsmen and small retailers in the middle ranks and lesser artisans, merchant seamen, and laborers below them learned to define their interests and identify the self-interested behavior of those they had been taught to believe acted for the good of the whole. We have seen them beginning to struggle around the issues that were most palpable in terms of their daily existence and, in the process of struggling, developing a consciousness about their separate roles and their antagonistic interests with others in their communities.

Liberal theory, as imbibed by historians, recognizes tension and conflict only in terms of the "explicit and unwarranted intrusion of authority upon individual [political] freedom." But on a wide ensemble of issues—including political rights, but extending beyond them to wages and prices, charity, taxes, market and labor relations, and evangelical religion—the urban lower orders formulated distinctly different points of view from the ones held by those above them. It is necessary to reiterate that there was no unified ideology among those who worked with their hands or among those who did not. Urban society was much too fluid for that. Nor can it be said that there were no important areas where interclass agreement prevailed. Nevertheless, within their own cognitive structures, merchant seamen, artisans, and the poor, as well as merchants, shopkeepers, and professional men, saw their world changing. This led, as the Revolution approached, to the rise of a radical consciousness among many and to an interplay between calls for internal reform and insurgency against external forces that adversely affected the lives of city people. Challenges to the concentration of economic, political, and cultural authority ultimately shattered the equilibrium of the old system of social relations.

Although no social revolution occurred in America in the 1770s, the American Revolution could not have unfolded when or in the manner it did without the self-conscious action of urban laboring people—both those at the bottom and those in the middle—who became convinced that they must create power where none had existed before or else watch their position deteriorate, both in absolute terms and relative to that of others. Thus, the history of the Revolution is in part the history of popular collective action and the puncturing of the gentry's claim that their rule was legitimized by custom, law, and divine will. Ordinary people, sometimes violently, took over the power and the procedures of the constituted authorities. With wealth becoming far more concentrated at the top of urban society, plebeian urban dwellers forced their way into the political arena, not so much through the formal mechanisms of electoral politics as through street demonstrations, mass meetings, extralegal committees that assumed governmental powers, the intimidation of their enemies, and, in some cases, spirited defenses of traditional norms. This reordering of political power required a mental breakthrough, for it had to be accomplished in the face of a model of social relations, set by the elite, which claimed the superior wisdom and public mindedness of the educated and wealthy and prescribed deference as the customary and proper role of "inferior" people.

This shattering of the habit of obedience, advanced by the Great Awakening, proceeded far more rapidly in Boston in the second third of the century than in the other towns. Yet it relapsed after 1765, as traditional leaders, aided by the descent of a red-coated enemy on the community, reasserted themselves and as the people closed ranks in a reaffirmation of the spirit of covenant. In New York and Philadelphia the political leadership of the elite was challenged only sporadically until the end of the Seven Years War, when economic derangements and internal factionalism set the stage for the rise of laboring men to political power. But in all the cities those who labored with their hands, especially those who found it most difficult to weather the changes that had overcome their society, formed a picture of the social arrangements by which they lived. It was a picture that was political in its composition and increasingly vivid in its portrayal of the port towns as places where men struggled against each other rather than working harmoniously for the mutual good of the whole society.

T. H. BREEN

T. H. BREEN (1942–   ) is the William Smith Mason Professor of American History at Northwestern University. He is the author of The Character of The Good Ruler *(1974),* Shaping Southern Society *(1980),* Puritans and Adventurers *(1980), and* Tobacco Culture *(1985).*

Over the last four decades historians of eighteenth-century England reworked the entire field. . . . The newer literature . . . draws attention back to Great Britain, to a highly commercial, modernizing North Atlantic world, and to a shifting relation between an expansive metropolitan state and a loosely integrated group of American colonies. More to the point, this scholarship invites juxtaposition of two separate topics, each of which alone has generated a rich and impressive literature, but that when brought together hold out the promise of a greatly revised interpretation of the coming of the American Revolution. First, the recent work fundamentally recasts how we

T. H. Breen, "Ideology and Nationalism on the Eve of the American Revolution: Revisions *Once More* in Need of Revising," *Journal of American History,* 84 (June 1997). Reprinted with the permission of the *Journal of American History.*

think about the origins and development of American nationalism. And second, it provides new insights into the character of popular political ideology on the eve of independence, suggesting why the natural rights liberalism associated with John Locke had broader emotional appeal during this period than did classical republicanism or civic humanism. . . .

Whereas we once concentrated on elite political life, on the activities of unstable factions in court and Parliament, we now read of the development and maturation of an impressive fiscal-military state. No doubt, a good many fox-hunting country gentlemen will survive. The monarch will surely remain a key political figure. But those characters must now share the historical stage with an articulate and powerful middle class. Instead of tracing the genealogies of the members of parliament, English historians examine topics such as the establishment of a vibrant consumer economy, the creation of a complex state bureaucracy, the rise of manufacturing towns and commercial ports, and the development of genuine ideological differences within the political community. Dynamism, growth, and modernity suddenly seem apposite terms to describe this not-so-traditional England of the late eighteenth century.

We should remember that colonial Americans viewed those striking developments from afar. . . . The colonists experienced the transformation of mid-eighteenth-century England in gross outline, but for all of that, the impact of those changes on their sense of identity within the empire was real and substantial. Four new elements in particular influenced how the colonists imagined themselves within the Anglo-American world: the developing military strength of Great Britain, the spread of a consumer-oriented economy, the creation of a self-conscious middle-class culture, and, most significant for our purposes, the stirrings of a heightened sense of British national identity.

Recent English historiography reminds us of something that probably should have been obvious all along: the British not only waged almost constant warfare against France and Spain throughout the world but also usually emerged victorious. In other words, they were remarkably good at it. . . . Unlike their continental adversaries, the British had learned how to pay for large-scale war without bankrupting its citizens and, thereby, without sparking the kind of internal unrest that frequently destabilized other ancien régime monarchies. . . . British rulers discovered the secret of fighting on credit; along with innovative banking and financial institutions, legions of new bureaucrats (tax collectors and inspectors) appeared throughout the country, persons who served as constant reminders of what Joanna Innes has termed "an impressively powerful central state apparatus."

A second element powerfully shaping the eighteenth-century colonial world was the rapid development of a new consumer marketplace.

A flood of exports linked ordinary people living on the periphery of empire to an exciting metropolitan society. Few people understood the cultural, and therefore the political, impact of the burgeoning consumer trade better than did Benjamin Franklin. In his *The Interest of Great Britain Considered* (1760), he observed that the vast quantities of British imports had the capacity to influence how colonists imagined themselves within a larger empire. Sounding much like a twentieth-century anthropologist, Franklin announced that Americans "must 'know,' must 'think,' and must 'care,' about the country they chiefly trade with." . . .

Prosperous English men and women, much like their American counterparts, bought what they had seen advertised in an expanding commercial press. And, significantly, people of more modest means also participated in that vibrant marketplace. . . .

Colonial Americans . . . too had tasted luxury and increasingly called it happiness. On the eve of independence one American clergyman even went so far as to insist that civil rulers had an obligation to defend subjects "in the quiet and peaceable enjoyment of their persons and properties, i.e. their persons and worldly goods and estates, &c. together with all their just advantages and opportunities of *getting more worldly goods and estates*, &c. by labour, industry, trade, manufactures, &c."

A third element in the rapidly changing world of the midcentury colonists would almost certainly have been the activities of a new social group in Great Britain, the so-called middle class. . . . While no one denies the existence of other middle classes in the development of other nations, British historians make a strong and well-documented case for the invention of a distinct middle class in Georgian England. Educated, professional, and prosperous people with no claim to aristocracy established, for the first time, what Langford terms a "polite and commercial" society. "English society was given a basic fluidity of status," explain Lawrence Stone and Jeanne C. Fawtier Stone, "by the vigour, wealth, and numerical strength of the 'middle sort,' mostly rural but also urban, whose emergence between 1660 and 1800 is perhaps the most important feature of the age." This burgeoning middle group industriously copied the manners of its betters, fashioning self in ever more colorful and elaborate ways, celebrating consumer fads, purchasing the novels now marketed in large volume, and populating the spas and resort towns; perhaps most remarkable, even as it redefined the character of English popular culture, the new middle class never seriously challenged the traditional landed oligarchy for the right to rule the nation. It was those men and women who entertained visiting Americans, English families headed by lawyers, merchants, and doctors, who regularly proclaimed that the freest nation in the world was also the most prosperous. For the colonists, it was an exciting and convincing display.

These economic, cultural, and social transformations fed what for the midcentury American colonists would certainly have been the fourth and most striking feature of the age, the birth of a powerfully self-confident British nationalism. . . . Some time during the 1740s English men and women of all social classes began to express a sentiment that might be described variously as a dramatic surge of national consciousness, a rise of aggressive patriotism, or a greatly heightened articulation of national identity. To be sure, during the period of the Armada English people took intense pride in the defeat of the hated Spanish, and distinguished Elizabethan writers celebrated their Englishness. But the Georgian experience was quite different. Even if the eighteenth-century development represents an intensification of an imaginative project with ancient roots, it nevertheless involved a much broader percentage of the population. It was now sustained by a new commercial press that brought stories about the empire to urban coffeehouses and country taverns. . . .

If the social sources of a heightened sense of national identity are in doubt no one questions the character of the swelling patriotic movement. Ordinary people—laboring men and women as well as members of a self-confident middling group—who bellowed out the words to the newly composed "Rule Britannia" and who responded positively to the emotional appeal of "God Save the King" gave voice to the common aspirations of a militantly Protestant culture. Or, stated negatively, they proclaimed their utter contempt for Catholicism and their rejection of everything associated with contemporary France. . . . In time, . . . even members of the traditional ruling class came to appreciate the symbolic value of John Bull in mobilizing a population in support of war and monarchy. For most English people the expression of national identity seems to have been quite genuine. Indeed, by noisy participation in patriotic rituals, the middling and working classes thrust themselves into a public sphere of national politics. As Roy Porter reminds us, "English patriotism during the Georgian century should not be passed off as nothing but hegemonic social control, the conspiratorial ideological imprint of the ruling order; rather it signified a positive and critical articulation of the political voice of the middle class." . . .

Georgian historians have paid considerably less attention to the darker face of national identity: its powerfully exclusionary tendencies and its propensity to reduce the "other," however defined, to second-rate status. . . .

For persons of Celtic background, for example, the rise of "British" nationalism at midcentury drew attention to their own marginality. . . . As P. J. Marshall remarks, British nationalism had an extremely adverse impact on men and women who did not happen to live "at home." According to Marshall, "The eighteenth-century experience . . . revealed that 'imagined communities' of Britishness were parochial. English people could perhaps envisage a common community with the Welsh and, often with much difficulty, with the Scots, but they failed to incorporate the Irish or colonial Americans into their idea of nation." . . .

At midcentury, therefore, colonial Americans confronted what must have seemed a radically "new" British consciousness. It radiated outward from the metropolitan center, providing officials of a powerful, prosperous, and dynamic state with an effective vocabulary for mobilizing popular patriotism. It was in this fluid, unstable context that colonists on the periphery attempted to construct their own imagined identity within the empire. Although the process of defining identity had begun as soon as European settlers arrived in the New World, the conversation across the Atlantic Ocean changed dramatically at midcentury. Americans found that they were not dealing with the same nation that their parents or grandparents had known. Confronted with a sudden intensification of British nationalism, the colonists' initial impulse was to join the chorus, protesting their true "Britishness," their unquestioned loyalty to king and constitution, and their deep antipathy to France and Catholicism. As one American pamphleteer proudly announced, "Britain seems now to have attained to a degree of wealth, power, and eminence, which half a century ago, the most sanguine of her patriots could hardly have made the object of their warmest wishes."

With due respect to Edmund Burke—and to the many colonial historians who have echoed the phrase—"salutary neglect" fails utterly to describe the complexity of the changing American situation. Although the number of crown officials in the colonies was always small, Britain aggressively intruded into the colonial world of the mid-eighteenth century: the metropolitan center spoke insistently through the flow of consumer goods that transformed the American marketplace, through the regulars who came to fight the French and Indians along the northern frontier, through celebrity itinerants such as George Whitefield, who brought English evangelical rhetoric to anxious American dissenters, and, for most literate colonists, through a commercial press that depicted the mother country in most alluring terms, indeed, as the most polite and progressive society the world had ever seen.

This revised perspective on eighteenth-century Britain, one that focuses on the dynamic character of the metropolitan center, has major implications for how we think of the colonies within the empire. First, the new literature suggests that we should situate the American experience firmly within a broad comparative framework, within an Atlantic empire that included Scotland as well as Ireland. People living in all three regions suddenly found themselves at midcentury confronting an England different from any that they had previously known. While London piped the tune, the outlying provinces and colonies accommodated themselves as best they could to England's heightened sense of national purpose. In each area the relationship raised hard questions. Did being "British" mean that one was also "English," or that people who did not happen to live in England could confidently claim equality with the English within a larger empire? Although each region brought different resources and perceptions to the conversation, we should appreciate that Scots, Irish, and Americans were in fact engaged in a common interpretive project, and however we choose to view the coming of the American Revolution, we should pay close attention to what recent historians of Scotland and Ireland have discovered about the construction of eighteenth-century imperial identities. . . .

However much midcentury Americans knew about the politics of contemporary Scotland and Ireland, they too found themselves struggling to comprehend the demands of a powerfully self-confident imperial state. We must pay close attention here to chronology, to the different phases in a developing conversation with England as the colonists moved from accommodation to resistance, from claims of Britishness to independence.

Like the Scots, the Americans initially attempted to demonstrate, often in shrill patriotic rhetoric, their loyalty to almost everything associated with Great Britain. Before the 1760s they assumed that popular British nationalism was essentially an inclusive category and that by fighting the French in Canada and by regularly proclaiming their support of the British constitution, they merited equal standing with other British subjects who happened to live on the other side of the Atlantic. The colonists were slow to appreciate the growing conflict between nation and empire, between Englishness and Britishness. Like the Irish, they conflated those categories within a general discourse of "imperial" identity.

A narration of the construction of identity *within the British Empire* properly begins in the 1740s. European settlers of an earlier period had, of course, struggled with some of the same issues, alternately celebrating and lamenting the development of cultural difference. But whatever the roots of the challenge, dramatic changes in English society, several of which we have already examined, forced provincial Americans for the first time to confront the full meaning of "Britishness" in their lives. The response was generally enthusiastic. . . . They believed that the English accepted them as full partners in the British Empire, allies in the continuing wars against France, devout defenders of Protestantism, and eager participants in an expanding world of commerce. Insomuch as Americans during this period spoke the language of national identity, as opposed to that of different regions and localities, they did so as imperial patriots, as people whose sense of self was intimately bound up with the success and prosperity of Great Britain. . . .

Consider a single example of this midcentury imperial patriotism. In 1764 the editor of the newly founded *New-Hampshire Gazette* lectured his readers on the social function of newspapers. "By this Means," he rhapsodized, "the spirited *Englishman*, the mountainous *Welshman*, the brave *Scotchman*, and *Irishman*, and the loyal *American*, may be firmly united and mutually RESOLVED to guard the glorious Throne of BRITANNIA. . . . Thus Harmony may be happily restored, Civil War disappointed, and each agree to embrace, as *British Brothers*, in defending the Common Cause."

Many other Americans shared the New England editor's assumptions about the inclusive character of the British imperial identity. Some of them were quite distinguished. Appearing before the Committee of the Whole House of Commons in 1766, Benjamin Franklin argued for unity within the empire. When a member of Parliament pointedly asked him whether expanding the frontiers of the British Empire in North America was not in fact just "an American interest," Franklin shot back, "Not particularly, but conjointly a British and an American interest." The Reverend Jeremy Belknap, a talented historian and the founder of the Massachusetts Historical Society, also captured the spirit of eighteenth-century colonial nationalism. Like Franklin, Belknap assumed that England and America were equals. The success of one contributed directly to the success of the other. Both found fulfillment in their common Britishness. According to Belknap, the brilliant leadership of William Pitt during the Seven Years' War "had attached us more firmly than ever, to the kingdom of Britain. We were proud of our connection with a nation whose flag was triumphant in every quarter of the globe. . . . We were fond of repeating every plaudit, which the ardent affection of the British nation bestowed on a young monarch [George III], rising to 'glory in the name of Briton.'" . . .

In point of fact, however, the Americans were not really *"British Brothers."* As became increasingly and distressingly obvious during the run-up to independence, heightened British nationalism was actually English nationalism writ large. . . . To be sure, categories lower than free white colonists existed in this midcentury status hierarchy, but for the Americans such unflattering distinctions hardly mattered.

"We won't be their Negroes," snarled a young John Adams in 1765, writing as "Humphry Ploughjogger" in the *Boston Gazette*. Adams crudely insisted that Providence had never intended the American colonists "for Negroes . . . and therefore never intended us for slaves. . . . I say we are as handsome as old English folks, and so should be as free." Ploughjogger's shrill, uncomfortably racist response to the Stamp Act revealed the shock of rejection. The source of anger was not so much parliamentary taxation without representation as it was the sudden realization that the British really regarded white colonial Americans as second-class beings, indeed, as persons so inferior from the metropolitan perspective that they somehow deserved a lesser measure of freedom.

The substance, if not the tone, of Ploughjogger's bitter complaint echoed throughout the colonial press on the eve of revolution. To be sure, the popular print materials contained other themes—religious and constitutional arguments, for example—but in many cases, the raw emotional energy of the performance came from the American writers' abrupt discovery of inequality. Like the anonymous writer of a piece that appeared in the *Maryland Gazette*—actually an essay originally published in a Boston journal—colonists throughout America found themselves asking the embarrassing question, "Are not the People of *America*, BRITISH Subjects? Are they not *Englishmen?*"

That the response to such questions was now in doubt became an issue of general public concern. Consider the defensive, pathetic, frequently querulous attempts by American writers during this period to demonstrate self-worth in relation to the men and women who happened to live in Great Britain. The Reverend Samuel Sherwood of Connecticut protested that colonists were "not an inferior species of animals, made the beast of burden to a lawless, corrupt administration." Other Americans heard similar tales of alleged colonial inferiority. James Otis Jr., the fiery Boston lawyer who protested the constitutionality of the Stamp Act, responded with heavy-handed irony. "Are the inhabitants of British America," he asked rhetorically, "all a parcel of transported thieves, robbers, and rebels, or descended from such? Are the colonists blasted lepers, whose company would infect the whole House of Commons?" The answer was more problematic than Otis would have liked. Arthur Lee encountered similar difficulty during a heated debate with "Mr. Adam Smith." The son of a wealthy Chesapeake tobacco planter, Lee insisted that, whatever the great economist might think, the original founders of Virginia had been "distinguished, even in Britain, for rank, for fortune, and for abilities." And yet, as Lee remarked with obvious resentment, despite superior family background, the Virginians of his own generation "are treated, not as the fellow-subjects but as the servants of Britain." . . .

As Adams well understood when he wrote as Ploughjogger, the simple New England farmer, ordinary Americans were not particularly interested in crafting a separate identity, at least not in the mid-1760s. It was the English who had projected a sense of difference and inferiority upon the colonists. In other words, "American" as a descriptive category seems in this highly charged context to have been an external construction, a term in some measure intended to be "humiliating and

debasing." In an exhaustive survey of the contents of all colonial
newspapers during the period immediately preceding national independence, Richard L. Merritt discovered that "available evidence indicates that Englishmen began to identify the colonial population as
'American' persistently after 1763—a decade before Americans themselves did so." The full implications of Merritt's pioneering work have
largely gone unappreciated. Indeed, it was not until quite recently that
P. J. Marshall again reminded us that "the rise of the concept of 'American' owed quite a lot to British usage." The exclusionary rhetoric
broadcast from the metropolitan center was a new development, a surprising and unsettling challenge to the assumptions of equality that
had energized colonial nationalism until the Stamp Act crisis; since it
came after an intense burst of imperial loyalty during the Seven Years'
War, the colonists felt badly betrayed. . . .

Shifting constructions of identity within the empire involved
more than simple miscommunication. England's assertion of its own
Englishness shocked Americans, and the element of surprise helps to
account for the strikingly emotional character of colonial political
writing. Indeed, if one attempts to explain the coming of revolution as
a lawyer-like analysis of taxation without representation or as an enlightened constitutional debate over parliamentary sovereignty, one
will almost certainly fail to comprehend the shrill, even paranoid, tone
of public discourse in the colonies.

Other historians have addressed this curious problem. In *The Ideological Origins of the American Revolution*, for example, Bernard Bailyn analyzed the disjuncture between popular rhetoric and statutory
reality. The American reaction to various parliamentary regulations
seemed to him far more rancorous than one might have predicted on
the basis of actual levels of taxation. Bailyn concluded that over the
course of the eighteenth century Americans had borrowed a highly in-
flammatory strand of English political discourse, one that warned in-
cessantly against corruption and conspiracy, the loss of civic virtue,
and a restoration of Stuart despotism. When Parliament attempted to
tax the colonists without representation, Americans assumed the
worst. Events appeared to be fulfilling their ideological nightmares.
And in this situation, they employed a strident "country" language
employed originally by English politicians critical of "court" corruption to translate imperial regulatory policy into a dangerous plot
against provincial liberty and property.

While that interpretation of the apparently irrational political
rhetoric of the colonists is entirely plausible, it does not seem sufficient to account for the sudden sense of personal humiliation. The extraordinary bitterness and acrimony of colonial rhetoric requires us to
consider the popular fear that the English were systematically relegat-
ing Americans to second-class standing within the empire. To be sure,
the colonists may have found in the borrowed "country" rhetoric a

persuasive language in which to express their emotional pain. That is certainly part of the story. What we tend to forget, however, is that they also complained that their *"British Brothers"* had begun treating them like "negroes," a charge that cannot be easily explained as an American echo of English political opposition.

The racism that accompanied fear of exclusion appeared in the writings of several distinguished colonial patriots. Like John Adams, these were men who demonstrated that they could communicate successfully to a growing audience of unhappy Americans. Few were better at it than James Otis Jr. During the 1760s, he publicly lectured an imagined representative of English society: "You think most if not all the Colonists are Negroes and Mulattoes—You are wretchedly mistaken—Ninety nine in a hundred in the more northern Colonies are white, and there is as good blood flowing in their veins, save the royal blood, as any in the three kingdoms." And Daniel Dulany, a well-educated Maryland lawyer, sounded a lot like "Ploughjogger" when he protested in 1765 against how English officials regularly characterized American colonists. "What a strange animal must a North American appear to be," this enlightened gentleman explained in one of the most reprinted political pamphlets written before the Revolution, "from these representations to the generality of English readers, who have never had an opportunity to admire that he may be neither black nor tawny, may speak the English language, and in other respects seem, for all the world, like one of them!" . . .

Within this radically evolving imperial framework, the Stamp Act seemed an especially poignant reminder for the Americans of their new second-class status. . . .

As the constitutional crisis with Parliament evolved and as the possibilities for political reconciliation became less promising, the American sense of humiliation slowly transformed itself into bemused reflection on having been pushed out of an empire that once seemed to guarantee liberty and prosperity. Even at the moment of independence, the colonists still could not quite explain why the ministers of George III had decided systematically to dishonor a proud people. "Had our petitions and prayers been properly regarded," the Reverend Henry Cumings preached in 1781 at the site of the Battle of Lexington, "and moderate pacific measures pursued, we should have entertained no thoughts of revolt." This was hardly an expression of the kind of self-confident patriotism that one might have expected in that situation. But Cumings played on the theme of rejection. "It was far from our intention or inclination to separate ourselves from Great-Britain; and that we had it not even in contemplation to set up for independency; but on the contrary, earnestly wished to remain connected with her, until she had deprived us of all hopes of preserving such a connection, upon any better terms than unconditional submission." . . .

If assertion of English national superiority forced colonists to imagine themselves as a separate people, it also profoundly affected the substance of American political ideology. During the 1760s the colonists took up the language of natural rights liberalism with unprecedented fervor. That they did so is not exactly a momentous discovery. In recent years, however, historians of political thought have discounted the so-called Lockean tradition in prerevolutionary America. According to Bernard Bailyn, for example, the liberal discourse of this period lacked persuasive impact. "We know now," Bailyn insisted, "that Enlightenment ideas, while they form the deep background and give a general coloration to the liberal beliefs of the time, were not the ideas that directly shaped the Americans' responses to particular events." To some extent, Bailyn had a point. An earlier generation of historians had treated natural rights claims as sacrosanct principles, as self-evident and timeless truths whose popularity required no social explanation. When the case for Lockean ideas was stated in such reverent terms, it was very hard to understand why ordinary men and women might have found the natural rights argument so emotionally compelling, indeed, why they would have risked their lives on the field of battle for such beliefs. . . .

The explanation for the popularity of natural rights arguments in late colonial America now seems clear. Within an empire strained by the heightened nationalist sentiment of the metropolitan center, natural rights acquired unusual persuasive force. Threatened from the outside by a self-confident military power, one that seemed intent on marginalizing the colonists within the empire, Americans countered with the universalist vocabulary of natural rights, in other words, with a language of political resistance that stressed a bundle of God-given rights as "prior to and independent of the claims of political authority." The Locke of the *Second Treatise* seemed to the Americans to embody common sense precisely because he abstracted consideration of human rights and equality from the traditional rhetoric of British history. He liberated the theory of politics from the constraints of time and custom, from purely English precedent. As Ian Shapiro, a historian of political thought, explains, "Locke shifted the basis of antiabsolutist conceptions of political legitimacy away from history and toward a moral justification based on an appeal to reason." Those who still maintain that the republican ideology described in such detail in J. G. A. Pocock's *The Machiavellian Moment* would have served the colonists just as well are hard pressed to explain how a fundamentally historical justification for the Ancient Constitution spoke effectively to the problem of preserving timeless human rights.

However logical championing natural rights liberalism may have been, it was for the colonists a profoundly defensive move. Americans invoked "transhistorical arguments of natural equity and human liberty" because, in the words of one student of Anglo-Irish patriotism, "they did not have much of a historical leg to stand on." In their recent study entitled *Colonial Identity in the Atlantic World*, Nicholas Canny and Anthony Pagden came to a strikingly similar conclusion. The eighteenth-century Americans, they declared, "could only make their demands in terms either of claims of some set of political traditions that they shared with the metropolitan culture or, as most were ultimately to do, of claims of a body of natural rights shared by all men everywhere." What that suggests is that American liberalism may have owed much of its initial popularity to its effectiveness as a rhetorical strategy, as the political language of a colonial people who had not yet invented a nation and, therefore, who had not yet constructed a common history.

Everywhere in the public political debates, one encounters the language of rights and equality. Arguments for the dominance of a particular political discourse during any period, of course, are bound to be somewhat impressionistic. Although we can appreciate the echoes of classical republican thought and the inspiration of evangelical Protestantism, we most frequently encounter an angry, shrill, often nervous insistence on natural rights. During the 1760s and early 1770s, colonial writers repeatedly invoked the authority of John Locke, and even when the name of the great philosopher did not appear, his ideas still powerfully informed popular public consciousness. The appeal to natural rights sounded not only in the labored pamphlets that learned university-trained lawyers seem to have written for other learned lawyers but also in the more popular journals and sermons. Throughout pre-revolutionary America, men and women responded to what they perceived as English arrogance with a truculent cry: we are as good as any English person. . . .

Natural rights liberalism was so pervasive that a colonial town meeting could quickly transform itself into a public seminar on Lockean philosophy. On November 20, 1772, the Boston Town Meeting charged a committee of twenty-one persons "to state the Rights of the Colonists, and of this Province in particular, as Men, as Christians, and as Subjects." In due time the committee report received the approval of Boston freeholders and other inhabitants. They agreed that "All Men have a Right to remain in a State of Nature as long as they please." No government could compel the subject to surrender his rights. On that central point the authors specifically cited Locke. From him, the Boston committee had learned that "The *natural* Liberty of Man is to be free from any superior Power on Earth, and not to be under the Will or legislative Authority of Man; but only to have the Law of Nature as his Rule." And finally, in a statement clearly intended to mobilize broad popular support, the authors of the report insisted that "All Persons born in the British American Colonies, are by the Laws of GOD and Nature . . . entitled, to all the natural, essential, inherent, and inseparable Rights, Liberties and Privileges of Subjects born in Great-Britain, or within the Realm." Whatever else this document may contain, its character does not seem particularly religious, nor, for that matter, the stuff of classic civic humanism. Like so many other Americans of this period, the members of the Boston committee demanded inclusion within an empire that seemed to have become increasingly exclusive; they understood instinctively that historical arguments drawn from a shared British past would not have much purchase against the claims of a nationalizing mother country.

A newly aggressive English state forced the Americans to leap out of history and to defend colonial and human equality on the basis of timeless natural rights. English national sentiment did not transform Americans into natural rights liberals, but it was a necessary catalyst. . . . By situating our interpretation of the run-up to revolution in the recent historiography of eighteenth-century England—we discover why the forgotten "Ploughjoggers" of colonial America were so angry and defensive, colonial liberals so fearful of rejection, and, above all, a people so profoundly confused by changing perceptions of identity within the British Empire. It was not until after the Revolution, when Americans confronted the exclusionary and racist logic of their own nationalism, that ordinary men and women had reason to be thankful that whatever their country had become, it had commenced as a society committed to rights and equality, radical concepts then and now.

6

THE CONSTITUTION: CONFLICT OR CONSENSUS?

The Constitution remains one of the most controversial documents in all of American history. Generations of Supreme Court justices have reinterpreted the document according to their own predilections when handing down constitutional decisions. Presidents and political parties in power traditionally have viewed the Constitution in the light of their own interests, pursuits, and philosophies of government; historians, too, have presented conflicting interpretations of the Constitution and of the intentions of its framers. This changing outlook of historians has tended to coincide with changes in the intellectual climate of opinion within America.

From the Convention of 1787 to the close of the Civil War the Constitution was considered a controversial document by historians because of the questions it raised about two opposing doctrines: states' rights versus national sovereignty, or a strict versus a loose construction of the Constitution. The outcome of the Civil War seemed to settle the issue in favor of the national theory of the Constitution.

In the century since the Civil War, however, six distinct groups of historians have arisen to offer differing interpretations of the constitutional period. The first, the nationalist school, emerged in the 1870s and 1880s; it approached the Constitution influenced by the intense nationalism marking American society in the Gilded Age. Around the turn of the century there appeared the Progressive school, which viewed the document and its framing in light of the Populist-Progressive reform movements of the 1890s and early 1900s. Charles A. Beard, the leading Progressive scholar, saw the Constitution as a document that was intended to protect private property and that reflected the interests of privileged groups in postrevolutionary America. Since World War II three groups of historians—the neoconservatives, the "new intellectual historians," and the neo-Progressives—arose either to revise or to refine the Beardian interpretation. Then in the 1990s the sixth group arose, the new social historians, including women's historians, who offered perspectives on those affected by the Constitution but left out of deliberations about it.

The nationalist school, which developed in the decades after the Civil War, was best represented by George Bancroft and John Fiske.

Both believed in the racial superiority of white Anglo-Saxon Protestant peoples. They subscribed to the idea that the orderly progress of mankind in modern times toward greater personal liberty was due largely to the preeminent political ability of Anglo-Saxon peoples to build strong and stable national states. According to these two writers, America's democratic institutions could be traced all the way back to the ancient political practices of Teutonic tribes in the forests of Germany. The Constitution, in their eyes, represented the high point in world history in the efforts of human beings to civilize and govern themselves.

Bancroft visualized the years 1782 to 1788 as a single period with the ratification of the Constitution coming as a climax of the Revolution itself.[1] The Articles of Confederation, ratified in 1781, were too weak to cope with external threats from Britain and Spain and internal problems such as Shays's Rebellion. The American people demanded a new and better instrument of government. Since America was divinely ordained to create the first perfect republic on earth—according to Bancroft—the Constitution symbolized the crowning success of the movement for a more popular government that had started with the Revolution.

Around the turn of the twentieth century the Populist and Progressive reform movements brought about a marked change in attitude toward the Constitution. Progressive reformers, concerned with the problems that had arisen from the nation's increasing industrialization, became convinced that unless the imbalance in wealth and political power in American society could be redressed, democracy in the United States was doomed. In response to such demands, state governments in the 1890s and early 1900s began extending their laws regulating various aspects of the economy. Congress at the same time was making efforts to regulate certain industries, such as the railroads, and to break up monopolies and trusts. To check the growing maldistribution of wealth, income tax measures were passed by both the state and federal governments. When the Supreme Court declared much of this state and national legislation unconstitutional, however, many persons began to view the Constitution as an undemocratic document whose purpose was to protect the rich and powerful and to frustrate the democratic aspirations of the people.

To Progressive historians, the Constitution represented a reactionary document—one written by the conservatives at the constitu-

---

[1]George Bancroft, *History of the Formation of the Constitution of the United States of America,* 2 vols. (New York, 1882). The glowing praise of John Fiske in *The Critical Period of American History, 1783–1789* (New York, 1888), p. 223, is typical of this period.

tional convention to thwart the radicals who held visions of completely reforming American society. These scholars pointed to the undemocratic features of the Constitution—the system of checks and balances, the difficult procedure for adopting amendments, and the idea of judicial veto—which made majority rule all but impossible. Unlike the nationalist historians who had seen the Constitution as a forward step for democracy, the Progressive historians saw it as a setback in the movement for popular government.

Many writers of the Progressive school reflected a major trend in historical circles at the time—the tendency toward an economic interpretation of history. Such scholars thought that economic factors were the major determinants in shaping the course of history. The Progressive interpretation of the Constitution, then, was based upon class conflict along economic lines—a point of view that had grown out of Carl Becker's interpretation of the American Revolution as a dual revolution posing the questions of home rule and who would rule at home. In the internal class struggle that took place, the lower classes, made up of small farmers in the interior and workingmen in the eastern seaboard towns, gained dominance over the upper classes, composed of merchants, financiers, and manufacturers. Once the lower classes were in control, the Progressive version continued, they proceeded to democratize American society by writing radical state constitutions and the Articles of Confederation. They set up democratic governments that passed cheap paper money legislation, debtor laws, and measures that favored the small farmers.

Members of the upper classes whose economic stake was in personal property—holdings in money and public securities or investments in manufacturing, shipping, and commerce—became particularly alarmed because the democratic governments seemed to be discriminating against their kind of property and in favor of those who owned land and real estate. It was they who conspired to undermine the democratic Articles of Confederation and instituted instead the more conservative Constitution.

This Progressive point of view was most ably expressed in Charles A. Beard's *An Economic Interpretation of the Constitution*, published in 1913. The key to Beard's path-breaking study was a person-by-person examination of the economic holdings and status of the framers of the Constitution. Using the Treasury records Beard was able to show that most of these men held public securities—a form of personal property that would increase dramatically in value if a new Constitution were written to strengthen the government and thus improve the nation's credit standing. Beard concluded, "The movement for the Constitution of the United States was originated and carried through principally by four groups of personalty interests which had been adversely affected under the Articles of Confederation: money, public securities, manufactures, and trade and shipping."[2] Those opposed were mostly small farmers and workingmen so far in debt that they could not qualify to vote for delegates to the Constitutional Covention.

Beard's book was perhaps the most influential work in American history of all time. Vernon L. Parrington's *Main Currents in American Thought*, published in 1927, and Louis M. Hacker's *Triumph of American Capitalism*, which appeared in 1940, echoed Beard's point of view. Although adversaries sprang up quickly, Beard remained convincing. Textbooks in history and political science repeated Beard's thesis verbatim. Even today's constitutional scholars contend with Beard's ghost. Almost all interpretations of the Constitution written since Beard's book have been forced into a pro- or anti-Beard position. Until World War II Beard, though often contested, reigned.

Since World War II, however, historians have launched strong challenges at Beard's interpretation. Although they often disagreed in their interpretations of the Constitution, they all agreed that Beard's study did not offer a satisfactory explanation of the document.

The first of these challengers, the consensus historians, rejected two of Beard's basic assumptions. First, they viewed the Constitution as evidence of a consensus rather than a class conflict among the American people. Second, they believed that the revolutionary and constitutional periods represented a line of continuous growth; they dismissed Beard's idea of a period of radical revolution followed by one of conservative reaction.

These two themes were reflected in the suggestive title—*Consensus and Continuity, 1776–1787*—of a book written by Benjamin F. Wright in 1958. Wright, a political scientist, viewed the Constitution as a political, not an economic document. The most striking characteristic of the delegates at the Constitutional Convention, he claimed, was the broad agreement among them regarding what they considered to be the essentials of good government, including such basic issues as representation, fixed elections, a written constitution, which is a supreme law and contains an amendment clause, separation of powers and checks and balances, a bicameral legislature, a single executive, and a separate court system. These principles could have been taken for granted in no other country in the eighteenth century, nor could they in combination have been accepted in any other country even after discussion and vote. The nature and extent of this basic agreement better indicates the thought of Americans in 1787 than do the disputes over matters of detail or those based largely upon sectional disagreement, or upon the size of the states.[3]

---

[2]Charles A. Beard, *An Economic Interpretation of the Constitution of the United States* (rev. ed., New York, 1935), p. 324.

[3]Benjamin F. Wright, *Consensus and Continuity, 1776–1787* (Boston, 1958), p. 36.

Wright showed also an essential continuity between the Revolution and the constitutional periods so far as men and ideas were concerned. The same men who held responsible public offices in 1787 held them in 1776. Wright noted, moreover, that the political ideas of the Revolution were expressed best in the state constitutions, which were, in many instances, framed by the very same men who had written and signed the Declaration of Independence. How could the constitutional period be considered a reaction to the Revolution? For Wright, as for most consensus historians, the Constitution was seen as the fulfillment of the Revolution.

Robert E. Brown in his study, *Charles Beard and the Constitution*, published in 1956 took another line of attack on the Beardian thesis. Brown challenged Beard's evidence. He showed that Beard had consulted Treasury records dated several years after the Constitutional Convention in order to substantiate the point that the founding fathers had held public securities at the time they framed the document.

Brown's study also challenged one of Beard's underlying assumptions, that the "propertyless masses" made up of small farmers and workingmen were unable to participate in the political process. American society in the 1780s, according to Brown, was basically democratic because the majority of the population were small farmers who owned enough land to qualify for the right to vote. To Brown, then, the Constitution represented the wishes of a democratically minded middle class rather than those of an aristocratically minded upper class. Brown did not find class conflict at work.

Most historians in the post–World War II period, like Wright and Brown, emphasized the Constitution as a consensus document. The attitude toward the framers of the Constitution was far more favorable than it had been a generation earlier. Constitutional historians such as Henry Steele Commager declared that the Constitution was primarily a political document, focusing mainly on the problem of federalism, and not an economic document. Many historians praised the constitutional period as a constructive era rather than a destructive age in which a propertied minority robbed the majority of the American people of their rights. These historians were reflecting a response to the challenges of communism abroad. To bolster America's position as preeminent leader of the free world, historians sought to show that the United States had been a strong and united country throughout its history and one free from class-based oppression.

The second challenge to the Beardian interpretation came from a generation of "new intellectual historians" whose work first appeared in the mid-1950s. These historians emphasized ideas. This renewed interest in ideas as an explanation of the revolutionary era led such scholars as Bernard Bailyn, Gordon Wood, Douglass Adair, and Cecelia Kenyon to view the confederation period and the writing of the Constitution in a new light. Many of these intellectual historians cast their work within a much broader framework of America's intellectual inheritance from Europe. Scholars like Caroline Robbins and Bernard Bailyn, writing in the 1960s, demonstrated the importance of British antiauthoritarian thought and how it influenced the formulation of America's republican ideology.

One major problem facing the founding fathers was how to erect a republic whose representatives were elected by the people and, at the same time, to prevent the formation of a majority faction that might undermine the government. Republican governments in the past had inevitably succumbed to the tyranny of a majority faction. Douglass Adair, one of the new intellectual historians, wrote an article pointing out that James Madison's thoughts on the subject—contrary to Beard's presentist interpretation—could be traced back to Hume.[4] America's enormous size and the multiplicity of factions and interests arising from that size, Madison had said, would make it less likely that this country would suffer the fate of earlier republics. The existence of so many diverse interests would make it difficult, if not impossible, for factions to reconcile their differences and to come together to form a majority faction.

Cecelia Kenyon took issue with Beard's view of the debate between the Federalists, who supported the Constitution, and the Antifederalists, who opposed it. Beard had portrayed the Antifederalists as majority-minded democrats. Kenyon argued that the Antifederalists were as much antimajoritarians as the Federalists, and shared a common Whig mistrust of governmental power—legislative as well as executive. The Antifederalists believed, however, citing the French philosopher Montesquieu, that a successful republic must be geographically small and composed of a homogeneous population. What really distinguished the Antifederalists from the Federalists, Kenyon concluded, was their lack of faith in the ability of Americans to create and sustain a republic continental in size.[5]

The single most important work representing the point of view of these intellectual historians was *The Creation of the American Republic, 1776–1787* by Gordon S. Wood, published in 1969. A student of Bailyn, Wood explicitly connected the conceptual scheme of the American patriots to the classical republican tradition that existed in England. Wood portrayed American leaders as idealists at the start of the Revolution—men who dreamed of setting up a utopian commonwealth along lines English thinkers had earlier set forth. It was a radical ideology,

---

[4]Douglass Adair, "'That Politics May Be Reduced to a Science': David Hume, James Madison, and the Tenth Federalist," *Huntington Library Quarterly*, 20 (1957): 343–60.

[5]Cecelia M. Kenyon, "Men of Little Faith: The Antifederalists on the Nature of Representative Government," *William and Mary Quarterly*, 3d ser., 12 (1955): 3–43.

with moral implications. Revolutionary leaders, believing there was a direct relationship between the type of government a nation had and the character of its people, hoped that a republican government would morally regenerate the American people and thereby enable them to sustain a republic of continuing virtue.

Events of the late 1770s and early 1780s dashed these high hopes. The Revolution unleashed democratic forces that accelerated the breakdown of the existing hierarchy. What emerged in the 1780s was a society characterized by excessive egalitarianism, a contempt for the law by state legislatures bent on abusing their supremacy, oppression of minorities by the majority, and an increasing love of luxury that undermined the people's virtue. The 1780s was a "critical period" in moral terms, Wood said, because it shattered the dreams American leaders had in 1776 of creating a republican government along traditional lines.

The writing of the Constitution, then, was an attempt to save the Revolution from possible failure by restraining some of its democratic excesses. To Wood the Constitution developed into a struggle between forward-looking Federalists and old-fashioned Antifederalists. Instead of the old idea of mixed government, in which the Antifederalists believed, the Federalists proposed that sovereignty resided in the people rather than in any single branch. Hence government should be divided into separate parts not because each part represented a different social constituency, as the Antifederalists supposed, but simply because it would serve as a check upon the other branches of government. Every branch of government, in effect, represented the people. The result was the creation of a governmental system more modern, more realistic about political behavior, and that marked, according to Wood, the "end of classical politics in America."[6] The Federalists, troubled by the need to slow disorder in America during the Confederation period, clung to a notion of political representation that emphasized deference and an elitist conception of republicanism. Wood's book dominated much of the profession for a decade and a half after its publication in 1969. The first selection in this chapter is from Wood's volume.

It remained for J. G. A. Pocock in 1975 to round out what came to be called "the republican synthesis." This synthesis, which encompassed both the Revolution and the Constitution, incorporated the writings of Bailyn and Wood. Pocock demonstrated how republican ideas distilled from the philosophers of ancient Greece and Rome, Renaissance Italian writers such as Machiavelli, seventeenth-century re-

---

[6]Gordon S. Wood, *The Creation of the American Republic, 1776–1787* (Chapel Hill, N.C., 1969), p. 606.

publicans such as Harrington, and eighteenth-century English "country party" authors contributed to the American intellectual outlook.[7]

Embodied in this ideology was a constellation of ideas: the view of an inherent republican character in the American people; their desire for virtue; their fear of tyranny, corruption, and luxury; and particularly their dread of power. British policies intensifying these beliefs helped to bring on the Revolution. Experience under the Articles of Confederation gave Americans new perspective on them and led to the writing of the Constitution. This idealist approach was obviously at odds with the old Progressive interpretation that had downplayed the role of ideas.[8]

From the mid-1960s, beginning with the publication of Bailyn's book, until about the mid-1980s, the slowly emerging republican synthesis exercised a strong sway over the profession. But before, during, and after the Bicentennial of the Constitution, the synthesis came under increasing criticism.

It is impossible to summarize the vast literature appearing during the Bicentennial, but at least three major trends were discernible. First, there were the battles over the republican synthesis and its alleged shortcomings: its overemphasis of ideology and its deemphasis of interests, its slighting of other important intellectual influences besides classical republicanism, including classical liberalism, Scottish commonsense philosophy, and English common law, its failure to address ideas and practices regarding the political economy, and its omission of religion as a meaningful force in shaping political ideology. Second, there appeared a discernible trend away from the preoccupation with ideology toward a more integrative approach, one that incorporated institutional, intellectual, political, social, and economic history as well as ideology. Third, there was a considerable amount of writing about the framing of the Constitution by scholars in other disciplines—political scientists, law professors, and legal theorists.[9]

---

[7]Robert Shalhope, "Toward a Republican Synthesis: The Emergence of an Understanding of Republicanism in American Historiography," *William and Mary Quarterly,* 3d ser., 29 (1972): 49–80; Shalhope, "Republicanism and Early American Historiography," ibid., 39 (1982): 334–56. For Pocock's works see *The Machiavellian Moment* (Princeton, N.J., 1975); *Politics, Language, and Time* (New York, 1960), and *The Ancient Constitutions and Feudal Law* (Cambridge, Mass., 1957).

[8]Gordon Wood in a penetrating essay in the mid-1960s himself called for a synthesis of the two historiographical traditions—the idealist and Progressive—but they continued on their separate paths. See Wood, "Rhetoric and Reality in the American Revolution," *William and Mary Quarterly,* 3d ser., 23 (1966): 3–32.

[9]The best historiographical essay on writings during the Bicentennial was Peter Onuf's "Reflections on the Founding: Constitutional Historiography in Bicentennial Perspective," *William and Mary Quarterly,* 3d ser., 46 (1989): 341–75—a piece that not only reviews the literature but contains many original insights. See also Richard Bernstein, "Charting the Bicentennial," *Columbia Law Review,* 87 (1987): 1565–1624, and Jack P. Greene, *A Bicentennial Bookshelf* (Philadelphia, 1986). For a work that shows the popular neglect of the Constitution and its meaning, see Michael Kammen, *A Machine That Would Go of Itself* (New York, 1986).

Many of the criticisms of the republican synthesis were high-lighted in a symposium held on Wood's book in 1987. Ruth Bloch was critical of Wood's contention that classical republicanism had ended by 1790; she noted that Pocock, Lance Banning, John Murrin, and Drew McCoy had all demonstrated that this concept had continuing vitality beyond that decade. Edward Countryman criticized Wood for writing his book as though a single intelligence lay behind the quotations he employed to draw the composite portraits of the Federalists and Antifederalists rather than focusing on single individuals and their distinctive intellectual positions. John Patrick Diggins took exception to the picture of consensus politics he felt was portrayed in Wood's description of the period. John Howe concluded that Wood had not emphasized enough the role of either religious beliefs or views on political economy in forming political convictions in the constitutional era. Howe's article is the second selection in this chapter.[10]

Wood defended his position on two grounds. First, he claimed that many of his critics had assumed a different role of ideas in human experience than he had intended. Their assumptions were that there is "a sharp separation between beliefs and behavior, between ideas and actions, [and] between culture and society." Wood, on the other hand, believed that "all human behavior can only be understood and explained, indeed can only exist, in terms of the meanings it has. Ideology creates behavior." Second, in response to those who argued that classical republicanism may have played less of a part in late-eighteenth-century thought and action, Wood responded that republicanism and liberalism were historical constructs created by scholars. In the preface to his 1998 edition of the *Creation of the American Republic, 1776–1787,* Wood has argued that historians, eager to label and explain, have wielded the concepts in too mechanical a fashion—republican and liberal traditions coexisted comfortably in the minds of eighteenth-century Americans. In the end, despite Wood's defense it was clear that in the future the republican synthesis would have to address itself to certain issues he had either omitted or deemphasized: the political economy, religion, those left out of citizenship, and interests such as sectionalism.[11]

A major debate sparked by Wood's book during the Bicentennial was whether the Constitution had indeed marked "the end of classical politics in America." Some scholars held that classical republicanism was supplanted by another tradition—liberalism—either before, dur-

---

[10]"*The Creation of the American Republic, 1776–1787:* A Symposium of Views and Reviews," *William and Mary Quarterly,* 3d ser., 44 (1987): 550–657. Other critics included Jackson Turner Main, opposing the notion that ideas were the only motive of the framers, and Gary Nash objecting to the omission of social groups such as artisans, women, and blacks,

[11]Ibid., 628, 631, and 634. Quotation from p. 631; Gordon Wood, *The Creation of the American Republic, 1776–1787* (1998 ed.), Preface.

ing, or after the adoption of the Constitution. This shift was said to signal the transition from premodern to modern America. Under classical republicanism citizens presumably had followed the precepts of civic humanism within a premodern society—the pursuit of the public good, the upholding of virtue, and the hatred of luxury and corruption. With liberalism there appeared instead the pursuit of self-interest, a sense of personal acquisitiveness, and greater individual striving and competitiveness—in short, the attributes of modern America had all appeared. The debate, which reflected contemporary political differences between scholars who worried about the advent of capitalism and those who favored it, focused on the relative intensity of the two outlooks and which became dominant and at what time. By the end of the 1980s, it was generally agreed that both were present in the new republic, that both were very influential, and that neither tradition appeared to have had undisputed primacy during the decades of the 1780s or 1790s.[12]

Another controversy over Wood's book arose over what intellectual traditions besides republicanism and liberalism had influenced America during the constitutional period. Garry Wills in *Explaining America: The Federalist* made a case for David Hume and the Scottish moral philosophers. The writings of Sacvan Bercovitch and others on Puritanism, and of Alan Heimert and Rhys Isaac on evangelical Protestantism, demonstrated the importance of religion to America's political culture in that period. Forrest McDonald showed in an insightful way the bearing that certain English and European traditions had upon the framing of the Constitution. Wood, to be sure, had acknowledged certain of these intellectual traditions, as well as the role of religion, but it was felt that his thesis regarding the framing of the Constitution would be incomplete unless such emphases were addressed more forcefully.[13]

Historians, including Wood, also contended with controversies from scholars in other disciplines who were writing about the Constitution. One such challenge came from political scientists and legal theorists who did not accept the historians' methodologies. This was particularly true of the followers of the political theorist Leo Strauss. The Straussians, as they were called, condemned historicism, which

---

[12]Lance Banning, "Quid Transit? Paradigms and Process in the Transformation of Republican Ideas," *Reviews in American History,* 17 (1989): 199; Wood, *Creation* (1998), Preface.

[13]Garry Wills, *Explaining America: The Federalist* (New York, 1981); Sacvan Bercovitch, *American Jeremiad* (Madison, Wisc., 1978); Alan Heimert, *Religion and the American Mind* (Cambridge, Mass., 1966); Rhys Isaac, *Transformation of Virginia, 1740–1790* (Chapel Hill, N.C., 1982); Forrest McDonald, *Novus Ordo Seclorum* (Lawrence, Kans., 1985); and Isaac Kramnick, "'The Great National Discussion': The Discourse of Politics in 1787," *William and Mary Quarterly,* 3d. ser., 45 (1988): 3–22.

located ideas in their time and context, and resorted to a conservative interpretation that was based on timeless truths and hostile to what they considered to be the historians' preoccupation with contextual problems that gave ideas a relativistic cast. Historians, despite their disagreements with Straussians, found them useful for making all scholars more aware of the intellectual complexities involved in evaluating the constitutional period.[14]

Yet another challenge to historians came from present-minded members of the Reagan administration—such as Edwin Meese, the United States attorney general—who claimed that the Supreme Court should show greater respect for the "original intent" of the framers. Meese and other conservative public officials argued that if judges could freely ignore the intentions of both the framers and later legislators, they could substitute their own preferences of values for the decisions of popularly elected officials. Jack Rakove in an article written in 1986 replied that the relationship between the meaning of the Constitution and the actual intentions of its framers could never be taken for granted; for a variety of reasons it was often too difficult to discern or pinpoint.[15]

As a result of these developments—the writings of the new intellectual historians and other scholars during the Bicentennial, the challenges to the republican synthesis, the intrusion of contemporary politics into an academic debate—the constitutional period and early national era both became exciting and creative areas of American historical scholarship.

With the help of these fresh perspectives, scholars were able to create a new periodization that revolutionized American historiography. Although they disagreed on just when the transition from premodern to modern America took place, the "new intellectual historians" and others had raised and tried to answer one of the most pressing questions in our nation's history: just when did modern America emerge, and what were the forces that led to that emergence?[16]

Meanwhile, the neo-Progressive scholars, the third group writing since World War II, saw modern America emerging in early and continuing struggles over economic questions. They continued to refine the

---

[14]See Gordon S. Wood, "The Fundamentalists and the Constitution," *New York Review of Books*, 35 (February 18, 1988): 33–40.

[15]Jack Rakove, "Mr. Meese, Meet Mr. Madison," *Atlantic*, 258 (December 1986): 77–86.

[16]In tracing the evolution of republican ideology, several biographical studies showed that republicanism meant different things to different men. See, for example, Gerald Stourzh, *Alexander Hamilton and the Idea of Government* (Stanford, 1970); John Howe, *The Changing Thought of John Adams* (Princeton, N.J., 1966); George Athan Billias, *Elbridge Gerry: Founding Father and Republican Statesman* (New York, 1976); and Pauline Maier, *The Old Revolutionaries* (New York, 1980).

old Progressive interpretation as an alternative to the republican syn-thesis. This grouping lumps together historians who often disagreed as much with one another as they did with certain findings of the older Progressive school. The one characteristic they held in common was their belief that economic and social forces were the crucial determi-nants in the positions men took for or against the Constitution. Some neo-Progressives agreed with Beard in stressing class conflict, while others pictured divisions along more pluralistic lines.

The most prominent neo-Progressive scholar was Merrill Jensen. In two major works—*The Articles of Confederation* (1940) and *The New Nation* (1950)—Jensen rewrote the history of the period from 1774 to 1789 in terms of a socioeconomic division between two well-defined groups: the "nationalists" or conservative creditors and mer-chants who favored strengthening the central government versus the "federalists," radical agrarian democrats who controlled the state leg-islatures. The latter supported state sovereignty, of course, and favored rural and debtor interests.

The struggle between these two groups defined the entire revolu-tionary era, according to Jensen. During the early 1770s the radical agrarian democrats led the fight against both Britain and the entrenched colonial commercial aristocrats, achieving self-government with the Articles of Confederation. In the 1780s they became apathetic, failing to maintain their political organizations. The commercial elite used this opportunity to mount a conservative counterrevolution. They wrote the Constitution in order to create a strong central government that would protect their political and commercial interests. Thus Jensen, like Beard, pictured American society split into polarized groups throughout the period and viewed the Constitution as a repudiation of the Revolu-tion. Jensen charged nationalists with deliberately undermining a gov-ernment that might have served the United States well.[17]

The leading neo-Progressive scholars of the 1960s and 1970s—Jack-son Turner Main and E. James Ferguson—carried on Jensen's tradition and made original contributions of their own. Main pictured the strug-gle over the Constitution as a fight within each state between two fairly cohesive parties: "commercial cosmopolitans," on the one hand, and "agrarian localists" on the other. Main reaffirmed the older Pro-gressive view of the Antifederalists as democrats and small farmers, but he revised Beard's term "realty," meaning property owners, by de-scribing the farming population not as subsistence farmers but as non-commercial elements of the population. Ferguson's careful research

---

[17]Jensen continued the neo-Progressive tradition in the documentary history of the ratification of the Constitution, which he was in charge of editing until his death in 1980. Merrill Jensen, et al., eds., *The Documentary History of the Ratification of the Constitution*, 15 vols. to date (Madison, Wisc., 1976–).

aided Main's by casting doubt upon Beard's clear-cut distinction between personalty and realty interests.[18]

Neo-Progressive Forrest McDonald tested Beard's famous study by redoing his work and reanalyzing the economic interests of the delegates in both the federal and state constitutional conventions. He concluded that Beard's use of polarized categories—lower classes versus upper classes, real property versus personalty, creditors versus debtors, and commercial versus agricultural interests—to explain the framing and ratification of the Constitution simply did not work. McDonald found pluralistic rather than polarized political and economic interests at work on the local, state, and regional levels. The Antifederalists, for example, held much more in the way of personalty interests than Beard realized.[19]

By the end of the 1980s, most scholars found the debate over economic interests and the Constitution along Beardian lines unrewarding. Scholarly interests had shifted to an analysis of the American political economy as a whole, or to the links between society, economics, and politics. With the appearance of the new social historians, more attention was being paid to the social bases of the Federalists and Antifederalists and less to their economic holdings in securities.

Some historians increasingly applied social science concepts in their efforts to understand behavior during the period. Older scholars, such as Oscar and Mary Handlin, Lee Benson, Stanley Elkins, and Eric McKitrick, had employed concepts from sociology and psychology to revise the findings of the Progressive historians. Elkins and McKitrick, for example, argued that a particular shared psychology deriving from their circumstances led the Progressives to support Beard's conspiratorial view of the framers, but true understanding of them had little to do with their economic circumstance and much to do with their similar ages and experiences guiding a revolution and imagining a new nation's needs. The struggle was not "fought on economic grounds; it was not a matter of ideology; it was not, in the fullest and most fundamental sense, even a struggle between nationalism and localism. The key struggle was between inertia and energy, with inertia overcome, everything changed."[20]

---

[18]Jackson Turner Main, *The Antifederalists* (Chapel Hill, N.C., 1961) and *Political Parties Before the Constitution* (Chapel Hill, N.C., 1973), among many other works. See E. James Ferguson, *Power of the Purse* (Chapel Hill, N.C., 1961) and "The Nationalists of 1781–1783 and the Economic Interpretation of the Constitution," *Journal of American History*, 56 (1969): 241–61.

[19]Forrest McDonald, *We the People* (Chicago, 1958) and *E Pluribus Unum* (Boston, 1965).

[20]Oscar and Mary Handlin, "Radicals and Conservatives in Massachusetts after Independence," *New England Quarterly*, 17 (1944): 343–55; Lee Benson, *Turner and Beard* (Glencoe, Ill., 1960); Stanley Elkins and Eric McKitrick, "The Founding Fathers: Young Men of the Revolution," *Political Science Quarterly*, 76 (1961): 181–216, quotation from pp. 215–16.

In political science, practitioners had analyzed documents like *The Federalist* in terms of general ideas, whereas more recent scholars explored conceptual changes in the political language of such documents within more specific contexts. Some political scientists in departments of government continued the older tradition of analyzing certain constitutional ideas—federalism, sovereignty, separation of powers, and judicial review—though they often failed to connect these ideas with specific historical events. For historians, context was the order of the day.[21]

Two major historiographical controversies about the constitutional period emerged prominently during the post–World War II era. One was the question on which scholars remained divided: just how critical was the so-called critical period? John Fiske back in the 1880s had done the labeling, but Merrill Jensen, writing in the 1950s, concluded that the picture was a mixed one—progress in certain areas and backsliding in others. Forrest McDonald, writing in the 1960s, ridiculed the idea of a critical period, and Michael Lienesch in an article in 1980 charged that the Federalists created the myth of the critical period to make certain the Constitution would be written and ratified. Herbert Storing, who published in 1981 his superb edition of Antifederalist writings, found the crisis was real and acute. Even the Antifederalists conceded that conditions were bad. Richard B. Morris, writing in 1987, agreed that the postwar years were very critical indeed. To Gordon Wood the critical period was mainly a moral crisis, rather than a political and economic one: American elites faced a moral dilemma in trying to create a republican government—one premised on the notion of a virtuous people—with an American public that these leaders considered not virtuous. In short, the historiographical controversy has yet to be settled satisfactorily.[22]

---

[21]See also Martin Diamond, "Democracy and *The Federalist:* A Reconsideration of the Framers' Intent," *American Political Science Review,* 53 (1959): 53–61; Terence Ball and J. G. A. Pocock, eds., *Conceptual Change and the Constitution* (Lawrence, Kans., 1988); Patrice Higonnet, *Sister Republics* (Cambridge, Mass., 1988). For the older tradition of scholars in departments of government and law schools interested mainly in constitutional ideas in terms of political theory, see Andrew C. McLaughlin, *A Constitutional History of the United States* (New York, 1955); Edwin Corwin, "Progress of Constitutional Theory Between the Declaration of Independence and the Meeting of the Philadelphia Convention," *American Historical Review,* 30 (1925): 511–36. For a work by a historian who posits the continuing constitutional dilemma of reconciling the claims of "center" and "periphery" within an extended imperial model and the independent American polity, see Jack P. Greene, *Peripheries and Center* (Athens, Ga., 1986).

[22]Merrill Jensen, *The New Nation* (New York, 1950), passim; Forrest McDonald, *E Pluribus Unum,* p. 154; Michael Lienesch, "The Constitutional Tradition: History, Political Action, and Progress in American Political Thought, 1787–1793," *Journal of Politics,* 42 (1980): 13; and Herbert Storing, ed., *The Complete Anti-Federalist,* 7 vols. (Chicago, 1981), Vol. 1, p. 26; Richard B. Morris, *Forging of the Union* (New York, 1987); Gordon S. Wood, *Creation of the American Republic, 1776–1787,* pp. 393–429.

A second theme that became more pronounced during the period was the sectional basis of politics that influenced the creation of the Constitution. H. James Henderson in the mid-1970s produced the most exhaustive account of politics during the Confederation to appear since Jensen's work in the 1950s. Employing a voting-bloc analysis of the members of the Continental Congress, Henderson described the parties within that body as sectional in nature and with various sections becoming dominant at different times. New England radicals controlled the Congress from 1776 to 1779, but from 1780 to 1783 the middle-state nationalists prevailed. After 1783 there existed a period of three-way sectional tension—among the New England, middle, and southern states—that was partly alleviated by the adoption of the Constitution. Although the three sections pulled and tugged in different directions they were united in their belief in a republican ideology. Henderson's ideological-sectional interpretation was distinctly at odds with Jensen's neo-Progressive interpretation.[23]

Sectionalism likewise played an important part in Peter Onuf's important work, *Origins of the Federal Republic,* published in 1983. Onuf demonstrated that the thinking of the founders about an American union was profoundly shaped by the experience of interstate conflict, the difficulties of defining congressional authority, and the promotion of national interests under the Confederation. New York's northeastern counties, Pennsylvania's Wyoming Valley, and the trans-Ohio region all either sought to become separate states (as in the case of the New York counties that became Vermont) or were the source of a quarrel over conflicting western land claims (as, for example, Connecticut's invasion of Pennsylvania's Wyoming Valley). Only the newly formed Congress, Onuf argued, could settle such overriding issues. The states had come to recognize that a central authority was needed to resolve these problems. Thus, instead of the orthodox story, which pictured the new federal government and the states locked in a power struggle over sovereignty, Onuf showed there was an expansion of central authority and reinforcement of state sovereignty simultaneously. Sectionalism as an interpretive principle in the writing of the Constitution had come into its own after years of relative neglect.

The most recent significant historical work has been in two major areas. First, social historians used tools like deconstruction and gender analysis to deepen our understanding of the groups that the Constitu-

---

[23]H. James Henderson, *Party Politics in the Continental Congress* (New York, 1974). For sectional tensions during the period, see also William Crosskey and William Jeffrey, Jr., *Politics and the Constitution in the History of the United States,* 3 vols. (Chicago, 1953–1980), which argues that Madison and some of the other principal framers deliberately sought to create a government with a broad grant of power under the commerce clause. See also Jack N. Rakove's brilliant *The Beginnings of National Politics* (New York, 1979).

tion marginalized: blacks, women, and Indians. Second, intellectual historians worked to integrate political, economic, and biographical insights. They struggled with two large themes. First, an emphasis on understanding the original meanings of the Constitution as it was written, debated, and implemented rather than as a set of abstract ideas, and second, growing evidence of harmony between ideas about commerce and republicanism as more and more scholars worked to heal what they saw as an artificial breach between republicanism and liberalism.

In the 1990s, the transformations of the Soviet Union and China into capitalist economies suggested to many that the search for a continuing radical tradition needed to be blended with the realities of capitalism triumphant. Thus, the trend to find liberalism in republicanism and vice versa, which grew dramatically in this period, seemed to reflect a move on the part of some historians to find a past that had been elastic enough to contain and integrate conflict rather than one that had been characterized by continual confrontation. This did not mean that the by now not-so-new-social historians would not continue to spotlight Americans left out of the republican-liberal constitutional settlement.

Looking for those left out of the Constitution, Carroll Smith-Rosenberg in 1992 composed from the magazine rhetoric of the eighteenth century a portrait of the "subjectivity" or the identity of the male American citizen whom the Revolution and the Constitution had constructed. She found strains of liberal and republican rhetoric overlapping to create a figure who took his definition largely from his differences from stereotyped characteristics of females, Africans and Indians. Linda Kerber's 1998 study, *No Constitutional Right to Be Ladies*, explores the various meanings citizenship has had for women since the ratification of the Constitution. In the late eighteenth century a woman's dependence on and loyalty to her husband superseded her obligations as an American citizen. And Gary B. Nash, in *Race and Revolution*, has seen northerners as equally responsible as southerners, if not more so, for the constitutional stamp of approval on slavery. Other historians looking at the deliberations, however, have found southern intransigence on this issue.[24]

One of the dominant recent trends in more broadly based studies has been toward a synthesis—one of liberalism and republicanism. In a collection of essays published in 1992, a variety of scholars made a case for a new hybrid, "liberal republicanism," or a republicanism that was

---

[24]Carroll Smith-Rosenberg, "Dis-Covering the Subject of the 'Great Constitutional Discussion,' 1786–1789," *Journal of American History*, V. 79, No. 33: 841–73; Gary B. Nash, *Race and Revolution* (Madison, Wisc., 1990); Stanley Elkins and Eric McKitrick, *The Age of Federalism, The Early American Republic, 1788–1800* (New York, 1993).

modern rather than frightened and backward-looking. Liberal republicanism, which, these scholars claimed, characterized both the revolutionaries and the framers, "accepted self preservation and self-interest as fundamental to human nature." Furthermore, liberal republicanism saw the protection of natural rights and the acquisition of property and its protection as the proper purposes of government. Contributor John Murrin argued that the Constitution was a device for establishing republican government over liberal Americans. Jean Yarborough argued that framers saw commerce as producing its own virtues. Since they did not consider these sufficient to sustain a nation's virtue, they also looked to religion, but remained silent about this in the Constitution. The states, which shared sovereignty with the national government—indeed, as Peter Onuf argued, which depended upon the national government for their sovereignty, were to be responsible for morality and religion.[25]

Bernard Bailyn offered another assessment of the blend of liberalism with republicanism in his 1990 essay, "The Ideological Fulfillment of the American Revolution: A Commentary on the Constitution." He also, as the title suggests, saw the Constitution as the natural expression of the ideas of the Revolution, not a betrayal of them. His essay shows how the Federalists were able to devise arguments to refute longstanding republican fears such as that of a standing army and of acquisitiveness. In Bailyn's view, Federalists assessed the American situation in a creative and original fashion and came up with realistic responses to republicanism's traditional worries.[26]

Were the proponents of the republican synthesis correct in believing that Americans shared a basic ideological consensus? Or was this a generalization that failed to describe the diverse people of the new nation? History students continue to come to grips with the problem of evaluating the Constitution and the developments that led to its writing and ratification. Was the Constitution a fulfillment or a repudiation of the ideals of the Revolution expressed in the Declaration of Independence? What was the nature of the Constitution, and in what ways did its framing reflect the developments in political thought dur-

---

[25]Herman Belz, Ronald Hoffman, and Peter J. Albert, eds., *To Form a More Perfect Union, The Critical Ideas of the Constitution* (Charlottesville, Va., 1992); Peter Onuf, *Origins of the Federal Republic* (Philadelphia, 1983). See also his *Statehood and Union* (Bloomington, Ind., 1987); Joseph Davis, *Sectionalism in American Politics* (Madison, Wisc., 1977); and Drew R. McCoy, "James Madison and Visions of American Nationality in the Confederation Period: A Regional Perspective," in Richard Beeman, Stephen Botien, and Edward Carter, *Beyond Confederation: Origins of the Constitution and American National Identity* (Chapel Hill, 1987), pp. 226–58.

[26]Bernard Bailyn, *Faces of the Revolution, Personalities and Theme in the Struggle for American Independence* (New York, 1992).

ing the 1780s? Were the differences that divided those who favored and those who opposed the Constitution based more on ideology or interests? Was the Constitution, as Beard and some neo-Progressive historians argued, an undemocratic document—the work of a political and propertied minority who drafted it as an instrument to suit their own purposes? Were the Antifederalists tradition-minded classical republicans or enterprising protoliberals who glimpsed the future of America as Wood suggested? Only by raising such questions can the student decide whether the Constitution was a document that reflected conflict or consensus.

GORDON S. WOOD

*GORDON S. WOOD (1933–   ) is Alva O. Way University Profes-
sor and Professor of History at Brown University. He is the author of*
The Creation of the American Republic 1776–1787 *(1970), which won
the John H. Dunning Prize of the American Historical Association,
and* The Radicalism of the American Revolution *(1991).*

The division over the Constitution in 1787–1788 is not easily analyzed. It is difficult, as historians have recently demonstrated, to
equate the supporters or opponents of the Constitution with particular
economic groupings. The Antifederalist politicians in the ratifying
conventions often possessed wealth, including public securities, equal
to that of the Federalists. While the relative youth of the Federalist
leaders, compared to the ages of the prominent Antifederalists, was
important, especially in accounting for the Federalists' ability to think
freshly and creatively about politics, it can hardly be used to explain
the division throughout the country. Moreover, the concern of the
1780s with America's moral character was not confined to the proponents of the Constitution. That rabid republican and Antifederalist,
Benjamin Austin, was as convinced as any Federalist that "the luxurious living of all ranks and degrees" was "the principal cause of all the
evils we now experience." Some leading Antifederalist intellectuals
expressed as much fear of "the injustice, folly, and wickedness of the
State Legislatures" and of "the usurpation and tyranny of the majority" against the minority as did Madison. In the Philadelphia Convention both Mason and Elbridge Gerry, later prominent Antifederalists,
admitted "the danger of the levelling spirit": flowing from "the excess
of democracy" in the American republic. There were many diverse
reasons in each state why men supported or opposed the Constitution
that cut through any sort of class division. The Constitution was a single issue in a complicated situation, and its acceptance or rejection in
many states was often dictated by peculiar circumstances—the preva-
lence of Indians, the desire for western lands, the special interests of
commerce—that defy generalization. Nevertheless, despite all of this
confusion and complexity, the struggle over the Constitution, as the
debate if nothing else makes clear, can best be understood as a social
one. Whatever the particular constituency of the antagonists may have

---

Gordon S. Wood, *The Creation of the American Republic*, 1776–1787 (Chapel Hill: University of North Carolina Press, 1969) pp. 485–492, 494–499, 506–508, and 513–518.
Reprinted with omissions by permission of the University of North Carolina Press and
the Institute of Early American History and Culture.

been, men in 1787–1788 talked as if they were representing distinct and opposing social elements. Both the proponents and opponents of the Constitution focused throughout the debates on an essential point of political sociology that ultimately must be used to distinguish a Federalist from an Antifederalist. The quarrel was fundamentally one between aristocracy and democracy. . . .

The disorganization and inertia of the Antifederalists, especially in contrast with the energy and effectiveness of the Federalists, has been repeatedly emphasized. The opponents of the Constitution lacked both coordination and unified leadership; "their principles," wrote Oliver Ellsworth, "are totally opposite to each other, and their objections discordant and irreconcilable." The Federalist victory, it appears, was actually more of an Antifederalist default. . . .

But the Antifederalists were not simply poorer politicians than the Federalists; they were actually different kinds of politicians. Too many of them were state-centered men with local interests and loyalties only, politicians without influence and connections, and ultimately politicians without social and intellectual confidence. In South Carolina the up-country opponents of the Constitution shied from debate and when they did occasionally rise to speak apologized effusively for their inability to say what they felt had to be said, thus leaving most of the opposition to the Constitution to be voiced by Rawlins Lowndes, a low-country planter who scarcely represented their interests and soon retired from the struggle. Elsewhere, in New Hampshire, Connecticut, Massachusetts, Pennsylvania, and North Carolina, the situation was similar: the Federalists had the bulk of talent and influence on their side "together with all the Speakers in the State great and small." In convention after convention the Antifederalists, as in Connecticut, tried to speak but "they were browbeaten by many of those Cicero'es as they think themselves and others of Superior rank." "The presses are in a great measure secured to *their* side," the Antifederalists complained with justice: out of a hundred or more newspapers printed in the late eighties only a dozen supported the Antifederalists, as editors, "afraid to offend the great men, or Merchants, who could work their ruin," closed their columns to the opposition. The Antifederalists were not so much beaten as overawed. . . .

[F]ear of a plot by men who "talk so finely and gloss over matters so smoothly" ran through the Antifederalist mind. Because the many "new men" of the 1780s, men like Melancthon Smith and Abraham Yates of New York or John Smilie and William Findley of Pennsylvania, had bypassed the social hierarchy in their rise to political leadership, they lacked those attributes of social distinction and dignity that went beyond mere wealth. Since these kinds of men were never assimilated to the gentlemanly cast of the Livingstons or the Morrises, they, like Americans earlier in confrontation with the British court, tended to view with suspicion and hostility the high-flying world of style and connections that they were barred by their language and tastes, if by nothing else, from sharing in. In the minds of these socially inferior politicians the movement for the strengthening of the central government could only be a "conspiracy" "planned and set to work" by a few aristocrats, who were at first, said Abraham Yates, no larger in number in any one state than the cabal which sought to undermine English liberty at the beginning of the eighteenth century. Since men like Yates could not quite comprehend what they were sure were the inner maneuverings of the elite, they were convinced that in the aristocrats' program, "what was their view in the beginning" or how "far it was Intended to be carried Must be Collected from facts that Afterwards have happened." Like American Whigs in the sixties and seventies forced to delve into the dark and complicated workings of English court politics, they could judge motives and plans "but by the Event." And they could only conclude that the events of the eighties, "the treasury, the Cincinnati, and other public creditors, with all their concomitants," were "somehow or other, . . . inseparably connected," were all parts of a grand design "concerted by a few *tyrants*" to undo the Revolution and to establish an aristocracy in order "to lord it over the rest of their fellow citizens, to trample the poorer part of the people under their feet, that they may be rendered their servants and slaves." In this climate all the major issues of the Confederation period—the impost, commutation, and the return of the Loyalists—possessed a political and social significance that transcended economic concerns. All seemed to be devices by which a ruling few, like the ministers of the English Crown, would attach a corps of pensioners and dependents to the government and spread their influence and connections throughout the states in order "to dissolve our present Happy and Benevolent Constitution and to erect on the Ruins, a proper Aristocracy."

Nothing was more characteristic of Antifederalist thinking than this obsession with aristocracy. Although to a European, American society may have appeared remarkably egalitarian, to many Americans, especially to those who aspired to places of consequence but were made to feel their inferiority in innumerable, often subtle, ways, American society was distinguished by its inequality. . . . In all communities, "even in those of the most democratic kind," wrote George Clinton (whose "family and connections" in the minds of those like Philip Schuyler did not "entitle him to so distinguished a predominance" as the governorship of New York), there were pressures—"superior talents, fortunes and public employments"—demarcating an aristocracy whose influence was difficult to resist.

Such influence was difficult to resist because, to the continual annoyance of the Antifederalists, the great body of the people willingly submitted to it. The "authority of names" and "the influence of the great" among ordinary people were too evident to be denied. "Will any one say that there does not exist in this country the pride of family, of wealth, of talents, and that they do not command influence and respect among the common people?" "The people are too apt to yield an implicit assent to the opinions of those characters whose abilities are held in the highest esteem, and to those in whose integrity and patriotism they can confide; not considering that the love of domination is generally in proportion to talents, abilities and superior requirements." Because of this habit of deference in the people, it was "in the power of the enlightened and aspiring few, if they should combine, at any time to destroy the best establishments, and even make the people the instruments of their own subjugation." Hence, the Antifederalist-minded declared, the people must be awakened to the consequences of their self-ensnarement; they must be warned over and over by the popular tribunes, by "those who are competent to the task of developing the principles of government," of the dangers involved in paying obeisance to those who they thought were their superiors. The people must "not be permitted to consider themselves as a grovelling, distinct species, uninterested in the general welfare."

Such constant admonitions to the people of the perils flowing from their too easy deference to the *"natural aristocracy"* were necessary because the Antifederalists were convinced that these "men that had been delicately bred, and who were in affluent circumstances," these "men of the most exalted rank in life," were by their very conspicuousness irreparably cut off from the great body of the people and hence could never share in its concerns nor look after its interests. It was not that these "certain men exalted above the rest" were necessarily "destitute of morality or virtue" or that they were inherently different from other men. "The same passions and prejudices govern all men." It was only that circumstances in their particular environment had made them different. There was "a charm in politicks"; men in high office become habituated with power, "grow fond of it, and are loath to resign it"; "they feel themselves flattered and elevated," enthralled by the attractions of high living, and thus they easily forget the interests of the common people, from which many of them once sprang. By dwelling so vividly on the allurements of prestige and power, by emphasizing again and again how the "human soul is affected by wealth, in all its faculties, . . . by its present interest, by its expectations, and by its fears," these ambitious Antifederalist politicians may have revealed as much about themselves as they did about the "aristocratic" elite they sought to displace. Yet at the same time by such language they contributed to a new appreciation of the nature of society.

In these repeated attacks on deference and the capacity of a conspicuous few to speak for the whole society—which was to become in time the distinguishing feature of American democratic politics—the

Antifederalists struck at the roots of the traditional conception of political society. If the natural elite, whether its distinctions were ascribed or acquired, was not in any organic way connected to the "feelings, circumstances, and interests" of the people and was incapable of feeling "sympathetically the wants of the people," then it followed that only ordinary men, men not distinguished by the characteristics of aristocratic wealth and taste, men "in middling circumstances" untempted by the attractions of a cosmopolitan world and thus "more temperate, of better morals, and less ambitious, than the great," could be trusted to speak for the great body of the people, for those who were coming more and more to be referred to as "the middling and lower classes of people." The differentiating influence of the environment was such that men in various ranks and classes now seemed to be broken apart from one another, separated by their peculiar circumstances into distinct, unconnected, and often incompatible interests. With their indictment of aristocracy the Antifederalists were saying, whether they realized it or not, that the people of America even in their several states were not homogeneous entities each with a basic similarity of interest for which an empathic elite could speak. Society was not an organic hierarchy composed of ranks and degrees indissolubly linked one to another; rather it was a heterogeneous mixture of "many different classes or orders of people, Merchants, Farmers, Planter Mechanics and Gentry or wealthy Men." In such a society men from one class or group, however educated and respectable they may have been, could never be acquainted with the "*Situation* and Wants" of those of another class or group. Lawyers and planters could never be "adequate judges of tradesmen concerns." If men were truly to represent the people in government, it was not enough for them to be for the people; they had to be actually of the people. "Farmers, traders and mechanics . . . all ought to have a competent number of their best informed members in the legislature."

Thus the Antifederalists were not only directly challenging the conventional belief that only a gentlemanly few, even though now in America naturally and not artificially qualified, were best equipped through learning and experience to represent and to govern the society, but they were as well indirectly denying the assumption of organic social homogeneity on which republicanism rested. Without fully comprehending the consequences of their arguments the Antifederalists were destroying the great chain of being, thus undermining the social basis of republicanism and shattering that unity and harmony of social and political authority which the eighteenth century generally and indeed most revolutionary leaders had considered essential to the maintenance of order.

Confronted with such a fundamental challenge the Federalists initially backed away. They had no desire to argue the merits of the Constitution in terms of social implications and were understandably reluctant to open up the character of American society as the central issue of the debate. But in the end they could not resist defending those beliefs in elitism that lay at the heart of their conception of politics and of their constitutional program. All of the Federalists' desires to establish a strong and respectable nation in the world, all of their plans to create a flourishing commercial economy, in short, all of what the Federalists wanted out of the new central government seemed in the final analysis dependent upon the prerequisite maintenance of aristocratic politics. . . .

The course of the debates over the Constitution seemed to confirm what the Federalists had believed all along. Antifederalism represented the climax of a "war" that was, in the words of Theodore Sedgwick, being "levied on the virtue, property, and distinctions in the community." The opponents of the Constitution, despite some, "particularly in Virginia," who were operating "from the most honorable and patriotic motives," were essentially identical with those who were responsible for the evils the states were suffering from in the eighties—"narrowminded politicians . . . under the influence of local views." "Whilst many *ostensible* reasons are assigned" for the Antifederalists' opposition, charged Washington, "the real ones are concealed behind the Curtains, because they are not of a nature to appear in open day." "The real object of all their zeal in opposing the system." agreed Madison, was to maintain "the supremacy of the State Legislatures," with all that meant in the printing of money and the violation of contracts. The Antifederalists or those for whom the Antifederalists spoke, whether their spokesmen realized it or not, were "none but the horse-jockey, the mushroom merchant, the running and dishonest speculator," those "who owe the most and have the least to pay," those "whose dependence and expectations are upon changes in government, and distracted times," men of "desperate Circumstances," those "in Every State" who "have Debts to pay, Interests to support or Fortunes to make," those, in short, who "wish for scrambling Times." Apart from a few of their intellectual leaders the Antifederalists were thought to be an ill-bred lot: "Their education has been rather indifferent—they have been accustomed to think on the small scale." They were often blustering demagogues trying to push their way into office—"men of much self-importance and supposed skill in politics, who are not of sufficient consequence to obtain public employment." Hence they were considered to be jealous and mistrustful of "every one in the higher offices of society," unable to bear to see others possessing "that fancied blessing, to which, alas! they must themselves aspire in vain." In the Federalist mind therefore the struggle over the Constitution was not one between kinds of wealth or property, or one between commercial or noncommercial elements of the population, but rather represented a broad social division between those who believed in the right of a natural aristocracy to speak for the people and those who did not.

Against this threat from the licentious the Federalists pictured themselves as the defenders of the worthy, of those whom they called "the better sort of people," those, said John Jay, "who are orderly and industrious, who are content with their situations and not uneasy in their circumstances." Because the Federalists were fearful that republican equality was becoming "that *perfect equality* which deadens the motives of industry and places Demerit on a Footing with Virtue," they were obsessed with the need to insure that the proper amount of inequality and natural distinctions be recognized. . . . Robert Morris, for example, was convinced there were social differences—even in Pennsylvania. "What!" he explained in scornful amazement at John Smilie's argument that a republic admitted of no social superiorities. "Is it insisted that there is no distinction of character?" Respectability, said Morris with conviction, was not confined to property. "Surely persons possessed of knowledge, judgment, information, integrity, and having extensive connections, are not to be classed with persons void of reputation or character."

In refuting the Antifederalists' contention "that all classes of citizens should have some of their own number in the representative body, in order that their feelings and interests may be the better understood and attended to," Hamilton in *The Federalist,* Number 35, put into words the Federalists' often unspoken and vaguely held assumption about the organic and the hierarchical nature of society. Such explicit class or occupational representation as the Antifederalists advocated, wrote Hamilton, was not only impractical but unnecessary, since the society was not as fragmented or heterogeneous as the Antifederalists implied. The various groups in the landed interest, for example, were "perfectly united, from the wealthiest landlord down to the poorest tenant," and this "common interest may always be reckoned upon as the surest bond of sympathy" linking the landed representative, however rich, to his constituents. In a like way, the members of the commercial community were "immediately connected" and most naturally represented by the merchants. "Mechanics and manufacturers will always be inclined, with few exceptions, to give their votes to merchants, in preference to persons of their own professions or trades. . . . They know that the merchant is their natural patron and friend; and . . . they are sensible that their habits in life have not been such as to give them those acquired endowments, without which in a deliberative assembly, the greatest natural abilities, are for the most part useless." However much many Federalists may have doubted the substance of Hamilton's analysis of American society, they could not doubt the truth of his conclusion. That the people were represented better by one of the natural aristocracy "whose situation leads to extensive inquiry and information" than by one "whose observation does not travel beyond the circle of his neighbors and acquaintances" was the defining element of the Federalist philosophy.

It was not simply the number of public securities, or credit outstanding, or the number of ships, or the amount of money possessed that made a man think of himself as one of the natural elite. It was much more subtle than the mere possession of wealth: it was a deeper social feeling, a sense of being socially established, of possessing attributes—family, education, and refinement—that others lacked, above all, of being accepted by and being able to move easily among those who considered themselves to be the respectable and cultivated. It is perhaps anachronistic to describe this social sense as a class interest, for it often transcended immediate political or economic concerns, and, as Hamilton's argument indicates, was designed to cut through narrow occupational categories. The Republicans of Philadelphia, for example, repeatedly denied that they represented an aristocracy with a united class interest. "We are of different occupations; of different sects of religion; and have different views of life. No factions or private system can comprehend us all." Yet with all their assertions of diversified interests the Republicans were not without a social consciousness in their quarrel with the supporters of the Pennsylvania Constitution. If there were any of us ambitious for power, their apology continued, then there would be no need to change the Constitution, for we surely could attain power under the present Constitution. "We have already seen how easy the task is for *any character* to rise into power and consequence under it. And there are some of us, who think not so meanly of ourselves, as to dread any rivalship from those who are now in office."

In 1787 this kind of elitist social consciousness was brought into play as perhaps never before in eighteenth-century America, as gentlemen up an down the continent submerged their sectional and economic differences in the face of what seemed to be a threat to the very foundations of society. Despite his earlier opposition to the Order of the Cincinnati, Theodore Sedgwick, like other frightened New Englanders, now welcomed the organization as a source of strength in the battle for the Constitution. The fear of social disruption that had run through much of the writing of the eighties was brought to a head to eclipse all other fears. Although state politics in the eighties remains to be analyzed, the evidence from Federalist correspondence indicates clearly a belief that never had there occurred "so great a change in the opinion of the best people" as was occurring in the last few years of the decade. The Federalists were astonished at the outpouring in 1787 of influential and respectable people who had earlier remained quiescent. Too many of "the better sort of people," it was repeatedly said, had withdrawn at the end of the war "from the theatre of public action, to scenes of retirement and ease," and thus "demagogues of desperate fortunes, mere adventurers in fraud, were left to act unopposed." After all, it was explained, "when the wicked rise, men hide themselves." Even the problems of Massachusetts in 1786, noted General Benjamin Lincoln, the repressor of the Shaysites, were not caused by the rebels, but by the laxity of "the good people of the state." But the lesson of this laxity was rapidly being learned. Everywhere, it seemed, men of virtue, good sense, and property, "almost the whole body of our enlighten'd and leading characters in every state," were awakened in support of stronger government. "The scum which was thrown upon the surface by the fermentation of the war is daily sinking," Benjamin Rush told Richard Price in 1786, "while a pure spirit is occupying its place." "Men are brought into action who had consigned themselves to an eve of rest," Edward Carrington wrote to Jefferson in June 1787, "and the Convention, as a Beacon, is rousing the attention of the Empire." The Antifederalists could only stand amazed at this "weight of talents" being gathered in support of the Constitution. "What must the individual be who could thus oppose them united?"

Still, in the face of this preponderance of wealth and respectability in support of the Constitution, what remains extraordinary about 1787–1788 is not the weakness and disunity but the political strength of Antifederalism. That large numbers of Americans could actually reject a plan of government created by a body "composed of the first characters in the Continent" and backed by Washington and nearly the whole of the natural aristocracy of the country said more about the changing character of American politics and society in the eighties than did the Constitution's eventual acceptance. It was indeed a portent of what was to come. . . .

If the new national government was to promote the common good as forcefully as any state government, and if, as the Federalists believed, a major source of the vices of the eighties lay in the abuse of state power, then there was something apparently contradictory about the new federal Constitution, which after all represented not a weakening of the dangerous power of republican government but rather a strengthening of it. "The complaints against the separate governments, even by the friends of the new plan," remarked the Antifederalist James Winthrop, "are not that they have not power enough, but that they are disposed to make a bad use of what power they have." Surely, concluded Winthrop, the Federalists were reasoning badly "when they purpose to set up a government possess'd of much more extensive powers . . . and subject to much smaller checks" than the existing state governments possessed and were subject to. Madison for one was quite aware of the pointedness of this objection. "It may be asked," he said, "how private rights will be more secure under the Guardianship of the General Government than under the State Governments, since they are both founded in the republican principle which refers the ultimate decision to the will of the majority." What, in other words, was different about the new federal Constitution that would enable it to mitigate the effects of tyrannical majorities? What would keep the new federal government from succumbing to the same pressures that had beset the state governments? The answer the Federalists gave to these questions unmistakably reveals the social bias underlying both their fears of the unrestrained state legislatures and their expectations for their federal remedy. For all of their desires to avoid intricate examination of a delicate social structure, the Federalists' program itself demanded that the discussion of the Constitution would be in essentially social terms.

The Federalists were not as much opposed to the governmental power of the states as to the character of the people who were wielding it. The constitutions of most of the states were not really at fault. Massachusetts after all possessed a nearly perfect constitution. What actually bothered the Federalists was the sort of people who had been able to gain positions of authority in the state governments, particularly in the state legislatures. Much of the quarrel with the viciousness, instability, and injustice of the various state governments was at bottom social. "For," as John Dickinson emphasized, *the government will partake of the qualities of those whose authority is prevalent.*" The political and social structures were intimately related. "People once respected their governors, their senators, their judges and their clergy; they reposed confidence in them; their laws were obeyed, and the states were happy in tranquility." But in the eighties the authority of government had drastically declined because "men of sense and property have lost much of their influence by the popular spirit of the war." "That exact order, and due subordination, that is essentially necessary in all well appointed governments, and which constitutes the real happiness and well being of society" had been deranged by "men of no genius or abilities" who had tried to run "the machine of government." Since "it cannot be expected that things will go well, when persons of vicious principles, and loose morals are in authority," it was the large number of obscure, ignorant, and unruly men occupying the state legislatures, and not the structure of the governments, that was the real cause of the evils so much complained of.

The Federalist image of the Constitution as a sort of "philosopher's stone" was indeed appropriate: it was a device intended to transmute base materials into gold and thereby prolong the life of the republic. Patrick Henry acutely perceived what the Federalists were driving at. "The Constitution," he said in the Virginia Convention, "reflects in the most degrading and mortifying manner on the virtue, integrity, and wisdom of the state legislatures; it presupposes that the chosen few who go to Congress will have more upright hearts, and more enlightened minds, than those who are members of the individual legislatures." The new Constitution was structurally no different from the constitutions of some of the states. Yet the powers of the new central government were not as threatening as the powers of the state governments precisely because the Federalists believed different kinds of persons would hold them. They anticipated that somehow the new government would be staffed largely by "the worthy," the natural social aristocracy of the country. "After all," said Pelatiah Webster, putting his finger on the crux of the Federalists argument, "the grand secret of forming a good government, is, to put good men into the administration: for wild, vicious, or idle men, will ever make a bad government, let its principles be ever so good." . . .

In short, through the artificial contrivance of the Constitution overlying an expanded society, the Federalists meant to restore and to prolong the traditional kind of elitist influence in politics that social developments, especially since the Revolution, were undermining. As the defenders if not always the perpetrators of these developments— the "disorder" of the 1780s—the Antifederalists could scarcely have missed the social implications of the Federalist program. The Constitution was intrinsically an aristocratic document designed to check the democratic tendencies of the period, and as such it dictated the character of the Antifederalist response. It was therefore inevitable that the Antifederalists should have charged that the new government was "dangerously adapted to the purposes of an immediate *aristocratic tyranny*." In state after state the Antifederalists reduced the issue to those social terms predetermined by the Federalists themselves: the Constitution was a plan intended to "raise the fortunes and respectability of the *well-born few*, and oppress the plebians"; it was "a continental exertion of the *well-born* of America to obtain that darling domination, which they have not been able to accomplish in their respective states"; it "will lead to an aristocratical government, and establish tyranny over us." Whatever their own particular social standing, the Antifederalist spokesmen spread the warning that the new government either would be "in practice a *permanent* ARISTOCRACY" or would soon "degenerate to a complete Aristocracy." . . .

Aristocratic principles were in fact "interwoven" in the very fabric of the proposed government. If a government was "so constituted as to admit but few to exercise the powers of it," then it would "according to the natural course of things" end up in the hands of "the natural aristocracy." It went almost without saying that the awesome president and the exalted Senate, "a compound of *monarchy* and *aristocracy*," would be dangerously far removed from the people. But even the House of Representatives, the very body that "should be a true picture of the people, possess a knowledge of their circumstances and their wants, sympathize in all their distresses, and disposed to seek their true interest," was without "a tincture of democracy." Since it could never collect "the interests, feelings, and opinions of three or four millions of people," it was better understood as "an Assistant Aristocratical Branch" to the Senate than as a real representation of the people. When the number of representatives was "so small, the office will be highly elevated and distinguished; the style in which the members live will probably be high; circumstances of this kind will render the place of a representative not a desirable one to sensible, substantial men, who have been used to walk in the plain and frugal paths of life." While the ordinary people in extensive electoral districts of thirty thousand inhabitants would remain "divided," those few extraordinary men with "conspicuous military, popular, civil or legal talents" could more easily form broader associations to dominate elections; they had family and other connections to "unite their interests." If only a half-dozen congressmen were to be selected to represent a large state, then rarely, argued the Antifederalists in terms that were essentially no different from those used by the Federalists in the Constitution's defense, would persons from "the great body of the people, the middle and lower classes," be elected to the House of Representatives. "The Station is too high and exalted to be filled but [by] the *first* Men in the State in point of Fortune and Influence. In fact no order or class of the people will be represented in the House of Representatives called the Democratic Branch but the rich and wealthy." The Antifederalists thus came to oppose the new national government for the same reason the Federalists favored it: because its very structure and detachment from the people would work to exclude any kind of actual and local interest representation and prevent those who were not rich, well born, or prominent from exercising political power. Both sides fully appreciated the central issue the Constitution posed and grappled with it throughout the debates: Whether a professedly popular government should actually be in the hands of, rather than simply derived from, common ordinary people.

Out of the division in 1787–1788 over this issue, an issue which was as conspicuously social as any in American history, the Antifederalists emerged as the spokesmen for the growing American antagonism to aristocracy and as the defenders of the most intimate participation in politics of the widest variety of people possible. It was not from lack of vision that the Antifederalists feared the new government. Although their viewpoint was intensely localist, it was grounded in as perceptive an understanding of the social basis of American politics as that of the Federalists. Most of the Antifederalists were majoritarians with respect to the state legislatures but not with respect to the national legislature, because they presumed as well as the Federalists did that different sorts of people from those who sat in the state assemblies would occupy the Congress. Whatever else may be said about the Antifederalists, their populism cannot be impugned. They were true champions of the most extreme kind of demo-cratic and egalitarian politics expressed in the revolutionary era. Con-vinced that "it has been the principal care of free governments to guard against the encroachments of the great," the Antifederalists be-lieved that popular government itself, as defined by the principles of 1776, was endangered by the new national government. If the Revolu-tion had been a transfer of power from the few to the many, then the federal Constitution clearly represented an abnegation of the Revolu-tion. For, as Richard Henry Lee wrote in his *Letters from the Federal Farmer,* "every man of reflection must see, that the change now pro-posed, is a transfer of power from the many to the few."

Although Lee's analysis contained the essential truth, the Federal-ist program was not quite so simply summed up. It was true that through the new Constitution the Federalists hoped to resist and even-tually to avert what they saw to be the rapid decline of the influence and authority of the natural aristocracy in America. At the very time that the organic conception of society that made elite rule comprehen-sible was finally and avowedly dissolving, and the members of the elite were developing distinct professional, social, or economic interests, the Federalists found elite rule more imperative than ever before. To the Federalists the greatest dangers to republicanism were flowing not, as the old Whigs had thought, from the rulers or from any distinctive mi-nority in the community, but from the widespread participation of the people in the government. It now seemed increasingly evident that if the public good not only of the United States as a whole but even of the separate states were to be truly perceived and promoted, the American people must abandon their revolutionary reliance on their representa-tive state legislatures and place their confidence in the highmindedness of the natural leaders of the society, which ideally everyone had the op-portunity of becoming. Since the Federalists presumed that only such a self-conscious elite could transcend the many narrow and contradic-tory interests inevitable in any society, however small, the measure of a good government became its capacity for insuring the predominance of these kinds of natural leaders who knew better than the people as a whole what was good for the society.

The result was an amazing display of confidence in constitutional-ism, in the efficacy of institutional devices for solving social and politi-cal problems. Through the proper arrangement of new institutional structures the Federalists aimed to turn the political and social develop-ments that were weakening the place of "the better sort of people" in government back upon themselves and to make these developments the very source of the perpetuation of the natural aristocracy's dominance of politics. Thus the Federalists did not directly reject democratic politics as it had manifested itself in the 1780s; rather they attempted to adjust to this politics in order to control and mitigate its effects. In short they offered the country an elitist theory of democracy. They did not see themselves as repudiating either the Revolution or popular government, but saw themselves as saving both from their excesses. If the Constitution were not established, they told themselves and the country over and over, then republicanism was doomed, the grand experiment was over, and a division of the confederacy, monarch, or worse would result.

Despite all the examples of popular vice in the eighties, the Federalist confidence in the people remained strong. The letters of "Caesar," with their frank and violent denigration of the people, were anomalies in the Federalist literature. The Federalists had by no means lost faith in the people, at least in the people's ability to discern their true leaders. In fact many of the social elite who comprised the Federalist leadership were confident of popular election if the constituency could be made broad enough, and crass electioneering be curbed, so that the people's choice would be undisturbed by ambitious demagogues. "For if not blind to their own interest, they choose men of the first character for wisdom and integrity." Despite prodding by so-called designing and unprincipled men, the bulk of the people remained deferential to the established social leadership—for some aspiring politicians frustratingly so. Even if they had wanted to, the Federalists could not turn their backs on republicanism. For it was evident to even the most pessimistic "that no other form would be reconcilable with the genius of the people of America; with the fundamental principles of the Revolution; or with that honorable determination which animates every votary of freedom, to rest all our political experiments on the capacity of mankind for self-government." Whatever government the Federalists established had to be "strictly republican" and "deducible from the only source of just authority—the People."

J O H N   H O W E

JOHN HOWE (1935–   ) is professor of history at the University of Minnesota. He is the author of The Changing Political Thought of John Adams *(1966) and* From the Revolution Through the Age of Jackson *(1973).*

John Howe, "Gordon S. Wood and the Analysis of Political Culture in the American Revolutionary Era," *William and Mary Quarterly,* 44 (1987): 569–75. Reprinted with the permission of John Howe.

Seldom has a book exerted such powerful and lasting influence on the interpretation of early American history as Gordon S. Wood's *The Creation of the American Republic*. Probably no other single work has so dominated the political and constitutional historiography of the American Revolutionary and constitutional eras during the past two decades. Why has the book had such a profound effect, and how is it to be regarded, nearly twenty years after its publication, in the historiographical context of 1987?

Part of the explanation for the book's initial impact lies in the timing of its publication and its association with the work of Wood's mentor, Bernard Bailyn. In the early 1960s Bailyn published two major works that dramatically altered historians' interpretations of the Revolution. In the introduction to his volume of Revolutionary pamphlets, and then at greater length in *The Ideological Origins of the American Revolution*, Bailyn argued, eloquently and persuasively, that the key to an understanding of American Revolutionary behavior lay in the controlling influence of a powerful political culture centered in the English dissenting or country tradition. Neither conflicts within colonial society nor British efforts at imperial reform, Bailyn argued, fully explain the onset of the Revolution. Rather, one must look to distinctive colonial habits of mind, assumptions about history and human nature, notions of power and liberty, and theories of conspiracy to understand why the colonists broke with England.

In conceptualization as well as content, *Creation of the American Republic* can be seen as an extension, elaborate and creative in its own right, of Bailyn's work, for in it Wood explains how that dissenting tradition was transformed during the years following Independence into a distinctive American republican ideology and how, under the forcing pressure of Revolutionary events, that ideology evolved from its original, utopian formulation of 1776–1778 into the quite different federalist republicanism of the late 1780s. Taken together, Wood's and Bailyn's work, mutually reinforcing though not always in detailed agreement with each other, offered a compelling, encompassing interpretation of the nation's founding and the beginning of a distinctive national politics.

Wood's work found a congenial historiographical environment in another way as well. At the time of *Creation*'s publication in 1969, Revolutionary historiography was at something of a standstill. The once-dominant Progressive interpretation of the Revolution was under siege, its dichotomous, class-based view of Revolutionary politics attacked as oversimplified and inconsistent with historical evidence. In place of the Progressives' conflict-based model of politics, the so-called neo-whig historians substituted a model that emphasized political consensus based on a broadly participatory politics and a shared commitment to political liberty. Wood extended that neo-whig argument by offering an

interpretation that downplayed social conflict, stressed the causal importance of ideas, and emphasized the predominantly ideological character of Revolutionary change, while at the same time deepening the
analysis of connections between ideas and behavior, and locating the
main theme of Revolutionary politics in a continuing tension between
the advocates of egalitarian and hierarchical politics. In the process, he
fashioned a dramatic interpretation of the nation's origins and explored
in remarkable detail the central course of political/constitutional development during the Revolutionary era.

Historiographical breakthroughs, of course, are not fundamentally a matter of fortuitous timing, for countless historiographical
opportunities go unexploited. Ultimately, *Creation* succeeded so
handsomely because of its remarkable qualities: its erudition; its
comprehensiveness of theme and chronology; its interpretive control
over a sprawling, volatile period of history; the complexity and yet organizational clarity of its argument; the far-reaching importance of its
subject matter to an understanding of the nation's history; and the
provocative interpretation it offers of the central role of political culture in the nation's founding. It is this last point, the book's analysis
of political culture—its content, connections with its historical environment, and relationships to political behavior—that I wish to examine in this essay.

In an important article entitled "Rhetoric and Reality in the
American Revolution," published in 1966 in the *William and Mary
Quarterly*, Wood criticized what he called the traditional "idealist"
interpretation of Revolutionary thought for its failure to go beyond
the analysis of formal, rational bodies of theory—doctrines of liberty
and natural rights, of mixed and balanced government—to examine
the underlying, often implicit, but nevertheless powerful cultural
values that informed them. This call for enlarging the agenda of intellectual history—for dealing with the full range of subconscious as
well as conscious, affective as well as rational modes of understanding—was closely connected with Wood's search for a more subtle interpretation of connections between belief and behavior—that is, of
human motivation.

If we are to understand the Revolution, Wood explained, we must
transcend the colonists' stated intentions and recognize that "the purposes of men, especially in a revolution, are so numerous, so varied,
and so contradictory that their complex interaction produces results
that no one intended or could even foresee." Historical explanation
that "relies simply on understanding the conscious intentions of the
actors," he argued, is severely limited. Instead, historians must recognize that "men act not simply in response to some kind of objective reality but to the meaning they give to that reality," a meaning that is

shaped by a wide range of beliefs, values, fears, and predispositions—
exactly the stuff of which political cultures are made.

Finally, Wood argued that in order to understand the language of a
political culture and grasp its meaning, the analyst must locate the
culture in its social, economic, and political environment, for culture
is shaped by, as well as gives shape to, human experience. Thus the
"frenzied rhetoric" of Revolutionary political culture "reveals as nothing else apparently can the American Revolution as a true revolution
with its sources lying deep in the social structure." It was "the natural,
even the inevitable, expression of a people caught up in a revolutionary situation . . . and . . . involved in a basic reconstruction of their political and social order."

Wood took his own invocations seriously in the major work upon
which he was already well embarked. One of *Creation's* most impressive strengths is the skill with which it weaves together themes of
Anglo-American constitutionalism and the powerful, emotive assumptions about power, equality, virtue, and historical change that derived from the English dissenting tradition and fed directly into
Revolutionary republicanism. Wood proved sensitive as well to the in-
determinacy of political and constitutional debate, to inconsistencies
of thought, confusions of intention, and the difficult, drawn-out
processes of intellectual clarification. While tracing the evolving complexities of constitutional argumentation, Wood made wonderfully
clear the ways in which constitutionalism was grounded in and shaped
by political culture.

As rich as his conception of political culture is, however, it can be
seen, when viewed from the historiographical perspective of our own
time, as lacking two essential components. The first is American religious belief. The connections between religion and politics in Revolutionary America are difficult to unravel, as a sizable and disputatious
body of scholarship reveals. Yet taken together, the works of Sacvan
Bercovitch and Rhys Isaac, Alan Heimert and William G. McLoughlin, Harry S. Stout and Catherine L. Albanese, among others, make
clear the intimate and powerful connections between religious and
political belief. One cannot, for example, fully grasp the Revolutionary generation's understanding of equality, human liberty, or America's historic mission without taking religious beliefs into account,
whether they were expressed within the covenant structure or by Baptists and other dissenting enthusiasts. Nor can one adequately explain
the spread of Revolutionary doctrine or the force of political commitment among the American people without considering the mobilizing
power of religion.

At several points Wood acknowledges the place of religion (he
terms it scripture) along with history and Enlightenment rationalism

in "the Whig science of politics" (p. 3). But the Revolutionary generation, he asserts, turned above all to secular rationalism and its promise of access to the "scientific" principles of social and political behavior. Perhaps so; no doubt Wood's preoccupation with constitutional debate encouraged that conclusion. Yet his broader concern with political culture, it now seems clear, should have generated a more careful examination of the connections between religious and political/constitutional thought.

Recent work by Joyce Appleby and Drew R. McCoy calls attention to another important dimension of Revolutionary political culture—what Appleby and McCoy refer to as political economy—that is largely missing from Wood's analysis. Wood discusses at length the Revolutionary generation's fascination with the interdependence of the economic, social, moral, and political orders. He understates, however, the importance to eighteenth-century Americans of economic arrangements in shaping the essential character of a republic, as well as the extent to which government was viewed as an instrument for fashioning a republican socioeconomic order.

This is especially surprising because Wood is fully aware of how large the linked themes of commercialism, wealth, debt, dependence, luxury, and political corruption loomed in the dissenting tradition's critique of England. When he turns to the analysis of Revolutionary republicanism, however, he focuses attention on constitutional issues and loses sight of the fact that conflicting responses to the accelerating commercialism of the American economy shaped much of the argument over constitutional structures, governmental power, and the meaning of republican liberty.

This becomes most evident in Wood's discussion of the political crisis of the 1780s, the drive for a stronger national government, and the Constitution. Though one learns in part four that issues such as debt relief, paper money, tax policy, and commercial development kept state politics in an uproar during the 1780s, Wood fails to explain that those issues were so volatile, first, because of the economic and social turmoil generated by revolution and war, and, second, because they brought to a focus sharply conflicting social visions and theories of political economy. Recent works such as David P. Szatmary's study of Shays's Rebellion, Ronald Hoffman's book on Revolutionary politics in Maryland, and Edward Countryman's study of New York reveal how closely tax, price control, and monetary policies were tied not only to clashing economic interests but to different visions of what republican society and government should be.

In part five Wood offers a vivid comparison of the contrasting political philosophies of Federalists and Antifederalists—the Antifederalists harkening back to a locally based, democratic polity guided by the principles of 1776; the Federalists reaching forward to a new, energetic, elite-led national government capable of fashioning an expanding republican empire. In reading Wood's analysis, however, one is struck again by how little attention he gives to Federalists' and Antifederalists' notions of political economy, their sharply conflicting attitudes toward manufacturing and commerce, credit and wealth, and their views of the government's role in national development.

A careful rereading of *Creation* raises questions as well about Wood's handling of two other thorny and closely related problems of historical interpretation: the connections between political culture and its socioeconomic context, and the sources of cultural change.

One of the book's major strengths is its remarkably effective rhetorical structure. Part one offers a clear point of departure via a description of "The Ideology of Revolution," a body of thought fixed in colonial minds well before 1776 and ultimately responsible for persuading Americans that England was bent on enslaving them and that Independence was their only recourse. Parts two through four, which form the heart of the book, deal with the processes of historical change that transformed this ideology into republican utopianism, which, during the decade following Independence, was in turn debated, clarified, applied to the tasks of constitution making, evaluated against the changing realities of Revolutionary life, and ultimately transmuted into the distinctive federalist republicanism of 1786–1787. That "fundamental transformation of political culture" into an "entirely new conception of politics" that took the American people "out of an essentially classical and medieval world of political discussion into one that was recognizably modern" constitutes Wood's main story (p. viii). In parts five and six these processes of historical change find resolution in a new cultural paradigm that Wood titles the "federalist persuasion," an ideology once again fixed and stable, ready to guide national development.

The book's design is rhetorically effective because it provides both dramatic tension and cathartic resolution. At the same time, it gives an exaggerated impression of ideological fixedness at both ends of the Revolution, as if at these two moments consensus had been reached and all essential questions answered. One need only consider the violent philosophical debates of the 1790s to realize that such was not the case. Of greater concern is Wood's treatment of the process of cultural change between 1776 and 1787, for his explanation of that fundamental transformation remains unclear.

Wood addresses the issue head on, explaining in the preface that the transformation of republican ideology resulted from "the strongest kinds of polemical and experiential pressures" (p. viii). By that he means both the relentless, clarifying logic of constitutional debate and the reciprocal encounter between political culture and its rapidly changing environment. Fair enough, for surely both were at work. The problem is that by book's end Wood has told us a great deal about constitutional argumentation but surprisingly little about the interactions between republican political culture and its socioeconomic and political contexts. In a sense, the book's greatest strength, its interior analysis of republican political culture, is also its greatest liability, for Wood ties his discussion of that culture only loosely to the economic, social, and political revolutions of which it was a part.

We are told in part one, for example, that the "opposition" or "country" view of politics exerted such a powerful influence in late colonial America because of "widespread anger and frustration with the way the relationships of power and esteem seemed to be crystallizing" (p. 79), yet the sources and extent of those social and political tensions are not explored. At one point, Wood acknowledges his lack of clarity on the matter with the blunt statement: "Whatever the social reality prior to the Revolution may have been . . ." (*ibid.*).

Again, we read in chapters two and six about the explosive debates between Republicans and Constitutionalists in Pennsylvania over political equality and the appropriate design of state government, and Wood tells us that those debates reflected deep-seated social conflict. "Nowhere else," he writes; "was there more social antagonism expressed during the Revolution" (p. 84). He offers little more by way of explanation, however, than a vague reference to "the new men . . . socially outside the establishment" who now challenged the old whig elite for control (p. 85). Nowhere does he undertake the kind of social and economic analysis of political divisions that, for example, Eric Foner offers in his book on *Tom Paine and Revolutionary America.*

Even more jarring is Wood's treatment of Federalist and Antifederalist politics in *Creation*'s closing chapters, for though he develops a surprisingly Progressive-like interpretation of the Constitution, he offers only the most rudimentary explanation of the socioeconomic bases of Federalist and Antifederalist political support. Federalism, he explains, represented "the profoundest disillusionment with the great hopes of . . . 1776," a "conservative" movement mounted, in Federalist minds, to protect "the worthy against the licentious" (pp. 472, 475). Which elements of American political society responded to this conservative agenda, or to the other agendas addressed by the Constitution (for example, commercial expansion), is never made clear.

One can hardly fault Wood, of course, for not having written comprehensive social and political histories of the Revolution before undertaking his own work. As *Creation* stands, it is herculean enough! At the same time, it is important to note the difficulties Wood has in unraveling the ties between culture and its environment, explaining the causes of cultural change, and detailing the role of culture in guiding political behavior, because those are the analytical problems he set out to explore. Nor can Wood be held accountable for work produced after his own. Such work, however, provides the essential perspective by which we can judge the continuing importance of what he has done.

Where then does *Creation of the American Republic* stand today in the historiography of the Revolution? Though less dominant than before, its place remains secure as one of a handful of works demanding the attention of anyone seeking to know what the American Revolution was about. To have survived the shifting historiographical tides so long—and serve as the focus of a symposium such as the one in which this essay appears—attests to its remarkable strength. Every historian dreams of someday producing her or his "great book." Gordon Wood is one of the precious few who has turned that dream into reality.

7

THE EXPANDING NATION:
PIONEERS OR PLANNERS?

Mutually reinforcing economic and spatial expansion characterized the first half of the nineteenth century. What is now called the market revolution created a momentous change in the United States sometime between the end of the Revolution and the 1830s. It continued to transform America through the nineteenth century, but in these early years citizens—whether farmers, professionals, or entrepreneurs—all felt its tremors. In throwing off Great Britain, the new republic had also thrown off the economic restraints on manufacturing and trade that had tied the two countries together in a mutually beneficial but, at least on the part of the colonies, theoretically exclusive relationship (considerable colonial smuggling made it less exclusive in practice than on paper). After the Revolution, the United States was no longer limited to producing the cheap raw materials that Britain had sought from its colony. It could now market its goods as far and wide as its vessels could carry them.

While the market revolution was driven in part by expanding manufacturing, it was also driven by expanding population and more and more land under cultivation for profit. In enacting the Proclamation Act of 1763, part of the settlement of the Treaty of Paris ending the Seven Years War, London prohibited settlement by colonists beyond the Appalachians. This immensely unpopular legislation attempted (but failed) to prohibit new settlers, particularly from the British Isles, from pouring west and settling what Bernard Bailyn has called the Great Inland Arc: "the massive periphery that swung west and south from Nova Scotia to the Appalachian plateaus and the Florida borderlands."[1] Bailyn's Arc included the lands in western Pennsylvania and what would become Ohio as well as the lands that Virginia still claimed but that would become Kentucky. Farther south, the Arc covered lands on which the Cherokee and Creek lived: western North Carolina, and what would become Tennessee and Georgia. The British tried to stop settlement beyond the Appalachians because the British troops stationed in the West were

---

[1]Bernard Bailyn, *Voyagers to the West, A Passage in the Peopling of America on the Eve of the Revolution* (New York, 1988).

inadequate to protect land-hungry settlers and Indians from each other. Furthermore, London had the notion that the unsettled lands belonged to the British government and should be disposed of in some orderly way, producing substantial revenues and encouraging compact settlement. This was not what most Americans wanted, and self-government insured all-but-unrestricted westward movement, rapid agricultural growth, and an expanding market for goods.

Andrew Jackson and the Democratic party dominated antebellum economic and territorial growth from 1828 to 1836. Jackson differed from his predecessors in his open, rambunctious campaigns, his rhetorical embrace of the "common man" and disdain for governmental power, his insistence on the right to cheap or free land, and the extremity of his proclivity for violence, particularly against Indians. Jackson's political opposition, the Whig party, endorsed more governmental activity, including a national bank, the construction of roads and canals, and a national policy for the orderly sale of land and establishment of communities. Although Whigs adopted Democratic campaign techniques, including the mobilization of women supporters, they were associated with a more restrained, deferential style, and a more aristocratic outlook. The development of the country and the images of the two parties provided various themes for historians of the early republic to pursue.

Initially historians of the period discussed the politics. Nineteenth-century nationalist historians (except Bancroft), who were Whigs or were sympathetic to them, hated Jacksonian politics, Jackson, and the people he represented. At the turn of the century, the Progressives, frightened by the poverty and misery caused by industrial capitalism, reevaluated Jackson and found him a populist hero, fighting the forces of nascent capitalism. One Progressive, Frederick Jackson Turner (the son of one Andrew Jackson Turner), saw Jacksonian politics as an extension of the experience of westward migration rather than in isolation. This view prevailed until such conservative, consensus historians as Richard Wade and Daniel Boorstin described the time without such stark conflict. In some instances, the progressive view persisted alongside the consensus historians'. Conservative historians built on Turner's themes and put westward migration at the heart of the American, egalitarian character. They felt that pioneers, eager to work the land and make a good living, expressed an essential middle-class accord that Americans still shared.

At the same time as the consensus historians were reflecting the postwar need for a united, homogeneous America, economic historians were presenting a view of America as a nation whose proper business was and had always been business. If the consensus historians were responding to Cold War pressures to minimize conflict and present a unified America, business historians were glorifying capitalism in contrast to Soviet socialism. By the early sixties revisionists began to look at Jackson's presidency as more rhetoric than substance and to take seriously his personal flaws. Some also viewed the advance of capitalism with more subdued enthusiasm than that of the consensus or business historians.

By the early seventies, Jackson and politics were no longer at the center of research on the period. Protest against racism, poverty, and the imperialistic war in Vietnam had eroded much of the remaining enthusiasm for capitalism among the New Left historians, who turned their analyses to the dynamics of the country's transformation from a premodern to a modern economy. The new social historians turned away from the study of prominent men to look at the poor, women, blacks, and Indians left out of Jackson's embrace. These historians' interests lay in the cultural and social changes that accompanied antebellum capitalism. By the 1980s and 1990s social historians focused more on sexual and racial differences in the westward migration than differences between Whig and Democrat. And New Left historians no longer treated migration and the market revolution separately, but tried to reveal their profound interdependence. This essay tracks the development of historical thinking through those who emphasized a kind of unfettered westward expansion of democratic pioneer-farmers as basic to the rapid growth of the new nation as opposed to those who emphasized the capitalists and developers who planned for profits, not democracy.

Most nineteenth-century historians, who were, by and large, members of the elite, disliked both westward migrants and Jacksonian politics—and saw in them both a dangerous transfer of power from the worthy elite to the great unwashed. The fledgling historian Francis Parkman recorded for the popular press the continuing exodus of western migrants in 1848. Parkman, who held the immigrants in low esteem and thought them crazy and doomed to misery, reflected that he had "often perplexed [himself] to divine the various motives that give impulse to this strange migration . . . whether an insane hope of a better condition in life, or a desire of shaking off restraints of law and society, or merely restlessness."[2] Parkman's response to the migrants reflected his Whig politics, his distaste for disorder, large crowds, poverty, and the settlers' intrusive manners.

Whig historians like Parkman did not like how politics was transformed in the years between 1820 and 1840 when the vote was extended to almost all white men, so that the propertyless could exercise the franchise for the first time. Democrats were in the forefront of changing methods of politicking from the restrained promotion of a

---

[2]Francis Parkman, *The Oregon Trail* (New York, 1991), pp. 12–13.

candidate by his allies to boisterous self-peddling. Candidates who once would have hidden from overtly pressing their own cases initiated the tradition of making speeches, kissing babies, and pressing the flesh. Jackson the Democrat had ridden to power on the backs of illiterate and unpropertied men who no longer behaved deferentially to their social betters. For James Parton, author of an unflattering biography of Jackson, and Parkman, the fact that elite, well-educated men no longer automatically commanded authority at the polls was a sad corollary of Jackson's accession to power.

By the late nineteenth century, the view of Jackson's pioneers and their presumed politics had changed dramatically. The Progressive historian Frederick Jackson Turner in his famous essay "The Significance of the Frontier in American History," delivered in 1893, saw this wave of settlers as responsible for much that was distinctive, and indeed, much that was good about America. In Turner's view, Americans moving to unsettled lands ("free," he called them, invisibly annihilating their Indian proprietors) adopted for a time the dress and demeanor of "uncivilized" people while they cleared their acres, built log homes, and established small communities. After evolving from the savage frontier stage, they quickly went through pastoral and ranching stages, winding up in the urban and manufacturing stage. In this sense, each western American community recapitulated the growth and evolution of civilization. "The first frontier had to meet its Indian question, its question of the means of intercourse with older settlements, of the extension of political organization, of religious and educational activity."[3] These settlers were, he argued, not characteristically southern or Yankee, but rather from the middle Atlantic states—with middle-state tolerance and prosperity-seeking as defining qualities. Wherever they came from, their frontier experience shaped them, working against sectionalism and helping to glue the country together. Turner believed that pioneering produced pragmatic, voluntaristic Americans, developed a desirably martial spirit in those forced to defend themselves and families from Indian attacks, and honed their skills in working with one another. All of this resulted in strong, flexible, no-nonsense institutions.

For Turner, the economic programs passed during Jackson's presidency reflected the needs and desires of the frontier settlers for better transportation, distribution of land and a system of tariffs. Turner described the centrally organized Whig land distribution ideas of one-term president John Quincy Adams going down to defeat before the ideas of Missouri's first senator, the Democrat Thomas Hart Benton.

---

[3]Frederick Jackson Turner, "The Significance of the Frontier in American History," in *The Frontier in American History* (Tucson, Ariz., 1920, 1947, 1986), p. 9.

Benton replaced Whig Henry Clay's American System, whereby land was to be a national—not a local—resource and would be distributed and priced to make sure that settlements were compact and laid out in an orderly and systematic way, with a system of easy, locally run distribution. Turner wrote approvingly of a distribution administered not by the federal government, but by the states, which were free to give land away or sell to speculators. In his evolutionary model, this was a necessary step along the way to "civilization": agrarian-minded Democrats would eventually turn into Whigs whose interests were in a developing economy, but first they would divvy up the land and share the frontier experience.

Turner regarded with satisfaction the western migration as a democratic movement of moderate people, trained in ruggedness. These were community builders, creating America as they went along, and eventually bringing the whole continental United States under the tolerant, individualistic control, of shared values "rooted strongly in commercial prosperity." There were some problems, he thought, with excessive individualism and an underdeveloped community spirit. He also disapproved of wildcat banking practices and the knowing circulation of inflated paper currency. Turner saw these as reflections of corrupt business practices and selfishness. Nevertheless, from his perspective, the egalitarianism, the extended franchise, and the movement to extend land to all (white) men who wanted it indicated a growth of a wholesome leveling spirit and the emergence of a practical and tolerant American ready to defend his rights but also ready to cooperate with his neighbor across ethnic differences.

Turner's positive view of this migration, which in many ways confirmed the migrants' own view of themselves, persisted through the First World War and found some resonance with the later Progressive Vernon Parrington. But Parrington focused more clearly on what he saw as the inevitable, and in his view, pernicious development from Democrat to Whig. "The coonskin individualism that created Jacksonian democracy was gradually undermined by a middle-class individualism that inclined to the Whiggery of Henry Clay. The former was a spontaneous expression of the frontier spirit, the latter a calculating expression of the maturing settlement. The one discovered its native habitat on the backwoods farm, the other in the county seat town. The one was agrarian *laissez faire*, the other was exploitative and paternalistic."[4]

For Parrington, the egalitarian, rough-living pioneer inevitably become the bourgeois, who, by definition, exploited others and created hierarchies. The leading Whig spokesman, Henry Clay, Parrington

---

[4]Vernon Parrington, *The Romantic Revolution in America, 1800–1860* (New York, 1927), Vol. II, pp. 132–133.

thought honest but misguided, incapable of understanding the evil consequences of embracing the market. He had not read or studied enough, and his breathtaking rhetorical skills only managed to keep him from thinking straight about the future that nascent capitalism would produce. By contrast, Jackson was our first "great popular leader, our first man of the people," a man of unimpeachable integrity, if little learning. Jackson's lack of learning, even more marked than Clay's, was not a flaw but contributed to his egalitarianism. In office Jackson grew in understanding—and in detestation—of how government can be used to increase the profits of the elite. For Parrington, Democrats struggled with the Whigs from "class-feeling" or "the will to destroy the aristocratic principle in government."[5] In Parrington's view Democratic pioneers fought with Whig planners in an all-important class struggle that would be reproduced in graver circumstances in succeeding periods of American history.

The historian Arthur Schlesinger, Jr., argued in his influential *The Age of Jackson* (1945) along the same lines as Parrington. For Schlesinger the Jacksonian era was characterized by one of the periodic swells of democratic rebellion against the business interests that normally dominate American politics. Schlesinger, like Parrington, located Jackson's supporters in the South and West, but also found them among the growing numbers of wage earners. In Schlesinger's view Jacksonian democracy was working-class protest against people and policies trying to shape the young republic to the interests of a manufacturing and financial elite. Parrington's and Schlesinger's views, emphasizing class struggle and stark differences between the Democrats and Whigs, between the pioneers and the planners, dominated the field for several decades.

By the late 1950s and early 1960s the consensus historians had supplanted Progressive historians such as Schlesinger. These scholars found little conflict in the Jacksonian era and portrayed it as one in which Americans of all kinds agreed that working hard to improve one's standard of living was the most important goal. People participated in politics to find the best ways to get ahead. The political parties, like the Americans who constituted them, agreed on the important issues, and they worked the details out peacefully.

In 1959, Richard Wade pictured the West as a collection of liberal, profit-oriented communities. His *The Urban Frontier* described such cities as Pittsburgh, Cincinnati, Lexington, St. Louis, and Louisville as preceding and facilitating rural settlement. Wade saw the migration of Americans as an unstoppable "flood." The Continental Congress had tried to regulate this migration with the first Northwest Ordinance of

---

[5]Ibid., pp. 139, 140.

1785, which provided for government surveys before land sales. Before any surveys were completed, however, urban frontier cities had come into being. Institutions followed needs, as urban centers grew in population, their governmental structures improvised to keep up with rapid expansion. People, profit-oriented by nature, settled in Wade's cities to make a good living. Commercial development and planning arrived with the entrepreneurially minded settlers. Early Pittsburgh residents, for example, made money outfitting the thousands of travelers who passed through the city on their way west.

In Wade's view, the western cities had an uncomfortable, colonized economic relationship with the East. Like the colonies and Great Britain before the Revolution, western urbanites sent most of their hard currency east to pay debts and hence were always short of cash. They also shipped raw materials east and thus were inhibited from developing manufacturing for a time.[6]

The picture Wade painted of the relation between city and agrarian life was one of meshing interests. The western cities grew economically faster than the surrounding countryside and provided farmers with products, financial services, and cultural life. "They speeded up the transformation of the West from a gloomy wilderness to a richly diversified region. Any historical view which omits this dimension of Western life tells but part of the story." In Wade's mature city, the best urban leaders, like St. Louis' first mayor, William Carr Lane, tried to represent all the people, not just commercial and business interests. But, at the same time, Wade's was a classless story, or rather one in which the middle class stood in for all Americans. Thus the pioneers were planners from the start, eager to use urban governmental machinery to further their prosperity. In Wade's view, men of both parties were motivated by the same liberal vision—a vision that for Wade was unquestionably wholesome.

Following in Wade's footsteps was Daniel Boorstin, who, in *The Americans, The National Experience* (1965) wrote a paean to the mobile American, whom he called "The Transient." "Where," he demanded rhetorically, "had so many people of their own accord taken one-way passage? Where had so many men moved to unknown, remote places, not to conquer or convert or fortify or even to trade, but to find and make communities for themselves and their children? New institutions grew as the transients traveled. In order to travel they had to make new communities. They had to devise laws quickly and enforce them swiftly, without benefit of books or lawyers. They had to leave things and people behind. Above all, they had to be willing to go ahead anyhow, forming new communities, without waiting

---

[6]Richard C. Wade, *The Urban Frontier* (Chicago, 1959), p. 42.

for God or government to prepare the way."[7] These communities, Boorstin argued, were "expressly designed to serve private interests, and private interests were preserved only by the express construction of effective communities." While Parrington and Schlesinger saw the liberals' association of public good with private profit as corrupt and leading to the exploitation of the many by the few, Boorstin saw it as what was quintessentially American—and good. In his view, pioneers arrived at liberalism through their experience; they were, in some sense, pioneers *and* planners, where planning had no negative connotations of dominance or exploitation.

Like the Progressives, Boorstin thought that Democratic-designed land distribution schemes demonstrated pragmatic democracy and protected squatters."[8] Similarly, a powerful democratic ethos, Boorstin argued, prevailed in mining camps, agricultural communities, and the gold rush towns of California. Egalitarianism was the rule, at least, he thought, until women arrived. Women, he argued brought with them invidious distinctions—fancy clothes and furnishings pointed up status differences. Boorstin wrote that "along with their morality they brought inequality."[9] Thus, it was with family life and a relatively equal ratio of men to women that social differences manifested themselves on the frontier. Hierarchies grew from something innate in the female constitution, not the possibilities for exploitation contained within liberalism. Subsequent historians would challenge this view of sex and the westward migration.

Boorstin's transients were pioneers who planned minimally, but they planned. Settlers believed their government was responsible for giving them title to land, protecting their title to that land against Europeans and Indians, and increasing that land's value by building canals, roads, and, somewhat later, railroads. As Boorstin wrote, "While the particular source of government aid was frequently shifting, expectations of some form of public assistance never died."[10]

Meanwhile, a new contingent of economic historians began to see the Jacksonian period from the standpoint of businessmen, who, they argued, had always been central in the development of the New World. Thomas Cochran, author of *Basic History of American Business*, wrote that "from the beginning, business considerations, as distinct from feudal or religious, had a secure and honorable place in American life, and businessmen enjoyed far more prestige than in the aristocratic

[7]Daniel J. Boorstin, *The Americans, The National Experience* (New York, 1965), p. 50.

[8]Ibid., p. 74.

[9]Ibid., p. 92.

[10]Ibid., p. 253.

monarchies of the Old World."[11] In this view, commercial values had always and unabashedly influenced the direction and growth of North America. In Cochran's interpretation the merchant community instigated the Revolution with help from aggrieved laboring people. The Proclamation Act had not only inhibited the designs of would-be pioneers but, more important, had impeded land speculators like George Washington from asserting his claims to large quantities of land west of the Appalachians. The most important opposition to British and then to U.S. central governmental control of the sale of land came from wealthy businessmen intending to speculate, not from pioneers eager to buy small parcels cheaply. "The joint-stock companies, led by prominent citizens of many states, wanted to buy land wholesale with depreciated Continental securities and turn it over at a profit. This combination of state and private interests explains one of the first successful attempts to keep the central government from conflicting with business. A land ordinance was passed with both minimum acreage and price set so high, and conditions of purchase so difficult, that direct sale to small farmers was virtually prevented."[12]

Thus planning directed the development of the American frontier from the very start. For example, real estate speculators introduced democratic procedures into the plans for governing the Old Northwest not out of ideology but to make settlement attractive to democratic-minded farmers. The business of business was to get the government to support its projects.

A darker and more complex vision of planning emerged from Howard Lamar's immensely influential *The Far Southwest, 1846–1912*, published in 1970. Lamar wrote about a later period of settlement and different conditions, that is, the settlement of a land on which there was already a large Hispanic population. That settlement looked less like a folk migration and more like a "conquest of merchants who worried little about extending the glories of free government to their captive customers."[13] Lamar's detailed study revealed a violent and often deadly struggle for control of land and water. In his portrait of the Southwest, politics was one of the methods wealthy men used to try to create conditions favorable to their economic schemes.

Marvin Meyers came at the question of what was fundamentally shaping America in the early national period from a different direction, revising the consensus view. His interpretation revealed aspects of the Jacksonian phenomenon that had previously been obscure. In

---

[11]Thomas Cochran, *Basic History of American Business* (Princeton, N.J., 1959), p. 15.

[12]Ibid., p. 36.

[13]Howard Lamar, *The Far Southwest, 1846–1912: A Territorial History* (New York, 1970), p. 63.

The Jacksonian Persuasion (1957), he refused to take at face value how Whigs and Democrats *described* Jackson. Meyers, looking for meanings behind the meanings Democrats and Whigs articulated, saw Jackson *symbolizing* rather than really representing democratic-agrarian values. This was a bold and imaginative move, which drew on social psychology and psychology. Meyers pointed out that Jackson did not actually behave like an agrarian, but mobilized, with heated rhetoric, popular support for symbolic issues like his war against the Bank. Jackson's violent language convinced voters that something essential was at stake, but Meyers rated the programs of Whigs and Democrats as not widely divergent. The nation was on the road to capitalism, and while committed to this course, it was simultaneously afraid of the moral consequences of this development. Jackson, who was on an essentially Whig trajectory, along with the rest of the country, was nevertheless able to make many voters believe that their traditional values would be safe with him as president. Meyers's book tried to "convey the effort[of] Jacksonian Democracy to recall agrarian republican innocence to a society drawn fatally to the main chance . . . to the revolutionizing ways of acquisition, emulative consumption, promotion, and speculation—the Jacksonian struggle to reconcile again the simple yeoman values with the free pursuit of economic interest, just as the two were splitting hopelessly apart."[14] For Meyers, planning was dominant from the earliest years of the United States' development, and the ethos of pioneering served mainly rhetorical and symbolic purposes, even in Andrew Jackson's day. The market had triumphed. Pioneers were planners from the start, but suffered from misgivings and guilt about it. While there was a kind of consensus-in-denial in this view, there was little triumph.

Two years later, Glyndon G. Van Deusen took a more typical consensus stand, arguing that the Whigs and Democrats both had strengths and defects, and each commanded the support of about half the country. Van Deusen's task was to show how the parties from 1828 until 1848 compromised, horsetraded, and emerged sustaining "the improvement of society through the expression of the will of the people. Viewed in this light, the political history of these twenty years presents a hopeful rather than a gloomy picture of American democracy."[15]

In 1967 Robert Remini, in a return to the Progressive view of Jackson, analyzed his war over the Bank. He considered Jackson wrong to kill the Bank because the country needed a stable source of currency and a ballast against wild swings of the economy. While Jackson's con-

---

[14]Marvin Meyers, *The Jacksonian Persuasion, Politics and Belief* (Stanford, Calif., 1957), p. 15.

[15]Glyndon Van Deusen, *The Jacksonian Era, 1828–1848* (Prospect Heights, Ill., 1959), pp. vii, xi, xii, 266.

cern for the laissez faire market was ideologically in line with agrarian thinking and gained him wide popularity with working men, in practice, Remini argued, it benefited powerful members of the business community when he killed the Second National Bank. The Bank, by controlling currency and lending rates, had a stabilizing effect on the economy and inhibited speculators from more disruptive economic practices. Killing the Bank made Jackson look like an agrarian populist, but actually left the national economy open to the manipulation and profiteering of speculators, which in turn guaranteed that American cycles of bust and boom would continue with more and more damaging effects, especially on the poor.

Despite this, Remini maintained that Jackson's populism—even if more rhetorical than real—had a very real effect. The Constitution had provided for a dangerously weak Executive, and Jackson's responsiveness to the will of the people and his victory simultaneously increased both presidential strength and democracy. Jackson's assertion of power was essential to increasing the power of the will of the people who supported and guided the president. In this and other works on Jackson, Remini revived the Progressive view of the president, in which he contributed to enlarging democracy.[16]

Edward Pessen, sharply revising Remini and the consensus historians, was among the last to engage directly in the debate over how democratic was Jacksonian democracy. His *Jacksonian America*[17] assessed Jackson as a shrewd, dangerously violent opportunist in tune with the ugly materialism of the era in which American politics came of age. The franchise expanded in Jackson's presidency but voters had little or no real influence on how power was exercised. People were willing to mistake the political shadow for the substance and were, in any case, mostly busy trying to make a buck. Pessen argued that the modern politics born in the Jacksonian era was, and still is, characterized by a refusal to deal with important, that is, ethical issues, a willingness to have concerns dumbed down and a continuing preoccupation with money. A few insiders exercise real power; the rest is show.

In the 1970s, young social historians, influenced by the protests of the 1960s and continuing evidence of racial, gender, and economic in-

---

[16]Robert Remini, *Andrew Jackson and the Bank War* (New York, 1967), pp. 1–49, 176–78. See also Robert Remini, *Andrew Jackson and the Course of American Empire, 1767–1821* (New York, 1977); *Andrew Jackson and the Course of American Freedom, 1822–1832* (New York, 1981); *Andrew Jackson and the Course of American Democracy, 1833–1845* (New York, 1984).

[17]Edward Pessen, *Jacksonian America: Society, Personality, and Politics* (Homewood, Ill., 1969), pp. 2, 37, 179, 347–51. See George M. Frederickson's essay "Nineteenth-century American History" for how the question of growing democracy gave way to other, less self-congratulatory themes, in Anthony Molho and Gordon S. Wood, eds., *Imagined Histories, American Historians Interpret Their Past* (Princeton, N J., 1998), p. 164.

justice, renewed Progressive questions about class struggle but saw the era through a much darker glass than Progressives had. The concerns of historians influenced by the New Left overlapped with those of Pessen: failures of inclusion in democratic promise, an overriding emphasis on making money, and questions about how and where the reform movements fit into the wider framework. Planners had won, and the country was populated with winners and losers—not Americans sharing a vision.

Paul Johnson's *Shopkeeper's Millennium, Society and Revivals in Rochester, New York, 1815–1837,* looked at the evangelical awakening in Rochester in the 1820s through the lens of the political transformations that took place during the age of Jackson and asked how and why it had happened. Like the great English historian of the working class, E. P. Thompson, Johnson was interested in the steps that make and justify wage labor in a country where independence had been a central value and had been tied to land ownership from the first colonial landings. Johnson was among the first to see the construction of the Erie Canal as a site for investigating the ways pioneering and planning worked together. In the growing cities along the canal, Johnson found manufacturers and upwardly mobile working men participating in the revivals and adopting all the characteristics that would come to define the middle class, such as temperance, frugality, industriousness, and self-control. These bourgeois and Whiggish characteristics, he argued, helped secure the rule of the new middle class through the semblance of universality and ethical credibility they gave their possessors. In Johnson's interpretation, evangelical perfectionism helped legitimate the new status of free laborers—men who were selling their work "voluntarily" and were no longer living as indentured servants in the homes of their masters. As he put it, "Nascent industrial capitalism became attached to visions of a perfect moral order based on individual freedom and self-government, and old relations of dependence, servility, and mutuality were defined as sinful and left behind. The revival was not a capitalist plot. But it certainly was a crucial step in the legitimation of free labor."[18]

Johnson saw Jacksonian democracy facilitating the rise of this new morally saturated middle class through politicians' and voters' resolute refusal to intervene actively in moral problems. For example, voters would tax liquor-selling establishments, but not close them. To fill this frightening ethical void, created by liberal live-and-let-live attitudes, evangelical religion and its emphasis on self-control promised order and stability that would emanate from the good character of converts in this new, morally chaotic world. Bosses and, in lesser num-

---

[18]Paul E. Johnson, *A Shopkeeper's Millennium, Society and Revivals in Rochester, New York, 1815–1837* (New York, 1978), p. 141.

bers, ambitious workers collaborated in revivals to give the winners in Jacksonian democracy sweepstakes a respectable moral code to replace republicanism with its now-outmoded emphasis on disinterestedness.

Mary Ryan in *The Cradle of the Middle Class* brought gender into focus in analyzing the role of evangelical religion in the formation of the bourgeoisie.[19] Her study of women and class in Utica built on some of Johnson's ideas and gave them a domestic framework. She followed prosperous urban and rural women from inviting evangelical preachers, to bringing their families to conversion, to perfecting middle-class child-rearing techniques. Utica women essentially invented a new inheritance—training and habits for success in the middle class—to replace the land that was no longer available to patriarchs to bestow on their children. In Ryan's view, pioneers became planners when opportunity and ambition converged. Like Meyers's Americans, many of Johnson's and Ryan's were ambivalent about the changes that the market revolution was producing, but however worried, they were nevertheless committed to planning and commercial growth. The background of the Erie Canal and the economic changes that came with it highlighted the ways developing capitalism was both the product and the producer of the evolving planners' mentality.

In an effort to synthesize a wide rage of insights on reform, Jacksonian politics, and evangelicalism. Daniel Walker Howe has argued that evangelicals became "champions of modernization, that is of changes in the structure of society and individual personality that emphasized discipline and channeled energies by the deliberate choice of goals and the rational selection of means." They created a distinctive (Whig) political culture and were opposed by Democrats who were "more skeptical about such transformations and the accompanying inequality and regimentation of human life."[20] Steven Mintz's recent book on evangelical reformers as modernizers elaborates on this theory.[21]

The tendency to study planning and pioneering as part of the same phenomenon became more pronounced as historians no longer saw Whigs and Democrats or agrarians and capitalists as polar opposites but rather as different components of the same process. John Mack Faragher reexamined the pioneer experience from the standpoint of gender and class, finding in *Women and Men on The Overland Trail* (1979) that pioneers were people of some economic means and that the emigrant experience reinforced the inequalities of patri-

---

[19]Mary Ryan, *The Cradle of the Middle Class, The Family in Oneida County, New York, 1790–1865* (Cambridge, Mass., 1981).

[20]Daniel Walker Howe, "The Evangelical Movement and Political Culture in the North During the Second Party System," *Journal of American History*, Vol. 77, No. 4 (March 1991): 1216–39. The quotation is taken from pp. 1216–17.

[21]Steven Mintz, *Moralists and Modernizers, American Pre–Civil War Reformers* (Baltimore, 1995). See Chapter 8.

archy and capitalism. "For men, the overland emigration was an archetypal nineteenth-century event, for it was conceived in the spirit of progress, publicly designated to fulfill economic goals, yet infused and overlaid with male projections and identifications."[22] Women were almost never included in the decision to emigrate. The traditional sexual inequality of farming life when permeated by market concerns became even more so. Women were not liberated by the pioneering experience. Nor did they bring inequality and status worries to the egalitarian frontier as Boorstin had argued. The frontier stripped them of the benefits of the "cult of domesticity" without offering anything but hard labor in return.[23] Other historians focusing on gender and the westward experience did find some possibilities for new freedom for women in small western communities where class lines were relatively fluid and gender prescriptions looser.[24] However, even these historians made it clear that women's experience emphatically did not fit the individualistic portrait of the pioneer, who had always been assumed to be male.

By the 1990s, most historians had moved away from the more polarized idea of the frontier story as one of democratic pioneering or Whiggish planning and looked instead to the interplay of these forces. Harry L. Watson, author of *Liberty and Power, The Politics of Jacksonian America* (1990), reaffirmed the idea that there were differences between the Whigs and the Democrats that voters responded to, and that these differences did conform to Jackson's portrayal of the class struggle he was leading and that he successfully identified with the common white man. But Watson's close look at the programs, experiences, and personalities of Jackson and Clay demonstrates that this was a transitional period in the American economy and that the main players sometimes had a weak grasp of the implications of their actions— especially when Jackson vetoed the Bank. These years, in which agrarians and capitalists were most at odds, were also a time of high hopes for the potential of the market revolution to bring most Americans—at least the white ones—to a higher standard of living. In this volatile period of high immigration and migration, Democrats worried that increasing political democracy was not being accompanied by increasing economic equality. In fact, quite the reverse: Whigs worried that increasing democracy—which meant to them leadership by the ignorant masses—might inhibit the ways in which the market revolu-

---

[22]John Mack Faragher, *Women and Men on the Overland Trail* (New Haven, Conn., 1979), p. 183.

[23]Joan Cashin, *A Family Venture, Men & Women on the Southern Frontier* (New York, 1991). Cashin found a similar pattern in the southern migration from the coast to the rich cotton-growing lands of Alabama and Mississippi.

[24]See Sandra Myres, *Westering Women and the Frontier Experience* (Albuquerque, N. Mex., 1982).

tion should advance. Jacksonian Democrats, in this view, were advancing their class interests against the Whig elite and succeeding in politics if not in economic power.

At the same time, New Left historians had been engaged in charting the growth of the market and the market mentality across the country. Christopher Clark's discussion of eighty years in western Massachusetts, for example (*The Roots of Rural Capitalism*), showed such a mentality developing extremely slowly.[25]

Alan Kulikoff, in *The Agrarian Origins of American Capitalism*,[26] offered a new interpretation of the relationahip of early capitalism to western migration. Kulikoff saw merchants as the prime movers in the eminently bourgeois American Revolution. The result of throwing off colonialism was to free the economy from restraints on manufacturing and to encourage state governments to invest in internal improvements, accelerating capitalist development to a dizzying speed. Kulikoff's view of the Revolution and subsequent economic development is remarkably similar to Cochran's and the other entrepreneurial historians' except that he sees business as inherently destructive of the human spirit and human relationships.

Kulikoff argued of the early nineteenth-century migrants that while a few were planners, wanting to improve their circumstances, most "wanted merely to escape the threat of wage labor."[27] Only merchants or skilled craftsmen looked to urban areas as places of possibility. "All migrants wanted land and the independence it brought," he insists.[28] Most of his settlers wanted to participate in the market and "sought improved transportation . . . [and pursued] increased farm output." While the wealthier could purchase land and thereby independence, the poorer became "a new western rural proletariat, building internal improvements, harvesting crops or trees, operating canal or river boats, tramping from job to job from farm to frontier city."[29] Pioneers managed, for a short time, against the tide of capitalist development, to establish communities "meshing political individualism with strong communal goals."[30] But by the 1850s the Whigs had won out, in Kulikoff's analysis, and bourgeois culture and agricultural specialization for the market dominated the Old Northwest. Kulikoff's view of the inherent class struggle between the developer-planners and

---

[25]Christopher Clark, *The Roots of Rural Capitalism: Western Massachusetts, 1780–1860* (Ithaca, N.Y., 1990).

[26]Alan Kulikoff, *The Agrarian Origins of American Capitalism* (Charlottesville, Va., 1992).

[27]Ibid., p. 208.

[28]Ibid., p. 209.

[29]Ibid., p. 215.

[30]Ibid., p. 217.

the pure pioneers recapitulates the Progressives' and Schlesinger's idea that Jacksonian politics was about substantial class issues, not symbols. But in Kulikoff's story the capitalists win. The pioneers who refused to adapt to the new capitalist order could register their resistance only in one way—by not selling their own labor, by moving on, once again, to the next frontier.

Michael Merrill, in a 1995 article, reviewed the literature on the development of the market and the accompanying mentality. He called for a stricter understanding of capitalism as not just a market economy, which, he argues, characterizes any number of systems, but an economy in which capitalists have political control and use it to further their interests. Using this definition, many of Kulikoff's agrarian participants in the market economy would not yet be engaged in full-fledged capitalism.[31] Francois Weil has argued that local dynamism in small Massachusetts communities rather than Boston capitalists initiated the first textile industries, as historians have believed for decades. She adds another refinement to our understanding of the way a market economy, as opposed to capitalism, evolved.[32]

In *Sugar Creek* (1986), excerpted in this section, Faragher portrayed the growth of a community in southern Illinois that combined the themes of pioneering and planning over time. He skillfully blended contemporary perspectives on sex, Native Americans and class struggle, but the story of Sugar Creek's growth retains Turner's idea of pioneering as a uniquely American crucible from which emerged ideas about community, cooperation, pragmatism, and the strains and rewards of individualism. But Faragher corrected Turner for describing the Illinois land as "free." Migrants spent many years and lives wresting it from the Kickapoo Indians. But in other ways he described in rich detail experiences that Turner had only sketched. Rather than stress transience, he studied the growth of a stable community where inequality grew more pronounced over time as the market became a greater presence in agricultural life. Pioneering here, as on the overland trail, was a first stage in planning. Settlers in southern Illinois arrived in waves from the south—before the surveyors, they squatted and herded cattle, recapitulating, as Turner had said, steps along the path toward urban industrial society.

A very recent view of this same migration to Ohio offers a startlingly new perspective on Turner as well as the advent of capitalism. Eric Hinderaker's *Elusive Empires* studied attempts to control the Ohio Valley, concluding with the single success: postrevolutionary

---

[31]Michael Merrill, "Putting Capitalism in its Place," *William and Mary Quarterly*, 3rd ser., Vol. LII, No. 2 (1995): 315–26.

[32]Francois Weil, "Capitalism and Industrialization in New England, 1815–1845," *Journal of American History*, Vol. 84, No. 4):1334–54.

America. In his analysis, American settlers pouring in after the Revolution were fiecely independent, hard to control, and interested in subsistence, not farming for profit. They were, as Hinderaker says, "unpromising constituents for a nation-building project." They were firm in their desire for land but not in their loyalty to the new United States. The federal government originally posted the army there to prohibit squatting before the arrival of federal surveyors, but found itself forced to protect these unruly Americans from the attacks of Indians enraged at American disregard for their long-standing claims to the valley. The government had initially not wanted to sell land to speculators but, finding it too difficult to deal directly with each settler, it began selling large blocks of land to wealthy men interested in making real estate profits. Through this the federal government also created an elite that it hoped would bring stability and leadership to the territory. In other words, after 1787, settlers did not find free land, but a free market in land. Market prices, although low, forced them into participation in the agrarian market if they wished to hold on to their acres.

Simultaneously, constant warfare with the Indians pushed recalcitrant settlers and the federal government into an alliance. "In the Indian wars of the 1780's and 1790's," wrote Hinderaker, "the national government established a foothold in the region and shaped its early development in fundamental ways."[33] In his eyes, western migrants resembled Kulikoff's fugitives from the market; it was only Indian warfare that allied them with the federal government.

Three important books have dramatically revised Turner's ideas and been responsible for the new interest in western history. They, too, see pioneering and planning as linked enterprises with sometimes surprising results. William Cronon, an ecological historian, a student of Howard Lamar, and author of *Nature's Metropolis: Chicago and the Great West,* like Richard Wade, focused on the links between urban and rural development.[34] But, instead of seeing cities as the energetic nuclei of positive commercial growth, Cronon portrayed the massive environmental casualties caused by this development. His analysis of the entrepreneurial ventures of Chicago planners illustrates his theme that individual profit-making schemes combined to create the out-of-control metastasis of late-nineteenth-century capitalism.

Another of the best-known revisers of Turner, and another student of Lamar's, Patricia Limerick, a new western historian, described the history of the West as the ferocious struggle for property rights in natural resources. While Boorstin had celebrated collapsing public interest into private interest, Limerick quoted western writer Louis

---

[33]Eric Hinderaker, *Elusive Empires, Constructing Colonialism in the Ohio Valley, 1673–1800* (Cambridge, Mass., 1997), pp. 246, 244.

[34]William Cronon, *Nature's Metropolis: Chicago and the Great West* (New York, 1992).

L'Amour on the consequences: "People never worry about these things until it's too late." And while Turner had stressed the tolerance and flexibility of pioneer communities, Limerick investigated their ethnic and racial tensions.[35]

Finally, Stephen Aron looked at the history of Kentucky with Daniel Boone and Henry Clay as his temporal parameters. His title, *How the West Was Lost*, suggests ways in which he reversed Turner. He focused on losses and failures, not the triumphal march of democracy. "Henry Clay's Kentucky displaced hunters and held no place for Indians. The proliferation of tenancy, itinerant wage labor, and slavery denied men the independency they wanted and marked Kentucky as a broken promised land. For women, dependence was a given, and the transformation of *this* world offered little hope." The land that Boone had designated good for poor men no longer fit the description by the time of Henry Clay. It had been transformed from a destination for the poor to a place from which families migrated farther west.[36]

Carol Sheriff's *The Artificial River* (1996) is a sophisticated view of planning and its dense and complex relations with pioneering. She returned to the much-studied site of middle-class formation, the Erie Canal, and looked at how farmers behaved in this vortex of state and business planning. Her narrative documented the clashing of liberal and republican ideologies that informed farmers' thinking about the way both government and market were intruding on their lives. She identified the fears of those whose economic positions had improved as well as their fears of the ever-increasing number of wage earners living along the canal. One of her central themes was the farmers' belief in their government's responsibility to protect them from the corruption and greed of the rich. She poignantly recorded the growing fears of these victim-participants in planning, and recorded a contemporary-sounding lament, that the government had become not an advocate for small farmers, but an arm of the capitalists. Sheriff's intimate picture of life along and with the canal showed the market revolution at high speed throwing pioneers and planners together in a process neither completely controlled. Sheriff would agree with Charles Sellers and others surveyed here, including Parrington, Schlesinger, Paul Johnson, and Harry Watson, that "contrary to liberal mythology, democracy was born in tension with capitalism, and not as its natural and legitimating political expression."[37]

Pioneers and planners represent two strands of American development woven tightly together. For the most part, historians no longer

---

[35]Patricia Limerick, *The Legacy of Conquest, The Unbroken Past of the American West* (New York, 1987).

[36]Stephen Aron, *How the West Was Lost, The Transformration of Kentucky from Daniel Boone to Henry Clay* (Baltimore, 1996), pp. 4, 192–200.

[37]Charles Sellers, *The Market Revolution* (New York, 1991), p. 32.

see America and the American character as developing from one or the other, but as the complicated product of the two points of view. Historians comfortable with economic individualism and liberalism do not see the two in conflict. For historians worried by the intrusion of the market into more and more aspects of human life, they represent contradictory and incompatible values. Can democratic freedoms survive in an economy with few or no restraints on the market? At what point in the rapid economic development of the early nation did people's values to shift from communal to individualistic? Were westward migrants fleeing involvement in the market or looking for it? To what extent do the politics of the era reflect anxieties about the transtion to capitalism? As we try to chart our political, economic, and ethical way in the third millennium, the debates over these and other questions will continue.

JOHN MACK FARAGHER

JOHN MACK FARAGHER (1945–   ) is Arthur Unobskey Professor of American History at Yale University. He is the author of Men and Women on the Overland Trail *(1979), which won the Frederick Jackson Turner Award,* Sugar Creek *(1986), winner of the Society for the History of the Early Republic Award, and* Daniel Boone *(1992).*

In October of 1817, Robert Pulliam left his wife and children in southern Illinois and, accompanied by four men and one woman, led his string of cattle north into unsettled country. Moving at a grazer's pace, Pulliam's party spent at least ten days covering the hundred miles to Sugar Creek, and arrived there after autumn had set the prairie and timber ablaze with color. The herd grazed on the rich grass flourishing in the prairie meadows, while, a mile into the creek's timber in the midst of a large grove of sugar maple, the party built a rude log shelter to protect them from the winter. The men spent their winter days hunting and trapping the abundant small game of the river country; Mrs. Strickland, a sister of one of the hands, spent hers cooking over an open fire and tending to the domestic needs of camp. When snow covered the prairie, the drovers felled budding elm trees at the edge of the timber for the browsing cattle. Then, as spring approached, Pulliam set his men to work tapping the maples, rendering the sweet sap into sugar over the fire in the cabin. In April 1818, the party headed south, with fat stock, furs, and several hundred pounds of maple sugar to trade. Pulliam remained with his relations on the Kaskaskia River in St. Clair County until he and his family made a permanent move to Sugar Creek, in the spring of 1819.

Pulliam's story has provided the opening tale for the history of Sangamon County, Illinois, since 1859. That year a group of prominent local citizens formed an "Old Settlers' Society" and in order to begin the task of writing their history, appointed a committee to investigate the competing claims of several families to the honor of being the first to settle. The committee announced, after considerable deliberation, that although other settlers had broken ground for planting a full year before Pulliam brought his family in 1819, the 1817 sugarhouse was the first "local habitation" of Americans in the country of the Sangamon, so the committee awarded Pulliam the title "pioneer of Sangamon County."

Robert Pulliam typified his generation of pioneers. He was born in Henry County, Virginia, on the eastern slope of the Blue Ridge near the "dividing line" with North Carolina, in 1776. His father, John Pulliam, the son of Scotch-Irish emigrants, had emigrated there in the early 1770s after a childhood in the Shenandoah Valley, and there he fought with the county militia during the Revolution. But when the fighting ended, John led his wife (whose name was not recorded for posterity) and three children through the Cumberland Gap in the Appalachians into Kentucky, where Robert, his firstborn son, grew to young manhood. John Reynolds, a neighbor of the Pulliam family in Illinois and later governor of the state, described John as "a man of good mind, and more energy and activity than ordinary."

The Pulliam household and the Kentucky population grew apace. By 1800 the new state counted nearly a quarter-million residents; for her part, Mrs. Pulliam counted six more children. Poor settlers squatted on Kentucky land, hoping to accumulate the purchase price through their own labor, but, caught in the inflation of land values that accompanied development, many found themselves unable to raise the necessary cash. Many emigrated once again, and John Pulliam was one of these. After nearly two decades in Kentucky, he moved his family northwest across the Ohio River into the Illinois Country in 1796.

The Pulliams first settled at New Design, a community of Virginians located on the bluffs overlooking "American Bottom," a narrow strip of rich Mississippi floodplain running for a hundred miles along the east side of the river, south of its confluence with the Missouri. At American Bottom, French trappers and Jesuits built settlements in the eighteenth century, and there Americans began to settle after their conquest of the Illinois Country during the Revolution. There, in 1797, during an epidemic of what was probably malaria, Mrs. Pulliam died, leaving her oldest daughter, Nancy, to mother the five youngest children, while Robert and two half-grown brothers worked with their father in the fields. Over the next several years, John Pulliam farmed several sites both in Illinois and across the Mississippi in Spanish Missouri before finally settling his family at the outermost frontier of American settlement in Illinois, on Kaskaskia River bottomland ten miles above the Mississippi bluffs. In 1808 he sold his rights to the improvements on this place and followed the frontier of American settlement another ten miles upriver, where he spent the last years of his life operating "Pulliam's Ferry" across the Kaskaskia. Federal land sales did not begin in Illinois until 1815, so when John died in 1812 he had not secured title to the land he farmed along the river. It is likely, in fact, that John Pulliam had spent his whole life farming without ever owning land.

Raised on the frontier, and often in transit, John Pulliam's oldest son, Robert, was no stranger to moving. The boy never attended school, never learned to read or write (although he did master his signature). "The circumstances of his life prevented his obtaining an education from books," his neighbor John Reynolds wrote. Instead, his "natural good sense" was trained in woodlore and weather sign, in the oral traditions of song and story, in the ways of backwoods farming, herding, hunting, and the ways of squeezing a small cash income from a subsistence economy. Addicted to the "rude sports of the time"—wrestling, animal baiting, and horse racing—young Pulliam achieved a wide reputation as a "pretty considerable" drinker and gambler. Along the banks of the Mississippi, folks told the tale of the time Pulliam won a two hundred-dollar bet by beating a bragging Missourian in a reckless horse race run on the frozen surface of the great river.

When Robert left home for the first time at the age of twenty-six, he headed for the frontier, just as his father had. In the spring of 1804, not far from the base camp of the cross-continental expedition then being mounted by Merriwether Lewis and William Clark, Robert staked a claim along Wood River, a stream that feeds the Mississippi across from the mouth of the Missouri. In the American settlement there he met, courted, and wed Mary Stout, daughter of another frontier family. For the next twelve years Robert and Mary Pulliam squatted on the bluffs overlooking the confluence of the Missouri and Mississippi rivers, where they farmed, herded cattle, and raised three daughters and two sons.

Life on the frontier was pretty rugged. Local game, a patch or two of Indian corn and a few other vegetables, and a few hogs running wild in the woods living off the acorn and hickory nut mast supplied the family's subsistence. The nearest government authority was fifty miles south; the nearest mills, stores, and craftsmen were better than a day's ride away. In 1808, while on a hunting trip, Pulliam seriously injured his leg, and by the time he got to Cahokia, on American Bottom, it was so badly infected that his only hope was amputation. "The patient possessed such courage that he held his body as firm as a rock without assistance,"wrote John Reynolds, who watched as an army surgeon sawed through the bone, with no more anesthetic to ease the poor man's pain than liberal doses of corn liquor. Robert Pulliam's pegleg stood as a lifetime symbol of frontier isolation.

There were other dangers in Wood River. Kickapoo Indians had been coming to the area for many years to garden, gather, and hunt. In 1804 explorer William Clark noted a camp of Kickapoo on the Illinois side of the Mississippi, not five miles from Wood River, and just before he and Clark set out with their exploring party, a Kickapoo tribal band paid a visit to their base camp. When Americans moved into the area, settlers and Kickapoo contended for the same ground, and the resulting violence continued for the next twelve years, finally culminating in the struggle for the possession of Illinois during the War of 1812. In

1814, as part of that war, the Kickapoo murdered and scalped Mrs. Reason Reagan and six children as they were walking through the timber one sunny Sunday afternoon, just a mile from the Pulliam farm. Pulliam's son Martin, seven years old at the time, remembered hearing settlers' terrifying tales of American women tomahawked as they were making soap in their farmyards, and their screaming babies hurled into the boiling kettles by the Indians.

After the war the United States opened a land office at Edwardsville, county seat of newly established Madison County, and began the public sale of Wood River lands. But Pulliam did not buy land in Wood River. In 1816, after the crops were in, he and his family moved back to where his relations were at the Kaskaskia ferry, where he bought a small herd of American Bottom cattle. Settlers of American Bottom had raised cattle for over half a century, and herders frequently preceded farmers, exploring new areas with their cattle and searching for a free winter feed and a possible place for new settlement. Pulliam's 1817 reconnoiter of the possibilities one hundred miles north on Sugar Creek was part of a family and social pattern, a move to the frontier to stake out new lands ahead of the surveyors and land officers.

In the historic lore of Sangamon County, however, Robert Pulliam became something more than simply a typical frontiersman. At the first gathering of the Old Settlers' Society, held in October 1859 on the site of Pulliam's Sugar Creek homestead, James H. Matheny, a successful attorney, the best man at Abraham Lincoln's wedding, and a recently defeated candidate for Congress on the new Republican party ticket, described the pioneer of Sugar Creek as a latter-day Moses.

> Forty-two years ago the stillness of the unbroken forest was startled by the clangor of an axe in a strong man's hands. That day he had rested from a weary journey, but as he stood and gazed upon the beauty of the strange wild scene about him, there arose a longing in his heart to linger here. With that class of men to whom he belonged, to decide was to act. Soon his weary team was loosened from their heavy load, . . . his axe rung out, wild and clear, and some brave old tree that had stood the storms of a hundred years, crashed headlong to the earth. We do not know whether in that stilly hour, when all alone with nature and nature's God, he formally kneeled down upon the green earth and offered up a prayer for protection through the lonely hours of that first night in the strange land to which he had come, but we feel sure that there must have been in his heart a calm and unshaken trust that the guardian care of a kind Providence was around about him, to shield and protect him from every harm. This was a singularly marked characteristic of the early pioneers of the West. They had "faith in God"—an unswerving trust in His Providence . . . , an abiding faith that a kind Father is ever guarding, with a sleepless watchfulness, the welfare of his wandering children.

Matheny invoked the "God-is-on-our-side" sentiments that American politicians and pioneers have traditionally used to justify their move into other peoples' territories since the time of the Pilgrim fathers:

> We have a howling wilderness
> To Canaan's happy shore,
> A land of dearth and pits and snares
> Where chilling winds do roar.
>
> But Jesus will be with us,
> And guard us by the way;
> Though enemies examine us,
> He'll teach us what to say.

Matheny assigned Pulliam the part of discoverer and founder, forging alone into the howling wilderness of central Illinois, beckoning the chosen people to follow him and begin the course of history.

Matheny's version of the American past ignored the context and the setting for Pulliam's actions, substituting for them a mythic mission that lay outside the scope of temporal events. He ignored the Indian past, transforming everything that preceded Pulliam into natural history. Yet by setting out with his herds like some ancient patriarch, Pulliam acted with apparent knowledge of good grazing to the north. In packing the heavy kettles and other equipment necessary for sugaring, he seemed to anticipate the existence of a substantial stand of maple. These clues suggest that this trailblazer followed a well-marked path to the San-gam-ma Country (as Americans called the fertile land of central Illinois in the first decades of the nineteenth century,) a trail laid out by more than a century of human occupancy and history. The peg-legged pioneer of Sugar Creek played but one role in a panorama of thousands—Indian and American, female and male— who made history. Robert Pulliam depended on the Indians and Europeans who came before him, and the timing of his exploration places the pioneer of Sugar Creek at the culminating point of a decades-long struggle for American control of these Indian lands.

* * *

The American settlement of the San-gam-ma began in earnest in spring of 1818, three years before the surveyor Langham arrived. In meandering lines that at a distance must have looked very similar to the straggling bands of Kickapoo families moving west at the same moment, American families advanced north from Wood River, building cabins and breaking soil along the timbered rivers and creeks. Some carried their "truck and plunder" in wagons, but more used carts; some rode, but most walked. Theirs was a motley parade. One

Kentucky woman rode north on a mount to which she had lashed the family featherbed, with her babe in arms and leading another horse loaded unmercifully with household goods and farm implements; her husband walked ahead with their boy astride his shoulders. By 1819 approximately two hundred families had settled above the line of survey in Madison County, some as far north as the Sangamon River.

The first report of settlement along Sugar Creek itself, dated August 1819, was written by a German traveler, Ferdinand Ernst, who came up Edward's Trace to visit the San-gam-ma Country and explore the site of Kickapoo Town. Riding north along the east side of Sugar Creek timber, he found a newly arrived family building a log cabin, and three miles north of there he spent the night at an excellent spring where three other families had built huts and planted crops. The speed with which these pioneers had set about transforming the vista startled Ernst: "they have only broken up the sod with the plow and planted their corn, and now one sees these splendid fields covered almost without exception with corn from ten to 15 feet high." The maple groves of the San-gam-ma, Ernst noted, "gave those people the most promising prospect of a harvest of sugar." The German counted sixty families laying out farms along the timber margin from the source of the creek to its mouth on the Sangamon River and marveled at the number of "venturesome daredevils" who had risked coming north to this "beautiful land" even before the Kickapoo had ceded their proprietorship at Edwardsville. Now that Indian title was extinguished, he wondered, "how many will migrate hither, since everything is quiet and safe here!"

Only two years later, in 1821, the young geologist and ethnologist Henry Rowe Schoolcraft, coasting down the Illinois on a journey of exploration, heard such praise for the San-gam-ma among his boatmen that he pronounced it "a district almost proverbial for its fertility, and fast rising into importance." That same year, when surveyor Langham found forty-three households along upper Sugar Creek, the population of central Illinois was estimated at five thousand, and the state laid off a huge territory, from Sugar Creek on the south to Peoria on the north, as "Sangamo County," establishing a county seat at "Spring-field" on Spring Creek, south of the river, in the settlement of the populous Kelly family. During the fall of 1825, according to one report, each month over two hundred and fifty wagons, each carrying an average of five persons, rolled through southern Illinois headed for the Sangamo Country. By decade's end, although the county had been pared to about half its original size, it contained over 2,000 households and thirteen thousand residents, including 113 households filled with nearly nine hundred people along the upper creek. In 1840 the number of Sugar Creek households reached 134, the community's population nearly one thousand.

Three-quarters of the heads of household who immigrated before

1840 came directly from homes in Kentucky, Tennessee, or the up-country of Virginia and the Carolinas. Fewer than one in ten came from a state north of the Mason-Dixon line. The balance removed from southern Ohio, Indiana, or Illinois, but most of these men had lived north of the Ohio for only a few years. Nine in ten heads of settling families were born in the South—four in Virginia, three in Kentucky, two in the Carolinas. Farm wives were also southerners, the majority born in Kentucky.

Throughout central Illinois the great majority of residents before the Civil War were, in the jargon of the day, "white folks" from the South. "Our neighbors," New Englander Lucy Maynard wrote home from central Illinois, "are principally from Indiana and Kentucky, some from Virginia, all friendly but very different from our people in their manners and language and every other way." "They think," she noted, "that a boiled dish as we boil it is not fit to eat; it is true they boil their food, but each separate. It won't do to boil cabbage or turnips or beets, carrots or parsnips with their meat nor potatoes without pairing and the water that the meat is boiled in must be all boiled down so that there is nothing left but the fat and a very little of the water and that is taken up on the dish with the meat and answers for gravy." But despite the Southern distaste for the boiled dinners that Mrs. Maynard persisted in setting on her table, the goodwife found her neighbors a "very likely people."

"You would be diverted indeed, Julia, if you were to hear some of their uncouth and vulgar expressions," Sarah Aiken, another "Yankee," wrote home to New York about her Southern neighbors. A settler *toted* his *truck and plunder* to *Elanoy* with his *old woman* by his side, where, he *allowed*, they stood a *right smart chance* to break a *scrumptious* farm. He *reckoned* the time of day by the sun: *long before day, good light, about sun-up*, and, after rising, one, two, three hours *by sun*, and so on until *dinnertime*, when after working *tarnation* hard, he sat down to consume *a heap o'vittles*. He counted his afternoon labor four hours by sun, three, two, one, until sundown, followed by *early candlelightin'* an hour or so before *turnin' in*. To this farmer a large sum of money was *filthy lucre*, while the denominations commonly found in his purse consisted of *shillings* and *bits*. Much of this language harkened back to the vernacular speech of seventeenth-and eighteenth-century British colonists. "It really seems to me," Sarah Aiken concluded, "that I must be living the days of our forefathers over again." Commenting on their distinctive speech and customs, visiting Englishman William Oliver wrote that these Southern emigrants were "decent people of simple manners," as unlike Yankees "as if they were of different nations."

What lay behind this massive out-migration from the South? Many emigrants later suggested that opposition to slavery was an important factor in their decision to move north of the Ohio River. Sugar Creek settler James Wallace, born and raised in the backwoods of South Carolina in the era of the American Revolution, left home to seek his fortune as a young man and lived for some years in the Northeast, where he married, had twin sons, and accumulated some savings before he returned, expecting to settle near the family farm. But, according to Wallace family tradition, after "having lived where all men were free," Wallace found himself overcome by the feeling that slavery was "the sum of all villanies," so he and his brother George determined to move their families north. The Wallace clan arrived in Sugar Creek in 1822. Peter Cartwright, a Methodist lay preacher from western Tennessee and later a famous circuit rider in central Illinois, wrote in his autobiography that in part he moved to "carry the Gospel to destitute souls that had, by their removal into some new country, been deprived of the means of grace." But antislavery attitudes also propelled him; in a free state, he thought, "I would get entirely clear of the evil of slavery," "could raise my children to work where work was not thought a degradation," and "could better my temporal circumstances and procure lands for my children as they grew up." In 1824, the year Cartwright brought his family, Illinois voters rejected a referendum to permit slavery in the state by the relatively narrow margin of some seventeen hundred votes out of twelve thousand cast; Sangamo County voters like Wallace and Cartwright, however, overwhelmingly rejected the referendum by nearly five to one.

As Cartwright's comments suggested, emigrant antislavery sentiment had less to do with concern for Afro-Americans than with fears of the debasing effects of slavery on free white farmers. Simon O'Ferrall, a British traveler in the West in 1830, wrote that "during our journeys across Illinois, we passed several large bodies of settlers on their way to Sangamo and Morgan counties in that state. The mass of those persons were Georgians, Virginians, and Kentuckians, whose comparative poverty rendered their residence in slave states unpleasant." Despite the hatred of slavery among his southern Illinois neighbors, however, John Woods found that they had retained "many of the prejudices imbibed in infancy, and still hold negroes in the utmost contempt; not allowing them to be of the same species of themselves, but look on *negers,* as they call them, and Indians, as an inferior race of beings, and treat them as such." . . .

The objections were to the *system* of slavery, for, as a system, slavery offered a powerful symbol of the negative effects of economic progress in the South. In the eighteenth century the colonial administrators of Pennsylvania, Virginia, and the Carolinas encouraged the frontier settlement of migrant European peoples—principally English, Scotch-Irish, and Germans. These immigrants served two important colonial purposes, military and economic: wresting the frontier from the Indians and establishing a buffer to protect coastal populations from possible native attacks while at the same time inaugurating agricultural development. Then, as tidewater farmers, planters, and merchants prospered within the protected colonial seaboard, they expanded their operations inland, in many cases transforming the frontier economy from Indian trading and subsistence farming to slave-based, commodity-producing agriculture. In the interior South, one of the best indicators of the development of agriculture was the increasing Afro-American proportion of the population and the increasing proportion of household heads who owned slaves. Through this transition, some farmers prospered and became masters, others were less successful but found a niche as yeomen farmers amid the slave system; but over time the majority of residents chose to move, to extend the frontier, to begin the settlement process again. Farmers who felt constrained by the pressures of economic development, then, had to look no further than the slave for a potent symbol of what was forcing them out.

By the last quarter of the eighteenth century, when the squeeze of economic development began to press on backcountry communities in Virginia and Carolina, trans-Appalachia became a refuge. But as the history of Kentucky and Tennessee demonstrates, pioneers did not necessarily win title there either. By the end of the century, the development of the trans-Appalachian West forced thousands of families, unable to buy their farms, off the lands they had broken. Beginning the process again, these thousands "removed" to the next frontier. After Indian resistance ended in the Mississippi Valley in 1815, from Pennsylvania and Virginia, Kentucky and Tennesse, thousands of families poured into Alabama, Missouri, and Illinois, where, as English immigrant George Flower wrote, there was "good land dog-cheap everywhere, and for nothing, if you will go far enough for it." Contemporaries christened this mass movement "The Great Migration." Baptist preacher and educator John Mason Peck watched the procession of men and women from his southern Illinois porch and fancied that "Kentucky and Tennessee were breaking up and moving to the 'Far West.'"

Over half of the Sugar Creek emigrants before 1840 came directly from the Green River Country, several counties between the Green and Cumberland rivers in the southwestern part of Kentucky. Speculators and commodity farmers in Kentucky had originally considered this area a "barrens," both because of its sandy soil and its distance from market, concentrating their attention on the rich Bluegrass region near Lexington, where a plantation and horse-breeding economy quickly took root, leaving the Green River Country to hundreds of small farmers, particular Revolutionary War veterans who held land bounties entitling them to small plots. But as commodity agriculture expanded its operations, speculators moved into Green River Country, bidding up land prices, and yeoman farmers began to experience a familiar difficulty in securing title. Beginning in the 1790s and extending through the first several decades of the nineteenth century, the Green River Country exported thousands of farming families to Missouri and Illinois.

"Many of our neighbors are true backwoodsmen, always fond of moving," John Woods noted of his fellow southern Illinois farmers in 1820, and now some "wish to sell their land, with its improvements, to go to the Sangamond [sic] river, 150 miles towards the north-west." Among these "extensive travelers," he wrote, "to have resided in three or four states, and several places in each state, is not uncommon." Like Robert Pulliam, a number of Sugar Creek settlers were prodigious movers. Samuel and Isaac Vancil, for instance, were born in the 1760s into a German immigrant family in Lancaster County, Pennsylvania, and after the Revolution moved with their parents from that hearth of pioneers into Virginia, where in the 1790s they both married and began families. By 1800 the brothers and their growing kinship group were living in Kentucky; by 1811 in Ohio near Cincinnati; and, after a few more years, across the state boundary in Warren County, Indiana. When the Vancils came to the Sangamo in 1818, it was the eighth "remove" for them. Before settling in Sugar Creek, eight in ten heads of Sugar Creek households had made at least one interstate move, and 35 percent moved two or more times.

Patterns of family migration greatly affected the development of the Sugar Creek community. While communities in early-nineteenth-century New England were characterized by dicennial persistence rates of 50 to 60 percent of households, communities in the American West experienced rates of 30 percent or less. Sugar Creek was no exception to this western pattern. At least two-thirds of heads of household moved elsewhere during the course of each decade. The presence of surnames not found on the federal enumerations in Sugar Creek poll books, militia rolls, and local lists of roadwork crews, suggests that numerous other families came and departed between the dicennial census counts. Some of these families may have pushed further westward; others, defeated in the struggle against the wilderness, may have returned to their communities of origin. Transience was an important fact of life in Sugar Creek.

Historians of the American frontier generally emphasize the legacy of the settlers who followed what George Flower called "the old hunter's rule": "when you hear the sound of a neighbor's gun, it is time to move away." Frederick Jackson Turner, the influential historian of the American frontier, wrote that patterns of migration offered Americans "a gate of escape from the bondage of the past." "The advance of the frontier," Turner wrote, "has meant a steady growth of independence on American lines. And to study this advance, the men who grew up under these conditions and the political, economic and social results of it, is to study the really American part of our history." In Turner's judgment, the process of migration and resettlement, and the cultural attitudes and character they engendered, were peculiarly American, dramatically contrasting with the conservatism and persistence of traditional European societies.

Most early-nineteenth-century contemporaries, however, did not celebrate but feared such mobility; transience, they believed, encouraged backsliding into a lower social state. "This line of frontiersmen," wrote Englishman William Strickland, "affords the singular spectacle of a race, seeking and voluntarily sinking into barbarism, out of a state of civilized life." Yale clergyman Timothy Dwight lamented in 1819 that the pioneers, "impatient of the restraints of law, religion, and morality," were "too idle, too talkative, too passionate, too prodigal, and too shiftless to acquire either property or character."

Such fears had a long history. In the 1730s, planter William Byrd railed against hordes of Scotch-Irish pioneers flooding into southern Virginia "like the Goths and Vandals of old." Forty years later, British conservative Edmund Burke argued in Parliament that colonial authorities must encourage settlement in "fixed establishments" with "the ruling power" near at hand to encourage frontiersmen "to believe in the mysterious virtue of wax and parchment." Otherwise, he warned, the backwoodsmen "would wander without a possibility of restraint" and soon "would become hordes of English Tartars." Forty years later, according to Timothy Flint, a Yankee transplanted to the Ohio Valley, Burke's fears had materialized. "Everything shifts under your eye," he despaired; "the present occupants sell, pack, depart. Strangers replace them. Before they have gained the confidence of their neighbors, they hear of a better place, pack up, and follow their precursors. This circumstance adds to the instability of connexions." "The general inclination here," concluded Flint, "is too much like that of the Tartars."

By the time these critics were employing the labels "Vandals" and "Tartars," the words had come to refer not only to the Germanic and Mongol hordes of history but to contemporary vagabonds, thieves, and shiftless persons as well. With its connotations of violence and barbarism, this was a language of condemnation. But for pure evocation their language is preferable to Turner's, for whereas his sought to isolate the pioneer experience as unique and exceptional, theirs linked frontier settlement with the tradition of folk migration. Despite the obvious differences between Tartarian tribes and Americans, most successful folk migrations have been conducted by populations armed and organized to dispossess the native inhabitants. In this regard, the historian William H. MacNeill explicitly compares such otherwise disparate peoples and argues that "the American frontier was merely an extreme case of contact and collision between societies at different levels of skill—a pattern that runs throughout recorded history and constitutes one of the main themes of the human past."

Although during their periods of migration the Vandals and the Tartars—like the Celts, Angles, Saxons, and Normans—could be described as transient peoples, they soon turned to farming and settled in permanent communities. Likewise, though mobility played an important role in shaping the character of American society, and despite the regular "turnover" in the population of the creek, a stable community soon developed amid the timber and the prairie. The history of Sugar Creek is part of the history of folk migrations, the story both of a transient majority, the people called "movers" by contemporaries, and those men and women who persisted in the area and put down roots.

C A R O L   S H E R I F F

CAROL SHERIFF (1964–   ) is assistant professor of history at the College of William and Mary. She is the author of The Artificial River *(1996), winner of the New York State Historical Association Prize.*

The Erie Canal was a public enterprise, an unabashed effort at state-controlled economic development. After both the federal government and neighboring states rejected New York's requests for financial assistance, the state had taken sole responsibility for funding, constructing, and operating its artificial river. New York also undertook several additional canal projects in the years after 1825. Following the completion of the main Canal, the state constructed small channels linking land-bound communities to the main waterway; built the eight lateral canals running north or south from the Erie; and enlarged and rerouted the Erie Canal itself. More canal digging took place after the opening of the Erie Canal than before.

While a wide variety of New Yorkers joined in celebrating the Canal's accomplishments, many of them also knew from personal ex-

---

"The Politics of Land and Water" revised for publication from *The Artificial River: The Erie Canal and the Paradox of Progress, 1817–1862,* by Carol Sheriff. Copyright © by Carol Sheriff.

perience that the business of creating and then enlarging a canal might damage a property owner's land or buildings in a number of ways. Before laborers had even picked up their axes and shovels, the state legislature had taken for public use a strip of private property extending across the width of the state. Where the government did not receive outright property grants along the route, it appropriated land—without always paying for it. An important piece of canal legislation did require the state to compensate individuals for any appropriation of private property. But, in keeping with a general trend in legal reasoning across the country, that piece of legislation provided that if the state's appraisers deemed that the benefit a landowner would receive from proximity to the Canal outweighed the value of the land appropriated, then the state did not owe the proprietor any financial compensation.

Land had become a commodity whose value could be measured in terms of relative market value. The appropriation of farmland clearly constituted an "injury." But the Canal also increased the value of the owner's remaining contiguous property, conferring a certain "benefit." If, to take a typical case, an appropriated piece of a farm bordered on the site of a canal lock, where grocery stores and other businesses would thrive from the congregation of boats at that spot, then the appraisers usually argued that the increased value of the owner's remaining land was greater than the injury caused to the owner by the appropriation. Given that many farmers in the Mohawk Valley already feared that their relative market advantage would decline once the Canal provided easy access to less expensive western lands, these New Yorkers did not always accept the state's arguments that access to the waterway would compensate them for the loss of their property. . . .

The possibility of owning land, as we have seen, is what lured such large numbers of people to the upstate region in the first place; property offered economic security as well as political rights and social status. Few upstate farmers could afford to buy land outright, but rather gradually paid off their mortgages by selling produce on the market. By necessity, if not choice, these farmers' immediate aspirations were modest. They first had to clear their land—an arduous and labor-intensive task. The simplest way to remove trees was girdling, which meant killing a tree by cutting deep notches around its trunk with an ax. A few weeks later, the trees would lose their leaves, allowing sun to shine through on what would become fields. As soon as enough light shone through the remaining limbs, settlers would plant wheat or corn to feed their families for their first year on the frontier. After chopping down the trees during the off season, farmers planted their crops around the stumps. Thus, the average farm family could clear only between five and ten acres per year, depending on the number of family members who could girdle trunks, chop limbs, burn leaves and stumps, rake ashes, pull up roots, and remove rocks. With so much of

their time and energy invested in their land, modest farmers understandably resented the ways in which the state's improvements damaged their property. . . .

Settlers who bought land after the Canal's route had been laid out
believed that the value of their property lay in a combination of its
productive worth and its proximity to markets. The closer a piece of
land was to the Canal, the simpler it was to reach markets. As Cadwal-
lader Colden noted in his official memoir of the Erie's construction,
"Now, that the Canals are open, the distance from market may be almost computed by the distance from the Canal, or the distance from
the water communications with it . . ." Land along the waterway's
route fetched a higher selling price. When farm families decided to
move to western New York in the years after 1817, they calculated
whether the expense of land along the waterway would be balanced by
the benefits they would derive from such proximity. Because these
farmers often knew where the Canal would flow before they began
clearing their land, they planned their improvements to the land to
avoid or minimize construction damage. As a result, few of these property holders petitioned the state for compensation for damaged land.

Instead they argued that the state had the obligation to help them
take advantage of fresh opportunities the Canal had opened. Such arguments commonly emerged in requests for use of so-called surplus
water, water that state workers released from the Canal to prevent an
excess from weakening the banks. In 1825, the legislature passed a law
permitting canal officials to lease the right to these waters to private
concerns. When in 1827 inhabitants of the Genesee region petitioned
the Canal Board to channel such surplus water to the village of Holley,
where they would establish mills, they argued that such a policy
would benefit the population's struggling new settlers. "When it is remembered that most of the inhabitants . . . are new settlers & with
very few exceptions yet indebted for their land that a majority of them
are indeed, & in truth *poor* . . . ," the farmers of Holley remonstrated,
"it must be obvious that those severe privations & expences incident
to their remote situation from Mills necessarily come home to them
with superadded calamity." Without water to propel a mill near their
farms, the petition continued, settlers would have to rely on "a more
fortunate neighbor"—one with a wagon team or riverboat—to trans-
port their wheat to mills. If the state granted surplus water rights to
the town of Holley, it would allow these poor farmers to realize their
property's productive worth while relieving them of any dependence
on wealthier neighbors.

Poor people were not alone in thinking that the state had an obligation to foster their prosperity. In 1831, a group of prosperous farmers
insisted that the state build a lock that would allow them to move
their produce around a dam blocking their easy access to the Canal. . . .

Whether "poor" or "large"—and whether they measured their losses in terms of the productive or the market value of their property—farmers thought it reasonable to expect the state to promote their private economic interests.

Although New Yorkers regularly filed petitions with the Canal Board to serve their private interests, farmers (modest and substantial) tried to bolster their arguments by telling state officials that their own interests coincided with the public good. From the Canal's inception, its promoters had referred to its promised impact on the public welfare, a central component of both republican and liberal approaches to political economy. Perhaps remembering that the Canal corridor had been touted as a sort of middle landscape between the extremes of civilization and savagery, New Yorkers sometimes argued that the state should use its regulatory powers to shield the public from some of the potentially harmful forces of the expanding commercial world. Some of them accordingly asked the state to intercede to prevent the excesses of unfettered market competition as well as the contamination of nature.

Antebellum Americans generally feared that market expansion would intensify class stratification. . . . In trying to convince the Canal Board to adopt their own preferred policies, people of modest circumstances often made appeals based on what they articulated as the government's obligation to control the greedy intentions of wealthier members of society.

The Genesee farmers who petitioned for surplus water rights, for example, tried to bolster their case by pointing out that without the state's intervention they would be deprived of equal access to economic opportunity. When the villagers traveled to distant mills, they explained, they were often "compelled to return without their grist, those mills being in most cases too exclusively *Merchant* mills to perform *custom* work promptly . . ." Merchant mills ground large quantities of grain for their customers; they would not stop a well-paying job to grind a farmer's small load of wheat while he waited. By granting water power at Holley and thus allowing its residents to construct their own mills, the petitioners argued, the state would be acting both with equity and with the public interest in mind:

> far greater difficulties . . . have not deterred your Honorable Board from *controlling* & *dispensing* the surplus waters at all other points upon the canal, in such a manner as best to promote *public revenue* & the *greatest amount of accommodation* to the *inhabitants*, without regard to *individual cupidity*, or *sectional influence*.

While the market's invisible hand favored merchant grinding and "cupidity" on the part of commercial millowners, the petitioners demanded that the state intervene to protect its citizens' access to family grinding by channeling water to Holley; this, in turn, would promote the common good in at least two ways. Since residents paid the state for access to surplus water, the citizens of Holley would be contributing to the "public revenue." And because that water would serve more people, and less selfish ones, it would contribute to an abstract sense of good as well. . . .

By the mid-1830s, the landscape of upstate New York barely resembled its earlier appearance, complicating the state's efforts to promote internal improvements. Largely because of the influences of the Erie Canal, New York was now the Empire State. With each passing year, more and more western produce flowed through central New York on its way to the Hudson, helping to make New York City the nation's leading port. The western section of the state had been transformed into a thriving commercial and manufacturing corridor, with its population already more thickly settled than that of the Mohawk Valley. The waterway nurtured several of the state's largest cities, in areas that had been swamps or woodlands just decades earlier. Warehouses and mills dotted the Canal's banks, and wheat sprouted where formerly pine needles had collected on the forest floor.

This prosperity signaled the transformation of the "wilderness" into "civilization," and New Yorkers still had reasons to believe that they could avoid some of the corruption of older civilizations. Theirs seemed to be a land of social mobility, where a resident of Rochester could exclaim, "The Labourer feels himself as independent as the Esqr. we bow our heads to Nothing nor Nobody excepting the Lord above & the canal bridges as we pass under." Most white men could continue to aspire to economic independence as well, by mustering the cash either to purchase land or to become a workshop master.

With so many visible signs of progress, many New Yorkers actively campaigned to make the Erie Canal bigger and, they hoped, even better. In 1835, the state passed the Enlargement Bill, designed to widen the waterway to seventy feet from forty feet and to deepen it to seven feet from four feet (a tripling of volume.) By allowing larger boats to travel the waterway, the new construction would cut transportation costs even further by taking advantage of the economies of scale. It would allow farmers to market their produce more competitively while also decreasing the price of luxury goods imported from the East. Few farmers objected in theory to an enlarged Canal, though they certainly hoped the waterway could be widened without damaging their own buildings and land—property whose market value had increased along with the Canal's success. . . .

Upstate farmers' active participation in market-oriented production enmeshed them in a complex economic web that made international economic crises reverberate on even the most local level. A waterway that brought exotic goods to the hinterlands also created interdependent credit relationships among a vast network of economic actors. When financial panics hit the country in 1834, 1837, and again in 1839, they exploded New Yorkers' notions of inevitable economic growth. Shortages of cash almost halted business activity, casting many farmers back into debt and bankrupting others. When international merchants did not have cash to pay the forwarding merchant, that entrepreneur could not pay the local merchant, who, in turn, could not buy the farmers' apples. Everyone from farmers to speculators began to realize that economic mobility could move downward as well as upward.

Property owners feared slipping down the social ladder, a fear that the enlargement project exacerbated. While before they had snatched glimpses of what lay below them, now they looked more closely at where they could possibly land—and they did not like what they saw. By 1840, more—not fewer—New Yorkers worked for other people, and the Canal corridor provided tangible and daily reminders of this shift. With the start of the enlargement project, construction workers again overran the landscape, and this time they were more visible. Whereas much of the original construction had taken place in wilderness, the work on the enlargement was centered in heavily populated areas. And unlike the previous generation of canal diggers, this later group occasionally joined together to strike for higher wages, reminding residents of the class strife that Americans feared would accompany economic growth. If in the 1820s property owners believed that wage laborers would disappear once construction came to an end, by the 1830s they had too much evidence to the contrary.

Not only did businessmen set up large manufacturing and milling establishments right along the Canal's banks, but the operation of the waterway itself required the labor of tens of thousands of semiskilled wage earners. The boatmen had replaced the original canal diggers, and they seemed no better fit to become productive members of society than had the construction workers. Worse yet, their numbers promised to increase once the enlargement was completed and began carrying larger boats requiring additional hands. By the late 1830s, it became obvious that—promises of the Canal's sponsors notwithstanding—the artificial waterway had helped bring into being a more divided society, one that even state-funded canal bridges could not mend.

As the state's finances became more strained over time, reaching a true crisis in the early 1840s, residents of the Canal corridor grew increasingly suspicious of the state's ability to satisfactorily reconcile competing claims to its resources. This shift in popular mood did not arise from doubts about the state's ability to play a useful role in economic development. To the contrary, thousands of New Yorkers continued to petition for lateral canals that would be poor financial investments for the state but that petitioners justified as means to spur local enterprise. People's growing distrust of the state registered instead the fear—especially among Jacksonian Democrats—that scheming interests might too easily corrupt the state for their own selfish ends. If farmers and millers continued to welcome opportunities to participate in an expanded market economy, they came to fear that the state favored commercial over agrarian interests and well-connected politicos over ordinary citizens. . . .

As we have seen, whatever their party affiliation, New Yorkers often used the rhetoric of republicanism when they addressed state officials. Yet by the 1830s the meaning of republicanism had evolved even beyond the ideas articulated by the Canal's sponsors. After 1825, property owners no longer had an exclusive claim on voting rights, thanks to a change in the state constitution. The deference that DeWitt Clinton had extolled had also died; the laborer bowed his head to nobody but God. People still spoke of their republican rights, and they still lauded the common good or public interest. But to many of them, republicanism had come to mean "fairness." "Now I ask the State to build me a Brige," demanded one farmer whose lands had been cut in two by the enlargement. "[I]f they say they will not because it is there rules, I am a Jackson man & Will Try to Git my rites in a free republicking Govrment." More and more farmers began to question whether the government could be trusted to ensure those republican rights, their right—as this same farmer put it—"to have the State deel farly with me." . . .

No one felt more strongly about this issue than the farmers of Dansville in Livingston County. Although the original Canal had bypassed their town altogether, in the late 1830s the state had completed the lateral Genesee Valley Canal, a branch of which ran three-quarters of a mile from the center of their village. For years, the residents of Dansville petitioned first the legislature and then the Canal Board to remedy their lack of access to the lateral waterway. They offered to bear the cost of constructing a channel to that canal if the state would secure them a right-of-way to the land. Adopting the language of Jacksonian Democracy, they argued that the interests of the "many"—*their* interests—should take priority over the interests of the "few." They couched their own interests in terms of the common good. Meanwhile, the "few" had seen opportunity in the villagers' misfortune. Speculators purchased the land that lay between the village and the feeder to the Genesee Valley Canal, hoping that the village would expand toward the canal in order to take full advantage of its trading opportunities. Were that to happen, the market value of property that lay between the town and the canal could be expected to appreciate greatly. In order to protect their investments, these speculators refused to grant a right-of-way through their property, even though the farmers had already dug a slip to within a few hundred yards of the lateral canal.

When the farmers of Dansville brought their claim to the legislature in 1844, the assembly voted in favor of a bill granting them a right-of-way. But the bill did not pass the senate, and so did not become law. As it happened, Senator Faulkner, the state senator from Dansville, owned a portion of the land in question. According to the *Albany Evening Atlas,* he convinced some of his colleagues to vote against the bill and, as a result, the measure lost by a narrow margin. In this case, the farmers of Dansville could not trust even their own representative to avoid the temptations of greed.

The farmers now made their dissatisfaction known through action rather than rhetoric. When the state twice sent workers to fill in the farmers' slip, the villagers drove them away with raised shovels and spades. After the second rebuff, according to the *Atlas,* the farmers "proceeded to aggression, and assembling some three hundred strong, cut through the corner lots of the Senator, and made a union between the canal and their basin and slip." The newspaper labeled the farmers' actions "a riot." When the citizens of Dansville realized that all the rhetoric in the world could not make the state fulfill its mandate to represent what they saw as the common good, they took the law into their own hands. The state might need them to build its artificial river, but *they* did not need the state to build theirs.

Two years after the Dansville riot, the Democratic-controlled legislature issued a 866-page report outlining the frauds that state employees had committed while managing the Canal's construction and maintenance. These deceptions usually involved state employees and contractors charging the government for work they did not perform or could have performed more efficiently. Very much aware of such dishonest deals on the local level (deals that tempted members of all political parties), many New Yorkers submitted lengthy petitions to the Canal Board demanding that the state official in charge of their section of the Canal be dismissed. Evidence of widespread dishonesty, designed to line the pockets of men who had gotten their jobs through political patronage in the first place, only increased farmers' perceptions that the state disregarded their interests in favor of the wealthy and powerful. Many small landowners had come to see the state's failures as moral in nature.

When they pointed to the state's moral failings, most Canal Board petitioners concentrated on what they called violations of the public trust. These New Yorkers' willingness to risk offending the very officials whom they sought to persuade suggests that they may well have believed what they said. Such harsh rhetoric also reflects a more widespread decline in deference-based politics, but even so it is telling that people took the risk of insulting the state officials who most easily wielded immediate, tangible power over their lives. It is one thing to say that a Presidential candidate won office through a "corrupt bargain," as Jackson's supporters accused Adams of doing in 1824. It is quite another issue to insult the person charged with the responsibility of making sure that canal water does not destroy your crops, especially since a certain amount of canal damage was known to result from neglect and even vandalism.

Even if we remain skeptical of the farmers' rhetoric and assume that they chose to couch their claims in moral terms to strengthen their appeals for policies in which they held a self-interest, their rhetoric is nonetheless revealing. Their insistence that the government maintain a certain moral standard in a time of market expansion suggests a great deal about their broader conceptions of the state's obligations to its citizens. Whether or not they genuinely believed their own words, property owners cast their Canal Board claims in logic that they thought state officials would find compelling.

Levinus and Abraham Lansing were among those who used a combination of harsh language and moral reasoning in their attempts to win greater compensation for their damaged land. When the state argued that their land now held increased value as a potential tavern stand, the Lansings retorted that they did not want to open businesses, and surely, they insisted, not businesses profiting from "immorality." Taverns sold alcohol, which was consumed in tremendous amounts by antebellum Americans. Yet in reaction to what one historian has called the "alcoholic republic," other antebellum Americans considered the consumption of alcohol, and certainly its sale, a vice. "At the present day," Levinus Lansing contended, "it seems a libel upon the character of the State to say that a tipling shop is such a benefit to an individual or to a community that the State ought to compel persons to resort to the establishment of such places of immorality & vice to get pay for the land taken from them for the use of the public." While we have no way of knowing whether the Lansings truly believed that taverns were immoral, they did make their claim near the peak of the antebellum temperance campaigns. Either they truly believed that the state should not encourage immoral behavior, or they thought that state officials would be swayed by an appeal to their responsibility to uphold public morality. . . .

Some New Yorkers sensed that the state had violated its mandate not just by favoring the wealthy and well-connected but also by failing to follow through on its more general commitment to use internal improvements to promote its citizens' welfare. Property owners' distrust of the state government increased after the Democrats cut back on canal spending in a process that culminated in the 1842 "Stop and Tax" law. With this law, the legislature halted further work on internal improvements until adequate funds could be raised through taxation to support the work. Under severe financial stress, state officials decided that they could no longer finance internal improvements through loans, as they had done up to this point. Given the burden of the debt, the legislature voted to place property taxes on residents throughout the state to fund improvement projects. In theory, small property owners along the Canal's banks should have welcomed this shift in policy. In their eyes, they had been unduly "taxed" for the Canal all along, and the new law promised to spread the burden more broadly.

While most newspapers in the region endorsed the new policy, believing it necessary to maintain the state's solvency, they did not always speak for those who lived directly on the waterway's banks. These property owners objected not to the "tax" part of the bill but to its "stop" provision. For them, the abrupt stop in improvements caused them to lose additional faith in the state's willingness to meet its obligations to its citizens. Once the state began making changes in the landscape, it needed to carry through on them. If not, then, like Jacob Sanders, these residents would crave to be delivered from public justice, not because they doubted the state's ability to play a beneficial role in the economy but because they had misgivings about its abilities to be just.

Internal improvements were not supposed to disappear as quickly as they had sprung up. From the outset, the Canal's promoters had bragged about the durability and permanence of its structures. And in the intervening decades, the artificial river had in many respects become part of the natural topography. Having already had their property "injured" by the original and enlarged canals, some upstaters now faced new disruptions with the state's financial cutbacks. In 1838, for example, the owner of a grist mill near the Champlain Canal had expended $3,000 on repairs. In the early 1840s, when the canal commissioners removed the dam that fed his mill, he complained that he "was under the impression supported by the opinion of all [my] neighbors, that the big dam would never be abandoned . . ." According to the miller, the state had the obligation to keep the dam in repair to protect his investment as well as those of his neighbors. When millers depending on water from the Fort Miller Dam heard that the state intended to discontinue its use, they argued that "mills would not have been erected . . . if the owners had supposed that the Feeder would have Ever Closed up, by the State . . ." When they made material investments based on the artificial reshaping of the landscape, when they did what the state encouraged them to do by building the Canal, many New Yorkers thought they had struck a bargain with the state.

William Adams had literally done so. Instead of demanding damages for his farmland that the state appropriated for the enlargement project, Adams agreed to give the state the property in exchange for certain improvements to his remaining land. The state had consented to dig a ditch for him and to clean out the canal bed near his property. Rather than living up to his end of the deal, Adams charged, the state engineer intentionally neglected his duties and used the state's weak financial circumstances as an excuse for "this evasive break of . . . agreement on the part of the State [that] has destroyed my property and turned it into a nuisance." The state, Adams continued, "was wrong, rich or poor, so to use my release [of property rights] and I want this corrected. It is my right that it should be." He then argued that the state, as much as any individual, had an obligation to live up to its agreements, regardless of its financial strains. . . .

When property owners initially embraced the artificial changes in the landscape, they thought those changes would themselves be immutable. Instead, from their point of view, the state had continued its triumph over the landscape, now destroying productive agrarian property in favor of mercantile ventures. They began to distrust the state because, in a world of competing interests, the state seemed more often an adversary than an ally.

8

ANTEBELLUM REFORM:
DISCIPLINE OR LIBERATION?

"In the history of the world the doctrine of Reform had never such scope as at the present hour," confided Ralph Waldo Emerson in his journal in 1840 in mock fear.". . . Not a kingdom, town, statute, rite, calling, man, woman, or child, but is threatened by the new spirit."[1] Nothing and no one escaped the reformers' influence.

The reform movements that swept across America during the first half of the nineteenth century took a variety of forms. The most famous was the antislavery crusade, but there were also movements to improve the condition of people afflicted with blindness, intemperance, deafness, insanity, and poverty. Some of these reform movements were intended to help individuals and groups powerless to change their condition; others were even more ambitious, aiming to end war, remake society through utopian communities, establish greater equality between the sexes, and found a free system of universal education.

It is equally difficult to categorize the ideologies of the reformers. Some saw social evils arising out of improvident and immoral behavior on the part of the individual. Others believed that an imperfect environment was at fault and that a meaningful solution to the problem at hand involved structural changes in American society. Some viewed reform as diminishing class rivalries and antagonisms, thereby preserving a fundamentally good and moral social order; others saw reform in more radical terms and urged fundamental changes in the structure of society. Similarly, there was little agreement about the use of the state to effect reform; some regarded state intervention as an absolute necessity while others felt that reform efforts should be confined to private endeavors.

Although reform movements were heterogeneous in nature, there were a few themes common to them all. The reformers were optimists. In their eyes no problem was so difficult that it could not be solved; no evil was so extreme as to be ineradicable; no person was so sinful as to be unredeemable. Second, an extraordinarily large number

---

[1] *The Journals and Miscellaneous Notebooks of Ralph Waldo Emerson*, 16 vols. to date (Cambridge, Mass., 1960–82), Vol. 7, p. 403. This quotation was later incorporated into Emerson's essay entitled "Man the Reformer."

of them had been influenced by the revivals of the Second Great Awakening. Although uninterested in and even hostile to dispute about fine points of belief, most were evangelical Christians motivated by a firm sense of responsibility to God for their fellow man. Third, most reformers believed that science and reason complemented rather than contradicted religious faith. Indeed, reason and science provided the means of fulfilling the moral and religious obligations that bound all individuals. Finally, most reformers recognized the complexity and interdependency of society. Consequently, they were frequently involved in more than one type of reform. Horace Mann, for example, first came to national attention as a crusader on behalf of the mentally ill. But he turned later to educational reform partly out of his conviction that the evils and diseases that manifested themselves in later life could be minimized or prevented by proper education. Mann, like most activists, recognized that a multifaceted attack on existing evils was indispensable for social betterment.

The intended beneficiaries of reform, it should be noted, included a disproportionately high percentage of poor and helpless. Slaves, for example, needed allies to bring about their own liberation. The mentally ill, orphans, drunkards, and convicts could not agitate for the establishment or improvement of institutions that would benefit them. At the same time, reformers had to have both time and a sufficient income to pursue social activism. Reform movements, therefore, drew much of their inspiration and personnel from the ranks of the middle class and the well-to-do.

Reformers found it difficult to deal with an individual problem without bringing under scrutiny broader institutional structures. As a result, reformers typically developed moral judgments about the basic arrangements of American society, judgments certain to engender conflict.

Just as Americans between 1800 and 1860 argued and fought over various visions of what constituted a just and moral society, so historians have argued over the nature, sources, and intentions of reformers. The result has been a multiplicity of interpretations of the many reform movements that developed during the first half of the nineteenth century, interpretations that were likely to reflect the personal values of the historians writing about the problem. Viewing reform without evaluating its moral goals is a fairly recent development.

The first generations of students of reform were Progressives who looked on it favorably. Abolitionists were the exception. At the turn of the century, when Ulrich Phillips's view of slavery as benign prevailed, historians saw abolitionists as fanatics and agreed with antebellum southerners that they stirred up the Civil War needlessly. This view prevailed until racial prejudice began to erode. With the civil rights movement and the advent of social history and New Left scholarship, historians looked much more favorably on the abolitionists, but more critically upon reform as a whole, which some scholars saw as ineffective and failing to challenge the real problems of advancing capitalism, and others saw as efforts by the middle class to control the lower class. In 1975, David Brion Davis, influenced by the New Left, altered the study of reform dramatically by pointing out the ways in which abolitionism helped to solidify the ideology supporting the advent of capitalism. At about the same time, women's history and black history began to explore reform in new ways. The result has been continuing innovation in a field that seemed deadlocked in the 1970s.

Scholars who tended to interpret the past in terms of a struggle between the mass of people on the one hand and selfish special interests on the other have dominated the writing of American history in the twentieth century. It was not surprising, therefore, that they held reformers and reform movements in high esteem. "In that time, if ever in American history," wrote Alice F. Tyler in her comprehensive study of antebellum reform, "the spirit of man seemed free and the individual could assert his independence of choice in matters of faith and theory. . . . The idea of progress . . . was at the same time a challenge to traditional beliefs and institutions and an impetus to experimentation with new theories and humanitarian reforms."[2] The origins of reform, she argued, were to be found in the interaction of Enlightenment rationalism, religious revivalism, transcendentalism, and the democratization of society that resulted from the frontier experience.

Despite their generally liberal views, Progressive scholars differed over the nature and origin of early-nineteenth-century reform. Arthur E. Bestor, Jr., for example, insisted that the communitarian movement of this era was a unique historical event. Unlike Tyler, he did not trace the origins of the communitarian experiments to a frontier experience, nor did he perceive a shared tradition binding together reformers in different eras of American history. Instead, he compared the task for these activists with that of Progressive Era reformers who had to alter already established institutions. In the antebellum period, he argued, most Americans believed in the plasticity of institutions—hence the frequent formation of model communities seeking to revolutionize American society.[3]

Although most accounts were favorably disposed toward antebellum reform, they were often critical of specific movements. The temperance crusade, they believed was led by narrow-minded and bigoted

[2]Alice Felt Tyler, *Freedom's Ferment: Phases of American Social History from the Colonial Period to the Outbreak of the Civil War* (Minneapolis, 1944), p. 1.

[3]Arthur E. Bestor, Jr., "Patent-Office Models of the Good Society: Some Relationships Between Social Reform and Westward Expansion," *American Historical Review*, 58 (April 1953): 505–26. See also Bestor's *Backwoods Utopias: The Sectarian and Owenite Phases of Communitarian Socialism in America, 1663–1829* (Philadelphia, 1950).

individuals seeking to impose their own moral code upon the rest of the people. Indeed, Tyler, in her generally sympathetic survey of reform, noted that in back of the temperance crusade "lay the danger, ever present in a democracy, of the infringement by a majority of the rights of a minority and the further dangers inherent in the use of force to settle a moral issue." Equally distasteful to historians was the strong current of nativism—a movement that took a marked anti-Catholic turn during and after the 1830s and that entered politics in the form of the Know-Nothing or Native American party during the 1850s. Most scholars found it difficult to reconcile this movement and its accompanying intolerance with the general current of reform.[4]

Much the same pattern was true of abolitionism. Virtually no scholar defended slavery, yet a large number were extraordinarily critical of the abolitionist movement because of its inflexibility and zealotry. Indeed, abolitionism offers a dramatic illustration of the way in which historians have interpreted the past in terms of their own values and the concerns. To northerners writing in the 1870s and 1880s the abolitionists were courageous men and women who were so convinced that slavery was immoral that they were willing to dedicate their lives to its elimination in spite of being ostracized and even endangered by the hostility of their outraged countrymen. Many of these early writers, of course, had themselves been participants in the Civil War; their works in part represented both an explanation and a justification for their actions. Southerners, on the other hand, flatly laid the blame for the Civil War at the doorstep of the abolitionists. Some even charged that the intolerance and fanaticism of the abolitionists had aborted a moderate and sensible emancipation movement that had been under way in the South.

The southern view of abolitionism by the early part of the twentieth century had become the dominant tradition in American historiography. One reason for this was that a significant number of scholars came from the South. These southerners tended to treat the abolitionists as an irresponsible group who had stirred up sectional animosities to the point where an armed confrontation was all but inevitable. Thus in his discussion of the causes of the Civil War, Frank L. Owsley condemned the abolitionists in unequivocal terms. "One has to seek in the unrestrained and furious invective of the present totalitarians," he stated, "to find a near parallel to the language that the abolitionists and their political fellow travelers used in denouncing the South and its way of life. Indeed, as far as I have been able to ascertain, neither Dr. Goebbels . . . nor Stalin's propaganda agents have as yet been able to plumb the depths of vulgarity

---

[4]Tyler, *Freedom's Ferment*, p. 359. See especially Ray Allen Billington, *The Protestant Crusade 1800–1860: A Study of the Origins of American Nativism* (New York, 1938).

and obscenity reached and maintained by . . . Stephen Foster, Wendell Phillips, Charles Sumner, and other abolitionists of note."[5]

But not all the hostility of historians toward the abolitionists can be attributed to sectional partisanship, since many of these scholars came from other regions of the country. The dislike of these individuals arose out of a distaste for the singlemindedness of the abolitionists. Historians reflected some of the general apathy—even hostility—toward the plight of black Americans that was characteristic of the first three or so decades of the twentieth century, a fact that made it all the more difficult to attribute wisdom or sincerity to the abolitionist movement. A few scholars also noted that not all abolitionists were committed to the proposition that blacks and whites were equal. Consequently they alleged that abolitionists were "insincere" and "hypocritical." The result was a constant and subtle denigration of the abolitionist movement in historical literature.[6]

Scholars using insights borrowed from the social and behavioral sciences to inquire into the motives of reformers provided further ways to denigrate the abolitionists. Interpreting fanaticism in psychiatric terms could reduce abolitionism to pathology. Hazel Wolf, for example, described the behavior of individual abolitionists as obsessive and paranoic in nature. All of them, she wrote, were "eagerly bidding for a martyr's crown."[7] David Donald, in an essay that has become a classic since its publication in 1956, used social psychology and status anxiety to explain the behavior of the abolitionists as a reform group. They were born to lead in a world that was modernizing so fast that their leadership was in jeopardy. "Many of the young men were unable to overcome their traditional disdain for the new money-grubbing class that was beginning to rule. In these plebeian days they could not be successful in politics; family tradition and education prohibited idleness; and agitation allowed the only chance for personal and social self-fulfillment." Donald described them as complacent about capitalism, but unhappy with the transfer of power to slave owners and textile manufacturers. "An attack on slavery was their best, if quite unconscious, attack upon the new industrial system."[8]

---

[5]Frank L. Owsley, "The Fundamental Cause of the Civil War: Egocentric Sectionalism," *Journal of Southern History*, 7 (February 1941): 16–17.

[6]For example, Gilbert H. Barnes argued that abolitionists, influenced by evangelical religion, were more interested in rebuking slave owners than freeing slaves. See *The Antislavery impulse 1830–1844* (New York, 1933), p. 25.

[7]Hazel C. Wolf, *On Freedom's Altar: The Martyr Complex in the Abolition Movement* (Madison, Wisc., 1952), p. 4.

[8]David Donald, *Lincoln Reconsidered: Essays on the Civil War Era* (New York, 1956), pp. 33–34. For a critique of Donald's thesis see Robert A. Skotheim, "A Note on Historical Method: David Donald's 'Toward a Reconsideration of Abolitionists,'" *Journal of Southern History*, 25 (August 1959): 356–65.

While the majority of historians were unfriendly in their treatment of the abolitionists, the older and more favorable views held by northern writers in the 1860s and 1870s did not completely disappear. Indeed, by the late 1930s—especially when it began to be increasingly apparent that the problem of black-white relationships was becoming more and more tense and racist theory was being discredited—the beginnings of a change in portrait of abolitionism began to be evident. Dwight L. Dumond, for example, showed considerable sympathy for the abolitionists in his study of the origins of the Civil War in 1939.[9] The broadening of the civil rights movement and the struggle for equality in the 1950s and 1960s further shifted the framework of the debate, for it was difficult, if not impossible, for historians to avoid dealing with the tragedy of black-white relationships in America. Indeed, by the 1960s a significant number of historians sympathized with the abolitionists, and their approach became dominant. In a major study of antislavery in 1961 Dumond began by stating his own viewpoint in clear and straightforward language: "The course of the men and women who dedicated their lives to arresting the spread of slavery was marvelously direct and straightforward. They denounced it as a sin which could only be remedied by unconditional repentance and retributive justice. . . . These people were neither fanatics nor incendiaries. . . . They precipitated an intellectual and moral crusade for social reform, for the rescue of a noble people, for the redemption of democracy."[10]

To Merle Curti,[11] a scholar writing within the Progressive tradition of American history in the early 1940s, the roots of reform were to be found in a complex combination of Enlightenment beliefs—faith in reason, natural law, and the idea of progress—and a liberal humanitarian religion that assumed the goodness of humans and the perfectibility of the individual. Two other intellectual trends also played a role in stimulating reform: romanticism, with its enthusiasm for everyone as a human being without reference to status; and utilitarianism, which insisted that all institutions be judged by standards of social utility rather than tradition or custom.

Dumond and Curti were not alone in rehabilitating the abolitionists. In addition to the publication of numerous favorable biographies, there was a new tendency to write about the movement in friendly, even glowing, terms. One book of essays by various authorities in 1965 explicitly rejected earlier views of abolitionism as a movement of mal-

---

[9]Dwight L. Dumond, *Antislavery Origins of the Civil War in the United States* (Ann Arbor, Mich., 1939).

[10]Dwight L. Dumond, *Antislavery: The Crusade for Freedom in America* (Ann Arbor, Mich., 1961), pp. 417ff, v.

[11]Merle Curti, *The Growth of American Thought*, 3rd ed. (New York, 1964), especially Chapter 15. The first edition of this book appeared in 1943.

adjusted and evil fanatics. Indeed, in the concluding essay, Howard Zinn argued that abolitionist radicalism was highly constructive when compared with the extreme inhumanity of slavery.[12] Similarly, Donald G. Mathews, who analyzed the arguments and rhetoric of the abolitionists, concluded that they were neither irrational nor fanatic. The abolitionists as agitators were not attempting to change the values of Americans—rather they were trying to extend them to human beings who were generally considered to be outside society. Nor were the men and women who spent much of their lives fighting against slavery guilty of oversimplification, according to Mathews. They freely admitted that many slaveholders were good people, that not all were sinners, and that slavery was a complex institution. Nevertheless slavery involved the exercise of arbitrary and absolute power. The absolute power of whites over blacks corrupted not only individuals, but the South as a section as well as the entire nation. Mathews's interpretation reflected the more sympathetic views of abolitionism characteristic of historical literature during the last few decades.[13]

The problem with these assessments was, while they provided useful intellectual background to the reformers, they left historians stuck in a good-bad debate and seemed to offer no new views on the subject. In 1959, in his controversial study, *Slavery*, Stanley M. Elkins offered what he thought was a view without moral evaluation as well as a major reinterpretation of reformers in general. Instead of judging their movement, Elkins looked at their world and their world view. To Elkins the most distinctive feature of American society in the early nineteenth century was the general breakdown of a number of key social institutions. The older establishments that had stood for order and stability—the church, the bar, the Federalist party, the Eastern merchant aristocracy—had been stripped of their power by the 1830s and replaced by an almost mystical faith in the individual. With formal institutions losing their influence, a new kind of reformer emerged who did not rely upon such agencies to bring about social change. The pressures on such an individual were not the concrete demands of an institution or organization; there was no necessity to consider the needs of a clientele or spell out a program that was sound strategically. When abolitionists sought to abolish slavery, they did not feel impelled to discuss institutional arrangements in their proposed solutions to the problem. Protest, therefore, occurred in an institutional vacuum, and reformers were never called upon to test their ideas. Out of Elkins's interpretation emerged a more generalized description of the abstract

---

[12]Martin Duberman, ed., *The Antislavery Vanguard: New Essays on the Abolitionists* (Princeton, N.J., 1965), pp. 417–51.

[13]Donald G. Mathews, "The Abolitionist on Slavery: The Critique Behind the Social Movement," *Journal of Southern History*, 23 (May 1967): 163–82.

and moral nature of American reform and its failure to come to grips with concrete and specific problems.[14]

In an article, published in 1965, John L. Thomas attempted to synthesize many of the diverse and even conflicting interpretations of antebellum reform. Beginning with a romantic faith in perfectibility and confined to religious institutions, wrote Thomas, reform quickly overflowed its specific limits and spread across society and politics. Defining social sin as the sum total of individual sin, reformers worked to reeducate individuals. Reform therefore involved a broad moral crusade—but with a strong anti-institutional bias since it was based on the concept of the free and regenerate individual. In an important sense Thomas agreed with Elkins. Even the communitarian experiments, Thomas noted, were anti-institutional solutions, for they involved an abandonment of political and religious institutions in favor of an ideal society giving full rein to the free individual.[15]

Elkins's focus on antiinstitutionalism as well as the dramatic protests of the 1960s helped spur the development of new themes among historians studying pre–Civil War reform. Influenced by the New Left and the new social history, scholars explored new facets of antebellum reform in their examination of the legacy of unsolved problems in American society. An initial phase of studying the social control aspect of reform gave way to a more complex exploration of the relations between the reform movements and the emerging classes of the new capitalist order.

In the early 1970s historians began to suggest that the motivation behind the actions of many reformers, either consciously or unconsciously, was to impose some form of social control over those whom they were ostensibly trying to help. This interpretation arose in part from the understanding that the reformers were active at the same moment that class formation was taking place, and historians, particularly those influenced by the New Left, looked for class conflict and class interest expressed by the largely middle-class reformers.

Religious benevolence—clearly a major theme in mid-nineteenth-century America—also underwent a sharp reevaluation. Clifford S. Griffin, noting the phenomenal increase in the number of national societies

---

[14]Stanley M. Elkins, *Slavery: A Problem in American Institutional and Intellectual Life* (Chicago, 1959), pp. 140–222. Several historians, on the other hand, have argued that reformers and abolitionists were shrewd strategic thinkers. See in particular Aileen S. Kraditor, *Means and Ends in American Abolitionism: Garrison and His Critics an Strategy and Tactics, 1834–1850* (New York, 1969), and James M. McPherson, *The Struggle for Equality: Abolitionists and the Negro in the Civil War and Reconstruction* (Princeton, N.J., 1964).

[15]John L. Thomas, "Romantic Reform in America, 1815–1865," *American Quarterly,* 17 (Winter 1965): 656–81. See also Robert H. Walker's three-stage typology of reform, *Reform in America: The Continuing Frontier* (Lexington, Ky., 1985). In *American Reformers 1815–1860* (New York, 1978), Ronald G. Walters explored social and cultural conditions that permitted reformers to perceive reality as they did.

established for such benevolent purposes as education, conversion, temperance, peace, antislavery, moral reform, and the dissemination of the Bible, saw in them more than merely the disinterested exercise of charitable impulses. As more and more people confronted political and social upheavals of the early national period, and immigration shattered the homogeneity of American society before their very eyes, many turned to evangelical Protestantism as the only social force capable of restoring "stability and order, sobriety and safety." Both clergymen and laymen turned to new national societies to promote religious benevolence and charity. Most of the leaders of these societies were relatively well-to-do, and viewed religious benevolence as a means of social control. "Religion and morality, as dispensed by the benevolent societies throughout the seemingly chaotic nation," argued Griffin, "became a means of establishing secular order."[16]

In a similar vein Michael Katz was critical of those historians who had interpreted the educational reform movement as merely an outgrowth of mid-nineteenth-century humanitarian zeal and the extension of political democracy. "Very simply," he wrote, "the extension and reform of education in the mid-nineteenth century [was] . . . the attempt of a coalition of the social leaders, status-anxious parents, and status-hungry educators to impose educational innovation, each for their own reasons, upon a reluctant community."[17] Those community leaders promoting education sought a school system that would simultaneously harmonize America's economic growth with a business-oriented value system that would prevent the violent consequences that had accompanied the rise of industrialism in countries such as England. Educational reform, moreover, was not a consequence of a broad and diverse coalition of various social and economic groups; rather it was imposed on a society by leaders who identified education with their own interests and values. Consequently education did not gain the allegiance of working- and lower-class groups, who reacted negatively precisely because the schools did not serve their particular needs.

After analyzing a number of local case studies in Massachusetts, Katz concluded that urban school reformers failed to achieve their goals. "The schools failed . . . because . . . educational reform and innovation represented the imposition by social leaders of schooling upon a reluctant, uncomprehending, skeptical, and sometimes . . . hostile citizenry. . . . From on high the school committees, representing the social and financial leadership of towns and cities, excoriated the working-

---

[16]Clifford S. Griffin, *Their Brothers' Keepers: Moral Stewardship in the United States, 1800–1855* (New Brunswick, N.J., 1960), pp. x–xiii. Some historians have modified the social control interpretation of benevolence by emphasizing that the effort to establish a general standard of right conduct is characteristic of many groups. See Paul Boyer, *Urban Masses and Moral Order in America 1820–1920* (Cambridge, Mass., 1978).

[17]Michael B. Katz, *The Irony of Early School Reform: Educational Innovation in Mid-Nineteenth-Century Massachusetts* (Cambridge, Mass., 1968), p. 218.

class parents. They founded schools with a sense of superiority, not compassion. . . . Ironically, their ideology and style could not have been better designed to alienate the very people whom they strove to accommodate in a more closely knit social order. In making the urban school, educational promoters of the mid-nineteenth century fostered an estrangement between the school and the working-class community that has persisted as one of the greatest challenges to reformers of our own times."[18]

The themes of social control and imposition of reform were not confined to religious benevolence or education. Joseph R. Gusfield, a sociologist by profession, analyzed the temperance movement in much the same manner as Donald, Griffin, and Katz viewed their reform movements. Gusfield argued that cultural groups act to preserve, defend, and enhance the dominance and prestige of their own style of living. During the Federal Era temperance attracted a declining social elite bent on retaining its power and leadership. This elite "sought to make Americans into a clean, sober, godly, and decorous people"—a people who reflected their own values. By the 1840s those who favored temperance saw the curtailment of the use of liquor as a means "of solving the problems presented by an immigrant, urban poor whose culture clashed with American Protestantism." Similarly, David J. Rothman insisted that fear of social disorder in the early nineteenth century led elite groups to espouse institutional solutions in the hope of controlling deviant behavior by predominantly lower-class groups. Prisons, mental hospitals, and almshouses, he observed, were not the fruits of benevolent reform; they reflected rather a desire to control and to change behavior through the application of institutional solutions.[19]

In the first of this section's readings, Michael B. Katz attempts to explain the early-nineteenth-century origins of the "Institutional State." In relating social context, social position, ideology, and policy, he employs the concept of deviance. Deviancy, Katz argues, is a political or social construct. Its meaning was altered at precisely the same

----

[18]Ibid., p. 112. For an interpretation that stresses education for the new industrial society see David Nassau, *Schooled to Order, A Social History of Public Schooling in the United States* (New York, 1979).

[19]Joseph R. Gusfield, *Symbolic Crusade: Status Politics and the American Temperance Movement* (Urbana, Ill., 1963), pp. 5–6, and David J. Rothman, *The Discovery of the Asylum: Social Order and Disorder in the New Republic* (Boston, 1971). For a somewhat different interpretation from Rothman's, see Gerald N. Grob, *Mental Institutions in America: Social Policy to 1875* (New York, 1973), and Nancy Tomes, *A Generous Confidence: Thomas Story Kirkbride and the Art of Asylum-Keeping, 1840–1883* (New York, 1984). For an effort to synthesize all of the nineteenth century within a quasi-Marxian model that emphasizes a two-class system, see Michael B. Katz, Michael J. Doucet, and Mark J. Stem, *The Social Organization of Early Industrial Capitalism* (Cambridge, Mass., 1982).

time that the mercantile-peasant economy was being superseded by a commercial capitalist economy. As capitalism spread, social relations changed and a new dependent population was created. Traditional means of caring for dependent groups declined and were replaced by institutions devoted to the care of the casualties of the new social order. Reflecting their social origins, these institutions sought to reshape character along certain lines. The ideal components of character in a capitalist society, Katz notes, were sensual restraint, dependability, a willingness to work, and acceptance of the social order and one's position within it. Those who could not function within capitalism were swept into custodial institutions, branded unworthy. The dismal legacy of the institutional activists of the early nineteenth century, Katz concludes, is still with us.[20]

Students of abolitionism, influenced by the new social and intellectual history and the very recent efforts to reform instutitions and people, wondered about the social and cultural context of the movement and the concern of individual abolitionists with the realization of themselves. In 1976, for example, Ronald G. Walters published a study of antislavery after 1830 that emphasized the interplay between individuals and culture. Three years later Lewis Perry and Michael Fellman brought out a collection of essays representative of this trend. This work, together with several others, dealt with the desire of abolitionists to create a universe of free and autonomous individuals, each able to realize his own destiny, free from social constraints. And in 1982 Lawrence J. Friedman attempted to depict the inner experiences of abolitionists from their youthful beginnings to their later careers starting with inner psychology and moving outward to immersion in social and political conflicts.[21]

Meanwhile, some scholars pursued the relationship of abolitionism and developing capitalism, but rejected overt self-interest and social control as too reductive. Perhaps the most important step in finding the connections between the two trends came with David Brion Davis's masterful *The Problem of Slavery in the Age of Revolution, 1770–1823.* Davis explored in detail the various antislavery ideologies available in

---

[20]Katz, *School Reform.*

[21]Ronald G. Walters, *The Antislavery Appeal: American Abolitionism After 1830* (Baltimore, 1976); Lewis Perry and Michael Fellman, eds., *Antislavery Reconsidered: New Perspectives on the Abolitionists* (Baton Rouge, La., 1979); Peter F. Walker, *Moral Choices: Memory, Desire, and Imagination in Nineteenth-Century American Abolition* (Baton Rouge, La., 1978); Lewis Perry, *Childhood, Marriage, and Reform: Henry Clarke Wright 1797–1870* (Chicago, 1980); Lawrence J. Friedman, *Gregarious Saints: Self and Community in American Abolitionism 1830–1870* (New York, 1982). See also John R. McKivigan, *The War Against Proslavery Religion: Abolitionism and the Northern Churches, 1830–1865* (Ithaca, N.Y., 1984); and James H. Moorhead, *American Apocalypse: Yankee Protestants and the Civil War, 1860–1869* (New Haven, Conn., 1978).

the late eighteenth century. He posed the question, why was it not until the emergence of a capitalist order that a powerful abolitionist movement was able to excite the revulsion of people toward an institution that had existed throughout history? Davis's wide-ranging argument rescued abolitionists from being portrayed as self-interested, market-driven hypocrites, but retained the link between antislavery and capitalism. His argument, highly simplified, was that antislavery was able to grow powerful at a moment in which the new capitalist relations of employer and contractual wage earner or "free laborer" benefited from a flattering contrast with the evils of slavery.[22]

At more or less the same time, Paul Johnson, in *A Shopkeeper's Dilemma* (see Chapter 7 of this book), made the case that participation in evangelical religion for employers and ambitious laborers provided a stamp of powerful moral credibility for these new contractual relations in a world that was rapidly losing its old hierarchical controls. These views of religion and slavery posited a framework in which people made choices within moral systems they understood, but their actions also served different aims from those they could have understood at the time.

In direct response to Davis's thesis, Thomas Haskell wrote a two-part essay that appeared in the *Journal of American History* in 1985, linking humanitarianism to capitalism in an even more subtle way than Davis had.[23] Haskell argued that capitalism called forth a new, sharpened perceptivity to chains of consequences. The thinking required for participation in market societies, Haskell argued, focused people's attention on causality and the results of extended sequences of events and actions. This increased sensitivity heightened feelings of moral responsibility for distant events and made it much more difficult to shrug off the suffering of others. Two years later, John Ashworth in a forum with Haskell argued that Haskell had failed to explain why abolitionists focused their reformist zeal on attacking slavery rather than wage labor. He argued for more "interested" motives: that an assault on the violence slavery did to family, community, and individual conscience served to validate the emerging ideological justification for wage labor and capitalism in the sanctity of the family, community, and home in the antebellum North. Reformers did not have to see the connections between the two issues for the antislavery ideology to function as it did.[24]

While a more sophisticated view of reform and modernization was

---

[22]David Brion Davis, *The Problem of Slavery in the Age of Revolution, 1770–1823* (Ithaca, N.Y.,1975).

[23]Thomas Haskell, "Capitalism and the Origins of the Humanitarian Sensibility," *Journal of American History*, Vol. 90, Nos. 2, 3 (April, June 1985).

[24]John Ashworth, "The Relation Between Capitalism and Humanitarianism," in Thomas Bender, *The Antislavery Debate, Capitalism and Abolitionism as a Problem in Historical Interpretation* (Berkeley, Calif., 1992).

developing, the new social history encouraged the study of reformers previously neglected because of sex or race. Vincent Harding, in *There Is a River*, argued for the unflagging persistence and leadership of black abolitionists in the antislavery struggle. Subsequent research on women abolitionists has demonstrated that it was black women in Salem, Massachusetts, who founded the first antislavery society in the nation. Through biographies and collections of writings, the work and lives of many black abolitionists have come to light.[25]

Just as the civil rights movement helped to develop a more sympathetic portrait of the abolitionists, so the women's movement helped to transform the ways in which historians interpreted earlier efforts to further social change. Women's participation in the reform movements was vigorous and scholarship about female reform documented the high percentage of women in movements from abolitionism to Bible societies, to the establishment of Sunday Schools, sexual reform, temperance, and suffrage. One strain of historiography spotlights the empowerment women felt, the networks they created, the isolation they overcame, and the challenges they issued to male domination. Carroll Smith-Rosenberg's article, "The Beauty, the Beast and the Militant Woman" is a good example of how a primary focus on gender emphasizes women's struggle with men and tends to sideline issues of class and racial conflict with other women.[26]

Soon, however, such scholars as Christine Stansell pointed to class conflict and the effort of middle-class women to enforce their standards of motherhood and comportment on working-class women as the price of aid. Mary Ryan's *Cradle of the Middle Class*, one of the most sophisticated treatments of middle-class women and reform, studied women in the process of creating a middle class. Ryan emphasized the formation of a new class identity out of traditional religious materials, not class conflict or efforts to control the working class so much as the development of traits useful to a new bourgeoisie. Nancy Hewitt emphasized striations in the emerging middle class itself, which, she argued, divided people in more important ways than sex did.[27]

---

[25]Vincent Harding, *There Is a River, The Black Struggle for Freedom in America*, (New York, 1981); Anne Firor Scott, *Natural Allies, Women's Associations in American History* (Urbana, Ill., 1991), pp. 13–14, 46. See, for example, Nell Irwin Painter, *Sojourner Truth: A Life, a Symbol* (New York, 1996); Marilyn Richardson, ed. *Maria W. Stewart, America's First Black Woman Politicsl Writer: Essays and Speeches* (Bloomington, Ind., 1987).

[26]Carroll Smith-Rosenberg "The Beauty, the Beast and the Militant Woman: A Case Study in Sex Roles and Social Stress in Jacksonian America," *American Quarterly*, 23 (October, 1971): 562–84.

[27]Christine Stansell, *City of Women, Sex and Class in New York, 1789–1860*, (New York, 1986); Mary Ryan, *The Cradle of the Middle Class: The Family in Oneida County, New York, 1790–1865* (New York, 1981); Nancy Hewitt, *Women's Activism and Social Change, Rochester, N.Y., 1822–1872* (Ithaca, N.Y., 1984).

Recovering untold stories of women reformers continues apace. Most recently, such studies as Sandra Haarsager's *Organized Womanhood* and Julie Roy Jeffrey's *The Great Silent Army of Abolitionism* offered new information about the breadth and depth of women's participation all over the country in every kind of reform. Anne Firor Scott in *Natural Allies* described the myriad benevolent associations that sprang up across the country from 1800 on and analyzed their evolution into the widespread activism of the antebellum and eventually the Progressive period. She found reformist energy coming from a variety of backgrounds, including groups without an evangelical foundation. As to social control, "The evidence does not support any simple hypothesis." Reformers divided up the world in many ways, economic class not being a particularly significant marker. She concluded that "there is a difference, too, between trying to promote social order by keeping people 'in their place,' as the phrase went, and trying to help them develop characteristics that—if accomplished—might admit them to them middle class."[28]

Women' suffrage is a subject that has prompted a number of recent studies. After Eleanor Flexner's unsurpassed survey of the movement, published in 1959, little was written until Ellen Carol DuBois's *Feminism and Suffrage*, in which she argued for a new interpretation of the relationship between abolitionism and feminism. The assumption had been that women saw their own subordination through identification with slaves, and that this mobilized them. DuBois argued that they understood their subjugation perfectly well, but needed to learn organizing skills and free themselves from intellectual and moral dependence on the clergy before they could start their own movement.[29]

The second selection in this chapter, by Lori D. Ginzberg, studies the institutionalization of this initially spontaneous women's movement and its costs. In the 1830s women emphasized moral suasion in fighting for a wide array of feminist reforms including suffrage. Moral suasion's failure to eradicate social evils led them to focus on politics and institutional change by the 1850s. Ironically, this shift tended to narrow the goals of feminist activism, ending in a concentration on the vote at the expense of other, more wide-ranging and radical aims.[30]

Amy Dru Stanley has written on a related theme from a different

---

[28]Sandra Haarsager, *Organized Womanhod, Cultural Politics in the Pacific Northwest, 1840–1920* (Norman, Okla., 1997); Julie Roy Jeffrey, *The Great Silent Army of Abolitionism: Ordinary Women in the Antislavery Movement* (Chapel Hill, N.C., 1998); Anne Firor Scott, *Natural Allies, Women's Associations in American History* (Urbana, Ill., 1991), p. 4.

[29]Ellen Carol DuBois, *Feminism and Suffrage: The Emergence of an Independent Women's Movement in America, 1848–1869* (Ithaca, N.Y., 1978).

[30]See also Suzanne Marilley, *Woman Suffrage and the Origins of Liberal Feminism, 1820–1920* (Cambridge, Mass., 1996), and Rosalyn Terborg-Pen, *African American Women in the Struggle for the Vote, 1850–1920* (Bloomington, Ind., 1998).

theoretical perspective. Looking at the abolitionists' constant focus on the enslaved and violated female body as the symbol of all that was wrong with slavery, she believed, led women to a new understanding of gender differences and the individual rights of women. By emphasizing the figure of the female slave, for whom slavery meant the loss of control not only of her labor but of her sexuality, and arguing for a form of possessive individualism for both men and women, abolitionists contradicted contemporary middle-class notions of the completely different natures and rights of men and women.[31]

Recently, scholars have found other fascinating new ways to view reform, through other large changes in society. Building on Elaine Scarry's monumental study of pain and Thomas Haskell's idea that cognitive changes accompanied the advent of capitalism, Elizabeth Clark noted that with the advent of anesthesia and the rejection of the punitive Calvinist God, people no longer believed that suffering was a necessary evil. Thus they perceived the infliction of suffering as commensurately more heinous. These changes predisposed audiences to respond with new and deep anguish to abolitionists' array of stories of the horrific physical torture of slaves.[32]

Two very recent contributions further demonstrate the creativity of scholars of the last decade in moving on from the old good-bad debate and finding new ways to view the movements collectively as well as bringing new insights to individual movements. Steven Mintz, surveying all mid-nineteenth-century reform in *Moralists and Modernizers*, argues that reform arose in a moment of growing laissez faire in which reformers shared fears of capitalist development and believed in the need for a wide array of internal controls to guard against the system's obvious excesses. "Antebellum reformers played a critical role in establishing minimum standards of human dignity and decency, imposing limits of exploitation, and creating modern institutions to rescue and rehabilitate the victims of social change." Mintz presents the reformers in the round, their good intentions intertwined with repression and paternalism. He studies them in the larger framework that David Brion Davis first established (indeed, the book is dedicated to Davis) by asking about the connections between reform and capitalism.[33]

---

[31]Amy Dru Stanley, "The Right to Possess All the Faculties That God Has Given: Possessive Individualism, Slave Women, and Abolitionist Thought," in Karen Halttunen and Lewis Perry, eds., *Moral Problems in American Life, New Perspectives on Cultural History* (Ithaca, N.Y., 1998).

[32]Elizabeth Clark, "'The Sacred Rights of the Weak': Pain, Sympathy and the Culture of Individual Rights in Antebellum America," *Journal of American History*, Vol. 82, No. 2 (1995): 463–93; Elaine Scarry, *The Body in Pain, The Making and Unmaking of the World*, (New York, 1985). See also Karen Halttunen, "Humanitarianism and the Pornography of Pain in Anglo-American Culture," *American Historical Review*, Vol. 100, No. 2 (April 1995): 303–34.

[33]Steven Mintz, *Moralists and Modernizers, American Pre–Civil War Reformers* (Baltimore, 1995), p. xviii.

Finally, in a 1999 article, Mary Hershberger has traced the strong links among the movement protesting the removal of the so-called Five Civilized Tribes, the energizing and radicalizing of the antislavery movement, and the mobilization of women to the antislavery cause. Hershberger traces women's involvement in antiremoval activity through their support of missionary associations ministering to various Indian groups. Protesting removal soon led them to reject the colonization of former slaves in Africa and generally radicalized the first cohort of antislavery activists. Hershberger credits Jackson with enlarging democracy, not directly, but through the protest he provoked: "His determination to carry out Indian removal generated the deepest political movement that the country had yet witnessed."[34]

There are still wide gaps in our knowledge about who, exactly, the reformers were and what motives they had for their work. How did they view themselves? How did they view those they were trying to change? How do we evaluate their legacy? There also remains much to learn about the links among reform movements. As the protest movements of the 1960s and 1970s continue to influence our society, historians will continue to look for parallels and explanations capable of telling us more about the origins, dynamics, and failures of the American impulse to improve.

------

[34]Mary Hershberger, "Mobilizing Women, Anticipating Abolition: The Struggle Against Indian Removal in the 1830s," *Journal of American History* (June 1999): 15–40, p. 40.

MICHAEL B. KATZ

MICHAEL B. KATZ (1939–   ) is professor of education and history at the University of Pennsylvania. His books include The Irony of Early School Reform *(1968),* Class, Bureaucracy and Schools *(1971),* The People of Hamilton, Canada West *(1975),* The Social Organization of Early Industrial Capitalism *(1982), and* Poverty and Policy in American History *(1983).*

We live in an institutional state. Our lives spin outwards from the hospitals where we are born, to the school systems that dominate our youth, through the bureaucracies for which we work, and back again to the hospitals in which we die. If we stray, falter, or lose our grip, we are led or coerced towards the institutions of mental health, justice, or public welfare. Specialists in obstetrics, pediatrics, education, crime, mental illness, unemployment, recreation, to name only some of the most obvious, wait in the yellow pages to offer their expertise in the service of our well-being. Characteristically, we respond to a widespread problem through the creation of an institution, the training of specialists, and the certification of their monopoly over a part of our lives.

We accept institutions and experts as inevitable, almost eternal. That, after all, is the way the world works. It is hard—almost impossible—for us to recall that they are a modern invention.

In North America prior to the nineteenth century few experts or specialized institutions existed. The sick, the insane, and the poor mixed indiscriminately within relatively undifferentiated almshouses. Criminals of all ages and varieties remained in prison for fairly short periods awaiting trial. If guilty they were punished, not by long incarceration but by fine, whipping, or execution. Dependent or troublesome strangers did not receive much charity; they were simply warned out of town. Children learned to read in a variety of ways and attended schools irregularly. In short, families and communities coped with social and personal problems traditionally and informally.

Everything changed within fifty to seventy-five years. By the last quarter of the nineteenth century, specialized institutions were dealing with crime, poverty, disease, mental illness, juvenile delinquency, the blind, the deaf and dumb, and the ignorant. Institutions proliferated so rapidly that by the 1860s some states began to create Boards of State Charities to coordinate and rationalize public welfare.

Michael B. Katz, "Origins of the Institutional State," *Marxist Perspectives* 1 (Winter 1978): 6–22. Reprinted by permission of *Marxist Perspectives* and Michael B. Katz.

The treatment of crime, poverty, ignorance, and disease repeated the same story with different details. Institutions suddenly came to dominate public life in a radical departure in social policy. Aside from their sudden creation, most new public institutions experienced a similar cycle of development during their early histories: a shift from reform to custody. Mental hospitals, school systems, reformatories, and penitentiaries began optimistically with assumptions about the tractability of problems and the malleability of human nature. Early promoters expected them to transform society through their effect upon individual personalities. In some instances, as in the case of early mental hospitals or the first reformatory for young women, the optimism appeared justified for a few years. However, institutions, as even their supporters soon came to admit, could not work miracles. Rates of recovery remained low, recidivism high; school systems did not eliminate poverty and vice; ungrateful inmates even, on occasion, set their institutions on fire.

The public had invested heavily in new institutions that a reasonable person might conclude were failures. Nonetheless, the newly created institutional managers did not intend either to admit failure or to abandon the intricate hierarchical professional worlds they had created. Instead, they altered their justification: Mental illness and crime frequently arose from heredity and were incurable; lower-class children were incorrigible; paupers genetically unable and unwilling to work. Institutions existed to keep deviants off the streets; to prevent a glut on the labor market; to contain, not cure, the ills of society. This shift from reform to custody characterized the history of reformatories, mental hospitals, prisons, and school systems within the first two or three decades of their existence.

Social historians disagree about the impulse underlying institutional development. Why did the institutional State emerge at the time and in the manner it did? The question is straightforward, the answer complex and elusive. Actually, two sets of events must be explained: the origins and founding of institutions and the shift from reform to custody. Here, I shall consider only the former and attempt to show a connection between the origins of institutions and the early history of capitalism in North America.

First, consider the pattern and timing of institutional development. The new institutions of the early nineteenth century divide into various groups. Those on which historians have focused most sharply treated deviance: mental hospitals, poorhouses, reformatories, penitentiaries. The first mental hospital, the private McLean's, opened in 1818, followed by the first state hospital in Worcester, Massachusetts, in 1835. The first reformatory, also a private corporation, the New York House of Refuge, opened in 1825; the first state reform school incarcerated its first boys in 1848. Both Massachusetts and New York established a network of poorhouses in the 1820s as a result of the famous Quincy and Yates reports which urged the virtual abolition of outdoor relief. In Ontario the provincial penitentiary opened in 1835 and the lunatic asylum in 1850.

New institutions were not solely residential nor did they serve only those whom we today label deviant. The most notable of the non-residential institutions designed to service a clearly defined sector of more ordinary people was the public school. Nineteenth-century educational promoters equated ignorance with deviance and both with poverty, but they intended public schools to serve a broader portion of the population than the children of the slums. And public schooling became especially popular among the middle classes. Tax-supported schools of sorts certainly had existed for centuries. The novelty during the nineteenth century rested in the creation of systems of public education—age-graded, finely articulated, nominally universal institutions presided over by specially trained experts and administrators. In New York City the system of public schools began with the organization of the Free School Society in 1805. The first state board of education was established in Massachusetts in 1837 and the Superintendency of Public Instruction in the Provinces of Canada in 1841. By 1880 elaborate, hierarchical educational systems existed in most urban centers.

New or novel institutions served other groups as well. Private boarding schools for the children of the rich developed in the antebellum period in the United States. The most influential of them, according to their historian, was St. Paul's, started in Concord, New Hampshire, in 1855. Indeed, it is fascinating to observe the parallels between private academies and other institutions. In their educational philosophy, organizational ideal, and theory of human nature, early reform schools resembled nothing so much as academies for the poor.

Within New York City, as Alan Horlick has shown, merchants developed a series of institutions to control and socialize the incoming hordes of young, aggressive, and undeferential clerks. This effort gave rise during the early nineteenth century to the YMCA, the Mercantile Library Association, and similar organizations.

The first general hospitals opened in 1752 in Philadephia, in 1792 in New York City, and in 1821 in Boston. Construed primarily as charities, early hospitals were supposed to cure both the physical and moral afflictions of the poor who composed their patient populations. As with schools, prisons, or reformatories, the purposes of early hospitals included the reformation of character, and, like the sponsors of other institutions, hospital supporters compounded poverty, crime, ignorance, and disease into a single amalgam. Hospitals proved no more able than schools, prisons, or reformatories to uplift social character, and by the 1870s their purpose narrowed to the treatment of specific diseases. At the same time the internal development of hospitals traced a path similar to that followed in other institutions: a growth in size and complexity accompanied by an emphasis upon professional management increasingly divorced from lay influence.

At the most intimate level even the family reflected the thrust of institutional development in more public spheres. Decreasingly the place of both work and residence, with boundaries more tightly drawn between itself and the community, and decreasingly the custodian of the deviant and deficient, the family—the working-class as well as the middle-class family—became a sharply delimited haven, a specialized agency for the nurture of the young. Within families sex roles became more clearly defined, and by the mid-nineteenth century Catharine Beecher, among others, was attempting to certify the institutionalization of the home through the conversion of domesticity into a science.

In sum, the institutional explosion did not issue directly or solely from state sponsorship, nor were institutions directed only towards deviance or solely asylums. More accurately, institutional development during the early and middle nineteenth century should be described as the creation of formal organizations with specialized clienteles and a reformist, or characterbuilding, purpose.

Institutions were not in themselves novel. Poorhouses had existed in colonial New England. Indeed, Foucault labels the seventeenth century the age of the great confinement. Nonetheless, the use of institutions as deliberate agencies of social policy their specialization, and their emphasis upon the formation or reformation of character represented a new departure in modern history.

Most major social institutions originated in a two-stage process. They commenced as private corporations to serve public purposes but within a few decades were imitated, superseded, augmented, or expanded by the State. The transition from voluntarism to the State did not represent a simple evolution. Certainly, the magnitude of the problems undertaken by early voluntary corporations—the alleviation of poverty, mental illness, delinquency, ignorance—strained private resources. Financially, voluntary corporations, however, did not rely solely, or, in many cases, at all, upon private contributions. Rather, they commonly received public funds. The assumption of primary responsibility for the operation as well as the funding of institutions, consequently, represented a shift in generally acceptable models for public organization. Elsewhere, I have called this shift the transition from paternalistic and corporate voluntarism to incipient bureaucracy. Voluntarism upheld an ideal of organizations controlled by self-perpetuating corporations of wealthy, enlightened, public-spirited citizens, essentially limited in size, staffed by talented generalists. The shift to the State reflected a belief that public funding required public control, a commitment to expansion of scale, and an emphasis upon the importance of specialized, expert administration.

The shift from voluntarism to the State appears in the New York House of Refuge, the McLean Hospital, the New York Free School Society, and another interesting variant, the Boston Primary School Committee. When these voluntary corporations went public they often altered their purpose as well as their form. In the case of mental hospitals, the entrance of the State meant the extension of service from the well-to-do served by McLean's to the poor treated at Worcester; in the case of public schools the opposite occurred, as school promoters sought to incorporate the children of the affluent into the free schools, which in their early years had suffered from their association with pauperism and charity. Both the mental hospitals and the public schools illustrate an attempt to broaden the social composition of public institutions.

The early history of hospitals formed an instructive, if partial, exception to the shift away from corporate voluntarism. The great early hospitals in Philadelphia, New York, and Boston, to name three, remained under the control of private, nonprofit corporations. When public representatives wanted hospitals to expand their size, role, or scope, they could not bring them under State control. Rather, they sometimes had to establish parallel institutions. In Boston in the 1860s the board and staff of the Massachusetts General Hospital fought against the creation of Boston City Hospital, which they explicitly viewed as an institution more "democratic" and more accessible to public influence in such important ways as admission procedures and internal routines like visiting hours. The social group that wanted Boston City was not the very poor served by Massachusetts General but the skilled workers, petty proprietors, and clerks who were less welcome at the older hospital yet unable to afford easily the cost of medical care at home. The reason that hospitals remained under private control probably rests in their relation to the medical profession. Often, physicians instigated the founding of hospitals and played the principal roles not only in a strictly professional capacity but also in institutional design and administration. Hospitals differed from other major social institutions in that a prestigious, prosperous, and generally cohesive corps of professionals preceded their establishment. By contrast, mental hospitals and schools, to take two examples, created two new professions. The founding of mental hospitals and school systems, therefore, much more than of general hospitals, depended upon lay support, and they consequently remained much more susceptible to public influence during their early years.

Although private hospitals did not go public, they still reflected one process that characterized other institutions: the shift in the social origins of their clientele. For years hospital supporters had tried to broaden the social composition of the patient population, but, as in the case of early public education, the aura of charity clung to hospitals. In sharp contrast to public schools, however, hospitals were unable to shed that aura until a series of demographic changes and medical advances coalesced during the late nineteenth and early twentieth centuries. The transition from home to hospital care by the affluent was symbolized dramatically by the construction of the expensive and luxurious Phillips House as a branch of the Massachusetts General in 1817.

The supersession of corporate voluntarism reflected the increasingly sharp distinction between public and private, which formed part of a larger theme in social development: the drawing of sharp boundaries between the elements of social organization; the separation of family and community; the division of community into discrete and specialized functions.

The connection that exists between the emergence of modern society and the expansive specialization of both public and private institutions remains open to interpretation. How are we to account, in this case, for the origins of public institutions? What, precisely, did they signify?

Historians currently offer two principal, competing interpretations, which, put crudely, can be called the fear of social disorder versus the humanitarian impulse. The most notable exponent of the former is David Rothman, of the latter, Gerald Grob. Here I must risk some violence to their complex and subtle work in order to highlight the central point in contention and the problems left unresolved. Although Grob has attacked Rothman, the two share much common ground, as Rothman points out in a review of Grob's most recent book. Both tell a similar story and even stress many of the same factors, but they differ in the interpretation they give to events and, ultimately, in the meaning they assign to American history in the formative years between the Revolution and the Civil War.

Rothman argues that the fear of disorder arising from the breakdown of traditional communal controls spurred the discovery of the asylum. He writes, "The response in the Jacksonian period to the deviant and the dependent was first and foremost a vigorous attempt to promote the stability of the society at a moment when traditional ideas and practices appeared outmoded, constricted, and ineffective . . . all represented an effort to insure the cohesion of the community in new and changing circumstances." Elsewhere he asserts, "under the influence of demographic, economic and intellectual developments, they [Americans] perceived that the traditional mechanisms of social control were obsolete."

Grob emphasizes the individualist philosophy and humanitarian impulses that arose from the Second Awakening. Although he cannot deny the pervasive fear of social disorder or the manifest influence of class in the social origins of reformers, he argues:

> Since the absence of broad theoretical models relating to public policy made it difficult to gather or to use empirical data in a meaningful way, policy often reflected external factors such as unconscious class interests or similar social assumptions that were never questioned.

This is not to imply that mid-nineteenth century legislators and administrators were deficient in intelligence or malevolent in character. It is only to say that lack of theory and methodology often led to the adoption of policies that in the long run had results which were quite at variance with the intentions of those involved in their formulation.

Grob's arresting and partly true statement rests on the assumption that knowledge—hard data—scientific in character and free from bias does in fact exist and awaits discovery by students of deviance and dependence. It assumes further that the acquisition of scientific knowledge automatically leads to rational, humanitarian solutions framed in the best interests of the people to which they were directed. The history of social and behavioral science should make us skeptical.

Five problems, which appear in varying degrees in different accounts, underlie most formulations of both the social disorder and humanitarian interpretations, the very problems that appear in most attempts to explain early-nineteenth-century social reforms and institutional creation.

First, most interpretations do not provide a link between institutions created for deviants and the other institutional developments of the time. An adequate interpretation must encompass not only the asylum, not only prisons, mental hospitals, and poorhouses, but also public schools, academies, the YMCA, and, ultimately, the family. Striking parallels exist between the timing, theory, and shape of those developments which affect deviants, dependents, children, adolescents, and families. An understanding of any of them depends upon an exploration of their interconnection.

Second, definitions of disorder usually remain loose. Scholars invoke industrialization and urbanization, but these broad concepts mask as much as they reveal. What was it, exactly, about the development of cities that created social disorder? What type of mechanisms broke down, when, and why? The arrival of hundreds of thousands of impoverished immigrants might explain a heightened concern with poverty or account for some of the nervousness on the part of genteel natives, but it assists little in an attempt to comprehend the origins of academies or even the special attention paid to the mentally ill.

Third, the way in which historical context intersects with the perception of people differentially situated in the social order usually remains unclear. The exact relation between the periodization of socioeconomic and institutional development rarely is made explicit, and the identity of institutional sponsors and opponents—and opposition did exist—remains unclear in most accounts. We are left with David Rothman's "Americans," surely a category within which significant differences of opinion existed. But which Americans wanted the asylum? How did their perceptions influence public policy?

There are, however, few, if any, historical subjects more treacherous than human motivation—thus, the fourth problem with existing interpretations. They simplistically use models of individual behavior. They confuse, that is, the analysis of individual motivation with the analysis of class. Class analysis does not deny that individuals believe they do good works. It regards individual sincerity as irrelevant. Class analysis concerns the actions of groups and the relation between activity and class position. It does not deny the role of religion or tradition in the formulation and expression of class action. The theory of class is neither crudely reductionist nor contradicted by the existence of deeply felt humanitarian conviction. To argue that institutional promoters believed they were acting in the best interests of the poor, the criminal, the mentally ill, or the ignorant, and to leave the argument there, is not to refute a class analysis but merely to finesse it.

The reluctance to probe the interconnections between social context, social position, ideology, and policy underlies the fifth problem. Most accounts of institutional development and social reform uncritically accept the interpretation of problems offered by institutional promoters and social reformers. They fail to question the description of crime, poverty, mental illness, or illiteracy offered in official sources. Thus, Grob simply accepts the proposition that immigrants were more prone than others to insanity and does not probe the social characteristics shaping definitions of mental illness. Other historians similarly accept the proposition that crime increased disproportionately in early-nineteenth-century cities, that industrialization eroded the stability of the lower-class family, or that, as Oscar Handlin has written, the Irish were degraded.

The acceptance of official descriptions of reality ignores important considerations. First, deviance is at least partly a social or political category and cannot be defined as a universal. It is the product of prevailing laws, customs, and views. Second, institutional promoters sometimes gauged popular sentiments inaccurately. The poor occasionally used new institutions in ways that violated the purposes and perceptions of their sponsors. For example, parents themselves provided the largest source of commitments to reform schools. The working-class family, however, was not breaking down. Rather, poor parents turned to reform schools, which had not yet acquired their present stigma, precisely as other and more affluent parents turned to academies as places that would remove their refractory children from trouble and educate them at the same time. Other poor parents used reform schools in difficult periods as places in which children could stay safely during episodes of family crisis. The people at whom institutions were directed were not inert or passive. The image of degradation and helplessness that emerges from institutional promoters must be treated, always, with skepticism. Indeed, wherever historians have looked with care—and the recent historiography of slavery has been especially rich in this regard—severe disjunctions emerge between official perception of client populations and their actual behavior.

Thus, a new interpretation of the origin of the institutional State should be set within a revised framework of North American social development between the late eighteenth and the middle nineteenth century. In particular, it should rest on a substitution of a three-stage for the more familiar two-stage paradigm that underlies much of North American history. The focus of the revised framework should be the spread of wage labor and the values associated with capitalism rather than urbanization and industrialization.

Most North American history rests on a simple two-stage paradigm—a shift from a preindustrial to an industrial society or from rural to urban life—which obscures the relationship between institutions and social change. For, though the transformation of economic structures and the creation of institutions did take place at roughly the same period, attempts to construct causal models or to develop tight and coherent explanations usually appear mechanistic or vague.

When a three-stage paradigm replaces the two-stage one, the connection between social change and institutional creation becomes tighter. In the three-stage paradigm North America shifted from a peculiar variety of a mercantile-peasant economy to an economy dominated by commercial capital to industrial capitalism. Though the pace of change varied from region to region and stages overlapped each other, the most important aspect of the late eighteenth and early nineteenth centuries was not industrialization or urbanization but, rather, the spread of capitalism defined, in Maurice Dobb's words, as "not simply a system of production for the market . . . but a system under which labour-power had itself become a commodity and was bought and sold on the market like any other object of exchange." Capitalism was the necessary, though conceptually distinct, antecedent of industrialization.

Consider the following as reflections of the spread of capitalist relations prior to industrialization. Between 1796 and 1855, prior to industrialization, the most striking change in New York City's occupational structure, according to Carl Kaestle's figures, was the increase in the proportion of men who listed themselves simply as laborers—an increase from 5.5 percent to 27.4 percent. Moreover, apprenticeship, whose emphasis on bound labor is incompatible with capitalism, had ceased to function with anything like its traditional character well before industrialization. In both Buffalo, New York, and Hamilton, Ontario, prior to their industrialization, there were about eleven skilled wage workers and several semiskilled and unskilled ones for every independent master or manufacturer. From a different point of view one historian recently has pointed to an unmistakable increase in the wandering of the poor from place to place in late-eighteenth-century Massachusetts. The expansion of commerce in this period has been documented extensively, and it was in this era that state governments exchanged their essentially mercantilist policies for reliance upon competition and private initiative to regulate the economy.

The problem, thus, becomes one of formulating the connection between the development of capitalism and the spread of institutions. The drive towards institutional development preceded the industrial takeoff in the Northeast. Any interpretation based upon industrialization must fall simply upon considerations of time. A much better temporal connection exists between institutional origins and the spread of capitalist relations of production.

The most profound statement of the relation between capitalism and the institutional State occurs in the remarkable book by the late Harry Braverman, *Labor and Monopoly Capital*. It is worth considering in detail:

> The ebbing of family facilities, and of family, community, and neighborly feelings upon which the performance of many social functions formerly depended, leaves a void. As the family members, more of them now at work away from home, become less and less able to care for each other in time of need, and as the ties of neighborhood, community and friendship are reinterpreted on a narrower scale to exclude onerous responsibilities, the care of humans for each other becomes increasingly institutionalized. At the same time, the human detritus of the urban civilization increases, not just because of the aged population, its life prolonged by the progress of medicine grows ever larger; those who need care include children—not only those who cannot "function" smoothly but even the "normal" ones whose only defect is their tender age. Whole new strata of the helpless and dependent are created, or familiar old ones enlarged enormously: the proportion of "mentally ill" or "deficient," the "criminals," the pauperized layers at the bottom of society, all representing varieties of crumbling under the pressures of capitalist urbanism and the conditions of capitalist employment or unemployment. In addition, the pressures of urban life grow more intense and it becomes harder to care for any who need care in the conditions of the jungle of the cities. Since no care is forthcoming from an atomized community, and since the family cannot bear all such encumbrances if it is to strip for action in order to survive and "succeed" in the market society, the care of all these layers becomes institutionalized, often in the most barbarous and oppressive forms. Thus understood, the massive growth of institutions stretching all the way from schools and hospitals on the one side to prisons and madhouses on the other represents not just the progress of medicine, education, or crime prevention, but the clearing of the marketplace of all but the "economically active" and "functioning" members of society. . . .

Note that Braverman isolates three processes that link capitalism and institutions: (1) the absolute growth of a dependent population through underemployment, accidents, and other means; (2) the end of traditional ways of caring for dependents; (3) the creation of new types of dependents—not just the sick, poor, or criminal, but all who are economically unproductive and, as a consequence, put out of the way and out of sight. In fact, all three processes can be shown clearly at work in late-eighteenth- and early-nineteenth-century North America. Take some examples:

First, the rise in transiency. By the early nineteenth century a highly mobile class of wage laborers, cut off from close ties with any communities, drifted about and between cities. Living for the most part in nuclear families, with no personal or communal resources for the periods of recurrent poverty or frequent disaster that disfigured their lives, they swelled the dependent class.

The recognition that transiency had become a widespread way of life impelled the reform of the poor laws called for by the Quincy and Yates reports in Massachusetts and New York during the second decade of the nineteenth century. Previously, counties had retained legal responsibility for their own poor almost wherever they wandered. Poor strangers were warned out of town or shipped back to the communities from which they came. But after a point who could claim that any particular community could be considered home for the poor who wandered through it? The upsurge in population movement made obsolete the concept of a community of origin, and the very size of the problem meant that the customary practice would produce an endless stream of poor people shipped back and forth between countries. The sensible solution appeared to be to end the traditional practice and to require each county to support the poor within its boundaries, whatever their place of origin, in a new network of poorhouses strung out across the state.

The problem of the poor illustrates both the growth of dependency and breakdown of traditional ways of coping with poverty. Other developments underscore another process—the creation of new categories of dependency. One of these categories was youth. In earlier times the life cycle of young people had followed a clear and well-defined sequence. At no point in their lives were they uncertain how they should spend their time or in what setting they should live. But the erosion of apprenticeship and, contrary to popular belief, the lack of wage work for young men in the early phase of capitalist development, occurred before the creation of any set of institutions to contain or instruct them. In consequence, young people in the nineteenth-century city faced a crisis that cut across class lines. In the 1820s, for instance, a group of Boston merchants gathered at the home of William Ellery Channing to discuss their anxieties about their sons, no longer needed in the countinghouse or on shipboard at the age of fourteen. The result of that meeting was Boston English High School. In Hamilton, Ontario, the rapid creation of a public school system with special provisions for adolescent students followed the period in which the crisis of idle youth became most acute. Similarly, the disruption of traditional career patterns and living arrangements for young men in New York City provoked worried merchants to create new institutions to guide their behavior and refine their manners.

The nineteenth century's institutionalized population represented the casualties of a new social order: landless workers exposed without buffers to poverty and job-related accidents; men broken by the strain of achievement in a competitive, insecure world; women driven to desperation by the enforced repression inherent in contemporary ideals of domesticity; or even children—casualties on account of their age. But how did institutions assume the shape they did? Why did the response to problems take the form not simply of institutions but of ones specialized in organization and reformist in internt?

Peter Dobkin Hall offers an answer applicable to the early, voluntarist stage of institutional development. After the Revolution, he argues, merchants sought to expand the scope of their activities. To do so, they had to increase specialization, pool risks, create joint-stock corporations, and accumulate capital outside of family firms:

> The disengagement of capital from family firms was achieved through two fundamental innovations in the means of wealth transmission: the testamentary trust and the charitable endowment. Under testamentary trusts it became possible for testators to entirely avoid the partible division of their estates. . . . The charitable endowment was also a kind of trust. Through it moneys could be left in perpetuity to trustees or to a corporate body for the accomplishment of a variety of social welfare purposes—most of which had, in Massachusetts, been traditionally carried out through families. Once the merchants began to search for means of disengaging capital from familial concerns, they quickly recognized the usefulness of charitable endowments both for the accumulation of capital and for relieving their families from the burdens of welfare activity.

The specialization in mercantile life between institutions for credit, insurance, wholesaling, retailing, warehousing, and other activities reflected the division of labor that characterizes capitalist development. That division, as Marx observed, takes opposite forms in social life and in industry. Within manufacturing the division of labor results from the combination of previously distinct operations into one process. By contrast, the social division of labor requires the decomposition of tasks—all originally performed by the family—into separate organizations. "In one case," wrote Marx, "it is the making dependent what was before independent; in the other case the making independent what was before dependent." Equally, with cotton mills, foundries, or shoe factories, new social institutions—schools, penitentiaries, mental hospitals, reformatories—exemplified in their own way the division of labor as the dynamic organizational principle of their age.

The spread of what Christopher Lasch called the "single standard of honor" accompanied the early history of capitalism in North America. By that standard the unproductive became more than a nuisance; they became unworthy. In an attempt to raise their usefulness, the unproductive were swept into massive brick structures that looked distressingly like factories and there taught those lessons in social and economic behavior which, it was hoped, would facilitate their reentry into real workplaces. The depressing sameness about the look of schools, prisons, mental hospitals, and factories belied the sentimentality of the age. The romantic proclamation of the child's innocence, purity, and potential masked the disdain and exasperation that designed urban schools or reformatories. As in the case of children, a transmutation of disdain into purity justified the confinement of women in the institution called home. Indeed, the unwillingness to acknowledge confinement as nasty proved a remarkable feature of early nineteenth-century institutional promotion. But promoters protested too much: Their love for, or at least neutrality towards, those they would incarcerate sounds hollow when echoing through the halls of a nineteenth-century mental hospital, prison, or school. We do no better today, though our particular specialty is perhaps the aged. We construct ghettos for the aged, ostensibly because they want them. In fact, we want to have them out of the way. The single standard of honor remains our legacy and our trademark.

Early capitalist development was experienced by the immediate heirs of the Enlightenment and the Revolution—by people swept simultaneously by optimistic theories of human nature and evangelical religion. Their intellectual and religious heritage composed complex lenses through which people filtered their perceptions of social and economic change. The refraction undoubtedly contributed to their interpretation of crime, poverty, mental illness, ignorance, and youth as conditions of character. Imbued with a belief in progress and committed to either a secular or spiritual millennium, institutional promoters approached their work optimistically, defining their task as the shaping of souls. Nonetheless, characters were to be shaped to a standard with clear components: sensual restraint, dependability, willingness to work, acquiescence in the legitimacy of the social order, and acceptance of one's place within it—all serviceable traits in early capitalist America.

One example, sums up the problem of character, its relation to social institutions, to cultural definitions of deviance, and to the per-

sonal strain exacted by early capitalism: the trouble with the first patient admitted to the New York State Lunatic Asylum when it opened
on January 14, 1843. He thought he was Tom Paine.

L O R I   D .   G I N Z B E R G

*LORI D. GINZBERG (1957–   ) is assistant professor of history and
women's studies at Pennsylvania State University. She is the author
of* Women and the Work of Benevolence: Morality, Politics, and Class
in the Nineteenth Century United States *(1990).*

As a result of the Second Great Awakening of the 1820s and early
1830s, a millennial spirit pervaded efforts at transforming United
States society. Abolitionists, vegetarians, temperance activists, and
crusaders against "male lust"—"ultraists" in nineteenth-century
terms—sought not merely social change but spiritual transformation,
the moral regeneration of the world. That evangelical impulse, as numerous historians have argued, provided the framework in which radical social change was articulated in the antebellum period. American
middle-class radicalism in the 1830s and 1840s evolved in a religious
context, one in which the regeneration of individuals would precede—
and assure—the salvation of society.

Women played a central role both in the ideology and in the means
of the proposed national transformation. Viewed as inherently moral,
women were to instruct by example and to participate in movements
for social, or moral, change. Moral suasion, the chosen means for those
who sought nothing less than the transformation of the public soul,
conformed both to women's supposed qualities and to the nature of
their access to those in power.

For a brief period in the 1830s, ultraist women called on men to ad-
here to a single—"female"—standard of behavior in the interest of social change. Being voteless and, in theory, nonpartisan was part of the
radical vision, and votelessness was a choice made with pride. "Far be
it from me to encourage women to vote," declared Lucretia Mott in an

Lori D. Ginzberg, "'Moral Suasion is Moral Balderdash': Women, Politics, and Social Activism in the 1850s," *Journal of American History* 73 (December 1986). Reprinted with
the permission of the *Journal of American History.*

early speech asserting women's right to do so, "or to take an active part in politics in the present state of our government. . . . Would that man, too, would have no participation in a government recognizing the life-taking principle." "As to [women's] ever becoming partisans, i.e., sacrificing principles to power or interest," wrote Angelina Grimké, "I reprobate this under all circumstances, and in *both* sexes." Access to the political process itself—long assumed by relatively elite and conservative women who petitioned legislators for legal changes, state funds, and corporate status for their organizations—represented to more radical activists the privileges of class, the advocacy of a traditional cause, and narrowness of vision. For ultraists, the adoption of "practical" means for change represented a retreat from principle, from the ideal of an aggressively Christian and implicitly "female" identity that would be shared by all. To those who believed that governments were ineffective at implementing fundamental change, "moral" power was the only kind worth exerting.

By the late 1840s, however, all but a few of the most "ultra" of reformers agreed that moral suasion had failed to transform society. Increasingly, reformers turned to electoral means and to institutional settings through which to consolidate the work of the previous decades. For women, who had been at the heart of the earlier movements, the shifting context of reform was especially momentous.

Two trends in the 1850s helped redefine both the rhetorical and the actual association of women with benevolent change. First, women reformers faced a narrowing definition of political action that emphasized electoral activity rather than the traditional forms of lobbying in which women had participated. As moral suasion became a less convincing call to action, ultraist women's influence in benevolent movements declined. Women became less prominent in a number of activities, such as petitioning, in which they had participated fully in the earlier decades. Voteless, women discovered that benevolent work's growing dependence on electoral means had by the 1850s rendered "female" means for change less effective and thus less popular.

At the same time, more conservative benevolent activists increasingly sought to alleviate social and moral conditions by founding benevolent institutions, often in close alliance with men. Earlier, women had refused male offers of organizational "assistance": When an 1803 legislative committee suggested that the "ladies" of the Boston Female Asylum permit male trustees to control their funds, the female managers "firmly opposed" the attempt to limit their autonomy, and the suggestion was withdrawn, apparently with little dispute. But in 1849, for example, the American Female Guardian Society engaged an advisory board composed of men. Conservative women's new reliance on male advisers suggests that they too were finding traditional female avenues to political and economic favors inadequate.

Both trends affected reformers' commitment to broad social change, for the narrower focus on elections and on institutions corresponded to a declining faith in the moral transformation of American society. To many women in the "utilitarian" 1850s, who came to accept both the brick and stone of institutionalized benevolence and the new emphasis on electoral results, movements that called on slaveowners to free the slaves, drunkards to reject liquor, and seducers to protect the innocent had, quite simply, failed. Substantial changes in the work of activists across the benevolent spectrum signified a more limited, if perhaps more realistic, vision of the possibilities for social change, as benevolent activists sought to restrain the sins they had been unable to eradicate.

The changing nature of politics itself made the commitment to a nonvoting position increasingly anachronistic. Political parties organized unprecedented numbers of voters in the antebellum decades, and voters behaved as if voting mattered. Interest in presidential politics in particular increased greatly. The growing prestige of the vote is seen in the rising percentage of eligible voters who actually bothered to cast ballots. Fewer than 30 percent of adult white males, an unusually small percentage, voted in the presidential election of 1824; in 1828 more than 57 percent did. Voter turnout continued to rise dramatically. In 1840 more than 80 percent of eligible voters, which by then included virtually all white men, went to the polls. Only once more in the antebellum period did the percentage of voters casting ballots in a presidential election top 80 percent (81.2 percent in 1860), but only once did it fall below 70 percent (69.6 percent in 1852). Increased voter participation was even more pronounced in some northeastern states.

The editors of the *History of Woman Suffrage* recognized that a significant change in the popular perception of elections occurred in 1840, when women began to attend "political meetings, as with the introduction of moral questions into legislation, they had manifested an increasing interest in government." In keeping with the growing concern for electoral politics, activist movements increasingly framed their conception of social change in terms of electoral means and goals. The 1850s witnessed a burst of legislative activity on the part of women; hundreds and thousands demanded their civil and political rights and joined men in appealing for laws against alcohol, for removal of politicians and judges, and for corporate charters and funds for their organizations. Women's interest in legislation introduced them to a wider range of political issues. As one writer for the *Lily* commented sarcastically, "The women of Seneca Falls have so far dared to outstep their sphere as to go by scores and hundreds to the political meetings recently held to discuss the constitutionality of the Canal Bill, and to pass upon the conduct of the resigning Senators! And what is more strange still, the men consented to it. . . . Yes, our ladies have mingled at political meetings with the 'low rabble' who go to the polls." The *Una* published regular and varied reports from a correspondent in the visitors' gallery of the United States Senate. In 1854, for the benefit of its largely female readership, the paper added a column entitled "Acts of Legislatures."

Gradually ultraists among both sexes, including the most unyielding of "nonvoters," shifted their enthusiasm to elections in the decade or so before the Civil War. "I am rejoiced to say that Henry is heart and soul in the Republican movement," wrote Elizabeth Cady Stanton to Susan B. Anthony, adding that she herself had "attended all the Republican meetings." Such intense interest in electoral politics characterized the decade that Martha Coffin Wright feared for the attendance at the 1856 Woman's Rights Convention: "[The] engrossing subject of the coming elections," she wrote worriedly to Anthony, "will distract somewhat from the interest of anything not strictly political." Reformers' growing dependence on and interest in electoral politics underscored the powerlessness of a nonvoting position.

The temperance movement provides perhaps the best example of the decidedly "partisan political turn" taken by reformers in the late 1840s and the 1850s. Ironically, the shift toward electoral politics coincided with the entrance of significant numbers of women into temperance work and with the beginning of a long history of viewing temperance as a woman's issue. Its timing suggests that temperance women might have early become convinced of their own growing need for the ballot. Those women most identified with antebellum temperance—Mary C. Vaughan, Amelia Bloomer, and Susan B. Anthony— turned quickly to the emerging woman's movement's demand for suffrage for a new source of authority.

The *Lily,* Amelia Bloomer's paper, most self-consciously reflected the connection between the temperance movement of the 1850s and women's emerging recognition of the value of suffrage. "We have not much faith in moral suasion for the rumseller," the paper admitted in its third issue, as it advocated legislative solutions to problems associated with drunkenness. Over time, contributors—including the vociferous, although not typical, Elizabeth Cady Stanton—demanded that women have a share in the making of laws to restrict the sale of liquor and to permit wives to divorce intemperate men. The paper's tone broke sharply from that of the previous decade, when reformers had encouraged petitioning as a "moral" tool. "Why shall [women] be left only the poor resource of petition?" wondered one article. "For even petitions, when they are from women, without the elective franchise to give them backbone, are of but little consequence."

Because of the temperance movement's outspokenness about the importance of electoral politics, temperance women were indeed relatively willing to express what Amelia Bloomer called "a strong woman's-rights sentiment." In Buffalo, New York, she wrote, "all feel that the only way in which women can do anything effectually in this cause is through the ballot-box, and they feel themselves fettered by being denied the right to thus speak their sentiments in a manner that could not be misunderstood." As early as 1846 "fourteen hundred women from Monroe County [New York] 'bemoaned their lack of the ballot,' and 'petitioned voters to safeguard their welfare at the polls' by voting for candidates opposed to the liquor traffic." Indeed, it was through frustration with temperance men and the "senseless, hopeless work that man points out for woman to do" that Susan B. Anthony became a supporter of woman suffrage.

Many benevolent women, still convinced that the broadest possible social change would be achieved by "female" means, were dismayed by the trend toward electoral means and eschewed the demand for woman suffrage. Only a few women, such as Elizabeth Cady Stanton, had always been aware of the dual nature of moral suasion, its power and its weakness, and had labeled "nonpolitical" means a screen set up by conservative men who smugly advised more radical women to "'pray over it.'" More had doubted whether the vote was a tool that could advance a moral cause: "It is with reluctance that I make the demand for the political rights of women," admitted Lucretia Mott. Even as they moved into suffrage activity, some women continued to insist that only in moral suasion lay the possibilities for a major social transformation and for an enlarged female influence. By the 1850s, however, the radical possibilities of that analysis, like the evangelical fervor that had nurtured it, had been exhausted, and some advocates of social change looked more to the ballot for assistance.

Those who turned to electoral means and goals continued to express ambivalence about partisanship, that buzzword of moral compromise. Within the antislavery movement, for example, even abolitionists who embraced the idea of a third party worried over what partisanship would do to their souls. Women, who did not benefit directly from political victory, sought to take the moral high ground in the electoral contest. Antoinette Brown, who "like her father, was a 'voting abolitionist'" and who had campaigned actively for Gerrit Smith's election to Congress, told Lucy Stone that she "should hate to sink so low as to become a common vulgar politician. Let me first be a [nonvoting] Garrisonian ten times over. I say, Lucy, I pray you won't get converted to such politics as the world at large advocates." Brown had reason to worry; conversions to "such politics as the world at large advocates" were becoming more frequent every day. . . .

That transition was reflected in the work of individual women who consolidated decades-old benevolent organizations in new settings that signified both stability and more limited goals. For example, Abby Hopper Gibbons, abolitionist, prison reformer, and frequent and effective lobbyist, increasingly turned to institutional contexts in which to achieve her benevolent ends. In 1854, following a dispute with male colleagues over conflicting prerogatives, the Female Department of the Prison Association of New York, with Gibbons as president, formed an independent Women's Prison Association and Home. At the same time, Gibbons became president of the Industrial School for German girls, under the auspices of the Children's Aid Society of New York. Virtually all of her work in the 1850s was geared toward building and promoting those institutions. Gibbons was unusual in that she maintained contact with abolitionist and woman's rights circles. Her almost exclusive focus on institutional and legislative means, however, was characteristic of the time.

Even activists who united for the purpose of lobbying for legislation occasionally ended up building institutions. In January 1847 a group of women, leading ultraists such as Lucretia Mott, Abby Kimber Burleigh, Mary Grew, and Sarah Pugh among them, organized in Philadelphia to petition the state legislature for the abolition of capital punishment. After sending off almost twelve thousand signatures a mere six weeks later, the women eagerly applauded the suggestion made by one of their number that they "open a house for the reformation, employment, and instruction of females, who had led immoral lives." By October they had formulated a plan for the new undertaking, purchased a building, recruited 346 women as members, and opened a house of industry. By the following April they had acquired an act of incorporation and a $1,300 mortgage and were on their way to becoming a respected, established institution in the city. In 1854, as evidence of that status, the Pennsylvania legislature granted the Rosine Association an annual appropriation of $3,000.

More conservative and elite women avoided the questionable connotations of aiming their efforts at prostitutes and pursued the tradition of aiding the "worthy poor." Still they, like members of the Rosine Association, focused on establishing institutions. By mid-decade, industrial schools and houses of industry had sprouted throughout urban areas. The American Female Guardian Society (AFGS) alone sponsored a number of industrial schools in New York City and elsewhere in addition to its Home for the Friendless and House of Industry. Numerous older institutions celebrated their growth and stability by moving into larger buildings in the 1850s. The New Haven Orphan Asylum did so in 1853. The AFGS dedicated its first building in 1848 and opened a larger one in 1857. Sketches of those imposing structures constitute the frontispiece of many an annual report, capturing in a picture a changing intellectual and physical environment that the women saw little need to explain. . . .

Both the trend toward electoral means and that toward institutional structures tended to weaken women's overall position in benevolent movements and to narrow the goals of social activism. The rhetorical evidence of women's displacement is clear: Rarely does a student of the 1850s come across calls to men to adopt the standard set by "female" virtues and female votelessness. Even for women working in all or predominantly female institutions, the change in rhetoric signaled an altered context—a waning of authority based on the special morality of "female" values. Indeed, "female" virtue was coming to be seen as just that: an exclusively female quality to be applied within those settings that continued to be dominated by women rather than to be inculcated in the world at large. The prestige of female influence, so celebrated in the form of moral suasion a decade earlier, was seriously threatened at the same time that the focus on elections and on institutions narrowed the goals of benevolence itself. Increasingly those who had once called for the regeneration of the world through "female" virtues relied on asylums and on laws as pragmatic steps to a more limited transformation.

As the goals that activist women sought became more frequently confined to legislation and the issues that absorbed the nation increasingly focused on elections and on the federal government, some women came to feel acutely the limitations of their disfranchisement. The fact that activists recognized voting as an essential tool suggests a new interpretation of the call for woman suffrage made by a small group of women in 1848. The changing political context of the era, rather than simply a sudden awareness of the injustices of women's status, was central to women's demand for the ballot.

The most forward-looking movement of the day, the emerging woman's rights movements, constituted a wholly new route for women, one that advanced explicitly electoral rather than "moral" means for effecting social change. Women active in the movement understood the limitations placed on their work by the ideology of benevolent womanhood and by the strategy of moral suasion. At the same time, woman's rights activists engaged in a rhetorical displacement of "female" virtues: They demanded, in essence, that women's status be raised to a level of equality with men rather than that men should aspire to the standard supposedly set by women. Determined to use the essential tools of electoral change, they adopted a political rather than a moral definition of status. For them, the growing centrality of electoral politics underscored the irony of extolling the virtues of a nonvoting stance. Female influence seemed to have lost its power of persuasion. . . .

The Civil War and the immediate postwar decades would make even clearer how benevolence itself had changed. As their work in the 1850s anticipated, reformers became political activists in a secular society. The women who reached adulthood in the 1850s, launched their careers during the Civil War, and worked on postwar charity boards and committees composed of elite women and men virtually never used the imagery of gender in their public work. Indeed, the founders of postwar charity undermined those traditional images in their very dependence on the wartime principles of efficiency, order, and unsentimental discipline. The State Charities Aid Association of New York, for example, founded by Louisa Lee Schuyler, stressed its freedom from "weak or sickly sentimentality" so closely associated with "a gathering of sympathetic women." Benevolent workers had become liberals who, according to David Montgomery, "sought to bring under the sway of science the management of the social order itself." In close alliance with state governments, they set about creating institutional settings for the "social welfare" programs that would be the focus of a later generation.

By the postwar period the genteel Protestant reformers of antislavery heritage were no longer on the radical cutting edge of United States society. Organizations such as Josephine Shaw Lowell's Charity Organization Society, with its emphasis on science and business principles, helped recast benevolent discourse from a radical call for the moral transformation of society into a conservative defense of the class privilege of benevolent leaders. "Outraged respectability" found an outlet in the new journal the *Nation*, which, although founded by abolitionists James Miller McKim and William Lloyd Garrison, Jr., "opposed nearly all the political economic movements of that period." One of the *Nation*'s primary goals was to find "means of checking the popular passions, which it felt were largely manifestations of ignorance and sin" and which were increasingly defined in class terms.

Workers' and farmers' organizations came to represent the radical voice of United States society after the Civil War. Laying claim to the utopianism that the middle class had rejected, they often adopted the ideals of earlier reformers. "[T]he Christian perfectionism of pre-Civil War evangelical and reform movements," asserts Herbert G. Gutman, "lingered on among many discontented postbellum workers." Middle-class liberals, in contrast, found themselves defending a distasteful "procorporation credo." Depressions, strikes, corruption, and noticeably greater extremes of wealth—all played a role in transforming the context in which middle-class Protestants had once sought a grand moral change in society. Slavery no longer provided an issue around which ultraists could rally their moral forces. Battles between classes and regions cornered the middle class in a defense of privilege based on a growing conviction of human nature's imperfectability. Even the demand for woman suffrage was losing its radical associations as more conservative women became convinced of the value of the vote in their own work. The 1870s and 1880s were a conservative time, as the middle class engaged in a backlash against both prewar utopianism and the radical possibilities of abolition. "Many persons who have been Radicals all their lives," wrote the *Nation's* editor E. L. Godkin in 1871, "are in doubt whether to be Radical any longer.". . .

The ideology of women's unique moral calling thus seemed to have lost its radical potential as a means of social change. Virtue itself came to be treated as solely, even biologically, women's responsibility, rather than as a model to which men should aspire. The belief that human perfectibility was possible through female benevolence was as anachronistic in the postwar decades as the utopian impulse that had inspired it. Not until the Progressive decades would elite Protestant women such as Grace Hoadley Dodge and Jane Addams again infuse social reform with the rhetoric of female virtue and moral righteousness.

The reemergence of a radical voice among middle-class Protestants in the late 1880s suggests the cyclical nature of the history of social reform in the United States. Commonly, reform activity has moved from an agitational focus on the transformation of individuals to an emphasis on electoral and institutional solutions. For example, ultraist reform in the 1830s emerged in part as a reaction against the conservative political tactics of the Benevolent Empire, only to return to political strategies in the 1850s with the decline of moral suasion. Certainly the woman suffrage movement abandoned its concern for broad social change to campaign for suffrage alone. Mainstream suffragists defended their increasingly racist rhetoric and rigid class and ethnic bias on the basis of the difficulty of achieving their exclusively legislative goal.

Similarly, the Progressive movement of the turn of this century, the civil rights movement of the 1950s and 1960s, and the women's movement of the 1960s and 1970s experienced a shift in focus as each moved from an effort to achieve what might loosely be called a moral transformation to a narrower concentration on electoral politics. To the extent that those movements have been absorbed into the electoral process at the expense of other forms of action, they may have both limited their vision of social change and isolated less powerful groups within them.

That is not to say that a vision of social change that proscribes electoral politics—such as that advanced by many ultraists in the 1830s—can necessarily be productive of change in other political contexts. The belief that only in moral change lay the broadest female power, for example, is far less convincing in our own time than it was in the 1830s, when the power of government and other institutions was far less pervasive and the rigidity of class boundaries less daunting. Reformers' adoption of electoral means and goals, however, though it has seemed to democratize the holding of political power, has involved tradeoffs: As the history of benevolent reform during the 1850s illustrates, electoral politics has tended to isolate groups with limited access to those in authority, to redefine the nature of social reform, and to limit the vision of reformers themselves.

9

SLAVE CULTURE: AFRICAN OR AMERICAN?

Since the 1960s, research on slave culture has attracted some of the nation's best scholars. The evolution of the debate over slave culture, its existence, its roots, and its accomplishments is to a substantial degree intertwined with the continuing debate over race relations in the United States. At stake are ideas about race, the existence of autonomous black life and culture distinct from the impress of white institutions, the profile of the black family and the meanings attaching to it, the causes and cures for black poverty, and the role of Africa in the imagination and culture of African Americans. There are few areas of investigation so charged with contemporary significance. Taking a position on the nature of slave culture inevitably entails a vision of black life today.

The historiography of slave culture has focused on the degree of autonomy slaves were able to retain and hence how much room they had in which to construct a culture of their own. A related question is the degree to which slaves were able to use their African past as a source for cultural creation and continuity. A strong relation with Africa has come to suggest slaves' ability to maintain a vital and proud cultural tradition. Slave studies began around the turn of the century with Ulrich Phillips, a southern apologist with racist views who argued that slaves had a fair degree of autonomy, but no connection with Africa, from where, he thought, they were lucky to be gone. This view stood until the early 1960s when Stanley Elkins argued that the experience of slavery obliterated any connection with a usable past. The seventies saw an outpouring of scholarship designed to refute this view. Historians began to search for links with Africa. This quest became more sophisticated, using techniques from anthropology, linguistics, and archeology to prove that West Africans not only brought their culture with them, they also transmitted it in some degree to the surrounding white community. One contemporary scholar has managed to do what earlier historians believed impossible—to trace the American fate of various West African ethnic groups. He has shown that their cultures helped transform them into different occupational and status groups and that these new identities, in turn, structured their emerging understanding of themselves as black Americans. Current scholars of the slave experience may differ on the degree to which Africa shaped the American black experience, but none would deny its significance. Indeed, many historians regard ignoring the African background of slave culture as a glaring scholarly omission.

Interest in nineteenth-century black life is recent. Very few white historians saw anything to attract their attention to slave life until the second half of this century. As historian Nathan Huggins has written, "The social death implicit in slavery and racial caste was carried over into the writing of American history until the 1960s. Black historians aside, American history, almost universally, was written as if blacks did not exist and their experience was of no consequence."[1] The most influential exception was Ulrich B. Phillips, son of a plantation owner, who was intent on putting a humane face on slavery and slaveholders and to that end published *American Negro Slavery* in 1918 (See Chapter 4.) He portrayed slavery as a benign institution, not very profitable and something of a burden to slave owners who were responsible for looking after their charges. African Americans were inherently inferior to whites.

Despite, or because of, his racist view, Phillips's richly detailed work inspired other historians. Among them were the African American historians W. E. B. Du Bois and John Hope Franklin, who challenged different aspects of Phillips's work, and in 1945, the Marxist scholar Herbert Aptheker, who published a slim collection of essays attacking Phillips and his views, particularly the idea that blacks were submissive.

Aptheker's *Essays in the History of the American Negro*[2] listed numerous instances of resistance to slavery. Aptheker also restored blacks to their rightful place as Union soldiers, two hundred thousand strong, and as leaders and forceful participants in the abolitionist movement, whom historians had seen until then as dangerous (white) fanatics or liberal (white) reformers. Aptheker did not have a wide audience at the time, but scholars have had to contend with the issues he raised: the extent of black resistance to slavery and restoring to black people their contributions, forgotten by the wider culture, as abolitionists, saboteurs of slavery, and soldiers.

Despite Aptheker's combative work, Phillips's account remained the more widely accepted version of slavery, if only because no full-scale treatment of the subject appeared until Kenneth Stampp, in 1956, published *The Peculiar Institution: Slavery in the Antebellum South*. Stampp's earliest scholarly interests in showing that the Civil

---

[1]Nathan Irvin Huggins, *Black Odyssey, The African American Ordeal in Slavery,* (New York, 1977, 1990), p. xvii.

[2]Ulrich B. Phillips, *American Negro Slavery* (New York, 1918); Herbert Aptheker, *Essays in the History of the America Negro* (New York, 1945).

War was fought over slavery led him to study slavery itself. He researched *The Peculiar Institution* in archives that were still largely segregated during the volatile years surrounding the *Brown* v. *Topeka Board of Education* decisions and their immediate aftermath.

Stampp reversed Phillips's findings and, backed by meticulous archival research, asserted that slavery was an institution both of great severity and profitability. To Stampp race was without significance. "Slaves were merely ordinary human beings."[3] These findings found a receptive audience in the postwar years of renewed civil rights activism. However new his racial views, Stampp, like many others who came after him, followed Phillips's outline for the debate. Did planters treat slaves well or badly? What was the extent of paternalism on plantations? Was there a slave culture? If so, were its elements African or American? While Phillips had seen African Americans as imitating white culture, Stampp saw them suspended between the two, unable to use the past fruitfully and not yet able to create their own traditions. Influenced by the African American sociologist E. Franklin Frazier's *The Negro Family in the United States,* Stampp portrayed the slave family as too fragile to provide much respite from the rigors of slave life, as so fundamentally matriarchal that men contributed little or nothing of importance, and as a family in which even mothers could barely cook, clothe, or take care of their children.[4]

Just three years later, Stanley Elkins suggested in *Slavery: A Problem in American Institutional and Intellectual Life* that slavery had been a system of such complete and effective coercion that it reduced slaves to psychological helplessness. Elkins, who used social psychology to make his argument, had been influenced by Frank Tannenbaum's comparative work *Slave and Citizen.* Tannenbaum maintained that slavery in Iberian colonies had been a looser system than slavery in the United States, more subject to the moderating influences of the Catholic Church and feudal loyalties. Elkins, like Tannenbaum, insisted that in the United States, slavery had been a total system analogous to the concentration camps of World War II, producing radically dependent and foolish "Sambos" or damaged people capable of little in the way of resistance or creativity. Elkins declared his interest in substituting science and objectivity for the morality that he thought flawed Stampp's neoabolitionist view of slavery. He criticized Stampp and the anthropological scholarship on which he relied, for focusing

------

[3]Robert Abzug and Stephen Maizlish, eds., *New Perspectives on Race and Slavery in America, Essays in Honor of Kenneth Stampp* (Lexington, Ky., 1986,) pp. 1–3.

[4]E. Franklin Frazier, *The Negro Family in the United States* (Chicago, 1939): Kenneth M. Stampp, "The Daily Life of the Southern Slave," in Nathan Huggins, Martin Kilson, Daniel Fox, eds., *Key Issues in the Afro-American Experience* (New York, 1971), pp. 116–37.

on "examples of Negro courage, Negro rebelliousness, Negro hatred for the slave system, and so on—all the characteristics one might expect of white men who knew nothing of what it meant to be reared in slavery."[5]

Although Stampp was a forceful critic of racism, on other topics he echoed Phillips. Phillips insisted that slaves were able to carve out a space for themselves and were able to negotiate the system of slavery so that owners simply could not exercise anything like total control. For Phillips slave cooperation was part of his effort to give slavery a benign profile. Subsequent historians, such as Stampp, however, developed a theme of black helplessness and familial destruction in a well-intentioned attempt to prove that slavery was devoid of black complicity.

It is ironic that Elkins's thesis and E. Franklin Frazier's *Black Bourgeoisie: The Rise of a New Middle Class*, which elaborated on the theme of matriarchy, provided fuel for Daniel Patrick Moynihan's *The Negro Family: The Case for National Action*, published in 1965. Moynihan was Nixon's assistant secretary of labor and his book was intended as a liberal call for programs to ameliorate the poverty of urban ghetto life. Moynihan described what he saw as the "tangle of pathology" that stemmed from slavery and over a century of white supremacist policies under which families were matriarchal. The resulting mother-dominated family "seriously retards the progress of the group as a whole, and imposes a crushing burden on the negro male and, in consequence on a great many negro women as well."[6]

Elkins's book and Moynihan's report produced an extraordinary outpouring of criticism. Calling black women, perhaps the least powerful members of American society, matriarchs and placing the burden of black family pathology on their already overburdened shoulders as they struggled to raise children in ghettoes ravaged by unemployment and poverty was simply too much, however good Moynihan's objectives. This debate was partly responsible for mobilizing historians to research and revive, for a totally different reason, Phillips's depiction of a lively and to some degree autonomous slave culture.

Since the 1970s, no historian has claimed that slaves had been rendered incapable of creating a world of their own or that they did not resist the conditions of slavery. In the process of recreating aspects of slave initiative and creativity, historians have spent considerable time on slave family life and religion. In refuting the Sambo theory, histori-

---

[5]Stanley Elkins, *Slavery, A Problem in Institutional and Intellectual Life* (Chicago, 1959), p. 23; Frank Tannenbaum, *Slave and Citizen, The Negro in the Americas* (New York, 1946)

[6]Daniel Patrick Moynihan, *The Negro Family: The Case for National Action* (Washington, D.C., 1965); Lee Rainwater and William Yancey, *The Moynihan Report and the Politics of Controversy* (Cambridge, Mass., 1967), p. 29.

ans disagreed over how much autonomy slaves exercised, about what kinds of actions actually constituted resistance to their owners, and to what degree they were party to the paternalism of their masters. For the first time, historians asked about slave culture's precise relationship to the dominant culture and under what conditions it flourished or withered.

Elkins as well as E. Franklin Frazier had argued that slaves arrived traumatized by the horrors of capture and the middle passage and were sold without regard to their ethnicity. These experiences and subsequent sales meant that they retained little or nothing of their African past. Stampp's work also insisted on the extinction of any trace of African culture. Other historians, including Eugene Genovese, would argue that African culture and religion played a role in the lives of slaves and was a source of inspiration for an Afro-American culture. This argument had its roots in the work of the anthropologist Melville Herskovitz, who had tracked down "survivals" from Africa, such as musical instruments.

Where Moynihan and Elkins had emphasized damaged psyches and pathological behavior, historians responded with massive evidence detailing resilience, vitality, cultural coherence, and the presence of Africa in slave communities. Eugene Genovese, in *Roll, Jordan, Roll, The World The Slaves Made* (1972), initiated the first historical effort to look at slave life from the point of view of slaves. While Genovese was, in many respects, locked into Phillips's framework, and, ironically, came to a number of the same conclusions, he did so from the standpoint of respect for African Americans' dignity and their struggle to resist the conditions of slavery. Genovese essentially adopted Phillips's concept of paternalism, agreeing with Phillips that it allowed slaves a certain negotiating room, including the ability to force planters into accepting compromises with regard to the speed and conditions of their work. While Phillips had been interested in exonerating owners by emphasizing their paternalistic concerns, Genovese was interested in demonstrating that paternalism provided slaves with a substantial margin—contrary to Elkins—in which to manoeuver and create relationships and rituals to serve their social and cultural needs.[7]

Although he was criticized for ignorance of Africa, Genovese asserted the African basis of aspects of slave culture. He believed that Herskovitz had overstated his case for "survivals," but Frazier had similarly overstated his against the possibilities of African influences. "Black America's tie," he wrote, "with an African tradition . . . helped

---

[7]Eugene D. Genovese, *Roll, Jordan, Roll: The World the Slaves Made* (New York, 1974), pp. 3–7.

shape a culture entirely its own."[8] He used evidence from anthropologists and archeologists in describing African origins of a variety of burial customs and religious and magical beliefs. For contemporary scholars of black culture, Genovese's view of the importance of paternalism compromised the independence he claimed for slave culture, yet his massive work was the first since that of W.E.B. Du Bois in another context[9] had argued that the influences of culture went both ways, and that when whites and blacks interacted, the former did not merely impose their culture on the latter.

In the same year that Genovese's volume was published, the economic historians Robert Fogel and Stanley Engerman published *Time on the Cross*, a book as controversial as Elkins's had been. They used a quantitative approach to aspects of slavery to determine how profitable it was and how brutal. While their focus was not slave culture, they did try to describe the plantation atmosphere in which culture might or might not develop. For many their methodology—estimating the number of whippings on a plantation and the calories in a slave's diet—seemed inappropriate and offensive. That Fogel and Engerman's conclusions showed that slavery was a mild and profitable system of coerced labor, offering a range of worker incentives and promotions, seemed to many further evidence that their project was ill-conceived.[10] Herbert Gutman and Richard Sutch showed that Engerman and Fogel's arguments were flawed by over-reliance on their economic model rather than relying on substantial research and that they grossly underestimated punishments on plantations while overestimating planters' incentives to keep slaves healthy and motivated. Critics also argued that counting whippings did nothing to explain their psychological effects or contribute to a genuine assessment of the severity of slavery—that "cliometry" was the wrong tool for evaluating slavery. Despite, or rather because of, its critics, however, *Time on the Cross*, like Elkins's *Slavery*, provoked many refutations, which have enlarged our understanding of the living conditions of slaves. And it emphasized the importance of understanding how work shaped slave culture.

John Blassingame wrote *The Slave Community: Plantation Life in the Antebellum South* as a direct refutation of the Elkins thesis. He distinguished slave life in the quarters as the primary environment and slave life in contact with whites and during work as a secondary environment, which he argued "was far less important in determining his personality. . . . The more [he was] immune from the control of

---

[8]Genovese, *Roll*, p. 210; Michael A. Gomez, *Exchanging Our Country Marks* (Chapel Hill, N.C., 1998), pp. 248–49.

[9]W.E.B. Du Bois, *The Souls of Black Folk*, David W. Blight and Robert Gooding-Williams, eds. (1903; reprinted Boston, 1997).

[10]Peter J. Parish, *Slavery: History and Historians* (New York, 1989), pp. 32–37.

whites, the more the slave gained in personal autonomy and positive self-concepts."[11] He insisted that slavery and plantation life had not undermined the African American's ability to invent a life for himself out of a rich past and a meager present. As to African influence, "The sophisticated research of ethno-musicologists, anthropologists, and folklorists, coupled with the evidence in a large number of primary sources, suggests that African culture was much more resistant to the bludgeon that was slavery than historians have hitherto suspected."[12] Scholars have questioned how light the influence of the work environment could have been on slaves, whose lives were determined by the work they did. And women have challenged Blassingame's unswerving focus on males. But Blassingame's conclusions about Africa and the complexity of slave culture stand.

Herbert Gutman's *The Black Family in Slavery and Freedom, 1750–1925*, published in 1976, was another early and forceful response to the Elkins-Moynihan theses. He also criticized Genovese's emphasis on paternalism for shifting the focus from the development of an Afro-American culture to overemphasizing white influence. Gutman's work detailed the remarkable stability of slave marriages under the assaults of slavery and the persistent and poignant efforts of former slaves during Reconstruction to find those spouses and children who had been sold away or had disappeared during the war. In addition, Gutman found a strong knowledge of and preference among slaves for exogamy, which contrasted sharply with the frequency of first-cousin marriages among planters.[13] In a similar vein, Gutman traced naming patterns among slave parents to African customs, demonstrating not only the forceful efforts of slaves to hold their families together but also the long shadow African ways cast in the formation of kin ties in the New World. As Gutman wrote, "Slave exogamy as contrasted to planter endogamy is one reason to put aside mimetic theories of Afro-American culture, and so are the naming practices of slaves." Gutman was not just testifying to the persistence of cultural links between Africans and antebellum African Americans. He was simultaneously disproving the contention of Phillips and others that African Americans could do little but imitate white culture—in Phillips's view because they were incapable of creativity, in Elkins's because slavery rendered them psychologically impotent, and in Stampp's because their past was inaccessible to them.

---

[11]Blassingame, *Slave Community*, quoted in Peter J. Parish, *Slavery: History and Historians* (New York, 1989), p. 76; John Blassingame, *The Slave Community* (New York, 1972), p. 105.

[12]Blassingame, *Community* pp. 34–35. He revised his book to present a fuller picture of slave culture in a second edition.

[13]Herbert Gutman, *The Black Family in Slavery and Freedom, 1750–1925* (New York, 1976) p. 93.

Gutman's findings attracted some criticism from scholars who were afraid it was too rosy a picture of people living under a terrible regime. On the one hand, sociologist Orlando Patterson, in his wide-ranging exploration of slave systems throughout world history, found that slave owners *aspired* to accomplish what Elkins insisted they did accomplish—the destruction of the slave's individuality and sense of self-respect—but that by and large they failed. He agreed with Genovese and Gutman that the search for dignity and honor was omnipresent in slave communities, rendered more urgent because those were precisely what slave owners tried to monopolize. On the other hand, he disagreed with Gutman's reading of some of his particular evidence, for example, that most slaves managed to choose a surname other than their owners' and that this served to reject owners' overbearing intimacy and establish a degree of slave autonomy. Patterson found that most slaves had their owners' surnames after all and that those changed if they changed owners.

Although most scholarship on slavery would be of narrower scope than Gutman's or Genovese's, and would consist of investigations of communities at particular times, the discovery of autonomous cultures and African influence would continue.[14] Among the foremost of these explorations of African-influenced slave culture was Charles Joyner's *Down by the Riverside,* a study of Waccamaw Neck, All Saints Parish in South Carolina, one of the richest rice-growing communities in America, and source of a large number of South Carolina's secessionist leaders. South Carolina had the highest population of blacks in the country, and in Lower All Saints Parish the ratio was nine blacks to one white. Joyner meticulously recreated the work habits of residents of Waccamaw and their West African roots. He explained the invention and use of the Waccamaw residents' Gullah language, made up of English and West African words, primarily Wolof but also Igbo, Ewe, Mandinke, and Yoruba. Gullah was a creole language that had a completely different grammar from English and a distinctive vocabulary and form, evolving over the late eighteenth and nineteenth centuries.[15] In Joyner's view of Waccamaw just before the Civil War the slaves had created "out of African traditions as well as American circumstances . . . a new language, a new religion—indeed, a new culture—that not only allowed them to endure the collective tragedy of slavery, but to bequeath a notable and enduring heritage to generations to come."[16]

---

[14]Orlando Patterson, *Slavery and Social Death, A Comparative Study* (Cambridge, Mass., 1982), p. 56.

[15]Charles Joyner, *Down by the Riverside: A South Carolina Slave Community* (Urbana and Chicago, 1984), pp. 196–224.

[16]Ibid., p. 242.

As a result of studies like Joyner's few scholars today examine any aspect of pre–Civil War life without some attention to African pasts. This is true for works as different as Margaret Washington Creel's study of slave religion among the Gullahs and W. Jeffrey Bolster's *Black Jacks, African American Seamen in the Age of Sail,* in which he probed West African sailing and navigational experience to introduce African American mariners.[17]

The possibilities for thinking more broadly about slave culture also grew from the expansion of social history to include the history of women. In 1984 Deborah Gray White published *Ar'n't I A Woman?,* the first critique of sexism in the historiography of slavery. White's argument was twofold: not only had historians left women out of their accounts of slavery, but when they included them it was as matriarchs or helpless dependents. She criticized Blassingame, Genovese, Elkins, and Stampp for distorting or omitting enslaved women in their histories. She also raised the politically charged issue of black women as more vulnerable than any other group to stereotyping on both racial and gender grounds. In her first chapter she discussed two destructive stereotypes that derived from the slave trade and slavery: black women as promiscuous and black women as mammies.[18] She found continuity between West African marriage traditions and slave families, particularly in the strength of mother-child relationships and in the tracing of matrilineal ties. She also established the existence of a strong female network, which helped account for numerous examples of strong and resilient slave women.[19] White's contribution opened her to the criticism that fighting battles for black women's dignity was less important than, and sometimes counter to, the fight for equality for all black people. But it was a useful critique of the male bias attendant on most slavery studies and also led the way for other studies of slavery that explored the experience of women.[20]

Feminist criticism has also reinforced the idea that race, like gender, is socially constructed. In this view, as Kenneth Stampp posited, in and of itself race has no meaning; its meanings accrue from ideas the powerful attach to it. A dominant group gives racial characteristics social meaning when it is in their interest. Edmund Morgan's example was in the Chesapeake when elite Virginians stigmatized blackness when it became useful as a way to consolidate their bonds with poor

---

[17]Margaret Washington Creel, *"A Peculiar People," Slave Religion and Community-Culture Among the Gullahs* (New York, 1988), and W. Jeffrey Bolster, *Black Jacks, African American Seamen in the Age of Sail* (Cambridge, Mass., London, 1997).

[18]Deborah Gray White, *Ar'n't I A Woman?* (New York, 1984), pp. 23, 27–61.

[19]Ibid., pp. 91–141.

[20]Brenda Stevenson, *Life in Black and White, Family and Community in the Slave South* (New York, 1996), is a good example.

whites. Kathleen Brown, updating Morgan, in *Goodwives, Nasty Wenches and Anxious Patriarchs*, placed the social construction of gender *and* race at the heart of political relations in early Virginia. Whereas Edmund Morgan saw the development of racist legislation after Bacon's Rebellion as a way to secure the loyalty of poor white farmers to wealthy white planters against the black "other," Brown saw a more complex construction, not only of the male black other, but the *extremely* other black female. Building on White's point that black women are doubly vulnerable to stereotyping, Brown posited that African women were even more objectified than black men by their defeminization and their degraded status, which were secured through transformed legal and social meanings given to womanliness. Morgan had pointed out how white men profited and lost from stigmatizing blackness, and Brown showed how white women profited and lost from new, late-eighteenth-century requirements for what constituted a woman. The spread of gentility for white women furthered the degradation of black women and poor whites by the comparisons it continually provided.[21]

Another useful by-product of a gender analysis of slave culture has been the devaluation of paternalism as a practical way of understanding slavery. As historians, primarily women, have looked at plantation mistresses and their active participation in sustaining slavery, the paternalistic master shouldering his responsibilities toward "his people" has begun to disappear, along with debates over whether slaves compromised or collaborated with paternalism.[22]

In a parallel development, scholars continued to develop the links between the growing knowledge about African roots in slave culture to a militant contemporary black consciousness. George Rawick, Sterling Stuckey, and Lawrence Levine have all emphasized the autonomous growth of black culture. Rawick and Stuckey were interested in seeing the African dimensions of black nationalism. Stuckey wrote of the "centrality of the ancestral past to the African in America."[23] This claim was directly related to his account of the varieties of resistance of African Americans to the oppression of whites.

---

[21]Kathleen M. Brown, *Good Wives, Nasty Wenches and Anxious Patriarchs: Gender, Race and Power in Colonial Virginia* (Chapel Hill, N.C., 1996).

[22]Joyce Chaplin, "Berlin's Two Concepts of Slavery," in *Reviews in American History*, Vol. 27 (Baltimore, June 1999), pp. 192–93. See, for example, Elizabeth Fox-Genovese, *Within the Plantation Household, Black and White Women of the Old South* (Chapel Hill, N.C., 1988); Catherine Clinton, *The Plantation Mistress: Woman's World in the Old South* (New York, 1982). Most recently, Marli Weiner, *Mistresses and Slaves, Plantation Women in South Carolina, 1830–1880* (Urbana, Chicago, 1998), and Cynthia Kierner, *Beyond the Household, Women's Place in the Early South, 1700–1835* (Ithaca, N.Y., and London, 1998).

[23]Sterling Stuckey, *Slave Culture: Nationalist Theory and the Foundations of Black America*, quoted in Parish, *Slavery*, p. 77; Stuckey, *Slave*, p. 43.

Lawrence Levine, author of *Black Culture, Black Consciousness, Afro-American Folk Thought from Slavery to Freedom* (1977), focused on African traditions, folk tales, and beliefs at the center of his study of storytelling, music, and other aspects of Afro-American culture. In emphasizing African origins of slave music, Levine further discredited the Elkins thesis by establishing cultural persistence and the possibilities for creativity that remained despite slavery. He also wished to create an alternative understanding of resistance to include the evidence of spiritual resistance he found among African American Christians. He feared that scholars had defined resistance too narrowly, as violent rebellion or escape. Instead, he insisted resistance originated in an uncolonized imagination. "If mid-twentieth century historians have difficulty perceiving the sacred universe created by slaves as a serious alternative to the societal system created by southern slaveholders, the problem may be the historians' and not the slaves."[24] The sacred world view of slaves, Levine argued, invested *all* natural things with spiritual life. Slaves thus possessed a radically different attitude toward the environment and living creatures from their owners' (not to mention their historians').

Levine, like Genovese, emphasized that slave religion was the all-important center of black resistance, the heart of African American vitality and the spiritual fuel that helped them to endure their daily lives. The distinguished historian of southern religion John Boles, however, has argued that scholars may have exaggerated the degree of autonomy blacks experienced in practicing their religion. Instead, Boles stressed the degree to which black Christians adopted white values. John Blassingame has agreed, seeing the church more as a force for Americanizing slaves than as a site of cultural resistance.[25] The debate over the degree of religious autonomy slaves experienced is crucial to estimating how effectively they were able to establish positive, alternative ways of constructing their world.

Another important shift in the study of African American culture has been from the nineteenth to the seventeenth and eighteen centuries, which also has brought scholars into contact with Africa and Africans. One of the pioneers in that shift was Peter Wood. In *Black Majority, Negroes in Colonial South Carolina from 1670 Through the Stono Rebellion*,[26] published in 1974, he plumbed West African sources in discussing slavery in South Carolina. His ground-breaking study traced the partial immunity of many Africans to the worst ef-

---

[24]Lawrence Levine, "Slave Songs and the Slave Consciousness," in Allen Weinstein and Frank Otto Gatell, eds., *American Negro Slavery* (New York, 1973), p. 177.

[25]Parish, *Slavery*, pp. 83–84.

[26]Peter Wood, *Black Majority: Negroes in Colonial South Carolina from 1670 Through the Stono Rebellion* (New York, 1974).

fects of malaria, which made them unfortunately desirable as workers, particularly to rice planters who wanted workers to toil in hot, insect-infested bogs day after day. Wood argued that these planters actively sought slaves from West African regions with knowledge of rice culti-vation. (This was an early contradiction of ideas that ethnicity corre-lated poorly with colonial slave selection.) Wood also noted direct African carryovers, like the guinea fowl, guinea corn, the use of drink-ing gourds, and the most important carryover of all—the large percent-age of militant Angolans who participated in the Stono Rebellion.[27] Wood's erudite blend of research into Africa and colonial America in-spired scholars to investigate less timidly the African roots of African American practices, beliefs, and traditions and to imagine pre–Civil War America as a dynamic mixture of these influences.

In contrast, Albert J. Raboteau, in *Slave Religion: The Invisible In-stitution in the Antebellum South*, also looked at eighteenth-century African American culture and cosmology and argued that a variety of factors "tended to inhibit the survival of African culture and religion in the United States." What remained was to be found in spirituals, the ring shout and folk beliefs.[28] In studying black religion, Raboteau emphasized less the autonomy and Africanness of worship than the search for and insistence upon equality within Christianity. For exam-ple, in an essay on the impact of the Revolution on slave religion, Raboteau described Afro-American preachers "mediating between Christianity and the experience of the slaves, interpreting the stories, symbols, and events of the Bible to fit the day-to-day lives of those held in bondage." In his account, slaves turned not to traditional African sources of wisdom and solace but to Christianity for a useful and restorative understanding of daily life. And, although some schol-ars have criticized him for underestimating the significance of the African past in his search, others have sustained his findings.[29]

Mechal Sobel made imaginative use of West African philosophy in *The World They Made Together* (1978), an innovative view of the eigh-teenth-century Chesapeake. Although noting African influences, she set in relief those beliefs of blacks and whites in the Chesapeake which overlapped: beliefs about time, work, space, architecture, and the universe. She placed them in the early Baptist context where

---

[27]Ibid.

[28]Albert J. Raboteau, *Slave Religion: The Invisible Institution in the Antebellum South* (New York, 1978), p. 92.

[29]Timothy E. Fulop and Albert J. Raboteau, *African American Religion, Interpre-tive Essays in History and Culture* (New York, 1997), pp. 14–15; Margaret Washington Creel, *"A Peculiar People": Slave Religion and Community-Culture Among the Gul-lahs* (New York, 1988), pp. 6–7, Intro. ftn. 9; Albert J. Raboteau, "The Slave Church in the Era of the American Revolution," in Ronald Hoffman and Ira Berlin, eds., *Slavery and Freedom in the Age of the American Revolution* (Urbana and Chicago, 1983), pp. 205–206.

blacks experienced a measure of equality. While some scholars disagreed with her conclusion that whites and blacks formed something that could be truly called a community, her study of early, interracial Baptist congregations was of great importance in integrating African and Western thought. And she reasserted the important theme that African and white colonial cultures interpenetrated one another and that mutual shaping took place. Whites did not impose their values and traditions unilaterally on blacks, nor were blacks predominantly engaged in imitating white culture.[30]

Gwendolyn Midlo Hall, another scholar who went back to the eighteenth century, found a concentration of African survivals. By 1731 the French had imported into Louisiana about six thousand Africans, a large proportion of whom were Bambara from what is today Senegal.[31] The French had traded extensively in Africa with the Bambara, whose military traditions were so strong that the word Bambara, all along the western coast of Africa, came to mean slave soldier.[32] Bambara words made their way into French as their navigating skills and recipes shaped Louisiana culture. The unusual cultural uniformity of the Bambara population in Louisiana allowed Hall to find more predictable correspondences between African and New World customs and practices than most scholars have found elsewhere. The contributions of Sobel, Creel, Hall, Raboteau, and others have begun to fill a lamentable gap in our knowledge of the religious traditions of West Africans.[33]

In continuing efforts to understand the African influence on colonial culture, historians have reached out beyond history and anthropology for tools. Anne Elizabeth Yentsch, a historian-archeologist, explored West African–American cultural connections through an investigation of the material remains of an eighteenth-century Maryland family. Her work provided insight into the blended daily lives of blacks and whites. Through travelers' accounts, she traced seventeenth- and eighteenth-century West African eating habits, women's gardening methods, and cooking utensils and found much that corresponded with her archeological data from Maryland.[34]

---

[30]Mechal Sobel, *The World They Made Together* (Princeton, N.J., 1978).

[31]Gwendolyn Midlo Hall, *Africans in Colonial Louisiana: The Development of Afro-Creole Culture in the Eighteenth Century* (Baton Rouge, La., 1992), Chapter 1.

[32]Ira Berlin, *Many Thousands Gone, The First Two Centuries of Slavery in North America* (Cambridge, Mass., 1998), pp. 81–82.

[33]Michel Gomez has criticized scholars for studying the European roots of North American beliefs, but not affording Africans the same interest and attention. Michael Gomez, *Exchanging Our Country Marks* (Chapel Hill, N.C., 1998), p. 248.

[34]Anne Elizabeth Yentsch, *A Chesapeake Family and Their Slaves, A study in Historical Archaeology* (New York, 1994), pp. 196–215. See also John Michael Vlach, *Back of the Big House: The Architecture of Plantation Slavery* (Chapel Hill, 1993), for another example of this kind of work.

Studying the eighteenth century has inevitably led to looking at the impact of the American Revolution on slavery and the development of slave culture. It became increasingly clear that the Revolution's successes and its failures incised the fault lines that led to the Civil War. Furthermore, as Ronald Hoffman and Ira Berlin wrote, "The failure of scholars until recently to focus attention on the black experience and the role of slavery during the formative period of the American nation is difficult to explain. But one thing is clear—for too many years, historians were parties to the compromise of the founding fathers," that is, the compromise to leave Jefferson's proposed condemnation of the slave trade out of the Declaration of Independence for fear of splitting the colonial coalition.[35]

Across both time and region, historians had homogenized the experiences of slaves. By seeing the antebellum period as the culmination of an inevitable progression rather than simply another period of changing patterns, scholars had overlooked important phases in agriculture, labor, and slave life. In looking directly at the Revolution, historians realized that upheaval both solidified slavery in the South and hastened its demise in the North. As David Brion Davis has explained, the Revolution removed the British effort to control westward expansion. At the same time, it also fueled northern artisans' hatred of any form of bound labor.[36] Hence, the forces of slave expansion and free labor ideology unleashed by the Revolution were responsible for deepening the already evident divisions in the country.

A third theme which studying slavery and the Revolution invited was the way it affected blacks. It encouraged migration and hence destabilized the black family after a late colonial period of relative security.[37] Revolutionary ideology and the changeover from the year-round labor demands of tobacco to the seasonal needs of corn and wheat in the upper Chesapeake made manumission and flexibility of slave life more common there. On the other hand it made life in the low country, where slaves were numerous and crops produced much wealth, harder and less likely to result in manumission. In other words, it increased disparities in the living and working arrangements among blacks.[38]

Most important, perhaps, the Revolution provided black people

---

[35]Hoffman and Berlin, *Slavery*, p. xi; see also Sylvia Frey, *Water from the Rock: Black Resistance in a Revolutionary Age* (Princeton, N.J., 1991).

[36]David Brion Davis, "American Slavery and the American Revolution," in Hoffman and Berlin, *Slavery*, p. 273.

[37]Alan Kulikoff, "Uprooted Peoples: Black Migrants In the Age of the American Revolution," in Hoffman and Berlin, *Slavery*, pp. 143–44.

[38]Philip D. Morgan, "Black Society in the Low Country, 1760–1810," in Hoffman and Berlin, *Slavery*, p. 83.

with the ideal of equality to which they continued to hold their country accountable after the brief rush of postrevolutionary manumission had ceased. Benjamin Quarles, the great and venerable historian of blacks and the revolutionary experience, quoted Virginian St. George Tucker's observation that blacks who went to fight for the British to get their freedom in exchange for revolutionary military service thought of freedom as a good, but blacks who joined Gabriel Prosser's rebellion in 1800 thought of freedom as a right. Quarles concluded, "To a degree approaching unanimity, [blacks] clothed the War for Independence with meaning and a significance transcending their own day and time and not confined to the shores of the new republic. To them the full worth of the American Revolution lay ahead."[39]

Two immensely important studies by Ira Berlin and Philip Morgan place the eighteenth century at the heart of any understanding of North American slavery. These massive syntheses chart the changing faces of slavery and continue to attempt to capture the reasons for obdurate persistence of racial inequality in the United States. Berlin's *Many Thousands Gone* pulls together an enormous amount of research on slavery and starts with several unfamiliar premises: at the beginning of the nineteenth century most slaves did not live in the black belt, they were not Christian, and they did not cultivate cotton. Berlin contends that race and slavery were both transformed in the antebellum years. Racism grew in the North and the South for different reasons. In the North it bolstered the rights and prerogatives of the common man, who understood the value of "whiteness" in a society that consigned its most servile labor to blacks.[40] In the South, it grew to undergird planter control of the new, more taxing system of slavery, rapidly expanding in the black belt where short staple cotton grew. Slave owners transferred over a million slaves to the area stretching from Georgia on the east to what is now eastern Texas in the antebellum years. "The cotton revolution—like the earlier tobacco and rice revolutions—eroded the traditional constraints on the master's power. Limitations on the slaveholders' authority achieved through years of arduous negotiations disappeared in an instant, as planters used the new demands of cotton cultivation to revoke the long-established prerogatives, strip slaves of skills, and ratchet up the level of exploitation."[41]

Berlin's book exemplifies a number of trends that characterize the most recent literature on slavery. Stampp, Genovese, and others had argued for a picture of antebellum slavery that crystallized in the mid-

---

[39]Benjamin Quarles, "The Revolutionary War as a Black Declaration of Independence," Hoffman and Berlin, *Slavery,* pp. 294, 301.

[40]See David Roediger, *The Wages of Whiteness* (London, New York, 1991).

[41]Berlin, *Many Thousands Gone: The First Two Centuries in North America* (Cambridge, Mass., 1998), pp. 363–64; Philip D. Morgan, *Slave Counterpoint: Black Culture in the Eighteenth Century Chesapeake & Lowcountry* (Chapel Hill, N.C., 1998).

nineteenth century, but Berlin and more recent scholars saw the economic and ideological underpinnings of slavery as constantly in motion. Slavery was a process of renegotiation. It evoked varying responses from slaves, slaveholders, free blacks, and nonslaveholding white society. The changing market for staple crops and the shift from colonial notions of hierarchy and dependence to revolutionary ideas of individual liberty, to the Jacksonian concept of the essential whiteness of the democratic man all help account for the ways in which blackness has been constructed and reconstructed and the heritage of slavery perceived.

When Stampp published his work in 1956, the notion that scholars would accept the idea of the existence of a slave culture, much less be arguing about its shape, character, and elements would have seemed more than implausible. Like most scholars today, Berlin not only assumes a slave culture but also its expressly African characteristics. His book is rich in such detail. As of today, Africa and Africanness, like the Atlantic World, are an integral part of Afro-American history. The debate has proceeded well beyond the either-or phase and become one about how to delineate the mixing of cultures. To help refine their descriptions, historians have imported from anthropology the idea of syncretism, which occurs when colonized people adopt a new cultural belief or practice that overlaps and can disguise their continuing belief in an older, forbidden notion. African Americans in varying degrees adopted Christianity while retaining congruent spiritual beliefs from African culture.

Michael Gomez's, *Exchanging Our Country Marks*, published in 1998, is a dramatic example of the contemporary sophistication and depth of Afro-American studies. Gomez argues from extensive research on various African ethnic groups that these identifications and the specific abilities attaching to them were initially the way planters created occupational hierarchies within the slave community. Over time, ethnically motivated hierarchies gave way to occupational and color hierarchies as those who had inherited skills and mulatto slaves usually found themselves doing the most desirable work. In this original and imaginative work, Gomez, following the work of Sterling Stuckey and Lawrence Levine, has used folk tales to identify the period when ethnic divisions among slaves gave way to a shared sense of themselves as united by race. Gomez's rich knowledge of African ethnicity shows how African differences prefigured Afro-American fissures within the slave community. By tracing folk accounts of enslavement Gomez pinpoints the moment when slaves began seeing themselves as a race of Afro-Americans rather than as Africans of different ethnicities.[42]

The debate on the content of slave culture and its legacy is far

---

[42]Michael Gomez, *Exchanging Our Country Marks: The Transformation of African Identities in the Colonial and Antebellum South* (Chapel Hill, N.C., 1998), particularly Chapter 8.

from over. Edmund Morgan has criticized a recent book by Orlando Patterson for tracing the causes of poverty in black families to the irresponsibility of black men, and, in turn tracing that back to patterns derived from slavery. His review demonstrates how energized are the synapses connecting scholarship about slavery and the racial inequities that have persisted into the new millennium. Morgan chided the renowned scholar of slavery for not incorporating evidence about the stability of the majority of black families in slavery and its aftermath, and thus incorrectly reading the causes of the contemporary scene into a distant past, when, in Morgan's view, the continuing prejudicial treatment of American blacks in the twentieth century is more likely the reason.[43]

In the selected readings, the focus is on what many historians see as the core of vitality in the slave experience: the emergence of a distinctively Afro-American Christianity. Raboteau shows the liberatory and political meaning of Christianity for slaves, and although he has written about the African roots of slave religion, his interest is more in the ways in which Christianity nurtured and kept alive promises of equality and less with its parallels with West African beliefs. Sylvia Frey and Betty Wood, on the other hand, have steeped their account of the black experience of the First and particularly the Second Great Awakening in West African traditions. In their view, slaves adopted Christianity in part because it fit into West African ideas about the deities, the universe, and rebirth. Slaves brought a tradition of exuberant and ecstatic worship to Christianity that contributed uniquely to evangelical culture and became reflected in white patterns of worship. In this view, Christianity was not imposed on unwilling or empty "Sambos," but sought out by people who found resonance with their traditions in a new philosophy that offered both solace for their suffering and an explanation for the evil they endured. It also substantially changed the nature of white evangelical worship, giving it a more expressive and ecstatic character. The authors' differing emphases point in different directions, Raboteau toward the growth of black political aims and organization and Frey and Wood toward elaborating an American religious culture profoundly shaped by African Americans.

As a pluralistic society that recognizes its past in countless countries around the globe, white America has been reluctant to welcome Africa to that company. Yet Africa has been symbolic for generations of African Americans of the continuity and dignity of an Afro-American culture. In 1976 Alex Haley, author of *The Autobiography of Malcolm X*, reached an extraordinarily wide readership with *Roots*, his odyssey into his family's past in the Senegambia region. Such histori-

---

[43]"Plantation Blues," Edmund S. Morgan, *The New York Review of Books* (June 10, 1999): 30–33.

ans as W.E.B. Du Bois and such activists as Stokeley Carmichael decided to live there rather than go on combating racism in the United States. And recent historians are increasingly studying African nations with the same care so long lavished on Europe and the Middle East to better understand the mix that created the New World.

There is probably no field where the passions run higher than the study of slave culture. Historians evoking a past cannot avoid present-day voices. Elkins odious Sambo evoked a deeply damaged people. Recently, Daryl Scott, in *Contempt and Pity*, has argued that *Brown v. Board of Education*, the Supreme Court decision to desegregate schools that brought unsurpassed joy to the black community, unfortunately relied on an equally dangerous conception of a damaged black psyche.[44] But slavery was a damaging institution—how can historians portray its pervasive evil without registering it as harm? Most scholars accept the notion that while society gives meanings to race, biology does not. And yet books arguing for innate characteristics of blacks and whites, such as *The Bell Curve*, continue to be written and find wide audiences. The ever-present historical question—to what extent were blacks able to manage their lives within American slavery?—will continue to be mixed up with underlying feelings of pride, shame, guilt, and resentment because the history of slavery carries with it the weight of all our unresolved questions about race and justice.

---

[44]Daryl Michael Scott, *Contempt and Pity, Social Policy and the Image of the Damaged Black Psyche, 1880–1996* (Chapel Hill, N.C., 1997).

SYLVIA R. FREY (1935–   ) is professor of history at Tulane University and author of The British Soldier in America *(1979) and* Water from the Rock *(1991) and coauthor of* Come Shouting to Zion *(1998).* BETTY WOOD *is a fellow of Girton College, Cambridge, and is the author of* Slavery in Colonial Georgia *(1984) and* The Origins of American Slavery *(1997) and coauthor of* Come Shouting to Zion *(1998).*

For more than a century and a half the vast majority of Afro-Atlantic peoples had clung tenaciously to their ancient beliefs. Excluded from the ranks of human society by virtue of their status as chattel slaves, culturally isolated from society at large and from one another by multiple identities and disparate cultural practices, they had struggled against incredible odds to recreate the domestic and communal lives that were brutally shattered by slavery and to define a new cultural identity that would transcend ethnic and cultural differences. In the forty years preceding the American Revolution the number of Africans claiming a Christian identity had slowly increased. Yet, apart from a few small enclaves in Virginia and Georgia and scattered mission stations in the Caribbean, African Christians remained an insignificant minority in all of the British Atlantic plantation societies. Beginning in 1785, however, Christianity made rapid advances, becoming by 1815 a dominant religious influence among Afro-Atlantic peoples. By 1830 a new and highly visible Afro-cultural presence had emerged. It rested on the firm foundation of evangelical Christianity.

Evangelical religion provided a framework for the unprecedented social and cultural changes that mark this period of Afro-Atlantic history. As the only form of organized communal life available to slaves, evangelical institutions came to constitute important loci wherein African peoples could develop a sense of belonging and assert a cultural presence in the larger society through the creation of their own moral and social communities. Instead of a single, coherent movement, the process of conversion was a stepped transition that varied according to the local environment and in terms of temporal progression. The most critical factors affecting the timing and character of these disparate developments were the demographic configurations and the cultural and political frameworks in which religious cultures evolved. Despite these variations, the process had a global quality that derived in part from the fact that the evangelical missionaries who initially led the movement viewed themselves as emissaries of a universal church with the world as their mission field and in part from the movements of people within and between societies in the wake of the American Revolution. The migration of cultures thus forms an important and continuing link between increasingly different regions of the plantation world.

The American Revolution and political independence ushered in a series of changes that dramatically transformed the religious landscape of mainland North America. The demand for religious freedom that paralleled the movement for political freedom was especially strong in the South, where evangelical sects flourished. Beginning with Virginia, old denominations like the Anglicans were disestablished and new denominations like the Baptists and Methodists established themselves. Old and new congregations split over ostensibly inconsequential matters of religious practice and ritual, and entirely new sects arose out of the religious disorder. What issued from the chaos was a keen competition for souls between the bewildering array of denominations and sects. As English and American evangelists surveyed the moral landscape, they discovered African Americans, and African Americans discovered them. It was an enduring attraction. With their deeply rooted spirituality derived from Africa and their profound religious need for a sense of meaning in life, African Americans became a great prize in the evangelical contest for church membership and gathered souls.

In the newly formed Southern states there were two discrete phases of religious change: a brief but intense postwar phase from 1785 to 1790 that remained largely confined to the Chesapeake states of Virginia and Maryland, and a general post-1800 phase precipitated by the Great Revival and extending episodically to 1830. Each phase had certain distinctive characteristics, but as historical sequences they are connected by the migrant communities that furnished the personnel and the revival culture that fueled both phases. In the spring of 1780 Francis Asbury gave up the relative security of semiretirement in Delaware and set out on an arduous tour of Virginia and North Carolina that lasted five months and covered over 1,000 miles. The long rides on bad roads, through dense woods, over rocks, and across dangerous creeks and rivers, gave Asbury a discouraging view of the effects of war and confronted him with the enormous difficulties ahead for the itinerancy. Everywhere he found "broken" societies and the region in a state of decline. People, he complained, were "so distracted with the times" that they were afraid to leave their homes or ride their horses. White Southerners, he concluded, were "insensible," and preaching to them was "of little purpose."

A decade after Asbury made that discouraging assessment, two-thirds of all Methodists in the United States were located in three

Southern states, Maryland, Virginia, and North Carolina. Over half of all Baptists resided in five Southern states. The phenomenal advance of evangelical Protestantism was a product of several different but interrelated processes operating more or less simultaneously. The first was the great spiritual awakening that began on the banks of the James River in 1785, spread through the Chesapeake until the 1790s, and faltered and then reemerged with the spectacular rise of the camp meeting revivals after 1800. The second was the physical movement of people that began in the 1760s and culminated in the vast migrations of the post-Revolutionary era, which served as the vehicle for the transplantation of the evangelical movement into the expanding West and the Caribbean. The third was the organization of a national, independent Methodist church in the United States and the extension of the itinerant system throughout the South. Central to all of these developments was the embrace of evangelical Protestant Christianity by African Americans.

The postwar revivals serve as a kind of laboratory wherein one can observe how, step by step, the religious rituals associated with black and white evangelical worship developed and established themselves. By and large what they reveal is that in certain ways African American Christianity was derivative of European American Christianity, and that often European American Christianity unconsciously borrowed from African American patterns. The outcries, tears, and tremblings often associated with camp meeting behavior were common features of Separate Baptist worship during the 1760s and of Methodist quarterly meeting revivals during the 1770s. They continued to occupy a central place in the revivals of the 1780s as well. Until the advent of the carefully orchestrated camp meeting, no rigid format shaped revival services, although for the most part worship consisted of prayers, testimonies, exhortations, preaching, and singing. The open format allowed for innovation and highly participatory forms of worship. It was within this experimental environment that African Americans began to structure and organize their own ritual devotion and to construct a belief system of their own. These collectively shared beliefs and practices formed the cultural essence of a new identity.

With the outbreak of religious awakenings in Virginia in 1785, revivalism began to take on aspects of a mass movement. In the highly decentralized structure of the quarterly meeting, conversion was increasingly characterized by charismatic phenomena, such as shaking and trances. Accounts left by Methodist itinerants of the work of revival provide graphic evidence that early on enslaved women established a definite cultural presence in revival meetings. What this suggests is that the fervor of black women's conversion led scores of men and women, black and white, to the same deeply personal, highly emotional affirmation of the faith. . . .

Evangelical Protestant Christianity initially tolerated women as

religious intermediaries, in part because of the emotional nature ascribed to women, in part because ecstatic behavior functioned more as
ritual presence than active leadership and therefore did not represent
an open challenge to male authority. Religious enthusiasm did, however, represent an attempt on the part of women to empower themselves through mystical experiences, perhaps to establish a symbolic
domain of authority by emphasizing the equal access of women to the
spirit world. As a result, they had the potential to inspire reflections
on the capacities of women and thereby to challenge indirectly the notion of a divinely created order with strictly male leadership. But this
power was ephemeral because it was individual and dependent upon
charismatic power. Female leaders whose powers were based upon expressive leadership disappeared as rapidly as they emerged, not, however, before they had made their mark on revival culture and African
American worship. . . .

Another important feature of early revival culture was the intense
dialogue between black and white participants that formed the basis
for the creation of a sense of shared culture. Revival meetings provided
the most important institutional framework for African Americans to
gain exposure to white religious forms. Their participation in evangelical meetings of various kinds initiated them into aspects of white culture and therefore served as a crucial part of the assimilative process
that integrated them into the community. This is not to say, however,
that African Americans merely adopted white religious beliefs and ritual practices. Simultaneous with these developments African Americans were creating a religious culture of their own through the
appropriation and transformation of the worship service. An entirely
different sort of revival meeting witnessed by the Reverend Philip
Bruce, elder of the Methodist Episcopal Church, illustrates the point.

During a night meeting in Isle of Wight County "there arose a cry
among the poor slaves (of which there was a great number present)."
The noise and drama helped to build emotional excitement and to create the religious experience. Then "a number was on the floor crying
for mercy, but soon one and another arose praising God." Those who
had accepted conversion then provided collective support and approval
for others to attain the state of spiritual ecstasy: "Those who were
happy, would surround those who were careless, with such alarming
exhortations, as appeared sufficient to soften the hardest hearts. If they
could get them to hang down their heads, they would begin to shout
and praise God, and the others would soon begin to tremble and sink. I
saw a number brought to the floor . . . and there lie crying till most of
them got happy."

In this scene described by Bruce, an incipient form of the style of
expression known as "shouting" emerges uncertainly as part of the
conversion ritual. Early accounts of the First Awakening contain frequent references to vocalizations of various types, ranging from quiet

rapture to wild weeping, forms of ecstatic expression congruent with both African and Protestant patterns. . . .

Long after shouting had become institutionalized and ritualized as part of the structure of conversion, black shouting could still incite awe and fear in whites witnessing it for the first time. . . . Apparently derivative of African forms, the shouting ritual was neither what it had been, nor yet what it would become. It belonged neither to the old nor to the new, but to both. . . .

For African Americans, if not for all white evangelicals, conversion was often a ritual of collective catharsis and collective commitment that was performed collaboratively. The shout they had invented to help them reach the spiritual ecstasy of conversion also served to forge social relations. It produced such a highly evocative sound that it invited a response. The reciprocal nature of the shout united the black group as a unique and distinctive spiritual community, a part of but separate from the white religious community. While the evidence is admittedly sparse, it suggests the possibility that through a relatively brief period of sustained contact, the sort of possession behavior exhibited by black evangelicals may have carried over to white evangelicals. . . .

As the conversion experience became more widespread and acquired greater power, male participation became increasingly common. And, although Virginia was not the sole source for the black itinerancy, it nevertheless provided fertile ground for its development and played an important role in its subsequent proliferation elsewhere. The very first waves of religious enthusiasm engendered a penchant for moral experiments, and black and white preachers often worked together in spiritual companionship. Perhaps the most striking example of such a collaboration was the partnership between Francis Asbury and Harry Hosier, an illiterate but gifted speaker whose first appearance with Asbury created a sensation in Fairfax, Virginia. A regular companion of Asbury's, Hosier also itinerated with Thomas Coke and Freeborn Garrettson, attracting large crowds of blacks and whites, some of whom angrily objected to a black man preaching before white audiences.

Beyond the privileged few like Hosier were dozens of black preachers who went out on their own, quite independent of white ministers. Although most of them never rose above the rank of exhorter, the success of pioneer itinerants like Hosier encouraged a number of black men to venture into the formerly closed world of the ministry, thereby challenging at every turn the limited vision of a white clerical monopoly. . . .

These self-proclaimed preachers, sincere Christians intent on striking out on their own spiritual paths, were quick to seize upon and absorb the teaching authority of the preacher, as the Reverend James Meacham learned when he itinerated on Virginia's Greenville Circuit in 1789. Meacham opened one particular meeting as usual with prayers followed by an exhortation. Moved by the emotion of the moment, he "strove to encourage the black people out at the window."

Much to his chagrin, Meacham was made aware of the inadequacy of his own evangelical methods and the pronounced superiority of Africans in proselytizing their own people by "one poor slave beginning to move off a space and speak in Exhortation. The rest of the poor innocent delinquents immediately flocked around: while I myself could be suffered to preach and to pray in the church."

The incident between Reverend Meacham and the unnamed slave centered around one of the most crucial issues raised by lay evangelism: the control of preaching. A sense of the power of the spoken word as the voice of God was well understood by all concerned, black and white, male and female. Bondmen and -women, the progeny of oral-aural cultures, associated vocal communication with power—the power to establish presence, to evoke responses, to unite groups, and to create community. White church leaders also appreciated the importance of controlling sound—to discipline backsliders, to express spiritual power, to establish domination. But by the time white church leaders awoke to the incipient challenge to their authority posed by these self-proclaimed black preachers, a separate black ministry had already emerged. . . .

For all its power, by 1790 the revival movement seemed to be faltering, perhaps dying out. But the maturation of two separate processes, migration and the launching of missionary work, combined to give the movement new energy and power and contributed to its rapid diffusion after 1800. The story of Afro-Christianity is inextricably bound up with both of these processes. The local migration of black and white Virginians that began in the pre-Revolutionary years, expanded in the postwar period, lengthening westward across the mountainous wilderness into Kentucky and southward into the Caribbean. The migration carried the spirit and, in some cases, the personnel of revival religion. . . .

The march of Methodism into the Lower South was initially propelled by the movement of people that began in the 1760s and culminated in the vast post-Revolutionary migration of planters and enslaved people from Virginia and Maryland into South Carolina and Georgia. Asbury's epic preaching tour of 1785 had led to the establishment of the first—and predominantly black—Methodist society in Charleston, but the annual conference remained doubtful "whether it would be for the glory of God to send even one Preacher" to the "barren soil" of South Carolina. However, as Asbury discovered, many of the migrants "that had no religion in Virginia, have found it in their removal into Georgia and South Carolina." A petition of a group of migrants from Virginia persuaded the conference to send two "travelling preachers," Hope Hull and Jeremiah Maston, to the circuit then called Pee Dee, which included the coastal parishes and the region around the Great Pee Dee where enslaved people made up about 30 percent of the population.

Thereafter Methodism in South Carolina "increased beyond any formed example," as South Carolina's first historian, David Ramsay, put it. Methodism grew at a faster rate than any other denomination precisely because its preachers went out to the advancing frontier. In keeping with the Methodist strategy for implanting Christianity, the state was divided into twelve circuits and stations through which twenty-six itinerants rode daily, except on Mondays. According to Ramsay's calculations, between them the itinerants preached 156 sermons weekly, 8,112 sermons yearly, exclusive of night and informal gatherings. In addition to the traveling preachers there were ninety-three local preachers who preached on the average two sermons each a week for a total of 9,672 a year. The total number of Methodist sermons annually preached in South Carolina amounted to 17,784.

This highly organized missionary activity and the post-Revolutionary migration of peoples precipitated a different sort of cultural interaction and exchange on an international scale. Except for the Moravians, who in 1792 had 137 men and women at work in the West Indies and the trust estate operated by the Society for the Propagation of the Gospel on the Codrington estate in Barbados, there was no systematic attempt to convert slaves until the 1780s. But beginning in the 1780s the British sugar islands experienced an influx of American emigrants and British missionaries. After the American Revolution a number of black émigrés, acting independently of white missionaries, began evangelizing in parts of the Caribbean that had never before heard the Christian message.

Whether they were émigrés from the mainland or missionaries sent from Britain, the sugar islands presented the missionaries of every Protestant sect and denomination with a cultural and political framework that was fundamentally different from that of the American South. For one thing, the population of the islands was overwhelmingly black. . . . Moreover, compared to population of the American South, by the early nineteenth century the island population contained a significantly higher proportion of free black and free colored people, whose agendas did not always or necessarily conform to those of enslaved people. . . .

Unlike the scattered rural population of the American South, in most of the islands the creolized European population clustered together in towns or retreated to England, leaving the management of their estates in the hands of attorneys and overseers. Attorneys were an especially influential and powerful group who could admit or deny entrance to the estates they controlled, a power that would prove to be of critical and continuing importance in shaping the contours of formal missionary activity. However, although they might turn away white missionaries, neither attorneys nor overseers could totally prevent the transmission of religious ideas between and within estates. . . .

Despite the strenuous efforts of the more orthodox black Baptists and, during the late 1810s and 1820s, of British missionaries to quash a religious ideology they found both abhorrent and threatening, and to discredit influential black and free colored leaders whom with some justification they termed "Christianized obeahs," the "Native Baptists" not only survived but also assumed a critical religious and political role in "The Baptist War," the momentous Jamaican slave revolt of 1831.

All evangelical missions in the Caribbean, and not merely the Baptists, sought to follow the example of the pioneering Moravians, whose flourishing missions in Antigua reported a membership of 7,400 slaves and free people of color in 1791. Among other things, the Moravian experience had convinced white missionaries that a reliably trained and disciplined black missionary force could be put to productive advantage in instilling moral discipline and subordination in the large and potentially dangerous enslaved populations of the Caribbean. Nowhere perhaps was this more true than in Jamaica, whose 30,000 or so free white inhabitants were greatly outnumbered by enslaved people....

It was the Wesley Methodists who, despite the intense and often violent opposition they encountered from the planter class because of their reputation as opponents of chattel slavery, made the most effective use of the pedagogy of conversion pioneered by the Moravians. However, a planter hostility that often prevented their own licensing as preachers and decreed that of black and free colored people to be strictly illegal, meant that in a purely formal sense white Methodist missionaries had little choice but to make covert use of their black and colored converts. And this they did with a remarkable degree of success. Through the symbiotic efforts of white missionaries and local black and free colored converts Methodism's reach was extended from the towns, where small societies were originally formed, to the rural areas, where black slaves so heavily outnumbered whites....

There were striking similarities and fundamental differences in patterns of religious growth and development in the British Caribbean and the American South. In the British Caribbean most whites, who were not particularly renowned for their religiosity, shunned evangelical Protestantism in favor of the established Anglican Church. As a consequence the overwhelmingly black evangelical churches formed the primary context for growth. In the American South, the Second Awakening, the dramatic resurgence of revivalism whose explosive spirit was unleashed by the Great Kentucky Revival of 1801, was the principal vehicle for growth. The biracial character of Southern revivalism decisively shaped black and white religious culture.

After 1806 a decisive shift occurred in the character of Southern revivalism. The partnership between English missionaries and African itinerants had developed in a fashion that mirrored the ebullient freedom of early itinerant revivalism. In the more complicated geography of the Second Awakening, the white evangelical establishment sought to shore up the jagged boundaries of race, class, and gender by isolating

African men and women behind the walls of cultural segregation. While there were significant continuities between the First and Second Awakenings, the latter had certain novel features that both reflect and recapitulate key changes in race and gender relations that reverberated through Southern society in the late eighteenth and early nineteenth centuries, namely the accommodation reached by evangelical leadership and slaveholding society on the question of slavery; the formation of a proslavery version of Christianity and the acceleration of the movement toward evangelical Protestantism by the upper ranks of Southern society that accompanied it; and the emergence of a coherent patriarchal ideology based on the subordination of women and the enslavement of Africans. The special sense of racial and class superiority and the gender roles associated with the rapidly developing patriarchy were dramatically reproduced in the spatial arrangements of the camp meeting and of the biracial churches that proliferated after 1800.

Camp meetings were to a large extent but extensions of the Virginia revivals. Most of the inhabitants of Kentucky were migrants from Virginia, and many of the personnel of the revival movement had received their training in Virginia. However, camp meetings differed significantly from the Virginia revivals in size and duration and, most importantly, in certain aspects of the ritual setting. The meeting site was usually situated near a stream or other source of water to accommodate the needs of the 8,000 to 12,000 people who commonly attended. Horses and carriages and rows of closely lined tents formed an oblong or semicircular, theaterlike enclosure, at one end of which were ranged rows of preaching stands or stages from which several preachers officiated day and night without interruption. Facing the preaching stand were rows of plank seats that were divided by a central aisle into two sections, one for white men and one for white women. Near the foot of the preaching stands stood a large post-and-rail mourners pen, admission to which was monitored by guards. Behind the preachers stands and at some distance from the white assembly were rows of tents occupied by black participants.

The physical arrangement of seating represents the general direction of the Second Awakening: It destroyed the perception of a revolution in spiritual authority that had been perpetuated by spatially open meetings; and it delineated the fault lines of race, class, and gender and physically structured the idea that for men and women, and for blacks and whites, spiritual equality operated on different terms. Thus, while evangelical ideology continued to pronounce the doctrine of egalitarianism, the spatial arrangements of the meeting argued differently, reproducing as they did the race and gender hierarchies that had been temporarily suspended during the First Awakening. Beyond these new social and psychological walls, divergent forms of ritual behavior and a different constellation of worship patterns began to emerge.

From the beginning black and white evangelicals had drawn upon distinctive spiritual traditions, which in the intimacy of church and house revivals mutually reinforced one another. The separate spaces of the camp meeting encouraged the development of differences in the style and substance of the conversion ritual. Professional revivalists, who made their first appearance in the Great Revival, introduced a repertory of behaviors that took the white conversion ritual to remarkable and bizarre levels of expression known as "bodily exercises." The first appearance of a pattern that quickly became a recurring phenomenon was at a meeting of the Red River congregation in Logan County, Kentucky, in 1799. The meeting was presided over by a group of Presbyterian preachers locally known as the "Sons of Thunder," and John McGee, a Methodist preacher. Nothing unusual occurred until McGee rose to speak. Concluding that "it was his duty to disregard the usual orderly habits of the denomination," McGee "went through the house shouting, and exhorting with all possible ecstasy and energy, and the floor was soon covered with the slain; their screams for mercy pierced the heavens."

The paroxysms of ecstasy deliberately provoked by McGee became commonly known as the "falling exercise." The dancing exercise was added to the repertory at a meeting at Turtle Creek when John Thompson, a seceding Presbyterian preacher, danced around the preaching stand for over an hour, all the while chanting in a low voice, "This is the Holy Ghost—Glory!" Thereafter New Light Presbyterians began "to encourage one another to praise God in the dance, and unite in that exercise." . . .

These learned bodily techniques produced, or perhaps induced, a distinctive kind of motor behavior reminiscent of the patterned behavior exhibited during the Methodist revivals of 1758 at Cambuslang and Kilsyth in Scotland, and Everton and Bristol in England. In the American revivals of the Second Awakening, as in the earlier Scottish and English revivals, more men and a high percentage of children and youth were affected. In its most extreme forms the conversion ritual was characterized by the same eccentric repertory of motor behaviors seen in the Scottish and English revivals: violent contortions of the body and spasmodic jerkings, rolling and spinning, running and leaping. Sinners under conviction emitted deep groans and piercing shrieks, howled and growled, snapped and barked, their darkened and distorted faces revealing the horror and anguish of convicted sinners.

Although the Scottish and English revivals furnished the prototype for white ecstatic behavior, white evangelical Christians had neither a persistent cultural tradition nor a religious framework to accommodate ecstatic performance regularly. By contrast, emotional ecstasy formed the central core of the black Christian ethos. Black men and women in the throes of conversion did, on occasion, exhibit the same motor behavior as whites. Among African Americans, however, behavioral expectations were different and different performance rules prevailed with distinctive ritual results. Their relative isolation at camp meetings afforded black worshipers an opportunity to gradually embellish the ritual forms they had begun to create during the First Awakening. Far from abandoning ancestral structures and forms, they fused characteristically African aesthetic elements with Christian forms to create their own distinctive religious rituals, which were at once Christian and African.

The stimulus for the emotional ecstasy that marked the climax of the black conversion experience was more often than not rhythmic, accompanied by music or sermon. Whether or not African Americans forged original music forms from an essentially African musical heritage and transmitted them to white co-religionists or whether they adapted and perpetuated basically white liturgical forms to suit their own cultural and social needs has been the subject of extended debate among scholars. Most scholarship now recognizes that there were elements held in common by both cultures: for example, the Protestant tradition of lining-out songs and the analogous antiphonal structure, or the call and response characteristic of traditional West African music. Neither the ultimate origins nor the degree of musical interchange can be documented from the few shreds of evidence surviving from the eighteenth century. What is certain is that an Africanized spiritual was fashioned by early black Christians.

Anglican missionaries were the first to give religious instruction to Africans and to teach them to sing psalms. During the 1740s Isaac Watts hymns were reprinted in the colonies and were probably introduced to black Christians by the Reverend Samuel Davies during the First Great Awakening. Although musical styles probably varied according to denomination and geographic location, a white liturgical tradition was thus implanted among a very small proportion of the African population. Simultaneously with this development, African slaves began shaping their own unique music forms in the isolated slave quarters where they lived and in the fields where they worked. The work songs they created preserved many of the characteristics of West African music: offbeat phrasing, staggered accents, musical interpolations, repetition, and call and response.

During the Virginia revivals black and white Christians began to compose their own religious songs. "Some of [them]," the Reverend John Leland wryly observed, "have more divinity in them than poetry or grammar," some of them "have little of either." Contemporary sources have very little to say about the creative process or musical interchange, but in his history of early Methodism Jesse Lee affirms at the least the possibility of reciprocal influences. "It was often the case," Lee wrote, "that the people in their corn fields, white people, or black, and sometimes both together would begin to sing, and being affected would begin to pray, and others would join with them."

Camp meetings were, however, the primary environment for the creation of new religious music. Within a decade, the new music, and emotional worship in general, had become synonymous with black worship in the minds of some white evangelicals. Perhaps as a way of disparaging the popular repertoire of religious songs they found so distasteful, the increasingly vocal critics of revival culture associated the early gospel forms with the African part of the revival community. Among the Methodist "errors" the Reverend John E. Watson protested were the religious songs that were extemporaneously composed by black revivalists: "In the blacks' quarter the coloured people get together, and sing for hours together, short scraps of disjointed affirmations, pledges, or prayers, lengthened out with long repetition choruses." The "idle expletives" Watson scorned frequently were word or line fragments isolated from hymns or from Scriptures, a sample of which he preserved: "'Go shouting all your days,' in connection with 'glory, glory, glory,' in which go shouting is repeated six times in succession."

Watson was even more bothered by the unorthodox practice of fusing sacred songs with secular ones, a legacy of West Africa in which they "are all sung in the merry chorus manner of the southern harvest field, or husking-frolic method, of the slave blacks." Watson apparently recognized that the musical traditions of West African and European cultures shared certain features in common, among them the use of repetitive phrases, which he attributed to Welsh influence. Still, he implied that whites absorbed, perhaps unwittingly, the improvised religious music composed by black revivalists. "Merry airs, adapted from old songs, to hymns of our composing: often miserable as poetry, and senseless as matter" were, he wrote, "first sung by illiterate blacks of the society."

The power and exuberance of extemporaneously composed religious music provided the stimulation for a new expressive mode, a unique ritual known as the holy dance, or the ring shout. Given the poverty of sources, precise reconstruction of the development of ritual trance dancing is next to impossible. However, the first motions of the holy dance were apparently hand clapping, foot stamping, and leaping, which first appeared during the Virginia revivals. None of these acts was unique to West Africans, but because they were not a regular part of the white aesthetic experience they were greatly altered or they disappeared from the white repertoires of religious expression once acceptability of such behaviors declined.

Because they were intrinsic to African religious expression, these forms of musical behavior survived and heightened the rhythmic patterning of black worship. By the end of the first decade of the nineteenth century they had evolved into a choreography of sound and movement known as the ring shout, the ultimate refinement of the religious ceremony of shouting. . . .

Contemporary accounts suggest that the primary environment for the development of the ring shout was the camp meeting, although clandestine gatherings almost certainly nurtured ring dancing. The earliest written reports reveal that an elemental dance ritual had developed as part of black Methodist worship in the Upper South as early as 1809. One such account came from Benjamin Henry Latrobe, in which he reported that after witnessing what he considered the excesses of a revival meeting near Georgetown in August, he left in disgust. His son Henry remained at the camp until midnight and later reported that "the negroes after the Camp was illuminated sung and danced the methodist turnabout in the most indefatigable and entertaining manner." . . .

The degree to which traditional African dance survived varied throughout the Americas. Dance rituals like the santeria, candomble, cumina, and the petro are only a few of the countless forms of religious musical expression that proliferated in the Caribbean and throughout South America. In North America, the ring shout became highly ritualized and remained an integral part of African American worship throughout the antebellum period. For example, the Swedish traveler Frederika Bremer saw the "holy dance" performed by black women at a camp meeting near Charleston in 1850. A year later she witnessed a similar performance at a Methodist class meeting in New Orleans. And in his recollections of his childhood in South Carolina, Samuel Gourdin Gaillard described a black worship service that he witnessed in a plantation chapel. The ceremony, which Gaillard speculated "must have come with the slaves from Africa," began with a low, moaning hymn sung by a woman. As the congregation joined in, the singing gradually increased in volume and intensity and the movements became more hectic. "One by one of the congregation slipped out into the center of the floor and began to 'shout'—(that is whirl around and sing and clap hands, and so round and round in circles). After a time as this went on, the enthusiasm became a frenzy and only the able bodied men and women remained—the weak dropping out one by one, returning to the 'side lines' to clap and urge the 'shouters' on."

The liturgical traditions that emerged out of revival religious culture formed an important nexus in race relations within the biracial evangelical community. For black Christians the creation of specific and distinctive rituals like the ring shout was part of the process by which they established a definite presence in the religious community. Their attempt to claim a cultural space disturbed white Christians like John Watson, who publicly demeaned such behavior as noisy, crude, impious, and, simply, dissolute. Despite its mixed origins, emotional worship was increasingly characterized as "black" and, therefore, culturally inferior. Such an identification worked to reinforce the growing consciousness of racial distinction developing behind the rising wall of spiritual separation. White Christians rejected rituals that had an apparent African style or feeling and were associated with supposed racial inferiority in favor of the more carefully controlled European cadences with which they were familiar. For black Christians ritual music and dance became important cultural foci, symbols of their cultural independence and of their identity as a black group.

A L B E R T   J .   R A B O T E A U

ALBERT J. RABOTEAU (1943–   ) is the Putnam Professor of Religion at Princeton University and author of Slave Religion: The "Invisible Institution" in the Antebellum South *(1978) and* A Fire in the Bones: Reflections on African American Religious History *(1995). He is currently coediting, with David Wills,* African American Religion: An Interpretive History and Representative Documents *(forthcoming).*

Late in the eighteenth century, black Americans, slave and free, Southern and Northern, began to convert to Christianity in larger numbers than ever before. The type of Christianity that they joined and continued to join in mounting numbers during the next century was experiential, revivalistic, and biblically oriented. That is, it placed heavy stress upon the necessity of an inward conversion experience for Christian salvation; it institutionalized the revival as a means of converting sinners, extending church membership, and reforming society; and finally, it read the Bible literally and interpreted the destiny of America accordingly.

Black Evangelicals, no less than whites, sought conversion, attended revivals, and viewed their lives in biblical terms. There was a fundamental difference between the two, however. American slavery and the doctrine of white supremacy, which rationalized and outlived it, not only segregated evangelical congregations along racial lines, but also differentiated the black experience of evangelical Christianity from that of whites. The existence of chattel slavery in a nation that claimed to be Christian, and the use of Christianity to justify enslavement, confronted black Evangelicals with a basic dilemma, which may be most clearly formulated in two questions: What meaning did Christianity, if it were a white man's religion, as it seemed, have for blacks; and, why did the Christian God, if he were just as claimed, permit blacks to suffer so? In struggling to answer these questions, a significant number of Afro-Americans developed a distinctive evangelical tradition in which they established meaning and identity for themselves as individuals and as a people. Simultaneously, they made an indispensable contribution to the development of American Evangelicalism. If evangelical Protestantism has formed a major part of the cultural history of Afro-Americans, from the beginning black Evangelicals have troubled the conscience of Christian Americans.

A White Man's Religion?

The fires of revival that initially swept most of the British North American colonies in the 1740s flared up intermittently during the 1780s and 1790s particularly in the Chesapeake region of the upper South, and broke out anew on the Kentucky and Tennessee frontier around the turn of the century. These successive "Awakenings" inaugurated a new religious movement in America. Whether viewed as a renewed Puritanism, an extension of Continental Pietism, or as the rise of popular denominations on the expanding frontier, Evangelicalism was by the early decades of the nineteenth century the predominant voice on the American religious scene. By the 1830s, revival had linked with reform to institute an energetic and influential evangelical front that intended nothing less than the purification of the nation from sin in order to prepare for the coming millennium, which undoubtedly would begin in America. During these same decades, 1780–1830, Evangelicalism had been planted and had taken hold among enslaved Africans and their descendants, some free, but most of them slaves.

Initially, blacks had heard the message of evangelical Christianity from whites, but rapidly a cadre of early black preachers, licensed and unlicensed, took it upon themselves to convert and to pastor their own people. By 1830, these "pioneers" had been succeeded by a second and more numerous generation of black clergymen, so that blacks were no longer exclusively dependent upon whites for the Christian gospel, though white missionaries might think so. Separate black churches—mainly Baptist due to the congregational independence of that denomination—sprang up not only in the North, where emancipation gave blacks more leeway to organize institutionally, but also in the South, where an increasingly entrenched slave system made any kind of black autonomy seem subversive. In the North and upper South, two black evangelical denominations formed and chose bishops of their own to lead them. Already, black American missionaries had established Baptist and Methodist congregations in Nova Scotia, Jamaica, and Sierra Leone. In short, blacks showed no reluctance in taking a leading role in the spread of evangelical religion.

The opportunity for black religious separatism was due to the egalitarian character of evangelical Protestantism; its necessity was due, in part, to the racism of white Evangelicals. The egalitarian tendency of evangelical revivals to level the souls of all men before God had been one of the major attractions to black converts in the first place. Early white Evangelicals in the South, where the majority of blacks were, appeared to the Anglican establishment as a revolutionary rabble, a disorderly, "outlandish, misshapen sort of people," in the words of one Virginian. They threatened the established order, both in ecclesiastical and civil terms. The lower sort made up their church membership, and the unlettered, even including servants, spoke at their meetings. Racial and social status was overturned in the close communion of Baptist conventicles and Methodist societies in the 1780s and 1790s. Runaway slave advertisements in Virginia and Maryland newspapers complained that blacks were being ruined by the "leveling" doctrines of Baptist and Methodist sectarians. Not surprisingly, Anglican authorities in Virginia and North Carolina jailed evangelical preachers, and mobs frequently harassed or assaulted them. Some, but not all, eighteenth-century Methodists and Baptists concluded that holding slaves was sinful and encouraged converts either by legislation or admonition to emancipate their slaves.

Blacks were impressed by this gospel of freedom; and after white Evangelicals retreated from the antislavery principles and became more respectable, they acknowledged that Christianity and slavery were contradictory. In the North, it was possible for blacks to criticize slaveholding Christianity publicly; in the South, the message had to be muted. Whether their critiques were open or secret, by 1800, black Evangelicals, slave and free, had already scored a significant victory in the war to assert their "manhood." By that date, the black church had begun.

Because they converted, churched, and pastored themselves, black Evangelicals were able to deny, in effect, that Christianity was a white religion. Even in the South, where whites were legally in control of black congregations, their control was nominal, since black exhorts and deacons functioned in reality as the pastors of their people. At times black evangelical congregations challenged white authorities, and in some cases succeeded in preserving their independence from white domination, as did the African Methodists of Mother Bethel in Philadelphia and the black Baptists of First African in Savannah. The astute leadership of men like Richard Allen and Andrew Marshall was tangible proof of black competence and skill in the affairs of men. Of even greater symbolic value was the power of black preachers in the affairs of God.

Due to the emphasis on conversion, an awakened clergy was more important than a learned one, at least in the early days of American Evangelicalism. Blacks seized the opportunity afforded by the willingness of Methodists and Baptists to license them to "exercise their gift." Whites as well as blacks fell under the powerful preaching of eloquent "brethren in black." The sight of whites humbled in the dust by blacks was a spectacular, if rare, demonstration of the lesson that "God is no respecter of persons."

More common was the day-to-day presence of the black minister in his community, slave or free, preaching funerals, weddings, prayer meetings, Sabbath sermons, with a force that uplifted blacks and proved the ability of black men. The point was not lost on defenders of the slave system who saw the existence of black churches and the activity of black clergymen as dangerous anomalies. Racists in the North and South found it necessary to denigrate black churches and black preachers by ridicule and restriction in order to be consistent with the doctrine of white supremacy. The racial hierarchy was threatened by any independent exercise of black authority, even though spiritual in nature. While whites had tried to limit Christian egalitarianism to the spiritual realm, the wall between spiritual and temporal equality was too frequently breached (most conspicuously by Denmark Vesey and Nat Turner). Yet, despite the threat to slave control that black religious independence posed, the evangelical tradition insured that suppression could only go so far. To deny blacks the possibility of preaching or gathering for religious meetings would have violated the tradition of gospel freedom as understood by evangelical Protestants (in contrast to a hierarchical tradition, like Catholicism, which had no such problem). When legislators took this step, evangelical objections led to amendment or evasion of the law.

Thus black churches functioned as much more than asylums from the "spirit of slavery and the spirit of caste." As Bishop Daniel Alexander Payne of the A.M.E. Church put it, in the African Methodist and Baptist churches they "found freedom of thought, freedom of speech, freedom of action, freedom for the development of a true Christian manhood." Significantly, Payne and other black clergymen linked "True Christian manhood" with the exercise of freedoms that sound suspiciously like civil and political rights. The ineluctable tendency of the black evangelical ethos was in the direction of asserting "manhood" rights, which were understood as a vital form of self-governance. In this sense, long before emancipation the black evangelical churches were political, though in the slave South they could be only incipiently so. In the North, the free black churches clearly functioned as a political institution, not simply because they were the only institutions that blacks were allowed to control, but because black Evangelicals connected the concept of "Christian manhood" with the exercise of political rights. . . .

Black Jeremiads

American blacks made evangelical Christianity their own by assuming, whenever possible, leadership of their own religious life. By doing so they denied that Christianity was a white religion. But the assertion of institutional autonomy was not enough. History affords many examples of oppressed people internalizing and institutionalizing the ideology of their oppressors in their own social organizations. Some critics of the black church have accused it of precisely this failure; however, black Evangelicals went beyond institutional separatism: they denied the doctrinal basis of "slaveholding Christianity" by refusing to believe that God had made them inferior to whites. Though whites might appeal to scriptural texts, such as "Cursed be Canaan; a servant of servants shall he be until his brethren," or "Servants be obedient to them that are your masters," blacks rejected the notion that either the Bible or Christianity supported American slavery.

Among the first public protests by black "citizens" were pre-Revolutionary petitions from slaves in Massachusetts pointing out the contradictions between slavery and a "free and Christian land." Over the next century, black condemnation of the sin of slavery ranged from the assignment of individual slaveholders to hell, to the castigation of American Christianity as hypocritical and false, to the prophecy that the nation itself was doomed to God's wrath unless it repented its crime.

By far the most affecting condemnation to emerge from the antebellum period was the pamphlet published by David Walker, a free black of Boston, in 1829. Known as Walker's *Appeal*, this amazing document has been read by some scholars as an early manifesto of black nationalism. Essentially it is a religious pamphlet, a black jeremiad urging the nation to turn from the sin of slavery before it was too late:

> Are . . . Americans innocent of the blood and groans of our fathers and us, their children? Every individual may plead innocence, if he pleases, but God will, before long, separate the innocent from the guilty unless something is speedily done—which I suppose will hardly be, so that their destruction may be sure. Oh Americans! let me tell you, in the name of the Lord, it will be good for you, if you listen to the voice of the Holy Ghost, but if you do not; you are ruined!!! Some of you are good men; but the will of my God must be done. Those avaricious and ungodly tyrants among you, I am awfully afraid will drag down the vengeance of God upon you. When God almighty commences his battle on the continent of America for [because of] the oppression of his people, tyrants will wish they never were born.

Besides issuing apocalyptic warnings, Walker attacked the claims of whites to superiority. Summarizing the evils of Greek, Roman, British, and European societies (American civilization's fictive pedigree), he concluded that "whites have always been an unjust, jealous, unmerciful avaricious and blood-thirsty set of beings, always seeking after power and authority." He questioned whether whites, given the record of the past, "are *as good by nature* as we are or not." Walker then raised a topic that would be discussed by black theologians for at least another century after his death: "It is my solemn belief, that if ever the world becomes Christianized (which must certainly take place before long) it will be through the means, under God of the *Blacks,* who are now held in wretchedness, and degradation, by the white *Christians* of the world. . . ."

Walker contemplated a revolution, albeit couched in religious terms. He leaves the effecting of the revolution to God's designs, but has no doubt that it will happen in this world, not the next. His God is the biblical God of nations and wars "who rules in the armies of heaven and among the inhabitants of the earth, and who dethrones one earthly king and sits [*sic*] up another." Unless Americans speedily abandon slavery and oppression of blacks, "God Almighty," Walker warned, "will tear up the very face of the earth" and "you and your *Country are gone.*" Lest Walker's rhetoric make him seem like a religious eccentric, it should be remembered that the Psalms, prophets, and apocalyptic books of the Bible have fueled a long tradition of Christian protest against injustice. Walker's jeremiad was part of this tradition as well as an eloquent example of black American Christianity standing in prophetic judgment against the perversion of Christianity by whites.

Though they could not declare it publicly, slaves in the South, like their Northern brethren, distinguished between true Christianity and false. They knew that holding a fellow Christian in bondage was a blatant violation of the fundamental spirit of Christianity and they saw that white Christians failed to understand this or else refused to acknowledge it. They scorned the doctrine of slavery's preachers, "don't steal, obey your masters," and held their own meetings when they wanted some "real preaching," even when it was forbidden. When their master's authority contradicted God's, some slaves risked severe punishment by choosing the latter. White claims of superiority and white norms of morality collapsed in the context of slavery. "They always tell us it am wrong to lie and steal," recalled Josephine Howard, "but why did the white folks steal my mammy and her mammy?" "That the sinfullest stealin' there is."

Disdainful of the religious hypocrisy of whites, slaves protested in several ways. Some rejected Christianity outright as a sham. Others who were tired of the moralistic misuse of the gospel to make slaves better—that is, better slaves—focused on the experience of God's spirit in states of ecstatic possession as the essence of Christianity. When accused of immorality they defended their piety by denying that God was concerned about every little sin.

White (and Northern black) missionaries were shocked to find former slaves who valued the experience of God's power as the norm of Christian truth rather than the Bible. The Bible, for them, came *after* conversion. "They wanted to see their children and friends get religion as they did. They fell under the mighty power of God . . . after mourning many days, and then came out shouting, for an angel they said, told them their sins were forgiven. They said their masters and families were Bible

Christians, and they did not want to be like them." Undoubtedly the African heritage, which placed spirit possession at the center of religious worship, played a significant role in their interpretation of Christianity, but so did their reaction to the slaveowner's version of the Bible. At the other extreme, some slaves cherished obedience to a strict moral code, in part at least because it assured their moral superiority over whites.

Despite their condemnations of white Christianity, black Evangelicals acknowledge that there were some good whites and offered them the hand of fellowship. Northern Evangelicals, black and white, cooperated in the antislavery movement, though blacks were irked at the paternalism and prejudice of the best-intentioned whites. In the South some slaves took to heart the hard saying, "Forgive your enemies, do good to those who persecute and spitefully use you," and tried, incredibly, to put the lesson into practice. Human relationships being as complex as they are, there were occasions of religious fellowship between blacks and whites, no matter how fixed in law and custom race relations were supposed to be. Particularly in the first year of the evangelical movement in the South, during the emotional tumult of the revivals and protracted meetings, blacks and whites influenced one another in the liminal experience of conversion.

Even as both races shared many of the same doctrines, beliefs, and rituals, they differed fundamentally about God's will for black people and about the meaning of the black presence in America.

The Meaning of Slavery

Blacks could accept Christianity because they rejected the white version with its trappings of slavery and caste for a purer and more authentic gospel. They were certain that God did not condone slavery and that he would end it: the problem was how and when. While black Evangelicals believed that the issue was ultimately in God's hands, they also believed that God used instruments. What were black people to do to end slavery? Vesey and Turner had offered one option: since God is on our side, we strike for freedom, confident in his protection. The Reverend Henry Highland Garnet offered a similar solution: "To such degradation it is sinful in the extreme for you to make voluntary submission . . . Brethren arise, arise! Strike for your lives and liberties. Now is the day and the hour. . . . *Rather die freemen than live to be slaves.*"

Most blacks, slave and free, realized that revolt, even with God on one's side, was doomed to failure. Garnet's address, though stirring, was rejected by the National Negro Convention before which it was given. Black Evangelicals believed that the relationship between God's sovereignty and human action was more mysterious than Vesey, Turner, or Garnet appreciated. Still, it was their duty to act. Three movements formed the arenas for black organization and activism in the North—anti-slavery, anticolonization, and moral reform. Stressing solidarity with their slave brothers, Northern black clergymen, many of them refugees from the South, organized antislavery societies; agitated from pulpit, press, and platform against slavery and oppression; fostered boycotts of slave-produced goods; formed networks to assist fugitive slaves; and strenuously opposed the American Colonization Society's plan to repatriate Afro-Americans in Africa.

While they generally favored voluntary emigration of American blacks to civilize and Christianize Africans, most black clergymen decried the American Colonization Society as a hypocritical organization bent on pressuring Congress into deporting all free blacks in order to insure the permanent security of slavery. In freedom-day celebrations and annual sermons, the American identity of blacks, their contributions to the nation, and their sacrifices in its wars, were increasingly stressed by black ministers and other spokesmen to counter the threat of forced emigration. That descendants of Africans, forced to America against their wills, were now fighting against a forced return to Africa seemed a particularly galling irony.

Black Evangelicals in the North also viewed moral reform, self-help, and education as part of the campaign against slavery. Ignorance, poverty, crime, and disease not only enslaved nominally free blacks, they were also excuses employed by racists to argue that blacks were incapable of the responsibilities of freedom and citizenship. Thus for black Evangelicals, doing good and avoiding evil were proofs of racial equality as well as signs of justification or sanctification. In this context, bourgeois values of honesty, thrift, temperance, and hard work took on a social significance for free black communities in the North that they did not have for slave communities in the South. For slaves, dishonesty, theft, and malingering were moral acts if directed against whites but not fellow blacks.

Moreover, for slave Evangelicals the essence of Christian life was not ethics, but liturgy. The ecstatic experience of God's powerful presence and the singing, dancing, and shouting that accompanied it were central, not rules, duties, and obligations. Although religious ecstasy was not absent from black evangelical churches in the North, increasing stress on education and moral reform (represented most firmly by men like Daniel Alexander Payne) led to discordance between the tone of black evangelical piety in the North and South. This discrepancy would become clear when Northern black missionaries, some originally from the South, began to work among the freedmen. Payne, for example, could not abide the former slaves' ring-shout, which he ridiculed as a "voodoo dance," heathenish, a disgrace to the race. He was shocked to find how resilient the custom was; the former slaves declared it to be "the essence of religion."

Antislavery, anticolonization, and moral reform were three issues around which black Evangelicals organized in the North. In these causes they attempted to answer the question, "What must we do to end slavery?" Though they believed the final outcome was hidden in the providence of God, this belief did not lead them to fatalism or quietism but instead to activism.

In the South, slaves believed just as strongly that God would deliver them from bondage as he had the biblical children of Israel. Indeed, their situation seemed to be appropriately characterized in Moses' words to the Israelites at the Red Sea: "Stand still and see the salvation of God." According to testimony from former slaves, Christianity did foster quietism just as it fostered acts of resistance, sometimes claiming both in the same slave. External acts must be distinguished from internal attitudes, especially in a situation like American slavery where coercion and effective police power made rebellion futile in the majority of cases.

External accommodation did not necessarily entail internal acceptance, however. Oppression may easily force outward acquiescence, but internal dissent is virtually impossible to control. The inner world of slaves was the fundamental battleground and there evangelical Christianity served as an important weapon in the slave's defense of his psychological, emotional, and moral freedom from white domination. In a brutal system, Evangelicalism helped slaves resist brutalization.

In particular, conversion, a profound experience of personal acceptance and validation, reoriented the individual slave's view of himself and of the world. "The eyes of my mind were open, and I saw things as I never did before," recalled one, recounting his conversion experience. "Everything looked new," claimed another. The visionary experiences that occurred during the sometimes lengthy period of mourning and conversion moved the slave through a series of emotional transformations, from dread to security, from pressure to release, from depression to elation, from the danger of annihilation to the assurance of salvation. These "otherworldly" symbols clearly reflected "thisworldly" concerns.

In the *Narrative* of his life, Frederick Douglass articulated in romantic nature imagery that moment of internal transformation that convinced him that he was, though still enslaved, free. Many less famous former slaves described that same moment, but in the evangelical imagery of conversion. Contradicting a system that valued him like a beast for his labor, conversion *experientially* confirmed the slave's value as a human person, indeed attested to his ultimate worth as one of the chosen of God.

Like all "peak experiences" the intensity of conversion waned in the face of day-to-day drudgery and occasional brutality. Now and then the experience needed to be recaptured. Moreover, conversion was essentially an individualistic experience, though it certainly was influenced by and shared with others. It gave an invaluable sense of personal meaning and direction to the individual held captive in slavery, but it failed to explain why a just God allowed the innocent to be enslaved at all. In other words, evangelical conversion gave meaning *to* life in slavery; it did not explain the meaning *of* slavery. In the prayer meetings and worship services held in the quarters or the hush harbors of the plantation South, slaves sought a renewed vision of their worth and an answer to the riddle of slavery from the evangelical community.

Slaves did find tangible relief from the misery of slavery in the ecstatic worship of the praise meetings during which they literally "stood outside" their normal selves seized and refreshed by the spirit of God. One former slave vividly recreated the scene many years later: "They'd preach and pray and sing—shout too. I heard them git up with a powerful force of the spirit, clappin' they hands and walkin' round the place. They'd shout, 'I got the glory . . . in my soul.' I seen some powerful figurations of the spirit in them day." The extemporaneous form of these meetings encouraged participants to include references to individual misfortunes and problems in their prayers and songs, so that they might be shared by all. This type of consolation, which has taken on the pejorative connotation of "compensatory," should be seen more positively as the answer to the crucial need of individuals for community.

The communal identity of slave Evangelicals was based upon the story of biblical Israel's enslavement and exodus from Egypt. Without doubt, the Exodus story was the most significant myth for American black identity, whether slave or free. White Americans had always thought of themselves as Israel, of course, but as Israelites in Canaan, the Promised Land. Black Americans were Israelites in Egypt. And even after emancipation they found that Canaan was still a far way off. Even so, they were a chosen people, destined for some special task under the direct protection of God. Identification with Israel intensified during the emotional climaxes of the prayer meetings. As Lawrence Levine has suggested, slaves dramatically reenacted the events of the Bible in their worship, with the result that time and distance collapsed into the sacred time of ritual as the congregation imaginatively became the biblical heroes whom they sang, danced, and preached about.

So strong was their identification with Israel that the slaves thought of Jesus, according to one missionary, as "a second Moses who would eventually lead *them* out of their prison-house of bondage." Though the longing was there, and sometimes expressed, no historical figure emerged around whom the Moses-Messiah figure could coalesce. Freedmen sometimes referred to Lincoln, Grant, and other Union figures as deliverers and saviors like Moses and Jesus, but it seems to have been an analogy and not a literal or symbolic identification. Others were quite clear that it was God who had freed them and left little credit to any man at all.

Nor did the slaves develop millennarian expectations around the long-hoped-for emancipation. Certainly they envisaged it as a glorious event, the day of "Jubilo," but perhaps they were too realistic about the ambiguities of freedom in a land that they did not control to forecast emancipation as the beginning of a thousand-year reign of peace and justice. As one former slave put it, "De preachers would exhort us dat us was de chillen o'Israel in de wilderness an' de Lord done sent us to take dis land o' milk and honey. But how us gwine-a take land what's already been took?"

By thinking of themselves as Israelites in Egypt, the slaves assured themselves that the God who had delivered his people once would do so again. Understanding their destiny as a repetition of Exodus, slaves found hope and purpose, but at the same time deferred the underlying question: Why does God allow the innocent to suffer slavery? Similarly, free blacks in the North were preoccupied with the God of Israel who would someday soon overthrow the wicked and raise up the just as he had done in the past. However, they also were engaged in arguing for abolition and black manhood rights, intellectual tasks that forced them to face difficult questions about the past, present, and future destiny of the black race.

Emancipation proved that God was faithful to his people, that their trust had been justified, but it also sharpened the problem. As freedom turned out to be less than complete, as Reconstruction was overthrown, as civil rights legislation was declared unconstitutional, as terrorism and Jim Crow legislation mounted, the questions became all the more urgent: What was God's purpose in permitting Africans to be enslaved? What is his purpose for the colored race now? In the decades of the 1880s and 1890s black theologians and clergymen would confront these problems head-on. They would persist for the rest of the century and beyond.

During the last three decades of the nineteenth century, black Evangelicals (and other black Christians) articulated more fully than before systematic answers to the vexed problem of the destiny of black folk. Frequently their discussions revolved around the ubiquitous topic, "the Negro problem." Perhaps the most acceptable answer to the greatest number of Evangelicals was that God had permitted but not condoned slavery, so that enslaved Africans might accept Christianity and civilization and then return one day to Africa to convert the fatherland. . . .

Another not necessarily antithetical solution to the question of black destiny had been stated but not fully developed during the antebellum period. Actually, it had been implicit in all the critiques of white Christianity penned by blacks: American Christianity was corrupt and blacks would reform it (or replace it with a pure Christianity). As early as 1837, the American Moral Reform Society had employed a striking image to state just this belief: the descendants of Africa should multiply and increase in virtue in America so "that our visages may be as so many Bibles, that shall warn this guilty nation of her injustice . . . until righteousness, justice, and truth shall rise in their might and majesty . . . and without distinction of nation or complexion, she disseminates alike her blessings of freedom to all mankind." Blacks, in this view, are the leaven that will save Christian America, whose noble ideals have been sadly betrayed by whites.

A more radical version of this notion, explicated most fully by black theologians James Theodore Holly and Theopilus G. Steward in the late nineteenth century, declared that Euro-American Christianity and civilization were corrupt, violent, materialistic, and nearly at an end. Black Christianity, new and vital, would succeed white Christianity and usher in an age when religion would be practiced, not just preached.

Black Evangelicals supported all these theological opinions by appealing to Psalms 68:31, probably the most widely quoted verse in Afro-American religious history, "Princes shall come out of Egypt; Ethiopia shall soon stretch out her hands unto God." Whether interpreted as a divine commission to evangelize Africa, as a prophecy of the black Christian role in restoring Christianity, or as both of the above, it well represented the self-conscious identity of black Evangelicals as they struggled and suffered to build a separate tradition in search of the meaning of their distinct destiny in America. As the twentieth century approached, black Evangelicals, like their forerunners for a century, would look to revival, conversion, and the Bible for the strength to endure and to improve their lives.

Selected Bibliography for Further Reading

Boles, John B., ed. *Masters and Slaves in the House of the Lord: Race and Religion in the American South, 1740–1870.* Lexington: University of Kentucky Press, 1988.

Creel, Margaret Washington. *"A Peculiar People": Slave Religion and Community-Culture Among the Gullahs.* New York: New York University Press, 1988.

Mathews, Donald. *Religion in the Old South.* Chicago: University of Chicago Press, 1977.

Raboteau, Albert J. *Slave Religion: The "Invisible Institution" in the Antebellum South.* New York: Oxford University Press, 1978.

Sernett, Milton C. *Black Religion and American Evangelicalism: White Protestants, Plantation Missions, and the Flowering of Negro Christianity, 1787–1865.* Metuchen, NJ: Scarecrow Press, 1975.

10

THE CIVIL WAR: REPRESSIBLE OR IRREPRESSIBLE?

No event in American history has been studied more than the Civil War. Not a year passes that does not see the publication of a wave of books and articles dealing with the war and its causes and consequences. So widespread has been interest in the field that many organizations as well as journals have been founded expressly for the purpose of furthering additional research and stimulating popular and professional interest in this subject. The History Book Club sells more books on the Civil War than any other subject; Ken Burns's Civil War series on PBS is the most-watched television documentary of all time; Civil War enactments on battle sites from Pennsylvania to Georgia increase in number and popularity every year. Indeed, to refer to a "cult" of Civil War enthusiasts is not to exaggerate the intensity of interest in the subject.

Despite the vast body of published material dealing with the Civil War, dispute over its causes never ceases. "Historians, whatever their predispositions," noted Howard Beale, "assign to the Civil War causes ranging from one simple force or phenomenon to patterns so complex and manifold that they include, intricately interwoven, all the important movements, thoughts, and actions of the decades before 1861."[1] Disagreements among historians over what caused the Civil War, as well what consequences proceeded from it, are as sharp today as they were over a century ago. While Americans have debated the wisdom and meaning of every war in which they participated, the Civil War has undoubtedly been the most controversial of all.

One reason for the enduring interest in the Civil War undoubtedly lies in the fact that the conflict pitted Americans against Americans. No external foe, no set of factors beyond the control of Americans led to the cataclysm: the Civil War was our fratricidal tragedy. Both a symbolic and actual dividing line in American history, the Civil War bears a similar relationship to the American people as the French Revolu-

---

[1]Howard K. Beale, "What Historians Have Said About the Causes of the Civil War," in *Theory and Practice in Historical Study: A Report of the Committee on Historiography, Social Science Research Council, Bulletin,* 54 (1946): 55.

tion to the French, the English Civil War to the English, and the Russian Revolution to Russians. Questions involving vital national issues are at stake in any interpretation of the event: the status of African Americans in our society; the sovereignty of the nation-state and the competing claims of states' rights and sectionalism; the contest between a society shaped by urbanization and advanced industrial capitalism and one shaped by agriculture; the meaning of those ideals of freedom and democracy on which the nation was founded; and the very viability of a republic in a world of centralized nation-states.

A second reason for the depth and persistence of interest in the Civil War is related to the first: the sheer level of violence unleashed by the war is unprecedented in American history. The more than six hundred thousand who died in the Civil War exceed the total American deaths in the Revolution, the War of 1812, the Mexican War, the Spanish-American War, World Wars I and II, and the Korean War *combined.* A staggering *one out of every four* Civil War combatants was killed. "Future years will never know the seething hell" of that slaughter, Walt Whitman asserted at war's end. "Its interior history will not only never be written," he went on to say, it "will never even be suggested."[2] Moreover, unlike the American Revolution or World War II—whose results few ever questioned—American historians have never been unanimous about whether all the horror of the Civil War was necessary or worthwhile. Fixing responsibility for so great a calamity upon specific groups or institutions has therefore been a continuous—and continuously contentious—task.

In the three decades following the end of fighting in 1865, writers marked out most of the lines of argument that would shape interpretations of the war into the future. These lines separated those who saw one region or the other as more responsible for causing the war; those who saw the war as avoidable or unavoidable; and those who saw slavery as opposed to economic differences as the cause of hostility between North and South.

In the immediate aftermath of the war, Northern writers portrayed Southern secessionists as men dedicated to the advance of slavery, regardless of the harm to the rest of the nation. The "slave power," wrote Henry Wilson in a famous book published in the 1870s, "after aggressive warfare of more than two generations upon the vital and animating spirit of republican institutions, upon the cherished and hallowed sentiments of a Christian people, upon the enduring interests and lasting renown of the Republic organized treasonable conspiracies, raised the standard of revolution, and plunged the nation into a bloody

---

[2]From Whitman's *Specimen Days and Collect* (1882), excerpted in *The Union in Crisis,* Robert W. Johannsen, ed. (Acton, Mass., 1999), pp. 192–93.

contest for the preservation of its threatened life."[3] Thus, in the prevailing Northern view, an aggressive conspiracy of slave owners forced the North to defend the Union, the Constitution, and basic human rights. For Southern writers, the war was not a moral conflict over slavery. Rather, the war resulted from the unconstitutional and aggressive strategy of the North to use its growing economic power to reduce the Southern states to political subservience. The North's domineering attitude toward the South was based on its self-righteous sense of moral and cultural superiority. Convinced that their liberal, commercial values were the only basis for a modern civilization, Abraham Lincoln and the Republican party attacked the South. Like most partisans of the Union cause, partisans of the Confederacy saw the war as a noble struggle against an oppressive alien culture.

While Northern and Southern partisans attacked each other, a third school of writers began to argue that the Civil War had in fact been needless or avoidable. These writers blamed the war on the failures of statesmen, both Northern and Southern. For example, James Buchanan, the president on whose watch relations disintegrated, and thus a clearly interested party, portrayed himself as having been caught between rabid Northern Republicans and rabid Southern Democrats. He argued that the cause of the Civil War was to be found in "the long, active, and persistent hostility of the Northern Abolitionists, both in and out of Congress, against Southern slavery, until the final triumph of President Lincoln; and on the other hand, the corresponding antagonism and violence with which the advocates of slavery resisted these efforts, and vindicated its preservation and extension up till the period of secession."[4] There was no substantive issue important enough in 1861 to necessitate a resort to arms; the war had been brought on by the malice of a few and the folly and weakness of many more.

Although by the 1890s a postwar generation of historians could attempt serious explanations of the Civil War free from the bitterness of recent memory, many of the essential points of contention would remain. And, although these scholars had the benefit of distance, they had powerful biases of their own. They were influenced by the rising tide of American nationalism at the turn of the century. The phenomenal industrial growth of the United States in the decades after the Civil War[5] had made the nation a world power. Politicians, journalists, and intel-

---

[3] Henry Wilson, *History of the Rise and Fall of the Slave Power in America*, 3 vols. (Boston, 1872–77), Vol. 1, pp. vi–vii.

[4] James Buchanan, *The Administration on the Eve of the Rebellion: A History of Four Years Before the War* (London, 1865), p. iv.

[5] On industrialization, see Volume II, Chapter 3.

lectuals—including historians—increasingly turned their attention from the divisiveness of the past toward a newly nationalist future. Intent upon cementing the bonds of American nationality, they cast upon the Civil War a gaze that was, if less partisan, also highly selective.

One of the first and most influential works of the nationalist school was James Ford Rhodes's multivolume history of the United States from 1850 to 1877. In many ways Rhodes sounded like his Northern predecessors: slavery was the basic cause of the war; the Southerners' claim that they had been persecuted was false; the South had fought the war to extend slavery, which was an inherently immoral institution. The Civil War, Rhodes concluded, was, as leading antebellum Republican and Lincoln's secretary of state, William H. Seward, had said, an irrepressible conflict between North and South, and the South had been clearly in the wrong. Despite his obvious Northern sympathies, however, Rhodes modified considerably the Northern partisan approach to the South and its peculiar institution. Southerners were not monsters; they might very well have overseen the peaceful and gradual abolition of slavery, he argued, had it not been for the cotton gin. It was thus an unforeseen and fateful bit of technological progress that revived slavery by turning cotton into the economic backbone of the Southern economy. Moreover, both England and New England played an important role in the preservation of slavery, because their citizens regularly purchased slave-grown cotton without any moral compunctions. Rhodes also distinguished between the institution of slavery and individual slave owners. He absolved the latter of guilt, insisting they deserved sympathy rather than censure because they had inherited a burdensome institution they could not fully control. Indeed, Rhodes found much to praise in Southern life: its gallantry, its concern for nonmaterial values, its respect for tradition. To Rhodes, therefore, the Civil War was a tragedy, the collision of impersonal forces beyond the control of individuals, most of whom were personally honorable and whose moral and cultural loyalties commanded respect. Finally, the Civil War had yielded an unforeseen and undeniable good: a modern, united, and powerful America.[6]

Rhodes's nationalist approach proved especially attractive to Southern scholars. For them, the causes of war were less important than its results: sectional reconciliation and the integration of the South into national life, including the blessings of industrialization and prosperity. Sympathetic to the South, these historians (including future president Woodrow Wilson) were nonetheless critical of slavery and secession. But their condemnation of slavery did not rest on a belief in racial equality. Instead they blamed slavery for saddling the

_____

[6]James Ford Rhodes, *History of the United States from the Compromise of 1850 to the Final Restoration of Home Rule in the South in 1877*, 7 vols. (New York, 1893–1906).

South with a backward economy and a hopelessly unproductive work-force, thereby retarding Southern progress in industrial, economic, so-cial, and cultural matters. Because of slavery, they concluded, the South developed along lines increasingly different from the rest of the country and therefore remained outside the rising spirit of nineteenth-century nationalism. Echoing Seward, one of these nationalist histori-ans, Edward Channing, wrote, "Two distinct social organizations had developed within the United States . . . Southern society was based on the production of staple agricultural crops by slave labor. Northern so-ciety was bottomed on varied employments—agricultural, mechani-cal, and commercial—all carried on under the wage system. Two such divergent forms of society could not continue indefinitely to live side by side within the walls of one government. . . . One or the other of these societies must perish, or both must secure complete equality."[7]

Most of the nationalist historians approved of the outcome of the Civil War. The growth of industrial capitalism was an unambiguous good. A more integrated economy and more powerful federal govern-ment were indispensable for the flourishing of an expansive world power. Few of these historians took occasion to protest the abandon-ment of African Americans after Reconstruction, or to assert egalitar-ian racial views of any kind. Being self-consciously modern scholars, they buttressed conventional prejudice with contemporary pseudo-scientific findings about the supposed evolutionary differentiation of races. They therefore accepted the subordinate role of blacks in Ameri-can society as a natural development.

By the early twentieth century the nationalist school of Civil War historiography began to face a formidable challenge from the rising Progressive school. Like many of their reform-minded fellow citizens, Progressive historians were dismayed by the ill social effects of indus-trialism, especially the increasing maldistribution of wealth and power in the United States.[8] Looking to the past to provide solutions to problems in the present, they found in American history a continu-ous cycle of struggle between democracy and aristocracy, between have-nots and haves, between "the people" and "the interests." Led by Charles A. Beard, these scholars emphasized not the development of a beneficent and unified nationalism, but the emergence of a turbulent democracy with alternating periods of reform and reaction generated by class conflict and other kinds of social antagonism.

Perhaps the most lucid and influential Progressive interpretation of the Civil War appeared in *The Rise of American Civilization*, which Beard himself wrote with his wife Mary in 1927. To the Beards the

---

[7]Edward Channing, *A History of the United States*, 6 vols. (New York, 1905–25), Vol. 6, pp. 3–4.

[8]See Volume II, Chapter 6.

1861 secession crisis and its debates over slavery masked a much more deeply rooted conflict. Stripped of all nonessentials the Civil War was "a social war, ending in the unquestioned establishment of a new power in the government, making vast changes in the arrangement of classes, in the accumulation and distribution of wealth, in the course of industrial development, and in the Constitution inherited from the Fathers. . . . In any event neither accident nor rhetoric should be allowed to obscure the . . . [revolutionary] character of that struggle. . . . [It was a] social cataclysm in which the capitalists, laborers, and farmers of the North and West drove from power in the national government the planting aristocracy of the South."[9]

Unlike the nationalist historians, the Progressives condemned the results of the Civil War in no uncertain terms. Its major result had been to install a gang of ruthless and self-aggrandizing capitalists in a position of dominance over the American economy. To Progressive historian Matthew Josephson, the half-century that followed the Civil War was the era of the Robber Barons: "Under their hands the renovation of our economic life proceeded relentlessly. . . . To organize and exploit the resources of a nation upon a gigantic scale, to regiment its farmers and workers into harmonious corps of producers, and to do this only in the name of an uncontrolled appetite for private profit—here surely is the great inherent contradiction whence so much disaster, outrage and misery has flowed.[10]

While the Beardian economic interpretation of the Civil War grew in influence during the Depression decade of the 1930s, a small group of Marxist historians began to move beyond the Beards in stressing the importance of economic causes of historical events. The Marxist periodization of American history followed the stages of capitalist development from self-sufficient agriculture, through commercial and industrial revolutions, finally issuing in the inevitable proletarian revolution. The place of the Civil War within this framework was clear: it was indeed—as the Beards claimed—a "Second American Revolution." Unlike the Beards, however, Marxist historians did not condemn the results of war. The destruction of the slave power had been the necessary preparation for the triumph of the bourgeois capitalist class—which in its turn set the stage for the inevitable triumph of the proletariat. "The sectional nature of the conflict and the geographical division of the contending classes," wrote James S. Allen, "have obscured the essential revolutionary nature of the Civil War. But this conflict was basically a revolution of a bourgeois democratic character,

---

[9]Charles A. and Mary R. Beard, *The Rise of American Civilization,* 2 vols. (New York, 1927), Vol. 2, pp. 53–54.

[10]Matthew Josephson, *The Robber Barons: The Great American Capitalists 1861–1901* (New York, 1934), p. viii.

in which the bourgeoisie was fighting for power against the landed aristocracy. . . . The destruction of the slave power was the basis for real national unity and the further development of capitalism, which would produce conditions most favorable for the growth of the labor movement."[11]

While the Progressive and Marxist economic interpretations flowered during the Depression of the 1930s, two schools of historical scholarship emerged in sharp contrast to them. The first of these came out of the resurgence of interest of native Southerners in their own section. A loosely defined and generally romantic assortment, sometimes referred to as the Southern Agrarians, the movement attempted to portray the Southern way of life as superior to the urbanized and industrialized condition of the rest of twentieth-century America. The Southern Agrarians gained a national audience in 1930 with a publication they subtitled *I'll Take My Stand*. Drawn from a symposium of Southern intellectuals, the twelve essays explored variations on a theme: Southerners would no longer tolerate the condescension of Northern critics; in fact, the agrarian South was superior to the industrial North; and further, the nation was in desperate need of what the South could offer it—an alternative to the corrosive skepticism and materialism that were the fruits of liberal capitalist society.

The rise of Southern sectional feeling was sharply mirrored in the work of its native historians. Three of the most influential—Ulrich B. Phillips, Charles W. Ramsdell, and Frank L. Owsley—set out to renovate the prevailing historical portrait of the South. At the center of this revised story was the Civil War, and on that ground the Southern historians did indeed "take their stand." Sounding remarkably like Confederate apologists of the 1860s and 1870s, these twentieth-century scholars idealized a land of chivalrous planters, genteel mistresses, and pathetically helpless and loyal slaves, all bound together with the threads of honor and tradition. At the same time, inevitably, they portrayed the North as nasty, brutish, and short on culture, except for the most debased commercial sort. In odd ways, the broad-brush Southern critique of modern bourgeois society echoed that of Marxists and Progressives. Like the Progressives, the Southern historians pictured nineteenth-century Northern industrialists as cynically exploiting abolitionist sentiments in pursuit of their own economic motives. And like Marxists, they found the politics and culture of modern America as bankrupt as the corporate economy that seemed to lie in ruins during the Depression years of the 1930s. If in denying that slavery caused the Civil War they sounded like Progressive or Marxist his-

---

[11]James S. Allen, *Reconstruction: The Battle for Democracy 1865–1876* (New York, 1937), pp. 18, and 26–28. The quotations are taken from the 1955 edition of this work.

torians, however, the Southern apologists sounded quite otherwise in asserting the beneficence of Southern institutions, including slavery. The flavor of their racial animosities was unmistakable. The blacks of the South, one of them wrote, were "cannibals and barbarians."[12] Slavery was simply a system of racial discipline: necessary, albeit burdensome, and fully ethical.

The second school of Civil War historiography that flourished in the 1930s and 1940s was the so-called "revisionist" school. It rejected all approaches, whether nationalist, Progressive, or Marxist, that proposed a fundamental confrontation—economic, social, or cultural—between North and South. The Civil War, even more than most wars, they insisted, was profoundly evil. Not only had it inflicted unspeakable suffering upon millions, but it had been avoidable. Genuine political alternatives had been available to political leaders in both sections. In refusing to choose those alternatives, the leaders bore the enormous moral burden of having sent hundreds of thousands to their deaths and impoverished millions. Such views gained credibility in the 1930s because an entire generation had been disillusioned with the results of World War I. Cynical about all patriotic appeals, the revisionist historians, like many of their contemporaries, determined to keep out of any future conflict that might emerge from imperial arrogance, capitalist greed, or petty national rivalries. Thus, when these revisionists turned their gaze upon the Civil War, they saw a catastrophe like their own: a struggle that cost much, gained little, and had been fully avoidable.

The most mature formulation of the revisionist hypothesis came from the pens of Avery Craven and James G. Randall in the years just before Pearl Harbor. Both of these distinguished scholars believed that wars never attained the noble objectives for which they were supposedly fought, and both equated war with pathological emotionalism and irrationalism. Given such assumptions, they insisted that the Civil War had been a repressible conflict and that the coming of the war could be explained as the political failure of the generation of the 1850s and 1860s.[13]

Craven, for example, argued that sectional differences—economic, social, political—could not explain the causes of the war; many countries with pronounced sectional dissimilarities had avoided civil strife. Nor was slavery the cause of the war. "If it had not become a symbol—

---

[12]Frank L. Owsley, "The Fundamental Cause of the Civil War: Egocentric Sectionalism," *Journal of Southern History*, 7 (February 1941): 3–18, and "The Irrepressible Conflict," in *Twelve Southerners: I'll Take My Stand* (New York, 1930), pp. 77–78.

[13]See Philip G. Auchampaugh, *James Buchanan and His Cabinet on the Eve of Secession* (Lancaster, Pa., 1926); George Fort Milton, *The Eve of Conflict: Stephen A. Douglas and the Needless War* (New York, 1934); and Gilbert H. Barnes, *The Antislavery Impulse, 1830–1844* (New York, 1933).

first of sectional differences and then of southern depravity, or superiority, according to the point of view—it might have been faced as a national question and dealt with as successfully as the South American countries dealt with the same problem."[14] The war, Craven maintained, occurred because normal sectional differences—which could have been resolved through political means—were magnified and emotionalized until they could no longer be dealt with in rational terms: "For more than two decades these molders of public opinion steadily created the fiction of two distinct peoples contending for the right to preserve and expand their sacred cultures. . . . Opponents became devils in human form. Good men had no choice but to kill and to be killed."[15] To the men who erred so catastrophically, Randall gave the name "the blundering generation."[16]

Although the revisionist approach remained popular throughout the 1940s and even afterward,[17] historians began to attack its basic premises in sharp terms. While wars could never be good in themselves, these scholars argued, in certain cases avoiding war was a far greater evil. Pointing to World War II, Samuel Eliot Morison argued in his 1950 presidential address before the American Historical Association that "war does accomplish something, that war is better than servitude, that war has been an inescapable aspect of the human story."[18] Reflecting on the recent struggle against fascist totalitarianism—and the growing Cold War against communism—Morison and other scholars insisted that war was justified when it involved the defense of uncompromisable moral and ethical issues. Some historians were influenced by the writings of the prominent theologian Reinhold Niebuhr, who insisted that evil was an unavoidable part of reality and had to be taken into account in any adequate explanation of human experience. Finally, in the 1940s and early 1950s growing demands by African Americans for equal rights contributed to a reevaluation of the causes of the Civil War. Taking civil rights seriously in post–World War II America reinforced the tendency to take slavery seriously as a cause of the Civil War.

In 1949 Arthur M. Schlesinger, Jr., wrote one of the most cogent at-

---

[14]Avery Craven, *The Repressible Conflict 1830–1861* (Baton Rouge, La., 1939), p. 64.

[15]Avery Craven, *The Coming of the Civil War* (New York, 1942), p. 2.

[16]J. G. Randall, "The Blundering Generation," *Mississippi Valley Historical Review,* 27 (June 1940): 4–16.

[17]Two outstanding revisionist works published after the end of World War II are Roy F. Nichols, *The Disruption of American Democracy* (New York, 1948), and Kenneth M. Stampp, *And the War Came: The North and the Secession Crisis 1860–1861* (Baton Rouge, La., 1950).

[18]Samuel Eliot Morison, "Faith of a Historian," *American Historical Review,* 56 (January 1951): 267.

tacks on the revisionist historians. He asked one specific question: if the war could have been avoided, what course should American leaders have followed? None of the revisionists had ever spelled out a plausible scenario that might have avoided war. Schlesinger listed three possible alternatives: that the South might have abolished slavery by itself if left alone; that slavery would have died because it was economically unsound; or that the North might have offered some form of emancipation compensation. Finding all three of these possibilities either inadequate or unattainable, Schlesinger charged that revisionism "is connected with the modern tendency to seek in optimistic sentimentalism an escape from the severe demands of moral decision." The South, in defending its evil institution, had posed moral challenges too profound to be solved by political compromise. Only by ignoring the moral dimensions of humanity, he concluded, could historians ascribe the cause of the Civil War to mere blundering.[19]

At about the same time that Schlesinger was attacking the revisionists, another famous historian was trying to reconcile revisionist and nationalist approaches, while strongly rejecting the Progressives' economic interpretation. Allan Nevins's magisterial history of the United States from the 1840s through the 1860s, *The Ordeal of the Union*, sounded revisionist on the question of causation. The Civil War, wrote Nevins, "should have been avoidable." He went on, however, sounding like a nationalist, to say that "the problem of slavery *with its complementary problem of race-adjustment*"[20] involved basic differences between North and South. And finally, he returned to the revisionist argument that bad leadership—and, indeed, in his view, bad citizenship—caused the war. The first selection in this chapter, from Nevins's second volume, elaborates on this argument.

By the 1960s, as the debate over the avoidability of the Civil War had become fairly static,[21] a new generation of historians began to undermine traditional approaches and ask new questions. The rise of the "new political history" (an approach that emphasized the social basis of politics and employed quantitative techniques) led some scholars to minimize the significance of slavery in the development of nineteenth-century American society. Sounding like neo-Progressives, they insisted that the behavior of Americans and their political parties in the two decades preceding the Civil War involved more than merely a reaction to slavery. Unlike the old Progressives, however, these new

---

[19]Arthur M. Schlesinger, Jr., "The Causes of the Civil War: A Note on Historical Sentimentalism," *Partisan Review*, 16 (October 1949): 969–981.

[20]Emphasis in the original.

[21]Indeed, David Donald wrote in 1960 that historians were no longer concerned with the causes of the Civil War: "American Historians and the Causes of the Civil War," *South Atlantic Quarterly*, 59 (Summer 1960): 351–55.

historians paid less attention to class conflict than to "ethnocultural" conflict. Antebellum politics revolved around conflicts between natives and immigrants, Protestants and Catholics, proponents and opponents of temperance. Passions fired by these causes were more significant than differences over slavery.[22] Broadly speaking, it might be said that for these scholars the Civil War became just one event within the larger and more important story of the modernization of American society.[23]

One of the most sophisticated of the new political historians was Michael F. Holt. Combining a behavioral with an ideological analysis, he conceded that the sectional conflict over slavery was relatively important to antebellum Americans. Nevertheless, he insisted, most of those Americans were more preoccupied with what they saw as the threat of corruption to the survival of republican institutions. The threat manifested itself in excessive individualism and urban vice. In response, many Americans decried extreme personal ambition, devotion to material success, and political and social contentiousness; they demanded a halt to massive immigration, which turned once homogeneous communities into boom towns, and modest cities into alien and polyglot metropolises. Anti-Mason, anti-Catholic, and anti-immigrant movements, culminating in the Know-Nothing party of the 1850s, arose to explain these disturbing changes and to propose ways of combating them. But the normal political process proved inadequate to the task of relieving so widespread and multidimensional a sense of social anxiety. When the second party system collapsed in the 1850s amidst a sense of crisis that a once-republican "government was beyond control of the people, that it had become a threatening power dominated by some gigantic conspiracy," politicians North and South responded by scapegoating the other section: each became for the other the chief menace to republicanism. To prevent the triumph of the great "slave power conspiracy," or of the great "anti-slavery conspiracy," became a cause of supreme political and moral urgency. "The consequence was secession and a tragic Civil War."[24]

In Holt's version of the new political interpretation, analysis of ethnocultural conflict and the stresses of modernization was interwo-

---

[22]See the collected essays of Joel H. Silbey in *The Partisan Imperative: The Dynamics of American Politics Before the Civil War* (New York, 1985); also his *The Shrine of Party: Congressional Voting Behavior, 1841–1852* (Pittsburgh, 1967).

[23]See Eric Foner, "The Causes of the American Civil War: Recent Interpretations and New Directions," *Civil War History*, 20 (September 1974): 194–214.

[24]Michael F. Holt, *The Political Crisis of the 1850s* (New York, 1978), and "An Elusive Synthesis: Northern Politics During the Civil War," in James M. McPherson and William J. Cooper, eds., *Writing the Civil War: The Quest to Understand* (Columbia, S.C., 1998), pp. 112–34. See also Ronald P. Formisano, *The Birth of Mass Political Parties: Michigan, 1827–1861* (New York, 1971).

ven with the persistent view that slavery was somehow central to the coming of war. In a study of the ideology of the Republican party, Eric Foner moved from the opposite pole but in the same direction. He began with the basic assumption that conflict over the expansion of slavery into the western territories caused the Civil War. In order to connect that issue with the whole range of social and cultural concerns that political historians had shown to be so important to nineteenth-century Americans, he explored the concept of "free labor." Those who espoused the doctrines of free labor—most of whom eventually came together in the Republican party in the late 1850s—believed in an open and mobile society that rewarded individual work. Whatever their other differences, Republicans were united in their conviction that slavery was incompatible with such a free labor society and would sooner or later have to disappear. Most Northerners were willing to let it erode slowly in the old South, but they refused to allow the "slave power" to expand any farther. To do so would not only threaten the material interests of small farmers and traders intent on winning the West for small-scale capitalist development. Slavery's expansion would threaten the very survival of the American experiment in constitutional republicanism.

Unlike Holt and the other historians who stressed ethnocultural conflict, Foner saw nativism as only one, and not the most important, among many issues contributing to the crisis of the Union.[25] In the half-century following the adoption of the federal Constitution, he argued, the political system functioned "as a mechanism for relieving social tensions, ordering group conflict, and integrating the society." By the 1830s and 1840s new, more formalized party structures channeled voter participation in politics. In both North and South the dynamics of party competition inadvertently gave rise to sectional agitators who increasingly forced public opinion—and hence government—to confront the issue of slavery. The result was a polarization of American politics along ideological lines and a growing inability of normal political institutions to resolve basic differences between North and South. In each section an ideological coalition emerged that was antithetical to the idea of national unity on any terms other than its own. Slavery had indeed caused the Civil War, Foner concluded, because its expansion threatened the continued evolution of the society,

---

[25]Eric Foner, *Free Soil, Free Labor, Free Men: The Ideology of the Republican Party Before the Civil War* (New York, 1970). For other views on the evolution of Northern politics see James L. Huston, *The Panic of 1857 and the Coming of the Civil War* (Baton Rouge, La., 1987); Mark W. Summers, *The Plundering Generation: Corruption and the Crisis of the Union, 1849–1861* (New York, 1987); William E. Gienapp, *The Origins of the Republican Party, 1852–1856* (New York, 1987); Kenneth M. Stampp, *America in 1857: A Nation on the Brink* (New York, 1990); Jean H. Baker, *The Political Culture of Northern Democrats in the Mid-Nineteenth Century* (Ithaca, N.Y., 1983).

culture, and political ideology of free labor. Only a country dominated by the North, the home of free labor, could accomplish the goal originally envisaged by the framers: the creation and preservation of a single nation founded on republican principles. Conversely, as William Barney has shown, Southerners believed that only a nation in which slavery guaranteed white men's democracy could realize that same original goal.[26]

The work of these historians, and also of Richard Sewell and James McPherson,[27] firmly reset slavery in the center of Civil War historiography. In doing so they integrated elements of nationalist and Progressive approaches, while decisively rejecting revisionist ones. That is, like the nationalists they reaffirmed the character of the Civil War as tragic but morally unavoidable. Like the Progressives they acknowledged the economic divergence between North and South, even while insisting that a range of social, cultural, and ideological differences moved millions toward a war that would settle the issue between slave labor and free. After their work, perhaps the most important advance in efforts to narrate a large-scale and synthetic history of the Civil War involves the deployment of comparative history. Historians of slavery have been prominent in this endeavor for years. Eugene Genovese, Peter Kolchin, and many others have rightly insisted that an international phenomenon of such scale and endurance can only be properly understood in comparative terms.[28] Similarly, a few historians of the Civil War itself have sought to compare the American road to emancipation with that of nations in the Caribbean and South America.[29] Among their most important findings are those highlighted in the essay by William Freehling in this chapter. First, the American

---

[26]William L. Barney, *The Road to Secession: A New Perspective on the Old South* (New York, 1972).

[27]See Richard H. Sewell, *A House Divided: Sectionalism and the Civil War, 1848–1865* (Baltimore, 1988), and James M. McPherson, *Ordeal by Fire: The Civil War and Reconstruction* (New York, 1982), and *Battle Cry of Freedom: The Civil War Era* (New York, 1988).

[28]See Eugene D. Genovese, *From Rebellion to Revolution: Afro-American Slave Revolts in the Making of the New World* (Baton Rouge, La., 1979); *The World the Slaveholders Made: Two Essays in Interpretation* (New York, 1969); with Laura Foner, eds., *Slavery in the New World: A Reader in Comparative History* (Englewood Cliffs, N.J., 1969); and with Elizabeth Fox-Genovese, *Fruits of Merchant Capital: Slavery and Bourgeois Property in the Rise and Expansion of Capitalism* (New York, 1983); Peter Kolchin, *Unfree Labor: American Slavery and Russian Serfdom* (Cambridge, Mass., 1987). See also works discussed in Volume I, Chapter 4.

[29]See, for example, George M. Fredrickson, *White Supremacy: A Comparative Study in American and South African History* (New York, 1981); Rebecca Scott, "Comparing Emancipations: A Review Essay," *Journal of Social History*, 20 (Spring 1987): 565–83; Peter Kolchin, "Some Thoughts on Emancipation in Comparative Perspective: Russia and the United States South," *Slavery and Abolition*, 21 (December 1990): 351–67.

experience was notably bloody; only a few nations abolished slavery as the result of a civil war. And second, the United States found itself ensnared in fratricidal struggle precisely because of its decentralized and quite exuberant mass political democracy; no central state or authority could decree or enforce emancipation on the self-governing societies of North America. Freehling makes clear just how intimately and fatally interwoven was slavery with the institutions and values of local democracy and small-scale capitalism.[30]

In addition to comparative approaches, historians in the 1990s have explored several lines of social historical analysis that connect the Civil War with the intimate, small-group, and local history of the nineteenth century.[31] Women's history has significantly enriched Civil War historiography in recent years.[32] In the past women either were absent from Civil War history or appeared as heroic nurturers. Whether serving as nurses, fund raisers, or domestic managers, their role was auxiliary to the main action and distinctly sex-bound. Eventually feminist historians focused on the effects of the war on the trajectory of women's advancement in the late nineteenth and early twentieth centuries. Women's exertions in the war years contributed to the professionalization of nursing and other "helping" professions, and ultimately strengthened women's claim to equal political rights.

Recently historians have qualified this picture, noting that differences among women, especially in terms of race and class, sharply determined their Civil War experiences. For example, while many middle-class, Northern white women made significant gains in their quest for social and political equality, Susan Lebsock showed that in one Southern town the war confirmed women's subordination and reinforced the racial divide between white and black women.[33] Historians Drew Gilpin Faust and LeeAnn Whites showed the significant impact of women, and more broadly of the sexual system, on the conduct and outcome of the war. In their accounts, men's failure to "protect" their women and women's unpreparedness for the roles of slave manager and plantation administrator created a climate of sexual hostility within families and communities, weakened the Confederate

---

[30]See also Barney, *Road to Secession*; James Oakes, *The Ruling Race: A History of American Slaveholders* (New York, 1982).

[31]See, for example, the essays in Maris A. Vinovskis, ed., *Toward a Social History of the American Civil War: Exploratory Essays* (Cambridge, Mass., 1990).

[32]See Drew Gilpin Faust, "'Ours as Well as That of the Men': Women and Gender in the Civil War," in McPherson and Cooper, *Writing the Civil War,* pp. 228–240.

[33]See Susan Lebsock, *Free Women of Petersburg: Status and Culture in a Southern Town, 1784–1860* (New York, 1984); Similarly, see George C. Rable, *Civil Wars: Women and the Crisis of Southern Nationalism* (Urbana, Ill., 1989).

war effort, and speeded the dissolution of slavery.[34] And finally, with an even broader brush Anne C. Rose showed that Northern middle-class Americans could only understand the Civil War—its causes, experiences, and consequences—within the context of Victorian culture. She suggested that the religious values, sexual codes, and family practices that were at the heart of that culture played a role in leading Americans to and through that transformative event.[35]

But by far the most important advances in the social history of the Civil War have been made by historians of African Americans. For years historians from W. E. B. Du Bois to Benjamin Quarles and John Hope Franklin have written of the experiences of slaves and free blacks in the Civil War era.[36] But only recently has the black contribution to Union victory and to slaves' self-emancipation received sustained attention.[37] Dudley Taylor Cornish and Joseph T. Glatthaar, among others, have demonstrated the decisive contribution of black soldiers to the Union victory.[38] More recently, Ira Berlin and a team of coeditors have made clear beyond a doubt that the preservation of the Union, the destruction of slavery, and the reconstitution of Southern society all depended crucially on the contributions of African Americans.[39]

Appreciation for the indispensable contribution of blacks to emancipation and military victory may have led some historians to exagger-

---

[34]Drew Gilpin Faust, *Mothers of Invention: Women of the Slaveholding South in the American Civil War* (Chapel Hill, N.C., 1996); LeeAnn Whites, *The Civil War as a Crisis in Gender: Augusta, Georgia, 1860–1890* (Athens, Ga., 1995). Alice Fahs argues in "The Feminized Civil War: Gender, Northern Popular Literature, and the Memory of War, 1861–1900," *Journal of American History*, 85 (March 1999): 1461–94, that while Southern women may have lost the war, they "won the popular battle for its memory." See also Catherine Clinton, *The Other Civil War: American Women in the Nineteenth Century* (New York, 1984).

[35]Anne C. Rose, *Victorian American and the Civil War* (Cambridge, Mass., 1992).

[36]W. E. B. Du Bois, *Black Reconstruction in America* (New York, 1935); Benjamin Quarles, *The Negro and the Civil War* (Boston, 1953); John Hope Franklin, *The Emancipation Proclamation* (New York, 1963). See also Bell Irvin Wiley, *Southern Negroes, 1861–1865* (New Haven, Conn., 1938).

[37]A fine bibliographical essay is Peter Kolchin, "Slavery and Freedom in the Civil War South," in McPherson and Cooper, eds., *Writing the Civil War*, pp. 241–60.

[38]Dudley Taylor Cornish, *The Sable Arm: Negro Troops in the Union Army, 1861–1865* (New York, 1956); Joseph T. Glatthaar, *Forged in Battle: The Civil War Alliance of Black Soldiers and White Officers* (New York, 1990), and "Black Glory: The African American Role in the Union Victory," in Gabor S. Boritt, ed., *Why the Confederacy Lost* (New York, 1992), pp. 133–62. See also James M. McPherson, *The Negro's Civil War: How American Negroes Felt and Acted during the War for the Union* (New York, 1965).

[39]Ira Berlin, et al., eds., *Freedom: A Documentary History of Emancipation, 1861–1867*, 4 vols. (Cambridge, Mass., 1985–93), with further volumes forthcoming. A sample of their findings can be found in *Free at Last: A Documentary History of Slavery, Freedom, and the Civil War* (New York, 1992), and works cited in Kolchin, "Slavery and Freedom in the Civil War South."

ate the power of efforts toward self-liberation and to obscure the military and, increasingly, the ideological commitment of Lincoln and other white Americans to the cause of emancipation. The debate on this question is wide-ranging, but may be sampled in the exchange between Barbara Fields and James McPherson.[40] For Fields, only desperate necessity and continual prodding from black Americans pushed Lincoln and his government toward emancipation; and Reconstruction after the war proved short-lived and ineffective precisely because the original commitment to freedom was weak. For McPherson, Lincoln's evolving moral commitment to emancipation embodies the "new birth of freedom" that was, in the end, the central meaning of the Civil War. Beyond this particular debate, a number of historians, McPherson among them, have shown just how complex and enriching was the interaction of black and white Americans during the Civil War. As David Blight's study of the great black abolitionist Frederick Douglass and Garry Wills's recent meditation upon the significance of Lincoln's Gettysburg Address show in quite different ways, that interaction was at the heart of the struggle to redefine the American constitutional republic.[41] Nothing that came before escapes reinterpretation in light of the Civil War; nothing that has come after escapes its shaping influence. "The scale of the union's triumph and the sheer drama of emancipation," Eric Foner declared, "fused nationalism, morality, and the language of freedom in an entirely new combination."[42]

At the end of the twentieth century determining "the cause" of the Civil War is as daunting a task as ever. Many of the same problems that confronted historians for nearly a century continue to confront the student today. Were North and South diverging into two civilizations and therefore heading toward irrepressible conflict? What role did social and economic differences play in the coming of the war? Did the extremism and folly of politicians and citizens turn a serious quarrel into an irresolvable one? How did religion, ethnicity, culture and ideology shape political behavior on local, state, and national levels in

---

[40]Barbara J. Fields, "Who Freed the Slaves?" in Geoffrey C. Ward, ed., *The Civil War: An Illustrated History* (New York, 1990), pp. 178–81; James M. McPherson, "Who Freed the Slaves?" in *Reconstruction*, 2 (1994): 35–40, and reprinted in his *Drawn with the Sword: Reflections on the American Civil War* (New York, 1996), pp. 192–207.

[41]David W. Blight, *Frederick Douglass' Civil War: Keeping Faith in Jubilee* (Baton Rouge, La., 1989); Garry Wills, *Lincoln at Gettysburg: The Words that Remade America* (New York, 1992). On Douglass, see also Waldo E. Martin, Jr., *The Mind of Frederick Douglass* (Chapel Hill, N.C., 1984), and William S. McFeely, *Frederick Douglass* (New York, 1990). On Lincoln and the Union commitment to freedom, see LaWanda Cox, *Lincoln and Black Freedom: A Study in Presidential Leadership* (Columbia, S.C., 1981), and James M. McPherson, *Abraham Lincoln and the Second American Revolution* (New York, 1991).

[42]Eric Foner, *The Story of American Freedom* (New York, 1998), p. 99.

the years leading up to the conflict? Similar difficulties arise in trying to decide on "the meaning" of the Civil War.

Despite these differences, however, most historians seem to agree today that slavery was central to the crisis of the Union and the coming of the Civil War. They agree that the Civil War was a momentous event—perhaps the most consequential event—in American history. In abolishing slavery and confirming once and for all the question of the integrity of the national republic and the dominance of industrial capitalism, the Civil War set the stage for all that has followed. Thus, although many questions remain, a few of the biggest are settled.

Almost half a century ago, historian Thomas Pressly took note of "the strength of the emotions" with which historians and other citizens expressed their views on the Civil War. In trying to explain this passion, he suggested that as long as Americans found themselves addressing racial inequality in their society, or debating the wisdom of fighting wars, or pondering the tension between majority rule and minority rights, the causes and consequences of the Civil War would remain matters of dispute.[43] If that is the case, there can be no doubt that the Civil War will remain the most intensely researched and discussed subject in American history.

---

[43]Thomas J. Pressly, *Americans Interpret Their Civil War* (Princeton, N.J., 1954), pp. 321–23.

ALLAN NEVINS

ALLAN NEVINS (1890–1971) was professor of history at Columbia University. He was one of the most prolific American historians of the twentieth century. In addition to his multivolume study of the Civil War era, he also wrote biographies of John D. Rockefeller and Henry Ford, among many other books.

Great and complex events have great and complex causes. Burke, in his *Reflections on the Revolution in France,* wrote that "a state without the means of some change is without the means of its conservation," and that a constant reconciliation of "the two principles of conservation and correction" is indispensable to healthy national growth. It is safe to say that every such revolutionary era as that on which the United States entered in 1860 finds its genesis in an inadequate adjustment of these two forces. It is also safe to say that when a tragic national failure occurs, it is largely a failure of leadership. "Brains are of three orders," wrote Machiavelli, "those that understand of themselves, those that understand when another shows them, and those that understand neither by themselves nor by the showing of others." Ferment and change must steadily be controlled; the real must, as Bryce said, be kept resting on the ideal; and if disaster is to be avoided, wise leaders must help thoughtless men to understand, and direct the action of invincibly ignorant men. Necessary reforms may be obstructed in various ways; by sheer inertia, by tyranny and class selfishness, or by the application of compromise to basic principles— this last being in Lowell's view the main cause of the Civil War. Ordinarily the obstruction arises from a combination of all these elements. To explain the failure of American leadership in 1846–1861, and the revolution that ensued, is a baffling complicated problem.

Looking backward from the verge of war in March, 1861, Americans could survey a series of ill-fated decisions by their chosen agents. One unfortunate decision was embodied in Douglas's Kansas-Nebraska Act of 1854. Had an overwhelming majority of Americans been ready to accept the squatter sovereignty principle, this law might have proved a statesmanlike stroke; but it was so certain that powerful elements North and South would resist it to the last that it accentuated the strife and confusion. Another disastrous decision was made by Taney and his associates in the Dred Scott pronouncement of 1857.

Still another was made by Buchanan when he weakly accepted the Lecompton Constitution and tried to force that fraudulent document through Congress. The Northern legislatures which passed Personal Liberty Acts made an unhappy decision. Most irresponsible, wanton, and disastrous of all was the decision of those Southern leaders who in 1858–1860 turned to the provocative demand for Congressional protection of slavery in all the Territories of the republic. Still other errors might be named. Obviously, however, it is the forces behind these decisions which demand our study; the waters pouring down the gorge, not the rocks which threw their spray into the air.

At this point we meet a confused clamor of voices as various students attempt an explanation of the tragic denouement of 1861. Some writers are as content with a simple explanation as Lord Clarendon was when he attributed the English Civil War to the desire of Parliament for an egregious domination of the government. The bloody conflict, declared James Ford Rhodes, had "a single cause, slavery." He was but echoing what Henry Wilson and other early historians had written, that the aggressions of the Slave Power offered the central explanation. That opinion had been challenged as early as 1861 by the London *Saturday Review*, which remarked that "slavery is but a surface question in American politics," and by such Southern propagandists as Yancey, who tried to popularize a commercial theory of the war, emphasizing a supposed Southern revolt against the tariff and other Yankee exactions. A later school of writers was to find the key to the tragedy in an inexorable conflict between the business-minded North and the agrarian-minded South, a thrusting industrialism colliding with a rather static agricultural society. Still another group of writers has accepted the theory that the war resulted from psychological causes. They declare that agitators, propagandists, and alarmists on both sides, exaggerating the real differences of interest, created a state of mind, a hysterical excitement, which made armed conflict inevitable.

At the very outset of the war Senator Mason of Virginia, writing to his daughter, asserted that two systems of society were in conflict; systems, he implied, as different as those of Carthage and Rome, Protestant Holland and Catholic Spain. That view, too, was later to be elaborated by a considerable school of writers. Two separate nations they declared, had arisen within the United States in 1861, much as two separate nations had emerged within the first British Empire by 1776. Contrasting ways of life, rival group consciousness, divergent hopes and fears made a movement for separation logical; and the minority people, believing its peculiar civilization in danger of suppression, began a war for independence. We are told, indeed, that two types of nationalism came into conflict: a Northern nationalism which wished to preserve the unity of the whole republic, and a Southern nationalism intent on creating an entirely new republic.

It is evident that some of these explanations deal with merely superficial phenomena, and that others, when taken separately, represent
but subsidiary elements in the play of forces. Slavery was a great fact;
the demands of Northern industrialism constituted a great fact; sectional hysteria was a great fact. But do they not perhaps relate themselves to some profounder underlying cause? This question has
inspired one student to suggest that "the confusion of a growing state"
may offer the fundamental explanation of the drift to war; an unsatis-
factory hypothesis, for westward growth, railroad growth, business
growth, and cultural growth, however much attended with "confusion," were unifying factors, and it was not the new-made West but
old-settled South Carolina which led in the schism.

One fact needs emphatic statement: of all the monistic explanations for the drift to war, that posited upon supposed economic causes
is the flimsiest. This theory was sharply rejected at the time by so astute an observer as Alexander H. Stephens. South Carolina, he wrote
his brother on New Year's Day, 1861, was seceding from a tariff
"which is just what her own Senators and members in Congress made
it." As for the charges of consolidation and despotism made by some
Carolinians, he thought they arose from peevishness rather than a
calm analysis of facts. "The truth is, the South, almost in mass, has
voted, I think, for every measure of general legislation that has passed
both houses and become law for the last ten years." The South, far
from groaning under tyranny, had controlled the government almost
from its beginning, and Stephens believed that its only real grievance
lay in the Northern refusal to return fugitive slaves and to stop the antislavery agitation. "All other complaints are founded on threatened
dangers which may never come, and which I feel very sure would be
averted if the South would pursue a judicious and wise course."
Stephens was right. It was true that the whole tendency of federal legislation 1842–1860 was toward free trade; true that the tariff in force
when secession began was largely Southern-made; true that it was the
lowest tariff the country had known since 1816; true that it cost a nation of 30 million people but $60 million in indirect revenue; true that
without secession no new tariff law, obnoxious to the Democratic
party, could have passed before 1863—if then.

In the official explanations which one Southern state after another
published for its secession, economic grievances are either omitted entirely or given minor position. There were few such supposed grievances which the agricultural states of Illinois, Iowa, Indiana,
Wisconsin, and Minnesota did not share with the South—and they
never threatened to secede. Charles A. Beard finds the taproot of the
war in the resistance of the planter interest to Northern demands enlarging the old Hamilton-Webster policy. The South was adamant in
standing for "no high protective tariffs, no ship subsidies, no national

banking and currency system; in short, none of the measures which
business enterprise deemed essential to its progress." But the Republican platform in 1856 was silent on the tariff; in 1860 it carried a milk-
and-water statement on the subject which western Republicans took,
mild as it was, with a wry face; the incoming president was little interested in the tariff; and any harsh legislation was impossible. Ship subsidies were not an issue in the campaign of 1860. Neither were a
national banking system and a national currency system. They were
not mentioned in the Republican platform nor discussed by party de-
baters. The Pacific Railroad was advocated both by the Douglas Democrats and the Republicans; and it is noteworthy that Seward and
Douglas were for building both a Northern and a Southern line. In
short, the divisive economic issues are easily exaggerated. At the same
time, the unifying economic factors were both numerous and powerful. North and South had economies which were largely complementary. It was no misfortune to the South that Massachusetts cotton
mills wanted its staple, and that New York ironmasters like Hewitt
were eager to sell rails dirtcheap to Southern railway builders; and
sober businessmen on both sides, merchants, bankers, and manufacturers, were the men most anxious to keep the peace and hold the
Union together.

We must seek further for an explanation; and in so doing, we must
give special weight to the observations of penetrating leaders of the
time, who knew at firsthand the spirit of the people. Henry J. Raymond, moderate editor of the *New York Times*, a sagacious man who
disliked Northern abolitionists and Southern radicals, wrote in January 1860 an analysis of the impending conflict which attributed it to a
competition for power.

> In every country there must be a just and equal balance of powers in
> the government, an equal distribution of the national forces. Each
> section and each interest must exercise its due share of influence and
> control. It is always more or less difficult to preserve their just
> equipoise, and the larger the country, and the more varied its great in-
> terests, the more difficult does the task become, and the greater the
> shock and disturbance caused by an attempt to adjust it when once
> disturbed. I believe I state only what is generally conceded to be a
> fact, when I say that the growth of the Northern States in population,
> in wealth, in all the elements of political influence and control, has
> been out of proportion to their political influence in the Federal
> Councils. While the Southern States have less that a third of the ag-
> gregate population of the Union, their interests have influenced the
> policy of the government far more than the interests of the Northern
> States. . . . Now the North has made rapid advances within the last
> five years, and it naturally claims a proportionate share of influence
> and power in the affairs of the Confederacy.

It is inevitable that this claim should be put forward, and it is also inevitable that it should be conceded. No party can long resist it; it overrides all parties, and makes them the mere instruments of its will. It is quite as strong today in the heart of the Democratic party of the North as in the Republican ranks and any party which ignores it will lose its hold on the public mind.

Why does the South resist this claim? Not because it is unjust in itself, but because it has become involved with the question of slavery, and has drawn so much of its vigor and vitality from that quarter, that it is almost merged in that issue. The North bases its demand for increased power, in a very great degree, on the action of the government in regard to slavery—and the just and rightful ascendency of the North in the Federal councils comes thus to be regarded as an element of danger to the institutions of the Southern States.

In brief, Raymond, who held that slavery was a moral wrong, that its economic and social tendencies were vicious, and that the time had come to halt its growth with a view to its final eradication, believed that the contest was primarily one for power, and for the application of that power to the slave system. With this opinion Alexander H. Stephens agreed. The Georgian said he believed slavery both morally and politically right. In his letter to Lincoln on December 30, 1860, he declared that the South did not fear that the new Republican Administration would interfere directly and immediately with slavery in the states. What Southerners did fear was the ultimate result of the shift of power which had just occurred—in its application to slavery:

Now this subject, which is confessedly on all sides outside of the constitutional action of the Government, so far as the States are concerned, is made the "central idea" in the platform of principles announced by the triumphant party. The leading object seems to be simply, and wantonly, if you please, to put the institutions of nearly half the States under the ban of public opinion and national condemnation. This, upon general principles, is quite enough of itself to arouse a spirit not only of general indignation, but of revolt on the part of the proscribed. Let me illustrate. It is generally conceded by the Republicans even, that Congress cannot interfere with slavery in the States. It is equally conceded that Congress cannot interfere with slavery in the States. It is equally conceded that Congress cannot establish any form of religious worship. Now suppose that any one of the present Christian churches or sects prevailed in all the Southern States, but had no existence in any one of the Northern States,—under such circumstances suppose the people of the Northern States should organize a political party, not upon a foreign or domestic policy, but with one leading idea of condemnation of the doctrines and tenets of that particular church, and with an avowed object of preventing its extension into the common Territories, even after the highest judicial tribunal of the land had decided they had no such con-

stitutional power. And suppose that a party so organized should carry
a Presidential election. Is it not apparent that a general feeling of resistance to the success, aims, and objects of such a party would necessarily and rightfully ensue?

Raymond and Stephens agreed that the two sections were competing for power; that a momentous transfer of power had just occurred;
and that it held fateful consequences because it was involved with the
issue of slavery, taking authority from a section which believed slavery moral and healthy, and giving it to a section which held slavery
immoral and pernicious. To Stephens this transfer was ground for re-
suming the ultimate sovereignty of the states. Here we find a somewhat more complex statement of James Ford Rhodes's thesis that the
central cause of the Civil War lay in slavery. Here, too, we revert to the
assertions of Yancey and Lincoln that the vital conflict was between
those who thought slavery right and those who thought it wrong. But
this definition we can accept only if we probe a little deeper for a concept which both modifies and enlarges the basic source of perplexity
and quarrel.

The main root of the conflict (and there were minor roots) was the
problem of slavery *with its complementary problem of race adjustment;* the main source of the tragedy was the refusal of either section
to face these conjoined problems squarely and pay the heavy costs of a
peaceful settlement. Had it not been for the difference in race, the slavery issue would have presented no great difficulties. But as the racial
gulf existed, the South inarticulately but clearly perceived that elimination of this issue would still leave it the terrible problem of the Negro. Those historians who write that if slavery had simply been left
alone it would soon have withered overlook this heavy impediment.
The South as a whole in 1846–1861 was not moving toward emancipation, but away from it. It was not relaxing the laws which guarded the
system, but reinforcing them. It was not ameliorating slavery, but
making it harsher and more implacable. The South was further from a
just solution of the slavery problem in 1830 than it had been in 1789. It
was further from a tenable solution in 1860 than it had been in 1830.
Why was it going from bad to worse? Because Southern leaders refused
to nerve their people to pay the heavy price of race adjustment. These
leaders never made up their mind to deal with the problem as the progressive temper of civilization demanded. They would not adopt the
new outlook which the upward march of mankind required because
they saw that the gradual abolition of slavery would bring a measure of
political privilege; that political privilege would usher in a measure of
economic equality; that on the heels of economic equality would
come a rising social status for the Negro. Southern leadership dared
not ask the people to pay this price.

A heavy responsibility for the failure of America in this period rests with this Southern leadership, which lacked imagination, ability, and courage. But the North was by no means without its full share, for the North equally refused to give a constructive examination to the central question of slavery as linked with race adjustment. This was because of two principal reasons. Most abolitionists and many other sentimental-minded Northerners simply denied that the problem existed. Regarding all Negroes as white men with dark skins, whom a few years of schooling would bring abreast of the dominant race, they thought that no difficult adjustment was required. A much more numerous body of Northerners would have granted that a great and terrible task of race adjustment existed—but they were reluctant to help shoulder any part of it. Take a million or two million Negroes into the Northern States? Indiana, Illinois, and even Kansas were unwilling to take a single additional person of color. Pay tens of millions to help educate and elevate the colored population? Take even a first step by offering to pay the Southern slaveholders some recompense for a gradual liberation of their human property? No Northern politician dared ask his constituents to make so unpopular a sacrifice. The North, like the South, found it easier to drift blindly toward disaster.

The hope of solving the slavery problem without a civil war rested upon several interrelated factors, of which one merits special emphasis. We have said that the South as a whole was laboring to bolster and stiffen slavery—which was much to its discredit. But it is nevertheless true that slavery was dying all around the edges of its domain; it was steadily decaying in Delaware, Maryland, western Virginia, parts of Kentucky, and Missouri. Much of the harshness of Southern legislation in the period sprang from a sense that slavery was in danger from *internal* weaknesses. In no great time Delaware, Maryland, and Missouri were likely to enter the column of free states; and if they did, reducing the roster to twelve, the doom of the institution would be clearly written. Allied with this factor was the rapid comparative increase of Northern strength, and the steady knitting of economic, social, and moral ties between the North and West, leaving the South in a position of manifest inferiority. A Southern Confederacy had a fair fighting chance in 1861; by 1880 it would have had very little. If secession could have been postponed by two decades, natural forces might well have placed a solution full in sight. Then, too, the growing pressure of world sentiment must in time have produced its effect. But to point out these considerations is not to suggest that in 1861 a policy of procrastination and appeasement would have done anything but harm. All hope of bringing Southern majority sentiment to a better attitude would have been lost if Lincoln and his party had flinched on the basic issue of the restriction of slavery; for by the seventh decade of nineteenth-century history, the time had come when that demand had to be maintained.

While in indicting leadership we obviously indict the public behind the leaders, we must also lay some blame upon a political environment which gave leadership a poor chance. American parties, under the pressure of sectional feeling, worked badly. The government suffered greatly, moreover, from the lack of any adequate planning agency. Congress was not a truly deliberative body, and its committees had not yet learned to do long-range planning. The president might have formulated plans, but he never did. For one reason, no president between Polk and Lincoln had either the ability or the prestige required; for another reason, Fillmore, Pierce, and Buchanan all held that their duty was merely to execute the laws, not to initiate legislation. Had the country possessed a ministerial form of government, the Cabinet in leading the legislature would have been compelled to lay down a program of real scope concerning slavery. As it was, leadership in Washington was supplied only spasmodically by men like Clay, Douglas, and Crittenden.

And as we have noted, the rigidity of the American system was at this time a grave handicap. Twice, in the fall of 1854 and of 1858, the elections gave a stunning rebuke to the Administration. Under a ministerial system, the old government would probably have gone out and a new one have come in. In 1854, however, Pierce continued to carry on the old policies, and in 1858 Buchanan remained the drearily inept helmsman of the republic. Never in our history were bold, quick planning and a flexible administration of policy more needed; never was the failure to supply them more complete.

Still another element in the tragic chronicle of the time must be mentioned. Much that happens in human affairs is accidental. When a country is guided by true statesmen the role of accident is minimized; when it is not, unforeseen occurrences are numerous and dangerous. In the summer and fall of 1858, as we have seen, the revival of a conservative opposition party in the upper South, devoted to the Union, furnished a real gleam of hope. If this opposition had been given unity and determined leadership, if moderate Southerners had stood firm against the plot of Yancey and others to disrupt the Democratic Party, if Floyd had been vigilant enough to read the warning letter about John Brown and act on it, the situation might even then have been saved. Instead, John Brown's mad raid fell on public opinion like a thunderstroke, exasperating men everywhere and dividing North and South more tragically than ever. The last chance of persuading the South to submit to an essential step, the containment of slavery, was gone.

The war, when it came, was not primarily a conflict over state rights, although that issue had become involved in it. It was not primarily a war born of economic grievances, although many Southerners had been led to think that they were suffering, or would soon suffer, economic wrongs. It was not a war created by politicians and publicists who fomented hysteric excitement; for while hysteria was important, we have always to ask what basic reasons made possible the propaganda which aroused it. It was not primarily a war about slavery alone, although that institution seemed to many the grand cause. It was a war over slavery *and* the future position of the Negro race in North America. Was the Negro to be allowed, as a result of the shift of power signalized by Lincoln's election, to take the first step toward an ultimate position of general economic, political, and social equality with the white man? Or was he to be held immobile in a degraded, servile position, unchanging the next hundred years as it had remained essentially unchanged for the hundred years past? These questions were implicit in Lincoln's demand that slavery be placed in a position where the public mind could rest assured of its ultimate extinction.

Evasion by the South, evasion by the North, were no longer possible. The alternatives faced were an unpopular but curative adjustment of the situation by the opposed parties, or a war that would force an adjustment upon the loser. For Americans in 1861, as for many other peoples throughout history, war was easier than wisdom and courage.

WILLIAM W. FREEHLING

WILLIAM FREEHLING (1935–   ) teaches American history at the University of Kentucky. He is the author of The Reintegration of American History *(1994) and* The Road to Disunion *(1990) and the editor of* Secession Debated *(1993).*

It is a telling historical irony that of all the New World slavocracies, only slaveholders in the United States lived in an advanced republic, and only the United States required a civil war between whites to abolish slavery for blacks. . . .

The southern slaveholders' unique acceptance of trial by warfare demanded unique self-confidence. Secession required both nerve and the perception of power. The Brazilian and Cuban slavocracies could have no such nerve in the 1870s and 1880s, after watching U.S. slaveholders go down in flames in the 1860s. Nor did their nondominant position in their respective political power structures embolden Cuban or Brazilian slaveholders with the illusion that they could win a civil war. . . .

The divergent U.S. and Latin American roads toward emancipation began with dissimilar colonial settlements. During the seventeenth century, England, the most republican of the European colonizing nations, sent to the North American mainland by far the largest percentage of nonslaveholding settlers to be found in any New World area containing large numbers of slaves. Because of that comparatively huge white republican population, the thirteen colonies had special leverage to resist English metropolitan impositions on colonial republicanism, and out of that resistance came the American Revolution and the first New World liberation from Old World control. With the establishment of the federal Union, the Revolutionaries encased one of the most extensive slaveholder regimes in the Americas inside the most republican nation in the New World. . . .

As the eighteenth century gave way to the nineteenth, an invention and a law pressed U.S. slavery toward tropical habitats. Eli Whitney's invention of the cotton gin in 1793 impelled the movement of slaveholders toward Lower South frontiers. Fourteen years later, in 1807, the federal government's closure of the African slave trade contracted the Cotton Kingdom's source of slaves. Unlike mid-nineteenth-century tropical developers in Cuba and Brazil, the two other large New World slavocracies, cotton planters could not legally buy slaves from Africa. But only U.S. slaveholders could purchase slaves from their own northerly, relatively nontropical areas, which had concurrently fallen into chronic economic recession.

A slave drain ensued, especially from the more northern South to the more southern South. Between 1790 and 1860, some 750,000 Middle and Border South slaves traveled downriver to the Cotton Kingdom. The Lower South, which had had 21 percent of U.S. slaves in 1790, had 59 percent in 1860. Maryland and Virginia, with 60 percent in 1790, had 18 percent in 1860. Thirty-seven percent of Lower South white families owned slaves in 1860, compared to only 12 percent in the Border South, down from 20 percent in 1790. . . .

With slavery swiftly concentrating southward and slowly fading northward, different social attitudes and political priorities developed. Lower South slaveholders came to call slavery a probably perpetual blessing, while Border South masters persistently called the institution a hopefully temporary evil. So too Lower South political warriors cared more about perpetuating slavery than the Union, while Border South leaders would compromise on slavery in order to save the Union. . . .

In the mid-nineteenth century, then, slaveholders overwhelmingly controlled the Lower South, which had been belatedly but massively developed. The slavocracy somewhat less solidly controlled the Middle and Border South, where percentages of slave owners were slowly dropping. But even in the Border South, vestiges (and sometimes defiant concentrations) of the old relatively nontropical slavocracy occasionally fought to salvage a fading system. The mature Slave South had a tropical base of states, containing large slave populations, and several layers of buffer zones to the north, with less tropical conditions and less proslavery commitments and fewer slaves in each successive tier above.

Yet despite this degree of geographic disunity, no other New World slavocracy could muster as united a front against worldwide antislavery currents. . . .

A more intense racism fueled the U.S. slaveholders' greater capacity to mobilize a united front. Because Latin American racial attitudes toward blacks were less hidebound than in the United States, greater tolerance for free-womb emancipation, for mulattoes, and for individual manumissions—and less willingness to fight a civil war over the issue—pervaded Latin American slavocracies. Because U.S. racism was so extreme, a more unified slaveholding class and more support from white nonslaveholders—and thus a greater capacity to fight a civil war—infused the Slave South.

Behind the more severe U.S. racism lay in part a different heterosexual situation, itself another result of the largest white migration to an important New World slavocracy. English colonists to the future United States migrated far more often in family groups and/or with equal numbers of unmarried males and females in the entourage than did colonists headed farther south, who more often sought their fortunes as unattached males, with only slaves available for sexual liaisons. More frequent and less taboo interracial sexual intimacies resulted south of British North America, which led to more mulattoes and less insistence that the world be rigidly separated into black and white. . . .

Some historians doubt that racism was more culturally deep-seated in the United States than south of the border. That position founders before the greater U.S. taboo surrounding miscegenation and the far greater desire to deport blacks from antebellum America than from any other New World slavocracy. . . . Uniquely in the United States, slaveholders had to mobilize nonslaveholders, and racism was their most potent weapon. . . .

The racial foundation of Southwide unity, however, was a two-edged sword. For racism to unite nonslaveholders and slaveholders, the black race had to be significantly present. With the slave drain to the Lower South and the movement of European whites to such northerly slave states as Maryland and Missouri, Border South blacks became steadily less visible. As for that highly visible group of blacks in northern Maryland and Delaware, the free blacks, their energetic labor and law-abiding deportment demonstrated that racial control hardly required slavery.

That conclusion had proved fatal to slavery in northern states where percentages of blacks had declined. . . . Mid-nineteenth-century Border South states were in no immediate danger of becoming a New York. . . . But given the Border South's waning percentage of blacks, its . . . manumissions, its propensity for thinking of slavery as a temporary evil, and its commitment to Union-saving compromises on the institution, could the Lower South rely on its northern hinterlands' future loyalty?

On the answer hung the Slave South's capacity to be that unique New World slave regime: the one that could defy an emancipating century rather than settle for a few more decades of slaveholder profits. . . . The Brazilian slavocracy could only postpone emancipation. . . . The Old South, in contrast, had various powers to command a majoritarian democracy despite its minority status—*if* all fifteen slave states hung together and the Border South did not go the way of New York. . . .

Numbers indicate how much was at stake in that *if*. The seven Lower South states of 1860 (South Carolina, Florida, Georgia, Alabama, Mississippi, Louisiana, and Texas, with 47 percent of their population enslaved) could not fight off the sixteen northern states (containing 61 percent of the American population) without the enthusiastic support of the four Middle South states (Virginia, North Carolina, Tennessee, and Arkansas, with 32 percent of their population enslaved) and the four Border South states (Maryland, Delaware, Kentucky, and Missouri, with 13 percent of their population enslaved). Those buffer areas above the Lower South could come under siege— the siege of democratic public opinion. Would the Border South remain foursquare behind slavery and the Lower South, even if the slavocracy's northern hinterlands came to possess scantier and scantier percentages of blacks?

That question transcended the Border South. The slaveholders' worst internal problem involved not a single localized place but a regionwide lopsided distribution of blacks. While the Border South was the most widespread locale with a relatively low percentage of slaves, some areas farther south also contained few blacks; and everywhere a paucity of slaves allowed more nonslaveholder hostility toward slaveholders. Wherever blacks were concentrated, whites drew together, however much the poor resented the rich, for lowly whites despised lowlier blacks even more than they resented lordly masters. But whenever blacks were scarce, race hatred intensified class hatred, for nonslaveholders preferred to have neither autocrats nor blacks around. A relatively slaveless situation, while most prevalent in the Border South, also predominated in western Virginia, in eastern Tennessee, and in piney woods and semimountainous areas of the Lower South. Here the Border South predicament came closer to home to worried Lower and Middle South slavocrats. Could upper-class ideology command lower-class loyalties in areas where no racial tensions united the whites? . . .

The North American dialogue about emancipation began with the foundation of U.S. republicanism, the Declaration of Independence. . . . Thomas Jefferson of Virginia, author of the Declaration and a large slaveholder, believed that all men would and should rise up against so antirepublican a horror as slavery. He thus feared that slave insurrection would disrupt white republics unless white republicans freed blacks. . . .

Yet if Jefferson called slavery antithetical to republicanism, he considered racism compatible with the Declaration of Independence. Whites and blacks, thought Jefferson, were innately different. Whites allegedly possessed a keener abstract intelligence; blacks, a keener sexual ardency. Ex-slaves, he further worried, would be eager for revenge and ex-masters determined to repress the avengers. If slaves were freed and remained in the United States, "deep-rooted prejudices entertained by the whites" and "ten thousand recollections by the blacks, of the injuries they have sustained" would "produce convulsions, which will probably never end but in the extermination of one or the other race."

Thus to preserve white republics, freed blacks had to be deported. The dangerous alternative was to keep blacks enslaved. Jefferson's conviction that emancipation must be conditional on removing blacks, the first thrust in the U.S. dialectic on abolition, was rare in Latin America. An insistence on race removal would have ill-suited Latin American nations, where individual bargains between masters and slaves slowly led to a third class of semifree blacks and a fourth class of free blacks. . . .

In the wake of Nat Turner's slave revolt, the most successful (although still abortive) slave uprising in the United States, Thomas Jefferson Randolph, Jefferson's favorite grandson, proposed to the Virginia legislature that slaves born after 1840 be freed on their eighteenth (women) and twenty-first (men) birthdays. Thus far Randolph's proposal was standard Latin American—style free-womb emancipation. But Randolph's bill added the condition, alien to Latin America, that the state must remove the freedmen to Africa. Randolph's speech for the historic proposal also featured the cynical prediction, more alien still south of the U.S. border, that many Virginia masters would sell slaves to the Lower South before emancipating birthdays. Thus, Randolph cheered, masters would profitably remove slaves from Virginia at no cost to state coffers.

Randolph's proposal led to a famous state crisis, for Virginia's largely nonslaveholding areas rallied behind Jefferson's grandson in defiance of slaveholding areas. Never before in the history of the Slave South, and never again until western Virginia seceded from Virginia during the Civil War, was the potentially dangerous antagonism between slaveless and slaveholding geographic zones more obvious, for here western Virginian nonslaveholders sought to impose emancipation on eastern Virginia planters. Earlier, eastern squires had built a bulwark against the nonslaveholder threat. They had insisted that slaveholders have more seats in the Virginia House of Delegates (lower house) than eastern Virginia's white numbers justified. The underrepresented western Virginians responded, like later Northerners, that the Slavepower thus enslaved *them*. These nonslaveholders preferred that all blacks depart the commonwealth. Then true white democracy would replace Slavepower dominion in Virginia. So western Virginians cheered Thomas Jefferson Randolph's black removal proposal.

After two weeks of debate, the Virginia House of Delegates rejected a variation of Randolph's proposal by a vote of 73–58. The margin against antislavery would have shriveled to one vote if the slaveholders had not held those extra legislative seats. The shaky anti-Randolph majority warned that even after masters had sold off some blacks, state-financed removal of other slaves would bankrupt the government. . . .

Thomas Jefferson had proposed a swifter way to deport blacks: a federal constitutional amendment that would authorize compulsory emancipation and colonization to be financed by federal land sales, a richer source of funds than state taxation. Throughout the nation, antislavery moderates perpetuated this scheme for liberating slaves while also whitening the republic. The persistent admirers of Jefferson's black removal plan included the Border South's favorite statesman, Henry Clay; the Republicans' favorite politician, Abraham Lincoln; and the North's favorite novelist, Harriet Beecher Stowe. A national volunteer organization, the American Colonization Society, used private donations to establish a rather unstable African colony, Liberia, to receive American blacks. In those unusual days of a federal budgetary surplus, the national government had excess funds to help with the financing. But South Carolina threatened secession if Congress even discussed the possibility. So the debate stopped before much was said. . . .

The more republican U.S. slavocracy ironically outdid their less republican Latin American counterparts in eradicating antislavery opinion. . . .

Nor could Border South whites altogether deter their most threatening black dissenters—fugitive slaves. Group insurrectionists in the

United States, though momentarily more terrifying than individual runaways, were less numerous. . . .

Thus fugitives achieved more than their own freedom in the seemingly apolitical act of running away from masters (and from millions of enslaved brethren). The runaways advanced the political process that led to war and emancipation. Particularly Border South fugitives illuminated the slavocracy's geographic area of weakness—an illumination that provoked border masters into initiating Union-shattering political controversies. The slaveholders' political answer to border fugitives lay in the national forum, for only national laws could consolidate the line between South and North, as well as the barrier between slavery and free democratic discourse.

The electoral numbers might seem to have forbidden slaveholders from wielding national governmental power to deter border fugitives or otherwise consolidate their outposts. During pre-Civil War controversies, around 70 percent of U.S. whites lived outside the Slave South, and around 70 percent of southern white families did not own slaves. In those overwhelming numbers lay the slaveholders' potential peril. But the democratic system, as ever both threatening and empowering for a besieged minority, long enabled the master class to protect its borderlands and dominate Yankee majorities.

The federal Constitution provided the minority's most obvious defensive weapon. Abolitionists often conceded that the Constitution protected slavery, not least because it authorized Congress to pass fugitive slave laws. The Constitution also contained many restrictions on majority antislavery action, including the ultimate one: a forbidding amendment process. Three-fourths of the states have to agree on a constitutional amendment before it becomes operative. . . .

This potential Border South problem illustrated the slaveholders' provokingly small margin for error. Totally to control 11/15 of slaveholders' territory and largely to control the other 4/15 of their world would have been a miracle in any other New World slaveholding regime. But U.S. slaveholders, unlike Latin American counterparts, were seeking to stonewall the Age of Emancipation; and the singular effort would fail if the slaveholders' large degree of control over their most vulnerable four states weakened. In part for that reason, southern extremists, including Calhoun, came to eschew the doctrine of federal hands off slavery and to urge that federal hands be heavily laid on, especially in the borderlands, to protect the slaveholders' interests there. National majorities must annex Texas on the Lower South's flank, admit Kansas on the Border South's edge, and ensure the return of fugitive slaves who escaped over any border.

Two more empowerments of the southern minority long enabled slaveholders to maneuver congressional majorities into fortifying southern outposts. First, the Constitution let the slaveholding states count three out of five slaves, in addition to all whites, when the number of southern congressmen and presidential electors was calculated. Thus in 1860 the Slave South, containing 30 percent of the nation's white citizens, had 36 percent of the nation's congressmen and presidential electors. That extra power (which had first prompted the coining of the word *Slavepower*) turned southern defeat into victory on key occasions, including the election of Virginia's Thomas Jefferson over Massachusetts's John Adams to the presidency in 1800, the Missouri Controversy, the Gag Rule Controversy, and the Kansas-Nebraska Controversy.

Second, national political parties gave a 30 percent popular minority with a 36 percent congressional minority the leverage to secure another 14 percent or more of congressional votes. Especially the dubiously titled Democratic Party became a bulwark of the slavocracy. . . . Jackson's egalitarianism, for white males only, won him huge majorities in the Lower South but progressively smaller majorities at every step northward and few majorities in New England. That voting distribution gave the Democratic Party a majority control in the nation and Southerners a majority control in the party. Thus when slavery controversies emerged in national politics, Southern Democrats could use the leverage of the nation's usually dominant party to demand that Northern Democrats help consolidate the slavocracy's frontiers.

Southern Democrats had to insist that Northern Democrats support the fullest proslavery protection. Southern Whigs also had to repel the Northern Whigs' slightest conditional antislavery overture. . . .

Ironically, northern extremists were southern extremists' best ally in these loyalty contests. Garrison's righteous denunciations, aimed at all who opposed unconditional emancipation, damned all Southerners, whether they hoped to remove or to retain slaves. Southern moderates, enraged at being called sinners, passionately joined proslavery extremists in resenting the slur on their honor. . . .

The Gag Rule Controversy, the first national slavery crisis after Garrison's emergence, introduced the deadly process. In 1835, antislavery zealots petitioned Congress to abolish slavery in Washington, D.C. The petitions inadvertently demonstrated that abolitionists constituted a fringe group outside the northern mainstream. Only a tiny fraction of Northerners signed the appeals, and a large number of signers were women, barred from the electorate.

Nevertheless, the petitioners reshaped national mainstream slavery politics. . . . That provocative response shook northern complacency about the slavery issue more than any abolitionist could.

The slaveholders' provocative demand was that petitions for congressional action against slavery must be barred from congressional deliberations. Antislavery must not be discussed in secret committees, much less publicly. . . . By attempting to gag congressional debate, Southerners tried to impose on the nation their regional version of republicanism: all ideas, *except* antislavery, were open to discussion.

Northerners responded that republicanism would lie in ruins unless *all* ideas could be debated. Representative republicanism especially would become a mockery, said Northerners, unless citizens could request that their representatives discuss whether slavery, an arguably antirepublican institution, should exist in the republic's capital city. The southern gag rule tactic, an irrelevant strategy in largely undemocratic Latin America, thus immediately produced the key non-Latin American question: Were slavery for blacks and democratic procedures for whites compatible? From that question, an otherwise rather isolated abolitionist movement would spread in the North, and the U.S. slavery controversy would assume its irrepressible—and non-Latin American—form. . . .

The most airtight of the Democratic Party's gag rules, passed in 1840, forbade the House of Representatives from receiving, much less considering, antislavery petitions. To the embarrassment of Southern Whigs, the Northern Whigs, led by Massachusetts's ex-President John Quincy Adams, refused to be gagged. Adams relentlessly attacked Northern Democrats as the Slave-power's slaves. The issue, he said, was not black slavery but white republicanism. The minority South must not rule the majority North. The slaveholding minority must not gag republican citizens. Northern Democrats must represent the majority North, sustain white men's democracy, and repeal the minority South's antidemocratic gag rule.

In December 1844, Northern Democrats finally acted to protect their home base. By voting down all gag rules, after eight years of caving in to ever-tighter gags, they signaled that the southern minority could push Northerners only so far. This denouement of the Gag Rule Controversy also signaled that northern and southern antiparty extremists had unintentionally collaborated to weaken their mutual foe: national party moderates. . . .

By demanding a gag on the discussion of that one issue, slaveholders had confirmed one aspect of the abolitionists' case: The preservation of southern-style black slavery meant the annihilation of northern-style white republicanism. These dynamics of northern consciousness raising ultimately forced those key northern appeasers, Northern Democrats, to join Northern Whigs and northern extremists in opposing all gags, just as the dynamics of southern consciousness raising forced southern moderates to join southern extremists in seeking ever-tighter gags. Then neither centrist national party could find a middle position between the two sections' different versions of republicanism. And in any democracy, the erosion of the vital center can be the first step toward civil war.

In 1844, an ominous second step was taken. Southern Democrats surrendered on the gag rules, partly to press Northern Democrats to support the annexation of the then-independent Republic of Texas . . . of whose population only 20 percent was enslaved in the early 1840s. That was a Border South percentage of slaves. But this time, the borderland with a low proportion of slaves abutted the slaveholders' south-western flank, thick with slaves . . . An annexed Texas, under U.S. control, would consolidate the Lower South frontier. . . .

A Southern Whig administration had proposed a border safeguard. But as usual, only the National Democratic Party could pass prosouthern legislation. Northern Whigs, as usual, denounced the southern proposal. Southern Democrats, however, induced reluctant Northern Democrats to replace the lukewarm annexationist New Yorker, Martin Van Buren, with the strongly annexationist Tennessean, James K. Polk, as the party's presidential candidate in 1844. After Polk won the election, Southern Democrats, now pressured by Southern Whigs to do still more for the South, successfully insisted that reluctant Northern Democrats not only admit Texas to the Union but also allow the annexed state, any time in the future, to divide itself into five slave states. Four years later, a resentful Van Buren bolted the Democratic Party, arguing that white men's majoritarian democracy must be protected from minority dictation. Van Buren ran for president on the Free-Soil ticket, hoping to stop slavery from spreading into federal territories.

At midcentury, while Van Buren sought to contain the Slavepower in the South, Southerners sought to stop the flight of slaves to the North. In 1850, border Southerners proposed a new fugitive slave law, especially designed to protect the South's northernmost hinterlands from northern slave raiders. The proposed law contained notorious antirepublican features. . . . Black fugitives were denied a jury trial. . . . Any nonslaveholder could be compelled to join a slave-chasing posse in the manner of a southern patrol—an outrageous requirement in the North.

In the face of the southern minority's latest attempt to impose on the nation southern-style republicanism, Northern Whigs again balked. But again Northern Democrats reluctantly acquiesced, and again the minority South, using the National Democratic Party as a congressional fulcrum, had gained protection of vulnerable frontiers. When Southerners subsequently attempted to extradite captured fugitives from the North, the new procedures returned the alleged slaves 90 percent of the time. But in the remaining cases, northern mobs blocked the return of the escapees. The well-publicized stories of rare fugitive slave rescues dramatized Garrison's most telling lesson: Southern-style power over blacks damaged northern-style republics for whites.

The Kansas-Nebraska Act of 1854 drove the lesson home. Once again a vulnerable slaveholders' hinterland, this time the Border South's Missouri, with only 10 percent of its population enslaved, demanded protection of its frontier. . . .

Before slaveholding citizens could come, Congress would have to repeal the Missouri Compromise of 1820, which had prohibited slavery in all Louisiana Purchase territories north of the 36° 30' line. That man-made geographic boundary continued westward from the latitude of Missouri's southern border, thus barring slaveholders from living west of Missouri, once Congress allowed settlement there. Stephen A. Douglas, the Northern Democrats' leader in the post-Van Buren era, warned Southerners that repeal of the Missouri Compromise would raise "a hell of a storm." . . .

Douglas was as convinced as any Southerner that supposedly superior whites should evict supposedly inferior Native Americans from the West and that the enslavement of supposedly inferior blacks was no Northerner's moral business. Yet Southern Democrats had to pressure Douglas to be Douglas, for their shared program bore the taint of Slavepower domination. And this astute majoritarian politician did not want to be labeled a tool of the minority.

Nevertheless, he had to risk the noxious designation. What became known as *his* Kansas-Nebraska Act, passed by a Douglas-rallied National Democratic Party plus a majority of Southern Whigs, repealed the Missouri Compromise ban on slavery in Kansas Territory, located due west of Missouri, and in Nebraska Territory, located due north of Kansas. Any settler with any form of property could come to these two territories, declared the law, and the majority of settlers in each territory would decide which institutions should thereafter prevail. This most important of all mid-nineteenth-century American laws authorized slaveholding migrants to move to Kansas, seek to make it a slave state, and thus protect the Border South's western flank, just as Texas Annexation had fortified the Lower South's western frontier and the Fugitive Slave Law guarded the Border South's northern extremities. Douglas's law also invited the Democrats' northern opponents to claim that the Slavepower minority, in its anxiety to quarantine border slavery from neighboring democratic currents, had again bullied a congressional majority in the manner of an imperious dictator. . . .

In the next six years the northern majority would revoke the minority's domination of the republic, making problems inside the southern outposts more threatening. . . .

In post-1854 politics, the South's most vulnerable instrument was the national party. Long useful in passing the slaveholders' favorite legislation, it had lately buckled under the weight of the minority's attempts to seek ever-more domination over the majority. . . .

In the early 1850s, however, the National Whig Party collapsed. Until the middle of the century, Lower South Whigs had hoped that Northern Whigs would relent on slavery-related matters. But after Northern Whigs said no to the Fugitive Slave Law, no to the Kansas-Nebraska Act, and, all too often, yes to the rescue of fugitive slaves, the Southern Democrats' charge rang all too true: Southerners who co-operated with Yankee Whigs might be secretly soft on slavery. After the Kansas-Nebraska Act, Whiggery lost all credibility in the Lower South.

Whiggery simultaneously lost some northern credibility. Old Whig rhetoric did not sufficiently convey many Yankees' twin indignations in 1854: hostility toward new immigrants and loathing for the Kansas-Nebraska Act. . . . A fusion of northern immigrants and southern slave-holders, many native Yankees thought, bid fair to destroy American republicanism, using as the agent of destruction the deplorably named Democratic Party.

A countervailing fusion swiftly transpired. Northern campaigns against immigrants and the Kansas-Nebraska Act, originally separate matters, partly funneled into one deliberately named *Republican* Party in time for the presidential election of 1856. The Republicans' first presidential campaign almost swept enough northern votes to win the White House, despite the lack of southern votes. Some Northerners especially welcomed most Republicans' secondary mission: to serve free laborers' economic interests. Republicans often saw southern and immigrant economic threats as similar. Impoverished immigrants could displace Yankee wage earners by accepting low wages, just as affluent slaveholders could displace Yankee farmers by making Kansas a slave territory. . . .

Republican rhetoric showed how much (and how little) William Lloyd Garrison had triumphed. Lincoln's mainstream rhetoric appropriated Garrison's extremist vocabulary about southern sinfulness, his conception that free-labor and slave-labor economies were antithetical, his demand for inclusion of blacks in the Declaration of Independence, his hopes for slavery's extinction, and his detestation of slaveholders' imperiousness. Still, Republicans' condemnation of the Slavepower's tyrannizing over whites, not Garrison's condemnation of slaveholders' tyrannizing over blacks, had been most responsible for spreading moral outrage about slave-holders from the northern extreme to the northern mainstream. The average Northerner rejected Slavepower imposition on *him*. But most Northerners were as fearful as ever that federally imposed abolition would break up the Union, jeopardize national commerce, and lead northern blacks to demand *their* egalitarian rights.

The Republicans' resulting caution outraged Garrison. He loathed Lincoln's political formula: Always emphasize containment of the Slavepower and occasionally add a vague hope of slavery's ultimate extinction. Garrison equally detested Lincoln's emphasis on the slow transformation of public opinion. . . .

The Southern Democratic majority on the U.S. Supreme Court provided the clearest protection for slaveholders' right to expand into the nation's territories. In its notorious Dred Scott decision (1857), the Court pronounced the Republican Party's containment program unconstitutional. Congress could not bar slavery from national territory, ruled the Court, for slaves were property and seizure of property violated the due process clause of the Constitution. Alarmed Republicans replied (and apparently believed) that a second Dred Scott decision would follow. Since citizens of one state had the rights and immunities of citizens of another state, the Court allegedly would next empower slaveholders to take (human) property into northern states!

If Republicans needed post–Dred Scott evidence that Southerners meant to extend slavery into northern latitudes, southern insistence on admitting Kansas as a slave state in 1857–58 seemed to provide it. The Kansas-Nebraska Act had allowed both Southerners and Northerners to come to the area, with the majority of settlers to decide on an eventual state's constitution and its labor arrangements. Three years later, when Kansans applied for admission to the Union as a state, northern settlers predominated. But the minority of southern settlers demanded admission as a slave state anyway, despite the majority of Kansans' frenzied objections. This time, Stephen A. Douglas defied the Southerners, for they were asking him to abjure his Popular Sovereignty principle that the majority of settlers should determine their own institutions. Despite Douglas's protests, the U.S. Senate voted 33–25 to admit Kansas as a slave state, with most Northern Democrats casting their usual prosouthern vote. The House then rejected a proslavery Kansas, 120–112.

Southerners, enraged at their first congressional loss on a major slavery issue since gag rule times, principally blamed the 40 percent of House Northern Democrats, admirers of Douglas, who had voted against them. Two years later, at the first of two 1860 Democratic National Conventions, Lower South Democrats insisted that the party platform contain anti-popular-sovereignty language on slaveholders' rights in the territories. Douglas and his supporters balked, just as Martin Van Buren had balked at southern control of the party during the Texas episode. But this time, when the key Northern Democrat said no to Slavepower rule, Lower South convention delegates walked out. At the subsequent Democratic convention, Northern Democrats barred those who had left from returning as accredited delegates.

With the split of the National Democratic Party, the minority South lost its long-standing leverage to secure majority laws protective of its hinterlands. The need never seemed greater. When the House of Representatives rejected a proslavery Kansas, six Upper South ex-

Whigs voted with the North. Had they voted with the South, the slave-holders' 120–112 defeat would have been a 118–114 triumph. The episode again illuminated one reason for southern defensive maneuverers' frantic quality: Even a small amount of southern internal disunity could destroy slaveholders' national dominion...

Other departures from proslavery solidarity arose. . . .

Antebellum Southerners intemperately clashed over the fastest rising Lower South political movement of the 1850s, the crusade to reopen the African slave trade. . . .

Reopening the African slave trade seemed to offer the most hopeful remedy yet for uncertain southern commitment. But hope swiftly gave way to a sinking realization: that instead of permanently fortifying a slightly shaky Border South, the proposed panacea drove the more northern and the more southern South further apart. Border South masters denied that slavery would be bolstered in their region if Lower South masters could buy cheap Africans. Instead, the more northern South would find its slaves devalued and its slave sales ended; and then its rationale for complicity in slavery would evaporate.

More ominous still for Lower South slaveholders who wished to import Africans in the 1850s, the Border South preference for exporting African Americans grew stronger. . . .

And in North Carolina, Hinton R. Helper's *Impending Crisis in the South: How to Meet It* was published in 1857. Helper urged the southern nonslaveholder majority to serve both its own economic interests and America's racial interests by deporting slaveholders' blacks. With this publication, the 1850s, not the 1830s, had become the Upper South's great age of dispute over removing slaves. . . .

Northern Republicans printed hundreds of thousands of copies of Helper's emancipation-by-removal scheme. Did Republicans, many Southerners wondered, thereby hope to provoke a southern white lower-class revolt against the slaveholding class? . . .

Lincoln . . . would have liked to build a national Whiggish party on this promising Border South foundation—a preference he later signaled by placing a couple of Border Southerners in his cabinet. But with no southern votes needed to gain the presidency, the biggest northern issue in the 1860 election remained the southern minority's domination of the white man's majoritarian republic. Upset over the recent southern triumph in the Dred Scott case and near-triumph on the Kansas issue, the majoritarian section now meant to rule like a majority. That determination could be seen in the Northern Democrats' rejection of the Lower South's demand for a proslavery platform at the party's conventions and in the northern electorate's sweeping affirmation of Lincoln's leading message: that the *Republican* Party must keep the South from destroying *republicanism*. Yet the question remained, after Lincoln's election in November 1860, would the southern minority now truly destroy the republic by withdrawing its consent to be ruled by the victorious majority?

Before southern secessionists could escape the northern majority, they had to win over their own majority. If some Southwide Gallup poll had inquired whether Southerners wished to secede immediately after Lincoln's election, the secessionists' vote likely would have been down in the 25 percent range. . . . In late November 1860, only Mississippi and Florida probably would have affirmed the expediency of secession, and only South Carolina assuredly would have done so. . . .

Lincoln's party did not have a majority in the Senate or in the House or on the Supreme Court. If Lincoln nevertheless managed to act against slavery, the South could *then* secede. Why secede now over an uncertain northern menace, thereby subjecting slavery to certain menace in a civil war?

Secessionists retorted that a stealthy northern majority would initially let Southerners do the menacing. Southern politicians would form a wing of the Black Republican Party, dedicated to agitating against slavery, especially in the Border South. South Carolina patricians, the most avid secessionists, considered all agitating parties dangerous . . . Patronage-hungry demagogues would stir up the masses and thus overwhelm disinterested paternalists.

In contrast, Lower South mainstream politicians beyond crusty South Carolina, having long happily participated in national parties, feared not democratic parties in general but a prospective Southern Republican Party in particular. They uneasily recalled Frank Blair's delivery of 10 percent of Missourians to Lincoln in the election of 1860, Delaware's 24 percent vote for Lincoln, the more northern South's Opposition Party's recent overtures to the Republicans, and Northern Republicans' publication of Helper's call for nonslaveholder war against slaveholders. They knew that Lincoln had patronage jobs at his disposal and that Border South leaders wanted them. They understood that Lincoln, like the Border South's hero, Henry Clay, carried on Thomas Jefferson's vision of emancipation with freedmen's removal financed by the federal government. Lincoln, in short, need not force abolition on the most northern South. He could instead encourage and bribe Border Southerners to agitate for their misty hope of, and his nebulous plan for, removing blacks from a whitened republic.

Nor, warned the secessionists, would Republican efforts for black removal be restricted to rallying a Border South *white* majority. Republicans would encourage slaves to flee the Border South. With white support melting away and black slaves running away, border slaveholders would dispatch their human property to Lower South slave markets. Then nothing could deter a Border South Republican Party. The Slave South, shrunk to eleven states or less and prevented from expanding into new territories, could only watch while northern free-labor states swelled from sixteen to thirty-three. In that forty-four-state Union, concluded secessionists, Republican emancipators would have the three-fourths majority to abolish slavery in eleven states by constitutional amendment. . . .

For the first time, many Lower South slaveholders felt power-less. . . . Their feeling of impotence rivaled that of Latin American colonists when European metropolitan centers abolished slavery and that of Brazilian coffee planters when sugar planters assaulted the institution. But if Lincoln's election seemed to revoke a democracy's unique invitation for slaveholders to control their fate, the U.S. republican system offered a final invitation for minority self-protection, unavailable in less democratic Latin America. The people of a single colony, the American Revolutionaries had declared, had a right to withdraw their consent to be governed. It was as if the Brazilian coffee provinces had a *right* to secede, which the sugar provinces might feel an obligation to defend.

A *right* of secession, held by a single one of the South's fifteen states! . . . But to force-feed secession to the antisecessionist majority, secessionists had to abort the southern Unionists' favorite idea: a regionwide southern convention, where a Southwide majority would veto immediate secession. Secessionists instead wanted the most secessionist state to call a convention to consider disunion. If the most secessionist state seceded, other southern state conventions would have to decide not whether secession was *expedient* but whether a seceded state could be denied its *right* of secession. Furthermore, other slave states might discern less expediency in remaining in the Union after several states with large slave populations had departed to form a proslavery confederacy. . . .

On December 20, 1860, the secessionists' stronghold, South Carolina, withdrew its consent to Union. South Carolina's neighbor, Georgia, was wary of secession. But with its neighbor out, could Georgia stay in? After a brilliant internal debate, Georgia decided, narrowly, to join South Carolina. And so it went, neighbor following neighbor, throughout the Cotton South. By the time Lincoln was inaugurated on March 4, 1861, the seven Lower South states had left the Union. But the eight Upper South states, containing the majority of southern whites, still opposed secession.

The balance of power changed in mid-April after the Civil War started. Now the more northern South had to decide not on secession per se but on whether to join a northern or a southern army. In making that decision, the Middle South affirmed that each state had the American right to withdraw its consent to be governed. These southern men in the middle also reaffirmed that Yankee extremists were more hateful than secessionist extremists. The Garrisonian insult, encompassing all Southerners who would not unconditionally and immediately emancipate, had long infuriated most Southerners. The Republican insult, encompassing all Southerners who sought to dominate or depart the Union, was equally enraging. To protect their self-respect and honor, Southerners usually felt compelled to unite against taunting Yankees. That duty had so often drawn together a region otherwise partially disunited. In April 1861, when Lincoln sent reinforcements to federal troops in Charleston's harbor, the old tribal fury swept the Middle South. By May 1861, eleven angry southern states had departed the Union. In that fury, parallel to Republican rage over an allegedly antirepublican Slavepower, lies the solution to the largest apparent puzzle about secession: why 260,000 men, whatever their initial preference for Union, died for the Confederacy.

11

RECONSTRUCTION:
CHANGE OR STASIS?

To students of American history the Civil War years stand in sharp contrast to those of the Reconstruction era. The war years represented a period of heroism and idealism; out of the travail of conflict there emerged a new American nationality that replaced the older sectional and state loyalties. Although the cost in lives and money was frightful, the divisions that had plagued Americans for over half a century were eliminated in the ordeal of fire. Henceforth America would stand as a united country, destined to take its rightful place as one of the leading nations in the world.

Reconstruction, on the other hand, had to address the problems of putting the nation back together again. The federal government had to bring the South back into the union on terms that permitted reconciliation, protect newly freed slaves from the wrath of angry whites, and construct a biracial society of free people. The era was marked by conflict, brutality, and corruption, and historians still do not agree on evaluating the results. To date there have been three schools of thought about Reconstruction: the Dunning school, the revisionists, and the neorevisionists.

The first dominant view of Reconstruction, called the Dunning school, after its founder, was forged in the widespread racism of both North and South in the years after the Civil War. It was reinforced by the worldwide European imperialism of the late nineteenth century and the racist ideology that intensified to justify it. Social Darwinism bolstered notions of white supremacy.

By the 1920s American historiography had come under the influence of the Progressive, or new history, school. Growing out of the dissatisfaction with the older scientific school of historians that emphasized the collection of impartial empirical data and eschewed "subjective" interpretations, this school borrowed heavily from the new social sciences. The new history sought to explain historical change by isolating underlying economic and social forces that transformed institutions and structures. In place of tradition and stability it emphasized change and conflict. Liberal and democratic in their orientation, Progressive historians attempted to explain the present in terms of the dynamic and impersonal forces that had transformed American society.

Economic issues, they maintained, were basic in shaping this era. The real conflict was not between North and South, white and black; it was between industrial capitalism and agrarianism, with the former ultimately emerging victorious. The question of the status of black people in American society was simply a facade for the more basic conflicts that lay hidden beneath the surface. Reconstruction, they concluded, was the first phase in the emergence of the United States as a leading industrial and capitalist nation.

The neorevisionist school, although owing much to the revisionists, was influenced by the egalitarianism of the period following World War II and the idealism and optimism of the civil rights movement. Equal rights for blacks, neorevisionists maintained, was complicated by economic and other factors but was, nevertheless, a potent issue in its own right. In a real sense the fundamental problem of Reconstruction was whether white Americans were prepared to accept the freedmen as equal partners. Even though the Radicals ultimately failed in achieving the egalitarian goals, they left an enduring legacy in the forms of the Fourteenth and Fifteenth amendments. That America did not honor these promises to political participation and equal protection under the law in the decades after Reconstruction in no way detracted from the idealism of those responsible for these amendments. Indeed, these amendments took on a new meaning as they gave legal sanction to civil rights after 1945. This is a broad school and today includes social historians whose work has been to broaden history to include the poor, blacks, other minorities, and women.

Led in the 1890s by Professor William A. Dunning of Columbia University—who literally founded the school of Reconstruction historiography that still bears his name—the historical profession set out to prove that the years following the Civil War were marked by tragedy and pathos because men of good will were momentarily thrust out of power by the forces of evil. This period, in the words of one historian, "were years of revolutionary turmoil. . . . The prevailing note was one of tragedy. . . . Never have American public men in responsible positions, directing the destiny of the Nation, been so brutal, hypocritical, and corrupt. . . . The Southern people literally were put to the torture."[1]

Underlying the interpretation of the Dunning school were two important assumptions. The first was that the South should have been restored to the Union quickly and without being exposed to Northern vengeance. Most Southerners, it was argued, had accepted their military defeat gracefully and were prepared to pledge their good faith and loyalty to the Union. Second, responsibility for the freedmen should

---

[1]Claude G. Bowers, *The Tragic Era: The Revolution After Lincoln* (Cambridge, Mass., 1929), pp. v–vi.

have been entrusted to white Southerners. Blacks, these historians believed, could never be integrated into American society on an equal plane with whites because of their former slave status and inferior racial characteristics.

Historians in the Dunning school tradition studied Reconstruction as a struggle between elements of good and evil. The forces of good—Northern and Southern Democrats and Republicans like Andrew Johnson—recognizing the necessity for compassion and leniency, were willing to forget the agonies of war and to forgive the South. Scalawags, carpetbaggers, and, above all, a group of radical and vindictive Republicans intent upon punishing the South by depriving the native aristocracy of their power and status constituted the forces of evil whose aim was to insure the dominance of the Republican party. The Radical Republicans, who had little or no real concern for the welfare of the freedman once he had left the ballot box, manipulated the helpless and ignorant blacks. According to the Dunning school, the Radical carpetbag state governments that came into power were totally incompetent—in part because they included illiterate blacks who were unprepared for the responsibilities of self-government. Still worse, these governments were extraordinarily expensive because they were corrupt. Most of them, indeed, left nothing but a legacy of huge debts.[2]

The decent whites in the South, the Dunning argument continued, united out of sheer desperation to force the carpetbaggers, scalawags, and blacks from power. In one state after another, Radical rule was eventually overthrown and good government restored. By the time of the presidential campaign of 1876 only three states remained under Radical control. When the dispute over the contested election was resolved, Hayes withdrew the remaining federal troops from the South, and the three last Radical regimes fell from power. Thus the tragic era of Reconstruction came to an end.

For nearly three decades after the turn of the century the Dunning point of view was dominant among most American historians. As late as 1942 Albert B. Moore, in his presidential address at the Southern Historical Association, argued that Reconstruction had the effect of converting the South into a colonial appendage of the North. The political enfranchisement of blacks, which laid the basis for carpetbag government, was to Moore perhaps the most incredible event of an incredible era. The South, he concluded, was still paying for the dark legacy of Reconstruction in the twentieth century.[3]

---

[2]E. Merton Coulter, *The South During Reconstruction 1865–1877* (Baton Rouge, La., 1947), p. 148.

[3]Albert B. Moore, "One Hundred Years of Reconstruction in the South," *Journal of Southern History*, 9 (May 1943): 153–65.

In the late 1920s, however, historians began to look at the events between 1865 and 1877 from a new and different perspective. These revisionists, influenced by Progressive thinking, particularly its emphasis on the importance of economic considerations, changed the interpretive framework of the Reconstruction era.

Generally speaking, the revisionists accepted most, if not all, of the findings of the Dunning school. The disagreement between the two groups arose because the revisionists did not view events between 1865 and 1877 in terms of a morality play that depicted Reconstruction as a struggle between good Democrats and evil Radical Republicans. Nor were the revisionists willing to accept the view that responsibility for the freedmen should have been entrusted to native white Southerners.

In 1939 Francis B. Simkins, a distinguished Southern historian who published with Robert Woody in 1932 one of the first revisionist studies, summed up some of the findings of the revisionist school. He emphasized many of the constructive achievements of this era. Simkins denied that the Radical program was radical; indeed, the Radicals failed because they did not provide freedmen with a secure economic base. Past historians, he concluded, had given a distorted picture of Reconstruction because they had assumed that blacks were racially inferior. The result was an approach to Reconstruction that was based on ignorance and prejudice. Only by abandoning their biases could historians contribute to a more accurate understanding of the past.[4]

While the revisionists often disagreed among themselves, there were common areas of agreement. For example, most viewed the problem of corruption in American society during these years as national rather than sectional in scope. To single out the South in this regard was patently unfair and ahistorical.[5] Revisionists also denied that the Radical governments in the South were always dishonest, incompetent, and inefficient. On the contrary, they claimed, such governments accomplished much of enduring value. The new constitutions written during Reconstruction represented a vast improvement over the older ones and often survived the overthrow of the men who had written them. Radical governments brought about many long-needed social reforms, including state-supported school systems for both blacks and whites, a revision of the judicial system, and improvements in local administration. Above all, these governments operated—at least in

---

[4]Francis B. Simkins, "New Viewpoints of Southern Reconstruction," *Journal of Southern History*, 5 (February 1939): 49–61.

[5]For a revisionist synthesis see J. G. Randall and David Donald, *The Civil War and Reconstruction*, 2d ed. (Boston, 1961). The first edition, written by Randall in 1937, was in the Dunning school tradition.

theory—on the premise that all men, white and black alike, were entitled to equal political and civil liberties.

Second, the revisionists drew a sharply different portrait of blacks during Reconstruction. They denied that developments in the postwar South resulted from black participation in government or that the freedmen were illiterate, naive, and inexperienced. In no Southern state, they pointed out, did blacks control both houses of the legislature. Moreover, there were no black governors and only one black state supreme court justice. Only two blacks were elected to the United States Senate and fifteen to the House of Representatives. Such statistics hardly supported the charge that the supposed excesses of Reconstruction were due to political activities of black Americans.

Indeed, the revisionists maintained that blacks, as a group, were quite capable of understanding where their own interests lay without disregarding the legitimate interests of others. The freedmen were able to participate at least as intelligently as other groups in the American political process. As Vernon L. Wharton concluded in his pioneering revisionist study of the Negro in Mississippi after the Civil War, there was "little difference . . . in the administration of . . . counties [having blacks on boards of supervisors] and that of counties under Democratic control. . . . Altogether, as governments go, that supplied by the Negro and white Republicans in Mississippi between 1870 and 1876 was not a bad government. . . . With their white Republican colleagues, they gave to the state a government of greatly expanded functions at a cost that was low in comparison with that of almost any other state."[6]

Revisionists refuted the Dunning school contention that state governments were controlled by evil, power-hungry, profit-seeking carpetbaggers and renegade scalawags who used black votes to maintain themselves in power. The stereotype of the carpetbagger and scalawag, according to revisionists, was highly inaccurate. Carpetbaggers, for example, migrated to the South for a variety of reasons—including the lure of economic opportunities as well as a desire to serve the former slaves in some humanitarian capacity. Among them were former Southern unionists and Whigs, lower-class whites who sought to use the Republican party as the vehicle for confiscating the property of the planter aristocrats, and businessmen attracted by the promise of industrialization. The Radical governments, then, had a wide base of indigenous support in most Southern states.[7]

---

[6]Vernon L. Wharton, *The Negro in Mississippi 1865–1890* (Chapel Hill, N.C., 1947), pp. 172, 179–80. See also Willie Lee Rose, *Rehearsal for Reconstruction: The Port Royal Experiment* (New York, 1964), and Joel Williamson, *After Slavery: The Negro in South Carolina During Reconstruction 1861–1877* (Chapel Hill, N.C., 1965).

[7]See Otto H. Olsen, "Reconsidering the Scalawags," *Civil War History,* 12 (December 1966): 304–20, and Allen W. Trelease, "Who Were the Scalawags?," *Journal of Southern History,* 29(November 1963): 445–68.

Finally, the revisionists rejected the charge that the Radical governments were extraordinarily expensive and corrupt, or that they had saddled the South with a large public debt. State expenditures did rise sharply after the war, but for good reasons. The war's destruction required an infusion of public funds. Deferring regular appropriations during the war years also meant that a backlog of legitimate projects had accumulated. Most important of all, the South for the first time had to build schools and provide other facilities and services for blacks, which did not exist before the 1860s and for which public funds had never been expended.

The revisionists also found that the rise in state debts, in some instances, was more apparent than real. Grants to railroad promoters, which in certain states accounted for a large proportion of the increase in the debt, were secured by a mortgage on the railroad property. Thus the rise in the debt was backed by sound collateral. The amount of the debt chargeable to theft, the revisionists maintained, was negligible. Indeed, the restoration governments, which were dominated by supposedly honest Southerners, proved to be far more corrupt than those governments controlled by the Radicals.

One idea on which the revisionists were united was their conviction that economic forces, which were related to the growth of an urban and industrialized nation, somehow played a major role during this period. Beneath the political and racial antagonisms of this era, some revisionists argued, lay opposing economic rivalries. Anxious to gain an advantage over their competitors, many business interests used politics as the vehicle to further their economic ambitions—especially since the South, like the North and West, was ardently courting businessmen. The result was that economic rivalries were translated into political struggles.[8]

Revisionists also emphasized the crucial issue of race. During Reconstruction many former Whigs joined the Republican party because of its probusiness economic policies. These well-to-do conservatives, at first, were willing to promise blacks civil and political rights in return for their support at the polls. Within the Democratic party, however, revisionists argued that lower-class whites, fearful of possible encroachments by blacks upon their social status and economic position, raised the banner of race. Conservatives found their affiliation with the Republican party increasingly uncomfortable, and they

---

[8]Recent historians have once again begun to study the importance of economic factors and rivalries in Reconstruction. See Mark W. Summers, *Railroads, Reconstruction, and the Gospel of Prosperity: Aid Under the Radical Republicans, 1867–77* (Princeton, N.J., 1984), and Terry L. Seip, *The South Returns to Congress: Men, Economic Measures, and International Relationships* (Baton Rouge, La., 1983).

slowly began to drift back into the Democratic party. The fact that both parties were under the control of conservatives made it easier for former Republicans to shift their political allegiance. This changed alignment left Southern blacks politically without white allies, which later made it easy to eliminate them from political life. This move came at a time when Northerners, tired of conflict and turmoil, became reconciled to the idea of letting the South work out its own destiny—even if it meant sacrificing black people. Northern businessmen likewise became convinced that only Southern conservatives could restore order and stability and thus create a favorable environment for investment.

The result polarized Southern politics along racial rather than economic lines and defined the Democratic party as the white man's party. Lower-class whites' primary goal was to maintain the South as a white man's country. And upper-class whites acquired the uncontested power to determine the future economic development of their section.

The end of Reconstruction, according to the revisionists, accompanied the triumph of business values and industrial capitalism. When the contested presidential election of 1876 resulted in an apparent deadlock between Rutherford B. Hayes, the Republican candidate, and Samuel J. Tilden, his Democratic opponent, some prominent Republicans saw an opportunity to rebuild their party in the South upon a new basis. Instead of basing their party upon propertyless former slaves, they hoped to attract well-to-do former Whigs who had been forced into the Democratic party to fight against Reconstruction governments. To accomplish this goal a group of powerful Republican leaders began to work secretly to bring about a political realignment. If Southern Democratic congressmen would not stand in the way of Hayes's election and would also provide enough votes to permit the Republicans to organize the House of Representatives, these leaders were willing to promise the South federal subsidies—primarily for railroads—and also to name a Southerner as postmaster general. The Compromise of 1877, as this political deal was called, was not fully carried out, but its larger implications survived unscathed.

Perhaps the most important, and certainly the most overlooked revisionist was W.E.B. Du Bois, who published *Black Reconstruction, 1860–1880*, in 1935. Du Bois, like the other revisionists, claimed that economics, not race, shaped Reconstruction and black-white relations. In his passionately argued volume he insisted that Reconstruction involved an effort to unite Northern workers with Southern blacks. The attempt failed because Southern conservatives employed racial animosity to fragment working-class unity and thus maintain their own class hegemony. Racism, in this view, was a tool that upper-class

whites used to their advantage, not an inherent, unchanging characteristic of poor whites, as most historians portrayed it. For Du Bois, Reconstruction was a valiant but shortlived attempt to establish true
democracy in the South, an opportunity quickly foreclosed. But, at
least in public education, black voters made a powerful contribution
to the region.

The *Journal of American History* ignored the book and most professional historians disparaged it. One complaint was that W.E.B. Du
Bois had based his work on secondary sources, not archival materials.
This was true, but it was also true that during Du Bois's research most
Southern archives were closed to blacks. Or, if they were allowed in,
they would have to hide themselves from view of the white scholars.
C. Vann Woodward was one of the few professional historians who rec-
ognized the value of Du Bois's work at the time. He wrote Du Bois in
1938 of his "indebtedness for the insight which your admirable book,
Black Reconstruction, has provided me."[9]

Woodward, the historian who propounded the thesis of the Compromise of 1877, concluded, the bargain "did not restore the old order
in the South, nor did it restore the South to parity with other sections.
It did assure the dominant whites political autonomy and noninterven-
tion in matters of race policy and promised them a share in the blessings of the new economic order. In return the South became, in effect, a
satellite of the dominant region. So long as the Conservative Redeemers held control they scotched any tendency of the South to combine forces with the internal enemies of the new economy—laborites,
Western agrarians, reformers. Under the regime of the Redeemers the
South became a bulwark instead of a menace to the new order."[10]

After the early 1950s a new school of Reconstruction historiography called "the neorevisionists" emerged. Many of these historians
had been affected by the racial injustice that the civil rights movement
demonstrated. They emphasized the moral rather than the economic
basis of Reconstruction. Generally speaking, while the neorevisionists
accepted many findings of the revisionists, they rejected the idea of interpreting Reconstruction in strictly economic terms. The Republican
party, the neorevisionists maintained, was not united on a probusiness
economic program; it included individuals and groups holding quite
different social and economic views.[11]

The neorevisionists stressed the critical factor of race as a moral is-

---

[9]W.E.B. Du Bois, *Black Reconstruction, 1860–1880* (New York, 1992), pp. x, xvi.

[10]C. Vann Woodward, *Reunion and Reaction: The Compromise of 1877 and the
End of Reconstruction* (Boston, 1951), p. 246.

[11]Robert Sharkey, *Money, Class, and Party: An Economic Study of the Civil War
and Reconstruction* (Baltimore, 1959), and Irwin Ungar, *The Greenback Era: A Social
and Political History of American Finance, 1865–1879* (Princeton, N.J., 1964).

sue. One of the unresolved dilemmas after the Civil War, they claimed, was the exact role that blacks were to play in American society. Within the Republican party a number of factions each offered their own solution to this question. Andrew Johnson, who had been nominated as Lincoln's running mate in 1864 on a Union party ticket despite his Democratic party affiliations, spoke for one segment of the party. To Johnson blacks were incapable of self-government. Consequently he favored the state governments in the South that came back into the Union shortly after the end of the war under his own plan of reconstruction and went along with the Black Codes that denied black Americans many of their civil rights.

Although Johnson was president as well as titular head of Lincoln's party, Radical Republicans fiercely opposed him. The Dunning school painted the Radicals as vindictive, power-hungry politicians; they were merely interested in blacks for their votes. To revisionists the Radicals represented, at least in part, the interests of the industrial Northeast—men who wanted to use black votes to prevent the formation of a strong, oppositional coalition of western and Southern agrarian interests.[12]

To the neorevisionists, on the other hand, the Radicals were a much more complex group. Many of the Radicals, they claimed, joined the Republican party in the 1850s for antislavery rather than economic motives. These men, before and after the war, demanded that blacks be given the same rights as white Americans. Their beliefs brought them to a confrontation with President Johnson in the postwar period. In the ensuing struggle the inept president soon found himself isolated. Taking advantage of the situation, the Radicals set out to remake Southern society by transferring political power from the planter class to the freedmen. The program of the Radicals was motivated in large measure by idealism and a sincere humanitarian concern.[13]

In 1965 Kenneth M. Stampp published an important synthesis that emphasized the moral dimension of the Reconstruction years. Stampp argued that the central question of the postwar period was the place of the freedmen in American society. President Johnson and his followers believed in the innate inferiority of blacks, rejecting any program based upon egalitarian assumptions. The Radicals, many of whom had been abolitionists, on the other hand, took seriously the ideals of equality, natural rights, and democracy. Stampp did not deny that the

---

[12]This point of view was best expressed by Howard K. Beale, one of the fathers of the revisionist school, in *The Critical Year: A Study of Andrew Johnson and Reconstruction* (New York, 1930).

[13]See James H. McPherson, *The Struggle for Equality: Abolitionists and the Negro in the Civil War and Reconstruction* (Princeton, N.J., 1964), and Hans L. Trefousse, *The Radical Republicans: Lincoln's Vanguard for Social Justice* (New York, 1969).

Radicals saw black Americans as valuable additions to the Republican party. But most politicians, he insisted, identify the welfare of the nation with the welfare of their party. To argue that the Radicals had invidious and selfish motives, Stampp concluded, does them a severe injustice and results in a distorted picture of the Reconstruction era.

The Radicals, according to the neorevisionists, ultimately failed in their objectives. Most Americans, harboring conscious and unconscious racial antipathies, were not willing to accept blacks as equals. By the 1870s the North was prepared to abandon blacks to the white South for three reasons: a wish to return to the amicable prewar relations between the sections; a desire to promote industrial investment in the South; and a growing conviction that the cause of black Americans was not worth further strife. The tragedy of Reconstruction, the neorevisionists maintained, was not that it occurred, but that it had ended short of achieving the major goal sought by the Radicals.

The struggle over Reconstruction, nevertheless, had not been in vain. In addition to the many achievements of the Radical governments, the Radicals had succeeded in securing the adoption of the Fourteenth and Fifteenth amendments. These amendments, in Stampp's words, "which could have been adopted only under the conditions of radical reconstruction, make the blunders of that era, tragic though they were, dwindle into insignificance. For if it was worth four years of civil war to save the Union, it was worth a few years of radical reconstruction to give the American Negro the ultimate promise of equal civil and political rights."[14]

During and after the 1970s neorevisionist scholarship began to take a more pessimistic turn even while interest in Reconstruction remained strong. The pervasiveness of inequality and racial friction after the civil rights movement seemed to highlight the failure of post–Civil War Americans to insure that blacks would be integrated into the social and political framework of the Union. Neorevisionist scholars continued to debate the same issues and problems as their predecessors. To what degree were Americans committed to an equal-rights ideology? Why were black Americans left in such a vulnerable position? What was the nature of such political events as the impeachment of Andrew Johnson? Why did Reconstruction come to an end far short of achieving its goals?[15]

To these and other questions neorevisionist historians gave varied answers that demonstrated that few differences had been conclusively resolved. In his study of the Ku Klux Klan, Allen W. Trelease argued

---

[14]Kenneth M. Stampp, *The Era of Reconstruction* (New York, 1965), p. 215.

[15]For a descriptive analysis of black Americans after slavery that does not deal with Reconstruction as a political event, see Leon F. Litwack's important *Been in the Storm So Long: The Aftermath of Slavery* (New York, 1979).

that Radical Reconstruction failed because the seeds of biracial democracy fell on barren soil in the South, and the federal government's artificial nurture was ephemeral and quickly discontinued. George C. Rable emphasized the counterrevolutionary guerilla warfare employed by white Southerners concerned with the destruction of the Republican party in the South. Michael Perman insisted that in the context of the political tensions that prevailed in the immediate postwar era, the very moderation that marked presidential and congressional Reconstruction was doomed to fail; only a coercive policy could have succeeded. In a subsequent work Perman emphasized the ways in which the center in both Republican and Democratic parties proved unable to hold together, thus permitting color to become the political line. And in a broad study of national politics, William Gillette observed that Reconstruction was so easily reversed because it had always been "fragmentary and fragile."[16]

Nor has interest in the role of Andrew Johnson flagged. Michael Les Benedict, for example, insisted that Johnson was impeached because he seemed to be violating the principle of the separation of powers and because he failed to carry out some key provisions in legislation pertaining to Reconstruction. Hans Trefousse emphasized the degree to which Johnson thwarted Radical policies and strengthened conservative forces, thereby facilitating the latter's eventual triumph in the 1870s. Of three other studies of Johnson, two (by Patrick W. Riddleberger and James E. Sefton) emphasized his commitment to sometimes incompatible principles, which rendered him impotent, and one (by Albert Castel) accentuated the degree to which his inordinate ambition and desire for power helped to destroy him.[17]

Robert J. Kaczorowski synthesized many themes that have resonated throughout Reconstruction historiography through the 1980s.

---

[16]Allen W. Trelease, *White Terror: The Ku Klux Klan Conspiracy and Southern Reconstruction* (New York, 1971); George C. Rable, *But There Was No Peace: The Role of Violence in the Politics of Reconstruction* (Athens, Ga., 1984); Michael Perman, *Reunion Without Compromise: The South and Reconstruction, 1865–1868* (Cambridge, 1973), and *The Road to Redemption: Southern Politics, 1869–1879* (Chapel Hill, N.C., 1984); William Gillette, *Retreat from Reconstruction 1869–1879* (Baton Rouge, La., 1979), p. 380.

[17]Michael Les Benedict, *The Impeachment and Trial of Andrew Johnson* (New York, 1973); Hans L. Trefousse, *Impeachment of a President: Andrew Johnson, the Blacks, and Reconstruction* (Knoxville, Tenn., 1975); Patrick W. Riddleberger, *1866: The Critical Year Revisited* (Carbondale, Ill., 1979); James E. Sefton, *Andrew Johnson and the Uses of Constitutional Power* (Boston, 1980); Albert Castel, *The Presidency of Andrew Johnson* (Lawrence, Kans., 1979). See also the following works: Michael Les Benedict's *A Compromise of Principle: Congressional Republicans and Reconstruction, 1863–1869* (New York, 1974) and *The Fruits of Victory: Alternatives in Restoring the Union, 1865–1877* (Philadelphia, 1975); Dan T. Carter, *When the War Was Over: The Failure of Self-Reconstruction in the South, 1865–1867* (Baton Rouge, La., 1985); and Richard N. Current, *Those Terrible Carpetbaggers: A Reinterpretation* (New York, 1988).

The Thirteenth and Fourteenth amendments represented a revolutionary change in American federalism, for citizenship was no longer within state jurisdiction. Consequently, Congress had authority to protect all citizens in their enjoyment of rights. This radical congressional Republican theory of constitutionalism, however, Kaczorowski argued, was altered during the 1870s by a Supreme Court bent on permitting partisans of states' rights in the South to reestablish their domination over former slaves.[18]

Using comparative history better to evaluate the American experience, George M. Fredrickson compared Reconstruction with the experiences of Jamaica and South Africa. He concluded that white Southerners—for a number of reasons—were less able than Jamaicans or South Africans to make even a limited adjustment to the concept of equality. The result was the development of a racist order in the United States that was not exceeded until the formal adoption of apartheid in South Africa after 1948. Although comparative history has yet to find a broad following, it clearly has the ability to transform in fundamental ways the manner in which Americans perceive themselves and their past.[19]

At the same time that interest in national politics remained high, monographs dealing with individual states continued to appear. Here too the traditional dichotomy was evident; some emphasized the degree to which Reconstruction succeeded while others pointed to its failures. Jon Wiener's study of postwar Alabama, excerpted below, argued that Reconstruction might never have happened for all the difference it made in the lives of black people. White elites retained control of the land and forced blacks into a form of tenant serfdom in which they were little better off than in slavery. In a novel study of black political leadership in South Carolina that used quantitative techniques, Thomas Holt argued that black leaders were divided among themselves by education and prewar status; their divisions contributed to the fall of the Republican party in the state. Holt's profile of black leadership demonstrated that most owned property and were literate, and 10 percent were professionally or college trained. And Barbara Fields, focusing on the changing economy in her study of Maryland, argued for eventual changes as the market slowly transformed the border

---

[18]Robert J. Kaczorowski, "To Begin the Nation Anew: Congress, Citizenship, and Civil Rights after the Civil War," *American Historical Review*, 92 (February 1987): 45–68.

[19]George M. Frederickson, "After Emancipation: A Comparative Study of White Responses to the New Order of Race Relations in the American South, Jamaica & the Cape Colony of South Africa," in *What Was Freedom's Price?* David G. Sansing., ed. (Jackson, Miss., 1978).

state. But the racist fallout from slavery persisted with such intensity that change came painfully slowly when it came.[20]

The 1988 publication of Eric Foner's massive *Reconstruction: America's Unfinished Revolution, 1863–1877*, excerpted below, was a milestone. The work represented an effort to restore cohesion to a field long fragmented by disputation. Foner's work in many ways hearkened back to W.E.B. Du Bois's *Black Reconstruction*. Like him, Foner centered his analysis on class and the political initiatives of newly freed black people. Unlike Du Bois and other earlier black scholars, Foner could and did make use of enormous archival material providing his political and economic history a deep base in vivid social history. Initially, he argued, Reconstruction was a radical attempt to destroy the South's antebellum social structure. But by the 1870s fear of class conflict in the North led that section's industrial leaders to evince greater sympathy for the South. The result was a resurgence of white domination below the Mason-Dixon line. Looking at the political and economic experience of blacks, Foner charted the demise by the 1870s of the free labor ideology that had brought the Republican party into existence. White fear of social conflict and concern to restrict the conditions of work for blacks led to a virtual abandonment of the equal rights and free labor ideology. Foner saw Reconstruction as a failure, but an immensely important one, and while it left much unfinished, it had made a beginning that would remain in such institutions as schools and in the memories of freed people.

After the publication of Foner's epic, the historian Michael Perman asked, "What is left to be done?",[21] a question that women historians, at least, had no problem answering. Nina Silber published *The Romance of Reunion* in 1992, a study of sex and the way the South, while losing the war itself, managed to win the interpretation of it. In her analysis, in the face of rapid postwar industrialization and immigration, Northerners and Southerners looked to antebellum Southern myths of manliness and femininity to give order to a fragmenting society. Romantic myths of prewar chivalry, delicate femininity, and interracial harmony blossomed in the stress of labor agitation, the violent retaliation of industrialists, the arrivals of millions of foreign poor and

---

[20]Thomas Holt, *Black over White: Negro Political Leadership in South Carolina during Reconstruction* (Urbana, Ill., 1977); Barbara Fields, *Slavery and Freedom on the Middle Ground, Maryland, 1860–?* (New Haven, Conn., 1985): See also Jerrell H. Shofner, *Nor Is It Over Yet: Florida in the Era of Reconstruction, 1863–1877* (Gainesville, Fla., 1974); Joe Gray Taylor, *Louisiana Reconstructed, 1863–1877* (Baton Rouge, La., 1974); William C. Harris, *The Day of the Carpetbagger: Republican Reconstruction in Mississippi* (Baton Rouge, La., 1979); Ted Tunnell, *Crucible of Reconstruction: War, Radicalism and Race in Louisiana, 1862–1877* (Baton Rouge, La., 1984).

[21]Brooks D. Simpson, *The Reconstruction Presidents* (Lawrence, Kans., 1998).

militant suffragists.[22] In 1995, LeeAnn Whites interpreted the Civil War and Reconstruction eras as a sexual crisis. In her study of Augusta, Georgia, Whites studied the conflicts for Confederate women as the war took their men away and called upon them to increase their domestic activities to help supply the troops. Moving women's traditional activities into the public sphere empowered them in a way that created tension when their defeated men came home. Emancipation exacerbated this because in its aftermath, white males could now legitimately dominate only their wives. Women's associational life after the war to memorialize it continued to give them public clout, but, with Reconstruction and redemption, men assumed these tasks and forced women back into the private sphere.[23]

Tera Hunter's *To 'Joy My Freedom* in 1997 was a rich and fascinating study of black women's lives in the South after the war, particularly in Atlanta. Combining social, urban, political, economic, and sexual history, Hunter portrayed labor conditions for freed women in postwar Atlanta, discovering widespread postwar labor agitation, particularly among militant African American laundresses. She also showed how real estate developers and city officials planned the city's neighborhoods and amenities to be sure blacks in Atlanta would get as few benefits, such as running water, as possible. In the same year Laura Edwards published *Gendered Strife and Confusion*, a subtle study of sex in Granville County in North Carolina. She argued that domestic institutions, particularly marriage, and social ideas of masculinity and femininity served new political and social functions in Reconstruction because of the demise of slavery as a method of control. Arguing that appealing to constructions of maleness, femaleness, and family sanctity provided freed people and poor whites with some new options for themselves, Edwards also describes how conservative Democrats could and did use the tool of sexual construction to bring about the expulsion of blacks from political life.[24]

Foner's inquiries into the ideology of free labor and ideas of contract prompted various studies of those topics. Foner himself addressed the issue in "The Meaning of Freedom in the Age of Emancipation" as well as in the book that grew out of that article.[25] He wrote "Recon-

---

[22]Nina Silber, *The Romance of Reunion, Northerners and the South, 1865–1900* (Chapel Hill, N.C., 1993).

[23]LeeAnn Whites, *The Civil War as a Crisis in Gender, 1860–1890* (Athens, Ga., 1995).

[24]Tera Hunter, *To 'Joy My Freedom: Southern Black Women's Lives and Labors after the Civil War* (Cambridge, Mass., 1997); Laura Edwards, *Gendered Strife and Confusion: The Political Culture of Reconstruction* (Urbana, Ill., 1997). See also Elsa Barkley Brown's "Negotiating and Transforming the Public Sphere: African American Political Life in the Transition from Slavery to Freedom," *Public Culture*, Vol. 7 (1994): 107–46.

[25]Eric Foner, "The Meaning of Freedom in the Age of Emancipation," *Journal of American History*, Vol. 81, No. 2: 435–460. See also Eric Foner, *The Story of American Freedom* (New York, 1998).

struction emerges as a decisive moment in fixing the dominant under-standing of freedom as self-ownership and the right to compete in the labor market, rather than propertied independence." Subsequently, Foner expanded on the transformation during Reconstruction of the meaning of the Fourteenth Amendment. In his view, it came to mean the freedom to contract, not equality before the law.

Legal scholar Peggy Cooper Davis came at the disappointment blacks experienced with postwar interpretations of the Fourteenth Amendment from a different tack. In *Neglected Stories, The Constitution and Family Values,* she recreated through stories from slavery and Reconstruction the problems the Fourteenth Amendment was at-tempting to address, particularly the complete absence of white respect for the rights of blacks to make and protect their families. The failure of the Supreme Court to interpret the Fourteenth Amendment in light of its framers' intent has had the effect of protecting industrialists' right to make and enforce unjust contracts with poor laborers, while not pro-tecting the rights of black men and women to a secure family life.[26]

Pursuing the sometimes paradoxical links between contract and freedom, Amy Dru Stanley's 1998 study, *From Bondage to Contract,* explored the tension implicit in the understanding that the Civil War and Reconstruction emancipated slaves to participate in freedom de-fined by the buying and selling of everything but people. In Stanley's view, prostitution remained the most flagrant violation of the postwar notion of freedom as self-possession.[27]

Julia Saville contributed another study of these themes. In her monograph on South Carolina from 1860 to 1870, she interpreted the activism of free people as rejecting the domination of their fomer own-ers, while at the same time contesting the notion of freedom as subjec-tion to landowners in particular and to market values in general.[28]

While there have been a few hardy souls publishing traditional po-litical studies in the wake of Foner's volume, perhaps the most original exploration of a Reconstruction theme is Mark Summers's *The Era of Good Stealing.*[29] The Dunning school claimed that Reconstruction governments cried out to be overthrown because of their massive cor-ruption. Revisionists and the neorevisionists claimed there was cor-

[26]Peggy Cooper Davis, *Neglected Stories, The Constitution and Family Values* (New York, 1997).

[27]Amy Dru Stanley, *From Bondage to Contract, Wage Labor, Marriage and the Market in the Age of Slave Emancipation* (New York, 1998).

[28]Julia Saville, *The Work of Reconstruction, from Slave to Wage Laborer in South Carolina, 1860–1870* (New York, 1994).

[29]Recent political studies include William C. Harris, *With Charity for All, Lincoln and the Restoration of the Union* (Lexington, Ky., 1997); Brooks D. Simpson, *The Reconstruction Presidents* (Lawrence, Kans., 1998); Mark Wahlgren Summers, *The Era of Good Stealings* (New York, 1993).

ruption in both the North and South, so the issue was a red herring. Summers, instead, argued that while there was serious but not paralyzing corruption nationwide, the question was not the amount but its significance in the minds of Americans. And there, he argued, it was sufficient to undermine the faith citizens had in government. Hence, the issue was not a red herring because citizen cynicism about government needs remedy even if the level of corruption is not crippling government's ability to function.

Although it is possible to demonstrate that particular interpretations grew out of and reflected their own milieu, historians must still face the larger and more important problem of evaluating interpretations.[30] Were the revisionists correct in emphasizing the fundamental economic factors? Were the neorevisionists justified in insisting that the major issue during Reconstruction was indeed moral in nature? Or were the two intertwined? Did the particular structural form of state and national politics preclude effective governmental action in dealing with the problems growing out of emancipation? What should have been the proper policy for both the federal and state governments to follow with regard to black Americans, and how were the voices of blacks to be heard during policy formation and implementation?

Was the American experience dissimilar from or similar to that of other nations that also experienced the transition from a slave to a free society? Was Reconstruction a meaningless experiment after which the Southern elite resumed business as usual complete with white supremacy? Or was Reconstruction a brave but shortlived attempt to fashion real democracy in the South—one that would lay the groundwork for the civil rights movement one hundred years later? How did the juggernaut of postwar capitalism affect the terrain on which Reconstruction was being attempted?

Although that period is more than a century from our own, many of the basic conflicts common to both remain unresolved and are as pressing as ever. Perhaps most fundamental of all is the question Reconstruction raised and did not answer. How can Americans give meaning to freedom in a market-driven society when those in power keep the market's rewards from blacks and other poor people?

---

[30]For a discussion of schools of Reconstruction historiography see Gerald N. Grob, "Reconstruction: An American Morality Play," in *American History: Retrospect and Prospect,* George A. Billias and Gerald N. Grob, eds. (New York, 1971), pp. 191–231; Richard O. Curry, "The Civil War and Reconstruction, 1861–1877: A Critical Overview of Recent Trends and Interpretations," *Civil War History,* 20 (September 1974): 215–38; Michael Les Benedict, "Equality and Expediency in the Reconstruction Era: A Review Essay," ibid., 23 (December 1977): 322–35.

JONATHAN M. WIENER

JONATHAN M. WIENER (1944–   ) is professor of history at the University of California, Irvine. He is the author of Social Origins of the New South *(1978),* Come Together: John Lennon and His Time *(1984), and* Professors, Politics and Pop *(1994).*

The postwar planters were a new class because they were in new social relations of production. But they were a new class made up of families which to a significant extent had been part of the antebellum elite. The old families persisted in a quantitative sense; in a qualitative sense, their relationship to production had been transformed. Yet they were not a fully modern bourgeoisie.

The development of the postwar southern economy can be understood first of all in terms of the relations between this planter class and the freedmen. After the war, the planters sought to preserve the plantation as a centralized productive unit, worked by laborers in gangs. The freedmen, however, wanted to own their own farms. These differences were resolved, not by the workings of the invisible hand of the free market, but rather by a process that can only be called class conflict. The planters used three tactics in particular: they sought informally to enlist the Freedmen's Bureau in preserving the gang labor plantation; they developed formal legal institutions to limit the free market in labor; and some turned from legalistic to illegal methods, from repressive law to terror, from the Black Codes to the Ku Klux Klan. The freedmen fought back in the only ways they could: they withdrew their labor, and they organized politically to demand the confiscation and distribution of plantations owned by rebels.

The outcome of this conflict gave the South its distinctive character, and indicates that the economic and political development of the South differed from that of the North not just in degree, but in kind. Postwar southern development was not following the same path as the North, in an evolutionary manner, because the landlord-tenant relation was of a different type than the capitalist-proletarian relation prevailing in the North. The key difference was the coercive mode of labor control the planters developed in their conflict with the freedmen. . . .

The Gang Labor Plantation

At the direction of the occupying Union army, slave labor was replaced by the "contract system"; the freedmen were to sign contracts
with planters specifying their duties and their pay. The contracts
with planters for 1865 and 1866 provided for gang labor for wages
rather than family tenancy. Because of the shortage of currency, wage
laborers were usually paid with a share of the crop rather than in
cash; this has led some to confuse the gang system of the immediate
postwar period with its successor, sharecropping. But it is the organization of production, rather than the form of payment, that is crucial:
wage laborers worked in a gang under an overseer, as they had under
slavery; their hours and tasks were clearly specified in their contract,
and carefully supervised; infractions, such as not showing up on time
or taking extra days off, were punished. . . . It must be clearly distinguished from the system of family tenancy where the rent was paid
with a share of the crop—"sharecropping." . . . The crucial difference
was the greater power of the planters over the daily lives of gang laborers, and the sharecroppers' greater independence from supervision
and control.

The Freedmen's Bureau reports on the reorganization of agriculture and labor in 1865 and 1866 described a system based on gang laborers receiving wages. . . .

While wage labor was ostensibly the basis of plantation agriculture
in 1865 and 1866, many planters avoided paying any wages at all to
their former slaves. One Alabama Freedmen's Bureau agent reported
incidents in which "the negro promises to work for an indefinite time
for nothing but his board and clothes," and Peter Kolchin has concluded that, in numerous places in Alabama, blacks were "working
without pay." The contracts were supposed to specify the tasks for
which the freedmen were to be paid, but many planters apparently
avoided this provision. . . . Indeed there is evidence that some planters
went so far as to try to sell their laborers as if they were still slaves. . . .

The planters not only tried to maintain many of the repressive aspects of slavery in the postwar wage system; they also tried to keep
their own former slaves as laborers. Colonel George H. Hanks, super-
intendent of Negro labor in the army's Department of the Gulf, told
the War Department's Freedmen's Inquiry Commission early in 1864
that the planters "make great endeavors to recover what they call their
own negroes." An extreme case was that of one of the "richest and
most extensive" planters, who refused to work his own plantation at
all "unless he could have his own negroes returned to him." . . .

The assumption behind this view could only have been that
planters would have more control over wage laborers who had been

their own slaves and then "stayed on." And the evidence is overwhelming that the freedmen were determined to avoid staying on for precisely this reason. Carl Schurz was one of the first to argue that leaving the old slave plantation was the most fundamental definition of "freedom" among the former slaves; "that they could so leave their former masters was for them the first test of the reality of their freedom," he told a Senate committee. . . .

The planters in these immediate postwar years formed organizations to protect their interests, class conscious efforts to place plantation agriculture on a firmly repressive basis. . . .

In Sumter County . . . a "meeting of citizens" discussing the "labor system" unanimously resolved that "concert of action is indispensable among those hiring laborers." They agreed that all planters should offer the same terms: one-fourth of the crop for the laborer when the planter supplied the provisions, or one-half the crop when the tenants paid half the expenses as well as their own provisions. "Tenants who don't comply with terms will be discharged," the meeting declared, and concluded "we pledge ourselves not to employ any laborer discharged for violation of contracts." . . .

A statewide "Planters Convention" met in the Alabama House of Representatives in February, 1871. Those who called for the convention announced that their purpose was for planters to "put their heads, and if need be, their means, together for mutual benefit and protection." . . . The convention, widely reported in the planter press, seemed to echo the sentiments of an Alabama planter who summed up his view of the labor situation for John Trowbridge in 1866: "The nigger is going to be made a serf, sure as you live. It won't need any law for that. Planters will have an understanding among themselves: 'You won't hire my niggers, and I won't hire yours;' then what's left for them? They're attached to the soil, and we're as much their masters as ever."

The planters' attempt to preserve the plantation as a centralized labor unit, using supervised gang labor, was a logical effort to preserve a mode of production that had evolved and developed over sixty years. The planters' desire to incorporate wage labor into the organizational structure of the antebellum plantation was not only an effort to preserve planter domination of the freedmen, but also to continue production along the lines of established agricultural methods and procedures. This effort, comprehensible as it was in economic terms, confronted an insurmountable obstacle: the freedmen's refusal to agree to it. Their widespread resistance to working in gangs for wages appears in the historical record as a "shortage of labor," and it played a crucial role in the reorganization of plantation agriculture after the war.

The Labor Shortage

. . . The most important cause of the labor shortage in 1865 and 1866 seems to have been the freedmen's refusal to work for wages, which was in turn based on their hope of becoming landowners. The Joint Congressional Committee on Reconstruction reported the freedmen had a "strong desire, amounting almost to a passion . . . to obtain land." In the words of the Montgomery *Advertiser,* "the negro is ravenous for land." . . . A Union officer wrote that "all concurred in the opposition to the contract system."

A convention of black leaders met in Montgomery in May, 1867, and issued an "address . . . to the People of Alabama," which expressed the blacks' desire to own land. They explained that blacks supported the Republican party, among other reasons, because "it passed new homestead laws, enabling the poor to obtain land." The convention said of their planter-antagonists that "the property which they hold was nearly all earned by the sweat of our brows—not theirs. It has been forfeited to the government by the treason of its owners, and is liable to be confiscated whenever the Republican Party demands it."

This expectation of land distribution was no idle fantasy in the black community, but one firmly based on political facts. General Nathaniel P. Banks, head of the military occupation of Louisiana, had provided small plots for freedmen in 1863 and 1864. John Eaton, who had jurisdiction over freedmen flocking to Grant's army, had 2,000 blacks on government-financed farms, and in January, 1865, Sherman provided for the establishment of homesteads for freedmen in the Sea Islands of South Carolina; this he did in direct response to requests from black leaders. The Freedmen's Bureau Bill, passed in March, 1865, provided that forty acres of abandoned and confiscated lands should be assigned to "every male citizen, whether refugee or freedman," to be rented for three years, and then purchased from the United States. Commissioner Howard of the Freedmen's Bureau had originally intended to turn over abandoned and confiscated land to freedmen, and it was only President Johnson's veto of this policy in the fall of 1865 that forced the bureau to begin returning confiscated land to its original owners. The following year, Congress passed the Southern Homestead Act, allowing blacks to file applications for homesteads in 1866, while most whites had to wait until 1867. . . .

Freedmen hesitated to work for wages in the immediate postwar period for additional reasons. The increasing refusal to work for wages corresponded to a decrease in the wages planters offered. According to Department of Agriculture statistics, the annual wages offered black men in Alabama fell from $117 in 1867 to $87 in 1868, a decline of 26 percent in one year.

The chief complaint of the freedmen working for wages, according to the Freedmen's Bureau, was "fraudulent division of the crops." Apparently planters were not only reducing wages, but also cheating on the shares paid to laborers—or at least the freedmen accused them of doing so. One authority reports that the number of such complaints rose "steadily.". . . .

A final cause of the labor shortage was the withdrawal of women and children from the labor force. As slaveowners, the planters had commanded the labor of black women and children; as employers of free labor, they found black women and children unwilling to work as they had under slavery. *DeBow's Review* reported in 1866 that, in contrast to slave times, "most of the field labor is now performed by men, the women regarding it as the duty of their husbands to support them in idleness," and that "there is a settled opposition on the part of the women to go into the fields again."

The Planters and the Freedmen's Bureau

The planters' bitter opposition to the presence first of the Union army and later of the Freedmen's Bureau in their own counties did not stop them from seeking to enlist the bureau in keeping the black labor force on the plantation. Their efforts tended to be successful; while the bureau opposed some of the more extreme proposals made on behalf of the planters, many bureau officials worked to perpetuate the planters' domination, and the bureau in some crucial respects became part of the repressive apparatus of the new agricultural system. . . .

Brigadier General C. C. Andrews, commander of Union forces in Selma, observed that the freedmen were filled with "restlessness and disquiet" over the persistence of the plantation system; this led him to issue a proclamation to the freedmen of the west Alabama black belt in May, 1865, in which he supported the planters' claims. "Quite a number of freedmen have complained to me," he told the blacks, but "planters have represented to me that the loss they have suffered . . . and the depreciation of their currency . . . have cramped their means . . . so that they cannot promise you much compensation." Andrews found that what the planters said was "true to a considerable extent," and told the dissatisfied freedmen, "you . . . appear misinformed of your real interests. [Therefore] I now offer you my advice: I do not believe you hazard your liberty by remaining where you are and working for such compensation as your employers are able to give." This was not a confidential memo to a superior; it was a public proclamation by the commander of U.S. forces in the area. . . .

Military authority over the freedmen gave way to the Freedmen's Bureau in Alabama officially in July, 1865. The assistant commissioner in charge of Alabama was Brigadier General Wager Swayne.

Swayne's view of the labor situation in Alabama was classically lais-sez-faire capitalist: "The system of annual contracts was regarded as a make-shift," he wrote in his 1866 report, "which it was hoped would disappear as confidence should grow out of experience on both sides, and leave to each the benefit of an appeal at any time to competition. The demand for labor promised a comfortable future for the freedmen on this basis." Swayne thought that legal regulation of labor was unde-sirable, that the free market in labor should be established, and that the high demand for black labor would assure the prosperity of the freedmen. In spite of these declarations of a laissez-faire policy, Swayne in practice intervened repeatedly on the side of the planters and against the freedmen. . . .

Upon his arrival in Alabama, Swayne took on the task of "remov-ing" from the freedmen the "belief . . . that they could live without la-bor." He candidly identified his task as "compelling the able-bodied to labor." And he commented that he was pleased by the "reasonable temper of the planters," a temper which was not surprising, given the bureau's declared purpose of compelling the freedmen to labor for wages on the plantations. . . .

Of course not all bureau agents worked closely with local planters. One Alabama agent, shocked at the bureau's pro-planter policy, wrote that his predecessor "worked with a view to please the white citizens, at the expense of, and injustice to, the Freedmen." The previous offi-cials "have invariably given permission to inflict punishment for inso-lence or idleness, and have detailed soldiers to tie up and otherwise punish the laborers who have, in the opinion of the employers, been 'refractory.'". . .

Why were the planters so successful in influencing the bureau? First of all, it was Swayne's policy to appoint "native whites" as bu-reau agents whenever possible, and to ignore the "tales of outrage" re-ported by agents who were northerners. Fleming suggests that the appointment of agents from the locality contributed to the closeness of the bureau to the local planter elite. . . .

Those bureau agents in Alabama who were neither local whites nor army officers met intense and calculated social pressure from the planter-dominated communities to which they were assigned. . . . The Montgomery *Weekly Mail* explained in 1866, "Union officers . . . who are gentlemen, are received into the best families in our city. It is true that they are taken in on probation. . . . Some [who] keep company with Negroes . . . could not get into society. . . . But all who are kind and considered gentlemen . . . will always be met by kind and consider-ate southern people." . . .

The bureau's free labor ideology made it thoroughly antagonistic to slavery. Nevertheless it supported planter interests in some crucial respects. The profoundly bourgeois conception on which bureau policy

was based regarded the lash of slavery to be both inhumane and inefficient as a form of labor discipline. The discipline of the market economy itself, however, was not only necessary, but a desirable way of
shaping a free laboring class. Freedom the bureau understood to be in
large part freedom to enter into a wage contract with a planter; and the
free man has an obligation to fulfill his terms of the contract. As for
the planters, the bureau insisted that they too needed to fulfill their
contracts, and to learn to use the market rather than the lash to discipline labor. The bureau and the planters, whatever their other differences, agreed that free labor was still labor, on the plantations and
under the planter class.

Legal Repression: The Black Codes

The passage of the Black Codes was the planters' attempt to end the
"labor shortage" by legal means—parallel to their informal effort to
enlist the aid of the Freedmen's Bureau in achieving the same goal.
The Black Code of Alabama included two key laws intended to assure
the planters a reliable supply of labor—a vagrancy law, and a law
against the "enticement" of laborers. The "Vagrant Law" defined va-
grants to include "stubborn servants . . . a laborer or servant who loi-
ters away his time, or refuses to comply with any contract . . . without
just cause." It provided as punishment for such hideous crimes a fine
of $50 plus court costs, and allowed judges to "hire out" vagrants until
their fines were paid, with a six-month limit. . . .

The second law, passed explicitly "for the purpose of regulating labor," made it a crime to "hire, entice away, or induce to leave the service of another" any laborer who had already contracted to work for
another. The penalty for those who "induce laborers . . . to abandon
their contracts, or employ such without the consent of their original
employer," was a fine of $50 to $500. If a laborer was found working
for "another," "that fact shall be *prima facie* evidence that such person is guilty of violating this act," unless the new employer "shall
upon being notified of such antecedent contract, forthwith discharge
said laborer." . . .

The law prohibiting enticement of labor was aimed not at the
blacks, but at the planters; it was intended to reduce conflict within
the planter class. It was also intended to stop agents from Mississippi
seeking to recruit Alabama blacks. Mississippi planters during the late
sixties were opening up new plantation areas in the western delta regions of the state, and had a severe shortage of black laborers there.
They needed blacks not only to raise cotton, but also to drain swamps,
build levees, clear cropland, and construct roads. Not only did private
agents of Mississippi planters recruit in Alabama, but Mississippi es-

tablished an official state bureau of immigration which sent agents
into Alabama. . . .

The planters' attempt to control black labor by legal means seems
to have backfired. Even Fleming found the Black Code provisions for
the regulation of labor to have been "carelessly drawn" and "technically unconstitutional." . . . The planters had proposed labor regulations whose repressive character was undeniable; the freedmen,
however, refused to end the "labor shortage," and some planters, increasingly desperate to preserve the large-scale plantation organization
based on wage labor, turned to terror, to the Ku Klux Klan.

The Social Base of the Klan

The extent to which the black belt Klan was an instrument of the
planter class, rather than of poor whites, is often overlooked. The two
white groups had conflicting interests, and the Klan in the black belt
worked in pursuit of the goals of the planters. The congressional investigation of the Klan focused on its political use of terror against Republicans; subsequent interpretations have tended to emphasize this
evidence. In so doing, they have underemphasized the role Klan terror
played in creating and perpetuating the South's repressive plantation
labor system.

The Ku Klux Klan was "more widespread and virulent" in the
black belt of western Alabama in 1869 and 1870 than in any other part
of the South, except perhaps for northern Alabama. . . .

The hill country whites used Klan terror to drive blacks off the
land, opening it to white small farmers. But the social base and strategy of the Klan in the black belt was "exactly the opposite," Fleming
wrote; there, "the planters preferred Negro labor, and never drove out
the blacks."

Planters used Klan terror to keep blacks from leaving the plantation regions, to get them to work, and keep them at work, in the cotton fields. Other sources support Fleming's interpretation that "the
best men" were members of the black belt Klan. John L. Hunnicutt
claims to have organized the Klan in the black belt of western Alabama; he wrote in his memoirs that he did so at the request of "some
of the best citizens." Richard Busteed, a U.S. district judge for Alabama, told the congressional investigating committee that "gentlemen of education and intelligence . . . compose the class called
Ku-Klux." . . .

Fleming, with typical directness, listed among the "causes of the
ku klux movement" the fact that "people in the Black Belt felt that labor must be regulated in some way." The Klan was necessary, Marengo
planter F. S. Lyon told the congressional committee, to counter the fact

that blacks "are told by some . . . that planters do not pay sufficient wages for their labor." . . . As early as 1866, masked bands in the black belt "punished Negroes whose landlords had complained of them." . . .

The ever-respectable Montgomery *Advertiser* often printed articles like the one which argued that "the negro's inherent sloth seems to communicate itself to domestic animals that live with him. His pigs are too lazy to root, his sneaking dogs won't bark, . . . his cabin looks more like a deserted dog kennel than a human dwelling." The Eutaw *Whig,* noting that northern white women were coming south to teach, wrote, "When they come the buck niggers will welcome them with ebony arms, to African couches, and then the next generation of Radicals in the South . . . will smell only half as bad as the present generation." It was cultured discourse of this kind, appearing in the most respected journals of the planter class, that was intended to justify Klan terror.

From Gang Labor to Sharecropping

In spite of the momentous political events taking place in 1867 and 1868—the attempted impeachment of the president and the beginning of Radical Reconstruction—Alabama planters were preoccupied first of all with their attempts to revive the plantation system. . . . The discussions increasingly came to one conclusion: the attempt had failed to preserve the plantation as a single, large-scale unit, cultivated by labor gangs paid in wages. The planters in increasing numbers were dividing their plantations into small plots, and assigning each to a single family, which was paid with a share of the crop; the old slave quarters were broken up and replaced with cabins scattered across the plantation. . . .

The "labor shortage" was a leading cause of this momentous decision by the planters, but it was not the only one. A series of bad cotton crops in 1865, 1866, and 1867 contributed to the planters' doubts that the plantations could be reorganized profitably on the basis of gang labor. The Radical constitutional convention met in December, 1867, and the Radical state constitution was ratified in February, 1868. The first Radical legislature gave agricultural laborers a lien on the crop in 1868. This could only have discouraged the planters further; giving the laborer the first lien meant that, in case of a dispute over wages, the laborer's claim had precedence over that of the planter. And the freedmen's most common complaint, it should be recalled, was fraudulent division of the crop.

Once the planters accepted the breakup of the antebellum plantation into small units, why did they not simply rent them? The key issue was the planter's control over his tenants. . . . The Selma *Southern*

Argus agreed, observing that if the black was permitted to rent, "the power to control him is gone." The wage system gave the planters a maximum of control over the daily activities of the freedmen, and it was precisely to this extensive control that the freedmen objected. . . .

The planters' argument was that black laborers required supervision because they were lazy and incompetent workers. Sharecropping contracts gave the planter specified rights to supervise the labor of his tenants, since he was "investing" his own capital in the crop as well as renting his land. The planters' claim that blacks were incapable of labor without supervision was an ideological justification of their own existence as a class and of their right to the surplus they acquired.

Although the move to sharecropping represented a substantial defeat for the planters, it was not without benefit for them. The *Advertiser* pointed to the benefits of the labor repressive aspects of the system. . . . Sharecropping offered the additional advantage of increasing the labor force considerably in comparison with the gang system; by making the family the unit of labor rather than the wage hand, it brought women and children back into the fields. . . .

Sharecropping and Economic Development

. . . For the dominant class in the immediate postwar South, there were two possible responses to a shortage of labor. One was to develop capital-intensive methods of production. The alternative to this classic capitalist road was to rely on the coercion of labor, to extract a larger surplus not by increasing productivity through improved technology, but by squeezing more out of the laborers. Because this intensification was likely to provoke resistance and flight, this second route required formal restrictions on labor mobility, laws that tied the workers to the land and restricted their access to alternative employment. This second route is not necessarily economically stagnant; it is capable of bringing economic development, but in a manner distinct from the classic capitalist method. Barrington Moore, mindful of European developments, has called it the "Prussian Road" to modern society: economic development that preserves and intensifies the authoritarian and repressive elements of traditional social relations.

The possibility that the South could take the classic capitalist road was not ignored in the immediate postwar period. Some of the most astute southerners pushed for precisely such a solution to the problems of postwar agricultural adjustment. The Selma *Southern Argus*, for one, argued tirelessly during the late 1860s that the planters should end their reliance on labor-intensive methods of producing cotton, and instead diversify crops, introduce stock raising, and substitute labor-saving machinery for black tenant labor.

The planter class, rooted as it was in the antebellum elite, chose the other solution, the Prussian Road. The Black Codes passed in 1865–1867 expressed that choice; temporarily abolished by the Radicals, many were resurrected by the planter regimes that regained power in the seventies. And once the institutions of a labor-repressive system of agriculture had been established, the planters had little incentive to mechanize or introduce more rational techniques to increase efficiency and productivity. Thus while wheat-growing capitalist farmers in the North were transforming their productive techniques with a technological revolution, southern sharecroppers in 1900 relied on hand tools and mule power; the result was southern economic stagnation, as crop outputs, yields per acre, and agricultural technology changed little from year to year.

Too much of the recent debate has treated southern economic and political development as separate questions. The South's characteristic poverty and political oppression arose out of the same social relations: the Prussian Road, with its dominant planter class and its labor-repressive system of agricultural production, which posed a major obstacle not only to economic development, but also to democracy, to the political freedoms present in the North and so glaringly absent from the South.

E R I C   F O N E R

ERIC FONER (1943–   ) is the DeWitt Clinton Professor of History at Columbia University. He is the author of Free Soil, Free Labor, Free Men (1970), Tom Paine and Revolutionary America (1976), Reconstruction: America's Unfinished Revolution, winner of the Bancroft Prize and Francis Parkman Prize (1988), and The Story of American Freedom (1998).

Thus, in the words of W.E.B. Du Bois, "the slave went free; stood a brief moment in the sun; then moved back again toward slavery." The magnitude of the Redeemer counterrevolution underscored both the scope of the transformation Reconstruction had assayed and the consequences of its failure. To be sure, the era of emancipation and Republican rule did not lack enduring accomplishments. The tide of change rose and then receded, but it left behind an altered landscape. The freedmen's political and civil equality proved transitory, but the autonomous black family and a network of religious and social institutions survived the end of Reconstruction. Nor could the seeds of educational progress planted then be entirely uprooted. While wholly inadequate for pupils of both races, schooling under the Redeemers represented a distinct advance over the days when blacks were excluded altogether from a share in public services.

If blacks failed to achieve the economic independence envisioned in the aftermath of the Civil War, Reconstruction closed off even more oppressive alternatives than the Redeemers' New South. The post-Reconstruction labor system embodied neither a return to the closely supervised gang labor of antebellum days, nor the complete dispossession and immobilization of the black labor force and coercive apprenticeship systems envisioned by white Southerners in 1865 and 1866. Nor were blacks, as in twentieth-century South Africa, barred from citizenship, herded into labor reserves, or prohibited by law from moving from one part of the country to another. As illustrated by the small but growing number of black landowners, businessmen, and professionals, the doors of economic opportunity that had opened could never be completely closed. Without Reconstruction, moreover, it is difficult to imagine the establishment of a framework of legal rights enshrined in the Constitution that, while flagrantly violated after 1877, created a vehicle for future federal intervention in Southern affairs. As a result of this unprecedented redefinition of the American body politic, the South's racial system remained regional rather than national, an outcome of great importance when economic opportunities at last opened in the North.

Nonetheless, whether measured by the dreams inspired by emancipation or the more limited goals of securing blacks' rights as citizens and free laborers, and establishing an enduring Republican presence in the South, Reconstruction can only be judged a failure. Among the host of explanations for this outcome, a few seem especially significant. Events far beyond the control of Southern Republicans—the nature of the national credit and banking systems, the depression of the 1870s, the stagnation of world demand for cotton—severely limited the prospects for far-reaching economic change. The early rejection of federally sponsored land reform left in place a planter class far weaker and less affluent than before the war, but still able to bring its prestige and experience to bear against Reconstruction. Factionalism and corruption, although hardly confined to Southern Republicans, undermined their claim to legitimacy and made it difficult for them to respond effectively to attacks by resolute opponents. The failure to develop an ef fective long-term appeal to white voters made it increasingly difficult for Republicans to combat the racial politics of the Redeemers. None of these factors, however, would have proved decisive without the campaign of violence that turned the electoral tide in many parts of the South, and the weakening of Northern resolve, itself a consequence of social and political changes that undermined the free labor and egalitarian precepts at the heart of Reconstruction policy.

For historians, hindsight can be a treacherous ally. Enabling us to trace the hidden patterns of past events, it beguiles us with the mirage of inevitability, the assumption that different outcomes lay beyond the limits of the possible. Certainly, the history of other plantation societies offers little reason for optimism that emancipation could have given rise to a prosperous, egalitarian South, or even one that escaped a pattern of colonial underdevelopment. Nor do the prospects for the expansion of scalawag support—essential for Southern Republicanism's long-term survival—appear in retrospect to have been anything but bleak. Outside the mountains and other enclaves of wartime Unionism, the Civil War generation of white Southerners was always likely to view the Republican party as an alien embodiment of wartime defeat and black equality. And the nation lacked not simply the will but the modern bureaucratic machinery to oversee Southern affairs in any permanent way. Perhaps the remarkable thing about Reconstruction was not that it failed, but that it was attempted at all and survived as long as it did. Yet one can, I think, imagine alternative scenarios and modest successes: the Republican party establishing itself as a permanent fixture on the Southern landscape, the North summoning the resolve to insist that the Constitution must be respected. As the experiences of Readjuster Virginia and Populist-Republican North Carolina suggest, even Redemption did not entirely foreclose the possibility of biracial politics, thus raising the question of how Southern life might have been affected had Deep South blacks enjoyed genuine political freedoms when the Populist movement swept the white counties in the 1890s.

Here, however, we enter the realm of the purely speculative. What remains certain is that Reconstruction failed, and that for blacks its failure was a disaster whose magnitude cannot be obscured by the genuine accomplishments that did endure. For the nation as a whole, the collapse of Reconstruction was a tragedy that deeply affected the course of its future development. If racism contributed to the undoing of Reconstruction, by the same token Reconstruction's demise and the emergence of blacks as a disenfranchised class of dependent laborers greatly facilitated racism's further spread, until by the early twentieth century it had become more deeply embedded in the nation's culture and politics than at any time since the beginning of the antislavery crusade and perhaps in our entire history. The removal of a significant portion of the nation's laboring population from public life shifted the center of gravity of American politics to the right, complicating the tasks of reformers for generations to come. Long into the twentieth century, the South remained a one-party region under the control of a reactionary ruling elite who used the same violence and fraud that had helped defeat Reconstruction to stifle internal dissent. An enduring consequence of Reconstruction's failure, the Solid South helped define the contours of American politics and weaken the prospects not simply of change in racial matters but of progressive legislation in many other realms.

The men and women who had spearheaded the effort to remake Southern society scattered down innumerable byways after the end of Reconstruction. Some relied on federal patronage to earn a livelihood. The unfortunate Marshall Twitchell, armless after his near-murder in 1876, was appointed U.S. consul at Kingston, Ontario, where he died in 1905. Some fifty relatives and friends of the Louisiana Returning Board that had helped make Hayes President received positions at the New Orleans Custom House, and Stephen Packard was awarded the consulship at Liverpool—compensation for surrendering his claim to the governorship. John Eaton, who coordinated freedmen's affairs for General Grant during the war and subsequently took an active role in Tennessee Reconstruction, served as federal commissioner of education from 1870 to 1886, and organized a public school system in Puerto Rico after the island's conquest in the Spanish-American War. Most carpetbaggers returned to the North, often finding there the financial success that had eluded them in the South. Davis Tillson, head of Georgia's Freedman's Bureau immediately after the war, earned a fortune in the Maine granite business. Former South Carolina Gov. Robert K. Scott returned to Napoleon, Ohio, where he became a successful real estate agent—"a most fitting occupation" in view of his involvement in land commission speculations. Less happy was the fate of his scalawag successor, Franklin J. Moses, Jr., who drifted north, served prison terms for petty crimes, and died in a Massachusetts rooming house in 1906.

Republican governors who had won reputations as moderates by courting white Democratic support and seeking to limit blacks' political influence found the Redeemer South remarkably forgiving. Henry C. Warmoth became a successful sugar planter and remained in Louisiana until his death in 1931. James L. Alcorn retired to his Mississippi plantation, "presiding over a Delta domain in a style befitting a prince" and holding various local offices. He remained a Republican, but told one Northern visitor that Democratic rule had produced "good fellowship" between the races. Even Rufus Bullock, who fled Georgia accused of every kind of venality, soon reentered Atlanta society, serving, among other things, as president of the city's chamber of commerce. Daniel H. Chamberlain left South Carolina in 1877 to launch a successful New

York City law practice, but was well received on his numerous visits to the state. In retrospect, Chamberlain altered his opinion of Reconstruction: a "frightful experiment" that sought to "lift a backward or inferior race" to political equality, it had inevitably produced "shocking and unbearable misgovernment." "Governor Chamberlain," commented a Charleston newspaper, "has lived and learned."

Not all white Republicans, however, abandoned Reconstruction ideals. In 1890, a group of reformers, philanthropists, and religious leaders gathered at the Lake Mohonk Conference on the Negro Question, chaired by former President Hayes. Amid a chorus of advice that blacks eschew political involvement and concentrate on educational and economic progress and remedying their own character deficiencies, former North Carolina Judge Albion W. Tourgée, again living in the North, voiced the one discordant note. There was no "Negro problem," Tourgee observed, but rather a "white" one, since "the hate, the oppression, the injustice, are all on our side." The following year, Tourgée established the National Citizens' Rights Association, a short-lived forerunner of the National Association for the Advancement of Colored People, devoted to challenging the numerous injustices afflicting Southern blacks. Adelbert Ames, who left Mississippi in 1875 to join his father's Minnesota flour-milling business and who later settled in Massachusetts, continued to defend his Reconstruction record. In 1894 he chided Brown University President E. Benjamin Andrews for writing that Mississippi during his governorship had incurred a debt of $20 million. The actual figure, Ames pointed out, was less than 3 percent of that amount, and he found it difficult to understand how Andrews had made "a $19,500,000 error in a $20,000,000 statement." Ames lived to his ninety-eighth year, never abandoning the conviction that "caste is the curse of the world." Another Mississippi carpetbagger, Massachusetts-born teacher and legislator Henry Warren, published his autobiography in 1914, still hoping that one day, "possibly in the present century," America would live up to the ideal of "equal political rights for all without regard to race."

For some, the Reconstruction experience became a springboard to lifetimes of social reform. The white voters of Winn Parish in Louisiana's hill country expressed their enduring radicalism by supporting the Populists in the 1890s, Socialism in 1912, and later their native son Huey Long. Among the female veterans of freedmen's education, Cornelia Hancock founded Philadelphia's Children's Aid Society, Abby May became prominent in the Massachusetts women's suffrage movement, Ellen Collins turned her attention to New York City housing reform, and Josephine Shaw Lowell became a supporter of the labor movement and principal founder of New York's Consumer League. Louis F. Post, a New Jersey-born carpetbagger who took stenographic notes for South Carolina's legislature in the early 1870s, became a follower of Henry George, attended the founding meeting of the NAACP, and as Woodrow Wilson's Assistant Secretary of Labor, sought to mitigate the 1919 Red Scare and prevent the deportation of foreign-born radicals. And Texas scalawag editor Albert Parsons became a nationally known Chicago labor reformer and anarchist, whose speeches drew comparisons between the plight of Southern blacks and Northern industrial workers, and between the aristocracy resting on slavery the Civil War had destroyed and the new oligarchy based on the exploitation of industrial labor it had helped to create. Having survived the perils of Texas Reconstruction, Parsons met his death on the Illinois gallows after being wrongfully convicted of complicity in the Haymarket bombing of 1886.

Like their white counterparts, many black veterans of Reconstruction survived on federal patronage after the coming of "home rule." P. B. S. Pinchback and Blanche K. Bruce held a series of such posts and later moved to Washington, D.C., where they entered the city's privileged black society. Richard T. Greener, during Reconstruction a professor at the University of South Carolina, combined a career in law, journalism, and education with various government appointments, including a stint as American commercial agent at Vladivostok. Long after the destruction of his low-country political machine by disenfranchisement, Robert Smalls served as customs collector for the port of Beaufort, dying there in 1915. Mifflin Gibbs held positions ranging from register of Little Rock's land office to American consul at Madagascar. Other black leaders left the political arena entirely to devote themselves to religious and educational work, emigration projects, or personal advancement. Robert G. Fitzgerald continued to teach in North Carolina until his death in 1919; Edward Shaw of Memphis concentrated on activities among black Masons and the AME Church; Richard H. Cain served as president of a black college in Waco, Texas; and Francis L. Cardozo went on to become principal of a Washington, D.C., high school. Aaron A. Bradley, the militant spokesman for Georgia's low-country freedmen, helped publicize the Kansas Exodus and died in St. Louis in 1881, while Henry M. Turner, ordained an AME bishop in 1880, emerged as the late nineteenth century's most prominent advocate of black emigration to Africa. Former Atlanta councilman William Finch prospered as a tailor. Alabama Congressman Jeremiah Haralson engaged in coal mining in Colorado, where he was reported "killed by wild beasts."

Other Reconstruction leaders found, in the words of a black lawyer, that "the tallest tree . . . suffers most in a storm." Former South Carolina Congressman and Lieut. Gov. Alonzo J. Ransier died in poverty in 1882, having been employed during his last years as a night watchman at the Charleston Custom House and as a city street sweeper. Robert B. Elliott, the state's most brilliant political organizer, found himself "utterly unable to earn a living owing to the severe os-

tracism and mean prejudice of my political opponents." He died in
1884 after moving to New Orleans and struggling to survive as a
lawyer. James T. Rapier died penniless in 1883, having dispersed his
considerable wealth among black schools, churches, and emigration
organizations. Most local leaders sank into obscurity, disappearing entirely from the historical record. Although some of their children
achieved distinction, none of Reconstruction's black officials created a
family political dynasty—one indication of how Redemption aborted
the development of the South's black political leadership. If their descendants moved ahead, it was through business, the arts, or the professions. T. Thomas Fortune, editor of the New York *Age*, was the son
of Florida officeholder Emanuel Fortune; Harlem Renaissance writer
Jean Toomer, the grandson of Pinchback; renowned jazz pianist
Fletcher Henderson, the grandson of an official who had served in
South Carolina's constitutional convention and legislature.

By the turn of the century, as soldiers from North and South
joined to take up the "white man's burden" in the Spanish-American
War, Reconstruction was widely viewed as little more than a regret-
table detour on the road to reunion. To the bulk of the white South, it
had become axiomatic that Reconstruction had been a time of "savage tyranny" that "accomplished not one useful result, and left behind it, not one pleasant recollection." Black suffrage, wrote Joseph
Le Conte, who had fled South Carolina for a professorship at the University of California to avoid teaching black students, was now seen
by "all thoughtful men" as "the greatest political crime ever perpe-
trated by any people." In more sober language, many Northerners, including surviving architects of Congressional policy, concurred in
these judgments. "Years of thinking and observation" had convinced
O. O. Howard "that the restoration of their lands to the planters provided for [a] future better for the negroes." John Sherman's recollections recorded a similar change of heart: "After this long lapse of
time I am convinced that Mr. Johnson's scheme of reorganization
was wise and judicious. . . . It is unfortunate that it had not the sanction of Congress."

This rewriting of Reconstruction's history was accorded scholarly
legitimacy—to its everlasting shame—by the nation's fraternity of professional historians. Early in the twentieth century a group of young
Southern scholars gathered at Columbia University to study the Reconstruction era under the guidance of Professors John W. Burgess and
William A. Dunning. Blacks, their mentors taught, were "children"
utterly incapable of appreciating the freedom that had been thrust
upon them. The North did "a monstrous thing" in granting them suffrage, for "a black skin means membership in a race of men which has
never of itself succeeded in subjecting passion to reason, has never,
therefore, created any civilization of any kind." No political order

could survive in the South unless founded on the principle of racial inequality. The students' works on individual Southern states echoed
these sentiments. Reconstruction, concluded the study of North Carolina, was an attempt by "selfish politicians, backed by the federal
government . . . to Africanize the State and deprive the people through
misrule and oppression of most that life held dear." The views of the
Dunning School shaped historical writing for generations, and
achieved wide popularity through D. W. Griffith's film *Birth of a Nation* (which glorified the Ku Klux Klan and had its premiere at the
White House during Woodrow Wilson's Presidency), James Ford
Rhodes's popular multivolume chronicle of the Civil War era, and the
national best-seller *The Tragic Era* by Claude G. Bowers. Southern
whites, wrote Bowers, "literally were put to the torture" by "emissaries of hate" who inflamed "the negroes' egotism" and even inspired
"lustful assaults" by blacks upon white womanhood.

Few interpretations of history have had such far-reaching consequences as this image of Reconstruction. As Francis B. Simkins, a
South Carolina-born historian, noted during the 1930s, "the alleged
horrors of Reconstruction" did much to freeze the mind of the white
South in unalterable opposition to outside pressures for social change
and to any thought of breaching Democratic ascendancy, eliminating
segregation, or restoring suffrage to disenfranchised blacks. They also
justified Northern indifference to the nullification of the Fourteenth
and Fifteenth Amendments. Apart from a few white dissenters like
Simkins, it was left to black writers to challenge the prevailing orthodoxy. In the early years of this century, none did so more tirelessly
than former Mississippi Congressman John R. Lynch, then living in
Chicago, who published a series of devastating critiques of the racial
biases and historical errors of Rhodes and Bowers. "I do not hesitate to
assert," he wrote, "that the Southern Reconstruction Governments
were the best governments those States ever had." In 1917, Lynch
voiced the hope that "a fair, just, and impartial historian will, some
day, write a history covering the Reconstruction period, [giving] the actual facts of what took place."

Only in the family traditions and collective folk memories of the
black community did a different version of Reconstruction survive.
Growing up in the 1920s, Pauli Murray was "never allowed to forget"
that she walked in "proud shoes" because her grandfather, Robert G.
Fitzgerald, had "fought for freedom" in the Union Army and then en-
listed as a teacher in the "second war" against the powerlessness and
ignorance inherited from slavery. When the Works Progress Administration sent agents into the black belt during the Great Depression to
interview former slaves, they found Reconstruction remembered for
its disappointments and betrayals, but also as a time of hope, possibility, and accomplishment. Bitterness still lingered over the federal gov-

ernment's failure to distribute land or protect blacks' civil and political rights. "The Yankees helped free us, so they say," declared eighty-one-year-old former slave Thomas Hall, "but they let us be put back in slavery again." Yet coupled with this disillusionment were proud, vivid recollections of a time when "the colored used to hold office." Some pulled from their shelves dusty scrapbooks of clippings from Reconstruction newspapers; others could still recount the names of local black leaders. "They made pretty fair officers," remarked one elderly freedman; "I thought them was good times in the country," said another. Younger blacks spoke of being taught by their parents "about the old times, mostly about the Reconstruction, and the Ku Klux." "I know folks think the books tell the truth, but they shore don't," one eighty-eight-year-old former slave told the WPA.

For some blacks, such memories helped to keep alive the aspirations of the Reconstruction era. "This here used to be a good county," said Arkansas freedman Boston Blackwell, "but I tell you it sure is tough now. I think it's wrong—exactly wrong that we can't vote now." "I does believe that the negro ought to be given more privileges in voting," echoed Taby Jones, born a slave in South Carolina in 1850, "because they went through the reconstruction period with banners flying." For others, Reconstruction inspired optimism that better times lay ahead. "The Bible says, 'What has been will be again'," said Alabama sharecropper Ned Cobb. Born in 1885, Cobb never cast a vote in his entire life, yet he never forgot that outsiders had once taken up the black cause—an indispensable source of hope for one conscious of his own weakness in the face of overwhelming and hostile local power. When radical Northerners ventured South in the 1930s to help organize black agricultural workers, Cobb seemed almost to have been waiting for them: "The whites came down to bring emancipation, and left before it was over. . . . Now they've come to finish the job." The legacy of Reconstruction affected the 1930s revival of black militancy in other ways as well. Two leaders of the Alabama Share Croppers Union, Ralph and Thomas Gray, claimed to be descended from a Reconstruction legislator. (Like many nineteenth-century predecessors, Ralph Gray paid with his life for challenging the South's social order—he was killed in a shootout with a posse while guarding a union meeting.)

Twenty more years elapsed before another generation of black Southerners launched the final challenge to the racial system of the New South. A few participants in the civil rights movement thought of themselves as following a path blazed after the Civil War. Discussing the reasons for his involvement, one black Mississippian spoke of the time when "a few Negroes was admitted into the government of the State of Mississippi and to the United States." Reconstruction's legacy was also evident in the actions of federal judge Frank Johnson, who fought a twelve-year battle for racial justice with Alabama Gov. George Wallace. Johnson hailed from Winston County, a center of Civil War Unionism, and his great-grandfather had served as a Republican sheriff during Reconstruction. By this time, however, the Reconstruction generation had passed from the scene and even within the black community, memories of the period had all but disappeared. Yet the institutions created or consolidated after the Civil War—the black family, school, and church—provided the base from which the modern civil rights revolution sprang. And for its legal strategy, the movement returned to the laws and amendments of Reconstruction.

"The river has its bend, and the longest road must terminate." Rev. Peter Randolph, a former slave, wrote these words as the dark night of injustice settled over the South. Nearly a century elapsed before the nation again attempted to come to terms with the implications of emancipation and the political and social agenda of Reconstruction. In many ways, it has yet to do so.

INDEX